GUIDE TO THE WEST SLAVONIC LANGUAGES

GUIDE TO THE WEST SLAVONIC LANGUAGES

(Guide To The Slavonic Languages,
Third Edition, Revised And Expanded, Part 2)

by

R. G. A. de Bray

1980

Slavica Publishers, Inc.

For a list of some other books from Slavica, see the last pages of this book. For a complete catalog with prices and ordering information, write to: Slavica Publishers, Inc.
P.O. Box 14388
Columbus, Ohio 43214

Published with the financial assistance of the United Nations Educational, Scientific, and Cultural Organization (UNESCO). The opinions expressed in this book are those of the author, and not necessarily those of either the publisher or UNESCO.

ISBN: 0-89357-061-3.

Copyright © 1951 by J. M. Dent & Sons Ltd., London; revisions copyright © 1969 and 1980 by R. G. A. de Bray. All rights reserved.

Printed in the United States of America by BookCrafters, Inc., Chelsea, Michigan 48118.

To the memory of
Robert Auty
Colleague, counsellor,
and friend

CONTENTS

PUBLISHER'S NOTE..7
PREFACE...9
LIST OF ABBREVIATIONS USED...............................13

INTRODUCTION

THE PURPOSE OF THIS BOOK................................. 15
THE PLAN AND ARRANGEMENT OF THIS BOOK.................... 16
THE METHOD OF USING THIS BOOK............................ 18
THE DISTRIBUTION OF THE SLAVONIC LANGUAGES............... 20
CHARACTERISTICS OF THE SLAVONIC LANGUAGES................ 22
THE IMPORTANCE OF OLD SLAVONIC........................... 23

BIBLIOGRAPHY

CZECH.. 25
SLOVAK... 27
POLISH... 28
LUSATIAN... 30
THE SLAVONIC GROUP....................................... 32

Section 1.
CZECH

INTRODUCTION... 33
ALPHABET... 37
PRONUNCIATION.. 39
DIALECTS... 45
VOWEL GRADATION AND VOWEL LENGTHENING.................... 50
SLAVONIC CHARACTERISTICS................................. 50
FEATURES CHARACTERISTIC OF CZECH......................... 54
FEATURES CHARACTERISTIC OF CZECH AND SLOVAK.............. 56
FEATURES CHARACTERISTIC OF CZECH, SLOVAK, AND
    POLISH... 57
MORPHOLOGY... 60
    Declensions of—
        nouns.. 60
        numerals... 71
        pronouns... 75
        adjectives... 81
    Adjectives (Comparison).............................. 84
    Adverbs.. 86
    Conjunctions... 91
    Prepositions... 93
    Conjugation of Verbs................................. 95
        Voices and tenses; Present and Infinitive.... 95
        Classification....................................... 99
        Future tense and aspects...................... 100
        Past tense................................... 103
        Pluperfect................................... 105

CONTENTS

    Conditional..................................106
    Past Conditional.............................106
    Imperative...................................106
    Gerunds......................................108
    Participles..................................110
    Verbal nouns.................................112
    Conjugation, examples........................112
    Irregular verbs..............................116
    Verbs of going and conveying.................120
WORD ORDER WITH ENCLITICS........................122
TEXTS..124

Section 2.
SLOVAK

INTRODUCTION....................................... 131
ALPHABET... 134
PRONUNCIATION...................................... 137
DIALECTS... 145
VOWEL GRADATION AND VOWEL LENGTHENING.............. 149
SLAVONIC CHARACTERISTICS........................... 149
FEATURES CHARACTERISTIC OF SLOVAK.................. 153
    (For Features of Czech and Slovak, and
      Features of Czech, Slovak, and Polish
      —refer to Chapter on CZECH.)
MORPHOLOGY... 155
    Declensions of—
        nouns...................................... 157
        numerals................................... 169
        pronouns................................... 175
        adjectives................................. 180
    Adjectives (comparison)........................ 182
    Adverbs.. 186
    Conjunctions................................... 190
    Prepositions................................... 192
    Conjugation of Verbs........................... 195
      Voice and tenses; Present and Infinitive.... 197
      Classification.............................. 200
      Future tense and aspects.................... 202
      Past tense.................................. 205
      Pluperfect.................................. 206
      Conditional................................. 207
      Past Conditional............................ 207
      Imperative.................................. 208
      Gerunds..................................... 209
      Participles................................. 210
      Verbal nouns................................ 212
      Conjugation, examples....................... 213
      Irregular verbs............................. 216
      Verbs of going and conveying................ 219

CONTENTS

WORD ORDER WITH ENCLITICS..........................221
TEXTS..222

Section 3.
POLISH

INTRODUCTION.......................................229
ALPHABET...234
PRONUNCIATION......................................236
DIALECTS...244
VOWEL GRADATION AND VOWEL LENGTHENING..............250
SLAVONIC CHARACTERISTICS...........................251
FEATURES CHARACTERISTIC OF POLISH..................255
    (For Features of Czech, Slovak, and Polish—
    refer to chapter on CZECH.)
MORPHOLOGY...263
    Declensions of—
        nouns..265
        numerals.......................................282
        pronouns.......................................287
        adjectives.....................................291
    Adjectives (comparison)........................296
    Adverbs..298
    Conjunctions...................................302
    Prepositions...................................303
    Conjugation of Verbs...........................304
      Voices and tenses; Present and Infinitive...304
      Classification..............................306
      Future tense and aspects....................308
      Past tense..................................311
      Pluperfect..................................312
      Conditional.................................312
      Past Conditional............................313
      Imperative..................................313
      Gerunds.....................................314
      Participles.................................315
      Verbal nouns................................317
      Conjugations, examples......................318
      Irregular verbs.............................319
      Verbs of going and conveying................324
WORD ORDER WITH ENCLITICS..........................326
TEXTS..328

Section 4.
LUSATIAN (or WENDISH)

```
INTRODUCTION...................................333
LUSATIAN LITERATURE............................338
UPPER LUSATIAN
  ALPHABET.....................................350
  PRONUNCIATION................................352
  VOWEL GRADATION AND VOWEL LENGTHENING........358
  SLAVONIC CHARACTERISTICS.....................359
  FEATURES CHARACTERISTIC OF UPPER LUSATIAN....363
  LUSATIAN DIALECTS............................370
    (including the Phonetic Features of Lower
      Lusatian.)
  MORPHOLOGY...................................375
    Declension of—
        nouns..................................375
        numerals...............................394
        pronouns...............................398
        adjectives.............................405
      Adjectives (comparison)..................411
      Adverbs..................................414
      Conjunctions.............................419
      Prepositions.............................420
      Conjugation of Verbs.....................423
        Voices and tenses; Present and Infinitive..424
        Classification.........................428
        Future tense and aspects...............429
        Compound Past (Perfect)................432
        Aorist.................................434
        Imperfect..............................435
        Pluperfect.............................436
        Conditional............................437
        Past Conditional.......................437
        Imperative.............................438
        Gerunds................................439
        Participles............................440
        Verbal nouns...........................442
        Conjugation, examples..................442
        Irregular verbs........................446
        Verbs of going and conveying...........457
WORD ORDER WITH ENCLITICS......................460
LOWER LUSATIAN
  MAIN DIFFERENCES IN MORPHOLOGY COMPARED WITH
      UPPER LUSATIAN...........................462
  WORD ORDER WITH ENCLITICS....................470
TEXTS: UPPER LUSATIAN..........................470
       LOWER LUSATIAN..........................479
```

PUBLISHER'S NOTE

Slavica is very pleased to be able to make available this Third, revised and expanded edition of Professor de Bray's work, which has been a standard reference for nearly thirty years. Eight of the twelve sections have been substantially revised for this edition, and considerable new material has been included.

In order to make the work even more useful, the author has recorded native speakers reading the texts at the end of each section. These recordings are available on cassettes or open-reel tapes from the publisher. For information and prices, please write directly to Slavica at P.O. Box 14388, Columbus, Ohio 43214.

Another innovation in the Third Edition is that the book has been split into three more manageable parts, each of which can be used individually, instead of a single book of over 1100 pages. One part is devoted to the South Slavic languages, a second to the West Slavic languages, and the third to the East Slavic languages. Since the parts are sold separately, students taking such commonly-taught courses as "Introduction to the South (West, East) Slavic Languages" will be able to use the appropriate volume, without having to buy and carry around the entire work.

Because the academic recession of the 1970's has so strongly depressed the market for scholarly books, it has been necessary to set this edition in more economical cold type, instead of the more elegant hot type with justified right margins which was used in the previous two editions. Slavica is grateful to UNESCO for a subvention which has met part of the costs of resetting the book. We are even more grateful to the typists who have done such a good job of coping with very difficult material. Eleanor B. Sapp typed the sections on Czech, Lusatian, Polish, and Slovenian. Karen L. Black typed the sections on Belorussian, Serbo-Croatian, Ukrainian, and much of the section on Old Church Slavonic. Debra E. Barco typed Bulgarian and Macedonian; Marcia Gauntt typed Slovak; David Birnbaum and Patricia Hansen typed Russian, and Joel and Monica Wilkinson typed part of the section on Old Church Slavonic. Dr. Black took overall responsibility for paginating, cross-referencing, checking corrections, and typing the Introduction and

Bibliography. I wish to thank her here for a complex job well done. Don D. Smith was in charge of checking the corrections from the second proofs and of making various other small but important corrections and improvements in the final camera-ready copy. I am grateful to him for careful attention to tedious and time-consuming work.

We have tried hard, by a system of double and even triple checking, to eliminate misprints, but some are bound to creep into a work of this complexity. Readers who find misprints are asked to send a list of them to the publisher at P.O. Box 14388, Columbus, Ohio 43214. A year or two after the publication of this work, we will publish a list of misprints in our journal, *Folia Slavica*, so that both individuals and libraries may correct their copies.

Columbus, Ohio
May 17, 1980

Charles E. Gribble
President and Editor

PREFACE TO THE FIRST EDITION

It is my pleasant duty to acknowledge with gratitude here the many useful suggestions and the generous encouragement of Professor N. B. Jopson, M.A., Professor of Comparative Philology in the University of Cambridge, Professor W. J. Rose, M.A., Ph.D., former Professor of Polish Literature and History and Director of the School of Slavonic and East European Studies, University of London, and Dr. W. A. Morison, B.A., Ph.D., formerly Lecturer in Comparative Slavonic Philology in the same institution. My sincere thanks are also due to Professor Sir Ellis Minns, Litt.D., F.B.A., of Cambridge, for looking through the first part of this text and making many valuable suggestions, especially as regards presentation, and also for his initial encouragement, without which this book might never have been offered for publication.

I also here express my sincere thanks to my numerous colleagues and friends for their invaluable help and advice with regard to the separate sections of this book: Professor G. Nandriş, Ph.D., Mr. A. Oleynyk, Professor S. Świaniewicz, Professor F. Ramovš, Miss Boža Anžič, Mr. Krum Tošev, Mr. Kiro Petrovski, Mr. D. M. Pavlović, Mr. A. Poberaj, Miss V. Jukova, Mr. K. Naumov, Mr. V. de S. Pinto, Mr. M. Kusseff, Dr. J. Pietrkiewicz, Dr. O. Kolman, Dr. V. Polák, Mrs. E. V. de Bray, Miss T. Ruppeldtová, Dr. E. M. Cyżowa, Dr. J. Rjenč, Rev. Dr. Č. Sipovič, and many others.

It gives me pleasure also specially to mention the tireless help, encouragement, and expert criticism of my wife, who also performed the stupendous feat of typing the entire work in preparation for printing. Her knowledge of several Slavonic languages and her understanding and sympathy with the aims of my work enabled her to make many valuable suggestions in shaping the book.

I would also like to thank my publishers, Messrs. J. M. Dent and Sons, Ltd., for their endless patience and unfailing encouragement in the writing of this work over a period of seven years and under various difficult circumstances.

Finally I warmly thank my printers, Messrs. Stephen Austin and Sons, Ltd., for their untiring perseverance and unfailing courtesy during the printing of my technically extremely difficult text and for the production of such excellent work.

The brief bibliography also serves the purpose of expressing my acknowledgments of indebtedness to the authors of the many valuable works which I have consulted. The list is not intended to be an exhaustive bibliography, but rather a guide to the student who wishes to start delving deeper for treasures which I here only indicate. (The purpose, plan, and method of using this book are explained in the following Introduction.)

Chalfont St. Giles
15. iv. 1950

PREFACE TO THE SECOND EDITION

In this edition the sections on Bulgarian, Czech and Polish have been corrected, revised and slightly expanded, where necessary. The section on Byelorussian has been fully revised and brought up to date in accordance with the new authoritative grammar of Byelorussian published by the Institute of Linguistics of the Byelorussian Academy of Sciences in Minsk. Some misprints have also been corrected in the section on Slovak.

A selection of the most important new practical works published since 1951 have been added to the bibliography.

I would like to express my warmest thanks to Dr. Václav Polák, Professor Ivan Duridanov, and Professor M. R. Sudnik and his colleagues in the Institute of Linguistics of the Byelorussian Academy of Sciences, Minsk, and to all my reviewers for their many helpful suggestions and criticisms.

New Barnet
11. x. 1968

PREFACE TO THE THIRD EDITION

For this edition the author has attempted to revise and bring up to date all the chapters that had not been thoroughly revised for the second edition, namely the chapters on Old Slavonic, Russian, Ukrainian, Macedonian, Serbo-Croätian, Slovenian, Slovak and Lusatian (Sorbian). A number of new grammatical tables have been added, especially in the chapters on Old Slavonic and Serbo-Croätian, and the introduction to the chapter on Russian has been considerably expanded. In the chapter on Ukrainian a more modern ap-

PREFACE

proach to the subdivision of the dialects has been adopted on lines suggested by Professor F. T. Zhylkó of the Institute of Dialectology in Kiev. The chapters on Macedonian, Slovak and Lusatian in particular have been revised so as to comply with modern orthographical and grammatical norms. The chapters on Byelorussian, Bulgarian, Czech and Polish, which were revised for the second edition, have only been lightly revised, where necessary.

It is my pleasant duty to thank all my colleagues and friends who have helped me with advice, opinions and information in connection with my work for this edition, and in particular Professor R. I. Avanesov, Professor V. A. Artemov, Professor O. S. Akhmanova, Dr. E. A. Bryzgunova, Mr. B. K. Yoondin, Dr. I. Miloslavsky, Professor A. M. Babkin, Professor L. R. Zinder, Mr. V. Swoboda, Professor F. T. Zhylkó (mentioned above), Professor M. Zhovtobriuch and other colleagues at the Institute of Linguistics of the Ukrainian Academy of Sciences in Kiev, Academic B. Koneski, Academic H. Polenakoviḱ, the late Professor Krum Toshev, Professor T. Stamatoski, Professor T. Dimitrovski, Professor B. Korubin and other colleagues at the Krste Misirkov Institute of the Macedonian Language, Skopje, Professor B. Vidoeski, Miss Olga Spirkoska, Professor M. Stevanović, the late Dr. B. Nikolić, Professor P. Ivić, Professor M. Ivić, Dr. I. Grickat-Radulović, Dr. O. Banković-Todorović and other colleagues of the Serbo-Croatian Language Institute of the Serbian Academy of Sciences, Academic L. Jonke, Dr. B. Finka, Dr. V. Putanec, Dr. D. Alerić and other colleagues of the Language Institute of the Yugoslav Academy of Sciences and Arts, Zagreb, Professor J. Jurančič, Dr. J. Rigler, Professor A. Bajec, Professor M. Tomšič, Dr. L. Legiša, and other colleagues of the Slovenian Language Institute of the Slovenian Academy of Sciences and Arts, Ljubljana, Professor J. Toporišič, Professor J. Zor, Professor J. Ružička, Professor L. Dvonč, and Professor V. Blanár of the L'udevit Štúr Institute of the Slovak Language of the Slovak Academy of Sciences, Miss Eva Ružičková, Dr. R. Pynsent, Dr. M. Corbridge-Patkaniowska, Professor H. Schuster-Šewc, Dr. L. Hajnec, Professor P. Nowotny, and Mr. J. Rjenč.

It is my pleasure also to acknowledge with sincere thanks the material help proffered by the Central Research Fund of the University of London and also by the Australian National University. Both generously helped me to make numerous visits to the Slavonic-speaking countries of Eastern Europe in pursuit of my research. I also express my gratitude to the then

Director of the School of Slavonic and East European Studies, University of London, Dr. G. Bolsover, to the Vice-Chancellor of the Australian National University in Canberra, Professor D. A. Low, and to the Dean of the Faculty of Arts, Dr. W. S. Ramson, for granting me study leave for research purposes between 1968 and 1976, without which I would not have had the opportunity to collect the necessary material for the completion of this work. To all the abovementioned, to my secretary of the Department of Slavonic Languages, the Australian National University, Ms. K. North, and to my publishers for their interest and continual support, I offer my most heartfelt thanks.

Finally, I wish to express my deep gratitude to the Slav Studies project of UNESCO, under the able guidance of Professor V. Tiourine, for their subsidy which enabled the project of the publication of this work to be realized.

If this work will in any way help its readers the better to understand the Slavonic languages, literatures and culture, and the peoples who have created them, it will have achieved its modest purpose.

> молю же вьсѣхъ почитаѭштихъ· не можете клати, нъ исправльше почитаите. тако бо и стꙑ апл паvл глеть· блте, а не кльнѣте. аминъ.

Canberra
1 July 1977

ABBREVIATIONS

A., Acc.	Accusative	g., gend.	genders
Act.	Active	G., Gen.	Genitive
adj.	adjective	Germ.	German
adv.	adverb	Gk.	Greek
an.	animate		
Aor.	Aorist	I., Instr.	Instrumental
approx.	approximate	I.E.	Indo-European
arch.	archaic	Imper.,	
art.	article	Imperat.	Imperative
aux.	auxiliary	Imperf.	Imperfect
		impers.	impersonal
b.	born	Impfve.	Imperfective
B-r.,		inan.	inanimate
Byelor.	Byelorussian	Ind.	Indicative
Bulg.	Bulgarian	indef.	indefinite
		Infin.	Infinitive
Card.	Cardinal	interrog.	interrogative
cf.	compare	intrans.	intransitive
Cl.	class	irreg.	irregular
coll.	collective	irr. vb.	irregular verb
colloq.	colloquial	Iter.	Iterative
Comp.	Comparative		
Comp. Past	Compound Past	L., Loc.	Locative
Cond.	Conditional		(= Prepositional)
conj.	conjunction	Lat.	Latin
cons.	consonant	L.L.,	
Cr.	Croätian	Lower L.	Lower Lusatian
C.S.	Common Slav	lit.	literally
Cyr.	Cyrillic	lit. lang.	literary language
Cz.	Czech	Lus.	Lusatian
d.	died	m., masc.	masculine
D., Dat.	Dative	Mac.	Macedonian
Demonstr.	Demonstrative	m. impers.	masculine impersonal
def.	definite	m. pers.	masculine personal
dial.	dialect	Mod. Gk.	Modern Greek
Distrib.	Distributive		
du.	dual	n., neut.	neuter
		N., Nom.	Nominative
ed.	edition	neg.	negative
encl.	enclitic	num.	numeral
Eng.	English		
		Obl.	Oblique (case)
fam.	familiar	Opt.	Optative
f., fem.	feminine	Ord.	Ordinal
Fr.	French	O.S.	Old (Church) Slavonic
Freq.	Frequentative		
Fut.	Future	p.	page

ABBREVIATIONS

p., pers.	person, personal	vol.	volume
pal.	palatal		
Part., Partic.	Participle	Zogr.	Codex Zographensis
Pass.	Passive	=	equals (translation)
Past Ger.	Past Gerund	>	into, becomes
Perf.	Perfect	<	from, derived from
Pers. Pron.	Personal Pronoun	><	as opposed to
Pfve.	Perfective	*	indicates a supposed, deduced form
phon.	phonetic script		
pl., plur.	plural		
Plup.	Pluperfect		
poet.	poetical		
Pol.	Polish		
Pos.	Positive		
Poss. Pron.	Possessive Pronoun		
P.P.A.	Past Participle Active		
P.P.P.	Past Participle Passive		
prep.	preposition		
Pres.	Present		
Pres. Ger.	Present Gerund		
pron.	pronounce(d)		
R., Russ.	Russian		
Reflex.	Reflexive		
reg.	regular		
Rel. Pron.	Relative Pronoun		
s., sg., sing.	singular		
Sb.	Serbian		
Sbcr., Serbocr.	Serbocroätian		
Slk.	Slovak		
Sln.	Slovenian		
Span.	Spanish		
st.	stem		
subst.	substantive		
Sup.	Superlative		
trans.	transitive		
Ukr.	Ukrainian		
U.L., Upper L.	Upper Lusatian		
V., Voc.	Vocative		
vb.	verb		
V.N.	Verbal Noun		

INTRODUCTION
The Purpose of this Book

This book is an attempt to simplify the task of learning the Slav languages as a group for those who know one of them already. It was originally conceived during the 1939-1945 war with a more limited programme.[1] It has a scientific, philological basis. But as it is not intended exclusively for philologists and university students it is written on as nearly "popular" lines as such a subject permits, with a minimum of specialized terminology. It is intentionally an effort at popularization, as the writer believes that all those knowing any one Slavonic language can with profit widen their linguistic horizon by the relatively easy method of learning other Slavonic languages. Those knowing Russian should interest themselves in the Balkans and/or Central Europe, and *vice versa*. A consciousness would thus grow up of the unity of Europe and the continuity, both geographical and cultural, of Russia with Western Europe by way of the intervening central region of Eastern Europe.

It has been the writer's experience that many officials and workers in various fields and even teachers and examiners are given the task of dealing with material in the Slav languages as a group on the strength of their knowledge of only one of them. It is to help this class of language worker, among others, that this work aims. It should be equally useful to the student (whether academic or not) of any of the Slav languages (even if he is a beginner), when his curiosity drives him to "look over the fence" and find out something about the other Slavonic languages beyond.

It is thus also an introduction to the comparative study of the modern Slavonic languages. In these three volumes we give a summary of every language of the group, including Old Slavonic—a synthesis of a very extensive field of knowledge, difficult to master just because of the closeness of one Slav language to another. For every language we try to give a list of its most characteristic phonetic and morphological features, thus showing where the main differences and similarities should be expected and observed.

---

[1] See p. 18.

INTRODUCTION

The Plan and Arrangement of this Book

For the sake of clarity and simplicity each language is treated in a separate section, giving the student a complete conspectus of a clearly defined subject—a single language. This is a new method of approach in dealing with comparative Slavonic grammar, calculated to suit the English beginner with only a modest experience in the Slavonic field. Many a student has found learned works from the Continent forbidding and confusing as an introduction to the comparative philology of the Slavonic languages, for these give as examples of the points they are illustrating rare and archaic words by the side of common words, words from obscure dialects by the side of words from the modern literary and conversational languages. From such works it is impossible to get a clear, working knowledge of any separate modern Slavonic literary or spoken language, for that is not what such books intend to impart. But the English student is often of a practical turn of mind and his needs may rightly be satisfied.

This book starts with a brief summary of the phonetics and grammar of Old Slavonic (also called Old Bulgarian). A knowledge of this dead language casts a great deal of light on the kinship of the modern Slavonic languages, just as a knowledge of Latin helps one to understand the Romance group of languages as a whole. But it must be borne in mind that Old Slavonic is not a "parent language," but rather an "elder sister" language of the *South* Slav group, preserved exclusively in Orthodox ecclesiastical texts. (The South Slav group also includes modern Bulgarian, Macedonian, Serbocroätian, and Slovenian.) Old Slavonic is the nearest we have today to "Common Slav," the "reconstructed" and supposed parent language of all three groups. The East Slav group consists of Russian, Ukrainian, and Byelorussian, while the Western group comprises Czech, Slovak, Polish, and Lusatian or Wendish. Old Slavonic differs from "Common Slav" in a number of important features, e.g. in the combinations of vowels and liquids. But on the whole it is sufficiently close to Common Slav to be used by the student as the essential pivot for passing from one Slavonic language to another.

Each section is built on the same plan:—
1. a brief history of the development of the language together with references to its main writers;

INTRODUCTION

2. a more detailed section on its script and sounds (orthography and descriptive phonetics);
3. a summary of its characteristic features, presented in historical perspective, i.e. compared with Old Slavonic or Common Slav and/or the closely related modern Slav languages—perhaps the most important part of each section. This is either preceded or followed by:
4. a brief summary of the main dialects. These are dealt with mainly from the point of view of their contributions to the formation of the literary language. They are not regarded as "languages" in their own right and of equal status to the generally recognized literary languages. The existence of a literature in a given language and the acceptance and use of the language in a cultured society have been taken as the criteria for dividing off languages from dialects;
5. a concise summary of the "grammar" of the language (its morphology).
6. a special section, where necessary, on word order with enclitics. This subject is always a stumbling block in the mastery of an *active* knowledge of those languages which have enclitics (i.e. South and West Slav here);
7. a few pages of selected texts (without any commentary) as samples of the language as it is printed for the native (i.e. without stress accents) to serve as illustration and reading practice for the student.

Each section also adheres as rigidly as possible to the same scheme and order of explaining the details in the above parts, so as to render the comparison of these details between any two or more of these languages as easy as possible. A minimum of directly comparative tables is included, thereby leaving the student to compare *any* language he likes of the group with any other. This overcomes the difficulty of different people starting out from a knowledge of different single languages.

For Old Slavonic, Byelorussian, Slovenian, and Macedonian till late there have been no text-books at all in English, while for Ukrainian, Bulgarian, and Slovak until recently aids have been only inadequate. For these languages, therefore, fresh material is presented to the English reader; but at the same time it is put *in perspective* and connected with knowledge previously available. The section on the recently recognized Macedonian language is an entirely new contribution to Slavonic studies in any West European language.

It will be seen, therefore, that this work also attempts to fill gaps in the knowledge of the English student, rather than cover familiar ground over again. For this reason less space is given to Russian (as already extensively treated and studied) and Serbocroätian for which grammars, similar to those for Russian, have been available. But Czech and Polish, owing to their complex morphology and the different arrangement of their grammars in the better works, have been rather more fully dealt with here to show their close connection with the other Slavonic languages. Relatively more space, therefore, is devoted to them and the languages named above for which material has so far been unavailable or only inadequate in English.

Any other disparities of length under the separate headings in each section are due to *(a)* the not sufficiently known lack of adequate material in this country, especially on the more obscure languages of this group; *(b)* the fact that the original wartime conception of the book covered only Old Slavonic, Russian, Serbocroätian, and Bulgarian, and that the greatest possible brevity for these was required.[1] The sections on these last-named languages have subsequently been revised and brought up to date, but not expanded to the length of the other sections, for the reasons given above.

As this book is mainly concerned with showing the general principles of phonetic and grammatical structure of each language rather than with the study of individual words, a word index has been deliberately omitted. In compensation, the contents have been tabulated as fully as possible to facilitate prompt comparison between the sections. Thus, for example, it is very easy to compare the behaviour of the adjectives in all the languages given by simply looking under the heading "The (Declension of the) Adjectives" under "Morphology" in the Contents List for each language.

The Method of Using this Book

The student should be warned that, as this book attempts a synthesis of a very vast field, the material given is necessarily very condensed. The student, therefore, and especially the beginner, should not attempt to absorb too much at a time. If he bites off

---

[1] See also p. 15.

a little at a time, he will more easily avoid mental indigestion.

As a general word of advice one may say that a person knowing one Slavonic language and approaching another for the first time is well advised to assume in the first place that he *knows* the new language in *outline*; and then—far more important and difficult—carefully and continuously to note and study all differences of phonetics, form, grammar, syntax, and meaning. He must always bear in mind that he is dealing with a really different language with different sounds, intonations, rhythms, and a different historical and sociological background, and different neighbouring influences. In the Slavonic field these languages are different and yet very similar and closely interlinked by linguistic, social and spiritual ties. Their literary vocabularies differ more than those in the Romance languages, and the "speech habits" in the conversational languages of the various Slavs are also very distinct. But the basic vocabulary for the ordinary things of everyday life is strikingly similar—a phenomenon which reminds one of the broad similarities of outlook and attitude to life which undoubtedly exist among the Slavs.

For the Englishman each Slavonic language presents its own difficulties and it would be fruitless to discuss which is the most difficult for him to master. But the difficulties to be met with can all be mastered in time by interest and enthusiasm, because the Slavs are, after all, distant cousins of the British, and often large passages of their languages can be translated literally and in almost the same word order and still make sense! This is impossible with more remote languages.

The importance also of using the brief section on Old Slavonic as a basis for learning another Slavonic language or for studying the whole group cannot be over-emphasized. The trouble of doing this will certainly be repaid and the task greatly facilitated. The student who takes this trouble will see in true perspective the relationship of one Slavonic language to another and gain a real mastery of several languages with an ease that will surprise him or her and give deep satisfaction.

Finally, the student is advised to make a careful study of the sound laws that can be inferred from the sections dealing with the characteristics of each language. Besides bringing out the salient differences of each tongue, these will explain many apparent irregularities and changes in the declensions and conjugations, etc. The importance of a patient study of the phonology (Lautlehre, or historical phonetics) can hardly be overstressed.

For a more detailed description of the languages and for adequate exercises the student is referred to the special grammars of the languages concerned, a list of which is appended in the brief bibliography which precedes each of the three main language groups. Complete lists, e.g. of exceptions, details of syntax, etc., have purposely been often omitted for the sake of brevity, as has all such information as, e.g., the names of the days and months, which can be found in dictionaries.

Each section is furnished with a short appendix of texts on which the student is urged to try his skill with the knowledge he acquires from the study of the preceding pages. He will find he has embarked on a journey of endless fascination.

*   *   *

The ultimate aim of this work is to enable a direct and reliable approach to be made to the wider issues reflected in the Slavonic literatures and their background, through an accurate knowledge of the Slavonic languages, and so help to create true understanding and friendship between the Slav peoples, great and small, and the English-speaking world. The student is urged always to have these "wider issues" in view and to remember that even an *accurate* translation, if it is torn from its context and background, can be totally misleading and distort the truth. To know the reality, truth, and beauty of the Slavonic world is an unforgettable experience. It enriches and brings hope.

ὄναρ ἀντ' ὀνειράτων
πολλῶν τε καὶ καλῶν

The Distribution of the Slavonic Languages

The greater part of Eastern Europe between Germany and the Urals is inhabited by Slavs. In the western part of this area Polish, Czech, and Slovak are spoken, as well as Lusatian, or Wendish, in a small linguistic island south-east of Berlin round the towns of Cottbus and Bautzen. Together these four languages form the West Slav group.

Adjoining these areas, to the east, Byelorussian —or White Russian—and Ukrainian are spoken, which together with Great Russian form the East Slav group. These linguistic areas are now in the U.S.S.R., but prior to 1939 they extended in the west to inside the frontiers of Poland for both languages, and into Czechoslovakia for Ukrainian only.

The Ukrainian language is essentially a unity, though in the west, in Galicia, it is naturally more influenced by Polish. The name Ruthenian came into English via German from non-classical Latin, being a corruption of the word "Rusin," meaning vaguely a Russian, more specifically a Ukrainian or "Little Russian," as they used to be called. This curious corruption of their name was a convenient cloak under the Austro-Hungarian Empire for disguising the essentially East Slav, or "Russian," character of their Ukrainian subjects (the name Russian really covers all three branches of the East Slav group, the people whom we know popularly as Russians being more precisely Great Russians). All Ukrainians now prefer the fairly modern name, Ukrainian. In more recent times "Ruthenian" came specifically to refer to Subcarpathian Russia, later called Transcarpathian Ukraine, at the extreme eastern end of pre-1939 Czechoslovakia and now incorporated into the Ukrainian S.S.R.—a convenient, but illogical, restriction of its meaning.

Byelorussian, a language even more akin to Great Russian than Ukrainian is to Great Russian, and with a very phonetic spelling, is even younger as a literary language and has also been called in some books White Ruthenian. In Polish the word "ruski" now means only Ruthenian or Ukrainian, whereas in Russian it means (Great) Russian. Owing to the political associations of the name "White Russian," Soviet authorities have also called it "Byelorussian," preserving the Russian word for "white".

North-east and east of the Byelorussian and Ukrainian speaking areas we find the Great Russian area, the language generally known loosely in English as Russian, the language of such great writers as Pushkin, Tolstoy, Dostoyevsky, etc. Geographically one might say that, whereas the Dniepr is the great river of the Ukraine, the Volga with its tributaries forms the chief artery of the Great Russian speaking area, but in its lower reaches it flows through territory peopled by many other nationalities besides the Great Russians. The Great Russian language spread across a sparsely populated Siberia from the seventeenth century onwards with the comparatively peaceful expansion of the Russian Empire across Northern Asia.

South of Austria, Hungary, and Romania, we have the area of the third, Southern, group of Slav tongues.

In the very north-west corner of it, Slovenian, or Slovene, is spoken by not quite two million people, still not all included in Yugoslavia. East and south of this area we have the Serbocroätian speaking region, corresponding roughly with Yugoslavia's northern, eastern, and south-western frontiers. By the Catholics of Croätia, Dalmatia, etc., and the Moslems of Bosnia, Serbocroätian is generally written in the Latin alphabet, whereas in Serbia the Cyrillic alphabet is prevalent; but as explained later, these and dialectical differences cannot be regarded as forming either racial or linguistic boundaries (the different alphabets are only an indication of a difference of religion), as the language is essentially one, i.e. mutually intelligible without previous study. This cannot truthfully be said of any other two Slav languages considered together except "Serbian" and "Croätian". In Southern Yugoslavia, Northern Greece and South-Western Bulgaria, the Macedonian dialects are prevalent. Linguistically they are somewhat more than a transitional stage to Bulgarian. Since 1944 the Macedonian literary language has been officially recognized for all purposes in the territory of the federative Macedonian People's Republic in Yugoslavia. Bulgarian is the fourth separate literary language of this (South Slav) group, spoken over an area pretty well corresponding to Bulgaria's political frontiers; and, owing to its greater divergence from Serbocroätian, it is classed by some (with Macedonian) as East South Slav as opposed to West South Slav.

Characteristics of the Slavonic Languages

Apart from the Cyrillic and the adapted Latin scripts which are purely superficial characteristics, the main features of the Slavonic languages are:—

Pronunciation:—
1. Varying degrees of "palatalization," i.e. variants of the consonants obtained by using the palate to alter their quality.
2. Few true diphthongs.
3. Agglomerations of consonants (but no aspirated consonants).

Grammar:—
4. A high degree of inflection in nouns, pronouns, adjectives, and verbs, comparable to Latin in their complexity.

5. "Aspects" in verbs, a duality of forms presenting an action regarded as either completed or not, or else as single or habitual.

Sentence construction:—

6. Frequent inversion of sentence order, i.e. verb first and subject later, as in Spanish. In Slavonic, owing to the inflections, the word order is much more elastic and variable than in English, French, or German.

The Importance of Old Slavonic

The necessity of knowing Old Slavonic for acquiring a knowledge of the Slavonic group of languages is comparable to the need for knowing Latin for learning the Romance group. Old Slavonic is now a dead and purely ecclesiastical language, but its knowledge gives one an immense insight into, and understanding of, the reasons for the differences between the Slavonic languages. Hence it is very much worth while getting familiar with it, if one wishes to learn more than one language of the Slavonic group, or to study any of these languages at all seriously in its historical aspect, or again to study the group as a whole—a by no means impossible, even if exacting, task.

BIBLIOGRAPHY
(Aids to further study)

The following list is not intended to be an exhaustive bibliography of all the books written on every aspect of the Slavonic languages. In conformity with the introductory and descriptive character of this work, we give below under the headings for the separate languages a selected list of some of the best and most modern grammars, books on their orthography and phonetics, the easier historical grammars, and the most useful dictionaries for each language (in this order). Precedence is given to works in English, after which works in French and German follow—with works in the Slavonic languages themselves given last. This is done purely on the assumption that the English student will be, to start with, more at home in the West European languages, as is usually the case.

The author and title are given as in the original work except in the case of dictionaries, where the title is translated into English. The script of the author's name helps to indicate the origin of dictionaries published in the Slav countries and aiming primarily at assisting natives of those countries. Such works naturally do not contain all the information an English student needs, but can be very useful to him nevertheless.

For the sake of brevity we give preference to latest editions where advisable. We have excluded most works not completed at the time of our writing, and also very large works such as the average student would find inaccessible or beyond his means.

We conclude with a very brief list of the main works on the Slavonic languages as a group.

It will be seen that the student has at his command a very rich variety of aids, if works in the Slavonic languages are included.

CZECH

M. HEIM. Contemporary Czech. Ann Arbor, 1976.
M. SOVA. A Modern Czech Grammar. London, 1944.
O. ŠTĚPÁNEK. Czech (Bohemian) Grammar. Omaha, 1933.
B. E. MIKULA. Progressive Czech. Chicago, 1940.
A. MAZON. Grammaire de la langue tchèque. 2nd edition. Paris, 1931.
V. ŠMILAUER. Nauka o českém jazyce. Praha, 1972.
M. ŠÁRA, I. ŠÁROVÁ, A. BYTEL. Čeština pro cizince. Praha, 1970.

ved ## BIBLIOGRAPHY

I. POLDAUF, K. ŠPRUNK. Čeština jazyk cizí. Praha, 1968.
B. HAVRÁNEK, A. JEDLIČKA. Česká mluvnice. Praha, 1963.
F. TRÁVNÍČEK. Mluvnice spisovné češtiny. 2 vols. Praha, 1947, 1949.
———. Pravidla českého pravopisu. Praha, 1977.
A. FRINTA. A Czech Phonetic Reader. London, 1925.
B. HÁLA. Výslovnost spisovné češtiny. Praha, 1967.
B. HÁLA. Uvedení do fonetiky češtiny. Praha, 1962.
V. ŠMILAUER. Novočeská skladba. 1947.
F. TRÁVNÍČEK. Historická mluvnice československá. Praha, 1935.
O. HUJER. Úvod do dějin jazyka českého. 2nd edition. Praha, 1946.
J. GEBAUER. Historická mluvnice jazyka českého. Praha, 1894-1909.
S. E. MANN. Czech Historical Grammar. London, 1957.

Dictionaries

I. POLDAUF. Czech-English Dictionary. Praha, 1965.
A. ČERMÁK. Czech-English, English-Czech Dictionary. Třebíč, 1932.
F. KRUPIČKA, J. HOKEŠ, H. and J. PROCHÁZKA. Czech-English, English-Czech Dictionary. London, 1941.
H. CHESHIRE, V. JUNG, L. KLOZNER, J. PROCHÁZKA, R. RYAN, A. ŠRÁMEK. Czech-English Dictionary. 2 vols. Prague, 1933.
*F. KABESCH. Czech-German, German-Czech Dictionary. Langenscheidt, Berlin, 1929.
H. H. ДУРНОВО. Czech-Russian Pocket Dictionary. Moscow, 1933.
L. KOPECKIJ. Russian-Czech Dictionary. Prague, 1937.
П. Г. БОГАТЫРЁВ. Czech-Russian Dictionary. Moscow, 1947.
Т. БРЯНЦЕВА, Г. БОРЕК, Л. КЕЛЛЕР, Е. Л. ОУТРАТА. Russian-Czech Dictionary. Moscow, 1947.
K. HORÁLEK, B. ILKA, L. KOPECKÝ. Czech-Russian Dictionary. Prague, 1958.
A. И. ПАВЛОВИЧ. Czech-Russian Dictionary. Moscow, 1967.
Й. ВЛЧЕК (J. VLČEK). Russian-Czech Dictionary. Moscow, 1968.
*L. V. KOPECKÝ, J. FILIPEC, O. LEŠKA. Czech-Russian Dictionary. 2 vols. Prague-Moscow, 1973.
L. V. KOPECKÝ, O. LEŠKA. Russian-Czech Dictionary. 2 vols. Moscow-Prague, 1978.
Slovník spisovné češtiny pro školu a veřejnost, Praha, 1978.
*With references to grammatical tables.

F. TRÁVNÍČEK. Slovník jazyka českého. Prague, 1952.
———. Slovník spisovného jazyka českého. 4 vols. Prague, 1960, 1964, 1966, 1971.
ADAM, JAROŠ, HOLUB. Český slovník pravopisný a tvaroslovný. Prague, 1955.
J. HOLUB, F. KOPEČNÝ. Etymologický slovník jazyka českého. Prague, 1952.
J. HOLUB, S. LYER. Stručny etymologický slovník jazyka českého. Prague, 1967.
V. MACHEK. Etymologický slovník jazyka českého a slovenského. Prague, 1957.

SLOVAK

J. J. KONUŠ. Practical Slovak Grammar. Pittsburgh, 1939.
J. BARTOŠ, J. GAGNAIRE. Grammaire de la langue slovaque. Paris-Bratislava, 1972.
P. BALÁŽ, M. DAROVEC, et al. Slovak for Slavicists. Bratislava, 1977.
A. MACHT. Praktisches Lehr- und Übungsbuch der slovakischen Sprache. 2 vols. Hartleben, Vienna-Leipzig, 1931.
A. MACHT. Sústavná mluvnica slovenská. Třebechovice, 1938.
J. ORLOVSKÝ, L. ARANY. Gramatika jazyka slovenského. Bratislava, 1946.
E. PAULINY, J. RUZIČKA, J. ŠTOLC. Slovenská gramatika. Martin, 1955.
L. DVONČ, and others. Morfológia slovenského jazyka. Bratislava, 1966.
———. Pravidlá slovenského pravopisu. Matica slovenská, 1967.
H. BARTEK. Správna výslovnost slovenská. Bratislava, 1944.
J. DVONČOVÁ, G. JENČA, Á. KRAL'. Atlas slovenských hlások. Bratislava, 1969.
E. PAULINY. Fonologický vývin slovenčiny. Bratislava, 1963.
E. PAULINY. Štruktúra slovenského slovesa. Bratislava, 1943.
S. CZAMBEL. Rukovät' spisovnej reči slovenskej. 3rd edition, 1919.
J. STANISLAV. Československá mluvnica. Praha, 1937.
E. PAULINY. Dejiny spisovnej slovenčiny. Bratislava, 1948.
J. STANISLAV. Dejiny slovenského jazyka. 3 vols. Bratislava, 1956, 1958, 1957.
V. ERTL. Stručná mluvnice česko-slovenská. Praha, 1919. Comparative tables useful, but not up to

date in orthography.
V. VÁŽNÝ. Stručná mluvnice slovenská pro Čechy. 2nd edition. Praha, 1948.
J. BĚLIČ, and others. Slovenština. Praha, 1964.

Dictionaries

J. VILIKOVSKÁ, P. VILIKOVSKÝ, J. ŠIMKO. Slovak-English Dictionary. Bratislava, 1964.
J. KONUŠ. Slovak-English Phraseological Dictionary. Passaic, NJ, 1969.
A. FILO, J. DETRICH. Slovak-English Dictionary. Ružomberok, 1946.
J. SCHULTZ, E. ŠKVÁRA. Slovak-German, German-Slovak Dictionary. Bratislava, 1937.
D. KOLLÁR, V. DOROTJAKOVÁ, M. FILKUSOVÁ, E. VASILIEVOVÁ. Slovak-Russian Dictionary. Bratislava-Moscow, 1976.
A. V. ISAČENKO. Slovak-Russian Dictionary. 2 vols. Bratislava, 1950, 1957.
A. V. ISAČENKO, and others. Concise Russian-Slovak Dictionary. Bratislava, 1952.
J. DETRICH, P. KIRILČUK. Slovak-Russian Dictionary. Ružomberok, 1945.
J. SCHULTZ. Russian-Slovak Dictionary. Bratislava, 1945.
Z. GAŠPARÍKOVÁ, A. KAMIŠ. Slovak-Czech Dictionary. Prague, 1967.
V. ŠEDIVÝ. Small differential Czech-Slovak Dictionary. Prague, 1937.
P. TVRDÝ. Slovenský frazeologický slovník. 2nd edition. Prague, 1933.
M. KÁLAL. Slovenský slovník z literatúry aj nárečí (Slovak literary and dialect dictionary). Banská Bystrica, 1924.
Š. PECIAR, and others. Slovník slovenského jazyka. 6 vols. Bratislava, 1959-1965.
Á. KRÁĽ. Príručný slovník slovenskej výslovnosti, Bratislava, 1979.

POLISH

M. Z. BROOKS. A Polish Reference Grammar. The Hague-Paris, 1975.
M. PATKANIOWSKA. Essentials of Polish Grammar for English-speaking Students. Glasgow, 1944.
M. CORBRIDGE-PATKANIOWSKA. Teach Yourself Polish. London, 1948.
J. A. TESLAR. A New Polish Grammar. 4th edition. Edinburgh and London, 1944.
A. M. SCHENKER. Beginning Polish. Vol. 1. New Haven, London, 1966.

BIBLIOGRAPHY

Z. M. AREND-CHOIŃSKI. A Polish Phonetic Reader. London, 1924.
A. MEILLET, H. de WILLMAN-GRABOWSKA. Grammaire de la langue polonaise. Paris, 1921.
H. GRAPPIN. Grammaire de la langue polonaise. Paris, 1942. 2nd edition. Paris, 1949.
T. LEHR-SPLAWIŃSKI, R. KUBIŃSKI. Gramatyka języka polskiego. Kraków, 1946.
S. SZOBER. Gramatyka języka polskiego, I. 3rd edition. Warszawa, 1931.
H. GAERTNER. Gramatyka współczesnego języka polskiego. 1931.
W. DOROSZEWSKI. Podstawy gramatyki polskiej. Pt. I. Warszawa, 1963.
———. Pisownia polska, XII. Wroclaw, 1957.
S. SŁOŃSKI. Historja języka polskiego w zarysie. Lwów-Warszawa, 1934.
J. ŁOŚ. Krótka gramatyka historyczna języka polskiego. 1927.
T. LEHR-SPŁAWIŃSKI. Język polski. Warszawa, 1947.
J. ŁOŚ. Gramatyka polska. 3 vols. Lwów, 1922, 1925, 1927.
Z. KLEMENSIEWICZ, T. LEHR-SPŁAWIŃSKI, S. URBAŃCZYK. Gramatyka historyczna języka polskiego. Warszawa, 1955.

Dictionaries

J. STANISŁAWSKI, W. JASSEM. English-Polish Dictionary. 2 vols. Warsaw, 1975.
K. BULAS, L. L. THOMAS, F. J. WHITFIELD. Polish-English Dictionary. The Hague, 1961.
K. BULAS, F. J. WHITFIELD. English-Polish Dictionary. The Hague, 1959.
J. STANISLAWSKI. English-Polish Dictionary. Warsaw, 1964.
T. GRZEBIENOWSKI. English-Polish, Polish-English Dictionary. Warsaw, 1958.
J. STANISŁAWSKI. Polish-English, English-Polish Dictionary. London, 1940.
W. KIERST. Polish-English, English-Polish Dictionary. Warsaw, 1926.
*A. ZIPPER, E. URICH. Polish-German, German-Polish Dictionary. Langenscheidt, Berlin, 1921.
*R. STYPUŁA, G. KOWALOWA. Polish-Russian Dictionary. Moscow-Warsaw, 1975.
D. HESSEN, R. STYPUŁA. Polish-Russian Dictionary. Moscow-Warsaw, 1967.

*With references to grammatical tables.

BIBLIOGRAPHY

N. I. GREKOW, M. F. ROZWADOWSKA. Polish-Russian Dictionary. Warsaw, 1950.
И. Х. ДВОРЕЦКИЙ. Russian-Polish Dictionary. Moscow, 1953.
M. РОЗВАДОВСКА, Б. Г. МАРХЛЕВСКА. Polish-Russian Dictionary. Moscow, 1941.
В. ЧЕРНОБАЕВ. Russian-Polish Dictionary. Moscow, 1941.
Ю. КРАСНЫЙ. Polish-Russian Dictionary. Moscow, 1931.
Ю. КРАСНЫЙ. Russian-Polish Dictionary. Moscow, 1933.
A. OBRĘBSKA-JABŁOŃSKA, M. BIRYŁA. Polish-Byelorussian Dictionary. Warsaw, 1962.
M. ARCT. Słownik ilustrowany języka polskiego. 1st edition. Warsaw, 1916; 3rd edition. Warsaw, 1929.
M. ARCT. Słownik ortograficzny języka polskiego. 6th edition. 1936.
S. JODŁOWSKI, W. TASZYCKI. Słownik ortograficzny i prawidła pisowni polskiej. Wrocław, 1954.
S. SKORUPKA, H. AUDERSKA, Z. ŁEMPICKA. Mały słownik języka polskiego. Warsaw, 1974.
W. DOROSZEWSKI, H. KURKOWSKA. Słownik poprawnej polszczyzny. Warsaw, 1973.
ed. T. LEHR-SPŁAWIŃSKI. Słownik języka polskiego. A-K. Warsaw, 1948.
S. SZOBER. Słownik poprawnej polszczyzny. Warsaw, 1948.
A. BRÜCKNER. Słownik etymologiczny języka polskiego. Warsaw, 1927.
A. LABUDA. Słowniczek kaszubski. (Small Kashubian-Polish Dictionary.) Warsaw, 1960.

LUSATIAN

М. И. ЕРМАКОВА. Очерк грамматики верхнелужицкого литературного языка. Москва, 1973.
H. ŠEWC. Gramatika hornjoserbskeje rěče. Budyšin, 1968.
P. ŠOLTA, H. PETRIK, H. JENČ, I. ŠĚRAKOWA. Gramatiske tabele hornjoserbsce. Budyšin, 1974.
V. MOHELSKÝ. Mluvnice hornolužické srbštiny a slovník hornosrbsko-český. (Vocabulary, pp. 103-233). Olomouc, 1948.
J. PÁTA. Krátká příručka hornolužické srbštiny. Praha, 1920.
J. WJELA. Lehrgang der sorbischen Sprache. Bautzen, 1949.
P. WOWČERK. Kurzgefasste obersorbische Grammatik. Leipzig, 1951.
J. KRAL. Grammatik der wendischen Sprache in der Oberlausitz. 3rd edition, 1925.

BIBLIOGRAPHY

P. VÖLKEL. Hornjoserbska ortografija a interpunkcija prawidła. Budyšin, 1974.
P. JANAŠ. Niedersorbische Grammatik. Budyšin, 1976.
H. NOWAK. Powědamy dolnoserbski. Budyšin, 1976.
B. ŠWELA. Grammatik der niedersorbischen Sprache. Bautzen, 1952.
G. SCHWELA (ŠWELA). Lehrbuch der niederwendischen Sprache. Vol. I. Heidelberg, 1906; Vol. II. Cottbus, 1911.
E. MUCKE (MUKA). Historische und vergleichende Laut- und Formenlehre der niedersorbischen (niederlausitzisch-wendischen) Sprache. Leipzig, 1892.
B. ŠWELA. Vergleichende Grammatik der ober- u. niedersorbischen Sprache. 1926.
B. ŠWELA. Dolnoserbski prawopis. 1903.
J. PÁTA. Serbska čitanka (Upper Lusatian and a few Lower Lusatian texts). Praha, 1920.

Dictionaries

P. VÖLKEL. Upper Lusatian-German Dictionary. Budyšin, 1970.
K. PANIG, P. WOWČERK. Upper Lusatian-German, German-Upper Lusatian Dictionary. Budyšin, 1966.
K. К. ТРОФИМОВИЧ. Upper Lusatian-Russian Dictionary. Moscow-Budyšin, 1974.
H. ZEMAN. Upper Lusatian-Polish Dictionary. Warsaw, 1967.
*F. JAKUBAŠ. Upper Lusatian-German Dictionary. Budyšin (Bautzen), 1954.
A. MITAŠ. Upper Lusatian-German Dictionary. Budyšin, 1952.
A. MITAŠ. German-Upper Lusatian Dictionary. Bautzen, 1953.
J. PÁTA. Kapesní slovník lužicko-česko-jihoslovanský a česko-lužický (Upper Lusatian-Czech-Serbocroätian and Czech-Upper Lusatian pocket dictionary). Prague, 1921.
K. B. PFUL. Łužiski serbski słownik (Lusatian Dictionary). 1866.
F. RĚZAK. Němsko-serbski wšowědny słownik hornjołužiskeje rěče (German-Upper Lusatian dictionary). 1920.
J. KRAL. Serbsko-němski słownik hornjo-łužiskeje rěče (Upper Lusatian-German dictionary). 1927.
B. ŠWJELA. Lower Lusatian-German Dictionary. Budyšin, 1963.
B. ŠWJELA, A. MITAŠ. German-Lower Lusatian Dictionary. Bautzen, 1953.

*With references to grammatical tables.

A. MUKA. Słownik dolnoserbskeje rěcy a jeje narěcow
   (A dictionary of Lower Lusatian and its dialects).
   I-III, 1911-1928.

THE SLAVONIC GROUP

W. J. ENTWISTLE, W. A. MORISON. Russian and the Slavonic Languages. London, 1964.
A. MEILLET. Le slave commun. 2nd edition. Paris, 1934.
A. VAILLANT. Grammaire comparée des langues slaves, I. Lyon, vol. I, 1950; vol. II, 1958; vol. III, 1966.
W. VONDRÁK. Vergleichende slavische Grammatik. 2 vols. Göttingen, 1924, 1928.
V. HRUBÝ. Vergleichende Grammatik der slavischen Sprachen. Hartleben, Vienna-Leipzig. Sketchy and out of date.
А. М. СЕЛИЩЕВ. Славянское языкознание, I: Западнославянские языки. Москва, 1941.
Н. КОНДРАШОВ. Славянские языки. Москва, 1956.
С. Б. БЕРНШТЕЙН. Очерк сравнительной грамматики славянских языков. Москва, 1961.
K. HORÁLEK. Úvod do studia slovanských jazyků. Praha, 1962.
T. LEHR-SPŁAWIŃSKI, W. KURASZKIEWICZ, F. SŁAWSKI. Przeglad i charakterystyka języków slowiańskich. Warszawa, 1954.
ed. W. WEINGART. Slovanské spisovné jazyky v době přítomné. Praha, 1937.
R. NAHTIGAL. Slovanski jeziki, I. Ljubljana, 1952.
O. BROCH. Slavische Phonetik. Heidelberg, 1911.
ed. T. LEHR-SPŁAWIŃSKI. Chrestomatia slowiańska. I (South Slav). Kraków, 1949; II (West Slav). Kraków, 1950.
E. BERNEKER. Slavische Chrestomathie. Trübner, Strasburg, 1902.
E. BERNEKER. Slavisches etymologisches Wörterbuch (to "morǔ" only). Heidelberg, 1908-1914.
F. MIKLOSICH. Dictionnaire abrégé de six langues slaves. 1885. Reprinted.

   The attention of students is also drawn to the articles on the Slavonic languages in the various encyclopedias and, for samples of the spoken language, to the various series of records available in Great Britain and elsewhere.

SECTION 1. CZECH

INTRODUCTION

It is only too little realized in Western Europe how ancient Czech culture is and how powerful and prosperous the Kingdom of Bohemia was in the Middle Ages. It is to those ancient sources of inspiration that the Czechs looked back at the time of the great National Revival at the beginning of the nineteenth century; and it is partly they that explain the maturity and balance of Czech culture as it exists to-day. The Czechs, who are among the most loyal Slavs and often the most conscious of their kinship with other Slavs, are yet at the same time deeply connected, spiritually and culturally, with Western Europe. Their culture forms an ideal synthesis of East and West. Let the incredulous go to Bohemia and Moravia and see for themselves. Dvořák's opera *Rusalka* is a perfect example: an essentially Slavonic legend, with a Slav atmosphere of mystery and longing, set to Dvořák's rich, melodious music, Slav in spirit, if you will, but western in technique and harmony.

From very early times the Czechs came under western influence. Their proudest and earliest memories, it is true, are of the mission of SS. Cyril and Methodius, who came from Salonika to convert them to Eastern Christianity. The Legend of St. Václav and the "Kiev Leaves", as well as the ancient hymn "Lord, have mercy on us" all bear witness to the Slavonic nature of their early culture and even show traces of the Czech language in their Old Slavonic texts. But in the eleventh century the Roman Church was already in the ascendant in Bohemia, and with the growth of its strength Latin came to be used more and more as the language of literature and culture, and Latin (and also German) words crept into the Czech language, e.g. kostel (<Lat. castellum) = church. Till the thirteenth century Czech words appear only as glosses in Latin texts. With the gradual growth of Czech political power, more favourable conditions were created for the formation of a Czech literary language. The Hymn to St. Václav, one of the earliest examples, dates from the thirteenth century. The "Chronicle of Dalimil", the "Alexandreis" and the "Legend of St. Catherine" are some of the outstanding examples from the fourteenth century.

It was at this period that the Czech vowel sounds began to change (the so-called "česká přehláska" = the Czech vowel mutation); and these

changes finally differentiated Czech from all other
Slavonic languages, even from Slovak, which is so
closely akin. (See "Features Characteristic of Czech
only".) But such archaic features as the Dual number
and the use of the Aorist and Imperfect tenses and
participial clauses still survived. The spelling at
this period was composite, like that of Polish at the
present day, e.g. *cz* for *č*, *sz* for *š*, etc.

The reign of Charles IV (1346-1378) was the
zenith of the first period of Czech culture, with the
foundation by him of Prague University and the monarch's favour for the Czech language. It is the literature of this period which makes Czech the most
ancient Slavonic literature and the greatest of the
period. The Czech beacon illuminated the surrounding
lands. The influence of Czech culture extended to
Slovakia, Poland, and elsewhere. The writings of
Ondřej z Dubé on law and of Tomáš ze Štítného on
philosophy and religion as well as the delightful
satires from this period bear witness to the eminence
it reached.

The great religious reformer and martyr, Master
Jan Hus (1369-1415), ushers in the second period of
Czech literature. He introduced the living language
of Prague as the literary language, purging it of
archaisms and foreign, especially German, loan-words.
He also introduced the modern "phonetic" spelling,
using one letter per sound, and originally writing
(a dot) over letters representing sounds not existing
in Latin, such as $\dot{s}$ (= *š*), $\dot{z}$ (= *ž*) (cf. modern Polish
ż), and distinguishing the long and short vowels. He
published his teaching in *De orthographia bohemica*
probably in 1406. No less important were his purely
literary and religious writings.

Later Petr Chelčický (*c*. 1390-1460) and the
first founders of the Moravian Brethren (Jednota
bratrská) wrote many religious and philosophical
works in Czech (Tolstoy considered Chelčický as his
predecessor), and also made a new translation of the
Bible (the Kralice Bible, 1579-93). Jan Blahoslav,
who published his *Deklarace* or Elucidation of Czech
Grammar in 1571, was one of the most eminent of the
Brethren from the linguistic point of view.

The first printed book in Czech— the *Kronika
trojanská*— came from the Catholic press at Plzeň in
1468. The first scientific dictionary of Czech, the
Lexicon symphonium, appeared in 1537, from the pen of
one of the Czech humanists, Zikmund Hrubý z Jelení.

By the sixteenth century the Aorist and Imperfect tenses had already disappeared from use, also
the Dual number in verbs, and declensions and

conjugations then took on their present form. The
Czech vowel mutation (přehláska) had also advanced to
its second stage, and was thus completed, e.g. Bóh,
having become Buoh, finally became Bůh, so also
súd > saud > soud. In 1603 a Slovak, Vavrinec
Benedikt Nudožerský, published a complete grammar of
Czech.

The final defeat of the Czech patriots at the
Battle of the White Mountain in 1620 ushered in the
darkest period for Czech literature, a period of decay
and stagnation which very nearly saw the final eclipse
of the Czech language under the zealous persecution
of the Counter-Reformation. Bohemia's most eminent
scholars, such as Jan Amos Komenský (Comenius, 1592-
1670), the great Protestant educationalist, had to
flee from their native land. Komenský lived for a
time in Poland and Sweden and was even invited to
England. In the Czech homeland the period of baroque
saw the growth of poetry under Romance influence from
the pens of Catholic writers, such as F. Bridel and
A. V. Michna; and from this period date many Czech
folksongs, noted also for the beauty and purity of
their language. But few educated people could pro-
duce pure Czech in those times, as the grammars of
Václav Rosa (1672) and Jan Václav Pohl (1756) show.
After 1774 German, instead of Latin, became the language in schools in Bohemia and the other Czech
lands.

But the persecution of the Czech language, together with intensified centralization in the Austro-
Hungarian Empire, in the age of rationalism and en-
lightenment at the end of the eighteenth century,
brought about a powerful and healthy reaction among
the Czechs, which was to bring with it complete
national revival. The inaugurator of the new period
(from about 1780) was Josef Dobrovský (1753-1829)
who, in 1809, brought out his *Ausführliches
Lehrgebäude der böhmischen Sprache*. In this work he
held up as models both the ancient Czech writings of
the late Middle Ages and the language of folk songs
and tales; he also laid down certain laws of Czech
grammar and orthography (such as the correct uses of
i and *y*). He tried to abolish the use of new words
as well as of German words in Czech, preferring to
revive old Czech words or borrow from other Slavonic
languages. Josef Jungmann and Antonín Marek, his
disciples, introduced such words as *pud* (= instinct),
rozlehlý (= extensive), and borrowed from Russian:
vzduch (Russ. воздух = air), *příroda* (Russ. природа
= nature), *nudný* (Russ. нудный = boring), etc. Naturally these various reforms met with resistance and

criticism; but it can safely be said that Josef
Jungmann's brilliant translation of Milton's *Paradise
Lost* laid the foundations of future Czech poetry.
Dobrovský wrote in German, as did many other patriot-
ic Czech noblemen in the early stages of the national
revival, when Czech was less widely known and perfected and efforts were being made to revive it as a
literary language. In fact "Němčina se
vybíjela němčinou" (= German was used to drive out
German).

A little later the (Slovak) reformer and scholar,
P. J. Šafárik, introduced further reforms, e.g. the
use of *j* instead of *g*, *í* for *j* (e.g. *její* for *gegj* =
her), *ej* for *ey*. In 1849 *v* was substituted for *w*,
ou for *au*.

Jungmann's big Czech-German dictionary, which
was to become the foundation of modern Czech lexi-
cography, came out in the years 1835-39. Jan
Gebauer's *Historical Grammar of Czech* (1894) and his
concise grammar of Czech finally stabilized the modern Czech literary language.

On these linguistic foundations, throughout the
nineteenth century there was growing up a literature
of no mean interest to the outside world. One cannot
overlook such writers as F. Palacký (1798-1876), the
historian of his people, or the collectors of its
folk literature, F. L. Čelakovský (1799-1852) and
K. J. Erben (1811-1870). Jan Kollár (1793-1852), a
Slovak who wrote poetry in Czech, is the crystallizer
of the ideal of Slavonic brotherhood, but dimly felt
in previous ages. The short-lived but brilliant poet,
K. H. Mácha, in his *Máj* shows the summit of Byron's
influence in Bohemia. No less important is the publicist and satirist K. Havliček (1821-56). The later
part of the nineteenth century saw a remarkable
growth of poetry among the Czechs: Svatopluk Čech,
Jan Neruda, J. S. Machar, A. Sova, O. Březina, P.
Bezruč, V. Dyk and S. K. Neumann are only a few of
most brilliant stars in a resplendent firmament. The
remarkable genius of J. Vrchlický (1853-1912), translator from many languages as well as poet, is also a
figure of European stature. The foundation of the
National Theatre in Prague in 1883 gave a fresh in-
centive to the development of the Czech theatre: Dyk,
Neumann and the brothers Čapek have made among the
most notable contributions. Among the novelists,
Božena Němcová, K. Čapek-Chod and Karel Čapek are
only a few of the writers that should not go unmen-
tioned.

With such a tradition behind them, one can understand the pride and confidence in survival of the

Czechs even under the most bitter persecution under the "Protectorate" (1939-1945). It is now impossible for the Czech language to be relegated to the peasantry as was the case during the period of decline in the seventeenth and eighteenth centuries. The *rôle* of the country people as the preservers of the language during that period was of supreme importance. But during the periods of development and florescence it was the city of Prague, as the most powerful political and cultural centre, that played the leading part. From the time of Jan Hus onwards the dialect of the Prague region was used as the norm for literary Czech. Had the eastern (Moravian) dialects, which show a transition stage to Slovak, been chosen, it might not have been necessary to create a separate Slovak literary language. As it is, modern Czech is among the most distinctive of all the Slavonic languages, quite difficult for other Slavs to understand when spoken (unlike Slovak which has not undergone the Czech vowel mutation mentioned earlier). Modern Czech is a virile, forceful language, often sounding abrupt and ironical in its wit. It is a carefully tended garden, which has attained a high degree of development through assiduous work during many centuries and is a true reflection of the conscientious and hardworking and at the same time deeply idealistic character of the Czech people, good Slavs and also good Europeans.

THE CZECH ALPHABET

Czech.		*Approximate English equivalent.*
A	a(short)	*u* in S. English "but" or *a* in in N. English "man"
	á(long)	*a* in "father"
B	b	*b*
C	c	*ts* pronounced together, as in "bits"
Č	č	*ch* in "church" (hard)
D	d	*d* (dental)
D'	d'	*d* in (S. English) "dew"
E	e(short)	*e* in "met"
(É)	é(long)	[1]*e* in "there"
	ě(short)	*ye* in "yes"
F	f	*f* (mostly in words of foreign origin)
G	g	*g* in "go" (only in words of foreign origin)
H	h	[2]voiced *h*
Ch	ch	*ch* in "loch"

Czech.		Approximate English equivalent.
I	i(short)	³*i* in "it", *i* in Fr. "vif"
	í(long)	³*ee* in "meet", *i* in "machine"
J	j	*y* in both "yes" and "boy"
K	k	*k*
L	l	⁴*l* (medium) in "last"
M	m	⁴*m*
N	n	*n* (alveolar)
Ň	ň	*n* in (S. English) "new" (rare initially)
O	o(short)	*o* as in "for"
(Ó)	ó(long)	*oo* in "door"
P	p	*p* (unaspirated)
R	r	⁴*r* (rolled)
Ř	ř	*r* and *š* (Eng. *sh*; ʃ) or *ž*, (*s* in "pleasure", ʒ) pronounced simultaneously
S	s	*s* in "see"
Š	š	*sh*
T	t	*t* (dental)
T'	t'	*t* in (S. English) "tune"
U	u	*u* in "put"
Ú	ú	*oo* in "boot" (occurs initially)
	ů	*oo* in "boot" (occurs medially and finally)
V	v	*v*
(Y)	y(short)	³*i* in "bit", *i* in "Fr. "vif"
	ý(long)	³*ee* in "meet", *i* in "machine"
Z	z	*z*
Ž	ž	*zh*, *s* in "pleasure"

Q, W and X appear only in foreign words.

( ): letters with capital in brackets occur initially only in a few words of foreign origin.

dž is a digraph representing the single sound of English *j* (phon. ʤ). It occurs mainly in words of foreign origin, e.g. džungle (= jungle).

Slovak letters not occurring in Czech are ä, ĺ, Ľ', ľ, Ô, ô, ŕ.

Polish letters not occurring in Czech are ą, Ć, ć, ę, Ł, ł, ń (in this form), Ś, ś, Ź, ź and Ż, ż (in this form). Polish *w* = Czech *v*. Ó ó which sounds *u* (like *oo* in "boot", but shorter) in Polish, has a different sound in Czech.

Lusatian letters not in Czech are:—Upper: Ć, ć, Dź, dź, Ł, ł, ń, W, w; Lower: also ś, ź.

Croätian letters not in Czech are: Ć, ć, Đ, đ.

[1] Colloquially long *é* is often narrowed to sound like *é* in French "été", or even further to an *i* sound: so také (= also) sounds *taky*.

[2] The Czech (and Slovak) sound of *h*, like an English *h*, but *voiced* (cf. English "inhale"), is peculiar to these two languages and Lusatian, being less fricative than the г of Byelorussian and the South Great Russian dialects. Phon. ɦ.

[3] Short *i* and short *y* are pronounced identically in Czech, the only difference being that short *i* causes preceding dentals (*t, d* and *n*) to be pronounced palatalized, i.e. like Czech t', d' and ň, *without* this being indicated by any special diacritic sign or accent. Thus ty (= thou) is pronounced tɪ, but ti (= to thee) is pronounced t'ɪ, phon. cɪ. Similarly long *í* and long *ý* are pronounced identically, only *í* causes the palatalization of preceding dentals.

Colloquially there is a tendency to shorten long *í*, as in balík (= parcel).

[4] *l*, *r* and occasionally *m* can also be vocalic, i.e. form a syllable without any other vowel (cf. *r* in Serbocroätian and Slovenian, and *l* and *r* in Slovak). In Czech they occur only short (also finally!), e.g.: prst (= finger), obr (= giant), vlk (= wolf), padl (= he fell), osm (= eight, colloquially: *osum*).

PRONUNCIATION

The *Accent* in Czech is a purely stress accent which always occurs on the *first* syllable of a word *or word group*, e.g. Československo (= Czechoslovakia) is stressed on the first syllable. (There is a secondary stress on the third syllable.) But the group "do Československa" (= to Czechoslovakia) is stressed on the "do" in correct speech. (In colloquial speech one can notice a tendency to ignore this rule—which applies to monosyllabic prepositions, except dle (= according to), skrz (= through), and stran (= concerning), and to the negative ne, preceding the words they govern—especially when the prepositions occur before long words.)

The spelling of Czech, both of vowels and of consonants, is on the whole "phonetic" and consistent, if one bears in mind certain rules, explained below. Consonants, on the whole, follow a "historical" spelling, as in other Slavonic languages except Serbocroätian.

The Vowels.

As can be seen from the table of the alphabet above, all vowels in Czech, except ě, can be both long, marked with an acute accent, and short (written without accent). This occurs quite independently of the (always initial) stress accent (which is not marked). The unstressed long vowels are at first difficult to imitate for the foreign learner. For example, in a name like Dvořák, the *o* is stressed, but the unstressed *á* is nevertheless quite long; it is pronounced, approximately in English spelling— Dvòrzhāh̀k. The name Smetana, on the other hand, has no acute accents and consists, therefore, of three short syllables, the first of which is stressed. (There is no modification of unstressed vowels, such as occurs in Russian or English.)

Ě, ě, which represents both a former ѣ (ě) and a former ѧ (ę) when short, as in—

svět = world, O.S. свѣтъ
pět = five, O.S. пѧть

has no long counterpart phonetically. (ѣ is represented in Czech by *í* when long; e.g.:—

svítiti = to shine;

and ѧ when long develops in Czech into á:—

pátý = fifth.)

Ů, ů represents the Czech development of a long *o*, e.g.:—

dům < duom < dóm = house

A real long *ó* occurs in Czech only in words of foreign origin, e.g.:—

óda = ode
móda = fashion

The spellings with *i* on the one hand and *y* on the other (and, when long, *í* as opposed to *ý*) represent and preserve an historical difference of origin, the *i* going back to C.S. *i* (O.S. и), and the *y* going back to C.S. *y* (O.S. ъі). As explained above, they are pronounced identically except that *i* and *í* cause palatalization of preceding dentals (only). *í* sounds especially close or narrow after the palatal consonants *t', d', ň*, and *j*. The consonants *h, ch, k* and *r* are never followed by *i* in Czech, but always by *y*. This preserves an old feature of the velars in Slavonic, now lost in Russian, Byelorussian, and Upper Lusatian (and in Polish and Lower Lusatian for *k* and *g*), cf. O.S. хъітръ (= clever, cunning), Russ. хитрый (= cunning), Cz. chytrý (= clever, cunning). *y* occurs after *c* only in foreign words, e.g. cynik (= cynic). After *z* it occurs only in three words: brzy (= soon), jazyk (= tongue, language), nazývati (= to call).

All the vowels can be preceded by *j*, except *ě, é, ů, ú*.

All the vowels can form diphthongs with *j* as the second element, then like *y* in English "boy" (phon. i̯), except *é*, *ó*, *ý*, e.g.:—

    kraj   = region
    háj   = grove
    dej!   = give!
    nesměj! = don't you dare!
    pij!   = drink
    října   = of October (Gen. sing. of říjen)
    kroj   = costume
    ujma   = loss
    můj   = my
    myj!   = wash!

Vowel sequences with *u* (phon. u̯) as the second element can occur with *a* and *e* in words of foreign origin only, e.g.: auto (= car), neutrální (= neutral).[1] On the other hand the diphthong *ou* is very typical of Czech (it occurs besides only in Slovak from among all the other Slavonic languages) and sounds very like English -*ow* in "show," phon. ou̯, e.g.: vedou mou milou (= they are leading my beloved).

Ě, ě is pronounced as a full *je* only after the labials *m, b, p, v, f*, e.g.: běda! (= alas), svět (= world). After *m*, it can also be pronounced ɲɛ, e.g.: město (= town) is pronounced either: mjɛsto or mɲɛsto. *Ě, ě* is also *written* after the dentals *t, d, n*; it then causes these to be pronounced palatalized, i.e. *t', d', ň* respectively, followed by *e* (phon. ɛ), e.g.: děti (= children), pron. dʲɛtʲi; tělo (= body), pron. tʲɛlo. *Ě, ě* is replaced by *e* after *l*, the *chuintantes č, š, ž* and the sibilants *c, s, z* which absorb the jot element, e.g.:—

              na dubě = on the oak
    but
              v lese   = in the wood
              v kostele = in the church

Vowel Correspondences

A. The long vowels *á, é, í, ú* often alternate with the short vowels *a, e, ě, o* respectively in the course of declension, e.g.:—

    brána = gate, Instr. sing. branou, Gen. plur. bran
    chléb = bread, Gen. sing.   chleba
    sníh = snow,   "   "   sněhu
    dům   = house,   "   "   domu
    mráz = front,   "   "   mrazu

[1] Phon. [ˈneʔutraːlɲiː].

and in conjugation, e.g.:—

míti = to have, Past (masc.) měl = (he) had

B. (Vowel mutation after palatal consonants: "česká přehláska").

Characteristic of Czech is the changing of certain vowels after the palatalized consonants ďʼ, ťʼ, ň, řʼ, and j and the formerly palatalized consonants, č, š, ž, and c. When these occur as the final consonant of a stem, the vowels—

$$a, á, ě, é, o, u, ou, ů, y$$

change to—

$$e, í, i, í, e, i, í, í, i \text{ or } e$$

The correspondences a/e, á/í, é/í, u/i, ou/í and ů/í are peculiar to Czech only. The other existed in Old Slavonic.

These changes affect the entire system of declensions and conjugations, differentiating "hard" stems from "soft" (and formerly soft) stems. (See "Morphology" below for full examples.) Such changes also occurred medially. We give below a few of the commonest types:—

a/e   žena = woman, but duše = soul
á/í   ženám (Dat. pl.) = to women, but duším = to souls; pátý = fifth, but žíti = to reap
ě/i   v městě = in the town, but na moři = at sea
é/í   dobrého (Gen. sg. masc. and neut of dobrý = good), but prvního (Gen. sg. masc. and neut of první = first)
o/e   město = town, but moře = sea
u/i   ženu (Acc. sg.) = woman, but duši = (Acc. sg.) = soul; jih = south; nesu = I carry, but píši = I write
ou/í   ženou (Instr. sg.), but duší (Instr. sg.). nesou = they carry, but kupují = they buy
ů/í   bratrům (Dat. pl.) = to the brothers, but mořím (Dat. pl.) = to the seas
y/i   stromy (Nom. pl.) = trees, but ptáci (Nom. pl.) = birds
y/e   (from ą) ženy = (Nom. pl.) = women, but ulice (Nom. pl.) = streets
       hady (Acc. pl.) = snakes, but muže (Acc. pl.) = men

A peculiarity of Czech only from among all the Slavonic languages is the glottal stop occurring initially in a word beginning with a vowel after another word whether it ends in a vowel or (even) a consonant. There is thus no liaison in Czech, in contrast to other Slavonic (and Romance) languages, e.g.:—

    ta ulice = this street, pron. taʔulitsɛ
    váš otec = your father,   "   vaːʃʔɔtɛts
    já a on = I and he,   "   jaː ʔa ʔɔn

This even causes preceding voiced consonants to be pronounced unvoiced, e.g.:

    v Americe = in America, is pronounced fʔamɛritsɛ

When *i* occurs before another vowel in a word, a *j* sound is inserted between them in pronunciation but not in spelling, e.g.:—

    Anglie = England, pron. 'aŋglijɛ,
    fialka = violet,   "   'fijalka.

The Consonants.

    The Czech consonants are of the usual Slavonic type with unaspirated plosives (*p*, *b*, *k*, *g*) and true dentals (*t*, *d*). *n* becomes ŋ before velars as in South Slav and other West Slav languages and in contrast to East Slav.

    The *chuintantes* č, š, ž are now hard in Czech. But in the declensions and conjugations[1] (see the Vowel Correspondences B above) they function as soft consonants and require the corresponding front vowels after them, like the truly palatalized consonants.[1]

    Final voiced consonants become unvoiced, as in all other Slavonic languages, except Serbocroätian and Ukrainian. Thus:—

    hrad = castle, is pronounced hrat
    dub = oak,   "   dup
    lev = lion,   "   lef
    muž = man,   "   muš
    mráz = frost,   "   mrás

    Final *h* is pronounced like Czech *ch* (phon. x), which is its regular unvoiced correspondent in Czech, though it is not its true counterpart phonetically. Thus:—

    Bůh = God, is pronounced bůch, phon. buːx

    Regressive assimilation is the rule in Czech for groups of consonants, the final one (unless it be ř,

---

[1] In the Present tense only a few verbs with stems ending in -š, -ž and -č can have alternative forms with soft mutated endings in the 1st person singular and the 3rd person plural: e.g. píšu and (literary) píši = I write; píšou and píší (lit.) = they write.

v or the always voiced consonants *l*, *r*, *m*, *n*, *ň*, and *j*) deciding whether a group is voiced or unvoiced. This rule also applies to prepositions when they consist of a single consonant or syllable. Thus:—

    hezký   = pretty,   is pronounced hezký
    dívka   = girl,   "   dífka
    vstal   = he got up,   (f)stal
    z Prahy = from Prague,   "   s Prahy
while—
    kde?   = where?,   "   gde
    léčba   = cure,   "   lédžba
    s Bohem = goodbye,   "   z Bohem
but—
    tvůj   = your(sg.),   "   tvůj (tvuːi̯)
    tlupa   = crowd,   "   tlupa
    srovnati= to compare,   "   srovnati
                                                  (with s)
    sněm   = parliament, "   sňem (sɲɛm)
    písně   = songs   "   písňe
                                                  ('piːsɲɛ)

In the case of *ř* assimilation is *progressive*, the *first* consonant deciding whether the group is voiced or unvoiced, e.g.:—

    středa = Wednesday, is pronounced with *ř* unvoiced
    při   = near,   "   "   "
    but—
    dříve = before(adv.), is pronounced with *ř* voiced
    břeh = shore,   "   "   "

    (By itself, of course, *ř* is voiced unless final, e.g.:—

    voiced in: řeč = speech, peřina = eiderdown, unvoiced in: keř = bush.)

The historical spelling of Czech is even more conservative than that in other Slavonic languages. Hence the omissions of consonants in pronunciation and the simplifications of consonantal groups are rather numerous. Not only are *t* and *d* omitted in the pronunciation of e.g.:—

                šťastný = happy
                prázdniny = holidays

but *t* is also dropped in the group *stk*, e.g.:—
                švestka   = plum

čtv is simplified to štv, e.g. in čtvrtek = Thursday
džb   "   "   žb, e.g. in džbán   = jug
dc   "   "   c, e.g. in dcera   = daughter

j is omitted in the pronunciation of:—

jméno = name
jsem = I am, but not in: nejsem = I am not
jdu   = I go, "   "   " nejdu = I do not go

v is dropped in the pronunciation of the groups *vz* or *vs* plus a further consonant, e.g.:—

        vzhůru = up
        vzpomněl = he remembered

Initial *h* is dropped in pronunciation before ř, e.g.:—

        hřeben = comb

z is dropped in pronunciation before *s* and š, e.g.:—

        rozsvítiti = to light
        rozšířiti = to widen

nb becomes *mb* by assimilation, e.g.:—

    honba = hunting, is pronounced homba

The groups *tš*, *dš* both become simplified in pronunciation to č, e.g.:—

        větší = bigger, is pronounced věčí
        mladší = younger,   "   mlačí

Similarly *ts*, *ds* both become simplified to *c*, e.g.:—

dětský = childish,   pron. děcký (phon. ɟɛtski:)
hradský = castle(adj.), "   hracký(phon. ɦratski:)

Czech on the whole avoids the pronunciation of double consonants, e.g.:—

cenný   = valuable, pronounced with single *n*
oddělení = department,   "   "   "   *d*

Only in the sense of "separating" could oddělení be pronounced with a double *d*, to emphasize the meaning of the prefix. Such examples are rare.

THE CZECH DIALECTS

Czech dialects fall into six groups:—

    (1) The Central dialect, with Prague as its centre;
    (2) The North-Eastern dialects, north-east of this area;
    (3) The South-Western dialects, south-west of the Central dialects and cut off by these from any common boundary with the North-Eastern dialects.

(These three groups make up the dialects of Bohemia proper);

(4) The transition group of Czecho-Moravian dialects;

(5) The Hanák dialects of Moravia, centred round Brno and Prostějov; and finally

(6) The Lach dialects of Silesia, which form a transition to Polish and remind one also of the Eastern Slovak dialects.

From the point of view of Slavonic literary languages, the most important group for Czech is the *Central* group, which forms the basis of modern literary Czech and whose phonetic characteristics are those of colloquial Czech in general and also features of Prague speech in particular. The most notable and characteristic features are:—

1. The pronunciation of $\acute{y}$, also of $\acute{\imath}$ after c, z, $ž$, and s, as ej, e.g.:—

    bejt for býti   = to be
    nožejk for nožík = small knife

2. $\acute{\imath}$ for original Czech $\acute{e}$, e.g.:—
dobrí (pivo) for dobré (Nom. sg. neut.) = good (beer)
píct for péci   = to bake

3. ou for original Czech $\acute{u}$, e.g.:—
    ouřad for úřad   = (state) office
    outerej for úterý = Tuesday

4. prothetic v before initial o (see "Slavonic Characteristics", No. 6), e.g.:—

    voheň for oheň = fire
    vona for ona = she

5. sh pronounced as sch, e.g.:—

shořel = it (masc.) was burnt, pronounced schořel.

6. Acc. plur. of masculine nouns like Nom. plur., e.g.:—

    viděl hoši = he saw the boys

7. $-ama$ frequently used as ending of Instr. plur. of nouns, e.g.:—

Instr. plur. chlapama from chlap = fellow, chap
   "   "   ženama from žena   = woman

8.* u for literary i in 1st pers. sing. Pres./Fut. of verbs with "soft" stem, e.g.:—

             píšu = I write

*These features are now acceptable alternative endings in literary Czech.

ou for literary *í* in 3rd pers. plur. Pres./Fut. of verbs with "soft" stem, e.g.:—

    píšou = they write

9. Loss of *í* in 3rd pers. plur. Pres./Fut., e.g.:—

    volaj for volají = they call
    umněj for umějí = they know how to

10.* Infinitive in -*t*, e.g.:—

    d'elat for dělati = to do

11. Loss of *l* after another consonant in the masc. sing. Past Participle Active, used as the 3rd pers. sg. masc. of the Past tense, as in colloquial Polish, e.g.:—

    upek for upekl = he baked
    dones for donesl = he brought

The *North-Eastern* dialects have certain features in common with Slovak, such as the pronunciation of *v* after a vowel and before another consonant, and also finally after a vowel, as *u̯*, e.g.:—

    prau̯da for pravda = truth
    kreu̯ for krev = blood

As in Slovak again, after labials *e* is pronounced and not *ě* in colloquial speech, e.g.:—

pet = five, literary pět   Co se smeješ?
mesto = town, literary město   = Why do you laugh?

Initial *j* is lost before *i*, *í*, e.g.:—

    istej for jistý = certain
    ídlo for jídlo = food

Perhaps the most striking feature not shared with Slovak is the reduction of the Dat./Loc sing. ending of masculine nouns from -*ovi* to -*oj*, e.g.:—

    bratroj for bratrovi = to the brother

cf. Dat. sing. of masculine nouns in Lusatian.

The *South-Western* dialects also have *i* and *í* for initial *ji*, *jí*, but -*ov* for the ending -*ovi*.

They do not have prothetic *v*, but occasionally a prothetic *h*, e.g.:—

    hucho for ucho = ear

---

*These features are now acceptable alternative endings in literary Czech.

Labials have a *j* before *i*, e.g.:—
> pjivo for pivo = beer

When two dentals meet, the first becomes *j* by dissimilation, e.g.:—
> bej zubú for bez zubů = without teeth
> poj domem " pod domem = under the house

Intervocalic *d* becomes *r*, e.g.:—
> d'erek for dědek = gran'pa

Long syllables in the Gen. plur. of nouns, e.g.:—
> ríb for ryb = fish

and Imperatives in -*ite* for -*ěte*, e.g.:—
> řekňite for řekněte = say!

remind one of Slovak.

The *Czecho-Moravian* dialects form a transition stage from the Czech dialects to the Hanák dialect of Moravia (and to Slovak). Here the Czech "přehláska" or vowel mutation is unknown, and šč is used for šť, e.g.:—
> ešče for ještě = still

Soft dentals are preserved before *e* in the Past Participle Passive and Infin., e.g.:—
> mláťenej for mlácen = threshed
> haďet for házeti = to throw

The *Hanák* dialects are notable specially for their peculiar vowels. They have *o*, *ó* for original Czech *u*, *ú*, e.g.:—
> bodo for budu = I shall be
> pijó " pijú (now pijí in literary Czech) = they drink

é is used for *ý*, *í*, and *ej*, e.g.:—
> dobré stréc for dobrý strýc = kind uncle
> prosém   " prosím   = please
> véce   " vejce   = egg, and

e is sometimes used for *i* and *y*, e.g.:—
> očetel for učitel = teacher
> rebe   " ryby   = fish (Nom. plur.)

Both *h* and *v* are used prothetically. The Czech vowel mutation is unknown. And šč is used for šť.
Short vowels in roots agree with Slovak, e.g.:—
> skala for skála = rock;

CZECH

and likewise the -*ite* ending for the Imperative, e.g.:—

>nepadnite! = mind you don't fall!

The *Lach* dialects are clearly a transition to Polish and have features in common with Eastern Slovak, although the latter and the Lach dialects are not geographically contiguous. Such common features are the absence of long vowels, the fixed stress accent on the penultimate syllable, *dz* for Czech *z* from *dj*, e.g.:—

>medzy for mezi = between, cf. Pol. między,

soft *chuintantes* *ś* and *ź* for soft *s and z*, e.g.:—

huś for hus = goose, cf. Pol. gęś
suśed " soused neighbour, " sąsiad
źima " zima = winter, " zima (pron. źima);

soft affricates *ć* and *dź* for *t'* and *d'* occurring also before all *e*'s of whatever origin, e.g.:—

vedźeće for vedete = you lead, cf. Pol. wiedziecie
budźe " bude = he will be, " będzie
vydać " vydati = to give out, " wydać;

n also is always palatalized before all *e*'s, e.g.:—

>ňe for ne = not, as in Slovak, cf. Pol. nie.

y is pronounced as in Polish, e.g.:—

>dobry for dobrý = good

l is either soft (*l'*), or hard (*ł* or *u̯*) as in Polish.

Instrumental singular of adjectives ends in -*ym*, e.g.:—

>dobrym

šč is used for *št'*, as in other Czech dialects, Slovak and Polish, e.g.:—

>ešče = still

A vowel is inserted with vocalic *ļ* and usually with vocalic *ŗ*

o replaces *a*, as in the neighbouring Polish dialects, e.g.:—

>vołom for volám = I call

The Czech "přehláska" is not known.
As in Slovak, C.S. *ę* becomes *a* and *ia*, e.g.:—

kuřa = chicken, for kuře, cf. Slovak kurča, Pol. kurczę
trpią = they suffer, for trpí, cf. Slovak trpia, Pol. cierpią

Animates have Acc. plur. = Gen. plur., e.g.:—

synuv = sons, cf. Cz. syny, Slk, synov,
Pol. synów

These features all point to the fact that the Lach dialects of Czech are very archaic. Being far from the centre where the later changes originated, they escaped their influence and preserved many old features such as are also preserved in Polish and Slovak to-day.

Finally, there is the dialect known as *moravská slovenština*, spoken in southern Moravia in the region known as Slovácko, a transition dialect to Slovak.

VOWEL GRADATION AND VOWEL LENGTHENING

Czech affords as numerous examples of these features as do other Slavonic languages.

Vowel gradation is seen in the groups of words, e.g.:—

smrt = death, umříti = to die; umru = I shall die; umořiti = to exhaust, to "do to death".

duch = spirit, duše = soul, dech = breath, dechnouti = to take a breath, zdechnouti = to expire—of an animal

beru = I take; bráti = to take (Impfve.) from *bьrati.

téci = flow; útok = attack; tekutina = liquid.

Vowel lengthening is exemplified in:—

umru (<u-mьr-) (Pfve.) = I shall die; umírati (Impfve.) = to die.

dechnouti (also dýchnouti) (Pfve.) = to take a breath; dýchati (Impfve.) = to breathe.

téci = to flow; utíkati = to flee.

choditi (Freq.) = to go; vycházeti (Impfve.) = to go out.

napojiti (Pfve.) = to give to drink, napájeti (Impfve.).

SLAVONIC CHARACTERISTICS

1. The Slavonic metathesis of liquids. Here Czech has the same forms as South Slav, but the differences in quantity usually to be observed between Czech and Serbocroätian are noteworthy:—

cf. Czech.: vrána = crow   Sbcr. врȁна = crow
    "   hrad = castle   "   грȃд = city
    "   hlava = head   "   глáва = head
    "   břeh = shore   "   брȇг = hill

cf. Czech.: bříza = birch   Sbcr. бре́за = birch
 "   mlíti = to grind   " мле́ти = to grind

however—

 "   mříti = to die   " мре́ти = to die
      mléko = milk   " мле́ко = milk

    2. The 1st Palatalization of velars is a regular feature in Czech, *k*, *h* (!—from old *g*), *ch* changing to *č*, *ž*, *š* respectively, e.g.:—

    peku = I bake; peče = he bakes
    člověk = person, human being; Voc. sing. člověče! = my good fellow!
    mohu = I can; může = he can
    Bůh = God; Voc. sing. Bože!
    duch = spirit; Voc. sing. (Svatý) Duše! = (Holy) Spirit!

    Czech, like Polish in certain cases, gives the appearance of replacing the old 2nd Palatalization with the 1st Palatalization in the case of *ch*; this is arrived at by the hardening of a soft *s* (*š*) and is to be found in the earliest written Czech, e.g.:—

    hoch = boy; Nom. plur. hoši
    Čech = a Czech; Nom. plur. Češi
    moucha = a fly; Dat./Loc. sing. mouše

c and *z* also change to *š* and *ž*, e.g.:—

    chlapec = boy; Voc. sing. chlapče!
    kněz = priest; Voc. sing. kněže!

    A special feature of Czech is the change of *sk* to *št'* and of *ck* to *čt'* before *i* and *ě*, e.g.:—

český = Czech (adj.), Nom. plur. masc. čeští
anglický = English (adj.), "   "   " angličtí
lesk = lustre; leštění = polishing

    3. The 2nd Palatalization of velars survives in Czech in the case of *k* and *h* (and *g* in foreign words), e.g.:—

    voják = soldier, Nom. plur. vojáci, Loc. plur. vojácích
    jazyk = tongue, Loc. sing. (na) jazyce
    péci = to bake, Pres. 1st pers. sing. peku; Imperative 2nd pers. sing. pec!
    vrah = murderer, Nom. plur. vrazi
    noha = leg, Dat./Loc. sing. noze

and notice:—

    Olga (name— from Russian), Dat./Loc. sing. Olze.

4. The influence of the *j*-element (*yotation*) on preceding consonants is seen in the following changes:—

k, *h*, *ch* before *j* change to *č*, *ž*, *š* respectively, as in other Slavonic languages, e.g.:—

plakati = to weep: 1st pers. sing. Pres. pláču[1] = I weep
lháti   = to tell lies; "   "   "   lžu[1]   = I tell lies
dýchati = to breathe,   "   "   "   dýšu[1] = I breathe

t before *j* changes to *c* (a peculiarity of West Slav), while

d before *j* changes to *z* (a peculiarity of Czech and Lusatian only), e.g.:—

platiti   = to pay; Past Participle Passive
              placen = paid
naroditi se = to be born (Pfve.); Past Part Pass.
              narozen = born

s and *z* before *j* change to *š* and *ž* respectively, as in other Slavonic languages, e.g.:—

prositi = to request; Past Participle
          Passive prošen
ukázati = to show (Pfve.); 1st pers. sing.
          Future ukážu

n before *j* is softened to *ň*, e.g.:—

raniti = to wound; Past Part. Pass. raněn
         (= raňen)

r before *j* becomes *ř*, a peculiarity of Czech, e.g.:—

orati = to plough; 1st pers. sing. Present oru

l before *j* is not affected and *j* is lost, e.g.:—

chváliti = to praise; Past Part. Pass. chválen

The labials *p*, *b*, *v* and *m* also do *not* change before *j*, a characteristic of West Slav:—
the *j* is preserved in:—
    země   = earth
    trpěti = to suffer; Past Part. Pass. trpěn
             phon. 'trpjɛn
but dropped in:—
líbiti se = to please; líbený = liked, Past Part. Pass.
                                (adjectival)
mluviti = to speak; mluven = spoken, Past Part. Pass.

st, *zd* before *j* change to *št*, *žd'* respectively, the latter a peculiarity of Czech only, e.g.:—

pustiti = to let go; Past Part. Pass. puštěn

---

[1] The literary language here prefers the ending *-i*, though it is not in colloquial Czech.

CZECH

jezditi = to be conveyed, travel; ježdění = travel

sk before *j* also changes to *šť*, a peculiarity of Czech and Slovak, e.g.:—

vráska = wrinkle, vraštiti = to wrinkle, Past Part. Pass. vraštěn

sl before *j* becomes *šl*, e.g.:—

poslati (Pfve.) = to send; 1st pers. sing. Future pošlu

mysliti = to think; Past Part. Pass. myšlen

5. Disappearance of consonants. Besides the dropping of consonants such as we find to be common to all the Slavonic languages, as in Czech sen (= sleep) (Indo-European root *sup-*), the conservative historical spelling of Czech in regard to consonants offers numerous examples of the lag of the orthography behind the developments in the pronunciation of certain consonant groups. Examples have already been given under "Pronunciation" at the end of the section on "The Consonants" (see pp. 44-45).

6. Epenthetic and prothetic consonants are frequent in Czech.

Besides *n(ň)*, as in—

on = he; Instr. sing. jím, but s ním = with him
sněm = parliament (<sejíti se = to assemble)
snídaní = breakfast

we have in Czech an epenthetic *t*, e.g.:—

středa = Wednesday, from sředa
stříbro = silver

A prothetic *v* before *o* is very common in colloquial Czech, e.g.:—

von for on = he
vokno " okno = window

Before both *o* and other vowels, in certain words, it is an accepted feature of the literary language, e.g.:—

vosa = wasp
vous = whisker
vejce = egg
varhany = (mus.) organ

CZECH

FEATURES CHARACTERISTIC OF CZECH ONLY

1. Glottal stop at the beginning of words which start with a vowel (see "Pronunciation"— at the end of "The Vowels").

2. ě (from ѣ and ѧ) pronounced *je* after labials and pronounced *e* after dentals, which latter then become palatalized, i.e. tě is pronounced *t'e*, etc. (see "Pronunciation"), e.g.:—

        svět = world,   O.S. свѣтъ
        pět = five,   O.S. пать
        tělo = body,   O.S. тѣло
        těžký = difficult, O.S. тажькъ

3. *ů* [= u:] < uo < ó, e.g.:—

        dům < dóm = house

4. C.S. *l* represented by a single, unvarying medium *l*.

5. *ř* from soft *r'* (рь) before the C.S. front vowels *e*, *i*, *ę* (ѧ), before *j* and finally (before C.S. ь), e.g.:—

bratr   = brother, Voc. sing. bratře,
                           Nom. plur. bratři
řad (O.S. рѧдъ) = row
moře (O.S. морѥ) = sea
tvář   = creature; face

6. Vowel mutation (přehláska) after soft and formerly soft consonants (see "Pronunciation"— Vowel Correspondences D), e.g.:—

duše (<dušě) < duša = soul   Cf. O.S. доуша
Dat. plur. duším (<dušiem)<dušám   " доушамъ
Acc. sing. duši (<dušiu) <dušu   " доушѫ
Instr.sing. duší (<dušiú) <dušú   " доушек
Dat. plur. mořím (<mořiém)<moróm = sea " морѥмъ
Gen. sing. prvního <prvnieho = first

These mutations, together with the development of long ѣ to *í* and ьje also to ꙇ, e.g.:—

        cf. O.S. вѣра   = faith, Czech víra
           O.S. знамениѥ = sign, Czech znamení

seem to point to a Czech predilection for the closed vowels *i*, *í*.

7. Narrowing of *aj* to *ej*, e.g.:—

   dělej! from dělaj = do!
   nej-   Superlative prefix, from naj-
   vejce   from vajce = egg

8. *ou* as one of the developments of C.S. ǫ (O.S. ѫ), e.g.:—

   soud = court of Justice, O.S. сѫдъ   cf. Slk. súd
   jsou = they are,   "   сѫтъ   "   sú
   nesou = they carry,   "   несѫтъ   "   " nesú

The other possible developments of ѫ are exemplified in:—

Cz. Acc.sing. ženu from žena = woman, O.S. женѫ
                                        Slk. ženu
 " Instr.sg. ženou "   " (with contraction)
                          O.S. женоѭ Slk. ženou
 " Acc.sing. duši " duše = soul(with "přehláska"),
                          O.S. доушѫ Slk. dušu
 " Instr.sg. duší "   "   (with "přehláska"
                                    and contraction),
                   O.S. доушеѭ   Slk. dušou
so also:—
Cz. maži(literary) = I smear, from mazati,
                     O.S. мажѫ   Slk. (mažem)
 " maží   "   = they smear, from mazati,
                     O.S. мажѫтъ Slk. mažú

9. *ě* and *í* as developments from C.S. ę (O.S. ѧ), e.g.:—

   pět = five, O.S. пѧть, cf. Slk. pät'
   prosí = they request, from prositi, O.S. просѧтъ
                                    cf. Slk. prosia

The other possible developments of ѧ are seen in:—

Cz. řad = row, also in Slk. rad, O.S. рѧдъ
 " pátý = fifth, cf. Slk. piaty, O.S. пѧтъ; also
                                   Cz. napjatý = tense
 " se(Reflexive Pronoun) =-self, cf. Slk. sa,
                                   O.S. сѧ
 " duše Gen. sg., Nom. (Voc.) Acc. pl. of duše =
                     soul, cf. Slk. duše O.S. доушѧ
 " hledati = to look for, cf. Slk. hl'adat',
                     O.S. глѧдати (= to look at)

10. The ending of neuter nouns -ьje, contracted to -í, e.g.:—

   znamení = sign

11. Development of ъ to ě and í, e.g.:—
   svět = world; svíce = candle

12. Infinitives of verbs of Class I with root ending in velars g, k, in Czech end in -ci, e.g.:—
   moci (<mogti) = to be able
   péci (<pekti) = to bake
   říci (<rekti) = to say

13. Czech has changed back an original ъ after a *chuintante* (ž, š, or č) — (now a in other Slavonic languages) — to e, in accordance with the general Czech vowel mutations (přehláska), e.g.:—
   O.S. бѣжати = to run, Cz. běžeti

14. Development of C.S. dj to z (also in Lusatian), e.g.:—
   mez = boundary, narozen = born
   cf. Upper Lusatian: mjeza

FEATURES CHARACTERISTIC OF CZECH TOGETHER WITH SLOVAK ONLY

1. Initial stress in words and word groups (see "Pronunciation").

2. Long vowels (marked ´) and short vowels (without written accent) occurring independently of stress.

3. C.S. g develops into h (voiced aspirate fricative h), phon. ɦ.

4. The diphthong ou from оѫ, pron. (phon.) o$\underset{\circ}{u}$, e.g.:—
   Cz. and Slk. Instr. sing. ženou from žena = woman.

5. y or ý representing C.S. y, O.S. ы, preserved as distinctive in spelling, though in pronunciation distinctive only after dentals (see "Pronunciation").

6. True soft t' and d' (without the sibilant element as in Russian, and without the affricate element as in Polish and Serbocroätian), phon. c and ɟ.

7. Double consonants not generally pronounced, though often preserved in spelling, e.g. Cz. and Slk. povinný (= due, obliged to), pron. 'pɔvɪni:.

8. Partial preservation of C.S. vocalic $\underset{\circ}{l}$ and $\underset{\circ}{r}$ (O.S. лъ, ль, ръ), written l, r (in Slovak sometimes also ĺ, ŕ). In Czech a vowel (u or ou) is added after l except when labials originally preceded soft l'. In Slovak this is rare. With original $\underset{\circ}{r}$, in Czech the vowel e develops before the r after č, št' and ž; in Slovak only after č, e.g.:—
   Cf. O.S. влькъ = wolf, Cz. vlk, Slk. vlk

but
Cf. O.S. плъкъ = host, Cz. pluk = regi- Slk. pluk
army, ment,
" льгъ = long, " dlouhý " dlhý
" пръстъ = finger," prst, " prst
but
" урънъ = black " černý " čierny
" жръдь = rod " žerd' " žrd'

C.S. rъ, rь develop normally into *re*, *ře* in Czech and into *ŗ* in Slovak, while C.S. lъ, lь develop into *le* or *ļ* in both languages:—

O.S. кръвь = blood, Cz. krev, Slk. krv (phon. kru̯)
" кръстъ = cross, " křest " krst =
 = chris- christening
 tening,
" плъть = flesh, " plet' = " plet' =
 complex- complexion
 ion
" сльза = tear, " slza, " slza
 " hltati = to " hltat'
 swallow,

FEATURES CHARACTERISTICS OF CZECH, SLOVAK, AND POLISH

1. Development of C.S. *tj* to *c*, e.g.:—
Cz. svíce = candle, Slk. svieca, Pol. świeca

2. *t, d* retained before final *l*, e.g.:—
Cz. padl = he fell (colloquially pron. pat!), Slk. padol (with fill-vowel!), Pol. padł.
Cz. pletl = he wove, Slk. pletol, Pol. plótł.

3. Metathesis of liquids (see Slavonic Characteristics, No. 1). N.B. In Polish the vowels are different in some instances from those in Czech and Slovak.

4. Original C.S. *kv* retained, while *gv* becomes (quite regularly) *hv* in Cz. and Slk.; Polish has *gw'*, e.g.:—

Cz květ = flower, Slk. kvet, Pol. kwiat
 hvězda = star, " hviezda, " gwiazda

5. Labial consonants +*j* do not insert *l*, as they do in South and East Slav. Czech has a hard consonant with or without *j*, Slovak has hard labials, Polish— soft, e.g.:—

Cz. postaven = built, Slk. postavený, Pol.
  postawiony = placed, built
Cz. země = earth, Slk. (zem) zemetrasenie =
  earthquake, Pol. ziemia.

6. Both C.S. ъ and ь develop into *e*. In Slovak other vowels (*o* and *a*) are also possible. Polish has *ie* (= *'e*) for ь; e.g.:—

    O.S. сънъ = sleep, Cz. sen = dream,
    "   пьсъ = dog,   "   pes,
    "   вѣньць = wreath, " věnec,
    "   овьсъ = oats, " oves,
    "   вънъ   = out,   " ven,
    "   ръжь   = rye,   (" žito),
                           " (dial.) rež

    Slk. sen,   Pol. sen
    "   pes,   "   pies
    "   veniec, "   wieniec
    "   ovos,   "   owies
    "   von,   "   —
    "   raž,   (" żyto),
        Russ. рожь, Sbcr. pâж

7. C.S. *kt, gt* + *i, j* or ь become *c*, e.g.:—

Cz. noc = night, Slk. noc, Pol. noc (cf. Latin Gen.
                             sing. noctis from nox).
" moc = power " moc " moc (root *mog-*)

8. In Czech *e* is always used as the fill-vowel. (In Slovak and Polish other vowels are also used as fill-vowels.) E.g.:—

O.S. огнь   = fire, Cz. oheň, Slk. oheň, Pol. ogień
 " блазнъ = error, " blázen = madman, Slk. blázon,
                        Pol. błazen = fool, buffoon
Cz. modliteb, Gen. pl. of modlitba = prayer, Slk.
                   modlitba, Gen. pl.
                   modlitieb, Pol. modlitwa,
                   Gen. pl. modlitew or modlitw.
 " svateb, Gen. pl. of svatba = marriage, Slk.
                   svadba, Gen. pl. svadieb
 " sester, " " " sestra = sister, Slk. sestra,
                   Gen. pl. sestier or sestár,
                   Pol. siostra, Gen. pl.
                   sióstr.
 " ve světě = in the world, Slk. vo svete. Pol. we
                   wrześniu = in September.
 " ve vodě = in the water, Slk. vo vode, Pol. w(e)
                   wodzie
 " ke mně = towards me, Slk. ku mne, (Pol. ku—
                   always)

CZECH

9. In common with other West Slav languages and Serbocr., Czech preserves C.S. initial *je*, e.g.:—

Cz. jeden = one, Slk. jeden, Pol. jeden Sbcr. jèдан
" jezero = lake, " jazero, " jezioro, " jèзeро

10. Vowel contractions are frequent in Czech, as in other Slavonic languages, e.g.:—

*moje Nom./Voc./Acc. sing. neut.(= my) contracts to—
   Cz. mé   Slk. moje   Pol. (moje or)me
*mojého Gen. sing. masc. and neut. contracts to—
   Cz. mého   Slk. môjho   Pol. (mojego or) mego
*moja(e) Nom. sing. fem. contracts to—
   Cz. má   Slk. moja   Pol. (moja or) ma
*mojej Gen. Dat. Loc. sing. fem. to—
   Cz. mé   Slk. mojej   Pol. mej
*mojǫ Acc. sing. fem. to—
   Cz. moji, mou Slk. moju   Pol. mą
*mojich Gen./Loc. plur. to—
   Cz. mých   Slk. mojich   Pol. mych
*pojas = belt, to— Cz. pás, Slk. pás, Pol. pas
*ženojǫ, Instr.sg. = woman— Cz. ženou, Slk. ženou,
                                               Pol. żoną
*dobraja = good, Nom.sg.fem.— Cz. dobrá, Slk. dobrá,
                                             Pol. dobra
*dobroje = good, Nom.Acc.sg.neut.— Cz. dobré,
                                Slk. dobré, Pol. dobre
*dobrajego = good, Gen.sg.masc. and neut.—
        Cz. dobrého, Slk. dobrého, Pol. dobrego
*maje = has,   Cz. má Slk. má   Pol. ma
*dělaje = he does, " dělá "   —   " działa = acts
*uměje = he knows " umí "(roz)umie, " umie
         how to,
*sějati = to sow,   " síti, " siat',   " siać
*žitьje = life,   " žití, " žitie,   " życie
       living,   (two syllables!)
*pisanьje =writing, " psaní," písanie, " pisanie
                                                    (three syllables!)

11. The hard pronunciation of the *chuintantes*, in Czech and Slovak spelt— *š*, *ž*, *č*, *dž*, in Polish spelt— *sz*, *ż*, *cz*, *dż*, and *rz*.

(In Polish the hardness is particularly noticeable, contrasting with the softness of the palatalized *chuintantes ś*, *ź*, *ć*, *dź*.)

All these *chuintantes* were originally soft— a fact reflected in the orthographical rules of these three languages.

12. Nom., Voc., Acc. sing. of neuter adjectives ends in -é (Pol. -e), e.g.:—

   Cz. dobré = good, Slk. dobré, Pol. dobre
   " bílé = white, " biele, " białe

CZECH MORPHOLOGY

THE DECLENSION OF NOUNS

Czech has nouns of three grammatical genders, like other Slavonic languages, and has two numbers, the Dual having only left traces in the declension of certain nouns. All seven cases exist as in Old Slavonic, the Vocative singular having special forms in most masculine and feminine nouns.

In the neut. nouns Nom. = Voc. = Acc. in both sing. and plur., but for fem. nouns this is true of the plural only. All masc. and neut. nouns have the ending -em in the Instr. sing. (<-ъмь in the old $\check{u}$-stems), a feature shared with Polish, but not with Slovak or Lusatian. Before the ending -ě in all genders (Loc. sing. and Dat. sing. fem.) preceding dentals are regularly softened, r becomes $\check{r}$, and velars undergo the 2nd Palatalization.

The six old declensions, as seen in Old Slavonic, are better preserved in Czech than in other modern Slavonic languages. The fem. i-stems have become subdivided, as in Slovak, into pure i-stems and mixed i/ja-stems. The Czech consonantal stems actually preserve a few examples of $masc.$ stems with $-n-$ and $-t-$, e.g.: kámen (= stone) and loket (= elbow); but these cannot be regarded as regular models for large numbers of other nouns. In the neut. consonantal stems the $-t-$ type is the only one that is really alive. The $-n-$ type, being felt to be archaic, is replaced by o-stems ending in $-eno$ in the Nom. sing. Even the old long $\check{u}$-stems have left a few examples in fem. nouns ending in $-ev$, e.g. církev (= church), Gen. sing. církve, a remarkable archaism![1] The short $\check{u}$-stems have left numerous traces in the endings of masc. o- and jo-stems; Gen. sing. $-u$, Dat. sing. $-ovi$, Instr. sing. $-em$, Nom. plur. animate $-ové$, Gen. plur. $-\mathring{u}$ (<$óv$), Dat. plur. $-\mathring{u}m$.

Masc. o-stems are divided into animate and inanimate. For the animate the Acc. $sing.$ only! = Gen. sing. and regularly has the ending $-a$. In the Dat. and Loc. sing. the ending $-ovi$ is preferred. In the plural masc. animates have $-ové$, $-é$ or $-i$ in the Nom., and $-y$ in the Acc., an ending shared with the masc.

[1] Also in Slovenian.

inanimate *o*-stems. The endings -*ů* for Gen., -*ům* for Dat., and -*y* for Instr. are also shared by both categories and also by the neut. *o*-stems (cf. Slovenian Instr. plur. -*i*). The Loc. plur. ending for animate *and* inanimate *o*-stems is -*ech* after hard consonants except after velars which have -*ích*. Before -*ích* the 2nd Palatalization of the velars takes place, as it does before the -*i* in the Nom. plural animate.

Inanimate masc. *o*-stems prefer -*u* for the Genitive *and* Dative sing., and have Acc. sing. like Nom. sing. The Loc. sing. ends in -*ě* or -*u*. Nom., Voc. and Acc. plur. end in -*y*.

Neuter *o*-stems and fem. -*a*-stems keep very closely to the Old Slavonic endings. The Instr. sing. ends in -*em* and -*ou* respectively. The Dat. plur. of the neut. *o*-stems ends in -*ům* and the Instr. plur. in -*y*, as in masc. *o*-stems.

The corresponding soft stems, *jo*-stems masc. and neut. and *ja*-stems fem., have transformed their endings according to the rules of the Czech vowel mutation (přehláska) and only tolerate the vowels -*e*, -*i* or -*í* in most endings. Animate masc. *jo*-stems can have -*ovi* in Dat. and Loc. sing.,-*ové* in the Nom. plur., cf. -*e* Nom. plur. inanimate; and -*e*, -*ů*, and -*ům* are regular for the Acc., Gen. and Dat. plur. respectively. Both fem. and neut. soft stems have Gen. plur. in -*í*, Dat. plur. -*ím*, Loc. plur. -*ích*. Neut. *jo*-stems with endings going back to -*bje* or -*ije* form a special declension in Czech, characterized by a final -*í* arrived at by contraction. This is the ending in all cases of the sing., except the Instrumental.

Masc. nouns in -*a* decline like fem. nouns in the sing. in all cases except the Dat. and Loc. and like masc. animate *o*-stems in the plur., as in Polish. Masc. *ja*-stems, ending in Czech in -*e*, decline throughout like masc. *jo*-stems.

Some masc. long monosyllabic nouns shorten the root vowel when an ending is added (see "Pronunciation—The Vowels", Vowel Correspondences A), e.g.: Bůh (= God), Gen. sing. Boha.

Fem. nouns with a long vowel in the root can shorten it in the Instr. sing. and the oblique cases of the plural, sometimes only in the Gen. plur., e.g.: práce (= work), Instr. sing. and Gen. plur. prací; Dat. plur. pracím, etc.; hůl (= stick), Gen., Dat., Loc., Voc. sing. holi; moucha (= fly), Gen. plur. much.

Neut. nouns can shorten the root vowel in the Gen. plur. and sometimes in other cases, e.g.: dílo

(= a work), Gen. plur. děl; léto (= summer), Gen. plur. let, Dat. plur. letům, etc., or létům, etc.

The fill-vowel -e- appears in the Gen. plur. of many fem. and neut. nouns, e.g.:—

        barva = colour, Gen. plur. barev
        okno = window, "   "   oken.

A "movable" -e- is used in the Nom. sing. (only) of masc. and fem. nouns, e.g.:—

    Čapek   — a name, Gen.sing. Čapka
    špaček   = starling, " " špačka
    vrabec   = sparrow, " " vrabce
    krev(fem.) = blood,   " " krve
    píseň   = song,   " " písně

For purposes of declension *d, t, n, k, h, ch,* and *r* are counted as hard, while *č, š, ž, d', t', ň, ř, c,* and *j* are considered soft. The labials *b, p, m, v* and the sibilants *s* and *z,* and *l* can be either hard or soft.

1. *i*-stems, feminine only. In Czech these are subdivided into (*a*) true *i*-stems and (*b*) mixed *i/ja* stems which form a transition to the soft *ja*-stems (see below).

       (*a*) kost = bone   (*b*) síň[1] = hall

	Sing.		Plur.	
Nom.	kost	síň[1]	kosti	síně
Gen.	kosti	síně	kostí	síní
Dat.	kosti	síni	kostem	síním
Acc.	kost	síň	kosti	síně
Instr.	kostí	síní	kostmi	síněmi
Loc.	kosti	síni	kostech	síních
Voc.	kosti	síni		

It is not always certain whether a feminine noun ending in a consonant belongs to type (*a*) or (*b*) above. Some, e.g. nemoc (= illness), can follow either. But nouns ending in -*st,* -*č* and -*š* follow (*a*) kost.

      Notice: lež = lie, Gen. sing. lži
              zeď' = wall,   "   " zdi
              čest = honour, "   " cti
              lest = ruse,   "   " lsti
              veš = louse, "   " vši

---

[1]This declension differs from the *ja*-stems in the Nom., Voc., and Acc. sing. only.

CZECH

2a. Consonant stems, masc. with -n- and -t- (rare) and neut. with -t-.

kámen = stone   loket = elbow

SING.
Masc.

Nom.	kámen	loket
Gen.	kamene	lokte or loktu
Dat.	kameni or kamenu	lokti or loktu
Acc.	kámen	loket
Instr.	kamenem	loktem
Loc.	kameni or kamenu or kameně	lokti or loktě or loktu
Voc.	kameni	lokti or loktu

PLUR.

Nom.	kameny	lokty
Gen.	kamenů	loktů
Dat.	kamenům	loktům
Acc.	kameny	lokty
Instr.	kameny	lokty
Loc.	kamenech	loktech

Den (= day) and its compound týden (= week) are really irregular masc. n-stems and are declined as follows:—

	SING		PLUR.	
Nom.	den	týden	dni or dny	týdny
Gen.	dne	týdne	dní or dnů	týdnů
Dat.	dni or dnu	týdni or týdnu	dnům	týdnům
Acc.	den	týden	dni or dny	týdny
Instr.	dnem	týdnem	dny	týdny
Loc.	dni or dnu (ve dne)	týdni or týdnu	dnech	týdnech
Voc.	dni	týdni		

kuře = chicken

Neut.

	SING.	PLUR.
Nom. Voc.	kuře	kuřata
Gen.	kuřete	kuřat
Dat.	kuřeti	kuřatům
Acc.	kuře	kuřata
Instr.	kuřetem	kuřaty
Loc.	kuřeti	kuřatech

The original C.S. endings are preserved in kuře (with the usual developments) except in the Loc. sing. and Dat. plur.

Notice the difference of joining vowel in the sing. as opposed to the plur. in the declension of kuře. Similarly, when -ě is final in the Nom. sing., e.g.: kotě (= kitten), Gen. sg. kotěte, Nom. pl. kot'ata. This declension consists mostly of the names of the young of human beings and animals, but contains some others, e.g.: děvče (= girl), prase (= pig— *not* pigling), koště (= broom); also the masculine hrabě (= count), and kníže (= prince). Dítě (= child) is regular in the sing., but in the plur. is feminine and declined like kost:— Nom. děti, Gen. dětí, Dat. dětem, Acc. děti, Instr. dětmi, Loc. dětech.

One of the original fem. -*r*- stems survives in Czech: máti (= mother), used in serious language. Otherwise it is replaced by: matka. Dcera (= daughter) replaces the old: dci, but has the old Dat./Loc. sing. dceři. To this declension also belongs: net' (= niece), Voc. sg. neti!

	SING.	PLUR.
Nom. Voc.	máti	mateře[1]
Gen.	mateře	mateří
Dat.	mateři	(mateřem or) mateřím
Acc.	máteř	mateře
Instr.	mateří	mateřemi
Loc.	mateři	(mateřech or) mateřích

2*b*. The remnants of the old long *ū*-declension are seen in fem. nouns ending in -*ev*, e.g.:—

církev = (the) church

	SING.	PLUR.
Nom.	církev	církve
Gen.	církve	církví
Dat.	církvi	církvím
Acc.	církev	církve
Instr.	církví	církvemi
Loc.	církvi	církvích
Voc.	církvi	

krev, Gen. sg. krve (= blood) belongs to this declension in Czech.

3. *a*-stems, mostly feminine.

Owing to the existence in Czech of the regular vowel mutations after soft consonants (přehláska), *a*-stems in Czech have a declension apparently quite distinct from that of *ja*-stems. *ja*-stems show the regular modern Czech mutations (e.g. *a>e*), as well as those known in Old Slavonic (ѣ>н).

The variations of length in the root vowel should be watched and learnt individually, as no rules on this can be given.

---

[1]The plural forms of máti are now considered archaic and are not used.

The regular palatalizations (the 2nd for velars) take place before the ending -ě in the Dat. and Loc. sing.

(See also the general remarks under "The Declension of Nouns").

a-stem: žena = woman   ja-stem: duše = soul

	SING.	PLUR.		
Nom.	žena	duše[1]	ženy	duše
Gen.	ženy	duše	žen	duší[1]
Dat.	ženě	duši	ženám	duším
Acc.	ženu	duši	ženy	duše
Instr.	ženou	duší	ženami	dušemi
Loc.	ženě	duši	ženách	duších
Voc.	ženo	duše		

ruka (= hand) and noha (= leg, foot), when used in the sense of the two hands or feet of a person, have a special plural which is actually the remnants of the old Dual: Nom./Acc. ruce, nohy; Gen./Loc rukou, nohou; Dat. rukám, nohám; Instr. rukama, nohama.

Nouns with ě in Nom. sing. replace e with ě throughout their declension, e.g.: země, Nom., Gen., Voc. sing. and Nom., Acc., Voc. plur. (= earth). This noun has Acc. sing. zem only after prepositions.

The ending -yně is now used for fem. nouns formerly in -yni; thus: hospodyně (= housekeeper), is declined like země and duše. Gen. pl. -yní or -yň.

dveře (plur. tantum, = door), has irregular Instr. plur. dveřmi.

Paní (= lady, Mrs.), is irregular and declines as follows: Sing. all cases paní; plur. Nom. Gen., Acc., Voc. paní; Dat. paním; Instr. paními; Loc. paních.

Notice: Čechy fem. plur. = Bohemia, plur. tantum declined like ženy, Gen. plur. Čech, etc. Předseda *masc.* = president, has Dat., Loc. sing. předsedovi, Nom. plur. předsedové, etc. (see p. 61.)

4a. o-stems, masculine. (See also "The Declension of Nouns" above.)

As in the a-stems, owing to the Czech vowel mutations the jo-stems give the appearance of having a declension quite different from that of the o-stems.

---

[1] Nouns in -ice have no ending in Gen. plur., e.g.: ulice (= street) Gen. pl. ulic. Nouns of the type mříže or mříž (fem.) = net, šíře or šíř = breadth, follow the declension either of duše or of sîň, according to the Nom. sing. used.

Furthermore both *o*- and *jo*-stems are also subdivided into an animate and an inanimate declension, which have distinctive endings in certain cases. We thus have four main types:—

Hard *o*-stems:
had = snake   hrad = castle

Soft *jo*-stems:
muž = husband   klíč = key

SING.

	Animate	*Inanimate*	*Animate*	*Inanimate*
Nom.	had	hrad	muž	klíč
Gen.	hada	hradu	muže	klíče
Dat.	hadu	hradu	muži	klíči
Acc.	hada	hrad	muže	klíč
Instr.	hadem	hradem	mužem	klíčem
Loc.	hadu	hradě	muži	klíči
Voc.	hade	hrade	muži	klíči

PLUR.

Nom.	hadi	hrady	muži	klíče
Gen.	hadů	hradů	mužů	klíčů
Dat.	hadům	hradům	mužům	klíčům
Acc.	hady	hrady	muže	klíče
Instr.	hady	hrady	muži	klíči
Loc.	hadech	hradech	mužích	klíčích

Nouns ending in *s*, *z* and *l* can belong either to the *o*- or the *jo*-stems, e.g.:—

	osel	= donkey,	Gen. sg.	osla
	čas	= time,	" "	času
	úhel	= angle	" "	úhlu
but—				
	přítel	= friend,	" "	přítele
	městys	= small town,	" "	městyse
	uhel	= piece of coal	" "	uhle

The Genitive Singular

All *jo*-stems have Gen. sing. in -*e*.

In the *o*-stems there is considerable inconsistency with some common words, despite the general rule that animates take -*a* and inanimates -*u*.

Only pátek (= Friday), of the days of the week, and listopad (= November), of the names of the months, have Gen. sing. in -u: pátku, listopadu.

Other common inanimate nouns of ancient origin with Gen. sing. in -*a* are:—

kostel	= church	Gen. sg.	kostela
dvůr	= court,	" "	dvora
večer	= evening,	" "	večera
svět	= world,	" "	světa
les	= wood,	" "	lesa
potok	= brook,	" "	potoka

```
chléb  = bread,   Gen. sg. chleba
oběd   = dinner,   "    "  oběda
život  = life,     "    "  života
rok    = year,     "    "  roka (but "in the year
                                    1948" = roku
                                    1948...)
mlýn   = mill,     "    "  mlýna
```

The Dative Singular

The ending *-ovi* is frequent with animate nouns, for which it is reserved. In a string of nouns in apposition it is used only with the last, e.g.: panu Václavu Novákovi (= to Mr. Wencelas Novák).

The Locative Singular

Czech (and Slovak) have transferred the Dative sing. ending *-ovi* also to the Loc. sing., as an alternative ending to *-u/i* for animate nouns, both hard and soft. Inanimate nouns have either *-ě* (*e*) (for hard only) or *-u/i*.

Many nouns with velar stems avoid the 2nd Palatalization and have the ending *-u*, e.g.:—

```
hřebík = nail,   Loc. sing. na (= on) hřebíku
sněh   = snow,     "    "   v (= in) sněhu
prach  = dust,     "    "   v prachu,
```

Some have either ending, e.g.:—

```
potok = brook,    "    "   v potoku or potoce
jazyk = tongue,   "    "   na jazyce or jazyku
```

The Vocative Singular

Hard stems have *-e* (which causes the *1st* Palatalization of velars).

Soft stems have *-i* (from *-ju*).

Some velar stems avoid the 1st Palatalization and take *-u*, e.g.:—

   člověk = person, Voc. sg. člověče!

but

   voják = soldier,   "   " vojáku!

r changes to *ř* only if preceded by another consonant (in contrast to the regular change *r>rz* in Polish), e.g.:—

   doktor = doctor, Voc. sg. doktore!

but

   bratr = brother,   "   " bratře!

Nominative (and Vocative) Plural

-i is the regular ending for animate *o-* and *jo-* stem nouns. Before it dentals are softened and velars undergo the 2nd Palatalization, but proper names, the names of some nationalities and a few other nouns

take -*ové*, e.g.:—

Josef	= Joseph,	Nom. plur.		Josefové
Rus	= Russian,	"	"	Rusové
pán	= master,Mr.,gentleman	"	"	pánové
syn	= son,	"	"	synové

Nouns in -*tel* and some in -*an*, -*l*, -*t*, -*d*, take -*é*, e.g.:—

učitel	= teacher,	Nom. plur.		učitelé
Angličan	= Englishman,	"	"	Angličané
anděl	= angel,	"	"	andělé
host	= guest,	"	"	hosté
soused	= neighbour,	"	"	sousedé
Žid	= Jew,	"	"	Židé

Genitive Plural

Only place names with plur. endings and vánoce (= Christmas) and velikonoce (= Easter) have *no ending* instead of -*ů*, e.g.:—

Dráždany	= Dresden,	Gen. plur.		Drážďan
Karlovy Vary	= (Carlsbad),	"	"	Karlových Var
vánoce	= Christmas,	"	"	vánoc

Locative Plural

(Hard) velar stems, like the soft *jo*-stems, have -*ích*, which causes the 2nd Palatalization, e.g.:—

	voják	= soldier,	Loc. plur.		vojácích
	soudruh	= comrade,	"	"	soudruzích
	hoch	= boy,	"	"	hoších
also	les	= a wood,	"	"	lesích

but inanimate nouns with stem in velar *k* or *ch* can also have -*ách*, e.g. kousek = piece, L. pl. kouskách.

Important *irregular nouns* of this declension are:—

člověk = person, with its plural: Nom. lidé (= people), Gen. lidí, Dat. lidem, Acc. lidi, Instr. lidmi, Loc. lidech.

přitel = friend, with its plural: Nom. přátelé, Gen. přátel, Dat. přatelům, Acc. přátele, Instr. přáteli, Loc. přátelích.

kůň = horse, Gen. sg. koně, other cases of sg. as for muž; plur. Nom. koně, Gen. koňů or koní, Dat. koňům or koním, Acc. koně, Instr. koňmi or koni, Loc. koních.

švec = cobbler, Gen. sing. ševce, etc.

Notice:

Jan = John, Voc. sg. Jene! otherwise regular.
manžel = husband, Nom. pl. manželové >< manželé which means "a married couple".

Pán is shortened when used in agreement with other nouns in the singular, except the names of God, e.g.: pan doktor, but Pán Bůh = the Lord God, Kristus Pán = Christ the Lord.

křest = christening, Gen. sg. křtu, etc.
prs = breast, plur. N.V.A. prsa, Gen./Loc. prsou, Dat. prsům, Instr. prsy.
kněz = priest, Voc. sg. kněže, sing. otherwise as muž; plur. Nom/Gen./Acc. kněží, Dat. kněžím, Instr. kněžími, Loc. kněžích.
otec = father, Voc. sg. otče, Nom. pl. otcové, otherwise regular.
rodič = parent, Nom. pl. rodiče (or rodičové) = father and mother, otherwise: rodiči or rodičové.
keř = bush, Gen. sg. keře or kře.
peníz = coin, is declined regularly like klíč in sing. and plur. But when peníze means "money", it is declined: Nom./Acc. peníze, Gen. peněz, Dat. penězům, Instr. penězi, Loc. penězích.
tisíc = thousand, Gen. pl. tisíc after other numbers, otherwise tisíců.

4b. *o*-stems, neuter.

These, like the masc. *o*-stems, are also subdivided into hard *o*- and soft *jo*-stems, but neither type has any alternative endings.

o-stem: město = town   *jo*-stem: moře = sea

	SING.		PLUR.	
Nom.	město	moře	města	moře[1]
Gen.	města	moře	měst	moří[1]
Dat.	městu	moři	městům	mořím
Acc.	město	moře	města	moře
Instr.	městem	mořem	městy	moři
Loc.	městě	moři	městech	mořích

In the *Loc. sing.* the ending -*ě* becomes -*e* after *l*, *s*, or *z*, e.g.:—

maso = meat, v mase.

Some stems in -*r*, -*m*, -*v*, have -*u*, e.g.:—

[1]Nouns in -iště have no ending in the Gen. plur., e.g.: jeviště = stage, scene, Gen. pl. jevišt.

```
ministerstvo = ministry, Loc. sg. ministerstvu
vedro        = heat,       "    "   vedru
vědro        = pail,       "    "   vědru
jařmo        = yoke,       "    "   jařmu
```

Also: v právu = in the right.

Many nouns with stems in velars also avoid -ě in the Loc. sing., e.g.:—

```
jho    = joke, Loc. sg. jhu; notice its Gen. pl. jeh
                            and Loc. pl. jhách
ticho  = quiet, "   "   tichu
víko   = lid,   "   "   víku; notice its Loc. pl.
                            víkách
mléko  = milk,  "   "   mléku or mléce
vojsko = army,  "   "   vojsku
```

A few other nouns also have -u, e.g.: ve jménu = in the name (of), but o jméně = about the name.

koleno = knee,   has Gen./Loc. plur. kolenou (an old Dual form).
rameno = shoulder, has Gen./Loc. plur. ramenou (an old Dual form).
oko   = eye,   has Loc. sg. v oku and an irregular plur.: Nom. Acc. oči, Gen. očí, Dat. očím, Instr. očima, Loc. očích.
ucho   = ear,   has Loc. sg. v uchu and a similar irregular plur.: Nom./Acc. uši, Gen. uší, Dat. uším, Instr. ušima, Loc. uších.

Notice:

nebe = sky,   declined in Czech like moře, but in the plural it is the only survival in the declensions of the old consonantal s-stems, i.e. Nom. Acc. nebesa, Gen. nebes, Dat. nebesům, Instr. nebesy, Loc. (na) nebesích.

Like moře also: poledne = midday
                vejce   = egg, Gen. pl. vajec.

Neuter nouns ending in -í (<-ьje or -ije), including all Verbal Nouns and many collective nouns, e.g. obilí (= corn), zboží (= goods), have a special declension of their own in Czech, due to contraction:—

CZECH

psaní = writing, letter

	SING.	PLUR.
Nom.	psaní	psaní
Gen.	psaní	psaní
Dat.	psaní	psaním
Acc.	psaní	psaní
Instr.	psaním	psaními
Loc.	psaní	psaních

Datum (= date), museum (= museum), drama (= drama), are mainly declined like město: Nom. pl. data, musea, dramata; but Gen. sing. dramatu, Loc. sing. datu, etc. The plural of nouns in -*ium*, -*eum*, -*uum*, -*ion* follows moře: Gen. pl. museí, etc.

THE NUMERALS

Cardinal.

1-4 are adjectival numerals. Jeden (= one) still preserves its old pronominal declension which is the same as that of "ten" (= this). Dva (= two, masc.) has the form dvě for fem. *and* neut., and declines like an old Dual. Tři (= three) and čtyři (= four) also decline but do not vary according to gender. 2, 3, and 4 agree in case with the noun they govern, and take the verb in the plural; if the verb is the Past Tense the Past Participle goes in the appropriate gender.

The numerals from the five onwards are nouns, and nouns qualified by them are put in the Gen. plur., if the numeral is in the Nom. or Acc. In the oblique cases the numeral and noun agree in case. These numerals, when Nom., require the verb in the (neuter — for Past Tense) singular.

Compound numerals composed of tens and units can have either the form corresponding to "twenty-three", dvacet tři, or—equally common in Czech, the form corresponding to "three and twenty", třiadvacet. The glottal stop is heard before the first "a".

Jeden (= one) is declined as follows:—

	SING.			
	Masc.		*Neut.*	*Fem.*
Nom.	jeden		jedno	jedna
Gen.		jednoho		jedné
Dat.		jednomu		jedné
Acc.	= Nom. or Gen.		jedno	jednu
Instr.		jedním		jednou
Loc.		jednom		jedné

	PLUR. Masc. Anim.	Masc. Inanim. and Fem.	Neut.
Nom.	jedni	jedny	jedna
Gen.		jedněch	
Dat.		jedněm	
Acc.	jedny		jedna
Instr.		jedněmi	
Loc.		jedněch	

Nom./Acc.	Masc.	Fem.	Neut.	
1	jeden	jedna	jedno	
2	dva	dvě	dvě[1]	Gen./Loc. dvou Dat./Instr. dvěma
3	tři	(Nom./Acc. all Gend.),		Gen. tří, Dat. třem, Instr. třemi, Loc. třech
4	čtyři	(" " " ")		Gen. čtyř, Dat. čtyřem, Instr. čtyřmi, Loc. čtyřech
5	pět	(" " " ")		Gen./Dat./Instr./Loc. pěti

```
 6  šest  ⎫
 7  sedm[2] ⎬ declined like pět
 8  osm[2]  ⎭
 9  devět Gen./Dat./Instr./Loc. devíti
10  deset   "       "       "     desíti (or
11  jedenáct                              deseti)
12  dvanáct   ⎫
13  třináct   │
14  čtrnáct   │
15  patnáct   │
16  šestnáct  │
17  sedmnáct  │
18  osmnáct   │
19  devatenáct│
20  dvacet    ⎬ declined like pět
21  jedenadvacet    (or dvacet jeden)
22  dvaadvacet      (or dvacet dva)
30  třicet    │
40  čtyřicet  │
50  padesát   │
60  šedesát   │
70  sedmdesát │
80  osmdesát  ⎭
90  devadesát
```

[1] oba, obě (= both), is declined like dva.
[2] Also pronounced: sedum, osum.

```
      100 sto (neut.)
      102 sto dva
      200 dvě sté
      300 tři sta
      400 čtyři sta
      500 pět set
      600 šest set, etc.
      900 devět set
    1,000 tisíc (masc.)
    2,000 dva tisíce
    3,000 tři tisíce
    4,000 čtyři tisíce
    5,000 pět tisíc
1,000,000 milion or milión
```

Ordinal Numerals

The Ordinals are adjectives, all of which follow the adjectival hard declension (see below), except první (= first), třetí (= third), and tisící (= thousandth) which follow the adjectival soft declension. První has an alternative form which is hard: prvý. Notice the Czech for hundredth (= stý), and millionth (= miliontý). Compound Ordinals have all their elements ordinal.

```
 1st první or prvý
 2nd druhý
 3rd třetí
 4th čtvrtý
 5th pátý
 6th šestý
 7th sedmý
 8th osmý
 9th devátý
10th desátý
11th jedenáctý
12th dvanáctý
13th třináctý
14th čtrnáctý
15th patnáctý
16th šestnáctý
17th sedmnáctý
18th osmnáctý
19th devatenáctý
20th dvacátý
21th dvacátý první or jedenadvacátý
22nd dvacátý druhý or dvaadvacátý
30th třicátý
40th čtyřicátý
50th padesátý
60th šedesátý
70th sedmdesátý
```

        80th osmdesátý
        90th devadesátý
       100th stý
       102nd stý druhý
       200th dvoustý
       300th třístý
       400th čtyřstý
       500th pětistý
       600th šestistý
       900th devítistý
     1,000th tisící
     2,000th dvou tisící
 1,000,000th miliontý

Collective Numerals

These have two forms: A. the neut. sg. form used (*a*) with pluralia tantum, (*b*) to indicate things thought of in groups; B. the adjectival form used in the sense of "twofold, threefold" and "of two (three) different kinds".

A. 2 dvoje ⎫ The oblique cases are formed as from
    3 troje ⎬ dvojí, trojí (soft adj. declension)
           ⎭ in the *plural*, e.g.
                          Gen./Loc. dvojích
                          Dat.   dvojím
                          Instr.   dvojími

    4 čtvero ⎫
    5 patero ⎬ neut. + Gen. plur.
    6 šestero ⎪
      etc.   ⎭
   10 desatero Božích přikázání = the Ten Commandments

   100 stero   ⎫ díků = a hundred (thousand)
 1,000 tisícero⎭   thanks.

B. 2 dvojí svatba = twofold wedding
    3 trojí přání = threefold wish
    4 čtverý
    5 paterý
      etc.
   100 sterý
 1,000 tisícerý (tisíceré díky = a thousand thanks)

The forms dvé, Gen. dvého, etc., and tré are archaic and literary.

Half = půl, which is indeclinable and takes the Gen. sing.

Notice: půl druhého[1] měsíce, vědra = one and a half months, pails, but půl druhé tuny = one and a half tons (fem.)

[1] Less commonly: (půl) druha, čtvrta, páta.

půl třetího (m. and n.) = two and a half;
f. půl třetí
likewise půl čtvrtého[1] = three and a half; půl čtvrté
půl pátého[1] = four and a half; půl páté, etc.
cf. Polish, Byelorussian, Slovak and Lusatian.

Distributive Numerals are formed with *po* + Cardinal numerals in the Loc., e.g.:—

po třech = three each

The suffix -*krát* is used for forming numeral adverbs, e.g.:—

třikrát = three times

THE PRONOUNS

Czech preserves a few remarkably old forms in the pronominal declension, when compared with certain other Slavonic languages, most notably in the declension of ten (= this), the literary Relative jenž, the endings of všechen (= all), and ký (= what the ...— in exclamations), Gen kýho,— the only forms used. On the other hand it has several new formations, as in the contracted Possessive Pronoun-adjectives, e.g. můj (= my), Gen. sg. masc. mého, the oblique cases of ona: ji, jí, etc. As in other Slavonic languages, the adjectival declension is foreshadowed by that of the pronouns, from which it arose by composition. In Czech fewer pronouns have a purely adjectival declension than in certain other Slavonic languages, e.g. Slovak, Ukrainian and Polish.

The usual categories exist:—

Demonstrative:
```
ten   = this
tento = this here (= tenhle, colloquial)
onen  = that yonder
```

Interrogative:
```
kdo?    = who?
co?     = what?
který?  = which?         ⎫ (declined like hard adjec-
jaký    = of what kind?  ⎭  tives, see below)
čí      = whose? (interrog. only, declined like a
                  soft adj.)
```

Indefinite: (formed with prefixes or suffixes):—
```
někdo  = someone, a certain person
kdosi  = someone (more indefinite)
leckdo = anyone, various people
```

[1]Less commonly: (půl) druha, čtvrta, páta.

kdokoli = whoever

Relative:

jenž (literary)
který (conversational, declined like hard adjective) } = who
jehož (masc. or neut. possessor)
jejíž (fem. possessor) } = whose
jejichž (plur. possessor)
co (colloq.) = that

Possessive (pronoun-adjectives):

```
můj              = my, mine
náš              = our(s)
její             = her(s)(declined like a soft
                   adj., see below)
jejich(invariable)= their(s)
jeho       "     = his, its
```

Definitive:

```
všechen = all
každý   = every(declined like a hard adj.)
sám     = -self, alone
samý    = only, sheer, the very...(decl. like a
           hard adj.)
týž or  = the same (decl. like a hard adj. + ž:
 tentýž                          Gen. téhož, etc.)
jiný    = another   "    "   "   "    "
takový  = such      "    "   "   "    "
tak veliký = so great
```

Negative:

```
nikdo  = no one
nic    = nothing (declined like co)
žadný  = no, none (declined like hard adj.)
```

Personal:

```
on  = he
já  = I
ty  = you (sg. familiar)
vy  = you (plur. and polite)
```

We give below those declensions of pronouns which differ in any way from the adjectival declensions:—

ten = this (old hard model)

SING.	Masc.	Neut.	Fem.
Nom.	ten	to	ta
Gen.		toho	té
Dat.		tomu	té
Acc.	= Nom. or Gen.	to	tu
Instr.		tím	tou
Loc.		tom	té

PLUR.	Masc. anim.	inanim.	Neut.	Fem.
Nom.	ti	ty	ta	ty
Gen.		těch		
Dat.		těm		
Acc.	ty		ta	ty
Instr.		těmi[1]		
Loc.		těch		

Like ten: onen = that
Like ten with suffixes: ten-hle, ten-to = this here.

kdo = who?   co = what?, that

Nom.	kdo	co
Gen.	koho	čeho
Dat.	komu	čemu
Acc.	koho	co[2]
Instr.	kým	čím
Loc.	kom	čem

Notice also the emphatic forms with the suffix -ž (-že): kdož?, což?

všechen = all

SING.	Masc. anim.	inanim.	Neut.		
Nom.	všechen,	všecek	všechno,	vše,	všecko
Gen.		všeho			
Dat.		všemu			
	anim./inanim.				
Acc.	všeho/všechen,	všecek	všechno,	vše,	všecko
Instr.		vším			
Loc.		všem			

---

[1] A dual form: těma is used with nouns in the old dual form: rukama, nohama, očima = with hands, feet, eyes.

[2] Acc. sing. after the prepositions na, o, pro, ve, za is reduced to -č when interrogative only: proč? = what for?

CZECH

	SING	*Fem.*
Nom.	všechna, všecka	
Gen.	vší	
Dat.	vší	
Acc.	všechnu, vši[1], všecku	
Instr.	vší	
Loc.	vší	

PLUR.	*Masc. anim.*	*inanim.*	*Neut.*
Nom.	všichni, všickni	všechny, všecky	všechna, všecka
Gen.		všech	
Dat.		všem	
Acc.	všechny, všecky		všechna, všecka
Instr.		všemi	
Loc.		všech	

	Fem.
Nom.	všechny, všecky
Gen.	všech
Dat.	všem
Acc.	všechny, všecky
Instr.	všemi
Loc.	všech

můj = my

SING.	*Msc.*	*Neut.*	*Fem.*
Nom.	můj	mé, moje	má, moje
Gen.	mého		mé
Dat.	mému		mé
Acc.	= Nom. or Gen.	mé, moje	mou, moji
Instr.	mým		mou
Loc.	mém		mé

PLUR.	*Masc. anim.*	*inanim.*	*Neut.*	*Fem.*
Nom.	moji, mí	mé, moje	má, moje	mé, moje
Gen.		mých		
Dat.		mým		
Acc.	mé, moje		má, moje	mé, moje
Instr.		mými		
Loc.		mých		

---

[1] Now only used in a few petrified expressions, e.g.: nade vší pochybnost = beyond all doubt.

Like můj: tvůj = your(s) (fam.), svůj = own (referring to subject of sentence).

náš = our(s)

SING.	Masc.	Neut.	Fem.	PLUR.	Masc. anim.	Masc. inanim.	Neut.	Fem.
Nom.	náš	naše	naše		naši	naše	naše	naše
Gen.	našeho	naší	naší			našich		
Dat.	našemu	naší	naší			našim		
Acc.	= Nom.or Gen.	naše	naši			naše		
Instr.	naším	naší	naší			našimi[1]		
Loc.	našem	naší	naší			našich		

Like náš: váš = your(s), (polite sing. and familiar and polite plur.).

sám = -self, alone

SING.	Masc.	Neut.	Fem.	PLUR.	Masc. anim.	Masc. inanim.	Neut.	Fem.
Nom.	sám	samo	sama		sami	samy	sama	samy
Gen.	samého (sama)	samé	samé			samých		
Dat.	samému	samé	samé			samým		
Acc.	= Nom.or Gen.	samo	samu			samy	sama	samy
Instr.	samým	samým	samou			samými		
Loc.	samém	samém	samé			samých		

The Personal Pronouns

on = he, ona = she, ono = it (old soft model)

	SING.			PLUR.			
	Masc.	Neut.	Fem.	Masc. anim.	Masc. inanim.	Neut.	Fem.
Nom.	on	ono	ona	oni	ony	ona	ony
Gen.	jeho, ho[2]		jí	jich			
Dat.	jemu, mu[2]		jí	jim			
Acc.	jej, jeho, ho[2]	je, ho[2]	ji	je			
Instr.	jím		jí	jimi			
Loc.	něm		ní	nich			

The Gen. sing. masc. and neut. jeho is used for "his" and "its", when the possessor is masc. or neut., and is invariable.

Jej is used for the Acc. sing. masc. animate and inanimate. Jeho (ho), which is reserved for animate nouns in literary style, is used colloquially for

---

[1] A dual form: našima, is used with nouns in the old dual forms, as with ten, to, ta, q.v.

[2] The forms *ho, mu* are only used as enclitic, unemphatic forms. To express emphasis or contrast, one uses jeho, jemu instead. All the other forms of the oblique cases can be used either as enclitics or under emphasis.

inanimate and even neuter nouns (instead of je). Notice that je is also the correct Acc. plur. for all genders (in contrast to Slovak, Serbocr., Slovenian, and East Slav).

After prepositions a soft *n* is prefixed (to the long form, when there are two), e.g.: Instr. sg. m. jím, but—s ním (= with him). With the forms beginning with je, the combination ňje is written ně, e.g. do něho (= to it). All Loc. forms always have *n-*, as they are never used without a preposition. In the Acc. sing. masc. after the prepositions *na, o, pro, za*, and *ve*, něho can be reduced to *-ň*, written together with the preposition (cf. Slovak, Serbocr., and Slovenian), e.g.: mysli naň! (= think of him!).

After prepositions, only the "correct" forms are used:—

    na strom—na něj (not na něho or naň) = on the tree, on to it
    pro pivo—pro ně = for beer, for it

Sing. jenž (masc.), jež (fem. and neut.), plur. již (masc. anim.), jež (masc. inanim., fem., neut.) = who, is declined in its oblique cases exactly like "on" with the suffix *ž-*:—

    Gen. sg. jehož (masc., neut.) jíž (fem.)
    Dat. sg. jemuž ("   "   ) jíž ("   ), etc.

The forms: jehož, jejíž, jejichž are the *only* forms for the Relative "whose" (never: kterého, které, kterých, as in Slovak ktorého, etc.).

já = I, my = we, ty = you(fam.), vy = you, sebe = -self

Nom.	já	my	ty	vy	—
Gen.	mne[2]	nás	tebe	vás	sebe
Dat.	mně,[2] mi[1]	nám	tobě, ti[1]	vám	sobě, si[1]
Acc.	mne,[2] mě[1]	nás	tebe, tě[1]	vás	sebe, se[1]
Instr.	mnou	námi	tebou	vámi	sebou
Loc.	mně[2]	nás	tobě	vás	sobě

Sebe, se (= -self— referring to the subject) is like ty (without the Nom. sing.). Notice the frequently used enclitic Dative *si*, as in Slovenian, Bulg. and Slovak, but not in Pol. or Serbocr.

---

[1]Enclitic, unemphatic forms. See "Word Order with Enclitics", pp. 122-124.

[2]In colloquial Czech a form pronounced [mɲe] is used for Gen., Dat., Acc. and Loc., both as an enclitic and an emphatic form and after prepositions.

CZECH

In polite address to a single person in Czech, in contrast to South and East Slav and also Slovak, *vy* is used with the verb in the plural; but the complement and the Past Participle Active in the Past tense are put in the gender of the subject and in the *singular*: e.g.: (to a man) Vy jste byl nemocen? (= Have you been ill?), but (to a lady) Vy jste byla nemocna?

THE ADJECTIVES

The declension of ordinary adjectives in Czech is derived from the old compound, "Definite" declension and therefore reminds one of the declension of the pronoun on, ona, ono. Only the possessive adjectives have a (partly) substantival declension like the Indefinite Adjectives in Old Slavonic.

The ordinary adjectives are divided into those following the hard declension and ending in -ý (masc.), -á (fem.), -é (neut.), and those following the soft declension and ending in -í for all genders. The soft declension has a much smaller variety of endings owing to the contraction of many different vowel combinations all to -í-.

zdravý = healthy   cizí = foreign

Hard SING.	*Masc.*		*Neut.*	*Fem.*	Soft SING. *Masc.*	*Neut.*	*Fem.*
Nom.	zdravý		zdravé	zdravá	cizí (all genders)		
Gen.		zdravého		zdravé	cizího		cizí
Dat.		zdravému		zdravé	cizímu		cizí
Acc.	= Nom. or Gen.		zdravé	zdravou	= Nom. or Gen.	cizí	cizí
Instr.		zdravým		zdravou	cizím		cizí
Loc.		zdravém		zdravé	cizím		cizí

	Masc. anim.	inanim.	*Neut.*	*Fem.*	*All genders*
Nom.	zdraví	zdravé	zdravá	zdravé	cizí
Gen.			zdravých		cizích
Dat.			zdravým		cizím
Acc.		zdravé	zdravá	zdravé	cizí
Instr.			zdravými[1]		cizími[1]
Loc.			zdravých		cizích

Acc. = Gen. only for animate masc. nouns in the singular.

In the Nom. plur. masc. animate of *hard* adjectives the final consonant of the stem, if a velar, dental or *r* and the groups *sk* and *ck*, are softened

---

[1] The endings (hard) -ýma, (soft) -íma are used with nouns in the old Dual form: e.g. modrýma, rybíma očima = with blue, fish's eyes.

before the ending -í (cf. the similar softenings in Polish for adjectives qualifying masc. personal nouns in the Nom. plur.):—

Velars:
k +í>-cí   e.g. veliký   = great,big, Nom.pl.masc.an.   velicí
h +í>-zí   " drahý   = dear,   "   "   "   drazí
ch+í>-ší   " tichý   = quiet,   "   "   "   tiší

Dentals:
d +í>-dí (=dí̌)   " chudý   = poor,   "   "   "   chudí
t +í>-tí (=tí̌)   " bohatý   = rich,   "   "   "   bohatí
n +í>-ní (=ñí)   " krásný   = beautiful,   "   "   "   krásní

r +í>-ří   " dobrý   = good,   "   "   "   dobří
sk+í>-ští(=ští̌)   " český   = Czech,   "   "   "   čeští
ck+í>-čtí(=čtí̌)   " anglický = English,   "   "   "   angličtí

likewise:
čk+í>-čcí   " mladičký = very young,"   "   "   mladičcí

Notice that all surnames in -ský, -cký, etc., are declined like zdravý. So are certain nouns, such as:—

(masc.) hajný = gamekeeper, příbuzný = relative
(fem.) kopaná = football, dovolená = permismission, leave, holiday, krámská = saleswoman
(neut.) jízdné = fare, vstupné = entrance fee, charge

A few nouns are declined like cizí:

krejčí = tailor, Jiří = George.

A few adjectives have a "short" form, used predicatively only and not declined in modern speech. But with most adjectives it is little used in conversation and is replaced by the ordinary (attributive) form.

The Nom. sg. masc. of the predicative form has no final vowel but a fill-vowel (-e-) appears in difficult final consonant groups. The fem. sing. ends in -a (short!), and the neut. sing. in -o. The Nom. plur. ends in -i (short) masc. anim., -y masc. inan. and fem., -a (short) neut., cf. the a-stem and o-stem nouns. The commonest are:—

    stár, -a, o   = old
    sláb   = weak
    zdráv   = healthy
    bohat   = rich
    jist   = certain, sure
    nemocen   = ill
    zvědav   = curious

hladov	= hungry
vesel	= merry
smuten	= sad
šťasten	= happy
znám	= known
schopen	= able, apt
vinen, vinna, vinno	= guilty
laskav	= kind
svoboden	= single, unmarried
ženat	= married (of a man)
vdána	= married (of a woman)

Notice the lengthening of the vowel in the predicative form. Cf. the attributives: zdravý, starý, slabý and the variations of accent in Serbocr. Rád, ráda, rádo, pl. rádi, rády, ráda (= glad, happy) is used only predicatively. Mám rád + Acc. = I like.

Possessive adjectives formed from personal names and nouns referring to men end in -ův (masc.), -ova (fem.), -ovo (neut.); but those formed from nouns referring to, and names of, women end in -in (masc.), -ina (fem.), -ino (neut.) with palatalization of the preceding consonant (the 1st Palatalization for velars).

These are regularly declined like *o*-stem nouns (for masc. and neut.) and *a*-stem nouns (for fem.) in all cases of the sing., except the Instr., and in the Nom./Acc. plur. In the oblique cases of the plur. and in the Instr. sing. the endings are the same as those of ordinary, attributive adjectives. E.g.:—

bratrův = brother's

SING.	Masc.		Neut.	Fem.
Nom.	bratrův		bratrovo	bratrova
Gen.		bratrova		bratrovy
Dat.		bratrovu		bratrově
Acc.	= Nom. or Gen.		bratrovo	bratrovu
Instr.		bratovým		bratrovou
Loc.		bratrově		bratrově

PLUR.	Masc.		Neut.	Fem.
	anim.	inanim.		
Nom.	bratrovi	bratrovy	bratrova	bratrovy
Gen.		bratrových		
Dat.		bratrovým		
Acc.	bratrovy		bratrova	bratrovy
Instr.		bratrovými		
Loc.		bratrových		

Examples of palatalization before the endings *-in*, *-ina*, etc.:—

matka	= mother,	matčin	= mother's
sestra	= sister,	sestřin	= sister's
tetička	= auntie,	tetiččin	
Olga	(name),	Olžin	
Jitka	= Judith,	Jitčin	

The movable -e- disappears before the endings -ův, -ova, etc., e.g.:—

otec = father, otcův, otcova, etc. = father's
Janáček (name), Janáčkův, Janáčkova[1], etc.

THE COMPARISON OF ADJECTIVES

There are two alternative ways of forming Comparative adjectives in Czech, but there is no way of telling for most adjectives which one is used for any particular adjective. Only for a few adjectives is one at liberty to use either form.

1. The commonest way is by adding -ejší (after l, s, z and the chuintantes) and -ější (after labials and dentals) to the stem, i.e. the adjective minus the final -ý, -á, -é. This ending is derived from -ьйш- and causes palatalization of preceding consonants, the 1st Palatalization for velars, r becoming ř, ck>čt', sk>št', and the dentals— soft; -ň+ě- are written -ně-. Cf. the changes in the Nom. plur. masc. anim. of Positive adjectives, etc.

Hence we have:—

teplý	= warm	Comp.	teplejší
drzý	= insolent	"	drzejší
lysý	= bald	"	lysejší
známý	= (well-)known	"	známější
hloupý	= foolish	"	hloupější
divoký	= wild	"	divočejší
hořký	= bitter	"	hořčejší
ubohý	= poor	"	ubožejší
vetchý	= feeble, frail	"	vetšejší
chytrý	= clever	"	chytřejší
otrocký	= slavish	"	otročtější
lidský	= human	"	lidštější
šťastný	= happy	"	šťastější

Notice the vowel change in the root in:—

svatý	= holy	"	světější
bílý	= white	"	bělejší

---

[1] This is the regular ending of many street names in Czech, and in Slovak, when they are formed from proper nouns.

2. The other way is by adding -ší to the stem of the adjective, if it ends in d-, t-, b- or r-, e.g.:—

mladý	= young	Comp.	mladší (pron. mlačí!)
tvrdý	= hard	"	tvrdší
bohatý	= rich	"	bohatší (or: bohatější)
čistý	= clean	"	čistší
slabý	= weak	"	slabší
starý	= old	"	starší

Notice the consonantal charges due to assimilation in:—

drahý	= dear	Comp.	dražší (pron. draší)
tichý	= quiet	"	tišší (pron. tiší)

Adjectives ending in -oký, -eký and many in -ký lose these endings before adding -ší. Similar assimilative consonantal changes can take place:—

hluboký	= deep	Comp.	hlubší
daleký	= distant	"	další
široký	= wide	"	širší
hladký	= smooth	"	hladší
krátký	= short	"	kratší
těžký	= heavy, difficult	"	těžší
vysoký	= high	"	vyšší (pron. vyší)
úzký	= narrow	"	užší (pron. uší)
blízký	= near	"	bližší (pron. bliší)
nízký	= low	"	nižší (pron. niší)

But a small group of adjectives in -ký in their Comparative degree keep the k which then coalesces with the -ší to give -čí, e.g.:—

hezký	= pretty	Comp.	hezčí (pron. heščí)
měkký	= soft	"	měkčí
vlhký	= damp	"	vlhčí
trpký	= bitter	"	trpčí
křehk	= brittle	"	křehčí

(Cf. Russian мягче = softer, легче = lighter.)

Further adjectives, with alternative Comparatives, are:—

lehký	= light	Comp.	lehčí	or	lehčejší
krotký	= tame	"	krotší	"	krotčejší
krásný	= beautiful	"	krašší	"	krásnější (the commoner form)
snadný	= easy	"	snazší	"	snadnější
hustý	= dense	"	hustší	"	hustější
tenký	= thin	"	tenší	"	tenčí

A few common adjectives have irregular Comparatives for which a different root is used:—

dobrý	= good	Comp.	lepší (= better)
špatný }	= bad	"	horší
zlý			
malý	= small	"	menší
velký or veliký	= big, great	"	větší (pron. věčí)
dlouhý	= long	"	delší

The *Superlative* degree is formed with the prefix *nej-* added to the Comparative degree (of every type), e.g.:—

nejteplejší, nejmladší, nejhezčí, nejlepší = the warmest, the youngest, the prettiest, the best.

All Comparative and Superlative adjectives are declined like soft Positive adjectives, i.e. like cizí above.

Very = velmi *or* velice, colloquially: moc
Than = než (conjunction), (popular: jak)
The Genitive of comparison is only used in literature, e.g.:—

Železo je mocnější zlata (for: než zlato) = Iron is mightier than gold.

Rather better	= trochu lepší, o něco lepší
Much better	= mnohem lepší, o mnoho lepší (o moc lepší— colloquial)
Rather good	= dost dobrý
Less than	= méně než
The bigger...*the* better	= čím větší,...tím lepší
As (good) *as*	= (zrovna) tak (dobrý) jako
As soon as possible	= co nejdříve
As fast as possible	= co (možná) nejrychleji
The very best of all	= nejlepší ze všech
Too	= příliš
The same as	= stejný jako, právě takový jako
In the same way as	= stejně jako

ADVERBS

Adverbs formed from adjectives, except from those in *-ský*, *-cký*, end either in *-o* or in *-e/ě*. The latter alternating endings, derived from -ě, cause palatalization of preceding consonants: dentals are softened, *r* becomes *ř*, velars undergo the 2nd Palatalization, labials remain hard and are followed by *-ě-*:—

teplý	= warm,	adv.	teple
rychlý	= quick	"	rychle
drzý	= insolent	"	drze
bohatý	= rich	"	bohatě
chudý	= poor	"	chudě
pěkný	= beautiful	"	pěkně
dobrý	= good	"	dobře
měkký	= soft	"	měkce
drahý	= dear	"	draze (= dearly)
tichý	= quiet	"	tiše
hloupý	= foolish	"	hloupě
laskavý	= kind	"	laskavě
soukromý	= private	"	soukromě

But with *-o* only (a few):—

malý	= small	"	málo (= little, few)
častý	= frequent	"	často (= often)
mnohý	= many a	"	mnoho (= much)

Some adjectives can have adverbs either in *-o* or in *-e/ě*, with a difference of meaning. The ending *-o* gives a more literal meaning, while that in *-e* gives a figurative one, e.g.:—

dlouhý = long,	dlouho = a long time,	dlouze = at great length
široký = broad, wide	široko = widely,	široce = amply
vysoký = high	vysoko = high up,	vysoce = highly
drahý = dear,	draho = expensively,	draze = dearly
těžký = heavy, difficult,	těžko = with difficulty,	těžce = heavily
blízký = near(by),	blízko = near,	blízce = closely

etc.

Notice that chladno, teplo, horko, mokro, jasno, etc., in the expressions: je chladno, teplo, horko, mokro, jasno, etc. (= it is cold, warm, hot, wet, bright, etc.), are classified in Czech as adverbs making statements.

All adjectives in *-í* have adverbs in *-ě*:—

denní	= daily,	adv.	denně
měsíční	= monthly,	"	měsíčně

Adjectives in *-ský*, *-cký*, have adverbs in *-sky*, *-cky* (with short *-y* and *no* preposition, in contrast to other West Slav languages), e.g.:—

	český	= Czech,	česky	= in Czech
	anglický	= English,	mluvím anglicky	= I speak English
Notice:	hezký	= pretty:	je hezky	= it is a fine day

The Comparison of Adverbs

Comparative adverbs are formed from the corresponding Comparative adjectives.

Those adjectives which have a Comparative degree in *-ejší (-ější)* have Comparative adverbs in *-eji (ěji)*.[1] E.g.:—

```
rychlejší   = faster          adv.— rychleji
zdravější   = healthier         " — zdravěji
příjemnější = more pleasant     " — příjemněji
```

Most adjectives with Comparatives in *-ší* have Comparative adverbs in *-e*, which causes palatalization of the preceding consonant. The root vowel is also lengthened. E.g.:—

```
širší  = wider      — šíře
vyšší  = higher     — výše
další  = further    — dále
bližší = nearer     — blíže
dražší = dearer     — dráže
užší   = narrower   — úže
těžší  = heavier    — tíže
nižší  = lower      — níže
```

In colloquial speech this type of Comp. adverb is used without the final *-e*, e.g.:—

dál

But
```
kratší = shorter, has kratčeji
tišší  = quieter,  "  tišeji (tiše is the
                                 Positive adverb)
řídší  = rarer,    "  řidčeji
```

The few adjectives with Comp. in *-ší* have Comp. adverbs in *-čeji*, e.g.:—

```
lehčí = lighter, easier  — lehčeji
hezčí = more pretty      — hezčeji
měkčí = softer           — měkčeji
```

The following Comparative adverbs are irregular:-

```
dobře          = well       Comp. lépe (colloq. líp)
zle    }
špatně }       = badly        "   hůř(e)
mnoho          = much         "   víc(e)
trochu         = a little }
málo           = little   }   "   méně(colloq. míň)
dlouho         = long         "   dél(e)
brzo   }
brzy   }       = soon         "   dřív(e.)
```

[1] This ending becomes -ejc (-ějc) in popular speech.

CZECH 89

```
hluboko  = deep    ⎫ Comp.  hloub or hlouběji
hluboce  = deeply  ⎭
snadno   ⎫
snadně   ⎭ = easily   "    snáz(e) or snadněji
```

The predicative adjective rád (= glad) has an adverbial Comparative raději, colloquially radši.

Superlative adverbs are easily formed—by prefixing *nej-* to the Comparative adverbs of all types, e.g.:—

```
nejrychleji            = the fastest
nejlépe                = the best
nejvýše                = the highest
nejraději(nejradši)    = most gladly, etc.
```

Adverbs of time, place, manner, degree, etc. have the most various forms and origins. To those approaching Czech from other Slavonic languages, the Czech forms are often confusing. We therefore give a fairly full list. Some of the most peculiar and frequently used adverbs are:—

Place

```
zde(lit.) ⎫                    nikde   = nowhere
tu        ⎬ = here             uvnitř  = inside
tady      ⎭                    venku   = outside
tam         = there, thither   ven     = out
tudy        = this way         pryč    = (go)away!, gone
sem         = hither           potud   = as far as that
odsud       = hence            domů    = home(-ward)
od(tam)tud  = thence           nahoře  = upstairs
jinde       = elsewhere        dole    = downstairs
všude       = everywhere       zpět    = back(ward)
někde       = somewhere        zvenčí  = from outside
```

Time

```
nyní(lit.) ⎫                   dávno    = long ago
teď'       ⎭ = now             konečně  ⎫
tehdy        = then            nakonec  ⎭ = at last
dnes         = to-day          teprve   = only
zítra        = to-morrow       právě    ⎫
včera        = yesterday       zrovna   ⎭ = just, only just now
již(lit.)  ⎫                   až       = only, not before
už         ⎭ = already         ráno     = in the morning
ještě        = still           večer    = in the evening
už ne        = no longer       posud    ⎫
ještě ne     = not yet         dosud    ⎭ = up to now
(i)hned    ⎫                   včas     = in time
okamžitě   ⎭ = immediately     časem    = sometimes, at times
vždycky      = always          občas    = occasionally
nikdy        = never           jindy    = another time
někdy        = sometimes       zas(e)   = again
```

Time (contd.)

kdysi	= once upon a time	příště	= next time
jednou	= once	poslední	= last time
stále	⎫ = all the time	minule	= recently
pořád	⎭	letos	= this year
pozdě	= late	(v)loni	= last year
časně	= early	zároveň	⎫ = at the same time
často	= often	současně	⎭
zřídka	⎫ = seldom	brzo	⎫ = soon
málokdy	⎭	brzy	⎭
potom	= afterwards	zatím	= meanwhile
pak	= then	leckdy	= at times

Manner[1]

tak	= so, thus	výjimečně	= exceptionally
pomalu	= slowly	obyčejně	= usually
honem!	= quickly!	náhodou	= by chance
náhle	⎫ = suddenly	nějak	= somehow
najednou	⎭	jinak	⎫ = otherwise
úmyslně	⎫	jináč(e)	⎭
schválně	⎬ = on purpose	nikterak	= in no way
naschvál	⎭	vlastně	= actually, really
darmo	⎫ = gratis	skutečně	= truly
zdarma	⎭	zajisté	⎫ = certainly, surely
nadarmo	⎫ = in vain	jistě	⎭
zbytečně	⎭	nenadále	= unexpectedly

Degree

velmi	⎫	docela	⎫
velice	⎬ = very	zcela	⎬ = quite
moc(colloq.)	⎭	úplně	⎭
tuze	= a great deal	celkem	= altogether, in all
mnoho	⎫ = much	aspoň	⎫ = at least
moc(colloq.)	⎭	alespoň	⎭
trochu	= a little	rozhodně	= definitely
málo	= little	prý	= they say, it is said
tolik	= so or as much	snad	⎫ = perhaps, possibly
několik	= some	možná	⎭
sotva	= hardly	zvláště	= especially
dost(i)	= enough	asi	= roughly, approximately
pouze	⎫	(vše-)	⎫
jenom	⎬ = only	obecně	⎬ = generally, in general
toliko	⎭	vůbec	⎭
skoro	⎫ = nearly	vůbec ne	= not at all
téměř	⎭	nikoli	= by no means
částečně	= partly	dokonce	= even
málem	= almost	opravdu	= indeed, really
většinou	= mostly		

[1]Note also: ležmo, leže = lying; mlčky = silently.

Interrogative

zdali ...?	(interrogative particle starting a sentence, literary, more usual in indirect questions)	proč?	= why?
		jak?	= how?
		kolik?	= how much?, how many?
		vždyť?	= surely?
		přece?	= but surely?
kdy?	= when?	skutečně?	= really?
kde?	= where?	co(ž)pak?	= not ... really? (expecting the answer "no")
kam?	= whither?		
odkud?	= whence?	cože?	= what?, really?
kudy?	= which way?		

Not = ne- (written as a prefix with verbs, and stressed)

No = ne; on the contrary = naopak; not at all, in no way = nikoli; not at all! not likely! = kdepak! (very colloquial).

Yes = ano; of course, certainly = ovšem.

CONJUNCTIONS

We give below the most important and characteristic conjunctions. The true shades of meaning and emotion of some can only be learnt by experience.

Coördinating:

a	= and (also contrasting)
i	= and...too
i...i	= both...and
také, též	= also
ale	= but, however
(a)však	= however (však is enclitic)
(a)nebo, čili	= or
či	= or (in questions)
buď...anebo	= either...or
ani...ani	= neither...nor
jednak...jednak	= on the one hand...on the other hand
nejen...nýbrž i	= not only...but also
ba	= certainly, indeed
přece	= and yet; certainly, surely
vždyť	= indeed, still
a to, a sice	= that is, to wit
totiž, zejména	= namely
takřka	= so to speak, as it were
jako	= as, like
arci(že)	= certainly, surely
tedy, teda	= well then, so, therefore
ostatně	= anyway

sice	= otherwise; it is true
přes to	= nevertheless
zato	= but still, yet
proto	= therefore
neboť	= for

Subordinating (those different from the interrogative adverbs):—

kdežto	= while (contrasting)
protože poněvadž ježto (archaic) jelikož	} = because, as, since
když	= when; after; if (with Pres. or Past Tense)
až	= when (in the future); until
dokud ne	= until
kdykoli	= whenever
zatím co mezitím co	} = while (of time)
jakmile	= as soon as
(dříve) než	= before
od té doby, co	= since (of time)
jestliže or -li (enclitic) most often + Fut.	= if
kdybych (variable according to person, see Verbs, Conditional Mood)	= if (in unfulfilled conditions)
i kdyby	= even if
byť i	= even if
ač, ačkoli(v)	= although
třebas, třebaže	= although, despite
abych (variable— see kdybych above)	= in order that, that (after verbs of wishing, requesting, commanding, fearing)
že	= that (after verbs of saying, thinking, rejoicing, also to express consequences)
jakoby	= as if
kéž! + Conditional	= would that...!
aniž (udělal), i.e. +finite verb	= without...(doing)

CZECH

THE PREPOSITIONS

Czech prepositions, on the whole, agree as to the case they govern with other Slavonic languages. But they also preserve some interesting archaisms and idiosyncrasies. "Through", in the sense of "about, along, or over" a place, is rendered by the plain Instrumental:—

    Šel ulicí, polem = he was walking down the street, through the field
    Cestuje Prahou = he is travelling via (or through) Prague

"Do" is used for "to" and "into".

Some prepositions govern two or three cases according to their exact meaning.

With Genitive:

bez[1]	= without
dle, podle	= along, according to
vedle	= beside
do	= into, up to; to (with inanimates only)
z, ze[1]	= out of
od[1]	= from
u	= at, near, by
kolem, okolo	= round
kromě	= except
místo	= instead of
stran	= concerning, because of
za	= during, at, on (of unspecified time)
s, se[1]	= off z, ze[1] = from, out of, of
blízko	= near
daleko	= far from
uvnitř	= inside
vně	= outside

[1] Prepositions consisting of, or ending in, a consonant take the fill vowel -e before difficult consonant groups and before the same consonant in the next word, as double consonants are not pronounced in Czech. All monosyllabic prepositions containing a vowel and those with an added fill-vowel are stressed, except *dle*, *skrz*, and *stran*. E.g.:—

    ve Vídni = in Vienna
    beze mne = without me
    se sestrou = with (his) sister
    ke mně = to me
    but ku (before *p*) Praze = towards Prague
    se mnou = with me
    ve mně = in me
    ze zlata = of gold

With Genitive (contd.)

během	= in the course of
následkem	= in consequence of
ohledně	= with regard to
pomocí	= by means of
kraj	= to the edge of, on the edge of
prostřed	= in the middle of
podél	= along

With Dative:

k[1]	= to (of persons), towards (of persons and things)
proti	= against
naproti	= opposite
kvůli	= for (the sake of)
díky	= thanks to
vůči	= as regards, towards
po	(only in adverbial expressions) = according to, e.g.
po právu	= by rights, rightly
po vlčímu	= like a wolf

With Accusative:

pro	= for, because of, to fetch
přes[1]	= through (of place, time), over (of quantity)
skrz(e)[1]	= through (a hole, passage)
mimo	= beyond; past; besides, except
na	= on to
v[1]	= into (rare); at, on (of time)
o	= against (of place); about, for (prosím o něco = I ask for something)
nad[1]	= (motion to) above, over
pod[1]	= (motion to) under, (also of quantity)
před[1]	= (motion to) before
za	= (motion to) behind; for, instead of, (with)in (of time)
mezi	= (motion to) between, among
po	= up to; throughout
s[1]	in various idioms: býti s to = to be capable of something
ob[1]	= every other, alternately: ob den = every other day

With Instrumental:

nad[1]	= above (rest)
pod[1]	= under (rest)
před[1]	= before (rest)
za	= behind, beyond (rest)
mezi	= between, among (rest)
s, se[1]	= with, together with

[1]See footnote on p. 93.

With Locative:

při	= near, at
na	= on, at
v¹	= in.
o	= about, concerning; during, on, at
po	= after; about, over (of place); at (of price); by; according to

The verbal prefixes *vy-*, *pře-*, *roz-*, *vz-* are not used as prepositions.

k is not used as a verbal prefix.

THE CONJUGATION OF VERBS

The five main classes of verbs, classified according to the endings of the Present, are preserved in Czech, which clearly differentiates *-e-* from *-je-*. But as in other West and South Slav languages, verbs formerly in *-aju, -aješ*, etc., now form a new class in *-ám, -áš*, etc., arrived at by contraction, the *-m* in the 1st pers. sing. originating from the four old "athematic" verbs. These latter are preserved in Czech and are best learnt as irregular verbs. The type of verb formerly in *-ěju, -ěješ* (O.S. -ѣѭ, -ѣѥши) has also been contracted—to *-ím, -íš*, thus becoming an *-i-* category verb except in the 3rd pers. plur., where *-ějí* is preserved. This type is more common in Czech than in other Slavonic languages, having gained many recruits, especially in the spoken language. On the other hand, the consonantal stems of the old Class III of the type, e.g. O.S. пишѫ, писати, have been greatly reduced in numbers, many of them having gone over to, or having alternative forms of, the class in *-ám, -áš*, now.

Compared with Old Slavonic, the number of forms and tenses in Czech has been reduced. The Dual number has been entirely lost. And the Aorist and Imperfect tenses also no longer exist in the modern language, though they were freely used in old Czech. The Pluperfect is obsolescent.

The modern Past Tense is formed with the Past Participle Active in *-l* (from verbs of both aspects) together with the Present tense of *býti* (= to be), *jsem, jsi*, etc., used as a separable auxiliary verb, as in Slovak and South Slav.

The Future of Imperfective verbs is formed with the Future of *býti*: *budu*, etc., + the Infin., as in East Slav, Slovak, Lusatian and sometimes in Polish. But an important exception to this rule are the Imperfective verbs of going, leading, carrying, etc., some of

---

¹See footnote on p. 93.

which form their Imperfective Future with the prefix *po-*, e.g.: nésti = to carry (Impfve.), Future Imperfective: ponesu. This is a feature peculiar to Czech and Slovak.

The Imperative has a special form for the 1st pers. plur., as well as for the 2nd pers. sing. and plur., in contrast to Russian, Bulgarian and Macedonian.

The Conditional is formed with the *variable* and separable auxiliary: bych, bys, by, etc., + the Past Participle Active in *-l*. The Past Conditional is less frequently used.

Both the Present and Past Gerunds (verbal adverbs) vary in gender in Czech (but do not decline). This is a unique feature of Czech, reminiscent of the indefinite declension of the participles in Old Slavonic (which, however, did decline).

There are also the Past Participle Active in *-l*, already mentioned, and the Past Participle Passive, which ends in *-n*, *-na*, *-no* or *-t*, *-ta*, *-to* (with "indefinite" or predicative endings!). In most Czech grammars only these two are recognized as true Participles. Here, however, for the sake of uniformity, we shall keep to our definition of a participle as a verbal adjective and call participles also the verbal adjectives formed from the Past Participle Passive and ending in *-ný*, *-ná*, *-né* or *-tý*, *-tá*, *-té* as well as the verbal adjectives formed from the Pres. and Past Gerunds and ending in *-í* for all persons of the sing. and plur. E.g.:—

Past Part. Pass. nesen (predicative) and nesený
                (attributive) = carried
Pres. Part. Act. nesoucí = (who is) carrying ><Pres.
                Gerund masc. nesa, fem. and neut.
                nesouc,
Past Part. Act. davší = (who has) given ><Past
                Gerund masc. dav, fem. and neut.
                davši.

The Infinitive ends either in *-ti* or *-t*, even in the written literary language.[1] The Supine, which can end only in *-t*, can be said to survive in Czech in the sense that after verbs of going it would be wrong to write a form in *-ti*: jdu spat (not spáti) = I am going to bed (lit. to sleep). Otherwise the Supine no longer has any separate existence in Czech. (Purpose is usually expressed by abych, etc. + Past Part. Active in *-l*.)

The Passive Voice can be rendered in Czech in

---

[1] Always *pronounced* -t.

three ways:—

(1) By the verb býti (= to be), in any form, and the *predicative* Past Participle Passive, e.g.:—

On je chválen = he is being praised
Ona byla námi (or:
 od nás) chválena = she was praised by us
Pivo bylo vypito = the beer was drunk

(2) By using a reflexive verb[1]:—

To se nedělá = that is not done
To se řiká = that is said, one does say that

(3) By using an Active verb and making the former subject the object:

Nesmírně ho chválí = he is immensely praised (lit. they praise him immensely)
Chválíme ho = he is praised by us (lit. we praise him)

A feature of Czech (and Slovak) orthography is that the negative *ne-* which is always stressed, is written as a prefix together with the verb (which loses its stress) in all tenses, e.g.: nésti (= to carry), nenesu (= I am not carrying), nenesl jsem (= I was not carrying), nebudu kouřit (I shall not smoke).

The Present is the only simple tense in Czech, as in Polish, Slovak and Slovenian, and for Pfve. verbs it has a *future* meaning, as in all West and East Slav languages.

The personal endings of the Present in Czech are:—

Sing. 1 -u (after *j*, -*i* is commonly used in the written literary language), or -*m* (after -*á*- or -*í*-, see below).
2 -š
3 no ending.

---

[1]Reflexive verbs are formed by adding the enclitic and separable Accusative Reflexive pronoun *se* to all forms of the Active verb and for all persons. Certain verbs only exist in the reflexive form, e.g.: báti se = to fear, ptáti se or tázati so = to ask (a question).

Czech is also fond of verbs used with the *Dative* Reflexive pronoun *si* (corresponding partly to the Middle Voice in Ancient Greek and) meaning "to do something for oneself". This *si* is used mostly with verbs expressing a bodily action, e.g.: sednouti si = to sit down, zakouřiti si = to have a smoke, to start smoking, odpočinouti si = to have a rest, koupiti si = to buy (for oneself).

Plur. 1 -me¹
2 -te
3 -ou (after *j*, -*í* is commonly used in the written lit. language); -*jí* after -*a*- (short in this person) and after -*e*-/-*ě*-; -*í* for *í*-verbs (see below).

The endings of the 2nd and 3rd pers. sing. and of the 1st and 2nd pers. plur. are joined to the verb stem by the joining-vowel -*e*- in the first three classes, by -*á*- in the fourth class and by -*í*- in the fifth class.

Class II is characterized by an -*n*- preceding the -*e*- joining vowel, and Class III by a -*j*- preceding the -*e*-. All other verbs with an -*e*- joining vowel belong therefore to Class I.

The Infinitive, which ends in -*ti* or -*t* in the written language but only in -*t* in the normal spoken language, has no joining vowel in Class I: nésti (= carry). In Class II it has -*nou*- preceding the -*ti*: tisknouti (= to press, print), minouti (= to pass away). In Class III the stem may end either in a vowel; ží-ti (= to live), hrá-ti (= to play), or in a consonant, when joining vowel -*a*- is used: milov-ati (= to love), táz-ati se (= to ask). In Class IV the -*ti* is invariably preceded by -*a*-:dělati (= to do), while in Class V it can be preceded by either -*i*-, as in chváliti (= to praise), or by -*ě*-, as in viděti (= to see), uměti (= to know how to).

Notice that verbs with a root originally containing -*er*, metathesized in Old Slavonic, e.g.: in оумрѣти, in Czech have an Infin. in -*říti*, e.g.: umříti (= to die, Pfve.). Infinitives going back to a root with the nasal vowel ѧ, generally have -*íti*: začíti (= to begin); but přijmouti (= to accept)— under the influence of the Present: přijmu.

Only velar stems of Class I end in -*ci* instead of -*ti*, e.g.: péci (= to bake, <*pekti), moci (= to be able, <*mogti).

Most verbs with a long vowel in their dissyllabic Infin., shorten this stem vowel in all other forms: nésti (= to carry), Pres. nesu, Past Part. Active nesl. Some dissyllabic Infinitives with a long -*á*- in the stem have this vowel shortened when a prefix or the negative *ne*- is used, e.g.: dáti (= to give, Pfve.), prodati (= to sell, Pfve.), nedati (= not to give).

¹Verbs of Classes I, II and III (only) may shorten the ending of the 1st pers. plur to -*m*; in colloquial speech this ending is the commoner.

CZECH

As in other Slavonic languages, it is essential to learn both the Present and the Infinitive of every verb, the one being no sure guide to the form of the other. Most modern Czech grammars classify the verbs according to the Infinitive, the form given in most dictionaries. But as this form by itself gives no further guidance, and also for comparative purposes, it is more helpful for us to classify Czech verbs according to their Presents in the first place, with subdivisions according to their Infinitives.

Classification of Czech Verbs according to their Presents, with Subdivisions according to their Infinitives.

	3rd pers. sg. Pres.	Infinitive		
I. A.a.	nese	nésti	= to carry	Same stem in Pres. and Infin., consonantal stem.
	peče[1]	péci	= to bake	
Also:—				
	mře[1]	mříti	= to die Infin. in -řti, from *-erti	
	začne	začíti	= to begin (Pfve.) Infin in -íti, from -ATM	
b.	(no vowel stems)			
B.a.	bere	bráti	= to take Infin. in -ati, consonant stem.	
b.	rve	rváti	= to tear Infin. in -ati, originally a vowel stem.	
II.	tiskne	tisknouti	= to press, print (Impfve.)	n-stems.
	mine	minouti	= to pass (Pfve.)	

III. Presents with -je-
  1. Primary verbs.

	3rd pers. sg. Pres.	Infinitive		
A.a.	žije	žíti	= to live	Same stem in Pres. and Infin., vowel stem.
	seje	síti	= to sow	
	pluje	plouti (from Class I A.b.)	= to sail, float	

  b. (no consonantal stems. The single verb mele mlíti = to grind, owing to the hardening of *l* in Czech now belongs to Class I.A.a.).

---

[1] 1st pers. sing. peku or peču; 3rd pers. pl. pekou or pečou. 1st pers. sing. mru or mřu; 3rd pers. pl. mrou or mřou.

              3rd pers.   Infinitive
              sg. Pres.

   B.   (Infinitives in -*ati*.)
    a. taje   táti(<tajati) = to melt Infin. in -*ati*,
                                            vowel stem.
    b. oře   orati   = to plough. Infin. in -*ati*,
                                          consonantal stem
        also (with hardening of labial):
        sype[1]   sypati   = to pour, sprinkle

  2. Derived verbs. All vowel stems:—
   A.   šediví (by contraction), 3rd pers.
            plur.: šedivějí   } Pres. stem -*ě*-,
                   šedivěti = to grow grey } Infin. in -*ěti*/
        sází,sázejí sázeti(<sadjati)   } -*eti*.
                            = to set, plant
   B.   kupuje   kupovati = to buy (Impfve.) Pres. stem
                             -*u*-, Infin. in -*ovati*.
IV. New class, by contraction from -*aje*- in Pres.
     zná   znáti   = to know (Fr. connaître)
     dělá   dělati   = to do
V. A.   chválí (3rd pers. sg. and pl.)
                chváliti = to praise *i*-stem throughout.
       bdí (3rd pers. sg. and pl.)
                bdíti   = to keep vigil *i*-stem through-
                            out, except in Past: bděl
   B.   vidí (3rd pers. sg. and pl.)
                viděti   = to see   } -*i*- Pres. stem, Infin.
       leží (3rd pers. sg. and pl.)   } in -*ěti/eti*.
                ležeti   = to lie   }

Athematic verbs:
jím(1st pers.sg.Pres.) jí(3rd pers.sg.Pres.)jísti = to eat
vím   "   "   "   ví   "   "   "   věděti = to know
                                                    (Fr. savoir)
jsem   "   "   "   je   "   "   "   býti   = to be
See under Irregular Verbs for full conjugation.

    Note that dám, dá, dáti = to give (Pfve.), in Czech belongs entirely to Class IV, like dělati: 3rd pers. plur. Pres./Fut.: dají.

The Future Tense and the Aspects

    The Future of Imperfective verbs is formed by using the Future Tense of býti (= to be), followed by the Impfve. Infinitive, e.g.:

---

[1]Or: sypá, class IV.

Sing. 1 budu   dělati = I shall do,
      2 budeš   "   etc.
      3 bude   "
Plur. 1 budeme   "
      2 budete   "
      3 budou   "

The only exceptions to this rule are certain simple verbs of going, leading, carrying and conveying, which form their Future tense by prefixing *po-* to their Present form, e.g.:—

vésti[1] = to lead (Impfve.), 1st pers. sg. Pres. vedu, Fut. povedu

zavésti = to lead (Pfve.), Fut. zavedu

The other verbs with Impfve. Fut. formed only with *po-* are jíti[1] = to go (on foot), jeti[1] = to go (conveyed), nésti[1] = to carry, vézti[1] = to convey, vléci = to drag, Fut. povleku, běžeti = to run, Fut. poběžím; (other compounds use the form -běhnouti only, e.g. vběhnouti = to run in, Pfve., Fut. vběhnu).[2]

The following verbs can form their Impfve. Fut. either regularly with budu, budeš, etc., or with *po-* prefixed to their Present:—

Infin.		*Impfve. Fut.*
lézti	= to climb	polezu or budu lézti
kvísti (lit. kvésti)	= to flower	pokvetu " budu kvísti,
růsti	= to grow	porostu etc.
téci	= to flow	poteku
plouti	= to swim, float	popluji
táhnouti	= to pull	potáhnu
hnáti	= to drive	poženu
letěti	= to fly	poletím[2]

The Future of Perfective verbs is in form their Present, which always has a future meaning, as in other West Slav languages, East Slav and usually in Old Slavonic:

dělám = I do,   but udělám = I shall do (Pfve.)
písu = I write, " napíšu = I shall write (Pfve.)

---

[1]For fuller conjugation see below, "Verbs of going and conveying."

[2]Sometimes these futures with *po-* are used in a perfective sense, e.g.: půjdu tam a zabiju ho = I shall go there and kill him.

The *Perfective aspect* can be formed *from a simple Imperfective* verb (i.e. one without a prefix) in one of several ways:—

1. With a prepositional prefix, which is "perfectivizing", but otherwise "void of meaning", as in the last two examples above. Other such prefixes are *po-*, *s-*, *z-* and *za-*, e.g.:—

prosím = I request;   poprosím = I shall request (Pfve.)
hynu   = I perish;   zhynu   = I shall perish (Pfve.)
rozumím = I understand; porozumím = I shall understand (Pfve.)
platim = I pay;   zaplatím = I shall pay (Pfve.)

2. Sometimes the endings *-nouti*, *-nu*, etc., are used. (Many new verbs have been formed with these endings in Czech, but by no means all are Perfective!):

Impfve. padati   = to fall,   Pfve. padnouti
"   sedati si = to sit down, "   sednouti si
"   řezati   = to cut,   "   říznouti
"   sahati   = to seize,   "   sáhnouti

3. Some verbs change the ending:

Impfve. chytati = to catch, Pfve. chytiti
"   strkati = to push, "   strčiti

4. In a few cases a totally different root is used:

Impfve. bráti = to take, Pfve. vzíti
"   klásti = to put, "   položiti

The *Imperfective Aspect is formed from the Perfective* by some form of lengthening, i.e. (1) by lengthening (phonetically) the root vowel and changing the ending, or (2) by actual insertion of an extra syllable. These methods are used with the few simple verbs which are in origin Perfective in meaning and with compound verbs, Perfective because of their prefix, for forming further Imperfectives.

1. Pfve. hoditi   = to throw,   Impfve. házeti
   "   pustiti = to let go, "   pouštěti
   "   pomoci   = to help,   "   pomáhati
2. "   dáti   = to give,   "   dávati
   "   koupiti = to buy,   "   kupovati
   "   usmáti se = to smile, "   usmívati se
   "   umříti   = to die,   "   umírati

Pfve. začíti   = to begin,   Impfve. začínati
  "   usnouti = to fall asleep,   "   usínati
  "   poslati = to send,   "   posílati
  "   zabíti   = to kill,   "   zabíjeti
                                         (<zabijati)
  "   podplatiti = to bribe,   "   podpláceti
                                         (<podplatjati)

The first two examples in (1) and the last two examples in (2) show a typically Czech feature: the change of vowel from -*a*- to -*e*- after the *j* due to the Czech "přehláska" (vowel mutation). All these verbs now have Presents in -*ím*, -*íš*, etc., 3rd p. pl. -*ějí/ejí*. The regular changes of the *consonants* before the *j (yotation)* also take place, of course.

For certain verbs Czech has special Iterative or Frequentative forms and even has Double Frequentatives as well. They are, however, falling out of use. E.g.:—

Impfve.		*Freq.*	*Double Freq.*
jísti	= to eat	jídati	jídávati
čísti	= to read	čítati	čítávati
psáti	= to write	psávati	—
běžeti	= to run	běhati	běhávati
nésti	= to carry	nositi[1]	nosívati
hnáti	= to chase	honiti = to hunt	—

Pres. ženu, ženeš, etc.
  plouti = to float   plavati = to swim   —
Notice:
  býti = to be   bývati = to be   bývávati
                               usually   (comic)

Only extensive reading and listening can teach the foreign learner the correct form and use of the aspects for any particular verb in Czech.

The Past Tense.
This is formed with the Present tense of býti (= to be), used as an enclitic auxiliary verb in the 1st and 2nd pers. sing. and plur. + the variable Past Participle Active in: sing. -*l* (masc.), -*la* (fem.), -*lo* (neut.), plur. -*li* (masc. anim.), -*ly* (masc. inanim. and fem.), -*la* (neut.). In the 3rd pers. sing. and plur. there is no auxiliary verb. The participle is usually formed from the Infinitive by dropping the ending -*ti* and substituting the above endings:

---

[1]See also "Verbs of going and conveying".

CZECH

		Past. Part. Act. masc.
nésti	= to carry,	nesl (with root vowel shortened)
minouti	= to pass away,	minul (with shortened vowel)
žíti	= to live,	žil (" " ")
dáti	= to give(Pfve.),	dal (" " ")
dělati	= to do,	dělal
prositi	= to request,	prosil

Velar stem verbs of Class I with Infinitives in -*ci*, restore the velar in the Past Part. Act.:—

		Past Part. Act. masc.
péci	= to bake,	pekl (colloq. pron. pek)
moci	= to be able,	mohl (" " moch)

Dental stem verbs of Class I with Infinitives in -*sti*, revive the dental in the Past Part. Act.:

		Past Part. Act. masc.
krásti	= to steal,	kradl (colloq. pron. krat)
plésti	= to weave,	pletl (" " plet)

Verbs of the type umříti (= to die), Class I, have Past Part. Act. with -*řel*: umřel, (fem.) umřela, etc.

Verbs originally having a nasal ą in the root, such as začíti (= to begin), have Past Part. Act. in -*al*: začal, začala, etc.; títi (= to cut), Past Part. Act. ťal, etc.

Most verbs with a consonant preceding -*nouti*, drop the syllable -*nu*- in the Past Part. Act.:

říznouti	= to cut(Pfve.),	Past Part. Act. řízl,řízla,
tisknouti	= to press, print,	" " " tiskl

Only verbs with contracted roots keep a long vowel in the Past Part. Act., e.g.:—

báti se(<bojati se)	= to fear,	Past Part.Act. bál se
přáti(<přejati)	= to wish,	" " " přál

We then get a complete tense, such as:—

Sing.
masc. dělal jsem(= I was doing), fem. dělala jsem
      dělal jsi   dělala jsi
      dělal   dělala
                                                      neut. dělalo

Plur. masc. anim.	dělali jsme dělali jste[1] dělali	masc. inanim. and fem. dělaly jsme[1] dělaly jste[1] dělaly neut. dělala

jsi may be abbreviated to *s*. The Nominative Personal Pronouns are only used when emphasized or contrasted.

If the subject or other emphasized word precedes the verb, the enclitic auxiliary verb is put before the Past Part. Act., e.g.: já jsem dělal.

With the reflexive verbs in the 2nd pers. sing., jsi se is contracted to ses, and jsi si to sis.

ty jsi se myl = you were washing > ty ses myl
ty jsi si přál = you were wishing > ty sis přál

The auxiliary verb always precedes the Reflexive Pronoun. (See "Word Order with Enclitics" below.)

In contrast to South Slav languages, the negative particle *ne-* is prefixed to (and written together with) the Past Part. Act. and not the auxiliary verb:

nedělal jsem = I was not doing, cf. Serbocr. нисам радио.

In meaning the Impfve. Past sometimes corresponds to the English Imperfect (I was doing), while the Pfve. Past corresponds to the English Perfect and Past Definite (Preterite) tenses:

dělal jsem = I was doing, I used to do
udělal jsem = I have done, or did

The Pluperfect

This tense is no longer used colloquially, but may be met with in writing, especially in older writers. It is formed with the Past Participle of býti in the appropriate gender added to the Past tense:

byl jsem viděl = I (masc.) had seen
byla jsem viděla = " (fem.)   "   "
byli jsme viděli = we (masc.) had seen
byly viděly   = they (fem. pl.) had seen, etc.

---

[1]But, when addressing a *single* person in polite speech, the participle is put in the singular, e.g. dělal jste (m.), dělala jste (f.).

The Conditional

This is formed with the variable enclitic auxiliary:

Sing. 1. bych, 2. bys, 3. by, Plur. 1. bychom, 2. byste, 3. by, + the Past Part. Act. in -*l*, -*la*, -*lo*, etc., as for the Past tense (see footnote p. 105).

As in the Past tense, if the subject or other emphasized word precedes the verb, the auxiliary is put before the Past Part. Act.:

jedl bych = I would eat, but: já bych jedl (here já = I, is put in for emphasis) = *I* feel like eating.

With the conjunctions aby and kdyby the Conditional auxiliaries are "telescoped" and written as one word:

    abych = in order that I ...
    kdybychom věděli = if we should know, if we had known ...

The Past Conditional

This is formed by byl, byla, bylo, byli, byly, byla and the Conditional auxiliary verb bych, bys, by, etc. (a Conditional of býti) + the Past Part. Act. in -*l*, also varying according to gender:

    byl bych věděl = I should have known (if ...)
    byli byste viděli = you would have seen

For the verb býti itself, the Past Part. býval, from the Frequentative bývati, is used:

    byl bych býval = I should have been

This tense is often replaced in conversation by the ordinary Conditional when there is no danger of misunderstanding.

The Imperative

The Imperative in Czech is formed from the Present stem:

1. If this ends in a single consonant, the endings for *all* classes of verbs are:—

2nd pers. sg. — (the final consonant is softened if it is a dental or a velar— the latter by the 2nd or 1st Palatalization)
1st pers. pl. -me
2nd pers. pl. -te
    E.g.:

CZECH 107

				With softening	
2nd pers. sg. Pres.	bereš	prosíš	zhyneš (Pfve.)	platíš (Pfve.)
2nd pers. sg. Imperat.	ber! = take!	pros! = ask!	zhyň! = perish!	plať! = pay!
1st pers. pl. Imperat.	berme	prosme	zhyňme	plaťme
2nd pers. pl. Imperat.	berte	proste	zhyňte	plaťte

With 2nd Palatalization

2nd pers. sg. Pres.	pečeš	pomůžeš (Pfve.)
2nd pers. sg. Imperat.	peč!¹ = bake!	pomoz! = help!
1st pers. pl. Imperat.	pecme	pomozme
2nd pers. pl. Imperat.	pecte	pomozte

Long root vowels are regularly shortened in the Imperat.:

| Pres. or Fut. | chválí = he praises | slíbí = he will promise | táže se = he asks | píše = he writes |
| Imperat. | chval! etc. | slib! etc. | taž se! | piš! |

2. If the Present stem ends in more than one consonant, the endings for *all* classes of verbs are:—

2nd pers. sg. -i
1st pers. pl. -ěme
2nd pers. pl. -ěte
E.g.

2nd pers. sg. Pres.	čteš	tiskneš	pozveš (Pfve.)
2nd pers. sg. Imperat.	čti! = read!	tiskni! = press!	pozvi! = invite!
1st pers. pl. "	čtěme	tiskněme	pozvěme
2nd pers. pl. "	čtěte	tiskněte	pozvěte

After *l*, *ř*, and *ž*, the forms of the 1st and 2nd pers. plur. are the same in spelling (but, of course, not in intonation) as the corresponding persons of the Pres. (Fut.), as these consonants cannot be followed by *ě*:

2nd pers. sg. Pres.	pošleš (Pfve.)	zavřeš (Pfve.)	lžeš
2nd pers. sg. Imperat.	pošli! = send!	zavři! = close!	(ne)lži! = (don't) lie!
1st pers. pl. "	pošleme!	zavřeme!	(ne)lžeme!
2nd pers. pl. "	pošlete!	zavřete!	(ne)lžete!

3. If the Present stem ends in a vowel, the endings for *all* classes of verbs are:—

---

¹Or: peč, pečme, pečte. The forms with -*c* are more literary.

```
2nd pers. sg.   -j
1st pers. pl.   -jme
2nd pers. pl.   -jte
    E.g.
```

```
2nd pers. sg. Pres.       pi-ješ         milu-ješ
2nd pers. sg. Imperat.    pij! = drink!  miluj! = love!
1st pers. pl.      "      pijme!         milujme
2nd pers. pl.      "      pijte!         milujte
```

Notice that Class IV stems ending in -*á* change this vowel to -*e* before these endings, e.g.:

```
2nd pers. sg. Pres.       děláš
2nd pers. sg. Imperat.    dělej! = do!
1st pers. pl.      "      dělejme!
2nd pers. pl.      "      dělejte!
```

Furthermore, verbs with contracted Present ending in -*ím*, -*íš*, etc., 3rd p. plur. -*ějí/ejí* (Class III 2.A), have Imperative endings in -*ě-j*/ -*e-j*, -*me*, -*te*, e.g.:

```
3rd pers. pl. Pres.       rozumějí           sázejí
2nd pers. sg. Imperat.    rozuměj! =         sázej! = plant!
                           understand!
1st pers. pl.      "      rozumějme!         sázejme!
2nd pers. pl.      "      rozumějte!         sázejte!
```

The 3rd persons sing. and plur. are rendered periphrastically by: ať (less commonly by nechť) + Pres. Impfve. or Fut. Pfve., e.g.:

```
ať pije (Impfve.)  = let him drink!
ať vypije (Pfve.)  = let him drink (up)!
```

The Gerunds (Active)

The *Present* (indeclinable) *Gerund* is formed by adding to the Present stem the endings:

-a (masc.), -ouc(fem. and neut.), -ouce (pl. all genders) for hard stems (Classes I and II), and
-e/ě("   ), -íc ("   "   "), -íce (pl. all genders) for soft and formerly soft stems (Classes III, IV, and V), e.g.:

```
Hard: m. bera     = taking      f.,n. berouc,    pl. berouce
         tiskna   = pressing,        tisknouc,        tisknouce
Soft:    žije     = living,          žijíc,           žijíce,
         píše     = writing,         píšíc,           píšíce
         sypaje   = pouring,         sypajíc,         sypajíce,
         rozuměje = understanding,   rozumějíc,       rozumějíce
         sázeje   = planting,        sázejíc,         sázejíce
         táže se  = asking,          tážíc se,        tážíce se,
         kupuje   = buying,          kupijíc,         kupujíce,
```

```
dělaje    = doing,           f.,n. dělajíc,   pl. dělajíce,
prose     = asking,                prosíc,        prosíce
leže      = lying down,            ležíc,         ležíce
```

Notice: lháti (= to tell lies), 2nd pers. sg. Pres. lžeš, but Pres. Gerund lha, lhouc, lhouce.

The Present Gerund is only used in the written language. It expresses an action performed by the subject, simultaneous with another action in the present, past or future. It is formed from Impfve. verbs only.

A Present Gerund formed from Pfve. verbs has a future meaning like their "Present" tense, and is used to express an action preceding another action in the Future—a use peculiar to Czech, e.g.:

Přectouce noviny, dáme Vám je = Having read the newspaper, we shall give it you.

The *Past Gerund* is formed only from Pfve. verbs from their Infinitive stem (i.e. Infin. less -*ti*). The root vowel is regularly shortened. If the stem ends in a consonant (Class I A.a. only), the endings are:—

(none)(masc.), -*ši* (fem. and neut.), -*še* (plur. all genders), e.g.:

```
přinésti = to bring, Past Ger. přines,   přinesši,   přinesše
říci     = to say,       "   " řek,      rekši,      rekše
```

But notice the types:

```
začíti   = to begin,     "   " začav,    začavši,    začavše
umříti   = to die,       "   " umřev,    umřevši,    umřevše
```

For all other Classes the Infin. stem ends in a vowel and the endings used are: -*v* (masc.), -*vši* (fem. and neut.), -*vše* (plur.).

```
sebrati    = to collect,           Past Ger. sebrav, sebravši,
                                             sebravše
stisknouti = to press,        "   "          stisknuv,
                                             stisknuvši,
                                             stisknuvše
napíti se  = to have a        "   "          napiv se, napivši
             drink,                          se, napivše se
porozuměti = to understand,   "   "          porozuměv, poro-
             grasp,                          zuměvši, poro-
                                             zuměvše
udělati    = to do,           "   "          udělav, udělavši,
                                             udělavše
poprositi  = to request,                     poprosiv, poprosi-
                                             vši, poprosivše
```

The Past Gerund is used only in writing, to express an action in the past preceding another action *in the past* only.

The Participles
Verbal adjectives (i.e. participles) can be formed *from the feminine form* of both Gerunds, by adding -í to the Pres. Gerund. and by lengthening the final -i to -í of the Past Gerund, for all genders and numbers (soft declension). E.g.:—

Pres.: tisknoucí = who, or which, press(es);
         dělající = who, or which, do(es)
Past.: vytisknuvší = who, or which, has (have) squeezed out:
    udělavší = who, or which, has (have) done

Their use is purely adjectival. But those in -cí should be distinguished from the pure adjectives sometimes formed from the same roots and describing an instrument, e.g.:—

píšící = who writes, but psací stroj = typewriter
mluvící = who talks, " mluvicí film = talkie
šící = who is " šicí stroj = sewing machine
    sewing

The *Past Participle Active* in -l and its formation have already been dealt with under "The Past Tense", q.v. This participle is only used in the Past and Pluperfect Tenses and the Conditional Mood and is in form identical with the 3rd pers. sg. of the Past Tense (which has no auxiliary verb).

The *Past Participle Passive*. This is formed from the Infin. stem of transitive verbs with the endings:

Sing. -n(masc.), -na(fem.), -no(neut.); Plur. -ni(masc. anim.),
                                            -ny(masc. inanim.
or   and fem.), -na
                                            (neut.),

Sing. -t(masc.), -ta(fem.), -to(neut.); Plur. -ti(masc. anim.),
                                            -ty(masc. inanim.
                                            and fem.), -ta
                                            (neut.).

The endings with -t- are confined to (1) verbs of Class III 1.A.a. (-je verbs with vowel stems), e.g.:

    žíti = to live, Past Part. Pass. žit;
    mýti = to wash, Past Part. Pass. myt
(2) some verbs of Class II, e.g.:

CZECH

tisknouti	= to press, print,	Past Part. Pass. tisknut (or tištěn)
vinouti	= to wind,	" " " vinut
probodnouti	= to pierce,	" " " probodnut (or proboden)

but

táhnouti	= to pull,	" " " tažen

(3) the few verbs of Class I.A.a. with root vowels from original nasal ᴀ of the type:

začíti	= to begin,	Past Part. Pass. začat, also—
najmouti	= to hire, let,	" " " najat

(4) a few verbs with contracted roots:

ohřáti > ohřejati = to warm (Pfve.), Past Part. Pass. ohřát

All other verbs have the endings with -n. Those with Infin. in -ati, have -an, -ana, etc., with -a- preceding the n. Other verbs have -e-preceding the n: -en, -ena, etc. E.g.:

orati	= to plough,	Past Part. Pass. oran
udělati	= to do,	" " " udělan

but

nésti	= to carry,	" " " nesen, etc.
péci	= to bake	" " " pečen, etc.

The stems of most verbs of Class V undergo *yotation* before the endings -en, -ena, etc. E.g.:

prositi	= to request,	Past Part. Pass. prošen
zkaziti	= to spoil,	" " " zkažen
mysliti	= to think,	" " " myšlen
platiti	= to pay,	" " " placen
naroditi se	= to be born,	" " " narozen
čistiti	= to clean,	" " " čištěn
měniti	= to change,	" " " měněn

(See also No. 4 under "Slavonic Characteristics".)

It will be seen that the above Past Participles Pass. have the endings of predicative adjectives. They are, in fact, used only predicatively, mainly with the verb "to be" to express the Passive voice. Most Czech grammars recognize only these forms as true Past Participles Passive.

But these same participles can also be used with the endings of attributive adjectives: Sing. -ý, -á, -é; Plur. -í, -é,-á, and with the same function as attributive adjectives, e.g.:

```
umytý hoch      = a boy who has been washed
vypité pivo     = beer which has been drunk
orané pole      = a ploughed field
změněný způsob  = a changed way (of doing
                  something)
```

These attributive Past Participles Passive are fully declined in contrast to their predicative counterparts, which are only used now in the Nominative.

The Verbal Noun

The Verbal Noun is formed from the Past Part. Passive by adding the neuter ending -*í*:

```
šit    = sewn     — šití    = sewing
psán   = written  — psaní   = writing
myšlen = thought  — myšlení = thinking
```

Dissyllabic Verbal Nouns have their first syllable lengthened, when they are compounded with a prefix, e.g.:

braní = taking,   nabrání = taking (in).

Verbs with contracted or polysyllabic stems also have a long penultimate syllable, e.g.:

```
státi<stojati = to stand; Verbal Noun stání
volati        = to call;     "     "  volání
```

Verbal Nouns can be formed for intransitive verbs as from a non-existent Past Part. Pass. e.g.:

```
spáti  = to sleep, Verbal Noun spaní   = sleeping
boleti = to hurt,      "    "  bolení  = pains
seděti = to sit,       "    "  sedění or sezení (= a
                                 meeting, sitting)
```

In contrast to Slovak and Polish, Verbal Nouns formed from reflexive verbs normally lose the Reflexive pronoun *se*, e.g.: vyspati se = to sleep one's fill; Verbal Noun vyspání. But učení se cizím jazykům = the study of foreign languages, cf. učení cizím jazykům = the teaching of foreign languages.[1]

Examples of the three main Conjugations of Verbs

1. -*e*- type (Class I, II, and III, 1. and III 2.B).

Class I. nésti = to carry   Class III, 1.A.a krýti = to
             (Impfve.)   cover
Class II. tisknouti = to press, Class III, 2.B kupovati = to buy
             print

[1] After verbal nouns the case (for the object) normally governed by the verb is preserved, except that the Accusative becomes an (objective) Genitive.

Class I. nésti = to carry (Impfve.)
Class II. tisknouti = to press, print

PRESENT:
Sing.	1	nesu	tisknu
	2	neseš	tiskneš
	3	nese	tiskne
Plur.	1	nesem(e)	tisknem(e)
	2	nesete	tisknete
	3	nesou	tisknou

IMPERATIVE:
Sing.	2	nes	tiskni
Plur.	1	nesme	tiskněme
	2	neste	tiskněte

FUTURE:
Sing.	1	pones	budu tisknouti
	2	poneseš	budeš tisknouti
	3	ponese	etc.
Plur.	1	ponesem(e)	
	2	ponesete	
	3	ponesou	

GERUNDS:
Pres.   nesa, nesouc,   tiskna, tisknouc,
        nesouce   tisknouce
Past   (za-)nes, -nesši,   (s)tisknuv, -tisknuvši,
        -nesše   -tisknuvše

PARTICIPLES:
Pres. Act.   nesoucí   tisknoucí
Past Act.   nesl, nesla, neslo   tiskl, tiskla, tisklo
Past Pass.   nesen, nesena,   tisknut, tisknuta,
             neseno   tisknuto or tištěn,
                             tištěna, tištěno

VERBAL NOUN:
             nesení   tištění

Class III. krýti = to cover (Class III 1.A.a)
kupovati[1] = to buy (Cl. III 2.B).

[1]Like kupovati are conjugated the consonantal stems, with *yotation* in the Pres., of the type III.1.B.b.--orati (to plough); Pres. oŕu or oŕi, oŕeš, etc., or orám; Imperat, oŕ or orej, Pres. Ger. oŕe or oraje. Only a few verbs of this class do not have an alternative Pres. of the dělám type (Class IV). The most important are:

tázati se	= to ask a question,	Pres.	tážu se
poslati	= to send (Pfve.)	"	pošlu
ukázati	= to show,	"	ukážu
plakati	= to cry, weep,	"	pláču
mazati	= to smear, spread on,	"	mažu
kázati	= to preach,	"	kážu
česati	= to comb,	=	češu
psáti	= to write,	=	píšu

(cont. p. 114)

PRESENT:

Sing.	1	kryji(kryju)	kupuji(kupuju)
	2	kryješ	kupuješ
	3	kryje	kupuje
Plur.	1	kryjem(e)	kupujem(e)
	2	kryjete	kupujete
	3	kryjí(kryjou)	kupují(kupujou)

IMPERATIVE:

Sing.	2	kryj	kupuj
Plur.	1	kryjme	kupujme
	2	kryjte	kupujte

GERUNDS:

Pres.   kryje, kryjíc,   kupuje, kupujíc,
        kryjíce   kupujíce
Past   (za-)kryv, -kryvši, (na-)kupovav, -kupovavši,
        -kryvše   —kupovavše

PARTICIPLES:

Pres. Act.   kryjící   kupující
Past. Act.   kryl, kryla, krylo   kupoval, kupovala,
                                    kupovalo
Past Pass.   kryt, kryta, kryto   kupován, kupována,
                                    kupováno

VERBAL NOUN: krytí   kupování

2. -*a*- type (Class IV)
       dělati = to do

PRESENT: **GERUNDS:**

Sing.	1	dělám
	2	děláš
	3	dělá
Plur.	1	děláme
	2	děláte
	3	dělají

Pres.   dělaje, dělajíc, dělajíce
Past   (u-) dělav, -dělavši, -dělavše

PARTICIPLES:

Pres. Act.   delající
Past Act.   dělal, dělala, dělalo
Past Pass.   dělán, dělána, děláno

IMPERATIVE:

Sing.	2	dělej
Plur.	1	dělejme
	2	dělejte

VERBAL NOUN: dělání

(Footnote continued from p. 113)
         lháti   = to tell a lie, Pres. lžu
    Only verbs with Infin. in -*ova*ti are conjugated like
kupovati. Verbs with Infin. in -ívati, -ávati follow dělati.

3. *-i-* type (Class V and Class III.2.A.)

Class V. chváliti = to praise
Class III.2.A. sázeti[1] = to set, plant

PRESENT:

		Class V	Class III.2.A
Sing.	1	chválím	sázím
	2	chválíš	sázíš
	3	chválí	sází
Plur.	1	chválíme	sázíme
	2	chválíte	sázíte
	3	chválí	sázejí[1]

IMPERATIVE:

Sing.	2	chval[2]	sázej
Plur.	1	chvalme	sázejme
	2	chvalte	sázejte

GERUNDS:

Pres.   chvále, chválíc,   sázeje, sázejíc,
        chválíce   sázejíce
Past (po-)chváliv,   (za-)sázev, -sázevši,
        -chválivši,   -sázevše
        -chválivše

PARTICIPLES:

Pres. Act. chválící   sázící
Past Act.   chválil, chválila,   sázel, sázela, sazelo
            chvalilo
Past Pass. chválen, chválena,   sázen, sázena, sázeno
            chváleno

VERBAL NOUN:

chválení   sázení

---

[1]This is the model for (*a*) Iterative and Impfve. verbs, often compound, derived from other verbs, e.g. přicházeti = to come (Impfve.), and (*b*) verbs derived from nouns and adjectives and meaning "becoming something", e.g. šedivěti = to grow grey. Uměti (= to know how to) and směti or smíti (= to dare, to be allowed to) are two other important verbs in this class. So also rozuměti (= to understand). Some 32 verbs of this class have an alternative ending -í in the 3rd pers. pl. (cf. Class V); e.g. náležejí *or* náleží = they belong.

[2]The root vowel is usually shortened in the Imperative in this class (see p. 107).

Irregular Verbs
The Athematic Verbs:

	býti = to be	jísti = to eat (Impfve.)	věděti = to know
		snísti = to eat (Pfve.)	pověděti = to say (Pfve.)

PRESENT:

Sing.	1	jsem	jím	vím
	2	jsi	jíš	víš
	3	je[1] (or jest)	jí	ví
Plur.	1	jsme	jíme	víme
	2	jste	jíte	víte
	3	jsou	jedí	vědí

FUTURE:

Sing.	1	budu	sním(Pfve.)	budu věděti
	2	budeš	sníš	etc.
	3	bude	sní	
Plur.	1	budeme	sníme	
	2	budete	sníte	
	3	budou	snědí	

IMPERATIVE:

Sing.	2	buď[2]	jez	věz (pověz)[3]
Plur.	1	buďme	jezme	vězme
	2	buďte	jezte	vězte

GERUNDS:

Fut.	buda, budouc, budouce		
Pres.	jsa, jsouc, jsouce	jeda, jedouc, jedouce	věda,[3] vědouc, vědouce
Past	byv, byvši, byvše	(vy-)jed, -jedši, -jedše	(z-)věděv, -věděvši, -věděvše

PARTICIPLES:

Pres. Act.	jsoucí	jedoucí	vědoucí
Past Act.	byl, byla, bylo	jedl, jedla, jedlo	věděl, věděla, vědělo
Past Pass.	-byt, -byta, -byto	(vy-)jeden, -jedena, -jedeno	(po-)věděn, -věděna, -věděno[3]
VERBAL NOUN:	bytí	jedení	vědění

[1]Negative 3rd pers. sing. Pres.: není. "Jest" is colloquially only used in the phrases: tak jest (= that is so, that's right), and to jest (= that is, i.e.).

[2]Emphatic form: budiž, also = all right! (agreeing).

[3]But in compounds: zvěděti (do(z)věděti se) (Pfve.) = to find out, Imperative: zvěď (do(z)věď se); Present Gerund: dovědě se; zapověděti (Pfve.) = to forbid, Past Participle Pass.: zapověděn *or* zapovězen; so for other compounds.

Note that in Czech dáti (= to give, Pfve.) is regular and is conjugated exactly like dělati (see above).

Other Verbs
The other most important irregular verbs in Czech are:—

míti = to have   chtíti = to want

PRESENT:
Sing.	1	mám	chci
	2	máš	chceš
	3	má	chce
Plur.	1	máme	chceme
	2	máte	chcete
	3	mají	chtějí or chtí

IMPERATIVE:
Sing.	2	měj	chtěj
Plur.	1	mějme	chtějme
	2	mějte	chtějte

GERUNDS:
Pres.   maje,majíc,majíce   chtěje,chtějíc,
                              chtějíce or chtě,
                              chtíc, chtíce
Past   měv,měvši,měvše   chtěv,chtěvši,chtěvše

PARTICIPLES:
Pres. Act. mající   chtějící or chtící
Past Act.   měl, měla, mělo   chtěl,chtěla,chtělo

VERBAL NOUN: jmění   chtění

The following common verbs are irregular only in certain parts. Sometimes their Present is markedly different from their Infinitive. We give their most salient features, arranging them according to the five Classes:—

Infinitive.	Meaning.	Pres. 1st.3rd.p. sg. (3rd. p. pl.)	Imperat. 2nd. p. sg.
Class I.			
bráti(Impfve.)	= to take	beru, bere	ber!
		Past Part. Act. masc. sg. bral	Past Part. Pass. masc. sg. brán
vzíti(Pfve.)	= to take	vezmu,vezme vzal	vezmi! vzat
cf. najmouti (Pfve.)	= to hire	najmu,najme najal	najmi! najat
(najímati, Impfve., is regular)			

Class I. (contd.)

Infinitive.	Meaning.	Pres. 1st.3rd.p. sg. (3rd. p. pl.)	Imperat. 2nd.p. sg.
čísti(Impfve.)	= to read	čtu, čte	čti!
		Past Part.	*Past Part.*
		Act. masc. sg.	*Pass. masc. sg.*
		četl,-a(f.)	čten
hnáti(Impfve.)	= to chase	ženu, žene	žeň!
		hnal	hnán
lézti(Impfve.)	= to crawl is regular, but nalézti (Pfve.) = to find, has Future: naleznu, nalezne (Class II)		
lháti(Impfve.)	= to tell lies	*lžu*, lže, *lžou*	lži!
		lhal	lhán
moci(Impfve.)	= to be able	mohu, může, mohou	(pomoz! = help)
		mohl	-možen
přísti(Impfve.)	= to spin	předu, přede	před'!
		předl	předen
říci(Pfve.)[1]	= to say	(jářku)[1], řeknu, řekne	řekni!
		řekl	řečen
růsti(Impfve.)	= to grow	rostu, roste	rost'!
		rostl	—
stláti(Impfve.)	= to make a bed	stelu, stele	stel!
		stlal	stlán
títi(Impfve.)	= to chop	tnu, tneš	tni!
		t'al	t'at
tlouci (Impfve.)[2]	= to beat, pound	tluku or tluču, tluče	tluc!
		tloukl	tlučen
třásti(Impfve.)	= to shake	třesu, třese	třes!
		třásl	třesen
tříti(Impfve.)	= to rub	tru or třu, tře	tři!
		třel	třen
zváti(Impfve.)	= to call	zvu, zve	zvi!
		zval	zván

[1] jářku = mark you, mind you.
Cf. obléci (Pfve.) = to dress, Pres. obleku, obleču, or obléknu,
Imperat. oblec!, obleč! or oblékni!

[2] Similarly: vléci = to drag. Pres. vleku or vleču,
téci = to flow, Pres. teku or teču,
síci = to mow, Pres. seku or seču.

Class II.

Infinitive.	Meaning	Pres. 1st.3rd.p. sg. (3rd.p. pl.)	Imperat. 2nd.p. sg.
-pomenouti (Pfve.), e.g.:—			
zapomenouti·	= to forget	Fut. zapomenu, zapomene	zapomeň!
		Past Part. Act. masc. sg. zapomněl	Past Part. Pass. masc. sg. zapomenut
vzpomenouti	= to remember, similarly		
(vzpomínati	= to remember, Impfve., is regular)		
-pnouti (Pfve.), e.g.:—			
napnouti	= to stretch,	Fut. napnu,napne napjal	napni! napjat
vypnouti	= to switch off, similarly		
(vypínati	= to switch off, Impfve., is regular)		
státi se (Pfve.)	= to happen	Fut. stane se stalo se	staň se
(stávati se	= to happen, Impfve., is regular, like dělati)		

So also its compounds: dostati (Pfve.) = to receive
                      zůstati (") = to remain

zblbnouti(Pfve.) = to go crazy, is regular: zblbnu. The Past Part. Act. has a spelling remarkable to English eyes: zblbl (as well as zblbnul).

Class III (except III.2.A)

hřáti(Impfve.)	= to warm	hřeji, hřeje hřál	hrej! hřát
přáti(Impfve.)	= to wish	přeji, přeje přál	přej! přán
psáti(Impfve.)	= to write	píšu, píše psal	piš! psán
smáti se (Impfve.)	= to laugh	směji se, směje se smál se	směj se vysmán
váti	= to blow	věji, věje vál	věj! (pře-)vát
stonati	= to be ill	stůňu, stůně stonal	(ne)stonej! —

Class III.2.A.:

boleti(Impfve.)	⎯ to hurt (intrans.)	3rd. sg. bolí, 3rd pl. bolejí or bolí bolel	bol! —
bydleti(Impfve.) or bydliti	= to dwell	bydlím,bydlí, bydlejí bydlel	bydli! —
museti or musiti	= to have to, must	musím, musí, musejí or musí musel or musil	— —

Class V.:

Infinitive.	Meaning	Pres. 1st.3rd.p. sg. (3rd.p. pl.)	Imperat. 2nd.p. sg.
báti se (Impfve.)	= to fear	bojím se, bojí se	boj se!
		Past Part. Act. masc. sg. bál se	Past Part. Pass. masc. sg. (obávan)
státi (Impfve.)	= stand	stojím, stojí stál	stůj! —
spáti (Impfve.)	= to sleep	spím, spí, spí spal	spi! -spán
viděti (Impfve.)	= to see	vidím, vidí viděl	viz! viděn

Pres. Gerund: vida, vidouc

Its compounds are regular: nenáviděti = to hate: Imperat. nenáviď!

Pres. Gerund: nenávidě

Verbs of Going and Conveying

To go (on foot) = Impfve. and Pfve. jíti¹   Frequentative: choditi

Pres.	jdu, jdeš, jdou	chodím, chodíš
Fut. *Impfve. and Pfve.*	půjdu	budu choditi
Past Part. Act. *Impfve. and Pfve.*	šel, šla, šlo, pl. šli, šly, šla	chodil, chodila
Imper. (Impfve.)	jdi! jděme! jděte!	= chod'! *go!*
" (Pfve.)	pojď! pojďme! pojďte!	= *come!*
Pres. Gerund	jda, jdouc	
Past Gerund	(vy-)šed, -šedši	

To go (be conveyed) = Impfve. and Pfve. jeti   Frequentative: jezditi

Pres.	jedu, jedeš, jedou	jezdím, jezdíš
Fut. *Impfve. and Pfve.*	pojedu	budu jezditi
Past Part. Act. *Impfve. and Pfve.*	jel, jela	jezdil, jezdila
Imper. (Impfve.)	jeď! jeďme! jeďte!	jezdi!
Past Part. Pass.	přejet (= run over)	ježděn
Pres. Gerund.	jeda, jedouc	
Past Gerund	(od-)jev, -jevši	

N.B.— popojeti (Pfve.) means "to go (conveyed) a little further".

---

¹N.B.— pojíti (Pfve.) has two meanings: (1) to originate, come from, be derived from, and (2) to die (of animals). *Pres. and Fut.*: pojdu; Imper. pojď! Past Part. Act. pošel; Impfve. pocházeti, Class III.2.A, only in sense (1).

To come (on foot) = Impfve. and Freq. přicházeti   Pfve. přijíti
Pres.   přicházím, přicházíš,   Fut. přijdu,
                     přicházejí   přijdeš
Past Partic. Act.   přicházel, přicházela   přišel,
                                                          přišla
Imper.   přicházej!   přijd'!
To come (conveyed) = Impfve. and Freq. přijížděti   Pfve. přijeti
Pres.   přijíždím, přijíždíš,   Fut. přijedu,
                     přijížději   přijedeš
Past Partic. Act.   přijížděl, přijížděla   přijel
Imper.   přijížděj!   přijed'!

Similarly: to go away (on foot) = odcházeti; odejíti, Fut. odejdu,
           Imper. odejdi!, Past Part. Act. odešel, odešla
           to go away (conveyed) = odjížděti, odjeti
           to go out (on foot)   = vycházeti; vyjíti
           to go out (conveyed) = vyjížděti; vyjeti

    vyjezditi (Pfve.)   = to wear (a track) by driving
    jezdívati (Iterative) = to go occasionally (in a vehicle)

To carry = Impfve. nésti   Pfve. zanésti   Freq. nositi
Pres.   nesu, neseš   Fut. zanesu   Pres. nosím
Fut.   ponesu, poneseš   Fut. budu nositi
Past Part. Act. nesl, nesla   zanesl   nosil
Imper.   nes!   pones! zanes![1] nos!

To bring = Impfve. and Freq. přinášeti   Pfve. přinésti
Pres.   přináším, přinášejí   Fut. přinesu
                     (3rd p. pl.)

To lead = Impfve. vésti   Pfve. zavésti   Freq. voditi
                                (also = to mislead)
Pres.   vedu, vedeš   Fut. zavedu   Pres. vodím
Fut.   povedu   Fut. budu voditi
Past Part. Act. vedl, vedla   zavedl   vodil
Imper.   ved'!   zaved'!   vod'!
                                Past Partic. Pass. voděn,
                                but in compounds -vozen.

To bring (a person) = Impfve. and Freq. přiváděti Pfve. přivésti
Pres.   přivádím, přivádějí (3rd p. pl.) Fut. přivedu

To convey = Impfve. vézti   Pfve. zavézti   Freq. voziti
Pres.   vezu, vezeš   Fut. zavezu   Pres. vozím
Fut.   povezu   Fut. budu voziti
Past Part. Act. vezl, vezla   zavezl   vozil
Imper.   vez!   zavez!   voz!

---

[1]N.B.— pones to sem! = bring it here!
       zanes to tam! = take it there!

To bring (in a vehicle) = Impfve.and   Pfve. přivézti
                         Freq. přivážeti
Pres.   přivážím, přivážejí (3rd p. pl.)   Fut. přivezu

WORD ORDER WITH ENCLITICS

(See also "The Past Tense" and "The Conditional" under "The Conjugation of Verbs".)

In Czech there are two main types of enclitics:—
1. The *auxiliary* verbs of
   (a) the Past tense: jsem, jsi, jsme, jste.
   (b) the Conditional mood: bych, bys, by, bychom, byste.
2. The short forms of the Acc. and Dat. of (a) the Reflexive Pronoun, and (b) the Personal Pronouns:
   (a) se (Acc.), si (Dat.)
   (b) mě, tě Acc. sg., ho, masc. Acc., also m. and n. *Gen.* sg.
       mi, ti, Dat. sg., mu, masc. and neut. Dat. sg.

Other monosyllabic Personal Pronouns in the oblique cases (and "to" = this) are also treated as enclitics when they are not emphasized, e.g. nás, nám, vás, vám, jím, je, ji, jí, jich, jim. But they may also bear a stress and then come in any position in a sentence.

The conditional suffix-conjunction -*li* is always enclitic and always comes second in a sentence before other enclitics, e.g. chceš-li ho vidět,... (= if you want to see him,...).

The above auxiliary verbs (1) and pronouns (2) are the only permanently enclitic words in Czech and regularly follow the first word or word-group in a sentence (the "strong" word) in the following order:—
   1. the auxiliary verb,
   2. the Reflexive Pronoun, either Acc. or Dat.,
   3. the Dat. Personal Pronoun,
   4. the Acc. Personal Pronoun.

E.g.:—
Viděl jsem ho   = I saw him
Ukazal jsi mu ho?   = Have you shown him it *or* it (masc.) to him?
To se mi (or nám) nelíbí   = That does not please me (us). I (we) do not like it

(This order is in contrast to that in Serbocr., but agrees with that in Slovenian.)

Jak se Vám u nás líbí?	= How do you like it in our country
Dal bych ti ho (or jej)	= I would give it (masc.) to you
Koupil byste si ho?	= Would you buy it (for yourself)?
Styděl se ho (Gen.)	= He was ashamed before him
Chce se mi spát	= I feel like sleeping
Když jste si je koupili,...	= When you (pl.) bought it for yourselves,...
Proč (jsi si) sis je vzal?	= Why did you take them (for yourself)?

Enclitics may *occasionally* occur directly after an adverbial phrase or a subordinate clause, continuing the main clause, e.g.:

Dosud, ač to slíbil, mi nepsal	= Up to now, although he promised, he has not written to me

But if the final phrase consists of several words, it is preferable to put the enclitic second, as usual:

Dosud, ač to slíbil, ten dlouhý dopis mi nenapsal	= Up to now, although he promised, he has not written me that long letter.

The conjunctions však (= however), and prý (= they say, it is said), are usually used enclitically and then come second word in a sentence before other enclitics:

Je[1] prý nemocen	= They say he is ill
Brzo však jsme odešli	= But we soon went away

The negative, being always prefixed to the main verb, presents no difficulties:

To se nesluší = That is not done (*or* bad manners).

Notice that the co-ordinating conjunctions *a*, *i* (= and) and *ale* (= but) do not count as "strong" words starting a sentence. Therefore one says:

To je hezké a líbí se mi (or: ale nelíbí se mi)	= That is pretty and pleases me, i.e. I like it (or: but I do not like it).

After prepositions the long forms of the Personal Pronouns are always used:—

k tobě = to you
k němu = to him

[1] It will be observed that when the Pres. of the verb "to be" is used as a copulative verb, it is not an enclitic (in contrast to the usage in Serbocr.). So also: Je tma (= It is dark). Jsem spokojený (= I am satisfied).

(See also under "Pronouns" on -ň.)

The adverb už or již (= already) is also often unstressed.

TEXTS

I. Sv. Lukáš, VIII.

5. Vyšel rozsévač, aby rozsíval símě své. A když on rosíval, jedno padlo podlé cesty, i pošlapáno jest, a ptáci nebeští zzobali je. 6. A jiné padlo na skálu, a vsešlé uvadlo, proto že nemělo vláhy. 7. Jiné pak padlo mezi trní, a spoluzrostlé trní udusilo je. 8. A jiné padlo v zemi dobrou, a když vzešlo, učinilo užitek stý. To pověděv, volal: Kdo má uši k slyšení, slyš.

II. Jan Hus, 1415.

Mistr Jan Hus, v naději slúha boží, všem věrným Čechóm, jenž pána boha milují a budú milovati, žádost svú vzkazuje, aby pán buoh dal jim v své milosti přěbývati i skonati a v radosti nebeské na věky přěbývati. Amen.
Věrní a v bohu milí páni, panie, bohatí i chudí. Prosím vás a napomínám, aby pána boha poslúchali, jeho slovo velebili a rádi slyšeli a plnili. Prosím vás, aby pravdy boží, kterúž sem z božieho zákona psal a z řěčí svatých kázal a psal, aby sě té drželi. Prosím také, ač by kto ote mne slyšal na kázání neb súkromie co proti pravdě božie, aneb ač bych kde psal, jenž, ufám bohu, toho nenie, aby toho nedržal. Prosím také, ač kto viděl mé lehké obyčeje v mluvenie neb v skutciech, aby sě jich nedržal, ale aby za mě boha prosil, aby mi ráčil odpustiti. Prosím, aby kněží dobrých obyčejóv milovali a velebili a je ctili, a zvláště, jenž pracují v slově božiem. Prosím, aby sě varovali lstivých lidí a zvláště kněží nehodných, o nichž die spasitel, že sú v rúšě ovčiem a vnitř vlcie hltaví.
Prosím pánóv, aby své chudině milostivě činili a právě jie zpravovali. Prosím měšťanóv, aby své obchody právě vedli. Prosím řemeslníkóv, aby věrně své dielo vedli a jeho požívali. Prosím sluh, aby svým pánóm a paniem věrně slúžili. Prosím mistróv, aby, jsúce dobře živi, své žáky věrně učili, najprvé aby boha milovali, pro jeho sě chválu učili a pro prospěch obcě a pro své spasenie, ale ne pro lakomstvie ani pro světské zvelebenie. Prosím studentóv i žákóv jiných, aby mistróv svých v dobrém poslúchali i následovali a aby sě pilně pro boží chválu a pro spasenie své i jiných lidí učili.

III. F. L. Čelakovský

Slzy a vzdychání

Kdyby všecky slzičky
  pohromadě byly,
co jsou, milý, pro tebe
  oči moje lily:
věru by se louky naše
  všecky zatopily.

Ach, kdyby to vzdychání
  pohromadě bylo,
co mé srdce pro tebe,
  milá, vypustilo:
věru na věži by naší
  zvony rozvonilo.

IV. Svatopluk Čech.

Naše řeč

Moc, sláva, bohatství — co ze všeho nám zbylo?
  Naše řeč.
Co štítem jediným nás v boji těžkém krylo?
  Naše řeč.
Necht' rajskou hudbou zvoní, půlí světa vládne
  jiná řeč,
nám královnou je všech a neustoupí žádné
  naše řeč.
A necht' by popelkou a žebračkou jen byla
  naše řeč,
my chceme, by se v pyšnou kněžnu proměnila
  naše řeč.
Buď zřítelnicí oka, buď nám všeho dražší
  naše řeč,
ni stínem utrpěti nesmí vinou naší
  naše řeč.
Tu není smlouvy žádné, kde má cenu platit
  naše řeč.
vše dejme raději, než píď by měla ztratit
  naše řeč.
Ne, s vůlí naší nesmí v područí se vzdáti
  naše řeč,
té svaté řeči práva odvěká nám zkrátí
  leda meč.
Zde není ústupu, jen k předu musí jíti
  naše řeč,
vždy musí stoupat výš, vždy jasněji se skvíti
  naše řeč!

V. Antonín Sova.

Návrat domů

Když sousedé jdou vždycky v podvečeru
s kosami domů na mohutných zádech,
jich silhouetty ztrácejí se v šeru
pod nebem, jež má blankytový nádech;
na pasech brousky se jim kolébají.
Smích dívek zní, jež uzavřely řadu
a v štěkot psů a bukot z blízkých stájí
zní rachot vozů v mírném letním chladu.
A výminkář, jenž opatroval děti,
že tolik se mu po těch polích stýská,
o každém zvlášť si dá zas vyprávěti ...
A na časy se v dlouhých pruzích blýská.

VI. Karel Rais

Zimní večer

Zasypána sněhem šírá leží lada,
s plné luny tiše záře na ně padá

Prostřed bílé pláně osněžených polí
jenom z plané hruše pahýl zůstal holý.

Na zahradách bílých, dole po úvale,
přikrčeny dřímou naše domky malé.

V drobných oknech jejich jiskry světla není,
v tichých snech tam leží lidé unavení.

Nad sněhovou plání vzduch se vlní tiše—
to je česká země z hluboka tak dýše...

VII. Karel Hlaváček.

Hrál kdosi na hoboj

Hrál kdosi na hoboj, a hrál již kolik dní,
hrál vždycky navečer touž píseň molovou
a ani nerozžal si oheň pobřežní,
neb všecky ohně, prý, tu zhasnou, uplovou.

Hrál dlouze na hoboj, v tmách na pobřeží, v tmách,
na plochém pobřeží, kde nikdo nepřistál:
hrál pro svou Lhostejnost, či hrál spíš pro svůj
                                        Strach?
byl tichý Pastevec, či vyděděný Král?

Hrál smutně na hoboj. Vzduch zhluboka se chvěl
pod písní váhavou a jemnou, molovou...
A od vod teskně zpět mu hoboj vlhkem zněl:
jsou ohně marny, jsou, vždy zhasnou, uplovou.

VIII. T. G. Masaryk.

(Karel Čapek: Hovory s T. G. Masarykem.)

Já nemám rád prázdné mluvení o slovanství, jako nemám rád vlastenčení. Prosím vás, kolik pak z našich slavjanofilů dovede aspoň číst rusky, polsky, srbsky? Stejně tak jako ti lidé, co mají plná ústa, že jsme národ Husův: kdo z nich pročetl aspoň kousek Husa, a nejen Husa, aspoň jednu knihu bratrské reformace? A nač to mluvení: normální člověk nevytrubuje do světa, že miluje své rodiče, svou ženu, své děti; to se rozumí samo sebou. Když miluješ svou vlast, nemusíš o tom mluvit, ale udělej něco kloudného; o nic jiného nejde. Já vím dost dobře, jak veliký, ale také jak těžký program je slovanství; zabýval jsem se studiem Polska, studoval jsem Rusko, pracoval jsem politicky s Charváty a Srby; jsem víc než na půl Slovák a už před padesáti lety jsem přišel s programem Slovenska. To se rozumí, že bych to nedělal bez lásky, člověk už je takový, že rád poslouchá svého srdce; právě proto o lásce nemluví, ale hledá pomoci rozumem. Mně vždycky bránil jakýsi stud, abych říkal slova "vlast", "národ" a tak. Nevyvolávám-li o sobě, že jsem vlastenec, nekřičím o tom druhém, že je zrádce vlasti; musím trpělivě dokazovat, že jeho cesta je z těch a těch důvodů chybná. Takovými velkými hesly se mohou lidé opíjet, ale memohou se jimi naučit pracovat. Osvobodili jsme se od despotických pánů; teď ještě se musíme osvobodit od velkých a despotických slov. Pravda, lidé se drží slov nejen v politice, nýbrž ve všech oborech, v náboženství, vědě, filosofii. Proto jsem vždy kladl důraz na věci, na pozorováni a poznání faktů; ale *dobře* pozorovat a poznávat—k tomu je třeba lásky.

IX. Karel Čapek.

Z názorů kočky

Tohle je můj Člověk. Nebojím se ho.
Je velmi mocný, neboť jí velmi mnoho; je Všežeroucí. Co žereš? Dej mi!
Není krásný, neboť nemá srsti. Nemaje dosti slin, musí se umývat vodou. Mňouká drsně a zbytečně mnoho. Někdy ze spánku přede.
Otevři mi dveře.
Nevím, proč se stal Pánem; snad sežral něco vznešeného.
V mých pokojích zachovává čistotu.
Bere do tlapky černý ostrý dráp a ryje jím do bílých listů. Jinak si neumí hrát. Spí v noci místo

ve dne, nevidí po tmě, nemá žádných rozkoší. Nikdy
nemyslí na krev, nikdy nesní o lovu a boji, nikdy
nezpívá láskou.
   Často za noci, když *já* slysím tajemné a
kouzelné hlasy, když vidím, jak vše oživá tmou, *on*
sedí u stolu se skloněnou hlavou a stále, stále
drápe svým černým drápkem do bílých listů. Nemysli
si, že se o tebe starám. Slýším jen tiché šustění
tvého spáru. Někdy šustění umlkne, ubohá tupá hlava
už neví, jak si hrát, a tu mi ho přijde líto, i ráčím
se přiblížit a tiše mňouknu v sladkém a trýznivém
rozladění. To tedy můj Člověk mne pozvedne a ponoří
do mé srsti teplý obličej. V tu chvíli v něm na
okamžik procitne záblesk vyššího života, i vzdychne
blahem a přede něco, čemu je skoro rozumět
   Nemysli si však, že se o tebe starám. Ohřál jsi
mne, a teď zas půjdu naslouchat černým hlasům.

X. Karel Toman.

Březen

   Na naší studni ráno hvízdal kos.
Jde jaro, jde jaro.
A když jsem okno na sad otvíral,
šeptaly pukající pupeny:
   Jde jaro, jde jaro.

   Bez chvěje se a hrušně čekají.
Jde jaro, jde jaro.
Zas novým třpytem rozkvétá ti vlas
a nových kovů napil se tvůj smích
   Jde jaro, jde jaro.

   Bože můj,
obnoviteli, obroditeli,
   na srdce v sněhu pamatuj.

XI. Jiří Zhor.

Zemětřesení

Svět otřásá se v základech. Kdo vlastně zůstal zdráv?
Tu katastrofu kosmickou odnáší seismograf.
Svět otřásá se v základech. Prý roste nový svět.
Prý pracně bude budován zas miliony let.
Pak nový otřes. Nový pád. A po něm nový růst.
A smysl všeho? K čemu ten kosmický masopust?
A přece ten svět miluješ. A přece toužíš žít.
A přece hledáš pevný bod, kde chceš se uchytit.
Leč hypocentrum revolt všech je, brachu, v srdci tvém.
Nejmenším jeho otřesem už otřásá se zem.
A věčný neklid, věčný kvas, a věčný oheň v nás
tu katastrofu kosmickou přivodí zas a zas.

A písař dějin? S úsměvem napíše hrstku dat.
A tečku k nim, tu udělá buď hrobař nebo kat.

XII. S. K. Neumann.

      Lipová alej

 Lipová alej, lipová alej,
 cesta do hlubin míru.
 Polabský větřík hrouživá prsty
 v její medovou lyru.

 Člověk ji vsadil, země však zdvihla,
 kolonádu svých snění.
 Kdo tudy kráčíš, hleď, zda jsi hoden,
 hoden tohoto jmění.

 A jsi-li dravec v člověčí kůži,
 v krvežíznivé dálce,
 žiješ-li v džungli představ, z nichž prýští
 zločin od mzdy až k válce,

 kéž by tě rázem pohltil písek
 mírumilovné míle,
 by o vteřinu byla zas blíže
 sjednocující chvíle.

 Lipová alej, lipová alej.
 Prodloužíme ji kolem.
 Alejí míru spoutáme běsy
 nad městem i polem.

SECTION 2. SLOVAK
INTRODUCTION

High among the Tatra mojntains and in the surrounding foothills north of Hungary live the Slovak people who, by a miracle of endurance, have survived a thousand years of alien, Hungarian, domination and gained their freedom only with the birth of the Czechoslovak Republic in 1918. Since then, despite many political vicissitudes, they have developed to a surprisingly high state of culture if one bears in mind their initial handicaps.

The Slovaks have preserved a beautifully soft and musical language, which might well serve as a modern "Common Slav" or lingua franca among the Slavs today. For modern Slovak is the most comprehensible of the living Slavonic languages to all other Slavs. Just as the Slovaks occupy geographically a central position among the Slavs, so too their language, in its sounds and forms, is the nearest to an all-round compromise between the various Slavonic languages, having features which make it near both to East and South Slav, as well as to the other West Slav languages.

It is not true to say that Slovak was not written till the nineteenth century, as some assert. It is true that the modern literary language, as we know it today, was then first stabilized, but there are traces of the Slovak language in the local Latin documents from the eleventh to the fifteenth centuries, Latin being the official language in Hungary at the time. In the fourteenth century, Czech became the literary language of the Slovaks, many of whom studied at the university of Prague. Czech culture and language stood at a very high level of development at that period, and the Slovaks were able to appreciate this and also the fact that the Czech language was very near to their own (nearer than it is now) and much easier to learn and use than Latin. Later the Hussites and the Protestant reformers in the sixteenth century also furthered the use of Czech, as well as the churches and other self-governing bodies in Slovakia. There thus grew up a sort of Czechoslovak language, for into the Czech written by Slovaks at that time there inevitably crept in Slovak linguistic features. The national consciousness of the Slovaks was thus saved from obliteration. The earliest documents in this language date from the fifteenth century.

In the seventeenth and eighteenth centuries the Catholics, especially those centered round the university of Trnava, tried to introduce Slovak as opposed to Czech in their church books, as for example in the Catholic hymnal, *Canthus Catholici*, of 1655, which had no ř, ě, etc. In Trnava (Western Slovakia) there were also produced a big Latin-Slovak dictionary in 1777 and grammars of Slovak. At this period the dialects of Western Slovakia were used as a basis for the language. Jozef Ignác Bajza (1755-1836) followed this tradition, and certain Protestant writers too.

Anton Bernolák (1762-1813), a divine and Slavist, crowns this movement. Among other works he published, in 1790, a big Slovak Grammar; and after his death, in 1825, his Slovak-Czech-Latin-German-Hungarian dictionary started appearing. His phonetic orthography was later to guide the reforms of Štúr, and his linguistic teaching guided the Slovak poet Ján Hollý (1785-1849). In the churches the Catholics followed Bernolák, while the Protestants preferred to use Czech.

Ľudovít Štúr (1815-1856), a Protestant (Evangelical), and his two collaborators, Michal Miloslav Hodža (1811-1870) and Jozef Miloslav Hurban (1817-1888), finally broke this division by introducing the speech of *central* Slovakia as the basis of literary Slovak. Štúr's chief aim was to save the Slovak nation from extinction under the Hungarians by uniting them and educating them through and with their native language. Understanding the wide social basis of modern languages, he realized that it was no longer the time when a foreign language, however akin, could be used as a medium of social intercourse. The spread of education and democracy among the masses, he realized, must be made in their own language. He thus laid sure foundations for their liberation. Modern Slovak, therefore, dates from the time of the birth of the new literary languages also among all the Orthodox Slavs.

In 1846, Štúrs's decisive disquisition on the Slovak language and its use, "Nárečja slovenskuo alebo potreba písaňja v tomto nárečí" (= Slovak speech or the necessity of writing in this dialect), appeared in Bratislava; but such eminent Slovaks as Kollár and Šafárik still opposed him, preferring Czech and declaring the need of a unified language for all Czechs and Slovaks. Štúr succeeded in assuaging certain anxieties in Prague and published a new Slovak grammar, *Nauka reči slovenskej*, that year. He introduced a phonetic orthography partly on Yugoslav models. M.M. Hodža, however, was not satisfied with it and in the following year introduced a new etymological spelling in his grammar.

The whole group of leaders finally agreed on an etymological system of spelling, and the seal was finally set to it by Martin Hattala's short grammar in 1852, expanded in 1864-65. It was in this language that were subsequently created all the great works in prose and poetry in Slovak; and it was partly by and for this language that the finally victorious struggle for liberation was carried on. In the case of deficiencies in vocabulary the school of Štúr, like that of Bernolák before them, borrowed from Czech. They also borrowed from Russian and other Slav languages, e.g.: želať (= to wish), dejstvovať (= to act).

At the beginning of this century the chief scholars of Slovak were Jozef Škultéty (1853-1947), for a long time editor of *Slovenské pohľady* and *Národnie noviny* and later director of the national cultural institution *Matica slovenská* and professor of Bratislava university, and Samo Czambel, who published an orthography, a chrestomathy and studies of dialects. These and the Czech, Fr. Pastrnek, and others cultivated the Slovak linguistic field in their studies published in the journal *Slovenské pohľady*. Since the liberation in 1918, Ján Dámborský's grammar has been regarded as authoritative, as well as the orthography, published by the Matica slovenská, entitled *Pravidlá slovenského pravopisu* (last edition, 1970). Since 1918, Slovak has enjoyed full rights as an official, as well as literary, language in the Czechoslovak Republic; and its literary achievements, especially in poetry, have been remarkable.

The poetical tradition started by the followers of Štúr, such as Samo Chalupka, Janko Kráľ, Ján Botto, and Andrej Sládkovič, was continued in the writings of Svetozár Hurban-Vajanský (1847-1916), the son of J. M. Hurban, and Pavol Országh (1849-1921), better known as Hviezdoslav, a figure parallel to Vrchlický among the Czechs. Notable too is the realist prose writer, Martin Kukučín, who also lived in Dalmatia and South America and whose real name was Bencúr. The lover of Slavonic poetry should also be familiar with the works of the later poets, such as Krasko, Gall, Roy, Rázus, Jesenský—to mention but a few.

In modern times the full functional development of literary Slovak has taken place, especially during the last two or three decades, for science and technology have greatly developed as well as the various branches of literature in Slovak. In the universities and technical colleges and in the Slovak Academy of Sciences, Slovak is used for lectures and in all printed publications dealing with the problems of each scientific discipline. Scientific books and journals are published in large numbers. Literary Slovak has established itself as the general means of communication in a developed modern society, in all spheres of public and private life.

The stormy history of the Slovak people is imprinted on their imaginative and emotional character, so wonderfully expressed in their unique folk-songs which approach those of the Balkans in their freedom of rhythm and phrase. In literature, it is poetry that has appealed most strongly to the Slovaks and has best expressed their most passionate yearnings and ideals. How typical and full of colour is their national anthem composed by Janko Matuška: "Nad Tatrou sa blýska, hromy divo bijú...."

THE SLOVAK ALPHABET

Slovak.		Approximate English equivalent.
A	a(short)	u in S. English "but" or a in N. English "man"
(Á)	á(long)	a in "father"
	ä	a very open e, phon. ε or æ
B	b	b
C	c	ts pronounced together as in "bits"
Č	č	ch in "church" (hard)
D	d	d (dental)
D'	ď	d in (S. English) "dew"
E	e(short)	[1]e in "met"
(É)	é(long)	e in "there"
F	f	f (mostly in words of foreign origin)
G	g	g in "go"
H	h	[2]voiced h
Ch	ch	ch in "loch"
I	i(short)	[1]i in "it", or i in Fr. "vif"
Í	í(long)	[2]ee in "meet", i in "machine" (rare initially)
J	j	y in both "yes" and "boy"
K	k	k
L	l(short)	l (medium) as in "last", [3](vocalic) l (hard) as in "table"
	ĺ(long)	[3](vocalic) l (hard) as in "table" but longer
L'	ľ	l (slightly soft) in "least"
M	m	m
N	n	n (dental)

SLOVAK

Slovak.		Approximate English equivalent.
Ň	ň	*n* in (S. English) "new" (rare initially)
O	o (short)	*o* as in "for"
(Ó)	ó (long)	*oo* as in "door"
Ô	ô	*wa* in "war" (phon. u̯o), (rare initially)
P	p	*p* (unaspirated)
R	r	*r* (rolled), ³also vocalic
	ŕ (long)	³*r* (rolled), vocalic only
S	s	*s* in "see"
Š	š	*sh*
T	t	*t* (dental)
T'	ť	*t* in (S. English) "tune"
U	u	*u* in "put"
Ú	ú	*oo* in "boot"
V	v	*v*
(Y)	y (short)	¹*i* in "bit", or *i* in Fr. "vif"
	ý (long)	¹*ee* in "meet", *i* in "machine"
Z	z	*z*
Ž	ž	*zh*, *s* in "pleasure"

Q, W, and X appear only in foreign words.
( ) letters with capitals so bracketed occur initially only in a few words of foreign origin.

The digraph *dž* is used to represent the single sound of English *j* (phon. ʤ), which occasionally occurs in Slovak: džavotať (= to chatter), džungľa (= jungle), erdžať (= to neigh).

dz also represents a single sound, like the *dz* in Eng. "adze". It occurs fairly frequently in Slovak in contrast to Czech: medzi (= between), prechádzať sa (= to go for a walk).

Czech letters not occurring in Slovak are: ě, Ř, ř, ů.

Polish letters not occurring in Slovak are: ą, Ć, ć, ę, Ł, ł, ń (in this form), Ś, ś, Ź, ź, and Ż, ż (in this form). Polish w = Slovak v. Ô, ô has a different sound, (= u in Polish).

Lusatian letters not occurring in Slovak are: Upper: Č, č, Dž, dž, Ł, ł, ń, W, w; Lower: also ŕ, ś, ź.

(Serbo-)Croatian letters not occurring in Slovak are: Ć, ć, Đ, đ.

¹Slovak *i*, *í* and *y*, *ý* play the same rôle as in Czech, preserving a historical differentiation between Common Slav *i* and *y* (O.S. и and ы) but sounding the same, except that *i*, *í* cause the palatalization of preceding dentals, *d*, *t*, and *n** without this being indicated in the spelling. As in Czech,

ty (= thou) is pronounced tɪ, but
ti (= to thee) is pronounced t'ɪ , phon. cɪ.

    y only is written after the velars *h, ch, k,* and *g;* while after the formerly palatal consonants *š, ž, č, c, dz,* and after *j, ľ* and (generally) *z,* only *i* is written. Foreign words, however, may be written with *cy-*, e.g.: cylinder. *-zy-* occurs in jazyk (= tongue), nazývat' (= to call), prezývat' (= to nickname), as in Czech.

    But in contrast to Czech, all Slovak (short) *e*'s also cause the palatalization of preceding dentals* except in the words:—

ten	= this	temer	= almost
teraz	= now	teprv	= only (of time)
teďy	} = then, so	hoden	= worth
teda (arch.)		vinen	= guilty
vtedy	= then	žiaden (masc. sg.)	= no
		jeden (" ")	= one

and in shortened adjectival endings, as in:—

        krásneho (Gen. sing. masc. and neut.)
        krásnemu (Dat.   "   "   "   ")
        krásnej (Gen. Dat. Loc. sing. fem.)

from krásny (= beautiful).
    Thus:— ne- (= not)   is pronounced ňe
          tečie (= flows)   " " ťečie
          dedine (= to the village) " " ďeďiňe

[2] Slovak *h* is a *voiced* aspirate *h,* exactly as in Czech, and has no other exact equivalent in the Slavonic languages, except in Lusatian in certain positions and in Ukrainian. It is a *voiced* version of English *h,* and = phon. ɦ.

[3] *l* and *r* can be vocalic as in Czech and like *r* in Serbocroätian and Slovenian. And as in the latter languages for *r,* in Slovak both vocalic *l* and vocalic *r* can also be long: l̄, r̄:—

        tlstý (= fat);   tĺct' (= to pound, beat)
        prst (= finger); kŕmit' (= to feed)

    But in contrast to Czech, vocalic *l* and *r* never occur finally, as a vowel is always inserted, cf.:—

        Slk. viedol (= he led), Cz. vedl
         " vietor (= wind), " vítr

Vocalic *l* is more frequent in Slovak than in Czech:—

        Slk. dlhý (= long), Cz. dlouhý
         " čln (= boat), " člun

*According to the literary norm *ľ* also should be included here; but in modern Slovak, *ľ* is not *strongly* palatalized before *i* and *e*. These rules do not apply to the pronunciation of foreign words, in which *hard* dentals are pronounced before *i* and *e*.

SLOVAK

PRONUNCIATION

The *Accent* in Slovak is a purely stress accent occurring on the first syllable of a word or word-group, as in Czech. It is quite independent of the length of the vowels. Thus: Bràtislava is stressed on the first syllable; so is Trenčín, though the *i* is long. While dò Bratislavy (= to Bratislava) is stressed on the "do"; and nèrobím (= I do not do) is stressed on the "ne-" (pron. ɲɛ!). The prepositions dľa (= according to—better: podľa), kol (= round, about—poet. for okolo), and krem (= except—more often: okrem), and all polysyllabic prepositions are never stressed, unlike most prepositions, and are proclitics, being pronounced with the following word in a single group. A secondary stress occurs in long words and word groups, e.g. 'zeme‚trasenie (= earthquake).

Long vowels can occur both stressed and unstressed.[1] But according to a special rule of Slovak, generally they do not occur in two consecutive syllables (in contrast to Czech). The rising diphthongs *ia*, *ie*, *iu*, and also *ô* count as long vowels for this rule. The second of two consecutive long syllables is shortened except in the following main instances:—

1. with the ending *-ou* of the Instrumental sing. of feminine nouns, pronouns and adjectives, e.g.: krásnou bránou (= with a beautiful gate).

2. with the endings *-ie*, *-ia*, *-iu*, *-í*, etc., in the declension of neuter nouns ending in *-ie* (see "Morphology", Declension of Nouns, Neuter *o*-stems, No. 4b), e.g.:—

> prútie Nom. sg. = twigs, prútia Gen. sg.
> liatie   = pouring

3. with the ending *-í* in the Genitive plur. of nouns, e.g.:—

> básní (= of poems), from báseň
> piesní (= of songs), "   pieseň

4. with the ending *-ia* in the 3rd person plur. Pres./Fut. of *i*-verbs, and with *-iac* in the Pres. Gerund, and *-úci*, *-iaci* in the Pres. Participle Active of *e*- and *i*-verbs respectively, e.g.:—

> súdia = they judge, chváliac = praising

---

[1] Length alone can differentiate meaning, e.g. rad = row, file, rád = glad (m.).

but—

píšu = they write, yet: hádžúci = who throws
also:
kúpia = they will buy
lúpiac = plundering
kŕmiaci = who feeds

Also:—

after the indefinite prefix *nie-*, e.g.: niečí = someone's;
with the endings of adjectives formed from the names of creatures e.g.: vtáčí = bird's;
with the endings *-ár* (agent) *-áreň* (premises), e.g.: mliekár = milkman, mliekáreň = dairy;
with verbs formed from adjectives and denoting "becoming something", e.g.: zmúdrieť = to become wise, Fut. 1st pers. sing. zmúdriem;
with the endings *-ievať*, *-ievam*, etc. of Frequentative verbs, e.g.: chválievať = to keep praising;
with the multiplicative endings *-násobný*, *-krát*, e.g.: tisícnásobný = thousandfold, tisíckrát = a thousand times;
and in certain modern compound words, e.g.: zásielka = parcel, dispatch, súčiastka = part, component.

The spelling of Slovak is "phonetic" and consistent on the whole. The vowels are phonetically spelt, except that the distinction between *i* and *y*, explained above, is preserved, as in Czech. The consonants follow "historical" rules, but somewhat less so than in Czech, concessions being made to the actual pronunciation, e.g.:—

	Slk.	svadba	= wedding,	Cz.	svatba
	"	som	= I am,	"	jsem
	"	spievať	= to sing,	"	zpívati
	"	väčší	= bigger,	"	větší
	"	štvrtok	= Thursday,	"	čtvrtek

The Vowels

As has already been shown, the vowels in Slovak can be either long or short, as in Czech, the long vowels being marked ´. The only exception to this is *ä*, which can only be short in literary Slovak. It varies in the pronunciation of various speakers between phon. æ (rather closed) and phon. ɛ not distinguishable from ordinary Slovak short *e* (in spelling). Its origin is Common Slav ę (O.S. ᴀ) *after*

labials only.
O really has two long versions, *ó* in foreign words, and *ô*, which is a diphthong—phon. u̯o, in native words. Hence it often corresponds to Czech *ů*, cf.:—

    Slk. kôň = horse   Cz. kůň
    " rôzny = different,   " různý

But the student can never assume that in Slovak the same long vowels occur in the same places as in Czech. Slovak tends to preserve much more closely the original Common Slav vowels and has not undergone the Czech vowel mutation (česká přehláska). Furthermore, Slovak has preserved the rising diphthongs *ia*, *ie*, and *iu* which used to exist in Old Czech. Finally, Slovak sometimes has long vowels in the roots of words where Czech has short ones, and *vice versâ*.

Vowel Correspondences

In Slovak in some instances different long vowels correspond to the short vowels from those in Czech. For instance, in Czech *á* corresponds to *a*, while in Slovak *á* corresponds to *a except after formerly soft consonants*, when *ia* is the long equivalent of *a*, e.g.:—

    cf. Cz. pasu (= I graze), Infin. pásti;
    Slk. pasiem, pásť

    Cz. šalba (= deceit), šáliti (= to deceive, fool); but
    Slk. šaľba, šialiť[1]

In Czech *é* corresponds to *e*, except after palatal consonants when *í* corresponds to *e*; but in Slovak *ie regularly corresponds to e*, cf.:—

    Cz. nesu (= I carry), Infin. nésti;
    Slk. nesiem, niesť

    Cz. střeliti (= to shoot, Pfve.), stříleti (Impfve.);
    Slk. streliť, strieľať

In Czech *ů* corresponds to short *o*, while in Slovak *ô* corresponds to *o*:

    cf. Cz. nůž (= knife), nožík (= small knife);
    Slk. nôž, nožík.

---

[1]The corresponding "long vowel" to *ä* is also the diphthong *ia*, e.g. päť = five, but piaty = fifth, cf. Czech pět, pátý. (See p. 154, No. 16)

But very often Czech has *ů* where Slovak has short *o* and *vice versâ*:—

cf. Cz. dům (= house), bol (= pain); Slk. dom, bôľ.

This contrast of lengths applies to all the vowels:—

cf. Cz. hrách   = pea;   Slk. hrach
       vrata   = gate;   "   vráta
       řeka   = river;   "   rieka
       sníh   = snow;   "   sneh
       lípa   = lime tree;   "   lipa
       růže   = rose;   "   ruža (!)
       smutek = sorrow;   "   smútok
       sýr   cheese   "   syr

In Czech *ou* regularly corresponds to short *u*, while in Slovak *ú* corresponds to *u*, *ou* occurring only in the Instr. sing. of fem. nouns, pronouns, and adjectives:—

cf. Cz. pustiti (= to let, allow, Pfve),
        pouštěti (Impfve.), but—
    Slk. pustiť (= to let, allow, Pfve.),
         púšťať (Impfve.);

    Cz. pěknou ženu = a beautiful woman (Acc. sing.), but—
    Slk. peknú ženu = a beautiful woman (Acc. sing.);

but—

    Cz. s pěknou ženou = with a beautiful woman (Instr. sing.), and—
    Slk. s pekn*ou* žen*ou* = with a beautiful woman (Inst. sing.).

Initial j *and Diphthongs*

In contrast to Czech *j* can occur, initially in words and syllables, with:—

(a) the short vowels *a*, *e*, *o*, and *u* (not *i*), e.g.:—

ja   = I   joj! = oh! (otherwise *jo* occurs
                              in names and foreign
                              words only)
stoja = they stand   Jozef = Joseph
je   = is   juh   south
seje = sows   moju   my (Acc. sing. fem.)

(b) the long vowels *á* (in new formations and names and words of foreign origin) and *ú*, e.g.:—

```
vejár    = fan         júl  = July
Ján      = John        pijú = they drink
lojálny  = loyal
```

Diphthongs can be formed in Slovak:—

1. with *i* as the first *or* second element—pronounced glide *i̯*, and written j when occurring as the second element,

2. with *u* (phon. u̯) as the first element only in the pronunciation of *ô*, pronounced u̯o (see above), or—

3. with *u̯* as the second element, as in *ou* (see above), phon. ou̯.

After palatal and formerly palatal consonants the diphthongs ia, ie, iu are spelt *ia, ie, iu* (the second element is short!)—a feature of Slovak. They are pronounced with a distinct *i̯* (not as in Polish, q.v.), e.g.:—

```
polia = fields      žien     = of women (Gen. pl.)
čiara = line        miest    = of towns (Gen. pl.)
piaty = fifth       znameniu = to the sign (Dat. sg.)
dieťa = child       božiu    = God's (Acc. sg. fem.
                                 adj.)
```

With *j*, pronounced *i̯* with slight friction, as the *second* element, diphthongs can occur with:—

(a) the short vowels *a, e, o, u* (not *i* or *y*), e.g.:—

```
čaj    = tea             vojsko = army
hej    = yes             kupuj! = buy!
peknej = beautiful (Gen./Dat./Loc. sg. fem.)
```

All original diphthongs with *i* (*ij* and *i̯j*) and *y* in genuine Slovak words lose the *j*, e.g.:—

```
pi!  = drink!, cf. Cz. pij!
kry! = cover!,  "    "  kryj!
```

but—

študijná cesta = a journey for study

(b) the long vowels *á* and *ô* only, e.g.:—

háj = grove
môj = my (Nom. sg. masc.)

Diphthongs with *u̯* as the second element, apart from *ou* above, occur:—

(a) spelt with *u*—in words of foreign origin, with the vowels *a* and *e* only:—

```
                    auto   = car
                    eunuch = eunuch
```

(b) spelt with *v*, with the vowels *a, á, e, i, í, o, u, y, ý* and with the diphthongs *ia* and *ie* followed by *v* finally or + any other consonant (except *n* and *l*), unless the *v* starts a syllable. E.g.:—

```
kavka  = jackdaw              obuv     = footwear
dávka  = portion, dose        vplyv    = influence,
lev    = lion                            phon. fpl̯iu̯
div    = marvel               pokrývka = coverlet
painv  = of beer (Gen. pl.)   polievka = soup
ovca   = sheep                žeriav   = crane
```
pív = of beer (Gen. pl.)

but—

návrat (= return), is pronounced with v, not u̯.

Before *n* either v or u̯ can be pronounced, e.g. slávny = glorious, phon.: 'slaːvni or 'slaːu̯ni.

A kind of diphthong also occurs with vocalic *r* + *v*: krv (= blood) is pronounced phon. kr̯u̯.

In colloquial speech these same diphthongs occur with these vowels + *l* and even with *v* before *l*, but this is not admitted in the literary language. Cf. Slovenian.

There is *no glottal stop* in Slovak, so ja a on (= I and he) sounds ja‿a‿on (without breaks), and—

```
v Amerike   = in America,  is pronounced 'vamɛrɪkɛ
neistý      = uncertain,        "        'n̯ɛɪstiː
neobyčajný  = unusual,          "        'n̯ɛɔbɪtʃa̯ɪniː
```

Only in foreign words is *j* inserted in pronunciation between certain vowels to avoid *hiatus*. Hence:—

Anglia (= England), is pronounced 'aŋglija, cf. Cz. Anglie, pronounced 'aŋglijɛ.

Similarly:—

```
história  (= history),  phon. 'ɦistɔːrija;
štadión   (= stadium),  phon. 'ʃtadijɔːn.
```

The Consonants

The consonants in Slovak are of the usual Slav unaspirated type and very similar to those of Czech with a few exceptions.

Slovak has no *ř*. In place of Czech *ř*, Slovak has *r*, e.g.:—

more = sea, Nom. plur. moria;

dvere = door, rieka = river.

SLOVAK

Slovak has a soft *ľ*, as well as a (medium) *l*, but in the pronunciation of many speakers the difference between the two is very small. *ľ*, however, does not become u̯ after a vowel in colloquial speech. Yet it is far less palatalized than ль in Russian or љ in Serbocroatian.

A characteristic of Slovak is the change of *v* to u̯ after another vowel or diphthong at the end of words and syllables (cf. Ukrainian, Byelorussian, Lusatian, and Slovenian), explained already under "Diphthongs" above.

It is important also to note that *c* and *dz* and the *chuintantes* *č*, *š*, *ž*, though hard phonetically, count as soft for the orthography and hence also in flexion.

The labials are never followed by a full j (jot) sound, but only by i̯:—

cf. Slk. viera (= faith), pron. 'vi̯ɛra and
    Cz. Věra (= Vera), pron. 'vjɛra

(cf. also Cz. víra, = faith!).
Slovak usually has a plain *e* or an *ä* where Czech has *ě* (= je) after a labial, e.g.:—

cf. Slk. pekný = beautiful, Cz. pěkný
   "   päť = five,   "   pět

The soft dentals *t'*, *d'*, *ň* are identical in pronunciation in Slovak and Czech. But in Slovak they and also soft *ľ* occur regularly in pronunciation (but not in spelling) before *e* as well as before *i*. (See note No. 1 on pronunciation after the Alphabet, p. 135-36.)

The letter *g*, sounding like *g* in English "go", occurs in native as well as foreign words, and is not felt to be a foreign sound as it is in Czech, e.g.:—

    gajdy = bagpipes   glg = gulp
    gate = pants   guľa = bullet

Nevertheless Common Slav *g* is generally represented by *h* in Slovak and alternates in final position with [x], as in Czech. Hence: Boh (= God) is pronounced bɔx, while the Gen. sing. Boha (= of God) is pronounced 'bɔɦa.

The sound *dz* is fairly frequent in Slovak (as also in Polish), but is heard in Czech only in assimilation. It is pronounced as one sound, as in English "adze" (or *dds* in "adds"), and is derived from Common Slav *d* + *j*, e. g.:—

    medza = boundary

n becomes ŋ (like *ng* in English "sing") before

the velars *k* and *g*, as in other South and West Slav languages, : banka (= bank) is pronounced 'baŋka.

As in other Slav languages, except Serbocroätian and Ukrainian, voiced consonants (except *v*) become unvoiced finally, e.g.:—

mráz	= frost,	is pronounced mrás,	phon. mra:s
chlieb	= bread,	" " chliep,	phon. xli̯ɛp
chlad	= the cold,	" " chlat,	phon. xlat

In groups of consonants assimilation is regressive, the last element, unless it is *j*, *l*, *l'*, *m*, *n*, *ň*, *v*, or *r*,[1] deciding whether a group is to be pronounced voiced or unvoiced. This rule also applies to prepositions consisting of a single consonant or syllable. Hence:—

kresba	= drawing,	is pronounced krezba,	phon. 'krɛzba
liečba	= cure,	" " liedžba,	phon. 'li̯ɛdʒba
kde	= where,	" " gde,	phon. gɟɛ
s dievčatkom	= with the girl,	" "	z d....

while—

obchod	= business,	" " opchot,	phon. 'ɔpxɔt
vták	= bird,	" " fták,	phon. fta:k
odsúdiť	= to condemn,	" " otsúdiť,	phon. 'ɔtsu:ɟɪc

but—

tvoj	= your (sg.)	is pronounced	phon. tvɔj
tri	= three	" "	phon. trɪ, etc.

Certain groups of consonants are simplified in pronunciation.

z disappears in pronunciation before *s* and *š*, as in:—

    francúzsky = French
    rozšíriť = to extend, pron. 'rɔʃʃi:rɪc

d is silent in:—

    dcéra = daughter

---

[1] This exception does not apply to word juncture in Slovak, e.g. vták letí = the bird flies, is pronounced fta:g'l̯ɛci:; ovos rastie = oats grow, is pronounced 'ɔvɔz'rasci̯ɛ.

tsk, dsk sound like *ck*, phon. tsk, as in:—

detský = childish, is pronounced ďecký,
                            phon. 'ɟɛtski:
hradská = main road, "   "   hracká,
                            phon. 'ɦratska:

Double Consonants

In the literary language double consonants should be pronounced in Slovak, as in — povinný (= obliged to), which should be pronounced: 'pɔvɪnni:. Similarly in: oddaný (= devoted), vyšší (= higher), mäkky (= soft). But in ordinary speech Slovaks often fail to pronounce double consonants, even if divided between two words pronounced closely together, as in: pred divadlom (= in front of the theatre), which ordinarily sounds: predivadlom, phon. 'prɛɟɪvadlɔm.

Double consonants would probably be pronounced by a careful speaker in a case where confusion might otherwise arise, e.g.:—

poddaný = subjected   > < podaný = handed to
zajatcov = of prisoners > < zajacov = of hares

THE SLOVAK DIALECTS

The Slovak dialects are interesting because their geographical distribution when compared with their characteristic features seems to point to a migration in early times of the speakers of the present Central dialects from regions further south, probably in Pannonia (modern Hungary). Here before the Magyar invasion they probably mingled with the Southern Slavs. Some Slovak linguists, notably Samo Czambel, have gone so far as to see the origin of Slovak in the South Slav group, a theory which, when examined more closely, hardly seems justified in view of the far greater number of frequently occurring features which Slovak shares in common with Czech and the other West Slav languages. (See "The Characteristics of Slovak" below.)

The Central dialects further have great importance in that they were chosen by Štúr and the other "national awakeners" as the basis of modern literary Slovak, whereas former writers up to Bernolák in the eighteenth century based themselves on the Western Slovak dialects. These latter have certain features which bring them nearer the Moravian dialects of Czech and at the same time, together with the Eastern Slovak dialects, they form a transition to Polish. The Eastern dialects also have features which show a gradual transition to Carpathian Ukrainian, as one might expect.

Each of these three main groups is subdivided into numerous sub-groups, which fall outside our scope here. We give below a list of the characteristics of the three main groups.

The *Central group* is characterized by the following features:—

A. Features adopted in modern literary Slovak:—

1. Common Slav ъ, ь represented by *e, o* or *a*, e.g.:—

>   sen = sleep
>   ovos = oats
>   raž = rye

2. Common Slav ę becomes *ä* (phon. æ) after labials, e.g.:—

>   mäso = meat

3. No vowel mutation (= Cz. přehláska, Slk. prehláska).

4. Original long *o (ó)* becomes ṷo *(ô)* or *ó*, e.g.:—

>   kṷoň (lit. kôň) = horse

5. Diphthongs i̯a, i̯e, i̯u preserved.

6. *šť* preserved, e.g.:—

ešťe (lit. spelling: ešte!) = still

7. *v* after a vowel before another consonant becomes ṷ, e.g.:—

>   krivda = injustice

8. Dentals *t, d, n,* and *l* generally palatalized before *i* and *e*.

9. Long vocalic *l* and *r (ĺ, ŕ)*, e.g.:—

vŕba = willow
jablĺk (Gen. plur.) = of apples

10. Shortening of the second of two consecutive long syllables.

11. Instrumental sing. of feminine nouns and adjectives in *-ou*.

12. Genitive sing. of masculine nouns with Nom. sing. in *-a*, now *-u*, e.g.:—

sluha = servant, Gen. sing. sluh*u*.

13. Nominative plur. of masculine personal nouns in *-ia*, e.g.:—

    rodiča = parents

14. Nominative plur. of neuter nouns in (long) *-á*, e.g.:—

    mestá = towns

15. čo (not co) = what.

16. Long (diphthong) endings in the Pres. of verbs such as—

    nesiem = I carry, pron. ɲɛsi̭ɛm
    pečieš = you (sg.) bake

17. Locative sing. masc. and neut. of adjectives in *-om*, as in Serbocr., e.g.:— dobrom = good.

B. Features not consistently adopted in modern literary Slovak:—

1. Original Common Slav initial syllables *ȏrt-*, *ȏlt-*, (with falling, circumflex, intonation) become *rat-*, *lat-*, as in South Slav (irrespective of intonation), e.g.:—

    rakyta = willow, literary: rakyta
    lakeť = elbow, " lakeť

but *roz-* is the regular form of the prefix meaning "apart",[1] and literary: robota (= work), loď (= boat).

2. Dropping of dentals before *l*, as in South and East Slav, e.g.:—

    šilo for literary šidlo = awl
    pomelo " " pome(t)lo = broom
    cf. lit. omelo = stove brush

3. *-uo* as the ending of Nom., Voc., Acc. sing. neut. of adjectives, reminiscent of South Slav, e.g.:—

    dobruo for literary dobré (= good), cf. Serbocr. dobro

This feature, together with the *a* for C.S. ъ, the Slovak hard *r*, and the generalization of the ending *-m* for the 1st pers. sing. Pres./Fut., Czambel considered as pointing to the South Slav origin of

---

[1] Literary Slovak has a few words with this prefix *long* as *ráz-*: e.g. rázcestie = crossroads.

Slovak.
4. Reminiscent of Ukrainian is the ending *-enia* for the Nom., Voc. and Acc., as well as for the Gen., sing. of neuter nouns formerly ending in *-enie*, e.g.:—

znamenia (Nom., Voc., Acc. and Gen. sing.) = sign

The *Western Slovak dialects* have the following main characteristics, which they share with the literary language and other Slovak dialects:—
1. Lack of vowel mutation for *a, á* and *u, ú*.
2. Two varieties of *l (l, t* or *l', l* or *l', t/u)*.
3. *dz̑* for C.S. *dj*.
4. Acc. plur. = Gen. plur. for masculine animate nouns.
5. Preservation of *ú*.

In common with Czech many Western dialects pronounce *v* after a vowel and before another consonant as *f*. In the extreme West, towards Moravia, some have *ř*. Vážný enumerates 19 features for the dialects of the Morava valley which show a transition to Czech, such as *ú* for original *ó*, the preservation of the 2nd Palatalization in the Dat., Loc. sing. of feminine *a*-stems, co = what, sem = I am, short vowels in monosyllabic Gen. plurals: žen (= of women), ryb (= of fish), etc. Further east more features from central Slovakia appear in the Western dialects, such as the general softening of dentals before *e* of whatever origin.

The *Eastern Slovak dialects* have features which connect them with Polish and Ukrainian, which are spoken to their north and east. Most striking is the fixed accent on the penultimate syllable, as in Polish. The loss of all long vowels, the preservation of various forms of soft *s* and *z*, and the insertion of various vowels with original vocalic *l* and *r* are features also to be found both in Polish and Ukrainian. So also, though colloquial only in Polish, is the loss of the final *l* in the masculine Past Participle Active after another consonant, giving ɲis or ɲes besides ɲesol for lit. niesol = carried. Quite peculiar to Eastern Slovak are the change of *ch* to *h* and the generalization of the ending *-och* in the *Gen*. plur. of nouns of all genders. With Western Slovak, but not with Central Slovak, Eastern Slovak has many features in common, such as the initial syllables *rot, lot* by metathesis, e.g. in lokec for lit. lakeť (= elbow), šč for lit. šť, f for *v* or ṵ, Instr. sing. of feminine *a*-stem nouns in -*u*, Nom./Voc./Acc. sing. of neuter adjectives in -*e*, (not -*uo* as in Central Slovak).

Despite the superficial resemblance of Eastern Slovak to Polish and Ukrainian, it has none of those features in them which developed before the thirteenth century, but much in common with Western Slovak. This points to its Slovak origin and to the fact that the Central Slovak dialects moved in between the Eastern and Western Slovak dialects at a comparatively late period.

VOWEL GRADATION AND VOWEL LENGTHENING

These features, inherited from the common Indo-European stock, can be found in Slovak, too, in numerous examples.

Vowel Gradation

    smrť = death, umrieť = to die (Pfve.), umriem = I shall die, umoriť = to exhaust
    duch = spirit, duša = soul, dych = breath, dochnuť = to expire, perish
    beriem = I take, brať = to take (Impfve.)
    tok = flow, útok = attack, tekutina = liquid, útek = flight

Vowel Lengthening

    umrem (< umьr-) = I shall die (Pfve.), umierať = to die (Impfve.)
    dych = breath, dýchnuť = to take a breath, dýchať = to breathe
    tečie = flows, tiecť = to flow
    chodiť = to go (Freq.), vychádzať = to go out (Impfve.)
    napojiť = to give to drink (Pfve.), napájať = (Impfve.).

SLAVONIC CHARACTERISTICS

1. The Slavonic metathesis of liquids. Slovak, like Czech, has the same forms and vowels as the South Slav languages. (See "The Slovak Dialects" for the additional feature shared with South [and not West] Slav by the Central dialects of Slovak in the case of *initial* Common Slav. *ŏrt-*, *ŏlt-*). Slovak often shows differences of quantity when compared with Czech.

```
           cf. Slk. hrad    = castle,        Cz. hrad
                "   brány   = harrow,         "  brány
but—
                "   hrach   = pea,            "  hrách
                "   vrana   = crow,           "  vrána
                "   vráta   = gate,           "  vrata

               Slk. hlas    = voice,         Cz. hlas
                "   hlásiť  = to announce,    "  hlásiti
                "   hlava   = head,           "  hlava
but—
                "   blato   = mud,            "  bláto

               Slk. breh    = shore,         Cz. břeh
but—
                "   breza   = birch,          "  bříza

               Slk. mlieť   = to grind,      Cz. mlíti
                "   mlieko  = milk,           "  mléko
but notice—
                "   žľaza   = gland,          "  žláza
```

    2. The 1st Palatalization of velars, with k, h (from g), ch changing to $č$, $ž$, $š$ respectively, is regularly to be found in Slovak, e.g.—:

piecť = to bake; piekol = he baked; pečiem = I bake, as well as pečie = he bakes, and pečú = they bake, (i.e. throughout the Present!).

Similarly—

môcť = to be able; mohol = he was able, môžem = I can, môže, môžu.

hriech = sin; hrešiť = to sin, swear.

    As in other Slavonic languages, c and z when originating from k and g respectively alternate with $č$ and $ž$ before syllables originally containing front vowels:—

mesiac = month; mesačný = monthly
kňaz   = priest; knieža = prince; kňažná = princess

    3. The 2nd Palatalization of velars has been lost in Slovak in the Dat. and Loc. sing. of feminine a-stem nouns and in the Loc. plur. of masculine o-stem nouns, and in the Imperative of verbs. It survives only in the Nom. plur. of masculine nouns ending in k and ch, e.g.:—

```
    Slovák = a Slovak  — Slováci
    vojak  = soldier   — vojaci
    mních  = monk      — mnísi
    Čech   = a Czech   — Česi (in Czech: Češi!)
```

4. The influence of the *j* element (yotation) on preceding consonants can be seen in the stem changes of the *je*-class consonantal stem verbs and in the roots of certain nouns, but not in the Past Participles Passive which in Slovak have been re-formed from the Infinitive stem.

k, *h*, *ch* before *j* change to *č*, *ž*, *š* respectively, as in other Slavonic languages, e.g.:—

plakať = to weep;   1st pers. sing. Pres. plačem
luhať = to tell lies; "   "   "   "   lužem,
                                      as well as luhám
páchať = to commit;   "   "   sing. Pres. pášem,
                                      as well as pácham

t before *j* changes to *c*, as in other West Slav languages, while *d* before *j* changes to *dz*, a peculiarity of Slovak and Polish:—

svieca   = candle,   from C.S. světja,
pláca   = pay,   "   "   platja, cf. platiť
medza   = boundary, "   "   medja
vychádzať = to go out (Impfve.), cf. chodiť.

s and *z* before *j* change to *š* and *ž* respectively, as in other Slavonic languages:—

písať = to write, 1st pers. sing. Pres. píšem
viazať = to bind,   "   "   "   "   viažem

n before *j* becomes palatalized *ň*:—

vôňa = smell, aroma, from vónja

r before *j* has become hard in Slovak and in some cases the *j* has disappeared leaving traces only in the fact that the declension of certain nouns follows the soft *ja*-stems instead of the hard *a*-stems. Thus:—

the Gen. sg. of zora (= dawn) is zore, not zory.

In other cases the *j* figures as *i* (phon. i̯) after a hard *r*:—

orať = to plough, 1st pers. sing. Pres. oriem
more = sea, (Gen. sg. mora), Nom. plur. moria

l before *j* becomes palatalized *ľ* in Slovak:—

vôľa = will, from vólja

The labials *p*, *b*, *v* and *m* before *j* are not affected. They remain hard and the *j* is lost:—

zem = earth, cf. zemetrasenie = earthquake
kúpa = a purchase, cf. Cz. koupě and Russian ку́пля,
                                        from kúpja

st before *j* changes to *št'*:—

pustiť = to let go (Pfve.), púšťať (Impfve.)

sk before *j* also changes to *št'* in:—

doska = plank, doštený = of planks (adj.)

zg before *j* changes to *žd'* in:—

raždie = dry twigs, cf. rázga = twig

sl before *j* becomes *šl* in:—

poslať = to send, 1st pers. sing. Fut. pošlem

It will be observed that Slovak offers fewer examples of yotation than Czech, Russian, or Serbocroatian.

5. Disappearance of consonants. Apart from the loss of consonants in the early Common Slav period, such as is exemplified by the word sen (= dream), also in Slovak, in its historical period Slovak does not offer many illustrations of the dropping of consonants. Its spelling is more "phonetic" than that of Czech and it has few mute consonants. For the few examples of differences between spelling and pronunciation see the end of the section on the *pronunciation of consonants*, p. 144–45.

6. Epenthetic and prothetic consonants are found in Slovak in, e.g.:—

The 3rd person Personal Pronoun which, as in most other Slavonic languages, takes an initial *n* after prepositions:—

on = he, Gen. sg. jeho; but od neho = from him

Also in:—

snem = parliament

As in Czech, an epenthetic *t* appears in the original group *sr*:—

streda = Wednesday
striebro = silver, etc.

Prothetic *v* is not general in Slovak, even in dialects. It occurs in:—

vajce = egg

Notice:—

fúz = whisker, cf. Cz. vous, Russian ус.

SLOVAK

FEATURES CHARACTERISTIC OF SLOVAK

1. No two consecutive syllables can have long vowels or diphthongs, except in the instances enumerated above under "Pronunciation", e.g.:—

    dáva = gives, cf. Cz. dává

2. No vowel mutation (in Czech: přehláska).

3. The presence of the diphthongs *ia, ie, iu* (phon. i̯a, i̯e, i̯u) which cause preceding dentals to become palatalized.

4. Short *e* as well as *i* nearly always causes preceding dentals *t, d, l, n* to be pronounced palatalized, e.g.:—

    budete, pron. buďeťe = you will be

5. Labials lose *j* or palatalization in those cases where in Czech they are followed by *ě* (= je) < ь, e.g.:—

Slk. vo sv*e*te = in the world, cf. Cz. ve světě
" pekný = beautiful, " " pěkný

6. *ä* for C.S. *ę* (O.S. ѧ) after labials, e.g.:—

    päť = five
    mäso = meat

7. *ô* (phon. u̯o) from *ó*, where Czech generally has *ů*, e.g.:—

    kôň = horse, Cz. kůň

8. Survival of soft *l*, written *l'*.

9. Survival of long vocalic *l* and *r* (*ĺ, ŕ*), cf. Serbocr. for vocalic *r*.

10. Pronunciation of *v* after vowels at the end of words and syllables (including before other consonants) as u̯ or w, as in Lusatian, Slovenian, Ukrainian, and Byelorussian, e.g.:—

    stav = position, state, pron. stau̯
    stavba = building, " stau̯ba

11. Loss of the diphthongs *ij, íj, yj, ýj*, e.g.:—

    pi! = drink!, cf. Cz. pij!
    kry! = cover! " " kryj!

12. The 2nd Palatalization is confined to the Nom. plur. of masculine nouns, e.g.:—

vojak = soldier, Nom. plur. vojaci (as in Czech)

mních = monk, Nom. plur. mnísi (cf. Cz. mniši)

but—

v Amerike = in America, cf. Cz. v Americe; na nohe = on the leg, k muche = to the fly.

13. Infinitives of verbs of Class I with roots in a velar *(k* or *h)* end in *-ct'*, e.g.:—

piecť = to bake,   Past (3rd pers. sg. masc.) piekol,
môcť = to be able, "   "   "   "   "   mohol.

14. C.S. *d + j > dz*, as in Polish, e.g.:—

    medza = boundary, Pol. miedza.

15. The development of C.S. *ě* (O.S. ѣ) in Slovak should be noted, though it is not peculiar to Slovak:—

  ѣ when long becomes *ie*, e.g.:—

  svieca = candle

  ѣ when short becomes *e*, e.g.:—

  svet = world

16. The development of the C.S. nasal vowels *ǫ* and *ę* (O.S. ѫ and ѧ) in Slovak can be summarized in the following examples:—

ѫ regularly develops into *ú* or *u*, e.g.:—

Cf. O.S. несѫтъ = they carry   Slk. nesú
         женѫ   = woman   "   ženu
         (Acc. sg.)
         сѫдъ   = judgment   "   súd = court
                                          of justice

but N.B.

O.S. женоѫ   = woman   Slk. ženou (as
     (Instr. sg.)   in Czech)
     доушеѫ = soul   "   dušou (!)
     (Instr. sg.)

ѧ develops into *a, ia, ä,* or *e*, e.g.:—

Cf. O.S. рѧдъ   = row   Slk. rad
         сѧ   = -self   "   sa
         глѧдати = to look at   "   hľadať =
                                     to look for
         просѧтъ = they request "   prosia
         пѧть   = five   "   päť (to *ä*
                                     after labi-
                                     als only!)

пать = fifth   Slk. piaty
доуша = soul   "   duše (Nom. sg. duša!)
(Gen. sg., Nom.
Voc. Acc. pl.)

17. The development of the C.S. semi-vowels ъ and ь in Slovak shows several possibilities: both can develop into *e*, *o*, or *a*. For examples see "Features Characteristic of Czech, Slovak, and Polish", No. 6.

For "Features Characteristic of Czech together with Slovak only" as well as "Features Characteristic of Czech, Slovak, and Polish", see Section on *Czech* under these headings.

MORPHOLOGY

While the phonetic system of Slovak is more conservative than that of Czech and so is nearer to that of Old Slavonic and other Slavonic languages, its morphological system has developed further than that of Czech, its nearest relative, mainly through the workings of analogy and the generalization of certain standard endings, especially in the plural of nouns. Both the 1st and 2nd Palatalization of velars occur less frequently in the declensions than they do in Czech, owing to the workings of analogy, as in Russian and Slovenian. And in general Slovak morphology has fewer irregularities, exceptions, and archaic survivals, such as the declension of kámen (= stone) in Czech.

Slovak has lost the Dual category and only a very few old dual forms survive. It has also lost the Vocative case, like Russian, Byelorussian and Slovenian, except for a few masculine nouns in the singular. Like Czech, Polish, Slovenian, and the East Slav languages, it has no Aorist or Imperfect tenses. The ending -*m* has been generalized for the 1st pers. sing. Pres. of all verbs, as in Slovenian, cf. also Serbocroätian and Macedonian. In common with Czech, Polish, Lusatian, Serbocroätian and Slovenian both the 3rd pers. sing. and the 3rd pers. plur. Present have lost the original final -*t*. Slovak has also simplified its forms for the Conditional Mood and the Gerunds, which latter do not show gender, in contrast to Czech. All Infinitives end in -*ť*.

The whole flexional system of Šlovak is much simplified, when compared with that of Czech, owing to the absence in Slovak of the Czech vowel mutation (přehláska) after "soft" consonants. Consequently the differences between hard and soft declensions and conjugations are far less numerous and striking.

In the use of the cases, Slovak has two important differences, when compared with Czech:—

1. The Genitive is not regularly used after a negative verb, as it is supposed to be in Czech, e.g.:—

Daj mi nôž (Acc.) = Give me a knife
Nemám nôž (Acc.) = I have not got a knife

2. The Acc. plur. = Gen. plur. for masculine nouns indicating persons (and animals when they are personified only, as in a fable), e.g.:—

Poznám tých pekných mužov = I know these handsome men
(cf. Cz. znám ty krásné muže).
Pre tých chudobných sluhov = for those poor servants
(cf. Cz. pro ty chudé sluhy)

Another important difference between Slovak and Czech is that in Slovak adjectives and participles qualifying nouns in the plural of any gender, except those referring to masculine persons, all have the same endings in the Nom. and Acc., as in Polish and Upper Lusatian. But this does not apply to the Past Tense of verbs. E.g.:—

Tie chudobné ženy (fem.) šli = These poor women were going
Tie chudobné dievčatá (neut.!) šli = These poor girls were going

(Cf. Cz. Ty chudé ženy šly, but: Ta chudá děvčata šla; so also in Serbocr. and Slovenian).

Slovak is also fonder of the Dative of the Possessor, which is frequently used in South Slav, e.g.:—

Neviem mu mena = I do not know his name

(cf. Cz. Neznám jeho jména).

Only in the numerals, the declension of soft adjectives and of neuter nouns with ending going back to C.S. -ьje (O.S. -ьѥ or -нѥ) has Slovak a greater multiplicity of forms than Czech. E.g.:—

Cf. Slk. dvaja = two (masc. pers.) > < dva (masc. non-pers.), dve (fem. and neut.).
Cz. dva = two (masc.) > < dvě (fem. and neut.).

Similarly:—

Slk. piati = five (masc. pers.) > < päť (masc. non-pers., fem. and neut.).

SLOVAK

Slk. Nom. sg. masc. boží = God's, božia (fem.), božie (neut.), Nom. pl. boží (masc. pers.), božie (other genders).
Cz. boží (sg. and pl. all genders).
Slk. umenie = art (Nom., Acc. sg.), Gen. sg. umenia, Dat. sg. umeniu, Loc. sg. umení.
Cz. umění (Nom., Acc., Gen., Dat., Loc. sg.) = art.

DECLENSION OF NOUNS

1. i-stems, feminine only. As in Czech, these are divided into *(a)* true i-stems of the type kosť, Gen. sg. kosti (= bone), and *(b)* mixed i/ja-stems, e.g. dlaň, Gen. sg. dlane (= palm of the hand). The latter type probably originated from nouns like zem = earth (the *only* form of this word used in Slovak), Gen. sg. zeme, which lost its original ending in the Nom. sg. and comes from zem-ja.
In the Dat., Instr. and Loc. plural of both types the endings of the fem. ja-stems have been adopted for this declension.

(a) kosť = bone   *(b)* dlaň = palm of the hand

	Sing.		*Plur.*	
Nom.	kosť[1]	dlaň[2]	kosti	dlane
Gen.	kosti	dlane	kostí	dlaní
Dat.	kosti	dlani	kostiam	dlaniam
Acc.	kosť	dlaň	kosti	dlane
Instr.	kosťou	dlaňou	kosťami (-mi)	dlaňami
Loc.	kosti	dlani	kostiach	dlaniach

Some nouns may belong to type *(a)* or *(b)*. The modern tendency is to give preference to type *(b)* endings. E.g.:—

štvrť = a quarter, Gen. sg. štvrte (or, formerly, štvrti)

So also:

myseľ	= thought,	"	"	mysle	("	"	mysli)
loď	= boat,	"	"	lode	("	"	lodi)
plť	= raft,	"	"	plte	("	"	plti)
obeť	= sacrifice,	"	"	obete	("	"	obeti)

A few nouns may belong either to type *(b)* or to the feminine ja-stems of the type duša, e.g.: nádej

---

[1] All abstracts in -*osť* follow kosť.
[2] So also all fem. nouns in -*eň* or -*ňa*, e.g:—
  mliekareň = dairy, Gen. sg. mliekarne
  sukňa   = skirt,   "   " sukne

or nádeja = hope.

Notice that in Slovak cirkev (= church) and krv (pron. krṷ, = blood), originally long $\bar{u}$-stems, now belong to this declension, type *(a)*. Cirkev has an irregular plural, in the Dat., Instr. and Loc. reminiscent of Old Slavonic: Nom./Acc. cirkve, Gen. cirkví, Dat. cirkvám, Instr. cirkvami, Loc. cirkvách. Most other nouns which were originally $\bar{u}$-stems have taken the ending -*va* and belong to the fem. *a*-stems, e.g.: kaňva = can, cf. Cz. konev; vetva = branch, cf. Cz. vetev.

    Notice: hus = goose, Gen. sg. husi (Cz. husa, husy)
                   lož = a lie, " " lži
                   voš = louse, " " vši
                   česť = honour, " " cti

but—

                   lesť = ruse, " " lesti or ľsti
                   raž = rye, " " raži

Also:

    tvár = face, cheek, Gen. sg. tváre or tvári, Dat. pl. tváram, Loc. pl. tvárach, the last two cases with regular shortening of ending and hard *r*,

    dvere (Nom. and Acc. pl.—plurale tantum) = door, Gen. pl. dverí or dvier, Dat. dverám, Instr. dvermi *or* dverami, Loc. dverách.

    2. Consonant stems. The only complete declension preserved in spoken Slovak is the neuter *t*-stem type, dievča = girl, Gen. sg. dievčaťa. The endings are mostly those of the soft neuter *jo*-stems in the singular and of the hard neuter *o*-stems in the plural (see below). In the plural there are alternative forms in -*enc*- which are frequently used.

	Sing.	*Plur.*	
Nom.	dievča	dievčatá	dievčence
Gen.	dievčaťa	dievčat	dievčeniec
Dat.	dievčaťu	dievčatám	dievčencom
Acc.	dievča	dievčatá	dievčence
Instr.	dievčaťom	dievčatami	dievčencami
Loc.	dievčati	dievčatách	dievčencoch

    This declension includes many names of young creatures, e.g.:—

šteňa = puppy, žriebä = foal, Gen. sg. žriebäťa, kura = chicken, and kurča = chicken, prasa = pig or pigling, teľa = calf. These have plurals: prasce, Gen.

pl. prasiec; teľce, teliec, etc., declined like dievčence, as well as prasatá, teľatá (less common and technical). Also: zviera = animal, knieža¹ = prince, Acc. sg. knieža or kniežaťa. Dieťa (= child) is declined regularly like this in the singular, but its plural deti (Nom. and Acc.) has Gen. detí, Dat. deťom, Instr. deťmi, Loc. deťoch.

The neuter n- stems of the type semä (= seed), Gen. sg. semena, are occasionally still so written in the Nom. sg., but in the ordinary spoken language they have been replaced by Nominatives of the type: semeno, declined like mesto.

The old masc. n- and t-stems, which survive in Czech, have become masc. jo-stems in Slovak, e.g.:—

```
kameň = stone, Gen. sg. kameňa
lakeť = elbow,  "   "  lakťa
deň   = day,    "   "  dňa (see below)
```

The plural of nebo = sky (neuter o-stem), affords the only example in Slovak of the survival of an s-stem:—

Nom./Acc. nebesia or nebesá, Gen. nebies, Dat. nebesiam or nebesám, Instr. nebesami, Loc. nebesiach or nebesách. (The endings are those of neut. o-stems.)

Mati or mať (= mother) is the only r-stem surviving in Slovak. It is declined:—

Nom.	mati, mať, (mater)	matere
Gen.	matere	materí
Dat.	materi	materiam
Acc.	mater, mať	matere
Instr.	materou	materami
Loc.	materi	materiach

Dcéra (= daughter) now belongs entirely to the feminine a-stems in Slovak.

3a. a-stems, feminine only. In Slovak *masculino* nouns ending in -a are declined like masc. o-stems. (See below.)

As in other Slavonic languages, feminine a-stems are subdivided in Slovak into hard a-stems and soft ja-stems. Owing to the absence in Slovak of the vowel mutations which are to be found in Czech, there are far fewer differences between these two declensions. In the Gen., Dat., Loc. sg. and Nom., Acc. plur. the true descendants of the original soft endings survive in the ja-stems; their Gen. pl. ending -í is from the i-stems.

---

[1] This word has no plural in -ce.

SLOVAK

a-stem: žena = woman   *ja*-stem: duša = soul

	Sing.		Plur.	
Nom.	žena	duša	ženy	duše
Gen.	ženy	duše	žien	duší
Dat.	žene	duši	ženám	dušiam
Acc.	ženu	dušu	ženy	duše
Instr.	ženou	dušou	ženami	dušami
Loc.	žene	duši	ženách	dušiach

Note that if the root vowel of a noun of either hard or soft type is long, the long endings of the *Dat. and Loc. plural -ám, -ách* (soft *-iam, -iach*) are regularly shortened, e.g.:—

brána = gate,   Dat. pl. bránam, Loc. pl. bránach
lúka = meadow,   "   " lúkam,   "   " lúkach
vŕba = willow,   "   " vŕbam,   "   " vŕbach

In the *Gen. plur.* when there is no ending, the root vowel is regularly lengthened in both *a-* and *ja-* stems in Slovak, in contrast to Czech.[1] Hence, *žien* above. So also:—

brada	= beard,	Gen. plur.	brád
žaba	= frog,	" "	žiab
lipa	= lime tree,	" "	líp
ryba	= fish,	" "	rýb
srna	= doe,	" "	sŕn
ulica	= street,	" "	ulíc[2]
bohyňa	= goddess,	" "	bohýň
hora	= forest, hill,	" "	hôr
vlna	= wave,	" "	vĺn

To avoid a difficult group of consonants finally in the Gen. plur., the most usual fill-vowel used in Slovak is *-ie-*, e.g.:—

hra	= play(ing),	Gen. plur.	hier
hradba	= rampart,	" "	hradieb
matka	= mother,	" "	matiek
záhradka	= little garden,	" "	záhradiek
miska	= bowl, small dish,	" "	misiek

ô can be used before *k*, e.g.:—

kvapka = drop,   "   " kvapôk,
                                      also kvapiek, kvapák

---

[1] Nouns in *-ova* and a few others form an exeption to this rule, e.g.:—

        budova = building, Gen. pl. budov;
        potvora = monster,   "   " potvor.

[2] Nouns in *-ca*, although counting as soft, regularly have no ending in the Gen. plural.

á can occur before *k*, but is most favoured before *r* and *l* (it can often be replaced by *ie* or *ô*), e.g.:—

stovka = a hundred,   Gen. plur. stovák or stoviek
    (of something)
sestra = sister,   "   " sestár or sestier
metla = broom,   "   " metál or metiel

o is regularly used after a long vowel in the root and after *j*, e.g.:—

    slúžka = maid-servant, Gen. plur. slúžok
    túžba = longing,   "   " túžob
    spojka = conjunction,   "   " spojok

Notice that in Slovak the plural of ruka (= hand) and of noha (= foot, leg) are regular and have no remnants of the Dual, unlike in Czech:—

Nom., Acc. ruky, Gen. rúk, Dat. rukám, Instr. rukami, Loc. rukách.

Nom., Acc. nohy, Gen. nôh, Dat. nohám, Instr. nohami, Loc. nohách.

    Note: dvere = door (Nom., Acc. pl.), Gen. (pl.) dvier or dverí, Dat. dverám, Instr. dverami or dvermi, Loc. dverách.

    Notice the word for "children" used in the plur. only: Nom., Acc. dietky, Gen. dietok, Dat. dietkam, etc. Cf. p. 159, dieťa.

    Notice the unique declension of pani = lady, Mrs.:—[1]

	Sing.	*Plur.*
Nom.	pani	panie
Gen.	panej	paní
Dat.	panej	paniam
Acc.	paniu	panie
Instr.	paňou	paniami
Loc.	panej	paniach

    When in apposition to another noun pani is not declined, e.g.:—

Videl som pani matku = I saw (your or his, etc.) mother (respectful)

    3*b*. Masc. nouns ending in -*a* (hard and soft stems) follow the declension of masc. *o*-stems, e.g.:—

---

[1] For the adjectival type of fem. noun, e.g. gazdiná = housewife, see p. 181.

sluha = servant

	Sing.	Plur.
Nom.	sluha	sluhovia
Gen.	sluhu	sluhov
Dat.	sluhovi	sluhom
Acc.	sluhu	sluhov
Instr.	sluhom	sluhami
Loc.	sluhovi	sluhoch

Those ending in *-ista* or *-ita*, have Nom. plur. in *-i*, e.g.:—

huslista = violinist, Nom. plur. huslisti
husita = Hussite,   "   " husiti

4*a*. Masc. *o*-stems. (The endings of this declension have mostly already been anticipated in the declension of sluha, masc. noun ending in *-a*, above.)

This declension is subdivided into hard *o*-stems and soft *jo*-stems, as in other Slavonic languages. But in the Instrumental singular the characteristic Slovak ending *-om* is used for both types. They also both have the endings *-ovi* (Dat. and Loc. sing. personal), *-ov* (Gen. plur., pronounced ou!), *-om* (Dat. plur.), *-och* (Loc. plur.). These endings have become standardized in Slovak, as has the ending *-mi* (*-ami* after *m* and difficult groups of consonants) for the Instr. plur.; the ending *-y* (cf. Czech) is used only in fixed phrases which are archaic survivals, e.g. ostrými zuby = with (its) sharp teeth.

The Nom. plur. has several endings: *-ovia* is reserved only for certain masc. personal nouns, otherwise *-i* is used. Personal nouns ending in *-k* and *-ch* in Nom. sing., undergo the 2nd palatalization in the Nom. plur. before this *-i*, e.g.: vojak = soldier, Nom. pl. vojaci, mních = monk, Nom. pl. mnísi. Also: vlk (= wolf), has Nom. pl. vlci. Nouns ending in *-h* prefer the ending *-ovia* in Nom. plur.: súdruhovia = comrades. Inanimates and animals have *-y* for hard stems, and *-e* for soft stems. The ending *-ia* usually corresponds to Czech *-é*, e.g.:—

mešťania	= townsmen	(from mešťan)
židia	= Jews,	(" žid)
súsedia	= neighbours	(" súsed)
učitelia	= teachers	(" učiteľ)
hostia	= guest	(" hosť)
ľudia	= people	

Also:

rodičia = parents

SLOVAK

Owing to the absence in Slovak of the vowel mutations (přehláska) known to Czech, the differences between the declensions of the hard and soft type are fewer than in Czech, i.e. Dat. and Loc. sing.: a few animate hard stems have Dat. sing. in -*u* instead of -*ovi*, but *all* soft animates have -*ovi*,[1] Loc. sing. inanim. hard: -*e*; velar stems: -*u*; inanim. soft -*i*; Nom. Acc. (Instr.) plur. inanimate hard: -*y*, soft: -*e*.

In the Gen. sing. this declension prefers the ending -*a* for animate nouns and -*u* for inanimate (largely hard-stem) nouns, as in Czech; but there are inconsistencies in Slovak too. In the Dat. and Loc. sing. the ending -*ovi* is used for animate nouns more consistently than in Czech. Nouns in -*ár*, -*al*, -*er*, -*el*, have Loc. sing. in -*i*: v januári (= in January), v hoteli (= in the hotel). Acc. sing. = Gen. sing. only for masc. persons (and animals when personified). Likewise Acc. plur. = Gen. plur. for masc. persons only—in contrast to Czech!

The Voc. sing. survives in a few nouns only, e.g.:—

Bože!	= O God!	(Nom. sg.	Boh)
človeče!	= man!	(" "	človek)
Hospodine!	= O Lord!	(" "	Hospodin)
bratu!	= brother!	(" "	brat)
synku!	= sonny!	(" "	synok)
pane!	= Sir!	(" "	pán)

chlap = man, fellow   oráč = ploughman
hrad = castle   meč = sword

	Hard:		Soft:	
	Animate.	Inanimate.	Animate.	Inanimate.
SING.				
Nom.	chlap	hrad	oráč	meč
Gen.	chlapa	hradu	oráča	meča[2]
Dat.	chlapovi	hradu	oráčovi	meču
Acc.	chlapa	hrad	oráča	meč
Instr.	chlapom	hradom	oráčom	mečom
Loc.	chlapovi	hrade	oráčovi	meči

[1] Consecutive words with the ending -*ovi* are avoided, as in Czech.

[2] But: plač, Gen. sg. plaču = weeping
      čaj,   "   "   čaju = tea
      bôľ,   "   "   bôľu = pain, grief

Nouns in -*iar* follow this declension, e.g. požiar = a fire, Gen. sg. požiaru, Loc. sg. (v) požiari.

SLOVAK

	Hard:		Soft:	
	Animate.	Inanimate.	Animate.	Inanimate.
PLUR.				
Nom.	chlapi	hrady	oráči	meče
Gen.	chlapov	hradov	oráčov	mečov
Dat.	chlapom	hradom	oráčom	mečom
Acc.	chlapov	hrady	oráčov	meče
Instr.	chlapmi	hradmi	oráčmi	mečmi
Loc.	chlapoch	hradoch	oráčoch	mečoch

The moveable vowel, appearing only in the Nom. sing. of masc. nouns, in Slovak can be either -*e*- or -*o*-, -*o*- being more frequent. E.g.:—

pes	Gen. sg.	psa	= dog
ker	"	"	kra	= bush
šev	"	"	šva	= seam
smysel	"	"	smyslu	= sense
otec	"	"	otca	= father
oheň	"	"	ohňa	= fire
marec	"	"	marca	= March
koniec	"	"	konca	= end

but—

orol	"	"	orla	= eagle
ovos	"	"	ovsa	= oats
sväzok	"	"	sväzku	= volume, bond
nájom	"	"	nájmu	= hire
vietor	"	"	vetra	= a wind
obor	"	"	obra	= giant

Notice the retention of the vowel in:—

ľan	Gen. sg.	ľanu	= flax
domček	"	"	domčeka	= little house
pohreb	"	"	pohrebu	= burial
jazvec	"	"	jazveca	= badger

Monosyllabic nouns with a long vowel in the Nom. sing. sometimes shorten this vowel in declension. E.g.:—

stôl	Gen. sg.	stola	= table
chlieb	"	"	chleba	= bread
vôl	"	"	vola	= ox
kôň	"	"	koňa	= horse
nôž	"	"	noža	= knife
dážď	"	"	dažďa	= rain
kôš	"	"	koša	= basket

but—

SLOVAK

```
pôst   Gen. sg. pôstu  = fast
háj     "    "  hája   = grove, wood
```

Some nouns have a short vowel in the Nom. sing. in Slovak, in contrast to the corresponding word in Czech. E.g.:—

```
dom    Gen. sg. domu   = house,     Cz. dům
dvor    "    "  dvora  = court,      "  dvůr
hrach   "    "  hrachu = pea,        "  hrách
prah    "    "  prahu  = threshold,  "  práh
sneh    "    "  snehu  = snow,       "  sníh
loj     "    "  loja   = tallow,     "  lůj
hnoj    "    "  hnoja  = manure,     "  hnůj
```

Irregular nouns of this declension:—

človek = person, man, has an irregular plural: Nom. ľudia, Gen. ľudí, Dat. ľuďom, Acc. ľudí, Instr. ľuďmi, Loc. ľuďoch.

hosť = guest, has a plural: Nom. hostia, Gen. hosťov or hostí, Dat. hosťom, Acc. hosťov or hostí, Instr. hosťmi, Loc. hosťoch.

brat = brother, has an irregular Nom. plur. bratia.

peniaz = coin, has an irregular plur., when this means "money": Nom. peniaze, Gen. peňazí, Dat. peniazom, Acc. peniaze, Instr. peniazmi, Loc. peniazoch.

kôň = horse, has a regular Nom. plur. kone, but its Gen. plur. is koní.

priateľ = friend, has Nom. plur. priatelia; otherwise it follows the declension of oráč. Similarly: nepriateľ = enemy.

kňaz = priest, has Nom. plur. kňazi.

deň = day, is irregular in some cases. It is declined:—

    SING. Nom. deň, Gen. dňa, Dat. dňu, Acc. deň, Instr. dňom, Loc. dni (but: vo dne = by day).
    PLUR. Nom. dni, Gen. dní, Dat. dňom, Acc. dni, Instr. dňami, Loc. dňoch.

týždeň = week, Gen. sg. týždňa, follows the declension of meč.

čas = time, and
ráz = occasion, time, have Gen. pl. čias (or časov),
ráz (without ending).

So also: tisíc Nom. sg. *and* Gen. pl. = thousand
Košice (a town), Gen. pl. Košíc

sen = dream, has Loc. pl. (v) snách (or snoch).

Masc. nouns ending in *-o* in the Nom. sing. decline like chlap in the other cases, e.g.:—

strýko = uncle, Acc. Gen. sg. strýka
Jano = John,   "   "   " Jana

But surnames have *-u* in the Gen. sing.:—

Krasko, Gen. sing. Krasku

Words of foreign origin ending in *-us* usually drop this ending in the other cases and are then declined like hrad. A few retain the *-us*. E.g.:—

katechizmus = catechism, Gen. sg. katechizmu
                         Loc. sg. katechizme

but—

omnibus   = omnibus,   Gen. sg. omnibusu
                         Loc. sg. omnibuse

Names of Hungarian origin in *-ó*, *-ő*, *-ü*, etc. follow the declension of chlap. E.g.:—

Szabó, Gen. sg. Szabóa, Dat. sg. Szabóovi, etc.

4*b*. Neuter *o*-stems. These are also subdivided into hard *o*-stems and soft *jo*-stems. But owing to the absence of vowel mutations, the declensions of the two types really differ only in the:—

Nom. Acc. sing.: hard end in *-o*, soft in *-e*
Loc. sg.:   hard end in *-e*, soft in *-i*
Gen. pl.:   hard have no ending, soft have *-í*

In the other cases of the plural, hard stems have long *-á* (except in Instr.), while soft stems have *-ia*. The long *-á* in the Nom. and Acc. is a peculiarity exclusively of Slovak. The "standardized" endings of the Dat., Instr. and Loc. plur. have been transferred from the feminine *a*-stems.

Nouns ending in *-ie* in the Nom. sg. follow the soft declension, but have Instr. sing. in *-ím*, Loc. sing. in *-í*, Instr. plur. in *-iami*.

SLOVAK

```
                o-stem:  mesto = town
   jo-stems:    pole = field    znamenie = sign
```

	Singular			Plural		
Nom.	mesto[1]	pole	znamenie[2]	mestá	polia	znamenia
Gen.	mesta	poľa	znamenia	miest	polí	znamení
Dat.	mestu	poľu	znameniu	mestám	poliam	znameniam
Acc.	mesto	pole	znamenie	mestá	polia	znamenia
Instr.	mestom	poľom	znamením	mestami	poľami	znameniami
Loc.	meste	poli	znamení	mestách	poliach	znameniach

Long vowels in the endings are shortened if the vowel in the preceding syllable is long, as in the other declensions, e.g.:—

miesto = place, Nom. Acc. pl. miesta, Dat. pl. miestam, etc.
pľúca = lungs, Dat. pl. pľúcam, etc.

In the Gen. plur. of the *o*-stems, where there is no ending, the root vowel, if originally short, is usually lengthened, as in mesto above and in the feminine *a*-stems. Further examples:—

```
        pivo    = beer,      Gen. pl.  pív
        mäso    = meat,        "   "   mias
        lono    = lap,         "   "   lôn
        zrno    = grain,       "   "   zŕn
        jablko  = apple,       "   "   jablk
        plece   = shoulder,    "   "   pliec
but—
        slovo   = word,        "   "   slov
        vojsko  = army,        "   "   vojsk
```

N.B.—sto (= hundred) has Gen. pl. sto.

As in the fem. *a*-stems too, the fill-vowels -*ie*-, -*á*- and short -*e*-, -*o*- are inserted in the Gen. plur. to avoid difficult final consonant groups. E.g.:—

```
okno        = window,      Gen. pl.  okien
krídlo      = wing,          "   "   krídel or krídiel
jedlo       = food, dish,    "   "   jedál or jediel
mydlo       = soap,          "   "   mydiel
dievčatko   = girl,          "   "   dievčatiek
kuriatko    = chicken,       "   "   kuriatok
```

[1] Velar stems (hard) in *h*, *k*, *ch*, have -*u* instead of -*e* in the Loc. sing.: vo vojsku (= in the army), v uchu (= in the ear).
[2] This is the model for the declension of all Verbal Nouns in -*nie* and -*tie*, e.g.: videnie = seeing, pitie = drinking.

Nouns ending in *-stvo* have Gen. pl. in *-stiev* (formerly in *-ství*), e.g.:—

panstvo = gentry, estate, Gen. pl. panstiev

Nouns with the soft endings *-ce* and *-ište* have no ending in the Gen. plur., but lengthen the last vowel of the stem. E.g.:—

		Gen. pl.	
vrece	= sack,		vriec
srdce	= heart,	" "	sŕdc
ohnisko	= hearth,	" "	ohnísk

But—

vajce (= egg) has Gen. plur. vajec.

Nouns with hardened stem in *-r-* have a mixed declension, e.g.:—

more = sea

Nom.	more	moria
Gen.	mora	morí
Dat.	moru	moriam
Acc.	more	moria
Instr.	morom	morami
Loc.	mori	moriach

Irregular nouns

oko (= eye) and ucho (= ear) have irregular plurals when they mean "eyes" or "ears":

Nom./Acc.	oči	uši
Gen.	očí (or očú, dual)[1]	uší (or ušú, dual)[1]
Dat.	očiam	ušiam
Instr.	očami	ušami
Loc.	očiach	ušiach

oje (= shaft) has short endings in the plur., except in the Gen.:—

Nom./Acc. oja, Dat. ojam, etc., but Gen. ojí

vnútro (= inside), has Loc. sing. vnútri. Similarly: nebo (= sky), Loc. sing. na nebi.

Foreign words in *-um* are declined like mesto, losing the *-um* in the other cases:—

dátum = date, Gen. sg. dáta, Loc. sg. datu, Nom. pl. dáta.

---

[1] The old dual forms are only used in fixed expressions, e.g. pozrieť do očú = to look in the eyes.

SLOVAK

múzeum = museum, Gen. sg. múzea, Loc. sg. múzeu, Nom. pl. múzeá, Gen. pl. muzeí.

THE NUMERALS

The Cardinal Numerals. 1-4 are adjectival numerals and agree with the noun they qualify in case. Jeden = one, is declined like a hard adjective (see below) in all cases except the Nom.; it has the usual three genders. Dva = two, tri = three, štyri = four, distinguish the masculine personal gender from the rest in the Nom. and Acc.; for the other cases they decline without distinguishing gender.

Päť = five, onwards, are usually in the form of nouns and take the Gen. plur., e.g.: päť chlapov (= five boys), päť žien, stromov, miest (= five women, trees, towns). But these numerals have alternative forms of Nom. and Acc. for masculine personal nouns, and these forms are then adjectival, e.g. Nom. pl. piati chlapi (= five boys) *may* be used. Päť = 5, onwards, usually decline (with endings like the plural of the pronoun môj, as do also dva, tri, štyri) and they then agree in case with the noun they qualify, i.e. they also are then adjectival. E.g.: s piatimi chlapcami (= with five boys). They may also be left undeclined.

Numerals compounded with the tens have two alternative forms, as in Czech. The form "three and twenty" is literary and rarer.

Sto (= hundred) and its compound hundreds, 200, 300, etc., when used as qualifying numerals are not declined. Tisíc (= thousand) also need not be declined; or it may take the same endings as in the declension of päť, when referring to masculine persons.

2-4 take the verb in the plural, in the same form for all genders in the Past tense, e.g.:—

dve ženy boli tam = two women were there
tam boli dva stromy = there were two trees there

and—

dvaja chlapci boli tam = two boys were there

(The use of the masculine personal form of 2, 3, and 4 is obligatory.)

5 onwards take the verb in the neuter singular, e.g.:—

päť žien, stromov, chlapov bolo tam = five women, trees, boys were there.

The (non-obligatory) alternative masculine personal forms of five onwards, however, take the verb in the plur.: piati chlapci boli tam.

When compound numerals are used, the noun is in the Gen. plur. but the verb is in the neuter sing.; compounds with "one" also take the Gen. plur. and the verb in neuter sing., e.g.:—

triadvasať žien bolo tam
  and— } = 23 women were there
dvadsaťtri žien bolo tam

dvadsaťjeden žien
dvadsaťpäť žien   } bolo tam { = 21 / = 25 / = 20 } women were there
  and
dvadsať žien

Jeden (with hard d!) = one, is declined as follows:—

SING.

	Masc.	Neut.	Fem.
Nom.	jeden	jedno	jedna
Gen.	jedného		jednej
Dat.	jednému		jednej
Acc.	= Nom. or Gen.	jedno	jednu
Instr.	jedným		jednou
Loc.	jednom		jednej

PLUR.

	Masc. Pers.	Other Genders
Nom.	jedni[1]	jedny
Gen.	jedných	
Dat.	jedným	
Acc.	jedných	jedny
Instr.	jednými	
Loc.	jedných	

	Masc.	Fem.	Neut.
1	jeden	jedna	jedno

	Masc.	Masc. Pers.	Fem. and Neut.
2	dva	dvaja	dve

[1] Pronounced with hard n.

SLOVAK

Gen./Loc.	dvoch			
Dat.	dvom			
		Masc. Pers.	*Masc.*	*Fem. & Neut.*
Acc.		dvoch	dva	dve
Instr.	dvoma			

All Genders except Masc. Pers.   *Masc. Pers.*

3   tri   traja

Gen./Loc.	troch		
Dat.	trom		
		Masc. Pers.	*Other Genders*
Acc.		troch	tri
Instr.	troma or tromi		

All Genders except Masc. Pers.   *Masc. Pers.*

4   štyri   štyria

Gen./Loc.	štyroch		
Dat.	štyrom		
		Masc. Pers.	*Other Genders*
Acc.		štyroch	štyri
Instr.	štyrmi		

All Genders except Masc. Pers.   *Masc. Pers.*

5   päť   piati

Gen./Loc.	piatich		
Dat.	piatim		
		Masc. Pers.	*Other Genders*
Acc.		piatich	päť
Instr.	piatimi		

All Genders except Masc. Pers.   *Masc. Pers.*

6   šesť   šiesti

declines like päť

All Genders except Masc. Pers.   *Masc. Pers.*

7   sedem   siedmi

declines like päť

All Genders except Masc. Pers.   *Masc. Pers.*

8   osem   ôsmi

declines like päť

All Genders except Masc. Pers.   *Masc. Pers.*

9   deväť   deviati

declines like päť

SLOVAK

	All Genders except Masc. Pers.	Masc. Pers.	

```
10  desať              desiati   declines like päť
11  jedenásť                        "      "      "
12  dvanásť                       etc.
13  trinásť
14  štrnásť
15  pätnásť
16  šestnásť
17  sedemnásť
18  osemnásť
19  devätnásť
20  dvadsať
21  dvadsaťjeden¹ or jedenadvadsať for all genders
22  dvadsaťdva² or dvaadvadsať
23  dvadsaťtri² or triadvadsať
30  tridsať
40  štyridsať
50  päťdesiat
60  šesťdesiat
70  sedemdesiat
80  osemdesiat
90  deväťdesiat
100  sto
101  sto jeden
200  dvesto
300  tristo
400  štyristo
500  päťsto                       etc.
1,000  tisíc
2,000  dvetisíc
3,000  tritisíc
4,000  štyritisíc
5,000  päťtisíc
1,000,000  milión
```

    Oba and obidva (= both), are declined like dva.
    Sto (= 100), when used by itself is declined like mesto; Loc. sg. is (v) ste or sto.[3]
    Tisíc (= 1,000), when used by itself is declined like meč; Instr. pl. tisícami or tisícmi.
    Milión (= 1,000,000), is declined (always) like hrad.

---

[1] Indeclinable and invariable as to gender.
[2] Need not be declined.
[3] Gen. pl. is either sto or replaced by stoviek or stovák from stovka = a hundred (of).

SLOVAK

The Ordinals. These are adjectives, as in other Slavonic languages. They all belong to the hard declension (see below) except tretí (= third), and tisíci (= thousandth) and its compounds, which are soft.

1st	prvý, -á, -é
2nd	druhý, -á, -é
3rd	tretí, -ia, -ie
4th	štvrtý, -á, -é
5th	piaty, -a, -e, N.B. short endings
6th	šiesty, -a, -e
7th	siedmy etc.
8th	ôsmy
9th	deviaty
10th	desiaty
11th	jedenásty
12th	dvanásty
20th	dvadsiaty
21st	dvadsiaty prvý
22nd	dvadsiaty druhý
30th	tridsiaty
40th	štyridsiaty
50th	päťdesiaty
60th	šesťdesiaty
70th	sedemdesiaty
80th	osemdesiaty
90th	deväťdesiaty
100th	stý (stotý), -á, -é
101st	stoprvý
200th	dvojstý
300th	trojstý
400th	štvorstý
500th	päťstý
1,000th	tisíci
2,000th	dvojtisíci
1,000,000th	miliónty

Long compound Ordinals have only the last two elements as Ordinals:

1321st = tisíc tristo dvadsiaty prvý.

The Collective Numerals. These are chiefly used with persons, animals, or objects thought of in groups, and with pluralia tantum. Modern Slovak mostly uses them in the neuter sing. form in the Nom., followed by the noun qualified in the Gen. plur. Their oblique cases are used only with *pluralia tantum.*

Dvoje = 2, is declined as follows:—

All genders.

Nom.	dvoje
Gen.	dvojich
Dat.	dvojim
Acc.	dvoje
Instr.	dvojimi
Loc.	dvojich

Like dvoje: troje = three, obidvoje or oboje = both.

Pätoro = five, etc. are not declined.

Like pätoro: štvoro = four, šestoro = six, sedmoro = 7, osmoro = 8, devätoro = 9, desatoro = 10, etc. Examples:—

dvoje detí = a couple of children
štvoro chlapcov = four boys
Desatoro božích prikázaní = the Ten Commandments
dvoje vrát = two gates (vráta: plur. tantum)

Half = pol, which is indeclinable and governs the Gen. sing., as in Czech.

1½ = masc. and neut.: pol druha (litra vody = litres of water); fem.: pol druhej (fľaše = bottle)

2½ = masc. and neut.: pol treťa; fem.: pol tretej

3½ = "   "   "   pol štvrta; "   pol štvrtej

etc.

Cf. Czech, Polish, Lusatian and Byelorussian.

Distributive Numerals. These are now formed with *po* + Cardinal numerals in the Acc., e.g.: po dve koruny = two crowns each. But with jeden the Locative is used.   e.g.: po jednom jablku = one apple each.

Numeral adverbs are formed with raz (= time, Fr. fois), qualified by a Cardinal numeral governing its usual case. Hence we have:—

(jeden) raz = once
dva, tri, štyri razy = twice, three, four times
päť (etc.) ráz = five times

The suffix -*krát* is also used: trikrát = thrice.

SLOVAK

THE PRONOUNS

The Pronouns in Slovak are similar to those in Czech, but the student should note differences of length in certain of the declensions of the Personal Pronouns and of ten (= this). He will also observe a tendency in Slovak to make the pronominal declension more like the adjectival one, e.g. in the plural of ten and in the declension of všetok (= all). All the usual categories exist, e.g.:—

Demonstrative:—

```
ten   = this          tamten ⎫
tento = this here     henten ⎬ = that yonder
                      onen     = that (not of place)
```

Interrogative:—

```
kto = who?     ktorý? = which?          ⎫ declined
čo  = what?    aký?   = of what kind?   ⎬ like hard
                                        ⎭ adjectives
               čí?    = whose? interrog. only, de-
                                clined like soft
                                                 adj.
```

Indefinite (formed with prefixes or suffixes):—

```
niekto   ⎫
dakto    ⎬ = someone, a certain person
voľakto  ⎭
ktosi       = some (more indefinite)
ledakto     = any one, various people
ktokoľviek  = whoever
bárkto    ⎫
hocikto   ⎬ = anyone you like
(lecikto) ⎭
nejaký ⎫
akýsi  ⎬ = some kind of (decl. like hard adj.)
kadejaký = any kind of
```

Relative:—

```
ktorý = who, which, declined like hard adjective
čo    = that
```

"whose" is rendered by ktorého (masc. or neut. pos-
                                                sessor)
                      ktorej (fem. possessor)
                      ktorých (plur. possessor)

Possessive (pronoun-adjectives):—

```
môj  = my, mine
náš  = our(s)
jeho = his, its, indeclinable
jej  = her(s)           "
ich  = their(s)         "
```

Definitive:—

```
všetok = all
každý  = each, declined like hard adjective
sám    = -self, alone
samý   = only, sheer, the very; decl. like hard
                                         adjective
ten istý, tá istá, to isté = the same; istý is de-
       clined like hard adjective
iný    = another, declined like hard adjective
taký   = such,         "      "     "     "
toľký  = so great,     "      "     "     "
```

Negative:—

```
nik, nikto = no one
nič        = nothing, declined like čo
žiadny  ⎫
žiaden[1] ⎬ = no, none
nijaký  ⎭
```

Personal:—

```
on = he                 ty = you (sg. familiar)
ja = I                  vy = you (pl. and polite)
```

The following pronouns have declensions which differ in some way from that of the adjectives:—

ten = this

	SING.			PLUR.	
	Masc.	*Neut.*	*Fem.*	*Masc. pers.*	*Other genders*
Nom.	ten	to	tá	tí	tie
Gen.	toho		tej	tých	
Dat.	tomu		tej	tým	
Acc. = Nom. or Gen.		to	tú	tých	tie
Instr.	tým		tou	tými	
Loc.	tom		tej	tých	

Like ten with suffixes or prefixes: tento,[2] tamten, henten.

---

[1] With hard d!
[2] tohoto, Gen. sg. masc. and neut. and Acc. sg. masc. pers., is contracted to: tohto.

But: onen, oná, ono, pl. oní, oné = that, Acc. sg. fem. onú, Acc. pl. ových (masc. pers.), oné (other genders) now follows the hard adjectival declension.[1] (See p. 181.)

N.B.—Ten and its compounds and onen are pronounced with *hard t* and *n* throughout, even before *i* in tí, tie, oní.

kto = who? (like ten), čo[2] = what?, that

	kto	čo
Nom.	kto	čo
Gen.	koho	čoho
Dat.	komu	čomu
Acc.	koho	čo
Instr.	kým	čím
Loc.	kom	čom

-*že* can be suffixed for emphasis, as in Czech: ktože? čože?

všetok (= all) is declined like a hard adjective, except in the Nom. sing. and plur. We give its full declension for comparison with other Slavonic languages:—

| | SING. | | | PLUR. | | |
	Masc.	*Neut.*	*Fem.*	*Masc. Pers.*	*Other Genders*	
Nom.	všetok	všetko	všetka	všetci		všetky
Gen.	všetkého		všetkej		všetkých	
Dat.	všetkému		všetkej		všetkým	
Acc.	Nom. or Gen.	všetko	všetku	všetkých		všetky
Instr.	všetkým		všetkou		všetkými	
Loc.	všetkom		všetkej		všetkých	

môj = my

| | SING. | | | PLUR. | | |
	Masc.	*Neut.*	*Fem.*	*Masc. Pers.*	*Other Genders*	
Nom.	môj	moje	moja	moji		moje
Gen.	môjho		mojej		mojich	
Dat.	môjmu		mojej		mojim	
Acc.	Nom. or Gen.	moje	moju	mojich		moje
Instr.	mojím		mojou		mojimi	
Loc.	mojom		mojej		mojich	

Like môj: tvoj = your(s), svoj = own (referring to subject of sentence).

[1] The forms onoho Gen. s. m. and n., onomu Dat. s. m. and n. are archaic in Slovak.
[2] Written as one word with the prepositions: pre, na, za, when interrogative: prečo? = why?

The forms of mojeho, mojemu, tvojeho, tvojemu, svojeho, svojemu are considered archaic.
náš = our(s), really follows môj:—

	SING.			PLUR.	
	Masc.	*Neut.*	*Fem.*	*Masc. Pers.*	*Other Genders*
Nom.	náš	naše	naša	naši	naše
Gen.	nášho[1]	našej	našej	našich	
Dat.	nášmu[1]	našej	našej	našim	
Acc.	Nom. or Gen.	naše	našu	našich	naše
Instr.	naším	našou		našimi	
Loc.	našom	našej		našich	

Like náš, váš = your(s), (polite sing. and fam. and polite plur.)

sám -self, alone

	SING.			PLUR.	
	Masc.	*Neut.*	*Fem.*	*Masc. Pers.*	*Other Genders*
Nom.	sám	samo	sama	sami	samy
Gen.	samého	samej	samej	samých	
Dat.	samému	samej	samej	samým	
Acc.	Nom. or Gen.	samo	samu	samých	samy
Instr.	samým	samou		samými	
Loc.	samom	samej		samých	

Personal Pronouns.

on = he, ona = she, ono = it

	SING.			PLUR.	
	Masc.	*Neut.*	*Fem.*	*Masc. Pers.*	*Other Genders*
Nom.	on	ono	ona	oni	ony
Gen.	jeho, ho[2]	jej	jej	ich	
Dat.	jemu, mu[2]	jej	jej	im	
Acc.	jeho, ho[2]		ju	ich (nich)	ich (ne)
Instr.	ním	ňou		nimi	
Loc.	ňom	nej		nich	

The Gen. case sing. and plur. is used in its full form (but without *n-* prefixed) for the Possessive Pronoun-adjective of the 3rd person: his, her, its, their. It is indeclinable.

Notice that in Slovak the Instr. case, sing. and

---

[1]Pronounced naːʒɦɔ, naːʒmu.
[2]Forms used only as enclitic, unemphatic (unstressed) pronouns. Other forms can be used both stressed and unstressed. See "Word Order with Enclitics", pp. 221-222.

SLOVAK

plur., *always* has an initial n- (ň), as in Ukrainian, Lusatian, Polish, and Slovenian.

After prepositions a soft n (ň) is prefixed—to the long form when there are two alternatives:—

Dat. sg. masc.	jemu;	but:	k nemu
Gen. sg. fem.	jej;	but:	do nej
Acc. sg. fem.	na ňu.		

When the preposition ends in a vowel, e.g. do, na, pre, za, and is followed by neho (Gen. Acc. sg. masc. and neut.) the two words are generally contracted in the modern language, e.g.:—

do neho becomes doňho, or even doň = to it
na neho   "   naňho, "   "   naň = on to him

After the prepositions nad, pred and pod, a fill-vowel -e- (which leaves the d hard) is used before -ň, e.g.:—

podeň = (motion to) under him

(See "Prepositions".)

In the Acc. plur. them = ich, referring to all genders, animate and inanimate, and used both stressed and enclitically. But after a preposition nich refers only to masc. personal nouns, and ne is the correct form referring to all others, e.g.:—

na nich = on to them (men only), but—
na ne (masc. non-personal, fem. and neut.)

ja = I   my = we   ty = you (fam.)   vy = you

Nom.	ja	my	ty	vy
Gen.	mňa, ma[1]	nás	teba, ťa[1]	vás
Dat.	mne, mi[1]	nám	tebe, ti[1]	vám
Acc.	mňa, ma[1]	nás	teba, ťa[1]	vás
Instr.	mnou	nami	tebou	vami
Loc.	mne	nás	tebe	vás

Notice the short vowels in the Instr. plur. nami, vami, in contrast to Czech.

Like *ty* without Nom. sing.: seba, sa = -self (referring to the subject of a sentence). Dat sing. enclitic *si* is frequently used, as in Czech, Slovenian, etc. sa is Acc. only.[1]

Notice the root vowel -e- in Dat., Instr. and Loc. sing. of ty and seba, in contrast to Czech,

---

[1]Enclitic, unemphatic forms. See "Word Order with Enclitics", pp. 221-222.

Polish and Lusatian.

In polite address in Slovak, in contrast to Czech on the one hand and to East and South Slav on the other, *vy* is used with the verb in the plural; and in the Past tense the Past Participle Active is always in the plur. with the ending -*li*. The complement, however, is in the "correct" gender and number, i.e. that of the person addressed. E.g.:—

(to a lady) Vy ste boli chorá? }
(to a man) Vy ste boli chorý? } = Have you been ill?

THE ADJECTIVES

Ordinary adjectives in Slovak are divided into a hard and a soft declension, as in other Slavonic languages. There are far fewer soft adjectives in Slovak than in Czech, because in Slovak new derived adjectives end in -*ný*, not -*ní*. But adjectives formed from the names of animals have soft endings in Slovak, as in Czech, e.g.: psí = dog's.

The hard declension in Slovak is similar to that of Czech. It differs in the sing. only in the Loc. masc. and neut. (-*om* > < -*ém*), Acc. fem. (-*ú* > < -*ou*), and Gen. Dat. Loc. fem. with their characteristic -*ej* (Cz. -*é*). In the Nom. and Acc. plur. adjectives qualifying masc. personal nouns are distinguished from those qualifying all others, which have common endings, as in the declension of the pronouns and as in Polish and Upper Lusatian (but not Czech!). In the Nom. plur. masc. personal there are no changes of the final consonants of the stem before the ending -*í* (in contrast to Czech and Polish) and dentals are *not* pronounced soft before it.

The soft declension (as already mentioned) has a far greater variety of endings than the corresponding declension in Czech, owing to the absence of vowel mutations. In the Loc. sing. masc. and neut. the ending is -*om*; and in Instr. sing. fem. the ending is -*ou*, as in the soft *ja*-stem nouns.

When the root of an adjective contains a long vowel, all long vowels in endings of both declensions are shortened, except -*ou*, according to the regular law of Slovak phonetics which generally avoids two consecutive long syllables. E.g.: hard decl.: krásny (= beautiful), Gen. sg. masc. and neut. krásneho, Nom. sg. fem. krásna, Nom. pl. masc. pers. krásni, Gen. pl. krásnych, etc. Where a form krásne can also be an adverb, the two are distinguished only in pronunciation: the adj. has a hard *n*, while the adv. has a soft *n*. A *shortened* -*e*, just like a long

-é or -ej, does *not* cause a soft pronunciation of preceding dentals, e.g.: krásneho has a *hard* n. In the soft declension the long endings -í, -ia, -ie, -iu are shortened to -i, -a, -e, -u after a preceding long vowel, e.g.: svieži Nom. sg. masc. (= fresh), Nom. sg. fem. svieža, Nom. sg. neut. svieže, Acc. sg. fem. sviežu, Gen. sg. masc. and neut. svieževho. The last example also illustrates that Slovak can have a long root vowel, where the corresponding adjective in Czech has a short one: cf. Slk. ľúby = dear, Cz. libý; Slk. čierny = black, Cz. černý.

Acc. sing. masc. = Gen. sing. masc. for animate nouns, but = Nom. sing. masc. for inanimates.

Hard: zdravý = healthy

SING. PLUR.

	Masc.	Neut.	Fem.	Masc. Pers.	Other Genders
Nom.	zdravý	zdravé	zdravá	zdraví	zdravé
Gen.	zdravého		zdravej	zdravých	
Dat.	zdravému		zdravej	zdravým	
Acc. = Nom. or Gen.		zdravé	zdravú	zdravých	zdravé
Instr.	zdravým		zdravou	zdravými	
Loc.	zdravom		zdravej	zdravých	

Soft: cudzí = foreign

SING. PLUR.

	Masc.	Neut.	Fem.	Masc. Pers.	Other Genders
Nom.	cudzí	cudzie	cudzia	cudzí	cudzie
Gen.	cudzieho		cudzej	cudzích	
Dat.	cudziemu		cudzej	cudzím	
Acc. = Nom. or Gen.		cudzie	cudziu	cudzích	cudzie
Instr.	cudzím		cudzou	cudzími	
Loc.	cudzom		cudzej	cudzích	

Slovak, like other Slavonic languages, has a number of nouns and proper names (surnames in -*ský*, -*cký*, etc.), which follow the adjectival declension, e.g.: pocestný = traveller, gazdiná[1] = housewife, kráľovná[1] = queen, vstupné = entrance fee, Krušinský (masc. surname), Frýdecká (fem. surname).

Slovak has only five true adjectives with predicative endings:—

---

[1]These fem. nouns follow žena in the Gen., Dat., Instr., Loc. plur.

	SING.		PLUR.	
Masc.	*Fem.*	*Neut.*	*Masc. Pers.*	*Other Genders*
hoden[1]	hodna	hodno	hodni	hodny = worthy
vinen[1]	vinna (arch.)	vinno (arch.)	vinní	vinné = guilty
dlžen	dlžna	dlžno	dlžní	dlžné = owing
rád	rada	rado	radi	rady = glad

also its negative: nerád = unwilling

These adjectives are not declined and are only used predicatively. Only rád is not falling out of use and being replaced by the corresponding attributive form.

Possessive adjectives in Slovak have the endings of ordinary hard adjectives in all the oblique cases of the sing. as well as of the plur., in contrast to Czech. In the Nom. and Acc. sg. fem. and neut. and in the Nom. pl. they have short final vowels. In the Gen. and Dat. sg. masc. and neut. the endings *-ho* and *-mu* are joined straight on to the stem, which ends in *-v* or *-n*, without a joining *-é-*. Possessive adjectives formed from masc. nouns end in *-ov*, *-ova*, *-ovo*,[2] etc. while those formed from feminine nouns end in *-in*, *-ina*, *-ino*. Before the latter endings velars do *not* undergo palatalization, e.g.: matkin (from matka) = mother's, cf. Cz. matčin. The final *-n* of the stem is not softened before the short endings *-i*, *-e*, *-ej*. Example: bratov = brother's.

	SING.			PLUR.	
	Masc.	*Neut.*	*Fem.*	*Masc. Pers.*	*Other Genders*
Nom.	bratov	bratovo	bratova	bratovi	bratove
Gen.	bratovho		bratovej	bratových	
Dat.	bratovmu		bratovej	bratovým	
Acc.	Nom. or Gen.	bratovo	bratovu	bratových	bratove
Instr.	bratovým		bratovou	bratovými	
Loc.	bratovom		bratovej	bratových	

Matkin has exactly the same declension.

THE COMPARISON OF ADJECTIVES

The regular Comparative degree of adjectives in Slovak is formed either with the soft endings *-ejší*[3] or with the shorter *-ší*[3] added to the stem. Which

---

[1] Pronounced with hard *d* and *n*!
[2] Movable *e* disappears before these endings, as in Czech: otec = father, otcov = father's.
[3] fem. -(ej)šia, neut. -(ej)šie.

ending is used, is purely a matter of usage, and no unfailing rules can be given. The ending -ší is more frequently used in Slovak than in Czech. No Comparative adjectives end in -čí in Slovak, otherwise the usage of the two languages is usually similar. As in Czech, a few adjectives can have either ending and there are a few irregular formations. Also long root vowels are usually shortened in forming the Comparative with -ší.

1. The ending -ejší can be used for adjectives with a stem in a dental, l, r, p, or k, which last does not undergo any palatalization in Slovak, e.g.:—

príjemný	= pleasant,	Comp.	príjemnejší	pron. with soft n
pekný	= beautiful,	"	peknejší	
hustý	= dense,	"	hustejší	
svätý	= holy,	"	svätejší	pron. with soft t
čistý	= clean,	"	čistejší	
teplý	= warm,	"	teplejší	
múdry	= wise,	"	múdrejší	
hlúpy	= stupid	"	hlúpejší	
horký	= bitter, hot to taste,	"	horkejší	
rezký	= lively, brisk, alert,	"	rezkejší	
ľudský	= human,	"	ľudskejší	
trpký	= tart, bitter,	"	trpkejší	
krehký	= brittle, fragile,	"	krehkejší	
krotký	= meek, tame,	"	krotkejší	
vlhký	= damp,	"	vlhkejší[1]	

2. The ending -ší can be used with stems in a labial, a dental, r, or a velar (which is retained in Slovak, in contrast in Czech), e.g.:

slabý	= weak	Comp.	slabší
zdravý	= healthy,	"	zdravší
bohatý	= rich,	"	bohatší
mladý	= young,	"	mladší
tvrdý	= hard		tvrdší
plný	= full,	"	plnší
zelený	= green,	"	zelenší
starý	= old,	"	starší
suchý	= dry,	"	suchší

[1] Notice also: čierny = black, Comp. černejší, demokratický = democratic, Comp. demokratickejší.

tichý = quiet,   Comp. tichší
drahý = dear,   "   drahší
tuhý = stiff, hard,   "   tuhší
dlhý = long,   "   dlhší
 (this last adj. is regular, in contrast to Czech),
    also:
biely = white,   Comp. belší (with shortening of
                                    root vowel).

Adjectives ending in -*oký*, -*eký* and some in -*ký* lose these endings before adding -*ší*. *s*, *z* become *š*, *ž* respectively by assimilation before -*ší*. E.g.:—

hlboký = deep,   Comp. hlbší
široký = wide,   "   širší
ďaleký = distant,   "   ďalší
sladký = sweet,   "   sladší
riedky = rare,   "   redší (with shortening of
                                    root vowel)
hladký = smooth,   "   hladší
krátky = short,   "   kratší (with shortening
                                    of root vowel)
ťažký = difficult,   "   ťažší
         heavy
vysoký = high,   "   vyšší (with assimilation)
úzky   = narrow,   "   užší (with assimilation
                                    and shortening of
                                    root vowel)
blízký = near,   "   bližší (with assimilation
                                    and shortening of
                                    root vowel)
nízky = low,   "   nižší (with assimilation
                                    and shortening of
                                    root vowel)
mäkký = soft,   "   mäkší
ľahký = light, easy, "   ľahší
tenký = thin,   "   tenší

A few adjectives can have either -*ejší* or -*ší*, e.g.:—

milý   = dear,   Comp. milejší   or milší
tmavý = dark,   "   tmavejší   " tmavší
krásny = beautiful,   "   krásnejší[1] " krajší
                                           (irregular)

A few common adjectives have irregular Comparatives with a different root from that of the Positive

---

[1]This form is now archaic.

degree, e.g.:—

dobrý	= good,	Comp.	lepší
zlý	= bad,	"	horší
malý	= small,	"	menší
veľký	= big,	"	väčší

and—

pekný = beautiful, " krajší

The Superlative degree is formed by adding the prefix *naj-* to all types of Comparative adjectives, e.g.: najpeknejší, najslabší, najširší, najlepší = the most beautiful, the weakest, the broadest, the best.

All Comparative and Superlative adjectives are declined like soft Positive adjectives, i.e. like cudzí above.

Very = veľmi
Than = než or ako
    slová sladšie ako (*or* než) med = words sweeter than honey

The Genitive of comparison after *od* can also be used, e.g.:—

    susedov dom je väčší od nášho *or* ako náš = our neighbour's house is bigger than ours

Rather better	= o trochu ⎱ lepší o niečo ⎰
Much better	= omnoho lepší
Rather good	= dosť dobrý
Less than	= menej { ako než
The bigger...*the* better	= čím väčší...tým lepší
As (good) *as*	= rovnako ⎱ taký (dobrý) ako práve ⎰ (aký)
As soon as possible	= čo najskôr, čo najskorej, čo najskoršie
As fast as possible	= čo najrýchlejšie, čo najchytrejšie
The (very) best of all	= { najlepší zo všetkých najlepší zpomedzi všetkých
Too	= príliš
The same as	= { ten istý ako práve taký aký
In the same way as	= { práve tak ako, tak isto ako

ADVERBS

Adverbs of manner formed from adjectives end more frequently in -*o* than in -*e* in Slovak, in contrast to Czech. This particularly applies to labial and velar stems. E.g.:—

hrubo	= roughly,	cf. Cz.	hrubě
hlúpo	= stupidly,	" "	hloupě
tmavo	= dark,	" "	tmavě
nemo	= dumbly,	" "	němě
ticho	= quietly,	" "	tiše
krátko	= briefly,	" "	krátce

But: Czech and Slovak—

- mnoho = much
- nízko = low
- blízko = near
- ďaleko = far (Slovak) (Cz. daleko)
- práve = just (Slovak) (Cz.: právě)

But some adverbs from adjectives in -*vý* have either -*o* or -*e*, e.g.:—

spravodlivo, spravodlive = justly, cf. Cz. spravedlivě
skúmavo, skúmave = searchingly, cf. Cz. zkoumavě

A few liquid and dental stems, except those in -*ný*, can have either -*e* or -*o*, e.g.:—

rýchl-e, -o = fast,   cf. Cz. rychle

but only—

múdr-o	= wisely,	" "	moudře
hrd-o	= proudly,	" "	hrdě
hust-o	= densely,	" "	hustě
mil-o	= kindly,	" "	mile or milo
smel-o	= boldly,	" "	směle

But: Czech and Slovak—

- málo = little
- skoro (Slk.) = soon, almost (Czech: brzy = soon; skoro = almost)
- teplo = warmly

Adjectives ending in -*ný* mostly have adverbs in -*ne* (pron. -*ňe*):—

krásne = beautifully, cf. Cz. krásně
slobodne = freely,   " " svobodně

but—

    jasno = clearly, cf. Cz. jasně
    dávno = long ago, " " dávno

Adjectives ending in *-ský*, *-cký* have adverbs in *-sky*, *-cky*, usually preceded by the preposition "po", especially if referring to languages or nationality, e.g.:—

    Hovorím po slovensky = I speak Slovak
    po priateľsky   = in a friendly way
    po nemecky   = in German

The soft adjective peší (= foot) has adverbs peši, pešo, or pešky (= on foot).

The Comparison of Adverbs

The Comparative degree of all adverbs in Slovak, except for the few irregular ones listed below, is always equivalent in form to the Nom./Acc. sing. neut. of the corresponding Comparative adjective. E.g.:—

    dlhšie   = longer
    širšie   = more widely
    nižšie   = lower
    rýchlejšie   = quicker
    priateľskejšie = in a more friendly way
    múdrejšie   = more wisely
    krajšie   = more beautifully

The only irregular Comparative adverbs in Slovak are:—

    dobre   = well,   Comp. lepšie
    zle   = badly,   "   horšie
    málo   = little, ⎫
    trochu, trocha = a little ⎭   "   menej
    veľmi   = very,   "   väčšmi =
                                     more (of degree)
    pekne, krásne - beautifully, Comp. krajšie
    mnoho ⎫
    veľa   ⎭   = much,   "   viac(ej) =
                                                more
                (of quantity and generally)
    ďaleko   = far,   Comp. ďalej =
                                               further
    skoro   = soon,   "   skôr,
                                   skorej or skoršie
    neskoro   = late,   Comp. neskôr or
                                           neskoršie

The predicative adjective rád (= glad) has an

adverbial Comp. radšej.

The Superlative degree of all adverbs is formed by prefixing *naj-* to the Comparative degree:—

najkrajšie, najlepšie, najmenej, najviac, najskôr or najskorej or najskoršie, najradšej.

Other adverbs of manner as well as adverbs of time, place, and degree, are independent formations or else the petrified remains of various cases of nouns, adjectives, and pronouns, and even of a few verbs. They have the most varied endings and include some of the most distinctive words of the Slovak vocabulary. Some of the commonest are:—

PLACE

tu, tuná	= here	von, vonka, vonku	= outside
tam	= there, thither	von	= out
ta	= thither	preč	= away!, gone
tade, tadiaľ	= this way	potiaľ(to)	= as far as that
sem	= hither		
odtiaľto	= hence	domov	= home(ward)
odtiaľ	= thence	hore	= upstairs, above
inde, inokade	= elsewhere	dolu, dole	= downstairs, below
všade, všadiaľ	= everywhere	späť	= backward, back
niekde	= somewhere		
nikde	= nowhere	zvonku, zvonka	= from outside
dnu	= (also: to) inside	tamhľa	= over there
vnútri	= inside	obďaleč	= at a distance

TIME

teraz[1], včuľ	= now	konečne, nakoniec	= at last
vtedy[1]	= then	iba, len	= only
dnes	= today		
zajtra	= tomorrow	práve	= just
včera	= yesterday	až	= not before (only in the future)
už	= already		
ešte	= still	ráno	= in the morning
už nie	= no longer		
ešte nie	= not yet	večer	= in the evening
hneď	= immediately		

[1]With hard *t*.

SLOVAK

TIME

vždy, vždycky	= always	dosiaľ, posiaľ	= up to now
nikdy	= never	včas	= in time
niekedy	= sometimes	zavše, časom	= at times, sometimes
kedysi	= once (upon a time)	občas	= occasionally
raz	= once	zas, zasa, zase	= again
stále	= all the time	budúcne	= in future
neprestajne	= continuously	minule	= last time, recently
neskoro	= late		
časne	= early	toho roku	= this year
často	= often	vlani	= last year
zriedka, málokedy	= seldom	zároveň, súčasne	= at the same time
potom	= afterwards, then	skoro	= soon
dávno	= long ago	zatým, medzitým	= meanwhile
čoraz	= each time		

MANNER

tak	= so, thus	akosi, nejako, dajak, voľajako	= somehow
pomaly	= slowly		
rýchlo	= quickly		
zrazu, naraz	= suddenly	inakšie	= otherwise
úmyselne, schválne, náročky, naschvál	= on purpose	nijako	= in no way
		vlastne	= actually, really
nadarmo, zbytočne	= in vain	skutočne, (na)ozaj	= truly
výnimočne	= exceptionally	zaiste, iste, istotne	= certainly, surely
obyčajne	= usually		
náhodou	= by chance	nenazdajky	= unexpectedly
nevdojak	= unintentionally		
nechtiac	= unwillingly	navidomoči	= obviously
ležiačky	= lying		

DEGREE

veľmi	= very	úhrnom, spolu, celkom, dovedna	= altogether, in all
mnoho, veľa	= much		
toľko, toľme	= so much, as much	rozhodne	= definitely
niekoľko	= some	vraj	= they say, it is said
trochu	= a little		
málo	= little	aspoň	= at least

DEGREE

sotva ledva	} = hardly		snáď azda vari	} = perhaps
dosť	= enough		akiste,	
len iba	} = only		podistým	= probably, I would say
skoro temer[1] takmer	} = nearly		môžbyť možno	} = maybe
čiastočne	= partly		zvlášť najmä	} = especially
bezmála	= almost (with neg.)		asi	= roughly, approximately
zväčša	= mostly			
celkom úplne	} = quite		tobôž	= the more so
vskutku, veru,			napospol	= throughout, wholly
(na)ozaj	= indeed, really		vôbec	= in general
vonkoncom	= completely, (with neg.)		vôbec ne ba i dokonca	= not at all } = even
			hádam	= probably

INTERROGATIVE

kedy?	= when?		koľko?	= how much?
kde?	= where?		veď?	= surely?
kam? kde?	} = whither?		pravdaže? predsa?	= surely? = but surely...?
odkiaľ?	= whence?		skutočne?	= really?
prečo?	= why?		čože?	= what? really?
ako?	= how?		však?	= isn't it so? Fr.: n'est-ce pas?

Not = ne- (written as a prefix with verbs, and stressed; always pron. ňe, with *soft n!*).
No = nie; naopak = on the contrary.
Yes = áno, *or*: hej.
Pravda(že), akože = of course, certainly.

CONJUNCTIONS

The conjunctions, like the adverbs in Slovak, form a category of words which are distinctive and peculiar to the language. Their use is similar to that of the conjunctions in Czech. (Whole words in brackets indicate words to be met with, but not recommended by the highest authorities.)

---

[1]With hard *t*.

SLOVAK

Coordinating:—

a } aj }	= and
i	= and...too
i...i } aj...aj }	= both...and
tiež (enclitic) } taktiež }	= also
ale } no } lež }	= but, yet
(a)však	= however
alebo	= or
či...či	= either...or (in questions)
buď...alebo } alebo...buď } alebo...alebo } buď...buď }	= either...or
čiže	= that is, or
ani...ani	= neither, nor
jednak...jednak	= on the one hand...on the other hand
dielom...dielom } sčiastky...sčiastky }	= partly...partly
nielen...ale aj } nielen...lež i }	= not only...but also
ba	= certainly, indeed, even
jednako	= likewise
predsa } jednako }	= yet, but, nevertheless
veď	= still, but
a to } najmä }	= that is, namely
totiž	= that is to say
takrečeno	= so to speak
ako } sťa (poet.) } ani } čo }	= as, like
pravda(že)	= surely, it is true, really
Leda¹	= so, well now
ostatne	= anyway, after all
síce	= it is true, indeed
preto	= therefore
lebo, bo	= for
no	= well; (followed by an Imperative

---

¹With hard *t*.

Subordinating (those different from the Interrogative adverbs):—

kdežto medzitým čo	= while (contrasting)
keďže, pretože, lebo, bo	= because, since
keď	= when
až kým...ne dokiaľ...ne	= until
kedykoľvek	= whenever
kým zatiaľ čo medzitým čo	= while (of time)
len čo (akonáhle) sotva(že) ledva	= as soon as, scarcely
prv než prv kým skôr než skôr ako	= before
odkedy	= since (of time)
ak	= if
keby	= if (in unfulfilled conditions)
trebárs i keby bár čo (by) aj	= even if, even though
hoc, hoci	= although
aby žeby	= in order that, that (after verbs of wishing, requesting, commanding, fearing)
že	= that (after verbs of saying, thinking, rejoicing; also to express consequence)
akoby sťaby (poet.)	= as if
kiež(by) + Conditional	= if only, would that...!
bez toho, aby (žeby)	= without
či	= whether (introducing indirect questions)

PREPOSITIONS

The regularly used prepositions in literary Slovak are very similar in form, construction and usage to those of Czech. The colloquial language has a number of "improper" prepositions and prepositional

SLOVAK

expressions which are frowned upon by purists and not recommended for the foreign learner, e.g. behom in brackets below. Slovak uses compound prepositions more freely than Czech, e.g. zpomedzi, ponad. Prefixes whose use is optional are given in brackets. The prefix po- has the effect of making the meaning local, rather than abstract.

With Genitive:—

bez[1]	= without	(po)niže	= below
podľa	= according to	(po)vyše	= above, over, more than
(po)vedľa	= beside		
do	= into, up to, to (with inanimates only)	(po)mimo	= outside, past, except
z, zo[1]	= out of, from, off	(behom)	= in the course of
od[1]	= from	následkom	= in consequence of
u	= at, with		
okolo	= round, about	kraj	= near, by
okrem	= except	(u)prostred *or* (v)prostred	= in the middle of
(na)miesto	= instead of		
za, počas	= during, in (the time of)		
blízko	= near	pomocou, prostredníctvom	= by means of
ďaleko	= far from		
konča	= at the end of	(po)zdĺž	= along
spod, spopod	= from under		
spomedzi	= from among		
sponad, znad	= from over		
sponiže	= from below		
spoza	= from behind		
spred, spopred	= from before		

With Dative:—

k, ku[2]	= towards, to (of persons)
proti	= against; despite
naproti, oproti	= opposite
kvôli	= for (the sake of—a person)
voči	= towards, in relation to (Fr. envers)
napriek	= despite; (better: proti, or i pri + Loc.)
vďaka	= thanks to

[1] Prepositions consisting of, or ending in, a consonant take the fill-vowel -*o* (except *k*, which takes -*u*) before difficult consonant groups and before the same consonant starting the next word.

[2] Pronounced gu except before personal pronouns.

With Accusative:

pre	= for, because of, for (to fetch)
cez[1]	= through (of place, time), (despite)
skrz(e) (lit.)	
kroz (poet.)	= through, by means of
na	= on to
v[1]	= in, into (metaphorically); on (of points of time)
o	= against (of place); about, for; after, in (of time)
	prosím o niečo = I ask for something
nad[1]	= (motion to) above, over (also of quantity)
ponad	= (" ") above
pod[1]	= (" ") under (also of quantity)
popod	= (" ") under
(po)pred[1]	= (" ") before
za	= (" ") behind; for, instead of; (during, over, in—of time)
poza	= (" ") behind
(po-)medzi	= (" ") among, between
po	= for (to fetch); up to; for (of duration), up to (of time)
s, so[1,2]	= about (of numbers) (only in fixed expressions)

With Instrumental:—

nad[1]	= (rest) above
(po-)pod[1]	= (") under
pred[1]	= (") before
za	= (") behind, beyond
medzi	= (") between, among
s, so[1,2]	= with, together with
hore	= up
dolu, dole	= down

With Locative:—

pri, popri	= at, near, by (often used of place where Cz. has "u"), past (of place)
na	= on; at
v[1]	= in
po	= after; about, over (of place); according to
o	= about, concerning; at (of time)

[1] See footnote No. 1 on p. 193.
[2] Pronounced z, zo except before personal pronouns.

All monosyllabic prepositions and those with an additional fill-vowel are stressed and the following word loses its stress:—

	vò Viedni	= in Vienna
	bèzo mňa	= without me
	sò sestrou	= with (his) sister
		(pronounced: zo...)
	kù mne	= to me
and—	kù Prahe	= towards Prague
	sò mnou	= with me
	vò mne	= in me
	zò zlata	= of gold

Note that before the Acc./Gen. sing. masc. and neut. pronominal suffix -ň, prepositions ending in -d and -z take as a fill-vowel the vowel -e, which in this case does *not* cause palatalization of d, e.g.:—

nadeň = (to) above him, pron. 'nadɛɲ
cezeň = through him

The verbal prefixes ob-, vy-, pro- (rare), roz-, vz- are not used as prepositions.

The prefix z- is now written s- before unvoiced consonants, e.g. spracovať = to elaborate, skrátiť = to abbreviate.

THE CONJUGATION OF VERBS

The conjugation of verbs in Slovak is similar to that in Czech in most respects. But there are two phonetic rules which create noteworthy differences:

(1) Slovak does not tolerate consecutive long syllables, e.g.:—

pácha = he commits, cf. Cz. páchá
vráti sa = he will return (intrans.),
     Cf. Cz. vrátí se

(2) Slovak e causes palatalization of the preceding consonant, hence:—

tnem (= I cut), is pron. tňem
trhnem (= I shall tear), is pron. trhňem
idem (= I go), is pron. iďem

According to the latest orthography, all regular verbs of Class I (see below) except those with Pres. stem in a consonant followed by -n- (e.g. tnem, above) and all verbs of Class II (see below) with a vowel stem "lengthen" the endings of the Present to -iem, etc. (pron. i̯ɛm); hence we have:—

nesiem = I carry
beriem = I take
miniem = I pass

All the examples quoted so far also illustrate an important morphological feature of Slovak verbs, shared with those of Serbocroätian and Slovenian—the ending *-m* generalized for the 1st pers. sing. Present or Perfective Future of *all* verbs.

In the plural of the Past Tense the Past Participle Active always takes the ending *-li* for nouns of all genders.

The Conditional auxiliary is *by* for all persons + Present tense of byť (= to be): som, si, etc.

All infinitives end in *-t'* in Slovak:—

niesť = to carry
môcť = to be able
volať = to call, etc.

The Gerunds do not distinguish gender, in contrast to Czech.

The Past Participle Passive always has the attributive, adjectival endings *-ý*, *-á*, *-é*, etc.:—

nesen-*ý*, *-á*, *-é* = carried, Cf. Cz. nesen, nesen-a, -o, as well as nesený, etc.

Most of the other regular differences between Czech and Slovak verbs arise from

(a) regular vowel correspondences, e.g.:—

Slk. nesú   = they carry,   Cz. nesou
 "   trpia   = they suffer,   " trpí
 "   držať   = to hold,   " držeti
 "   mrieť   = to die,   " mříti
 "   minúť   = to pass,   " minouti
 "   daj!   = give!,   " dej!

(b) differences of length, e.g.:—

Slk. dať   = to give (Pfve.), Cz. dáti
 "   kryť = to cover,   " krýti

(All monosyllabic Infinitives of verbs with stems ending in a vowel have short vowels in Slovak.)

Slk. začať = to begin (Pfve.), Cz. začíti
 "   chváľ! = praise! (2nd pers. sg. Imperative), Cz. chval!
 "   niesol = he was carrying, Cz. nesl
 "   kupovanie = buying (Verbal Noun),
                              Cz. kupování

SLOVAK

(The penultimate syllable of Verbal Nouns in Slovak is short, except in verbs with contracted root: Slk. prianie = wishing, Cz. přání.)

In the classification of the verbs according to their Presents, the same method is applicable in Slovak as in Czech. Only three types give the appearance of being radically different in Slovak:—
Class III 2 A of Czech has, in Slovak, two types, distinguished according to their derivation:—

> rozumiem < rozumejem < rozumeju = I understand—
>   Slk. Class III, 3rd p. plur. rozumejú.
> vraciam < vratjam = I return—Slk. Class IV, 3rd
>   p. plur. vracajú.
> Cf. Cz. rozumím, 3rd pl. rozumějí; vracím, vracejí.

Iterative verbs can occasionally be formed with the peculiarly Slovak alternative endings: *-úvať*, Pres. *-úvam*, etc., e.g.:—

> vybehúvať = to keep running out (Freq.), as well as: vybehávať, vybiehať; Pres. vybehúvam (Class IV); cf. Cz. vyběhávati only.
> vyhľadúvať = to keep looking out
> prehrabúvať = to dig over and over

Slovak verbs, like those of Czech, have no Dual Number, nor Aorist or Imperfect Tenses. They also have no remnants of the Supine.

The Passive Voice can be rendered in Slovak in three different ways:—

1. With the verb "to be" (byť) and the Past Participle Passive:—

   On je chválený učiteľom, or ... od učiteľa = He is praised by his teacher

   bývať, the Frequentative of byť, is also occasionally used:—

   On býva chválený = He is often praised

2. By using a reflexive verb[1]:—

   Dom sa stavia = The house is being built
   Zemiaky sa vykopávajú = Potatoes are dug up

3. By using an Active verb in the third person plural and "turning the sentence round":—

---

[1] Reflexive verbs in Slovak are formed with the separable enclitic Accusative Reflexive pronoun sa (for all persons) used with the Active verb.

Ešte nás nevolajú = We are not being called yet
                     (lit. they are not calling
                     us yet)
Chytili zlodeja   = The thief was caught (lit.
                     they caught the thief)

Slovak, like Czech, also has reflexive verbs formed with the Dative enclitic Reflexive pronoun si (which is also separable):—

kúpiť si = to buy for oneself
všímať si = to pay attention

Note that the negative *ne-*, as in Czech, is stressed and written as a prefix with all verbs (except in Slovak with the Present of byť!). It is, however, pronounced with *soft n* in Slovak, in contrast to Czech; nejdem, etc. (= I am not going), conforms to this rule.

nevolá   = he is not calling
nebolo   = it was not
nerobil som = I was not doing
nebudem robiť = I shall not do

but—

nie som   = I am not

The Present is the only simple tense in Slovak, as in Czech; and as in all West and East Slav languages, the Present (in form) of Pfve. verbs is really their Future by meaning.

The personal endings of the Present in Slovak are:—

Sing. 1. *-m* (for *all* verbs)
      2. *-š*
      3. *-* (no ending)

Plur. 1. *-me* (always)
      2. *-te*
      3. *-ú/-u* after a consonant ⎫ *-e-* and *-a-*
         -jú after *a* and *e*   ⎬   verbs;
         -ia for all *i*-verbs, except *j*-stems:
            e.g. stroja = they arrange.
            (See below.)

The endings of the 1st, 2nd, and 3rd pers. sing. and of the 1st and 2nd pers. plur. are joined to the verb stem by the joining vowels *-ie-* or *-e-* in the first three classes, by *-á-* in the fourth class, and by *-í-* in the fifth class. These vowels are shortened if a long vowel occurs in the preceding syllable.

Class II is characterized by an -*n*- preceding the -*e*- or -*ie*- joining vowel, and Class III by a -*j*- preceding the -*e*-. Other verbs with -*e*- or -*ie*- as joining vowel belong to Class I.

ALL *Infinitives* in Slovak end in -*ť*. Examples:—

Class I with no joining vowel:	niesť	= to carry
	môcť	= to be able
Class II with joining syllable -*nú/nu*-:	sadnúť	= to sit down
	tiahnuť	= to pull
	minúť	= to pass
Class III vowel stem:	žiť	= to live
consonant stem:	písať	= to write
	kupovať	= to buy
Class IV with joining vowel -*a*-:	volať	= to call
Class V with joining vowel -*i*-:	chváliť	= to praise
with joining vowel -*ie*- (according to the latest orthography):	vidieť	= to see

Verbs with root originally having -*er*-, e.g. O.S. оумрѣти, in Slovak have -*rie*-, e.g.:—

umrieť = to die

Verbs with Infinitive stem ending in -ѧ in O.S. have Infinitive in -*ať*, but -*ät'* after a labial, e.g.:—

začať = to begin
but—zapäť = to button up, switch on

To be able to conjugate a Slovak verb in full, the foreign student must learn both the Present and the Infinitive. The Infinitive gives no sure indication of the endings of the Present. For practical and comparative purposes we classify Slovak verbs in the first place according to their Present, with subdivisions according to their Infinitive.

SLOVAK

Classification of Slovak Verbs according to their Presents, with Subdivisions according to their Infinitives.

3rd pers. sg. Pres.   Infinitive

I. A. a. nesie   niesť = to carry ⎱ Same stem in
       môže   môcť = to be able ⎰ Pres. and In-
       (with short *e*)¹   fin., conso-
                                        nantal stem.

   also:—

   umrie   umrieť = to die (Pfve.) Infin. in
                   -rieť from *-erti.
   začne   začať = to begin (Pfve.) Infin.
                   in -ať from -ати

   b. (no vowel stems)

B. a. berie   brať² = to take. Infin. in -*ať*,
                     consonant stem.
   b. ruve sa ruvať sa = to fight. Infin. in
                        -*ať*, originally a
                        vowel stem.

II.   trhne   trhnúť = to tear (Pfve.) ⎱ *n*-stems.
       minie   minúť = to pass, spend   ⎰
                      (Pfve.)

III. Presents with -*je*-
  1. Primary verbs.
   A. a. žije   žiť² = to live ⎱ Same stem in
         čuje   čuť = to hear ⎰ Pres. and In-
                                 fin., vowel
                                 stem.
      b. melie   mlieť = to grind. Same stem in
         (pron. ˈmɛl̦iɛ) Pres. and Infin., conso-
                         nant stem (or Class I.A.
                         a.)—a rare type.
   B. Infinitives in -*ať*:—
      a. seje   siať = to sow. Infin. in -*ať*,
                      vowel stem.

   (Most verbs originally of this type have gone
   over to Class IV.)

---

¹The 1st Palatalization of velar stems in the Present is extended in Slovak, as in Ukrainian, to the 1st pers. sing. and 3rd pers. plur., hence: môžem = I can, môžu = they can. So also, e.g.: piecť = to bake, pečiem, pečie, pečú, cf. Cz. peku *or* peču, peče, pekou.

²Notice the short vowels in infinitives of the types brať, žiť, kryť (= to cover), and in dať (= to give, Pfve.), byť (= to be), in contrast to Czech.

SLOVAK

3rd pers. sg. Pres.   Infinitive

    b. orie   orať = to plough   ⎫ Infin. in
       píše[1]   písať = to write   ⎬ -ať', con-
       sádže   sádzať = to plant, set.⎭ sonant stem.

2. Derived verbs. All vowel stems.
   A. šedivie   šedivieť = to grow grey ⎫ -ie- Pres.
      (by contraction)   ⎬ stem,
      3rd p. pl. šedivejú   ⎬ Infin.
      rozumie   rozumieť = to understand.⎭ in -ieť'.
      3rd p. pl. rozumejú
   B. kupuje   kupovať = to buy. -u- Pres. stem,
                      Infin. in -ovať'.

IV. New Class, by contraction from -aje- in Pres.
  1. Hard stems:—
     zná   znať = to know (Fr. connaître)
     volá   volať = to call
     víta   vítať = to welcome
  2. Soft stems—a peculiarly Slovak type (from stems in -ja-):—
     stavia   stavať = to build
     3rd p. plur. stavajú
     vracia   vracať[2] = to return
     3rd p. plur. vracajú

V. A. chváli   chváliť = to praise ⎫ i-stem
    prosí   prosiť = to request.⎭ throughout.

  B. vidí   vidieť = to see. -i- Pres. stem,
                Infin. in -ieť'.
    leží   ležať[2] = to lie. -i- Pres. stem,
               Infin. in -ať' from -ieť' after *chuintante*.

Athematic verbs:—

jem (1st pers. sg. Pres.) je   jesť = to eat
viem ("   "   "   ") vie   vedieť = to know (Fr. savoir)

som ("   "   "   "   je   byť = to be

See under Irregular Verbs for full conjugation.

N.B.—The verb dám, dá, dať (Pfve.) = to give, follows Class IV: 3rd pers. pl. Pres./Fut. dajú, Imperat. daj!

---

[1] Even more verbs originally of this type have in Slovak gone over to Class IV, when compared with Czech.
[2] These types end in *-eti* in Czech, because of vowel mutation.

The Future Tense and the Aspects

The Future of Imperfective verbs is ordinarily formed with the Future of the verb "to be" (byť) followed by the Infinitive. E.g.:—

    Sing. 1 budem robiť = I shall do
           2 budeš   "   etc.
           3 bude   "
    Pl.   1 budeme "
           2 budete "
           3 budú   "

Only simple verbs of going, leading, carrying, etc., as in Czech, have Impfve. Futures formed by prefixing *po-* to the Present, this giving the appearance of a Perfective Future. Pfve. Futures for most of these verbs are formed with some other prefix. E.g.:—

ísť[1]   (Impfve.) = to go, 1st p. sg. Pres. idem, 1st p. sg. Fut. pôjdem
niesť[1] (") = to carry, 1st p. sg. Pres. nesiem, 1st p. sg. Fut. ponesiem
viezť[1] (") = to convey, 1st p. sg. Pres. veziem, 1st p. sg. Fut. poveziem
viesť[1] (") = to lead, 1st p. sg. Pres. vediem, 1st p. sg. Fut. povediem
hnať   (" trans.) = to drive, 1st p. sg. Pres. ženiem, 1st p. sg. Fut. poženiem

A few other verbs *may* have Impfve. Futures of this type. E.g.:—

tiecť = to flow, 3rd p. sg. Pres. tečie, Fut. potečie

The *Perfective* Future of verbs in Slovak has the same simple form and the same personal endings as the Present of Impfve. verbs, but is formed from a stem that is altered in some way—either by a prefix or by a change of ending (i.e. joining vowel) or by using a different root.

Examples of these alterations to form the Pfve. aspect from a simple Impfve. verb can be seen in the following formations:—

(1) With a prepositional prefix which adds nothing to the meaning of the verb except the change of aspect:—

---

[1] See "Verbs of going and conveying" below for fuller list of forms.

SLOVAK

Impfve.		Pfve.	Pfve. Fut.
písať	= to write	napísať	napíšem
prosiť	= to request	poprosiť	poprosím
robiť	= to do	urobiť	urobím
hynúť	= to perish	zhynúť	zhyniem
rozumieť	= to understand	porozumieť	porozumiem
platiť	= to pay	zaplatiť	zaplatím

(2) Using the ending *-núť*.[1] (But not all *-núť* verbs are necessarily Pfve.!):—

sadať si	= to sit down	sadnúť si	sadnem si
siahať	= to reach	siahnuť	siahnem

(3) Changing the joining vowel:—

chytať	= to catch	chytiť	chytím

(4) Using a different root:—

brať	= to take	vziať	vezmem
klásť	= to put	položiť	položím
hýbať	= to move	hnúť	hnem

Certain simple verbs, few in number, are *Perfective* in meaning. Most compound verbs with "meaningful" prefixes are also Perfective in meaning. For both these types of verbs a new *Imperfective* has to be formed. This is done either by lengthening the root vowel and changing the ending or by inserting an extra syllable before the Infinitive ending (often a new one). Yotation frequently occurs in the formation of the new forms with *-ať*, *-am*.

	Pfve.		Impfve.	Pres.
(1)	hodiť	= to throw	hádzať	hádžem[2]
	pustiť	= to let go	púšťať	púšťam[2]
	pomôcť	= to help	pomáhať	pomáham[2]

[1]This method is also used with compound verbs: vybiehať = to run out: Pfve. vybehnúť.
[2]In contrast to Czech, nearly all these newly formed verbs in *-ať* have regular Presents in *-am*, *-aš*, etc. Hádzať (= to throw) and sádzať (= to plant), Pres. hádžem, sádžem, are two exceptions. Verbs in *-ovať* regularly have Present in *-ujem*, *-uješ*, etc. Before these endings only dentals undergo yotation in contrast to Czech: e.g. ohradzovať = to fence round, zarmucovať = to make sad, but vyprosovať = to ask for, beg, ohrozovať = to endanger. In many cases Slovak has alternative endings *-ať*, *-am*, where Cz. has only *-ovati*, *-uji*:—

Cf. Slk. poúčam = I instruct, Cz. poučuji
napĺňam = I fill, " naplňuji

Pfve.		*Impfve.*	*Pres.*
vrátiť	= to return	vracať	vraciam[1]
podplatiť	= to bribe	podplácať	
otvoriť	= to open	otvárať	
(2) dať	= to give	dávať	dávam[1]
kúpiť	= to buy	kupovať	kupujem[1]
usmiať sa	= to smile	usmievať sa	
umrieť	= to die	umierať	
začať	= to begin	začínať	
zaspať	= to fall asleep	zaspávať	
poslať	= to send	posielať	
zabiť	= to kill	zabíjať	

Iterative and Frequentative verbs are formed from Imperfective verbs by the insertion of a syllable, sometimes accompanied by a change of the Infinitive ending:—

mať	= to have	mávať
robiť	= to do	robievať
hovoriť / vravieť	= to speak	hovorievať / vravievať
čítať	= to read (Impfve.)	čítavať (Iter.)
písať	= to write	písavať
bežať	= to run	behať, Freq. behávať. Also: bežkať = to run about
vybiehať	= to run out	vybehúvať or vybehávať
niesť	= to carry	nosiť,[2] Freq. nosievať
ísť	= to go	chodiť,[2] Freq. chodievať
hnať	= to drive	honiť = to hunt
byť	= to be	bývať = to live, dwell, as well as: to be regularly / bývavať = to be frequently
piť	= to drink	píjať = to carouse
vidieť	= to see	vídať, also vídavať

As can be inferred from the above examples, there are no regular rules for the formation of aspects in Slovak. The student must learn what is the accepted way to do so for each verb.

Slovak is particularly rich in Frequentative forms, and they occur often.

---

[1] See footnote 2 on preceding page.
[2] See also "Verbs of going and conveying".

The Past Tense

The Past Tense in Slovak is formed with the Past Participle Active in -*l*, which varies in gender and number, and the Present tense of the verb "to be" used as an (enclitic) auxiliary verb, as in Czech, i.e. the auxiliary is omitted in 3rd pers. sing. and plur.

The auxiliary verb therefore conjugates:—

　　Sing. 1 som　　Plur. 1 sme
　　　　　2 si　　　　　　2 ste (with soft *t*!)
　　　　　3 —　　　　　　3 —

The Past Participle Active endings are the same as those of Czech in the sing.: masc. -*l*, fem. -*la*, neut. -*lo*; but in the plur. the ending -*li* is now used for all genders.

This Participle, which is not used except to form the Past and Pluperfect tenses and the Conditional mood (see below), is formed from the Infinitive by cutting off the final -*t'* and adding the ending in the appropriate gender. Verbs with Infin. in -*iet'* shorten the vowel to -*e*-l. E.g.:—

volať　= to call, P.P.A. sg. masc. volal, fem.
　　　　　volala, neut. volalo; pl. volali
začať　= to begin, P.P.A. sg. masc. začal, fem.
　　　　　začala, neut. začalo; pl. začali
hriať　= to warm, P.P.A. sg. masc. hrial, fem.
　　　　　hriala, neut. hrialo; pl. hriali
čuť　　= to hear, P.P.A. sg. masc. čul, fem. čula,
　　　　　neut. čulo; pl. čuli

but—

vidieť = to see, P.P.A. sg. masc. videl, fem.
　　　　　videla, neut. videlo; pl. videli
trieť　= to rub (so also other verbs with root <
　　　　　-*er*-). P.P.A. sg. masc. trel, fem. trela,
　　　　　neut. trelo; pl. treli

Those verbs of Class I, whose stem ends in a consonant directly before the -*t'* in the Infinitive and has a long vowel preceding it, e.g. niesť (= to carry), retain the long vowel in the Past Part. Active and in the masc. sing. put in the fill-vowel -*o* before the final -*l*. Velar and dental stems restore the original consonant, which is transformed in the Infin. E.g.:—

niesť = to carry, P.P.A. sg. masc. niesol, fem.
　　　　　niesla, neut. nieslo; pl. niesli

piecť = to bake, P.P.A. sg. masc. piekol, fem.
  piekla, neut. pieklo, etc.
klásť = to put, P.P.A. sg. masc. kládol, fem. kládla,
  neut. kládlo, etc.
viesť = to lead, P.P.A. sg. masc. viedol, fem.
  viedla, neut. viedlo, etc.

The verb môcť (= to be able), P.P.A. sg. masc. mohol, fem. mohla, etc. with short o, is an exception.
Verbs of Class II with a consonantal stem before the -*núť* of the Infin., normally drop the -*nu*- in the P.P.A. (cf. Czech). The fill-vowel -*o*- is used when the -*nu*- is dropped. E.g.:—

trhnúť   = to tear, P.P.A. trhol
pohnúť   = to move, P.P.A. pohol[1]
padnúť   = fall (Pfve.), P.P.A. padol
vzbĺknuť = to blaze up (Pfve.), P.P.A. vzbĺkol

We thus have as a complete Past tense, e.g.:—

Masc. sg.	*Fem. sg.*	*Neut. sg.*	*All genders*
niesol som	niesla som		niesli sme
niesol si	niesla si		niesli ste
niesol	niesla	nieslo	niesli

The Nom. Personal Pronouns are only used when emphasized or contrasted, e.g. *Ja* som niesol. The auxiliary then precedes the Past Part. Act., as in other cases when the subject or other emphasized word comes first.
The Reflexive Pronoun sa comes after the auxiliary verb: hrial si sa (= you were warming yourself) or ty si sa hrial.
The negative *ne*- is prefixed to the Past Part. Act., as in Czech:—

nehrial si sa   = you were not warming yourself
nenapísal som list = I have not written the letter,
                    or: I did not write the letter

For the rule of agreement in polite address see under (Personal) Pronouns, p. 180.

The Pluperfect Tense

The Pluperfect tense is more frequently used in Slovak than in Czech. It is formed by adding the

---

[1] But hnúť = to move (Impfve.), P.P.A. hnul;
  usnúť = to fall asleep (Pfve.), P.P.A. usnul.
Note that in the P.P.A. the -*u*- in the ending is *short*!

Past Participle of byť (= to be), in the appropriate gender, to the ordinary Past Tense. E.g.:—

bol som niesol	= I (masc.) had carried, or been carrying
bola si niesla	= you (fem. sg.) had carried
bol niesol	= he had carried
boli sme niesli	= we had carried
boli ste niesli	= you (pl.) had carried
boli niesli	= they had carried

The Conditional

The Conditional mood is formed in Slovak (in contrast to Czech) with the *invariable* auxiliary *by* added to the Past tense of all verbs. "by" precedes the auxiliary verb. E.g.:—

volal by som	= I (masc.) would call (Impfve.)
volala by si	= you (fem. sg.) would call (Impfve.)
volal by	= he would call
zavolali by sme	= we would call (Pfve.), ring up
zavolali by ste	= you (pl.) would call (Pfve.), ring up
nezavolali by	= they would not call (Pfve.), ring up

When an emphasized word, e.g. the subject, precedes, the order is reversed. E.g.:—

Ja by som volal = *I* would call

The Past Conditional

This form is created by simply adding the Past Participle of byť, bol, bola, etc., in the appropriate gender to the ordinary Conditional. Bol, etc., usually comes first, then "by" followed by the auxiliary and then the Past Part. Act. of the verb used. E.g.:—

Bol by som volal = I would have called.

The negative is prefixed to bol, bola, etc.

Nebola by si volala = you (fem. sg.) would not have called

The verb "to be" may borrow the Past Participle of bývať (Freq.) to form its Past Conditional. E.g.:—

Bol by som bol *or* } = I would have been
Bol by som býval

The Imperative

Special Imperative forms exist in Slovak for the 2nd pers. sing. and 1st and 2nd pers. plur., as in Czech, Polish, Serbocroatian, and Ukrainian.

The endings of the Imperative vary according to the ending of the Present stem:—

(1) If it ends in a single consonant, the endings are:—

    2nd pers. sg. — ('—dentals and *l* are softened)
    1st pers. pl. -*me*
    2nd pers. pl. -*te*

E.g.:—

	Pres.		
	nesiem	vediem	miniem
2nd pers. sg.	nes! = carry!	veď! = lead!	miň! = pass!
1st pers. pl.	nesme	veďme	miňme
2nd pers. pl.	neste	veďte	miňte

So also:—

	beriem		mažem
2nd pers. sg.	ber! = take!		maž! = smear
	prosím		trpím
2nd pers. sg.	pros! = ask!		trp! = suffer!

Notice that the 2nd Palatalization of velars does not take place in Slovak. Hence we have:—

Pres. pečiem = I bake,   Imperat. peč! = bake!
Pres. pomôžem = I shall help,   " pomôž! = help!

Long root vowels are retained in Slovak, in contrast to Czech. E.g.:—

    chválim = I praise, Imperat. chváľ!
    píšem = I write,   "   píš!

(2) If the Pres. stem ends in a group of consonants, the endings for most verbs are[1]:—

        2nd pers. sg.   -*i*
        1st pers. pl.   -*ime*
        2nd pers. pl.   -*ite*

---

[1] A few verbs with such stems more commonly have an Imperative without the -*i*: pustiť = to let go, Imper. pusť!; fajčiť = to smoke, nefajč! = don't smoke!

E.g.:—začnem = I shall begin, Imperat. začni!
  začnime! začnite!
  pošlem = I shall send,   "   pošli!
  pošlime! pošlite!
  myslím = I think,   "   mysli!, etc.
  tnem   = I cut,   "   tni!
  spím   = I sleep,   "   spi!

(3) If the Present stem ends in a vowel, as in Classes IV 1 and 2, III 1.A.a., III 1.B.a., and III 2 A and B, the endings are:—

        2nd pers. sg.   -j
        1st pers. pl.   -jme
        2nd pers. pl.   -jte

E.g.:—

volám   = I call (< vola-jem), Imperat. volaj! volajme! volajte! (with no change of vowel in contrast to Czech)
vraciam = I return, 3rd p. plur. uncontracted: vracajú, Imperat. vracaj! vracajme! vracajte!
čujem   = I hear, Imperat. čuj!, etc.
rozumiem = I understand, 3rd p. plur. uncontracted: rozumejú, Imperat. rozumej!, etc.
kupujem = I buy, Imperat. kupuj!, etc.

Verbs of Class III 1.A.a. with stem in -*i*- or -*y*- have no -*j*- in the Imperative:—

kryjem = I cover, Imperat. kry! kryme! kryte!
pijem = I drink,   "   pi! pime! pite!

The 3rd pers. sing. and plur. are rendered by nech + 3rd pers. sing. or plur. of the Pres. of Imperfective, or of the Future of Perfective, verbs. E.g.:—

nech píše!   = let him write! (Impfve.)
nech napíšu! = let them write! (Pfve.)
nech sa páči! = may it please (you)!—polite phrase

The Gerunds

In contrast to Czech, the Slovak Gerund does not vary in gender and has only one (indeclinable) form. It is hardly ever used in conversation.
The Present Gerund is formed from the 3rd pers. plur. Pres. (of Impfve. verbs mainly) by simply adding -*c*. It expresses an action (by the subject of the sentence only) contemporary with that of the main

verb. A long vowel in the ending of the 3rd pers. plur. is always preserved. E.g.:—

Píšuc fajčil (3rd p. pl. Pres. píšu) = While writing, he smoked

but:—

Volajúc ... sa rozhneval = Calling (to someone) he got angry
Išiel hovoriac celú cestu = He went talking the whole way

According to the latest rules of orthography, (long) -*ia* is *retained* in the Gerund after a long root vowel in the preceding syllable, as it is also in the Present tense. E.g.:—

súdim = I judge, 3rd pers. plur. Pres. súdia, Pres. Ger. súdiac; -*ac* occurs only after -*j*: e.g. stojac = standing

Perfective verbs occasionally have a Gerund that is Present in form but has the meaning of a Past Gerund. E.g.:—

Chlapec padnúc plakal (bude plakať) = The boy, having fallen, was crying (will cry)

[*The* (now **obsolete**) *Past Gerund* expressed an action (by the subject of the sentence) previous to that of the main verb (in any tense). It was formed from verbs of either aspect by adding -*vši* if the Infinitive stem ended in a vowel and -*ši* if it ended in a consonant.

Verbs with lengthened *root* vowel in the Infin. shortened it to form the Past Gerund. E.g.:—

vola-ť = to call, Past Ger.: volavši = having called
padnúť[1] = to fall (Pfve.), Past Ger.: padnuvši
niesť = to carry, Past. Ger.: nesši

In practice Past Gerunds were formed more frequently from Pfve. verbs. This obsolete form is now of importance only for the formation of the Past *Participle* **Active**.]

The Participles

Verbal Adjectives, declined like cudzí, can be formed from both Gerunds by adding -*i*, -*a*, -*e* to the

---

[1]Verbs with Infin. in -*núť*, retain -*nu*- here!

Pres. Gerund and changing the ending -*i* of the Past
Gerund to -*í*, -*ia*, -*ie*. These are true Slavonic participles (verbal adjectives).

The *Present Participle Active* (formed only from
Imperfective verbs) has shortened endings after the
long vowel of the final syllable of the stem. Hence
we have:—

   sing.: nesúc*i* (masc.), nesúc*a* (fem.), nesúc*e* (neut.)
          = who is carrying
          píšúci[1] (masc.), píšúca (fem.), píšúce
          (neut.) = who is writing
          kričiaci (masc.), kričiaca (fem.), kričiace
          (neut) = who is shouting

The (literary) *Past Participle Active*, formed
only from Perfective verbs whose Infinitive stem ends
in a vowel, has long final vowels, like cudzí:—

   sing.: napísavš*í* (masc.), napísavš*ia* (fem.),
          napísavš*ie* (neut.) = who has written

For the *Past Participle Active in* -*l*, used only
with the Past and Pluperfect tenses and the Conditional mood, see "The Past Tense".

The *Past Participle Passive* has only attributive
adjectival endings in Slovak, in contrast to Czech,
even when it is used predicatively. It is formed
from transitive verbs with the endings:—

sing. -*ný* (masc.), -*ná* (fem.), -*né* (neut.);
plur. -*ní* (masc. pers.), -*né* (masc. impers., fem.,
      neut.).

or—

sing. -*tý* (masc.), -*tá* (fem.), -*té* (neut.);
plur. -*tí* (masc. pers.), -*té* (masc. impers., fem.,
      neut.).

The endings with -*t*- are only used with:—

(1) verbs of Class III 1.A.a., e.g.:—

   bijem = I beat, Past Part. Pass. bitý = beaten

(2) verbs of Class II, which *retain* -*nu*-, e.g.:—

   ukradnúť = to steal (Pfve.), Past Part. Pass.
   ukradnutý = stolen
   zapriahnuť = to harness (Pfve.) Past Part. Pass.
   zapriahnutý

---

[1] The -*ú*- of the final syllable of the stem is never shortened.

dosiahnuť = to reach (Pfve.), Past Part. Pass. dosiahnutý

(3) a few verbs of Class I A.a. with root originally with nasal ѧ or with *-er-*, e.g.:—

začať = to begin, Past Part. Pass. začatý;
zavrieť = to shut, Past Part. Pass. zavretý

(4) a few verbs with contracted roots, e.g.:—

zohriať (< zohrejať) = to warm (Pfve.), Past Part. Pass zohriaty

All other verbs have the endings with *-n-*. Those with Infin. in *-at'* have *-aný*, *-aná*, etc.[1] The rest have *-ený*, *-ená*, etc., before which *only* velar stems undergo palatalization, (in contrast to Old Slavonic, Cz., Pol., Lusatian, East Slav, Serbocr., and Slovenian). E.g.:—

volaný	= called	platený	= paid
mazaný	= smeared	narodený	= born
nesený	= carried	držaný	= held
prosený	= requested	videný	= seen

but, with 1st Palatalization—

pečený = baked (Infin. piecť)

The Verbal Noun is formed absolutely regularly in Slovak by changing the ending of the Past Participle Passive to *-ie*, e.g.:—

bitý = beaten, Verbal Noun: bitie = beating
dosiahnutý = attained, Verbal Noun: dosiahnutie = achievement
zohriaty = warmed, Verbal Noun: zohriatie = warming up
volaný = called, Verbal Noun: volanie = calling
prosený = requested, Verbal Noun: prosenie = asking
pečený = baked, Verbal Noun: pečenie = baking
vyberaný = chosen, Verbal Noun: vyberanie = choosing

Verbal Nouns can also be formed from intransitive verbs (which have no Past Participle Passive), e.g.:—

---

[1] Verbs of Class I B.a., e.g. brať = to take, can also have the Past Participle Passive in *-tý*: braný *or* bratý. Notice:
 vydaná (kniha) = published (book),
 vydatá (žena) = married (woman).

SLOVAK

```
stáť    = to stand, Verbal Noun:  státie
spať    = to sleep,     "    "   spanie
sedieť  = to sit,       "    "   sedenie
bolieť  = to ache,      "    "   bolenie
```

Verbal Nouns formed from reflexive verbs retain their Reflexive Pronoun sa, where ambiguity would otherwise arise, e.g.:—

učenie sa = learning, > < učenie = teaching
trápenie sa = torment (suffered), troubling oneself
>< trápenie = torment (inflicted), tormenting (others)

Examples of the Three Main Conjugations of Verbs

1. -e- type (Classes I, II, III 1. and III 2.B. Also Class III 2.A—contracted).

    Class I   Class II

niesť = to carry (Impfve.)   trhnúť = to tear (Pfve.)

PRESENT

```
Sing. 1   nesiem
      2   nesieš
      3   nesie
Plur. 1   nesieme
      2   nesiete
      3   nesú
```

IMPERATIVE

```
Sing. 2   nes                  trhni
Plur. 1   nesme¹               trhnime
      2   neste                trhnite
```

FUTURE

```
Sing. 1   ponesiem             trhnem
          (or budem niesť, etc.)
      2   ponesieš             trhneš
      3   ponesie              trhne
Plur. 1   ponesieme            trhneme
      2   ponesiete            trhnete
      3   ponesú               trhnú
```

GERUND

Pres.   nesúc   trhnúc

PARTICIPLES

```
Pres. Act.   nesúci                —
Past Act.    —                     trhnuvší
Past Act. in -l   niesol, niesla, nieslo   trhol, trhla (minul,
                                            minula = passed)
```

¹Pronounced: ˈɲɛzmɛ.

Past Pass.	nesený, nesená, nesené	trhnutý
VERBAL NOUNS	nesenie	trhnutie

Class III 2.B.
kupovať[1] = to buy
(Impfve.)

Class III 2.A.
rozumieť = to understand
(Impfve.)[2]

PRESENT

Sing.	1	kupujem	rozumiem
	2	kupuješ	rozumieš
	3	kupuje	rozumie
Plur.	1	kupujeme	rozumieme
	2	kupujete	rozumiete
	3	kupujú	rozumejú

IMPERATIVE

Sing.	2	kupuj	rozumej
Plur.	1	kupujme	rozumejme
	2	kupujte	rozumejte

GERUND

Pres.	kupujúc	rozumejúc

PARTICIPLES

Pres. Act.	kupujúci	rozumejúci
Past Act.	kupoval, kupovala, kupovalo	rozumel, rozumela, rozumelo
Past Pass.	kupovaný, kupovaná, kupované	rozumený, rozumená, rozumené
VERBAL NOUNS	kupovanie	rozumenie

[1] Like kupovať are conjugated the consonantal stem verbs with yotation in the Pres. of the type III 1.B.b. - písať = to write, Pres. píšem, píšeš, etc., píšu, Imperat. píš!, Pres. Ger. píšuc. Verbs mostly with stems in -s, -z, -t, -d, -k, -b, -p, -m, -v, -r, can have Pres., Imperat., Pres. Ger. and Pres. Participle exclusively of this type. Some verbs with stems in dentals and labials have alternative Pres. and Imperat., etc., of Class IV -a- type verbs, e.g. rúbať = to chop, Pres. 1st pers. sg. rúbem *or* rúbam, cf. Cz. kopati = to dig, Pres. kopu or kopám. Some have gone over entirely to Class IV, e.g. kárať = to reproach, Pres. káram, cf. Cz. kářu or kárám.

[2] In contrast to Czech, many Iterative and Imperfective verbs, often with prefixes and derived from other verbs, e.g. prichádzať (= to come - Impfve.) follow volať, Class IV 1, or vracať, Class IV 2; while verbs derived from nouns and adjectives and meaning "becoming something", follow rozumieť, e.g. šedivieť = to get grey, Class III 2.A.

SLOVAK

2. -*a*- type (Class IV).

    1. volať = to call (Impfve.)   2. vracať[1] = to return (trans., Impfve.)

PRESENT

		1. volať	2. vracať
Sing.	1	volám[2]	vraciam
	2	voláš[2]	vraciaš
	3	volá[2]	vracia
Plur.	1	voláme[2]	vraciame
	2	voláte[2]	vraciate
	3	volajú	vracajú

IMPERATIVE

Sing.	2	volaj	vracaj
Plur.	1	volajme	vracajme
	2	volajte	vracajte

GERUND

Pres.   volajúc   vracajúc

PARTICIPLES

Pres. Act. volajúci   vracajúci
Past Act. volal, volala, volalo   vracal, vracala, vracalo
Past Pass. volaný, volaná, volané   vracaný, vracaná, vracané

VERBAL NOUNS   volanie   vracanie

3. -*i*- type (Class V)

    chváliť = to praise (Impfve.), vidieť = to see (Impfve.), držať = to hold (Impfve.)

PRESENT

Sing.	1	chválim
	2	chváliš
	3	chváli
Plur.	1	chválime
	2	chválite
	3	chvália[3]

IMPERATIVE

Sing.	2	chváľ
Plur.	1	chváľme
	2	chváľte

GERUND

Pres.   chváliac

PARTICIPLES

Pres. Act.   chváliaci
Past Act.   chválil, chválila, chválilo
            videl, videla, videlo
            držal, držala, držalo
Past Pass.   chválený, chválená, chválené
            videný, videná, videné
            držaný, držaná, držané

VERBAL NOUNS   chválenie, videnie

---

[1] See footnote 2 on preceding page.
[2] These endings can be shortened after a long vowel in the preceding syllable (see p. 137, 195), e.g. dávam = I give (Impfve.).
[3] See p. 137, No. 4, for the retention of long -*ia* after a long vowel in the preceding syllable.

Irregular Verbs

The Athematic verbs:—

byť = to be[1]   jesť = to eat   vedieť = to know
                 (Pfve. zjesť)

PRESENT

Sing.	1 som	jem	viem
	2 si	ješ	vieš
	3 je[2], jest[3]	je	vie
Plur.	1 sme[4]	jeme	vieme
	2 ste	jete	viete
	3 sú	jedia	vedia

IMPERATIVE

Sing.	2 buď	jedz	vedz[5]
Plur.	1 buďme	jedzme	vedzme
	2 buďte	jedzte	vedzte

FUTURE

Sing.	1 budem	zjem (Pfve.)	budem vedieť
		budem jesť (Impfve.)	
	2 budeš	zješ	etc.
	3 bude	zje	
Plur.	1 budeme	zjeme	
	2 budete	zjete	
	3 budú	zjedia	

GERUND

Pres.	súc	jediac	vediac

PARTICIPLES

Pres. Act.	súci	jediaci	vediaci
Past Act.	bol, bola, bolo	jedol, jedla, jedlo	vedel, vedela, vedelo

[1] Compounds of byť in Slovak either follow the model of:—
zabudnúť (Pfve.), Fut. zabudnem; zabúdať (Impfve.) = to forget
or they follow the model of:—
dobyť (Pfve.), Fut. dobyjem; dobývať (Impfve.) = to win.
[2] Negative 3rd pers. sg. Pres. niet + Gen. = there is no..., as in Russian: нет... E.g. niet vody = there is no water. Otherwise the negative is written separate from the Present: nie som = I am not, etc.
[3] The form 'jest' means 'exists'.
[4] Pronounced: zmɛ.
[5] Compounds of vedieť, e.g. vyzvedieť, have Imperatives in -veď (cf. viď from vidieť = to see); e.g. vyzveď! = find out! But the Imperatives from *Perfective* compounds of -vedať, e.g. odpovedať (Pfve.) = to answer, have -vedz, e.g. odpovedz! Pfve. Future: odpoviem, -vieš, etc.

PARTICIPLES

Past Pass.   -bytý, -bytá,   jedený, jedená,
             -byté   jedené

VERBAL NOUNS

       bytie   jedenie   vedenie

Dať = to give (Pfve.), wholly follows the model of volať, Class IV 1.

    Other important irregular verbs in Slovak are:—

chcieť = to want

PRESENT		GERUND	
Sing. 1	chcem	Pres.	chcejúc
2	chceš		
3	chce	PARTICIPLES	
Plur. 1	chceme	Pres. Act.	chcejúci
2	chcete	Past Act.	chcel
3	chcú	Past Pass.	chcený
IMPERATIVE		VERBAL NOUN	
Sing. 2	chci		chcenie
Plur. 1	chcime		
2	chcite		

(mať = to have, is regular, following volať, Class IV 1, in all its parts.)

    For ísť (= to go), see "Verbs of Going and Conveying".

Infinitive.	Meaning.	Pres. 1st p. sg.	Imperat. 2nd p. sg.	Past Part. Act. masc. sing.	Past Part. Pass. masc. sing.
Class I.					
brať (Impfve.)	= to take	beriem	ber	bral	braný or bratý
vziať (Pfve.)	= to take	vezmem	vezmi	vzal	vzatý
najať (Pfve.)	= to hire	najmem	najmi	najal	najatý
sňať (Pfve.)	= to take off	snímem	sním	sňal	sňatý
hnať	= to drive	ženiem	žeň	hnal	hnaný
klať	= to prick	kolem	koľ	klal	klaný
(luhať	= to tell lies, is regular in Slovak and belongs to Class III 1.B.b., like písať: 3rd p. sg. Pres. luže. But notice the insertion of the -u- in the **stem**!)				

SLOVAK

Infinitive.	Meaning.	Pres. 1st p. sg.	Imperat. 2nd p. sg.	Past Part. Act. masc. sing.	Past Part. Pass. masc. sing.
ťať	= to cut, beat	tnem	tni	ťal	(od)ťatý
mäť	= to rub	mnem	mni	mäl	mätý
miasť	= to muddle	mätiem	mäť	miatol	mätený
môcť	= to be able	môžem	(po)môž	mohol	(-možený)
-päť or pnúť	= to stretch	pnem	pni	päl[1], pnul	-pätý or -pnutý
priasť	= to spin	pradiem	praď	priadol	pradený
riecť (Pfve.) or rieknuť	= to say	rečiem rieknem	rec!	riekol	rečený or rieknutý
rásť	= to grow	rastiem	rasti	rástol	—
stlať	= to make a bed	steliem	steľ	stlal	stlaný
striezť	= to guard	strežiem	strež	striehol	strežený
tĺcť	= to beat, pound	tlčiem	tlč	tĺkol	tlčený
triasť	= to shake	trasiem	tras	triasol	trasený
trieť	= to rub	triem	tri	trel	trený or treťý
pozrieť (sa)	= to look	pozriem	pozri	pozrel	(prezretý)
zvať	= to invite	zvem	zvi	zval	zvaný

Class II.

stať sa (Pfve.)	= to happen	stane sa (3rd p. sg.)	staň	stalo sa	—

(Impfve. stávať sa, Class IV 1, is regular.) So also the compounds: dostať = to get, zostať = to remain.

zabudnúť (Pfve.)	= to forget	zabudnem	zabudni	zabudol	zabudnutý
kvitnúť	= to flower	kvitnem	kvitni	kvitol	(roz)kvitnutý

Class III.

hriať	= to warm	hrejem	hrej	hrial	hriaty
priať	= to wish	prajem	praj	prial	(do)priaty
smiať sa	= to laugh	smejem sa	smej sa	smial sa	(vy-)smiaty[2]
kliať	= to curse	kľajem	kľaj	klial	kliaty

[1] In compounds either: e.g. napäl, napäla or! napol, napla, etc.
[2] vysmiaty = (1) mocked, laughed at, (2) smiling.

SLOVAK

Infinitive.	Meaning.	Pres. 1st p. sg.	Imperat. 2nd p. sg.	Past Part. Act. masc. sing.	Past Part. Pass. masc. sing.
liať	= to pour	lejem	lej	lial	liaty
okriať	= to revive	okrejem	okrej	okrial	okriaty
siať	= to sow	sejem	sej	sial	siaty
viať	= to blow	vejem	vej	vial	-viaty
poslať (Pfve.)	= to send	pošlem	pošli	poslal	poslaný
vládať	= to be capable	vládzem	vládz	vládal	ovládaný
hádzať (Impfve.)	= to throw	hádžem	hádž	hádzal	hádzaný
mlieť	= to grind	meliem	meľ	mlel	mletý
plieť	= to weed	plejem	plej	plel	vypletý
zrieť	= to ripen	zrejem	zrej	zrel	(do)zretý
smieť	= to dare, to be allowed	smiem, smú (3rd p. pl.)		smel	—
sať	= to suck	sajem	saj	sal	saný

Class V.

bať sa (Impfve.)	= to fear	bojím sa, boja sa (3rd p. pl.)	boj sa	bál sa	—
stáť	= to stand	stojím, stoja (3rd p. pl.)	stoj	stál	(odstatý)
spať	= to sleep	spím, spia (3rd p. pl.)	spi	spal	-spaný (or vyspatý)
erdžať	= to neigh	erdžím	erdži	erdžal	—

Verbs of Going and Conveying

Slovak, in contrast to Czech, Polish, Lusatian and the East Slav languages, has no separate verb to express "to go (in a vehicle)" as opposed to "to go (on foot)", using isť for both meanings. Jazdiť only means "to ride", cf. Serbocr. jáхати. On the other hand, in the compound verbs formed with the (Imperfective) root chod-, it has separate forms for the Imperfective and the Frequentative aspects (although they are loosely used)—in contrast to Czech, Polish, and East Slav.

To go (on foot *or* conveyed):—

        Impfve. *and* Pfve. ísť[1]   Freq. chodiť

---

[1] The Infin. pôjsť is not recommended in the latest "Orthography" (*Pravidlá slovenského pravopisu*), in the sense of 'to go'. It means: to originate from, start off, or to die (of animals).

Pres.:	idem, 3rd pl. idú[1]		chodím
Fut. *Impfve.* and *Pfve.*:	pôjdem		budem chodiť
Past Part. Act.:	Impfve. (i)šiel, (i)šla (Pfve. pošiel)		chodil
Imperat.:	(Impfve. iď!—rare) poď, poďme, poďte		choď! (used also as Impfve. with negative)
Pres. Ger.:	idúc		
Verbal Noun:	idenie		

To come (on foot *or* conveyed):—

	Impfve. prichodiť	Pfve. prísť Fut.:		Freq. prichádzať
Pres.:	prichodím	prídem	Pres.:	prichádzam
Past Part. Act.:	prichodil	prišiel		prichádzal
Imper.:	(ne-)prichoď!	príď, -me, -te		prichádzaj!

Similarly:—

to go away = Impfve. odchodiť, Pfve.
  (on foot or conveyed)   odísť[2] (Fut. odídem[2], Past
    Part. Act. odišiel[2]),
    Freq. odchádzať.

to go out = Impfve. vychodiť, Pfve.
  (on foot or conveyed)   vyjsť (Fut. vyjdem,
    Imperat. vyjdi!, Past
    Part. Act. vyšiel, vyšla),
    Freq. vychádzať.

To carry:—

	Impfve. niesť	Pfve. zaniesť Fut.:		Freq. nosiť
Pres.:	nesiem	zanesiem	Pres.:	nosím
Fut.:	ponesiem *or* budem niesť			budem nosiť
Past Part. Act.:	niesol, niesla	zaniesol		nosil
Imperat.:	nes!	zanes!		nos!

To bring:—

    Impfve. and Freq. prinášať   Pfve. priniesť
        Pres.: prinášam   Fut. prinesiem

---

[1] Negative forms: nejdem, etc., nejdú.
[2] Imperat. odíď! All pronounced with first *d* hard!

To lead:—

	Impfve. viesť	Pfve. zaviesť Fut.:		Freq. vodiť
Pres.:	vediem	zavediem	Pres.:	vodím
Fut.:	povediem			budem vodiť
Past Part. Act.:	viedol, viedla	zaviedol		vodil
Imperat.:	veď!	zaveď!		voď!

To bring (a person):—

Impfve. and Freq. privádzať   Pfve. priviesť
Pres.: privádzam   Fut.: privediem

To convey:—

	Impfve. viezť	Pfve. zviezť Fut.:		Freq. voziť
Pres.:	veziem	zveziem	Pres.:	vozím
Fut.:	poveziem			budem voziť
Past Part. Act.:	viezol, viezla	zviezol		vozil
Imperat.:	vez!	zvez!		voz!

To bring (in a vehicle):—

Impfve. and Freq. privážať   Pfve. priviezť
Pres. privážam   Fut.: priveziem

WORD ORDER WITH ENCLITICS

The rules for the order of enclitics in Slovak are almost entirely the same as those in Czech. (See chapter with the same heading in Section on Czech.)

The exclusively enclitic words in Slovak are:—

1. The auxiliary verbs of the Past tense: som, si, sme, ste
2. The Conditional auxiliary: by
3. The short forms of the Acc. (and Gen.) and Dat. of—
   (a) the Reflexive Pronoun: sa, si
   (b) the Personal Pronouns: ma, mi; ťa, ti; ho, mu

Other monosyllabic and dissyllabic Personal Pronouns in the oblique cases[1] may also be treated as enclitics (and often are), and also the words:—

>   to   = this
>   vraj = they say
>   už   = already
>   tiež = also, and the emphatic particle
>   -že.

-*li* does not occur in Slovak. (Ak = if, is an ordinary conjunction.)
The Conditional auxiliary "by" precedes all other enclitics, e.g.:—

Urobil by som mu to   = I would do this to (or for) him
Zdalo by sa Vám to tak = This would seem so to you

[1]Namely:—
3rd pers. sg.

	Fem.	*Masc. and Neut.*	*Plur.*	*1st pers. sg.*	*1st pers. pl.*	*2nd pers. sg.*	*2nd pers. pl.*
Gen.	jej		ich		nás		vás
Dat.	jej		im		nám		vám
Acc.	ju		ich		nás		vás
Instr.	ňou	ním*	nimi	mnou	nami	tebou	vami

*Example:—
    Pohŕda ním úplne = He despises him utterly.

TEXTS

I. Sv. Lukáš. VIII.

   5. Vyšiel rozsievač rozosiať svoje semeno. A jako tak sial, niektoré padlo vedľa cesty a zašliapalo sa, a pozobali ho nebeskí vtáci. 6. A iné padlo na skalu a vzíduc uschlo, pretože nemalo vlahy. 7. A zase iné padlo medzi tŕnie, a tŕnie vzrastúc s ním udusilo ho. 8. A opäť iné padlo do zemi dobrej, a keď vzišlo, donieslo úžitok stonásobný. A to povediac zavolal: Kto má uši, aby počul, nech počuje!

II. Ľudovít Štúr.

   Nedávno, keď som bol tuná poľutovania hodný stav tej "miserae contribuentis plebis" podotkol, zaslúžilý vyslanec Peštianskej stolice (Kossuth) videl v potlačení tom "ľudu osud", spomenúc mne na odvetu, "je to beh sveta, keď sa ten, čo v obci nižšie stojí, potlačí a ťarchu dane niesť musí, naproti tomu ten, čo sa v občianskom živote povznesie, práva dostane a v zácti stojí". Ale ja v tomto vonkoncom žiaden osud nevidím a chráň Boh, aby v tom aj dáky osud ležal! Takýmto činom by sa stav potlačených v ľudskej spoločnosti ani nikdy polepšiť nedal. Vec sa má celkom inakšie. Osud je nevyhnutná potreba prirodzená, ale tejto v štátoch a v historii nieto, ani byť nemôže, bo tu na čele dejov stojí vôľa ľudská a sama historia nie je nič, než rozvíjanie a uskutočnenie tejto vôle. Ale nechže sa vyslovím o stave chudobného ľudu nášho a o potrebe poľahčenia a polepšenia jeho losu. To požadujú čím najsúrnejšie záujmy a budúcnosť našej vlasti, to požaduje prisluhovanie spravedlnosti a svätá vec človečenstva. Všetko toto hlasite k nám volá, aby sa už raz a naposledok los chudobného ľudu polepšil. Žiadame v krajine slobodu a trpíme roboty urbárske, čo sa s ňou vonkoncom nezrovnávajú! Nuž ale obzrimeže následky tohoto smutného stavu! Či taký človek, ktorý k osohu iných robotujúc miesto odmeny každým sa opovrhuje, všade odstrkuje, či taký človek má vlasť? Či nestane sa pri prvej príležitosti podlým nástrojom proti nej a proti slobode vôbec? Či pritúli sa taký k vlasti ako k sladkej make? Čo nemá, čo nezná, k tomu nemôže sa ani s láskou túliť. Takýto človek len rodisko má, ale vlasti, tej drahej vlasti, nemá.

III. Hviezdoslav.

Slovenská reč

Ó, mojej matky reč je krásota,
je milota, je rozkoš, láska svätá!
je, vidím, cítim, celok života!
môj pokrm dobrý, moja čaša zlatá
a moja odev, ktorej neviem ceny ...
Buď požehnaný, kto sa pohodil
v tom so mnou, trvá pri tom nepremenný!
buď kliaty! kto sa zaprel, odrodil ...

IV. Ivan Krasko.

Otrok

Som ten, ktorému v uši znela pieseň matky otrokyne.
Tá pieseň z mojej duše nikdy, nikdy nevyhynie.
Tak smutno znela, divným bojazlivým bôľom
sa tíško niesla naším úhorovým poľom,
až chytila sa v detskej trasúcej sa duši.

Som ten, čo dozrieval pod bičom otrokára,
pod bičom, ktorý nestrábené rany denne znovu pootvára,
že žiadna z nich sa nikdy, nikdy nezahojí.

Môj chrbát skrivený už narovnať sa bojí,
však vo sklopenom zraku posiaľ skrytá iskra horí...

Som ten, čo čaká na ston poplašného zvona,
bo ťažko zhynúť otrokovi, pokiaľ pomstu nevykoná.
Až potom vystrem chrbát, rumeň zbarví líce.
Dovtedy sadiť budem stromy, z ktorých rastú
                                            šibenice...
O, smutno znela pieseň matky-otrokyne!

V. Janko Jesenský.

    Na janičára treba janičár,
    Zažmúrte oči, čo sa v slzách máču,
    zakryte dlaňou umáganú tvár,
    zaduste v hrdle chabé slová plaču!

    Nie barana, na vlka treba vlk.
    Nie prosiaca dlaň, tvrdá päsť nám svedčí,
    nie smútok v tvári, ale pomsty blk,
    nie poklony, lež oceľové reči.

    Na výške svet ten vidno dokorán,
    v údolí úzko, samé vrchy, skaly.
    Len s výšky hľaďme, pozdraví sa pán,
    len kráľmi buďme, uctia si nás králi!

VI. Hviezdoslav.

        From "Hájnikova žena", Canto VI

        Či čuli ste už padať les?
    videli kedy, jak sa valí,
    videli pád a čuli ston?
    Ó, to zjav hrôzy neskonalý,
    to v rozštiepení sviatku zvon,
    to nárek, čo ti uberá
    dych, v tlkot srdca prieči hate,
    to dusot, ktorý ducha mätie,
    to ...!—Ó, ty ľuté, kruté plemä,
    i rúcho zvliekaš s matky-zeme,
    posledných chceš ju zbaviť krás,
    z temena drahý kmášeš vlas?
    Ó, keď tak víchor ostrý zhudie,
    jak zimomraveť, krahnúť bude;
    keď lejak zhučí, sšuští dážď:
    jak márne hľadať bude plášť,
    svoj plášť, plášť tkaný v brde-čude;
    i slnko o Jáne keď vzplane:
    nebude jedlicovej dlane...
    A s vtačou čosi počne jarom,
    kam umiestni ju osiralú?
    Čo zrobí s božím rosy darom,
    či ponúkne ním mŕtvu skalu?

VII. Ľudo Ondrejov.

V starej krčme

Zakvitol agát nemá kvieťa
nesedí na ňom vonný roj
a mesiac výšin smutné dieťa
polieva striebrom okruh svoj

Blúznenie mámor krásne ženy
dávno to bolo za mlada
Dnes sedím v krčme opustený
a mesiac v horách zapadá

Dnes nemám za kým zatúžil bych
a niet už koho milovať
Na srdca strunách potrhaných
zaľahla hustá inovať

Jesenná ruža matka bola
tú ľúbim stále bludný ja
však tá už na mňa nezavolá
tam leží v svete pokoja

Nalejže krčmár nalejže mi
nech zvonia spevy veselé
Len jeden život je na zemi
čo bolí raz sa zacelie.

VIII. Martin Kukučín.

From "Tichá voda"

Do mlyna som veľmi často chodieval. Najmä v zime. Keď som sa najedol pečených zemiakov so surovou kapustou, ktorá vržďala medzi zubmi, sťa remeň na kordovánkach—ja hybaj do mlyna, ktorý bol hneď za vodou. Obyčajne sedeli za stolom: mlynár, majstrová a syn Martin, a jedli vždy niečo múčneho. Ej, dobré halušky s vaječnicou varievala pani majstrová! Boh jej daj zdravia! Celý mlyn voňal od nich; samo palečné koleso muselo dostať chuť na ne, lebo sa mi zdalo, že volá na majstrovú: "Daj i mne—daj i mne!"

Ale ani raz mu nedala. Len mne vždy oddelila na mištičku a položila ju pod pec na lavicu. Ja som, pravda, jedol, hoci mi mať neraz povedala:

"Čo sa ta vlečieš, keď idú jesť? Ale ty nevieš, že je to mrzko oči na nich vyvaľovať a lyžky im čítať? Ešte sa nazdajú, že ťa hladom morím!"

Čo som mal robiť? Keď som ta prišiel, skoro vždy som ich zastihol pri stole. A keď mi dali—čo by nejedol?

Raz som tak dusil halušky, keď—málo veru chýbalo, že mi niektorá nezabehla!—keď vošla mať moja do izby.

"Poďte s nami!" núkal ju majster Brna, robiac

jej pri sebe miesto.
 Ale mať nešla. Odpovedala chladno: "No, len zdravi!" A zaraz do mňa:
 "Čože tu hľadáš, pačrev kadejaký? Pakuješ ho domov!"
 Ústa sa mi rozšírili, slzy vypadli na líce a halušky na kabaňu z úst. Večná ich škoda!
 "Ale, Katruška, dajte mu pokoj—nebožiatku!"
 "Ale sa nenajedol, či čo?" hromžila mať.
 "Veď viete, Katrenka, aké sú deti! V cudzom dome by i čerta zjedli ... "
 "Nuž ale toto je už mnoho!" nedala sa utíšiť mať.
 Od toho dňa som vo mlyne ani nepáchol. Mať ešte ako·mať. Ale otec mi prikrútol, že mi "hlavu na kláte odtne", ak len jednou nohou vstúpim do mlyna. A čo ešte, keby oboma!

IX. Daňo Okáli.

Dedina

Deň tíchne slnkom opitý
a večer vonia mliekom kráv.
V záhradu padá noci čierny splav
a cesta zvoní koňov kopyty
domov.

Vták skríkne zo sna,
oblaky bielych jabloní,
do oči spadne ti mesiac a zazvoní—
Na lásky krosná
v maštali
šliape tichý vol
a kočiš dievku pobaví,
keď kone vypriahol.

Dievka je jako nebe
a kočiš jarom opitý—
v páse ju uchytí
a medza ich zvedie.

Oči dievky kričia o mede a chlebe
ruky kočiša ju lámu—
posvätná hostina.

V maštali
vol zbožne žuje slamu
a hviezda—dievku ostríha.

X. Peter Jilemnický.

From "Kompas v nás"

Konečne i tu zaujúkala si jar po všetkých stráňach. V jarčekoch, okolo ktorých sa zazelenela prvá trávička, zurčali veselé pramene. Kde-tu na lúkach pod brehmi klokotali žriedla. A hľa — sneh nestačil ani dobre zmiznúť, už je tu plno stokrások! Dedina ako keby omladla. Radostne žmurkala malými oknami chalúp, i podstienky, sotva oschli, zdajú sa ako nanovo nalíčené. Mach na starých strechách odhodil bielu perinu snehu a ožil. Čuchrali ho a otierali sa okolo jeho teplé nočné vetry, teplé vetry, plné kriku vtáctva, čo vo veľkých kŕdľoch a dlhých frontoch tiahlo k severu. Niekedy sa medzi kaderavými mračnami ukázali dve-tri hviezdy. Už sa netriasli od mrazu. Stáli v tej čiernej vlažnej priehlbine pokojné a veľké.

V takýchto nociach, keď zem oddychovala v ústrety slnečnému ránu, spriadali gazdovia svoje smelé plány na výboj. Pod šopami stáli pluhy, z maštalí počuť ťažký vzdych kravy alebo kopnutie odpočinutého koňa s nepokojnými nozdrami.

Už ani ináč nemohlo byť: ako keby sa boli dohovorili—takmer všetci v jeden deň zapriahli a vyšli orať.

A bol to krásny deň.

Vendel zavčas rána pod kôlňou naposled pozeral pluh. Pohladkal dlaňou blýskavý lemeš, pohol kolieskom a keď počul, že zaškripelo, vzal kolomaž a namastil os. Okolo neho poskakovala Bertina. Ako myška—hneď tu a hneď zase tam, všade za otcom a všetko vidí, všetkému sa rozumie.

—Tato ... ?

Otec neodpovedá, rozmýšľa, že už je čas zapriahať.

—Tato ... ! Čujete? Tato!
—Čo je?—vyhŕklo z Vendela.
—Poháňať ... kto vám bude?
—Čo sa staráš?
—Išla by som ...

Vendel sa usmial. Bola mu práve po pás. Taká drobná, maličká—len oči mala veľké a rozumné. Povedal jej:

—Až keď budeš väčšia. Teraz si ako hrášok ... stratila by si sa v brázde. Veď ty ešte ani do školy nechodíš! Mama bude poháňať.

—Pôjdem s vami.
—Nemôžeš. Veď vieš ... hus každú chvíľu zbehne z vajec, taká nepodarená. Musíš byť doma. Dáš pozor na hus. A starú mamu poslúchaj!

XI. Laco Novomeský.

Slovo

Dopíš svoj verš, rozlúč sa ešte s nami
a potom odíď navždy, básnik ihravý.
Hodina odbila a čas je okovaný
a my v ňom chabí, tápaví.
S trpkami v hrdle zdržaného vzlyku
nás zdrví tento neúprosný vek.
Všetko je stratené?
Mám slovo na jazyku
Na bolesť myslel som a našiel na ňu liek.

XII. Dobroslav Chrobák

Drak sa vracia

Za Spárou ukázali sa nové dve plesá a nad nimi vrch, ktorý sa volá Hrubý. Obišli ho z ľavej strany ponad kosodrevie, a tu boli—i keď sa to v prvej chvíli zdalo neuveriteľné—ďalšie dve plesá, celkom podobné predošlým, takže Šimon sa začal nechápavo obzerať z Draka na plesá a z plies na Draka.
—Temné smrečiny,—povedal Drak a dotknúc sa Šimovho pleca, obrátil ho trochu doľava.
—Oheň...
Spomedzi hory pod nimi i proti nim na svahoch Krížnej vystupovali biele machnaté obláčky. Tmolili sa nad vrcholcami stromov, spájali a rozchádzali sa v nevinnej hre na kolembabu. Len nástojčivosť a vytrvalosť, s ktorou tam trčali a nerozplynuli sa, ani keď zadul vietor, prezrádzala ich pôvod a svedčila, že sú živené odspodu desivou potravou.
Inak sem nebolo cítiť nijakého zápachu, nebolo vidieť plameňa, neozval sa odtiaľ jediný zvuk, jediné zastonanie. Všetko sa odohrávalo v mŕtvolnom tichu, hlboko v lone lesa, v samotných jeho útrobách, rozhlodávaných nezadržiteľne postupujúcou ohnivou rakovinou.
—A črieda?—opýtal sa Šimon.
—Črieda? Črieda je tamto,—a Drak ukázal na nehybné červenkasté bodky na protiľahlom svahu, ktoré vyzerali odtiaľto ako promincle na medovníku.

SECTION 3. POLISH

INTRODUCTION

The Polish language, like the Polish land and people, has its own peculiar fascination. This is partly to be found in that special blend of the Slavonic and the European elements in both the Polish language and in Polish culture in general. This culture was largely maintained by the Polish nobility and gentry and by a small nucleus of townsfolk, until in the nineteenth century there was a more general spread of education and the industrialization of certain areas. Polish is the only Slavonic language where the 3rd person singular is to this day used as a polite form of address (i.e., for "you") among educated people, as in Italian and Spanish. Pan (= Sir) is used to a man, and Pani (= Madam, lady) to a woman. This slightly formal form of address, although to a native (unless he is a peasant) it has lost any connotation of ceremony or formality, seems to most foreigners (and certainly to other Slavs) to denote a certain attitude to other people and to reflect one ideal (that of "grzeczność" = politeness) of the Polish character. This feature can be found combined with keen intellect, imagination, and a lively sense of humour. Many Poles also show both an interest in things foreign and a preoccupation with national and social problems—an ever recurring theme in Polish literature. The national character is based on the healthy realism of a stock whose roots are still largely in the country and not in town life, and whose sense of nature and individuals is still far from blunted. Essentially Europeans with close on a thousand years of contact with western culture, and at the same time a nation of individualists, the Poles in their language faithfully reflect their character, one of surprising yet fascinating contrasts and many brilliant qualities.

The Polish language is characterized by the preservation of many archaic Slav features, such as palatalization and nasal vowels. These contrast with a series of purely Polish characteristics, such as the frequent occurrence of affricate and sibilant consonants both hard and soft, separate endings for the Nominative plural of adjectives and pronouns referring to masculine personal nouns in contrast to all other nouns (also in Slovak and Upper Lusatian—see below), and the use of "Pan" and "Pani" for "you" mentioned above. Polish also has many early loan words from Latin and medieval Czech and German, proving the close connection of medieval Poland with the general culture of Europe in the Middle Ages.

Poland was from very early times a Roman Catholic country. Catholicism probably first penetrated from Moravia into Southern Poland in the ninth century. Some old church expressions point to a Czech source. Poland's oldest bishopric, the see of Gniezno, was founded in the second half of the tenth century, under Mieszko I.

The literary language and pronunciation was originally based mainly on the dialects of Wielkopolska, i.e. western Poland centred around Poznań and Gniezno, even though Kraków (Cracow) in Małopolska (S. Poland) became the capital of Poland in the later Middle Ages, and later still—Warsaw in Mazovia, which has its own dialect.

The University of Kraków was founded in 1364 by Casimir (Kazimierz) the Great (sixteen years after the foundation of Prague University). This is a date of great importance for the subsequent development of Polish culture and learning.

Poland's oldest documents are in Latin, and some of these contain glosses and proper names in Polish written in Latin spelling, which provide valuable sources for the study of the early stages of the language. The earliest of such documents is the Papal Bull issued in 1136 by Pope Innocent II to the Archbishop of Gniezno, confirming his rights to certain landed property in his diocese, and giving a full list of names. But it contains no other words in Polish.

The oldest recorded sentence in Polish occurs as a gloss, translating a quotation, in a document of 1270 relating to the founding of a nunnery in Silesia.

Justly famous is the beautiful old hymn to the Virgin Mary, "Bogurodzica" (the music has also been preserved), which is the oldest song in Polish. This and other ancient documents show that long before the Reformation, hymns and sermons, etc., were composed in Polish for the benefit of women and of the masses who were not schooled in Latin. The most ancient of such documents are the Kazania Świętokrzyskie (sermons), whose original must have dated from the thirteenth century. From the following century we have the Kazania Gnieznieńskie (sermons), a fragment of a life of St. Blaise and the Psałterz Floriański (psalter). It is very instructive to compare the language of this last with the Psałterz Puławski of about a century later. These early documents throw much light on the pronunciation of Polish. Those from the fourteenth century have only one letter (ǫ or ǭ) for the two nasal vowels of modern Polish. Documents from the fifteenth century are more numerous and distinguish between ą (probably then a true nasal a) and ę (nasal e); (so in the Psałterz Puławski of about 1450).

The Treatise on Polish orthography (*Traktat o ortografii polskiej*) written by Jakub Parkoszowic about 1440, is very interesting and important in that it confirms the survival of long vowels in Polish up till that time by rendering them with double letters: aa for long a, ee for long e, etc. The author, a prominent divine and doctor of the Kraków Academy, also tried to introduce order into the Polish spelling of his day by recommending the use of round-shaped letters for palatalized consonants and angular letters for hard consonants, an ingenious idea which was not generally adopted!

The fifteenth century also saw the beginnings of Polish poetry with the verses "O chlebowym stole" (= on bread and board) and "The Satire on the Lazy Peasants."

The stir caused by the Renaissance and the Reformation created a great demand for books in Polish. Printing in Poland started at the beginning of the sixteenth century. It was centred chiefly in Kraków and done at first mostly by Germans such as Haller, Ungler, and Wietor, who had settled in Poland and become Polish subjects. They satisfied the demand by supplying books of secular as well as religious content. In doing so they tried to introduce some sort of system into the chaotic Polish orthography of their time. It is to this period that we owe the form of certain modern Polish letters, such as ć, ś, ź for the soft affricate and *chuintantes*, ż, and cz (also rendered cž) and sz (also rendered ss). ą and ę were distinguished as to-day, but there were still several variations in the use of i, j, and y, and c was rendered both tz and cz. In contrast to Czech, vowels were marked with ´ (acute accent) to distinguish differences of quality rather than length.

In 1542 Wietor, in a Preface addressed to his patron and added to a Polish translation of a work by Erasmus on language, commended the wider use and cultivation of Polish as a literary medium among Poles.

Soon after, Mikołaj Rej (1505-1569) asserted stoutly:—

> "A niechaj narodowie wżdy postronni znają
> Iż Polacy nie gęsi, że swój język mają"
> (Let other nations always know

that the Poles are not geese, but have their
         language too),
when advocating the wider use of Polish in literature
as well as in sermons and hymns in church. He was a
genial country gentleman and a Protestant. A prolific
writer in both prose and verse, he is perhaps best
known for his "Zwierciadło," a delightful treatise on
a gentleman's upbringing, life, and duties, dating
from 1567.

   In 1566, Łukasz Górnicki (1527-1603) published
in Kraków his charming *Dworzanin Polski* (= the Polish
Courtier), modelled on Castiglione's *Il cortegiano*,
which had appeared in 1528. The Polish work contains
many original passages, including a very interesting
treatise on the nobleman's language, the first of its
kind to be written in Polish. In it Górnicki stresses
the importance of using Polish words and expressions
whenever possible, and not interlarding Polish speech
with ostentatious borrowings from Latin, Czech, or
Western European languages, as was fashionable then.
Górnicki showed he was well aware of the relationship
of Polish to the other languages of the Western,
Eastern and Southern Slav groups, and recognized the
advanced state of development and refinement of Czech
in his day.

   At this period Poland was enjoying great economic
prosperity and political power. With the Union of
Lublin in 1569 her influence expanded greatly to the
East into Lithuania, Byelorussia and Ukraine. Polon-
ized Ukrainian noblemen brought traces of Ukrainian
into their Polish, which they adopted as their language of communication. On the other hand in Poland
proper the Polish language enjoyed its first Golden
Age towards the end of the sixteenth century, contemporary to the great Elizabethan period of English.
Its climax was reached in the poetry of Jan Kochanowski (1530-1584), whose moving *Treny* (Laments), *Psalmy*,
and other poems, can be read without difficulty by
those knowing modern Polish and truly deserve to be
more widely known. No less excellent is the Polish
of the Jesuit, Piotr Skarga (1536-1612), whose *Kazania
Sejmowe* (Sermons to Parliament) were a powerful early
warning to the Polish nobles against the abuses which
eventually contributed to Poland's downfall.

   The seventeenth century saw the rapid decline of
the Western Slavs in Europe. Ruinous wars with
Muscovy and the Swedes, the Thirty Years' War in
Europe, as well as internal dissention and stagnation
all helped to bring about this decline in Poland.
Literature likewise declined, and the high standards

of language attained in the previous age were not maintained. (This continued into the first half of the eighteenth century.)

The second half of the seventeenth century showed an increase of French influences in Polish literature. In the language some of the last phonetic changes occurred. The old form of the 2nd Palatalization ch > sz was abandoned in the Nom. plural of masculine nouns: the Nom. plural of Włoch = Italian, became Włosi with i on the analogy of other nouns, instead of Włoszy. The pronunciation of rz and ż became finally identical. And in the Nom. plural of adjectives and pronouns, masculine personal nouns were qualified by adjectives with a special ending.

But by the middle of the eighteenth century, before the first Partition in 1772, the forces of revival in Poland were already at work. The writings of Father Stanisław Konarski on politics and language reform are the best proof of this. His *De emendendae eloquentiae vitiis* appeared in 1741, and his *O skutecznym rad sposobie* (= "Effective Counsels") was published in 1760. A permanent national theatre was founded in Warsaw in 1765 and flourished shortly afterwards under Bogusławski. 1773, the year after the first Partition, saw the foundation in Poland of Europe's first Ministry of Education. And in 1778, Father O. Kopczyński's *Grammar for National Schools* started appearing. It showed the influence of the Rationalist movement, and was more concerned with regularizing inconsistencies and variants of spelling than truly reflecting the spoken language. Nevertheless, it broke with purely historical discrepancies between spelling and pronunciation and brought in rules where none had existed before. Its influence remained long felt, e.g. the Locative and Instrumental singular and Dative and Instrumental plural endings of masculine and neuter adjectives, in which until recently genders were distinguished.

Father Kopczyński was a member of the famous Towarzystwo Przyjaciół Nauk (= the Society of the Friends of the Sciences), which also counted among its prominent members Stanisław Staszic, an eminent geographer, historian, social and political thinker as well as poet, S. B. Linde, the author of a dictionary of the Polish language which might be compared to Johnson's dictionary in its influence, though it was much bigger (its eight volumes appeared from 1806 to 1814, and the second edition from 1854-60), and General J. Mroziński, who became a prominent authority on orthography.

By the beginning of the nineteenth century

the Romantic movement in Poland was in full swing. The first volume of poems by Mickiewicz (1798-1855), his *Ballads*, appeared in 1822. Their language was regarded as revolutionary and un-Polish by the older critics of his time, because it included many foreign expressions and was also much nearer the contemporary spoken language than the "correct" literary language of the day. But with these, his *Ode to Youth* and his famous longer poems such as *Dziady* (= Forefathers' Eve), *Konrad Wallenrod*, and *Pan Tadeusz*, he quickly won the day. The story of his wanderings in Russia and friendship with Pushkin and his final emigration and exile in Paris make significant and interesting reading. His writings, together with those of his great contemporaries, the introspective Juliusz Słowacki (1809-1849) and Zygmunt Krasiński (1812-1859), author of *The Undivine Comedy*, are evidence of a new zenith reached by the Polish language and its literature in the nineteenth century. Their language is practically modern Polish, as much as that of Pushkin can be considered to be modern Russian; and with them terminates at present the "history" of the development of the Polish language.

They were followed by a host of important and interesting writers, such as the dramatist Fredro, the famous novelists Sienkiewicz, Prus, Orzeszkowa, Żeromski and Reymont, and the poets Norwid, Lenartowicz, Asnyk, Kasprowicz and Wyspiański, who was also a dramatist and painter. From Romanticism Poland turned to Realism or "Positivism" as it was called in Warsaw. This in turn gave way to Naturalism and a growing interest in the Polish peasant and his dialects, as can be seen in Żeromski's rendering of Kashubian, Tetmayer's *Tatra Tales*, and Reymont's freely adapted peasant "dialect" in his *Chłopi* (= Peasants), which won a Nobel Prize for literature.

This literature merits deep and serious study in the English-speaking world, especially by all scholars in the Slavonic field. It continued to flourish between the two world wars in liberated Poland, and shows no signs of dying in the newly resurrected and nationally more homogeneous Poland of the present day.

THE POLISH ALPHABET

Polish.   *Approx. English equivalent*

A	a	(more open and forward than) *ah*
	ą	nasal *o*, like French "on"
B	b	*b* (unaspirated)

POLISH

Polish.		Approx. English equivalent
C	c	*ts* pronounced together
Ć	ć	soft *ch*, cf. vulg. "tune" = chune
D	d	(purely dental) *d*
E	e	*e* in "bet" (but can be more closed in pronunciation)
	ę	nasal *e*, like French *in* in "vin"
F	f	*f*
G	g	*g* in "go"
H	h	*ch* in Scots "loch," = Polish *ch*
I	i	*ee* in "meet"
J	j	*y* in "yet" and "boy"
K	k	*k* (unaspirated)
L	l	*l* in "last"
Ł	ł	*l* in "table" (very "correct"), more usually *w* or *ṷ*
M	m	*m*
N	n	*n*
	ń	*ni* in "onion"
O	o	*o* in "for"
Ó	ó	*oo* in "book," = Polish *u*
P	p	*p* (unaspirated)
R	r	rolled *r*
S	s	*s* in "see"
Ś	ś	soft *sh*
T	t	(unaspirated dental) *t*
U	u	*oo* in "book," = Polish *ó*
W	w	*v*
	y	*y* in "Mary," more forward than Russian ы
Z	z	*z*
Ź	ź	*s* in pleasure but softer, *zh*
Ż	ż	*s* in pleasure but harder, *zh*

Q and V are used only in quoting foreign words;
Qu is otherwise rendered *kw*, e.g.: kwestia = problem, question
X is rendered *ks*.

    1. B, F, G, H and CH, K, M, N, P, W can be both soft, if followed by i, and hard.
    2. C (pron. *ts*), CZ (pron. *ch*), DZ (*dz* pron. together), SZ (pron. *sh*), RZ (= Pol. sz or ż, i.e. pron. *sh* or *zh*), Ż (= *zh*), DŻ (= Eng. *j*) are, in pronunciation, hard only.
    3. Ć or Ci (= soft *ch*), Dź or Dzi (= soft *j*), Ś or Si (= soft *sh*), Ź or Zi (= soft *zh*) are soft only.
    4. Ć or Ci is the soft version of T,
        Dź or Dzi is the soft version of D,
            E.g.: chata = (peasant's) house, Loc. sing.
                                        w chacie

woda = water, Loc. sing. w wodzie
5. L is regarded as the soft version of Ł,
   E.g.: siła = strength, Loc. sing. o sile
6. Rz is the 'soft' counterpart of R, though it is now hard phonetically,
   E.g.: siostra = sister, Loc. sing. o siostrze
7. Ś or Si, Ź or Zi are the soft versions of S and Z respectively,
   E.g.: los = fate, Loc. sing. o losie
   wóz = cart, Loc. sing. o wozie
8. Ch, though representing one sound (the equivalent of Polish h) and like *ch* in Scots "loch," is *not* regarded as a separate letter of the alphabet as it is in Czech and Slovak.

9. The combinations szcz, żdż (both hard) and ść (or ści), źdź (or ździ) (both soft) are compound sounds: sz + cz, etc. E.g.:—

szczupak = pike
drożdże = yeast
kość = bone
źdźbło = stalk, mote

PRONUNCIATION

(In the following paragraphs, for the sake of simplicity, we give our explanations of Polish pronunciation in Polish spelling, except where specially indicated: phon. = phonetic script, Eng. = English.)

The Accent

The accent in Polish is a very moderate, purely stress accent and falls on the penultimate syllable in practically all words and word groups containing enclitics and proclitics (see below). E.g.:—

ksiązka = book
nowina = novelty
gotów = ready
sprawiedliwość = justice
do-nich = to them

but—

do Pana = to you

Exceptions to this rule are a few words of foreign origin, such as: Ameryka, matematyka; the expression w ogóle (= in general); the Past and Conditional of verbs, e.g.: byliśmy (= we were), byliby (= they would be), bylibyśmy (= we would be); and words with Past or Conditional endings attached to them, e.g.= jeżelibyśmy = if we would...

The Vowels

The vowels are not affected in their quality by the position of the stress in the word, as they are in Russian, Ukrainian and Bulgarian and, to a less extent, in Slovenian. They retain their full value and clear quality, as in Czech, Slovak and Serbocroätian. Thus the two *a*'s in the word "matka" (= mother) are of the same quality. In the pronunciation of some speakers, the vowel of the stressed syllable seems slightly longer than those of other syllables.

In contrast to Russian, the quality of a vowel in Polish is little affected by a following soft consonant, except in the case of *e*, which is noticeably more closed before such a soft consonant, but not as much as in Russian,

    cf. ten (phon. tɛn) = this,
    and dzień (phon. dzeɲ) = day.

i: All consonants are automatically soft before *i*, the palatalization (see below) not being indicated in any way.

y: On the other hand palatalization never occurs before *y*.

The Polish "nasal" vowels ę, ą: These are only pronounced like French nasal vowels when—

(1) followed immediately by a fricative consonant, i.e., *s, z, ś, ź, sz, ż, ch, f, w,* e.g.:—

wąs = whisker gęsi = geese fąfel = child, brat
węzeł = knot   więzić = to imprison
mięso = meat   mąż = husband
         zamężna = married (fem.)
         węch = (sense of) smell
         wąwóz = ravine

(2) ą is final, e.g.:—

    wodą, Instr. sing. = with water

Final ę is regularly pronounced e except in very careful speech, e.g.:—

    widzę wodę (= I see water), pron. widze wode

But—

(*a*) Before hard labials, *p, b,* they are pronounced em, om, e.g.:—

    gęba = mouth
    dąb = oak

(*b*) Before soft labials, p', b', they are sometimes pronounced em̂, om̂, e.g.:—

o gębie, Loc. sing. = about the mouth
rąbie = he hews

(c) Before hard dentals, *t, d, c, dz*, they are pronounced en, on (with dental n), e.g.:—

ląd = land
w ręce = in the hand
żądza = passion, desire

(d) Before alveolars, *cz, dż, trz, drz*, they are pronounced en, on with alveolar (English) n, e.g.:—

męczyć = to torment
na... piętrze = on the ... storey
pączek = bud

(e) Before the palatal alveolar affricates *ć, dź*, they are pronounced eń, oń, e.g.:—

będzie = will be
w kącie = in the corner

(f) Before velar (guttural) *k, g*, they are pronounced Eng. eng, ong. (phon. eŋ, oŋ), e.g.:—

ręka = hand
mąka = flour

(g) Before palatalized k', g', they are pronounced phon. eɲ, oɲ, e.g.:—

ręki (Gen. sing.) = of the hand
mąki (Gen. sing.) = of flour

(h) Before *l* or *ł* they are pronounced e, o (plain oral vowels), e.g.:—

wziął = he took, with o
wzięła = she took, with e
wzięli = they took, with e

Other nasal vowels may occur in Polish before a fricative consonant, but they are spelt with a vowel + m or n. The nasal pronunciation is *not*, however, obligatory in these cases, e.g.:—

tramwaj = tram, with nasal a
dystans = distance, " " a
winszować = to wish, " " i
triumf = triumph, " " u
rynsztok = gutter, " " y

Even foreign words with *en, em, on, om* before a fricative can have these syllables nasalized, e.g.:—

sens = sense, pron. sęs
komfort = comfort, pron. kąfort

Vowel Alternations

For the vowel alternation: ę/ą see Features characteristic of Polish Nos. 2, 5.

For the vowel alternation: o/ó see Features characteristic of Polish No. 5.

For the vowel alternations: ie/io (e/o) and ie/ia (e/a) see Features characteristic of Polish No. 6.

The Consonants

The consonants, as in other languages, go mostly in pairs: one voiced and one unvoiced. (The reader will already have observed that some single sounds are represented by two letters, contrary to the general practice in other Slavonic languages.) In the following table ' (apostrophĕ) represents "softness" or palatalization.

Unvoiced	p	p'	t	k	k'	f	f'	s	sz	ś	h(ch)	h'(ch')	c	cz	ć
Voiced	b	b'	d	g	g'	w	w'	z	ż	ź	γ	γ' (rare)[1]	dz	dż	dź

The following consonants have no unvoiced counterparts:—

    m, m', n, ń, (ŋ)   (nasals)
    ł, l, l'[2], r   (liquids)
    j   (palatal semi-vowel)

j is never written before *i* in words of Polish origin, though it occurs in pronunciation, e.g.:—

kleić = to glue, pron. klejić
kolej = a railway line, Gen., Dat., Voc., Loc. sing. and Gen. plur. kolei, pron. koleji, cf. Instr. sing. koleją, Nom. plur. koleje, etc.

But *ji* can occur in foreign words: we Francji (Loc.) = in France.

Palatalization

As will be seen from the table above, the consonants *p, b, k, g, f, w,* and *ch* or *h* can be pronounced palatalized, or soft, as well as ordinary, or hard (as are most English consonants). Palatalization is generally indicated by writing *i* after the consonant so affected, this *i* not being otherwise separately pronounced, unless no other vowel follows.

[1] E.g. Bohdan, phon. 'Boγdan (Christian name); klechdzie, phon. kleγ'dze, = legend, tradition Dat. Loc. sg.
[2] l is soft only before i, e.g. list (= letter), phon. ĺist.

But these particular consonants are never palatalized finally (in contrast partly to Russian), cf.:—

    Pol. gołąb, gołębia = a dove, pigeon
    Russ. голубь, голубя   "   "

A variety of palatalized *t, d, s, z* and *r* also occur in Polish, but only in the pronunciation of words of foreign origin, e.g.:—

    tiara   = tiara
    diabeł = devil
    Rosja   = Russia
    poezja = poetry
    historia = history

In most foreign words the combinations *ti-, di-, ri-* are avoided and replaced by *ty-, dy-, ry-*, e.g.:—

    polityk   = politician
    dystans   = distance
    arytmetyka = arithmetic
    liryka   = lyric poetry

In native Polish words the role of palatalized *t, d, s, z,* and *r* is played by ć (*ci*), dź (*dzi*), ś (*si*), ź (*zi*) and *rz* respectively. (See Nos. 4, 6, and 7 after "The Alphabet").

ć, dź, ś, ź and also ń only occur in writing finally, or medially and also initially before other consonants, e.g.:—

ćma   = darkness; moth przyjaźń   = friendship
niedźwiedź = bear   cień(*masc.*)= shadow
śmiały   = bold

The same sounds before a vowel, other than *i*, are rendered *ci, dzi, si, zi, ni*, e.g.:—

    cień = shadow   ziarno = grain
    dzień = day   niuch = pinch of snuff
    siano = hay

Before the vowel *i* the unaccented consonants are *written,* but they are pronounced as if they bore the accents, e.g.:—

    cisza = quietness, pron. ćisza
    siwy = grey,   pron. śiwy
    dziki = wild   etc.
    niwa = field
    zima = winter

The pronunciation of ś is most easily arrived at by English people by pronouncing the *h* in huge, Hugh, and then closing the jaws—a soft *sh* then resulting. ź is the voiced counterpart of this sound.

POLISH

rz can be voiced and then = ż, e.g.:—

    morze (= sea), pron. może (the same as może = he can),

and unvoiced, and then = sz, e.g.:—

    przy = near, pron. pszy

In a few words, such as marznąć (= to freeze), r and z are pronounced separately.

trz, drz should always be pronounced separately, e.g.:—

    trzy (= three), pron. t-szy > czszy, tʃʃɨ
    drzeć (= to rend), pron. d-żeć > dżżeć, ʤetc

as opposed to:—

    czy...? (interrogative particle)
    dżungla = jungle (with phon. ʤ)

On the other hand, dz, dzi, dź which are usually pronounced as one sound (See Nos. 2 and 3 after "The Alphabet"), are pronounced separately when they occur as part of the prefixes od-, pod-, nad-, etc., before a root beginning with z, zi or ż, e.g.:—

    odzyskać = to regain
    podziemny = underground (adj.)
    odżyć = to revive

The consonants c, dz, cz, dż, sz, ż and rz are called ex-palatals or "historically" or "functionally soft," because they were formerly soft and still play a special rôle in the flexion of nouns and verbs. cz, dż, sz, ż and rz are never followed by i, requiring y instead. The same applies to c (phon. ts), and dz (phon. ʣ), i.e. when they represent these hard sounds and not ć and dź, e.g.: cynik = cynic, cudzy = foreign.

The Assimilation of Consonants

The assimilation is generally regressive, the second consonant by its nature deciding whether a group of two consonants is pronounced voiced or unvoiced, thus:—

    odbiór = (wireless) reception, pron. ɔdbiur

but—

    odporność = resistance, pron. otporność

The same rule applies to prepositions preceding any other word, whether they consist of a single consonant like w, z, a monosyllable ending in a consonant like pod, bez, or two syllables like obok. These prepositions are always pronounced in a group together with the word they govern and assimilation *must* occur, e.g.:—

    w Gdyni = in Gdynia, phon. v gd...
    w Polsce = in Poland, phon. f p...

similarly:—

  pod ziemią   = under the ground, pron. pod zie...

    but—

  pod sosnami   = under the pines,   " pot s...
  obok domu   = near the house,   " obog d...
  obok tego domu = near this house,   " obok t...

When *w* or *rz* are the *second* half of such a combination of consonants, however, the assimilation is progressive, the nature of the *first* consonant then being decisive, thus:—

    brzeg = shore, pron. bżek (on the k see next para.)

but—

    przy = near,   "   pszy (see also trzy, drzeć above)

likewise:—

    dwa = two, phon. dva

but—

    twój is generally (esp. in W. and S. Poland) pronounced tfuj.

m, n, j, ł, l and *r* when occurring in groups of consonants do not play any part in causing assimilation. In this respect they are neutral.

Devoicing of Final Voiced Consonants

It is also very important to note that final voiced consonants become unvoiced in Polish. That is why brzeg above sounds like bżek.

Likewise: Kraków is pron. Kràkuf, wód (Gen. plur., = of waters) is pron. wut, dąb (= oak) is pron. domp, etc.

This rule is common to all the Slavonic languages except Serbocroătian and Ukrainian.

Double Consonants

Double consonants may occur in Polish in pronunciation *as well as* in spelling (in contrast to Czech and Slovak). Thus two *n*'s are heard in:—

    inny = another

two *k*'s in:—

     lèkki = light

and even two *cz*'s (= Eng. ch) in:—

     czczy = vain, useless

This also applies to consecutive words when the first ends and the second begins with the same consonant. Thus:—

    dom matki = the mother's house

has two distinct *m*'s (in contrast to Serbocroätian).

Enclitics

  These are unstressed monosyllabic words pronounced in a group with the *preceding* word. They include:—

  (*a*) the short forms of the Personal Pronouns such as—

    mi = to me
    cię = you (Acc. sing.)
    mu = to him
    ich = them

  (see "Pronouns" below), as in other West and South Slav languages.

  (*b*) the Demonstrative Pronoun—

    to = this, it (Acc. sing.)

  in constrast to S. Slav languages.

  (*c*) the Reflexive Pronoun—

    się = -self

  as in other West and South Slav languages.

  (*d*) the particles—

    no
    to
    (and -że)

  Polish prefers to put the enclitics early in the sentence, but there are no such strict rules in this respect as there are in Serbocroätian. (See "Word Order with Enclitics" below.)

Proclitics

  These, on the other hand, are unstressed monosyllables pronounced in a group with the *following* word. They are:—

  (*a*) the negative particle—

    nie = not

when not preceding a *monosyllabic* verb (which throws the stress on to the nie), e.g.:—
  nie-màmy (= we have not), but
  niè-mam (= I have not).

(*b*) the monosyllabic prepositions do, pod, bez, etc., when *not* followed by (1) monosyllabic pronouns (Personal, Interrogative or Demonstrative) which throw the stress back on to the preposition, e.g.:—

  bèz-wysiłku = without effort
  bèz-tego   = without this

but—

  nà-tym = on that
  ò-co?   = about what?

and (2) certain monosyllabic nouns in idioms, e.g.:—

  nà wieś = to the country

(*c*) monosyllabic pronouns:—
  (1) Demonstrative—
    ten, ta, to = this
  (2) Possessive—
    mój = my
    mym = (Instr. and Loc. sing. masc. and neut.) = my
    jej = her
    ich = their
    nasz = our
  (3) Interrogative (in form) co, e.g.:—
    co roku = every year

(*d*) monosyllabic conjunctions such as—

  i, a = and
  lecz = but
  że   = that
  choć = though
  bo   = because (which last can also be enclitic)

THE POLISH DIALECTS

Polish dialects fall into five main groups:—
1. The dialects of Wielkopolska with Poznań as centre, with the dialects of Kujawy with Inowrocław and Włocławek as centre;
2. The dialects of Małopolska and Kraków (Cracow)

as centre;
3. The dialects of Polish Silesia (Sląsk) with Katowice as the chief town;
4. The dialects of Mazovia (Mazowsze) with Warsaw as centre;
5. The Kashubian dialects, on the seabord west of Gdańsk (Danzig) and running inland in a narrow belt in a south-westerly direction from Gdynia.

North, west and south of Łódź there is a central area forming a transition or bridge between the three main Polish groups, Wielkopolska, Małopolska, and Mazovia. Here the pronunciation of the nasal vowels most nearly approaches the literary, $ę$ being pronounced ę, and $ą$ as om.

Kashubian has been considered by some scholars in the past, such as Vondrák, as a separate language from Polish. And indeed it is more distinct from literary Polish than the other dialects. But its speakers have been too few in numbers to build up a literary language of their own of any importance, let alone demand national independence. And very little has been printed in Kashubian. So, from the standpoint of this book, it is best to consider it as a dialect of Polish. It is easier to understand for someone knowing Polish than broad Scots English for an Englishman.

Kashubian has the following peculiarities:—

1. C.S. vocalic $\underset{\circ}{l}$ develops into ol, whether it comes from $\underset{\circ}{l}'$ or $\underset{\circ}{l}$, in contrast to Polish:—

    połnĭ = full, literary Pol. pełny
        (for ĭ see No. 5 below);
    wołk = wolf, lit. Pol. wilk;
    dołgie = long, lit. Pol. długi

2. Consonants are softened before -*ar*-, from C.S. soft vocalic $\underset{\circ}{ŕ}$, when this occurs before a hard dental:—

    ćwardĭ = hard, lit. Pol. twardy
    ḿartwĭ = dead, lit. Pol. martwy

3. Soft *ś, ź, ć, dź* become hardened to s, z, c, dz respectively:—

    sec = net, Pol. sieć
    sedzec = to sit, Pol. siedzieć
    cemnĭ = dark, Pol. ciemny

(But *sz, ż, cz, dż* are preserved.)

4. Soft k' g' become ć, dź respectively:—

    ćedĭ = when, Pol. kiedy
    ćij = stick, Pol. kij
    dłudźi = long, Pol. długi

5. *y* is pronounced like a hard i without palatalization of the preceding consonant (marked ı̇ in the examples above):—

> połnı̇, cẃardı̇, m̂artwı̇, cemnı̇, ćedı̇.

6. Initial *o* and *wo* (vo) are confused, both giving u̯o:—

> u̯oko = eye, Pol. oko
> u̯oda = water, Pol. woda

This is also a feature of the dialects of Wielkopolska. *o* often changes to u̯o and also u̯e.

7 *u* and *i* when in short position (see below) become ĕ, a back vowel between Polish e and y:—

> cud = a wonder, Gen. sing. cĕdu,
> cf. Pol. cud, cudu
> zĕma = winter, Gen. plur. zim,
> cf. Pol. zima, zim

8. Similarly the vowel ŏ represents in Kashubian the "long" version of short *a*:—

> ptŏk = bird, Pol. ptak
> trŏwa = grass, Pol. trawa

Kashubian can be considered as a transition to the old dialects of the now Germanized Slavs on the left bank of the lower Oder. With them it affords some examples of Slavonic words without the metathesis of liquids: bardawka (= wart), Stargard (a town).

The feature of vowel correspondences, originally based on length, referred to in points 7 and 8 above is shared by Kashubian with all the other Polish dialects and also with literary Polish. Cf. Kash. cud, cĕdu with lit. Pol. wóz (= wagon), Gen. sg. wozu; ząb (= tooth), Gen. sg. zęba; and the dialectical Polish: ptåk (= bird), Gen. sg. ptaka; chléb (= bread), Gen. sg. chleba. The vowels ó, ą, å and é, originally long, are called "narrowed" (in Polish ścieśnione, or pochylone = lit. slanting), in contrast to the ordinary, short vowels. å is a vowel between a and o, sometimes rendered ȧ.

é is a regular feature of almost all dialects, being pronounced i or y.

ó is pronounced u in the South, Małopolska and Silesia, and half-way betweeu u and o elsewhere.

å is pronounced ou̯ in Wielkopolska and Silesia and like o in Małopolska.

The *dialects of Wielkopolska* are particularly important, as some scholars, such as Lehr-Spławiński, hold that they formed the basis of modern literary

Polish, though others, e.g. Słoński, have questioned this. The most unique features of these dialects are:—

1. The pronunciation of ę is either ę or a nasal y or else as e finally and before fricatives and as em, en, etc., before stops, e.g.:—

bende = I shall be, for będę

2. The pronunciation of ą as a nasal u or else as o finally and before fricatives and as om, on, etc. before stops, e.g.:—

wochać = to smell, for wąchać

but—

mondry = wise, for mądry.

3. The pronunciation of the groups *sw, tw, kw* with a voiced w (phon. v).

4. The endings -ewi in the Dat. sing. of masc. soft nouns (for literary -*owi*), e.g.:—

kowalewi (Dat. sing.) = blacksmith

and -ewy for adjectives formed from soft stem nouns, e.g.:—

wiśniewy = cherry (adj.) for literary wiśniowy.

(Here the literary language follows the example of Małopolska.)

In common with Kashubian, Wielkopolska pronounces hard i for *y* and confuses initial *o* and *wo*, both becoming u̯o. It also preserves the *chuintantes* *sz, ż, cz, dż*, like Kashubian, i.e. these dialects have no "mazurzenie" (see below).

In common with Małopolska and Silesia, Wielkopolska pronounces *n* before velars as ŋ, in contrast to the pronunciation of Warsaw and Mazovia generally.

The northern dialects of Poland, both in Wielkopolska and Mazovia, also pronounce:—

p' as p'j or p'ś or p'ch'
b' as b'j or b'ź or b'ch'

and even—

f' as ś, and
ẃ as ź (Źisła for Wisła = Vistula!)

Also św becomes śf, and dźẃ—dźw, the second element, w, hardening in these dialects.

Finally, when one word ends in a consonant and the next word begins with a vowel or the continuants, *r, l, ł, m, n* or *j*, Wielkopolska dialects, like those of Małopolska and Silesia, are characterized by the voicing of that final consonant which is unvoiced in Mazovia, e.g.:—

kot idzie (= the tom-cat is going) is pronounced:

in Wielkopolska, Małopolska and Silesia: kod idzie
but in Mazovia: . . . . . kot idzie

Similarly only Mazovia pronounces brat niesie (= the brother is carrying) as brat niesie. Wielkopolska, Małopolska and Silesia pronounce: brad niesie. Likewise before the endings of the Past tense of verbs, Wielkopolska, Małopolska, and Silesia pronounce: zaniosłem (= I brought) as zaniozem, but Mazovia has: zaniosem. (These endings were once separate words.)

The termination -wa for -my in the 1st pers. plur. of verbs is not known in Wielkopolska alone of the Polish dialectal regions.

The *dialects of Kujawy* share all these features in various degrees, except the confusion of initial *o* and *wo*.

The *dialects of Małopolska* have various pronunciations of the nasal vowels ę and ą:

Western Małopolska has ę for ę, but om for ą;
Eastern Małopolska has e for ę, and an o approaching a for ą;
Southern Małopolska has either ǫ or a true nasal a [ã] for both *ę and ą*.

In feminine ja-stems, South-west Małopolska and Silesia have preserved the old endings in the Gen. and Acc. sing., -e and -ą respectively. South-west Małopolska also has k for final *ch*, e.g.: od nik (= from them), for od nich. The mountain dialect of Podhale has -byk and -ek for the endings of the 1st pers. sing. of the Conditional and Past Tense. Silesian dialects have Cond. -bych, and in the 1st pers. plur. both Silesia and Podhale have bychmy, cf. Czech -bych. Both Podhale and Silesia also have -wa and in some places -me for the termination of the 1st pers. plur. of verbs.

In common with the Mazovian and some Silesian dialects, Małopolska has the important feature of "mazurzenie," i.e. the pronunciation of *sz, ż, cz, dż* as s, z, c, dz respectively, e.g.:—

syja for szyja = neck
zyto for żyto = rye
capka for czapka = cap
jezdze for jeżdżę = I travel

But *rz* is generally pronounced ż (phon. ʒ).

Both Małopolska and Mazovia pronounce *sw*, *tw*, *kw* as sf, tf, kf respectively and distinguish initial *o* from *wo*.

In morphology the endings -owi for the Dat. sing. of masc. jo-stems and -owy for adjectives formed from soft stems are a characteristic of Małopolska adopted in the literary language.

The *dialects of Silesia* are chiefly characterized by the pronunciation of true nasals in all positions: ę or ã (nasal a) for ę and ǫ for what is spelt ą.

The *dialects of Mazovia* have the unique feature of not distinguishing soft k', g' from hard k, g, having in some places only the soft consonants, in others only the hard. They also preserve a true n before velars. As has already been explained, they do not voice final consonants before words beginning with a vowel or a continuant. They also distinguish initial *o* and *wo*.

They treat p', b', f', ŵ, ś̂w, dź̂w like the dialects of Wielkopolska (q.v.), but sw, tw, kw like those of Małopolska (q.v.). *y* is pronounced as hard i in Central and Northern Mazovia only. The nasal vowels vary: Western Mazovia has ę for ę and om for ą; Central Mazovia has ã for ę and nasal u (ų) for ą. The dialect of Puławy, South of Warsaw, keeps the verbal ending -wa for a true dual in meaning. Eastern Mazovia has the ending -m for the 1st pers. plur. of verbs, under the influence of Ukrainian and Byelorussian dialects.

The Poles from Western Ukraine and Western Byelorussia (L'viv and Vilnia, formerly Lwów and Wilno) show the influence of Ukrainian and Byelorussian dialects in their pronunciation. They "sing" their stressed vowels and confuse *o* with *u* and *e* with *y* and *i*.

Mazovia made no contribution to the formation of literary Polish, as Warsaw became the capital of Poland comparatively late in Polish history, under Zygmunt III in 1596. It is difficult to say whether Wielkopolska or Małopolska contributed more in the past to the formation of the literary language, as the dialects have changed since then. Certainly on the face of it, modern Polish has more important features apparently from Wielkopolska; nevertheless as Kraków was the capital and centre of culture during the formative period of the literary language, it is highly likely that Małopolska, whose dialects were doubtless less different then than they are now from those of Wielkopolska, also made important contributions to literary Polish and that of the educated classes.

VOWEL GRADATION AND VOWEL LENGTHENING

Polish affords numerous examples of both these phenomena, but the spelling and phonetic development of the language make them look a little surprising at first sight.

Vowel Gradation is seen in:—

śmierć = death, umrzeć (Pfve.) = to die, umrę = I shall die, umarł = he died, zamorzyć = to starve, mór = plague;

nieść (Impfve.) = to carry, nosić (Freq.) = to carry, also niosę = I carry,—see "Vowel Alternations";

dech = breath, duch = spirit, dusza = soul, tchnąć (Pfve.) = to breathe out, to blow;

bierze = he takes, brać (Impfve.) = to take, also biorę = I take,—see "Vowel Alternations," ubiór = attire;

ciec	= to run, pour	tok	= course
żąć	= to reap	żnę	1st pers. sing. Present
ciąć	= to hew, cut	tnę	1st pers. sing. Present
wisieć	= to hang (intrans.)	wieszać	= to hang up (trans., Impfve.)
świt	= dawn	świecić	= to shine
leżeć	= to lie	łoże	= couch
pleść	= to weave, plait	płot	= fence

Vowel Lengthening can be seen in:—

umrę	= (Pfve.) I shall die	umierać	= (Impfve.)
dech	= breath	oddychać	= to breathe; dyszeć = to pant
brać	= to take	wybierać	= to choose
tnę	= I hew	wycinać	= to hew out
prosić	= to ask, request	upraszać	= to beg, entreat
mówić	= (Impfve.) to say, speak	mawiać	= (Freq.)
posłać	= (Pfve.) to send	posyłać	= (Impfve.)
poić	= to give to drink, make drunk	upajać	= to intoxicate (fig.)
pleść	= to weave, plait	wyplatać	= to weave, plait

SLAVONIC CHARACTERISTICS

1. The metathesis of liquids. Polish, like Lusatian, has true West Slav forms, in contrast to Czech and Slovak, which in this case have many South Slav forms. The old lengths are reflected in the vowel alternatives o/ó:—

głowa = head	głód	= hunger	
wrona = crow	gród	= town, castle	
	proch	= dust	
brzeg = shore	brzoza	= birch	
mleko = milk	mleć	= to grind	
robota = work	łokieć	= elbow (former intonation ⌒)
ramię = shoulder	łabędź	= swan (" " ´)

2. The 1st Palatalization of velars, changing k, g, ch into cz, $ż$, sz respectively, is a regular feature of Polish:—

piec = to bake, 1st pers. sing. Pres. piekę, 3rd pers. sing. piecze; człowiek = human being, Voc. sing. (in lofty style) człowiecze! (otherwise człowieku!).

móc = to be able, 1st pers. sing. Pres. mogę,
2nd pers. sing. możesz
Bóg = God, Voc. sg. Boże!
strach = terror, straszny = frightful

2a. c and dz, when derived from k and g respectively, also change to cz and $ż$:—

chłopiec = boy, Voc. sg. chłopcze!
miesiąc = month, miesięczny = monthly
ksiądz = priest, Voc. sg. księże!

3. The 2nd Palatalization of velars is also alive in Polish. Here k, g change to c, dz respectively, while ch changes to sz (as in Czech, by hardening) as well as to $ś$ (written si, a fairly recently restored form). c and dz used to be pronounced soft too, but have now become quite hard.

ręka = hand,	Loc. sing.		(w) ręce
Polak = Pole,	Nom. plur.		Polacy
wysoki = high,	Nom. plur. masc. pers.		wysocy
noga = foot,	Loc. sing.		(na) nodze
Norweg = Norwegian,	Nom. plur.		Norwedzy (or Norwegowie)
ubogi = poor,	Nom. plur. masc. pers.		ubodzy
mucha = fly,	Loc. sing.		(o) musze
mnich = monk,	Nom. plur.		mnisi
Czech = a Czech,	Nom. plur.		Czesi
suchy = dry,	Nom. plur. masc. pers.		susi

4. *Yotation*. The changes of consonants when followed by a j ("yot"), in Polish take the following forms:—

k, g, ch + j become *cz, ż, sz*:—

płakać = to weep,   1st pers. sing. Pres. płaczę
strugać = to plane, 1st pers. sing. Pres. strużę
duch   = spirit,   dusza (< duch-ja) = soul
cichy   = quiet (adj.), cisza = quiet (noun)

t, d + j become *c* and *dz* respectively:—

wypłata = paying, płaca (< płatja) = pay
płacić = to pay (with soft *t'* > *ć* before *i*),
    1st pers. sg. Pres. płacę, zapłacony = paid
świeca = candle (< světja)
widać   = one can see, widzieć = to see (with
    soft *d'* > *dź* before *ie*), 1st pers. sg. Pres.
    widzę
miedza (< medja) = boundary, balk

s, z + j become *sz, ż* respectively:—
pisać = to write, 1st pers. sg. Pres. piszę
wiązać = to bind, 1st pers. sg. Pres. wiążę

ł + j becomes *l*, while soft *n* and *l + j* remain unchanged and absorb it:—

słać (< stłać) = to spread, 1st pers. sg.
                 Pres.   ścielę
pozwolić   = to allow, 1st pers. sg.
                 Pfve. Fut.   pozwolę
                 Past Part. Pass.   pozwolonv
gonić   = pursue, 1st pers. sg.
                 Pres.   gonię
                 Past Part. Pass.   goniony

r + j becomes *rz*:—
orać = to plough, 1st pers. sg. Pres. orzę, 2nd
       pers. sg. orzesz, etc.
morze (< morje) = sea

p, b, w, m + j become soft and are spelt *pi, bi, wi, mi*:—
tępy   = blunt, tępić   = to blunt, exterminate
                           1st pers. sg. Pres.
                           tępię
luby   = dear, lubić   = to like, 1st pers. sg.
                           Pres. lubię
postawa = posture, postawić = to place, 1st pers. sg.
                           Pfve. Fut. postawię
łamać   = to break, 1st pers. sg. Pres. łamię
ziemia = earth, cf. Russ. земля

st, zd + *j* become *szcz, żdż* respectively:—
chłostać = to whip,   1st pers. sg. Pres. chłoszczę,
           2nd p.s. chłoszczesz
gwizdać = to whistle, 1st pers. sg. Pres. gwiżdżę,
           2nd p. sg. gwiżdżesz

ść, żdż + *j* (the soft versions of *st, zd*) also be-
become *szcz, żdż* respectively:—
puścić = to let go, 1st pers. sg. Pfve. Fut. puszczę
jazda = cavalry, ride, jeździć = to travel, be con-
         veyed (Freq.), 1st pers. sg. Pres. jeżdżę

sk, zg + *j* also become *szcz, żdż* respectively:—
głaskać = to caress, 1st pers. sg. Pres. głaszczę
          (also głaskam)
miazga = pulp, miażdżyć = to crush
          Past Part. Pass. zmiażdżony = crushed

5. The spelling of Polish is largely "historical"; and though on the whole the consonantal system
of Polish is rather conservative, yet there are quite
a number of examples of losses of consonants.
The old Common Slav ones are evident in:—

      sen   = sleep, dream   from *sъpn-
      pot   = sweat   "   *pokt-
      utonąć = to drown(intrans.) "   *utopn-

Characteristic of all West Slav languages, including Polish, is the retention of the dentals before an l in terminations, e.g.:—
pleść = to weave, plait, 1st pers. sing. Pres.:
        plotę, Past: plótł, plotła
paść (Pfve.) = to fall, 1st pers. sing. Fut.: padnę,
        Past: padł, padła
(Colloquially the 3rd pers. sing. masc. forms
of the Past tense, ending in stop + ł, are generally pronounced without this ł, viz. plót, pat.
Cf. jabłko = apple, pron. japko.)

Simplifications of groups of consonants are
evident in:—

   miłosny   = (of) love (adj.), with loss of t,
               for miłostny
   świsnąć   = to give a whistle, whizz, with loss
     (Pfve.)   of t, for świstnąć
   posłać   = to spread, with loss of t, for
     (Pfve.)   postłać
   miłosierny = charitable, merciful, with loss of
                d, for miłosierdny
   błysnąć   = to flash, with loss of k, for
     (Pfve.)   błysknąć

bryznąć = to splash, gush, with loss of g,
(Pfve.)   for bryzgnąć
saski = Saxon, with loss of s, for sasski
francuski = French, with loss of z, for francuz-
    ski
włoski = Italian (from Włoch), with loss of
    sz, for włoszski
boski = divine (from Bóg), with loss of ż,
    for bożski
kozacki = Cossack (adj.), from Kozak
ptactwo = birds (collectively), from ptak
bractwo = brotherhood, from brat
świecki = worldly, secular, from świat = world

Note the spelling of:—

grodzki (pron. grocki) = town (adj.), from
    gród
ludzki (pron. lucki) = human, from lud =
    people

Notice also:—

trześnia = sweet cherry, for czrześnia
trzoda = flock, herd, for czrzoda
  cf. czereśnia = cherry tree, with *Polnoglasie*
    from Ukrainian
and czereda = throng, with *Polnoglasie* from
    Ukrainian.

Somewhat irregular, with anticipation of palatalization, are:—

ojciec, Gen. sing. ojca, = father (for ociec,
    oćca)
miejski = town (adj.), from miasto = town

and by analogy with the latter we have—

wiejski = country (adj.), from wieś = village

Adjectives and surnames ending in *-owski, -ewski*, are often pronounced -oski, -eski, e.g.:—

żydowski = Jewish

Adjectives and surnames ending in *-ński* are sometimes pronounced without a true ń, as if they ended in -jski preceded by a nasal vowel, e.g.:—

świński = piggish, pron. śwĩjski (~ indicates nasal
    vowel)
Wyspiański (surname), pron.
    wysp'ãjski   ("   "   "
                                    ")

6. Epenthesis and prothesis of consonants.

An epenthetic soft *n* is used with the 3rd person Personal Pronoun after prepositions:—

   on = he, do niego = to him, do nich = to them

   It also appears in śniadanie = breakfast (from s + ĕd)

A prothetic w is frequent before the nasal vowels, e.g.:

   wąski = narrow,   cf. Russ. у́зкий
   węzeł = knot,   "   у́зел
   wąchać = to smell   "   благоуха́ние = aroma
             (trans.),

FEATURES CHARACTERISTIC OF POLISH

1. The penultimate stress. (See "Pronunciation, the Accent".)

2. The preservation of the nasal vowels ę and ą. These, however, do not correspond in position to the Old Slav nasal vowels ѧ and ѫ. Their development, in the main outlines, is as follows (O.S. forms first for comparison):—

ę = ѧ, being a front vowel, developed into -*ię* in modern Polish when it used to be short in Old Polish, e.g.:—

O.S. сѧ   = self, Pol. się,   cf. Cz. se, Slk. sa,
              Serbocr. ce
"   пѧть = five, Pol. pięć, cf. Cz. pět, Slk. päť,
              Serbocr. пêт

and into -*ią* when it used to be long, e.g.:—

пѧтъ = fifth, Pol. piąty, cf. Cz. pátý, Slk. piaty,
         Sbcr. пêти
тѧгнѫти (Pfve.) = to pull, Pol. ciągnąć (Impfve.),
         Cz. tahnouti, Slk. tiahnut',
         Sbcr. (ис)те́гнути = to draw out.

Similarly, with ѩ initially:—

ѩзꙑкъ = tongue, Pol. język, Cz. and Slk. jazyk,
         Sbcr. jèзик
ѩдро = kernel, Pol. jądro, Cz. jádro, Slk. jadro,
         (Sbcr. jèзгра)

Similarly, ǫ = ѫ, being originally a back vowel, developed into ę when formerly short:—

рѫка   = hand, Pol. ręka, Cz. ruka, Slk. ruka,
            Sbcr. ру́ка, Russ. рука́
рѫкѫ   (Acc. sing.), Pol. rękę, Cz. ruku, Slk.
            ruku, Sbcr. ру̑ку, Russ. ру́ку
люб(л)ѫ = I love, Pol. lubię = I like

and into q when formerly long, e.g.:—

сѫтъ = they are, Pol. są, Cz. jsou, Slk. sú, Sbcr. cy

несѫтъ = they carry, Pol. niosą, Cz. nesou, Slk. nesú, Sbcr. до̀несу̂

сѫдъ = court of justice, Pol. sąd, Cz. soud, Slk. súd, Sbcr. су̂д

q was also the result when ѭ was contracted with another vowel, e.g.:—

женоѭ (Instr. sg.) = woman, Pol. żoną, Cz. and Slk. ženou, (Sbcr. жѐном), Slovenian: žéno̩

But when a syllable became closed with a final hard consonant, especially if voiced, in Polish it was originally lengthened, a fact now reflected in ę being replaced by ą, e.g.:—

дѫбъ = oak, Pol. dąb, Cz. dub, Slk. dub, Sbcr. ду̂б

but—

дѫба (Gen. sg.), Pol. dęba,[1] Cz. dubu, Slk. duba, Sbcr. ду̂ба

рѫкъ (Gen. pl. of рѫка), Pol. rąk, (Cz. rukou— from Dual), Slk. rúk, (Sbcr. ру̀кӯ), cf.—

rączka = handle; however, ręczny = hand (adj.), manual

cf. also—

jagnię = lamb, jagniątko = little lamb

Like dąb: błąd = mistake, Gen. sg. błędu
but— sęp = vulture, Gen. sg. sępa
sęk = knot(in wood), Gen. sg. sęka, etc.

In the Past Tense and Past Participle Active of verbs, the same change of vowel occurs as with dąb, e.g.:—

dął = he was blowing, fem. dęła, neut. dęło, plur. dęli, dęły.

In early Polish, e.g., in the Psałterz Floriański (XIV century) only one letter, ǫ, is used for the nasal vowels. It is supposed that this implied only one nasal vowel in the pronunciation of that time, with the preservation still of differences of length (quantity) which are known to have survived till considerably later. Later on, quantity decided, together with the nature of the subsequent consonant or consonants, whether ą should be pronounced for the long nasal vowel or ę for the short.

[1] dęba = of the oak tree; dębu = of oak (wood).

POLISH

Owing to differences in the original Common Slav and its subsequent development, it will be found that the ą does not *always* correspond to long vowels or diphthongs in Czech and Slovak. Serbocroatian is even less of a guide. Cf.:—

мѫка = torment, Russ. му́ка, Pol. męka, Cz. muka, Slk. muka, Sbcr. му̑ка
мѫка = flour, Russ. мука́, Pol. mąka, Cz. mouka, Slk. múka, Sbcr. му́ка (usually бра̏шно)

but—

Pol. mąż = husband, Cz. and Slk. muž = man, Sbcr. му̑ж
" nędza = misery, Cz. nouze, Slk. núdza
" pęto = tether, Cz. pouto, Slk. puto

again—

będę = I shall be, Cz. budu, Slk. budem

but—

bądź = be!, Cz. buď!, Slk. buď!

Analogy, especially in less common words, also tends to level out these alternations of vowels.

3. The development of the semivowels, ъ into *e*, ь into *ie*, in strong position, e.g.:—

O.S. сънъ = sleep, dream, Pol. sen, Gen. sg. snu
" пьсъ = dog, " pies, Gen. sg. psa
" вьсь = village, " wieś, Gen. sg. wsi

(Finally ь causes the preceding consonant to become palatalized, as in the last example.)

So also usually with the development of the C.S. combinations rъ, rь, lъ, lь when stressed, e.g.:—

O.S. кръвь = blood, Pol krew, Gen.sg. krwi
кръстъ = cross, " chrzest, " " chrztu = baptism
плъть = flesh, " płeć " " płci = sex

But (unstressed):—

O.S. сльза = tear, Pol. łza, Gen. pl. łez
cf. " pchła, " " pcheł = flea
also Russian: слеза́, блоха́.

4. The development of vocalic ļ and ŗ (O.S. лъ, ль, ръ, рь). Polish distinguishes between original hard and soft vocalic liquids, not properly distinguished in O.S.:—

hard ŗ regularly develops into -*ar*:—

O.S. трьгъ = market, Pol. targ
" гръбъ = hump, " garb

soft ę develops into *ar* only before hard dentals:—

O.S. тврьдъ = firm, Pol. twardy = hard
" мрьтвъ = dead, " martwy
" чрьнъ = black, " czarny

in all other cases ę becomes -*ier*- or -*ierz*:—

O.S. съмрьть = death   Pol. śmierć
" тврьдити = to make firm, " twierdzić =
                                              to affirm
" врьхъ = top,   " wierzch

Both l̥ and l̥' after dentals developed into *łu*:—

O.S. стлъпъ = pillar, Pol. słup = pole, pillar
" тлъкѫ = I knock, " tłukę = I pound
" длъгъ = long, " długi
" слъньце = sun, cf. słuńce in Old Polish,
                      modern Pol. słońce

l̥ after velars became -*eł*, e.g.:—

kiełbasa   = sausage, cf. Slovak klbása, as
                       well as klobása
zgiełk   = tumult
chełpić się = to boast

l̥ after labials became first *oł*, then *o*, and sometimes *eł*:—

mowa = speech, < mołwa, cf. Russ. молва́ = talk
-pełk in names: Świętopełk, cf. Russ. Святопо́лк

l̥' before hard dentals became *eł*:—

wełna = wool
pełny = full

but after *cz*, *ż*, *sz* l̥' has changed to *oł*, *ół*:—

czółno = boat
żółty = yellow

l̥' before other consonants becomes *il*:—

wilk = wolf
milczeć = to be silent

5. The vowel alternations *ę/ą* (see the development of the nasal vowels, No. 2 above) and *o/ó* (*io/ió*):—

o represents a former short vowel, while
ó represents a former long vowel which was also more closed in quality.
Cf. Cz, vůz, Gen. sg. vozu (= waggon).

o usually changed to *ó* when a syllable became closed, especially before a voiced consonant except a nasal (*n* or *m*):—

    plotła = she was weaving, but masc. plótł
    niosła = she was carrying, but masc. niósł
    krowa = cow   but Gen. pl. krów;
                                      krówka = little cow

but—

    sroka = magpie, sroczka—diminutive.

So also—

    robić = to do, Imperat. rób!

but—

    poprosić = to request, Imperat. poproś!
    bronić = to defend, Imperat. broń!
    (chodź = go! and woź = convey! are exceptions.)

Note also:—

    róg   = corner, Gen. sg. rogu, etc.
    kościół = church, "   " kościoła,
    lód   = ice,   "   " lodu

but—

    dom   = house   "   " domu, cf. Cz. dům,
                                                         domu.
    kot   = tom-cat, "   " kota

So also:—

    droga = road, Gen. pl. dróg
    pole = field,   "   pól

but—

    sroka = magpie, " srok
    strona = side,   " stron
    kosa = scythe, " kos

Cf. mowa = speech, mówić = to speak.

    6. The vowel alternations *ie/ia* (from ě, O.S. ѣ, —its regular development in Polish) and *ie/io* (from e, and sometimes from ь and ѣ).

ie (e) from ѣ regularly changed to *ia* (a) before *hard* dentals, e.g.:—

    bielić = to whiten, but biały = white, Comp.
                                        bielszy = whiter

Similarly:—

świat = world, Loc. sg. (na) świecie
las = wood, " (w) lesie, adj. leśny
lato = summer, " (w) lecie
miasto = town, " (w) mieście
miara = measure, " (w) mierze; mierzyć = to measure
wiatr = wind, but wietrzny = windy
  (rz, like the other *chuintantes*, was formerly soft)
jadę = I go (am conveyed), 2nd pers. sg. jedziesz, etc., but 3rd pers. plur. jadą
widział = he saw, but 3rd p. pl. masc. pers. widzieli
śmiał = he dared, but 3rd p. pl. masc. pers. śmieli

So also, from Infin. słyszeć:—

słyszał = heard, but 3rd p. pl. masc. pers. słyszeli

On the other hand, in the adjectives analogy has worked the other way:—

śmiały = bold, Nom. plur. masc. pers. śmiali (for śmieli)
  like biały, biali, etc. Cf. Bulg. бял = white, fem. бѣла, Pl. бѣли.

ie (*e*) from e (and occasionally from ь and ě = ѣ) becomes *io* (*o*) before hard dentals, while *io* (*o*) reverts to *ie* (*e*) before soft dentals:—

niesie = he carries, but niosę = I carry, niosą = they carry
nieśli = they were carrying (masc. pers.), but niosły for other plural nouns.
kościół = church, Gen. sg. kościoła, but Loc. sg. w kościele
  cf. Cz. kostel, from Latin castellum.
ożenić = to marry (of a man), żeński = feminine, but żona = wife.
  Analogy has made the Dat./Loc. sg. żonie for żenie.
imię = name, has Gen. sg. imienia, but Nom. pl. imiona, etc.
siedzieć = to sit, but siodło = saddle
ziele = herb, has Nom. pl. zioła
zielony = green, has Nom. pl. masc. pers. zieleni
Similarly all Past Particles Passive: in -*ony*, -*iony*:—
niesiony = carried (Past Part. Pass.), has Nom. pl. masc. pers. niesieni

POLISH

With ь and ѣ as the origin of *ie/io* we have:—

    wieś = village, diminutive: wioska; O.S. вьсь
    osieł or osioł = donkey (from ь); O.S. осьлъ
    pieśń = song, diminutive: piosnka; O.S. пѣснь
    sień = hall, diminutive: sionka; O.S. сѣнь

7. The sounds *ś* (*si*), *ź* (*zi*) (palato-alveolar fricatives) for soft *s* and *z*:—

    kosa = scythe, Dat./Loc. sg. kosie
    koza = goat,   "   "   " kozie

8. The sounds *ć* (*ci*), *dź* (*dzi*) (palato-alveolar affricates) from soft *t* and *d*. (Cf. Sbcr. ħ, ђ).

    cień = shadow
    życie = life, cf. Sbcr. пиħe = drink
    dziad = grandfather, cf. Sbcr. je-dialect: ђȅд
                                      as well as дјȅд

In Polish soft dentals are hardened when they become followed by other dentals:—

    osioł   = donkey, Gen. sg. osła
    orzeł   = eagle,   "   " orła
    marzec   = March,   "   " marca
    dzień   = day,   "   " dnia
    kwiecień = April,   "   " kwietnia
    ciąć   = to hew, 1st pers. sg. Pres. tnę

9. Soft *r* and *r* + *j* both become *rz* in Polish:—

    siostra = sister, Dat./Loc. sg. siostrze
    morze   = sea, O.S. морје
    orać   = to plough, 1st pers. sg. Pres. orzę

10. Three varieties of *l*: *ł* for hard l, *l* (medium) for soft l except before *i*,[1] when what is written also *l* is pronounced soft l (*ļ*, phon. λ), e.g.:—

               łapa = paw
               lato = summer
               list = letter

11. Infinitives (of class I) with roots in a velar *g* or *k*, end in *c*:—

   mogę = I can, Infin. móc cf. Upper Lusatian móc
   piekę = I bake, "   piec   "   "   pjec

12. As in Slovak, *d* + *j* becomes *dz* in Polish:—

        miedza = boundary, Slk. medza
        widzę = I see

---

[1] According to K. Nitsch, λ does not occur in N. Polish pronunciation.

13. As in Ukrainian in certain cases, *zd* + *j* becomes *żdż*:—

    jeździć = to travel (Freq.), Pres. jeżdżę, cf.
                  Ukr. приїжджа́ти = to arrive.

14. *g*, *k* are softened before *e* and original *y*, becoming *gie*, *kie*, *gi*, *ki*; cf. Russian, Byelorussian, and Lusatian for *y*:—

        ślad = trace,   Instr. sg. śladem
but— róg = horn,   "   rogiem
       buk = beech,   "   bukiem

Also— kiedy = when (from къ-), cf. Slovak ked'
       ginąć = to perish, O.S. гъібнѫти

        żona = wife, Gen. sg. żony
but— noga = foot,   "   nogi
       ręka = hand,   "   ręki

True -ke and -ge are heard, when -*kę* and -*gę* occur finally, as in the Acc. sg. of fem. *a*-stem nouns and the 1st pers. sg. Pres. of verbs:—

        rękę = hand, phon. 'rɛŋkɛ
        nogę = foot,   "   'nɔgɛ
        mogę = I can,   "   'mɔgɛ

15. Soft labials occur only medially; final labials, originally soft (in words and syllables), are hardened, as in Ukrainian, Byelorussian, and other West and South Slav languages:—

    gołąb   = pigeon, Gen. sg. gołębia
    modrzew = larch,   "   " modrzewia
    robić   = to do, Imper. 2nd p. sg. rób! 2nd p.
             pl. róbcie!
    stąpić (Pfve.) = to step, Imper. 2nd p. sg.
             stąp! 2nd p. pl. stąpcie!
    postawić(Pfve.) = to place, Imper. 2nd p. sg.
             postaw! 2nd p. pl. postawcie!
    łamać   = to break, Pres. łamię, Imper. łam!

16. C.S./O.S. ъі preserved as *y*, distinct from *i*, except after *k* and *g*, cf. Russian, Byelorussian and Lusatian, e.g.:—

  być = to be
  myśl = thought
  ty   = thou, but Dat.(enclitic) ci, cf. O.S. тъі, ти

Features common to Polish, Czech, and Slovak
    For "Features characteristic of Czech, Slovak, and Polish," see pp. 57-60 in the Czech Section.

POLISH

POLISH MORPHOLOGY

Its Peculiarities and Features

Both in the nouns and verbs Polish has lost the old Dual number as a grammatical category; but like other Slavonic languages, it has preserved the three genders.

In the declensions it preserves seven cases, the Vocative singular having a separate form from the Nominative singular in masculine and feminine substantives. Otherwise, Voc. = Nom. In the declensions there are hard and soft types, the latter having a special sub-type—the stems ending in a "functionally" or "historically" soft (or "ex-palatal") consonant, namely *c, cz, sz, rz, ż,* and occasionally *dż*. These consonants, which were originally palatal but are now hard, cannot be followed by the vowel *i*, but have *-y* instead. This causes a certain dislocation in the schemes of endings and creates in some cases almost a third category, to which the foreign learner has to pay special attention. This phonetic feature also creates special sub-types of verbs.

The vowel alternations (see Nos. 2, 5, and 6 of "Features characteristic of Polish" above) which occur both in the declensions and conjugations, are another feature of Polish which the student has to watch.

The most remarkable feature of all Polish declensions is the complete generalization for nouns of *all* genders of the old masculine *o*-stem ending of the Dative plural *-om*. While the Instrumental and Locative plural of almost all nouns end in *-ami, -ach*, respectively, as in East Slav. As in East and other West Slav languages, the old hard *a-* and *o*-stem endings have predominated in certain cases; but in no other Slav language have the old (short) *ŭ*-stems left such widespread, if irregular, traces in the declension of masc. *o*-stem nouns in the singular and Nom. and Gen. plural (the endings *-u, -owi, -owie, -ów*). The student should also watch the regular softening of consonants that takes place before the ending *-ie* (< ѣ = ě) in the Dat. and Loc. singular, e.g.:—

chata = (peasant) house, Dat./Loc. sg. chacie

The characteristic Polish spelling takes one by surprise at first.

In the declension of the plural of masculine substantives, numerals, pronouns, adjectives, participles and in the Past Tense of verbs, Polish has developed a new division of the genders, singling out masculine persons in contrast to all other nouns, viz. masculine animate (animals) and inanimate, feminine, and neuter nouns. Except in the substantives these "other genders" all have identical endings (case by case). Cf. Slovak and Upper Lusatian.

The complications in the numerals are especially unexpected to those who know other Slavonic languages.

Polish pronouns are characterized by the existence of enclitic alternatives, used when there is no emphasis on the pronoun—a feature unknown in modern East Slav languages. Polish has slightly fewer exclusively enclitic pronouns than other West and South Slav languages.

The adjectives have the peculiarly Polish ending -(i)ego in the Gen. sing. masculine and neuter, while in the Nom./Voc./Acc. sing. neuter they are characterized by the ending -e, a West Slav feature.

The most important peculiarities of Polish verbs are:—

1. The ending -my in the 1st pers. plur. of all tenses.

2. The ending -ą in the 3rd pers. plur. Pres. or Pfve. Fut. of *all* verbs, both of the old *e*-type (including modern *a*-types) and the old *i*-type. Cf. Bulg. -ат/-ят for both types.

3. In the 1st pers. sing. Pres. the old ending -ж, when preserved, always gives -ę (colloquially pronounced just *e*).

4. Like other West Slav languages, and Serbocroätian and Slovenian, Polish has lost the ending -t in both 3rd pers. sing. and 3rd pers. plur. Pres.

5. In the Future of Impfve. and Frequentative verbs the Future of the verb "to be"—będę, etc., is used with the Past Participle Active in -ł, -ła, -ło, a feature Polish shares only with Slovenian. But in Polish one can use the Infinitive, as in other West and East Slav languages, as an alternative, identical in meaning to the Past Part. Active in -ł, e.g.:—

      będę pisał (Freq. pisywał) = I shall write

or

      pisać (Freq. pisywać) będę

6. The Past Tense and Conditional are characterized by transferable personal endings in the 1st and 2nd pers. sing. and plur. These are remnants of enclitic auxiliary verbs, such as are used in other West and South Slav languages. As the Past Part. Active, which precedes them, also varies according to gender, this leads to a great multiplication of forms, as compared with East Slav. (The *3rd* pers.

sing. and plur. Past, which have no personal ending, are identical in form with the Past Part. Active). E.g.:—

    pisałem = I was writing; kiedym pisał = when I was writing
    wzięlibyśmy = we (masc.) would take, but—
    jeżelibyśmy wzięli = if we would take

7. The Infinitive in Polish regularly ends in -ć, as in Upper Lusatian, except in velar stems of Class I, which have special endings also in other Slavonic languages, e.g.:—

    pisać = to write, paść = to fall, but piec = to bake

8. Reflexive verbs are formed by using the Accusative enclitic Reflexive Pronoun się, which is written separately, in contrast to East Slav, with Active verbs.

9. się can be used with Verbal Nouns, as in Slovak.

DECLENSION OF NOUNS

1. i-stems, all feminine.
These fall into three main types:—

(a) soft stems with Nom. plur. in -i (this category includes all the abstract nouns ending in -ość, e.g. miłość = love.)

(b) soft stems with Nom. plur. in -e (spreading in modern Polish, but nouns coming into this category defy classification).

(c) ex-palatal stems (ending in c, cz, sz, rz, ż)—these can have Nom. plur. in -e or -y. In the other cases this class has the ending -y, where nouns of classes (a) and (b) have -i, according to the rules of Polish phonetics and orthography.

Sing. (a) kość = bone; (b) łódź = boat; (c) mysz = mouse

Nom.	kość	łódź	mysz[1]
Gen.	kości	łodzi	myszy
Dat.	kości	łodzi	myszy
Acc.	kość	łódź	mysz
Instr.	kością	łodzią	myszą
Loc. Voc.	kości	łodzi	myszy
Plur.			
Nom.	kości	łodzie	myszy

[1] noc (= night) follows the declension of mysz, but has the ending -e in Nom./Voc./ Acc. plural: noce.

Gen.	kości	łodzi	myszy
Dat.	kościom	łodziom	myszom
Acc.	kości	łodzie	myszy
Inst.	kośćmi (kościami)[1]	łodziami	myszami
Loc.	kościach	łodziach	myszach

Soft labials are not indicated in the Nom. sing., but nouns so ending follow the declension of either kość or łódź, e.g.:—

    brew = eyebrow (with movable *e*), Gen. sg. brwi, Nom. pl. brwi

    cerkiew = (Orthodox) Church (with movable *e*), Gen. sg. cerkwi, Nom. pl. cerkwie

A few nouns of this class end in *-j*, e.g. kolej = railway, track, succession. The final -j disappears before the *-i* in the Gen., Dat., Loc., Voc. sing. and Gen. plur.: kolei; Nom./Voc./Acc. pl. koleje, according to class (*b*).

Wieś (= village) belongs to class (*b*). It has a movable *ie* in Nom./Acc. sing.: Gen., Dat., Loc., Voc. sing. wsi, Instr. s. wsią; Nom./Voc./Acc. plur. wsie, Gen. plur. wsi, Dat. plur. wsiom, Instr. plur. wsiami, Loc. plur. wsiach.

2. Consonantal stems, neuter only.

In Polish both the *n*-stems and the *t*-stems survive, but they have the *endings* of neuter (soft) *jo*-stems in the sing. and neuter (hard) *o*-stems in the plural, i.e. the stem is soft in the sing. and hard in the plural.

    imię = (Christian) name; cielę = calf

Sing.		
Nom.	imię	cielę
Gen.	imienia	cielęcia
Dat.	imieniu	cielęciu
Acc.	imię	cielę
Instr.	imieniem	cielęciem
Loc.	imieniu	cielęciu
Plur.		
Nom.	imiona	cielęta
Gen.	imion	cieląt
Dat.	imionom	cielętom
Acc.	imiona	cielęta
Instr.	imionami	cielętami
Loc.	imionach	cielętach

---

[1] The Instr. plur. of kość is exceptional. Most nouns of class (*a*) have Instr. plur. in *-iami*, e.g.: sieć, (= net), sieciami.

książę (Nom., Voc. sg. *masc.*, = prince) follows cielę in the sing. in lofty style only; it is usually contracted, viz. Gen., Acc. sing. księcia, Dat., Loc. sing. księciu, Instr. sing. księciem. In the plur. it follows cielę: Nom., Voc. książęta, *Acc.*, Gen. książąt, etc.

niebo (= sky, heaven), a neuter o-stem in the sing., has an alternative s-stem plural: Nom., Voc., Acc. niebiosa, Gen. niebios, Dat. niebiosom, Instr. niebiosami, Loc. niebiosach.

3. a-stems, mainly feminine, soft and hard.

In the Gen. sing. the old a-stem ending has predominated, giving the ending -*i* in the soft stems and -*y* in the ex-palatal stems (*c, dz, cz, dż, sz, rz,* and *ż*). In the Dat. and Loc. sing. the old *ja*-stem ending -*i* has been preserved for soft stems, but in the Nom. Voc. Acc. plur. soft stems have -*e* (cf. *i*-stems).

To the soft stems belong nouns in -*ni*, which may be regarded as being irregular in the Nom., Voc. sing. only. (They actually preserve an old Slavonic ending.)

Masculine nouns in -*a* follow the *a*-stems in the sing. only. In the plural they (almost all) have the endings of masc. *o*-stems. The same is true of masc. proper names with -*o* in Nom., Voc. sing.

In the hard feminine *a*-stems, in the Dat. and Loc. sing. before the soft ending -*ie* the usual consonantal changes from hard to soft take place. Velar stems in *k* and *g* have -*i* instead of -*y* in the Gen. sing. and Nom., Voc., Acc. plur. and the 2nd Palatalization in the Dat. and Loc. sing. Velar stems in *ch* keep -*y* in Gen. sing. and Nom., Voc., Acc. plur. and have the *2nd* Palatalization in the Dat. and Loc. sing.: mucha (= fly), Gen. sg. and Nom./Voc./Acc. plur. muchy, Dat./Loc. sg. musze.

In the Gen. plur. the fill-vowel -e- is inserted in consonantal groups which would otherwise be difficult to pronounce.

Hard stems kobieta = woman; matka = mother

Sing.
Nom.	kobieta	matka
Gen.	kobiety	matki
Dat.	kobiecie	matce
Acc.	kobietę	matkę
Instr.	kobietą	matką
Loc.	kobiecie	matce
Voc.	kobieto	matko

POLISH

	Plur.	
Nom.	kobiety	matki
Gen.	kobiet	matek
Dat.	kobietom	matkom
Acc.	kobiety	matki
Instr.	kobietami	matkami
Loc.	kobietach	matkach

Notice the change of vowel in the Gen. plur. of, e.g.:—

noga = foot, leg, Gen. pl. nóg
księga = big book, Gen. pl. ksiąg

Soft stems

rola = soil, field; rôle; ziemia = earth, land; armia = army; poezja = poetry; gospodyni = lady of the house

Sing.					
Nom.	rola	ziemia	armia	poezja[1]	gospodyni[2]
Gen.	roli	ziemi	armii	poezji	gospodyni
Dat.	roli	ziemi	armii	poezji	gospodyni
Acc.	rolę	ziemię	armię	poezję	gospodynię
Instr.	rolą	ziemią	armią	poezją	gospodynią
Loc.	roli	ziemi	armii	poezji	gospodyni
Voc.	rolo	ziemio	armio	poezjo	gospodyni
Plur.					
Nom.	role	ziemie	armie	poezje	gospodynie
Gen.	ról	ziem	armii	poezji	gospodyń
		(-ij)	(-zyj)		
Dat.	rolom	ziemiom	armiom	poezjom	gospodyniom
Acc.	role	ziemie	armie	poezje	gospodynie
Instr.	rolami	ziemiami	armiami	poezjami	gospodyniami
Loc.	rolach	ziemiach	armiach	poezjach	gospodyniach

	Feminine Ex-palatal stem.	*Masculine Hard stem.*	*Masculine Ex-palatal stem.*	*Masculine Nom. in -o.*
	praca = work	poeta = poet	radca = councillor	Kościuszko (name)
Nom.	praca	poeta[3]	radca	Kościuszko
Gen.	pracy	poety	radcy	Kościuszki
Dat.	pracy	poecie	radcy	Kościuszce
Acc.	pracę	poetę	radcę	Kościuszkę

[1] In the latest orthography j occurs only after c, s, and z: lekcja = lesson, Francja = France, Rosja = Russia.
[2] Pani (= lady) has an irregular Acc. sing. panią.
[3] mężczyzna (= man) has Gen. plur. mężczyzn.

Instr.	pracą	poetą	radcą	Kościuszką
Loc.	pracy	poecie	radcy	Kościuszce
Voc.	praco	poeto	radco	Kościuszko

Plur.

Nom.	prace	poeci	radcy	Kościuszkowie
Gen.	prac	poetów	radców	Kościuszków
Dat.	pracom	poetom	radcom	Kościuszkom
Acc.	prace	poetów	radców	Kościuszków
Instr.	pracami	poetami	radcami	Kościuszkami
Loc.	pracach	poetach	radcach	Kosciuszkach

The plural of ręka (= hand) is irregular, showing survival of the Dual in the Nom., Voc., Acc., and Instr., and goes as follows:—

N., V., A.; rękę, G. rąk, D. rękom, I. rękami or rękoma, L. rękach. ręku is an alternative Loc. s. form.

Rzeczpospòlita (= republic) and Wielkanoc (= Easter) are really compounds and decline as follows:—

Nom.	rzeczpospolita	Wielkanoc
Gen.	rzeczypospolitej	Wielkanocy (or Wielkiejnocy)
Dat.	rzeczypospolitej	Wielkanocy (or Wielkiejnocy)
Acc.	rzeczpospolitą	Wielkanoc
Instr.	rzecząpospolitą	Wielkanocą
Loc.	rzeczypospolitej	Wielkanocy (or Wielkiejnocy)
Voc.	rzeczypospolita	Wielkanocy

The masculines sędzia (= judge), hrabia (= count) and a few others are declined like adjectives (sic) in the Gen./Acc., and Dat. sing., e.g.:—

Gen./Acc. sędziego, Dat. sędziemu.

4a. Masculine o-stems.

There are fundamentally two basic types of masculine declension in Polish: the hard-stem declension (e.g. pan = gentleman), and the soft-stem declension (e.g. koń = horse) together with the ex-palatal stems (such as: żołnierz = soldier). But the division between these is blurred by two factors: (1) the strong, but inconsistent influence on the endings of the old (short) ŭ-declension (e.g. O.S. сынъ)—stronger than in other Slavonic languages; (2) the characteristically Polish distinction of *personal* nouns as opposed to impersonal. In the singular other *animate* nouns, e.g. the names of animals, are classed with the personal nouns, but *not* in the plural (in contrast to the usage in Russian).

This distinction is particularly observable in the *Nom., plural*, where the ending -*owie* is used only with nouns indicating persons, usually implying a certain degree of respect, rank, etc., e.g. panowie =

gentlemen, profesorowie = professors, królowie = kings, etc. However, many old and frequently used nouns do not follow this general rule, e.g.:—

    sąsiedzi = neighbours
    Polacy = Poles
    kupcy = merchants
    nauczyciele = teachers

and forms like syny = sons (contemptuous).

The endings -*y* for hard stems and -*e* for soft stems are regular for nonpersonal nouns, e.g.:—

    dom = house, Nom. pl. domy
    koń = horse,   "   konie
    krzyż = cross,   "   krzyże

In the *Acc. sing.* the same distinction is made as in other Slavonic languages, i.e. Acc. sing. = Gen. sing. for all animate nouns, but Acc. sing. = Nom. sing. for inanimates. In the *plural* Acc. = Gen. only for masculine *personal* nouns.

In the *Gen. sing.* most nouns denoting inanimates have the ending -*u* instead of -*a*, such as:—

1. collectives and composites, e.g.:—

    lud = people
    miód = honey, mead
    piasek = sand
    pociąg = train
    dwór = court

2. abstracts, e.g.:—

    rozum = reason, sense
    powód = cause
    czas = time

3. senses, e.g.:—

    wzrok = sight
    węch = smell

4. sounds, e.g.:—

    dzwięk = sound
    głos = voice
    płacz = weeping
    śmiech = laughter

5. forms and directions, e.g.:—

    kształt = form
    bok = side
    szczyt = summit
    wschód = east
    zachód = west

6. motions and conditions, e.g.:—

>   stan   = condition, state
>   głód   = hunger
>   ból   = pain
>   sen   = sleep
>   spokój = peace
>   wiatr   = wind

7. days of the week, when masculine, e.g.:—

>   wtorek = Tuesday

8. some geographical names, e.g.:—

>   Ren   = Rhine
>   Dunaj   = Danube
>   Londyn   = London
>   Rzym   = Rome
>   Waszyngton = Washington
>   Kaukaz   = Caucasus

9. words of Latin or French origin, e.g.:—

>   honor   = honour
>   kolor   = colour
>   papier   = paper
>   portret   = portrait
>   teatr   = theatre
>   wagon   = waggon, railway carriage
>   instynkt = instinct
>   atrament = ink
>   gaz   = gas
>   hotel   = hotel

A few nouns such as zamek (= lock, castle) use the ending -*a* for one meaning, e.g. zamka (= of a lock), and -*u* for the other, i.e. zamku (= of a castle). But this is quite exceptional.

Only one name of an animal has a Gen. sing. in -*u*:—

>   wół = ox, Gen. sing. wołu,

but its Acc. sing. is woła!

According to some, the ending -*u* is "more elegant," hence its use in abstract and foreign words.

The ending -*u* also occurs in the *Dat. sing.* of about twenty old and "primitive" (mostly monosyllabic) nouns:—

>   panu = to the lord, gentleman
>   kotu = to the tom-cat

But the ending -*owi* is much more frequently used for the Dat. sing.

-u can also be used in the *Loc. sing.*; it is the only normal form in soft, ex-palatal and velar stems, e.g.:—

> o kraju = about the land
> o kupcu = about the merchant
> o Polaku = about the Pole

The same general rule applies for the use of *-u* in the *Voc. sing.*

In the *Instr. sing.* the ending is always *-em*, except after *k* and *g*, when it is *-iem*, e.g.:—

> strach = fear, Instr. sing. strachem,

but—

> róg = horn, corner, Instr. sing. rogiem.

In the *Gen. plur. -ów* is by far the commonest ending for nouns of all categories, *-i* being used for some soft nouns and *-y* for some ex-palatal stems. *-ów* is obligatory for nouns with Nom. plur. in *-owie*.

In the *Dat., Instr. and Loc. plur.* the endings in modern Polish are regularly *-om*, *-ami*, *-ach*, respectively. *Voc. pl.* = Nom. pl.

To the masc. *o*-stems also belong nouns indicating inhabitants of places ending in *-anin*, e.g.:—

> mieszczanin = townsman,

which lose the syllable *-in* in the plural, as in other Slavonic languages; also familiar proper names in *-io*, which are treated as soft stems, e.g.:—

> Józio = Joe

Soft labial stems give no clue of their softness in the Nom. sing. in modern orthography, e.g.:—

> gołąb = pigeon, Gen. sing. gołębia
> karp = carp, " karpia
> paw = peacock, " pawia
> Radom(a town) " Radomia

We have already noted the vowel alternations in the roots of nouns, as in: dąb (= oak), Gen. sing. dębu; Bóg (= God), Gen. sing. Boga; las (= wood), Loc. sing. w lesie; obiad (= dinner), Loc. sing. przy obiedzie (= at dinner); sąsiad (= neighbour), Nom. pl. sąsiedzi; anioł (= angel), Loc. and Voc. sing. aniele. We should also note the regular consonantal softenings before the soft endings in the Loc. and Voc. sing., as in the examples just quoted. We are also already familiar with the movable *e* or *ie*, e.g. palec (= finger), Gen. sing. palca; pies (= dog), Gen. sing. psa.

POLISH

The 1st and 2nd Palatalization also occur in this declension.

The 1st in the Voc. sing. of a few nouns:—

    człowiek = person, Voc. sing. człowiecze!
    (also człowieku!)
    Bóg = God, " Boże!
    chłopiec = boy, " chłopcze!

The 2nd in the Nom. plur. of personal nouns in -k:—

    Polak = Pole, Nom. plur. Polacy
    urzędnik = official, " urzędnicy

but—

    ptak = bird, " ptaki (in contrast to Czech ptáci!)

also of some nouns in -g:—

    Norweg = Norwegian, " Norwedzy (or Norwegowie)

but—

    róg = horn, " rogi

also of some in -ch:—

    mnich = monk, " mnisi

but—

    dach = roof, " dachy

To illustrate this enormous variety in the Polish masc. *o*-declension, unparalleled in other Slavonic languages, we give below a selection (only) of the main types. From the preceding it follows that the student has to learn for each, apart from the Nom. sing., at least the Gen. sing. and Nom. and Gen. plur. as well, and preferably also the Dat. and Loc. sing.

Hard stems: *animate* (person):—

pan = gentleman; chłop = peasant; profesor = professor; syn = son

Sing.				
Nom.	pan	chłop	profesor	syn
Gen.	pana	chłopa	profesora	syna
Dat.	panu	chłopu	profesorowi	synowi
Acc.	pana	chłopa	profesora	syna
Instr.	panem	chłopem	profesorem	synem
Loc.	panu	chłopie	profesorze	synu
Voc.	panie	chłopie	profesorze	synu

POLISH

```
Plur.
Nom.     panowie      chłopi       profesorowie   synowie
Gen.     panów        chłopów      profesorów     synów
Dat.     panom        chłopom      profesorom     synom
Acc.     panów        chłopów      profesorów     synów
Instr.   panami       chłopami     profesorami    synami
Loc.     panach       chłopach     profesorach    synach
```

sąsiad = neighbour; Polak = Pole, synek = sonny;
mieszczanin = townsman; Józio = Joe

```
Sing.
Nom.     sąsiad       Polak        synek         mieszczanin
Gen.     sąsiada      Polaka       synka         mieszczanina
Dat.     sąsiadowi    Polakowi     synkowi       mieszczaninowi
Acc.     sąsiada      Polaka       synka         mieszczanina
Instr.   sąsiadem     Polakiem     synkiem       mieszczaninem
Loc.     sąsiedzie    Polaku       synku         mieszczaninie
Voc.     sąsiedzie    Polaku       synku         mieszczaninie

Plur.
Nom.     sąsiedzi     Polacy       synkowie      mieszczanie
Gen.     sąsiadów     Polaków      synków        mieszczan
Dat.     sąsiadom     Polakom      synkom        mieszczanom
Acc.     sąsiadów     Polaków      synków        mieszczan
Instr.   sąsiadami    Polakami     synkami       mieszczanami
Loc.     sąsiadach    Polakach     synkach       mieszczanach
```

```
         Sing.                    Plur.
Nom.     Józio             Nom.   Józiowie
Gen.     Józia             Gen.   Ózió
Dat.     Józiowi           Dat.   Józiom
Acc.     Józia             Acc.   Józiów
Instr.   Józiem            Instr. Józiami
Loc.     Józiu             Loc.   Józiach
Voc.     Józiu
```

animate (animals):—

kot = cat; ptak = bird; bocian = stork

```
Sing.
Nom.     kot          ptak         bocian
Gen.     kota         ptaka        bociana
Dat.     kotu         ptakowi      bocianowi
Acc.     kota         ptaka        bociana
Instr.   kotem        ptakiem      bocianem
Loc.     kocie        ptaku        bocianie
Voc.     kocie        ptaku        bocianie
```

POLISH

```
         Plur.
         Nom.    koty      ptaki     bociany
         Gen.    kotów     ptaków    bocianów
         Dat.    kotom     ptakom    bocianom
         Acc.    koty      ptaki     bociany
         Instr.  kotami    ptakami   bocianami
         Loc.    kotach    ptakach   bocianach
```

Hard stems: *inanimate*:—

    wóz = cart; dom = house; świat = world; chleb = bread; bok = side; róg = horn, corner

```
Sing.
Nom.    wóz      dom      świat      chleb     bok       róg
Gen.    wozu     domu     świata     chleba    boku      rogu
Dat.    wozowi   domowi   światu     chlebowi  bokowi    rogowi
                                               (-u)
Acc.    wóz      dom      świat      chleb     bok       róg
Instr.  wozem    domem    światem    chlebem   bokiem    rogiem
Loc.    wozie    domu     świecie    chlebie   boku      rogu
Voc.    wozie    domu     świecie    chlebie   boku      rogu

Plur.
Nom.    wozy     domy     światy     chleby    boki      rogi
Gen.    wozów    domów    światów    chlebów   boków     rogów
Dat.    wozom    domom    światom    chlebom   bokom     rogom
Acc.    wozy     domy     światy     chleby    boki      rogi
Instr.  wozami   domami   światami   chlebami  bokami    rogami
Loc.    wozach   domach   światach   chlebach  bokach    rogach
```

Soft stems: *animate* (persons):—

    król = king; gość = guest; nauczyciel = teacher

```
    Sing.
    Nom.     król         gość         nauczyciel
    Gen.     króla        gościa       nauczyciela
    Dat.     królowi      gościowi     nauczycielowi
    Acc      króla        gościa       nauczyciela
    Instr.   królem       gościem      nauczycielem
    Loc.     królu        gościu       nauczycielu
    Voc.     królu        gościu       nauczycielu

    Plur.
    Nom.     królowie     goście       nauczyciele
    Gen.     królów(-i)   gości        nauczycieli
    Dat.     królom       gościom      nauczycielom
    Acc.     królów       gości        nauczycieli
    Instr.   królami      gośćmi       nauczycielami
    Loc.     królach      gościach     nauczycielach
```

animate (animals):—

koń = horse; gołąb = pigeon

	Sing.	
Nom.	koń	gołąb
Gen.	konia	gołębia
Dat.	koniowi	gołębiowi
Acc.	konia	gołębia
Instr.	koniem	gołębiem
Loc.	koniu	gołębiu
Voc.	koniu	gołębiu

	Plur.	
Nom.	konie	gołębie
Gen.	koni	gołębi
Dat.	koniom	gołębiom
Acc.	konie	gołębie
Instr.	końmi	gołębiami
Loc.	koniach	gołębiach

Soft stems: *inanimate*:—

kraj = country; cel = aim; korzeń = root;
jedwab = silk

	Sing.			
Nom.	kraj	cel	korzeń	jedwab
Gen.	kraju	celu	korzenia	jedwabiu
Dat.	krajowi	celowi	korzeniowi	jedwabiowi
Acc.	kraj	cel	korzeń	jedwab
Instr.	krajem	celem	korzeniem	jedwabiem
Loc.	kraju	celu	korzeniu	jedwabiu
Voc.	kraju	celu	korzeniu	jedwabiu

	Plur.			
Nom.	kraje	cele	korzenie	jedwabie
Gen.	krajów	celów	korzeni	jedwabi
Dat.	krajom	celom	korzeniom	jedwabiom
Acc.	kraje	cele	korzenie	jedwabie
Instr.	krajami	celami	korzeniami	jedwabiami
Loc.	krajach	celach	korzeniach	jedwabiach

Ex-Palatal stems: *animate* (persons):—   *animate* (animals):—

żołnierz = soldier; chłopiec = boy;   zając = hare
mąż = husband;

	Sing.			
Nom.	żołnierz	chłopiec	mąż	zając
Gen.	żołnierza	chłopca	męża	zająca
Dat.	żołnierzowi	chłopcu	mężowi	zającowi
Acc.	żołnierza	chłopca	męża	zająca
Instr.	żołnierzem	chłopcem	mężem	zającem
Loc.	żołnierzu	chłopcu	mężu	zającu
Voc.	żołnierzu	chłopcze	mężu	zającu

Plur.				
Nom.	żołnierze	chłopcy	mężowie	zające
Gen.	żołnierzy	chłopców	mężów	zajęcy
Dat.	żołnierzom	chłopcom	mężom	zającom
Acc.	żołnierzy	chłopców	mężów	zające
Instr.	żołnierzami	chłopcami	mężami	zającami
Loc.	żołnierzach	chłopcach	mężach	zającach

inanimate:—

deszcz = rain; krzyż = cross; palec = finger

Sing.			
Nom.	deszcz	krzyż	palec
Gen.	deszczu	krzyża	palca
Dat.	deszczowi	krzyżowi	palcowi
Acc.	deszcz	krzyż	palec
Instr.	deszczem	krzyżem	palcem
Loc.	deszczu	krzyżu	palcu
Voc.	deszczu	krzyżu	palcu
Plur.			
Nom.	deszcze	krzyże	palce
Gen.	deszczów(-y)	krzyżów(-y)	palców
Dat.	deszczom	krzyżom	palcom
Acc.	deszcze	krzyże	palce
Instr.	deszczami	krzyżami	palcami
Loc.	deszczach	krzyżach	palcach

Some of the commonest irregular masculine nouns are:—

Hard.

brat = brother; człowiek = person; dech = breath

Sing.			
Nom.	brat	człowiek	dech
Gen.	brata	człowieka	tchu
Dat.	bratu	człowiekowi	tchu
Acc.	brata	człowieka	dech
Instr.	bratem	człowiekiem	tchem
Loc.	bracie	człowieku	tchu
Voc.	bracie	człowieku(-cze)	tchu
Plur.			
Nom.	bracia	ludzie	
Gen.	braci	ludzi	
Dat.	braciom	ludziom	
Acc.	braci	ludzi	
Instr.	braćmi	ludźmi	
Loc.	braciach	ludziach	

Soft

przyjaciel = friend; dzień = day; tydzień = week

Sing.			
Nom.	przyjaciel	dzień	tydzień
Gen.	przyjaciela	dnia	tygodnia
Dat.	przyjacielowi	dniowi	tygodniowi
Acc.	przyjaciela	dzień	tydzień
Instr.	przyjacielem	dniem	tygodniem
Loc.	przyjacielu	dniu	tygodniu
Voc.	przyjacielu	dniu	tygodniu
Plur.			
Nom	przyjaciele	dni or dnie	tygodnie
Gen.	przyjaciół	dni	tygodni
Dat.	przyjaciołom	dniom	tygodniom
Acc.	przyjaciół	dni or dnie	tygodnie
Instr.	przyjaciółmi	dniami	tygodniami
Loc.	przyjaciołach	dniach	tygodniach

Ex-palatal

ksiądz = priest; ojciec = father;
pieniądz = coin, pl. = money

Sing.			
Nom.	ksiądz	ojciec	pieniądz
Gen.	księdza	ojca	pieniądza
Dat.	księdzu	ojcu	pieniądzowi
Acc.	księdza	ojca	pieniądz
Instr.	księdzem	ojcem	pieniądzem
Loc.	księdzu	ojcu	pieniądzu
Voc.	księże	ojcze	pieniądzu
Plur.			
Nom.	księża	ojcowie	pieniądze
Gen.	księży	ojców	pieniędzy
Dat.	księżom	ojcom	pieniądzom
Acc.	księży	ojców	pieniądze
Instr.	księżmi	ojcami	pieniędzmi
Loc.	księżach	ojcach	pieniądzach

rok (= year) has no plural of its own. For "years," the plural of lato (neuter, = summer) is used: lata, lat, etc. (see No. 4*b*, neuter *o*-stems).

Words of foreign origin in -*ans* have Gen. sing. in -*u* or -*a*, Nom. plur. in -*e*, e.g.:—

romans = romance, Gen. sing. romansu, Nom. plur. romanse

kwadrans = quarter of an hour, Gen. sg. kwadransa, Nom. pl. kwadranse

Some nouns of foreign origin ending in -*t* have an alternative Nom. plur. in -*a*, besides the regular one in -*y*, e.g.:—

   dokument = document, Gen. sing. dokumentu, Nom. plur. dokumenta or dokumenty.

4b. *Neuter o-stems*

   The neuter *o*-stems in Polish are far simpler than the masculine, as they have no alternative case endings. The soft (together with the ex-palatal) stems differ in endings from the hard stems only in the Nom. = Voc. = Acc. and Loc. sing. Velar hard stems have Loc. sing. in -u like the soft stems. Nom.= Voc. = Acc. as in other Slavonic languages, Latin and ancient Greek.

   In the *Gen. plur.* there is usually no ending, as in the fem. *a*-stems, a fill-vowel being inserted in difficult final consonant groups, e.g.: okno (= window), Gen. plur. okien. In other examples we find the familiar vowel alternations

   o/ó as in słowo (= word), Gen. plur. słów, and—
   ę/ą as in święto (= festival, holiday), Gen. plur. świąt.

Augmentatives in -*isko*, e.g. chłopisko (= big fellow), pejoratives in -*ysko*, e.g. chłopczysko (= urchin), and affectionate diminutives in -*unio*, e.g. oczunio (= little eye), have Gen. plur. in -ów. A few nouns only, mostly trisyllables, but not Verbal Nouns, take -*i*, e.g.: narzędzie (= tool), Gen. plur. narzędzi.

   Neuters ending in -*um*, of Latin origin, are indeclinable in the sing. In the plural they decline regularly like other neuter *o*-stem nouns except in the Gen. in which they take the ending -ów, e.g.:—

   gimnazjum = secondary school, Gen. pl. gimnazjów
   muzeum   = museum,   "   muzeów

Hard stems:—

   okno = window; miasto = city; wieko = lid

   Sing.
Nom.	okno	miasto[1]	wieko
Gen.	okna	miasta	wieka
Dat.	oknu	miastu	wieku
Acc.	okno	miasto	wieko
Instr.	oknem	miastem	wiekiem[2]
Loc.	oknie	mieście	wieku
Voc.	okno	miasto	wieko

[1] So all neuters (abstracts, etc.) in -stwo, -ctwo: Gen. pl. -stw, -ctw, eg. bogactwo (= riches), Gen. pl. bogactw.

[2] Note the soft ending after k.

	Plur.			
	Nom.	okna	miasta	wieka
	Gen.	okien	miast	wiek
	Dat.	oknom	miastom	wiekom
	Acc.	okna	miasta	wieka
	Instr.	oknami	miastami	wiekami
	Loc.	oknach	miastach	wiekach

Soft stems:—   *Ex-palatal stems:—*

pole = field; zdanie = opinion, sentence;   morze = sea;
         narzędzie = tool;   wybrzeże = sea-shore;

Sing.					
Nom.	pole	zdanie[1]	narzędzie	morze	wybrzeże
Gen.	pola	zdania	narzędzia	morza	wybrzeża
Dat.	polu	zdaniu	narzędziu	morzu	wybrzeżu
Acc.	pole	zdanie	narzędzie	morze	wybrzeże
Instr.	polem	zdaniem	narzędziem	morzem	wybrzeżem
Loc.	polu	zdaniu	narzędziu	morzu	wybrzeżu
Voc.	pole	zdanie	narzędzie	morze	wybrzeże
Plur.					
nom.	pola	zdania	narzędzia	morza	wybrzeża
Gen.	pól	zdań	narzędzi	mórz	wybrzeży
Dat.	polom	zdaniom	narzędziom	morzom	wybrzeżom
Acc.	pola	zdania	narzędzia	morza	wybrzeża
Instr.	polami	zdaniami	narzędziami	morzami	wybrzeżami
Loc.	polach	zdaniach	narzędziach	morzach	wybrzeżach

Dziecko (= child) has an irregular plural:—

Nom., Voc., Acc., Gen.	dzieci
Dat.	dzieciom
Instr.	dziećmi
Loc.	dzieciach

The regular plural is only used contemptuously, for "brats."

Ucho with the meaning "ear", oko with the meaning "eye" both have irregular plurals as follows:—

Nom., Voc., Acc.	uszy	oczy
Gen.	uszu[2] or uszów	oczu[2] or oczów
Dat.	uszom	oczom
Instr.	uszami or uszyma[2]	oczami or oczyma[2]
Loc.	uszach	oczach

The regular plurals have a different meaning: ucha = handles or lugs (of a basket, pitcher); oka = meshes (of a net).

---

[1] All Verbal Nouns are declined like zdanie.
[2] Old Dual forms.

Ziele (= a herb) has the root *zioł-* in the plural:—

Nom., Voc., Acc. zioła, Gen. ziół, etc.

Nasienie (= seed) has the root *nasion-* in the plural:—

Nom., Voc., Acc. nasiona, Gen. nasion, etc.

The irregular plural of niebo (= sky), Nom. plur. niebiosa, has already been mentioned under the consonantal stem declension.

Notice the following common "pluralia tantum":—

like *Masc.*

Nom.		Gen.
plecy	= shoulders	pleców
łowy	= hunting	łowów
organy	= organ(mus.)	organów
okulary	= spectacles	okularów
dzieje	= history	dziejów
finanse	= finances	finansów
grabie	= rake	grabi
spodnie	= trousers	spodni
drożdże	= yeast	drożdży

like *Fem.*

Nom.		Gen.
drzwi	= door	drzwi
skrzypce	= violin	skrzypiec
wakacje	= holidays	wakacji
sanie	= sleigh	sań
kajdany	= chains	kajdan
koszary	= barracks	koszar
urodziny	= birthday	urodzin
nożyczki	= scissors	nożyczek
suchoty	= tuberculosis	suchot

like *Neut.*

Nom.		Gen.
bliźnięta	= twins	bliźniąt
wrota	= gate	wrót
drwa	= firewood	drew
usta	= mouth	ust

Czechy	= Bohemia, has Gen.	Czech	and Loc.	Czechach
Niemcy	= Germany "	Niemiec	"	Niemczech
Prusy	= Prussia "	Prus	"	Prusach or Prusiech
Włochy	= Italy "	Włoch	"	Włoszech
Węgry	= Hungary "	Węgier	"	Węgrzech

THE NUMERALS

The *Cardinal Numerals* 1-4 are adjectival and agree in gender and case with the noun they qualify. Jeden (= one) declines like an adjective with a movable (second) *e* and a final *-o* in the Nom., Acc. sg. neut.

The words for two, three, and four, when Nominative, have two alternative forms for masculine personal nouns. One is in form like the Genitive, which is also used for the Accusative with masc. personal nouns. The other Nominative form is also the only form for the Voc. with masc. personal nouns: dwaj, trej, czterej mężowie! = o two (three, four) men!. For "two" there is a third alternative, dwu, as well as dwóch and dwaj. 2-4 are followed by a verb in the plural (for all genders). When they are in any other case but the Nom. or Acc., they have the same form for all genders and agree with the noun in case.

The numbers from five onwards are nouns and are followed by the noun they qualify in the Gen. plur. and take the verb in the (neuter) singular. For masc. personal nouns the common form of the Gen., Dat., Instr. and Loc. is used also for the Nom. and Acc. Only the Instrumental has an alternative form in *-oma*.

In counting the forms of the neuter-feminine are used except for "one," which is then jeden (masc.). These are italized below.

Adjectives (see below under "The Adjectives" for their declension) when combined with numerals always agree with the noun they qualify (not with the numeral, when in a different case): trzy piękn*e* kobiety (= three beautiful women), pięć piękn*ych* kobiet (= five beautiful women).

	Nom.			Gen.	
	Masc.	Fem.	Neut.	Masc., Neut.	Fem.
1	*jeden*	jedna	jedno	jednego	jednej

	Dat.	
	Masc., Neut.	Fem.
	jednemu	jednej, etc.

	Nom.			
2	Masc. Pers.		Fem	Neut., Other Masc.
	dwaj dwóch dwu		dwie	*dwa*

Gen. and Loc.	Dat.
All Genders.	All Genders.
dwu *or* dwóch	dwu *or* dwom

POLISH

	Acc.		
Masc. Pers.	Fem.	Neut., other Masc.	
dwu or dwóch	dwie	dwa	

	Instr.	
Masc. Neut. All Genders.		Fem.
dwu	dwoma	dwiema

	Nom.		Gen. and Loc.	Dat.
Masc. Pers.	Fem., Neut. and other Masc.		All Genders.	All Genders
3 trzej	trzech	*trzy*	trzech	trzem

	Acc.		Instr.
Masc. Pers.	Other Genders.		All Genders.
trzech	trzy		trzema

	Nom.		Gen. and Loc.	Dat.
Masc. Pers.	Fem., Neut. and other Masc.		All Genders.	All Genders
4 czterej	czterech	*cztery*	czterech	czterem

	Acc.		Instr.
Masc. Pers.	Other Genders.		All Genders.
czterech	cztery		czterema

	Nom.		Gen.,Dat.,Loc
Masc. Pers.	Fem.,Neut. and Other Masc.		All genders
5 pięciu	*pięć*		pięciu

	Acc.		Instr.,
Masc. Pers.	Other Genders.		All Genders.
pięciu	pięć		pięcioma or pięciu

6 sześciu	*sześć*	
7 siedmiu	*siedem*	
8 ośmiu	*osiem*	} decline like pięciu, pięć
9 dziewięciu	*dziewięć*	
10 dziesięciu	*dziesięć*	

		Gen.,Dat., Loc.	Acc.(and Voc.)		Instr.
		All Genders	Masc. Pers.	Other Genders	All Genders.
11 jedenastu	*jedenaście*	jeden-astu	jeden-astu	jeden-aście	jeden-astu or jeden-astoma

283

12	dwunastu	*dwanaście*	
13	trzynastu	*trzynaście*	
14	czternastu	*czternaście*	
15	piętnastu	*piętnaście*	
16	szesnastu	*szesnaście*	
17	siedemnastu	*siedemnaście*	
18	osiemnastu	*osiemnaście*	
19	dziewiętnastu	*dziewiętnaście*	
20	dwudziestu	*dwadzieście*	decline like jeden-
21	dwudziestu jeden[1]	*dwadzieścia jeden*[2]	astu, jedenaście
22	dwudziestu dwu (dwóch)[1]	*dwadzieścia dwa*[2]	
23	dwudziestu trzech[1]	*dwadzieścia trzy*	
30	trzydziestu	*trzydzieści*	
40	czterdziestu	*czterdzieści*	

	Nom. *and* Acc.	Gen.,Dat., Instr.,Loc. *All Genders*	Instr. (alternative) *All Genders.*
50	pięćdziesię- ciu[3]	*pięćdzie- siąt*[3]	pięćdziesię- ciu[3]	pięćdziesię- cioma[3]
60	sześćdziesię- ciu[3]	*sześć- dziesiąt*[3]	
70	siedem- dziesięciu	*siedem- dziesiąt*	
80	osiem- dziesięciu	*osiem- dziesiąt*	decline like pięćdziesiąt
90	dziewięć- dziesięciu	*dziewięć- dziesiąt*	

[1]Compound numbers for male persons are made up only with the forms dwu or dwóch, trzech, czterech (not the forms ending in -j).

[2]Compound numerals are declined in every part, except jeden. E.g. dla stu dwudziestu pięciu osób = for 125 people (Gen.). The case of the noun they qualify is determined by the unit element. But compounds with the (invariable) jeden govern the Gen. plur., like those compounded with five onwards, and are followed by a verb in the (neut.) sing., while compounds with two, three or four are followed by a verb in the plural. *All* compound numerals in the special masc. personal forms are followed by the verb in the *neuter* sing.

[3]The ć is not pronounced in these numerals in ordinary speech.

	Nom. and Acc.		Gen., Dat.,	Instr.
	Masc. Pers.	Other Genders	Instr., Loc. All Genders	(altern.) All Genders.
100	stu	*sto*	stu	stoma
101	stu jeden	*sto jeden*		
121	stu dwidziestu jeden	*sto dwadzieścia jeden*		
200	dwustu	*dwieście*	dwustu[1]	dwustoma Gen. (altern.) All Genders.
300	trzystu	*trzysta*	trzystu	trzechset
400	czterystu	*czterysta*	czterystu	czterechset
500	pięciuset	*pięćset*	pięciuset	
600	sześciuset	*sześćset*	sześciuset	
700	siedmiuset	*siedemset*	siedmiuset	
800	ośmiuset	*osiemset*	ośmiuset	
900	dziewięciuset	*dziewięćset*	dziewięciuset	

1,000 *tysiąc* (masc. o-stem) for all genders
2,000 *dwa tysiące*
5,000 *pięć tysięcy*
1,000,000 *milion* (masc. o-stem)

The *Ordinal Numerals* are adjectives. (See below under "The Adjectives" for their declension). Only trzeci (= third) has a soft stem, and drugi (= second), a velar stem. Compound Ordinals have the ordinal form in their last two parts, in contrast to E. and S. Slav. languages.

	Masc.	*Fem.*	*Neut.*
1st	pierwszy	pierwsza	pierwsze
2nd	drugi	druga	drugie
3rd	trzeci	trzecia	trzecie
4th	czwarty	-ta	-te
5th	piąty, etc.		
6th	szósty		
7th	siódmy		
8th	ósmy		
9th	dziewiąty		
10th	dziesiąty		
11th	jedenasty		
12th	dwunasty		
13th	trzynasty		
14th	czternasty		
15th	piętnasty		

[1] Alternative Gen. for male persons: dwóchset.

Masc.

16th	szesnasty
17th	siedemnasty
18th	osiemnasty
19th	dziewiętnasty
20th	dwudziesty
30th	trzydziesty
40th	czterdziesty
50th	pięćdziesiąty
60th	sześćdziesiąty
70th	siedemdziesiąty
80th	osiemdziesiąty
90th	dziewięćdziesiąty
100th	setny
200th	dwóchsetny *or* dwusetny
300th	trzechsetny
400th	czterechsetny
500th	pięćsetny
600th	sześćsetny
700th	siedemsetny
800th	osiemsetny
900th	dziewięćsetny
1,000th	tysiączny *or* tysięczny
2,000th	dwutysięczny
3,000th	trzechtysięczny
4,000th	czterotysięczny
10,000th	dziesięciotysięczny
100,000th	stutysięczny
1,000,000th	milionowy

The *Collective Numerals* are used:—

(1) for groups of persons, etc., of mixed gender, e.g.:—

dwoje młodych ludzi = a young couple

(2) for things regarded in pairs or groups, e.g.:—

dwoje oczu = two eyes
dziesięcioro prżykazań = the Ten Commandments

(3) pluralia tantum, e.g.:—

troje drzwi = three doors

(4) pronouns referring to groups of mixed gender, e.g.:—

pięcioro nas było = there were five of us

They have a special declension and govern the Gen. plur., except when they themselves are in the Dat. or Loc., as illustrated in the table below:—

```
Nom.    dwoje      czworo      (ludzi)
Gen.    dwojga     czworga     (ludzi)
Dat.    dwojgu     czworgu     (ludziom)
Acc.    dwoje      czworo      (ludzi)
Instr.  dwojgiem   czworgiem   (ludzi, ludźmi)
Loc.    dwojgu     czworgu     (ludziach)
```

Like dwoje, oboje = both (collective).

Oba or obydwa, masc. pers. obaj or obydwaj, fem. obie or obydwie (= both) also has a special declension:—

Nom./Voc. MASC. PERS. obaj, obydwaj; OTHER MASC. and NEUT. oba, obydwa; FEM. obie, obydwie
Gen./Loc. ALL GENDERS obu, obudwu, obydwóch
Dat. ALL GENDERS obu, obudwu
Acc. MASC. PERS. obu, obudwu, obydwóch; OTHER MASC. and NEUT. oba, obydwa; FEM. obie, obydwie
Instr. ALL GENDERS obu, oboma, obudwu, obydwoma (additional FEM. alternative obiema)

Note the special Polish expressions:—

kilkanaście = between ten and twenty, a baker's dozen
kilkadziesiąt = a few score
kilkaset = a few hundred

They are declined like the numerals with the corresponding endings.

Note also:—

półtora (masc. and   półtory   = one and a half
  neut.)   (fem.)
półtrzecia (masc.   półtrzeci   = two and a half
  and neut.)   (fem.)
półczwarta (masc.   półczwarty   = three and a half,
  and neut.)   (fem.)   etc.

These do *not* decline further.

Distributive Numerals are formed with the preposition po + Acc. of the Cardinal Numeral, e.g.:—

po dwa, trzy = two, three each

THE PRONOUNS

Only in the case of the Personal Pronouns and the words for "who" (= kto) and "what" (= co) does there exist in Polish a separate pronominal declension distinct from the declension of adjectives (see below), except in the Nom. sing. masc. Relative Pronouns are the same in form as the Interrogative Pronouns.

As in other Slavonic languages, we have in Polish the following categories:—

Demonstrative:	ten	= this
	tamten	= that
	ów	= that (distant in time, mostly)
Interrogative:	kto?	= who?
	co?	= what?
	czyj?	= whose?
	jaki?	= of what kind?
Indefinite:	ktoś	= someone
	kto bądź ⎫ ktokolwiek ⎭	= whoever, anybody
	byle co	= anything (whatever)
	nieco	= something
	pewien, pewna	= a certain
Relative:	kto *or* ten, co	= (he) who
	który	= who, which

Possessive (pronoun-adjectives):—

	mój	= my, mine
	nasz	= our(s)
Definitive:	(wszystek) ⎫ cały ⎭	= all, the whole
	każdy	= each
	wszelki	= every
	sam	= -self
	ten sam	= the same
	taki	= such
	inny	= another
Negative:	nikt	= no one
	żaden	= no, none
	nic	= nothing
Personal:	on	= he
	ja	= I
	ty	= thou, (fam.) you

Declension (except for Personal Pronouns and kto, co).

In the singular the usual three genders exist. In the plural, however, only two genders exist in the Nom., Voc. and Acc.: the masculine *personal* and the masculine impersonal—feminine—neuter ("general") plural. In the other cases the genders are not differentiated.

For masc. nouns Acc. sing. = Gen. sing. for animate nouns but = Nom. for inanimates, as in other Slavonic languages, but in the plural Acc. = Gen. only for masc. personal nouns (i.e. not animals).

Voc. = Nom. in singular and plural.

POLISH

Hard stem:—

	SING.			PLUR.	
	Masc.	*Neut.*	*Fem.*	*Masc. Pers.*	*Others.*
Nom.	ten	to	ta	ci	te
Gen.	tego		tej	tych	
Dat.	temu		tej	tym	
Acc.	= Gen./Nom.	to	tę [1]	tych	te
Instr.	tym		tą	tymi	
Loc.	tym		tej	tych	

Nasz, nasza, nasze follow ten except in the Nom./Voc./Acc. sing. neut. Also wasz = your (fam. pl.).

Soft stem:—

SING.

	Masc.	*Neut.*	*Fem.*
Nom.⎫ Voc.⎭	mój	moje, me	moja, ma
Gen.	mojego, mego		mojej, mej
Dat.	mojemu, memu		mojej, mej
Acc.	= Gen./Nom.	moje, me	moją, mą
Instr.	moim, mym		moją, mą
Loc.	moim, mym		mojej, mej

PLUR.

	Masc. Pers.	*Others.*
Nom.⎫ Voc.⎭	moi	moje, me
Gen.	moich, mych	
Dat.	moim, mym	
Acc.	moich	moje, me
Instr.	moimi, mymi	
Loc.	moich, mych	

The shorter forms are not used often in colloquial speech.

Like mój: twój = your (fam.), swój = (my, your, his, etc.) own, referring to the subject, and czyj = whose.

Velar stem:—

	SING.			PLURAL	
	Masc.	*Neut.*	*Fem.*	*Masc. Pers.*	*Others.*
Nom.	taki	takie	taka	tacy	takie
Gen.	takiego		takiej	takich	
Dat.	takiemu		takiej	takim	
Acc.	Gen./Nom.	takie	taką	takich	takie
Instr.	takim		taką	takimi	
Loc.	takim		takiej	takich	

---

[1] Acc. sing. fem. tą for tę is very frequent colloquially. Tamtą, Acc. sing. fem., is regular.

Like taki: wszystek = all, Nom. plur. masc. pers. wszyscy, "general" plur. wszystkie, but Nom., Acc. neut. sing. wszystko.

	kto = who?	co = what?
Nom.	kto	co
Gen.	kogo	czego
Dat.	komu	czemu
Acc.	kogo	co
Instr.	kim	czym
Loc.	kim	czym

These can also be used as Indefinite Pronouns.

Like kto: nikt = no one
Like co: nic = nothing

Notice the vowel change *o > ó* when -*ż* (= *że*, emphatic particle) is added, e.g. któż = who then?, cóż? = what then?.

The Personal Pronouns

on = he, ona = she, ono = it

SING.

	Masc.	*Neut.*
Nom.	on	ono
Gen.	jego, niego, go*	
Dat.	jemu, niemu, mu*	
Acc.	jego, niego, go*	je, nie,(go*)
Instr.	nim	
Loc.	nim	

PLURAL

	Fem.	*Masc. Pers.*	*Other Genders.*
Nom.	ona	oni	one
Gen.	jej, niej	ich, nich	
Dat.	jej, niej	im, nim	
Acc.	ją, nią	ich, nich	je, nie
Instr.	nią	nimi	
Loc.	niej	nich	

The forms marked * are enclitic (unemphatic) and cannot start a sentence.

go for Acc. sing. neut. is so frequent colloquially that it can hardly be regarded as incorrect.

The forms beginning with *n*- are only used after prepositions except the Instr. case which has an initial *n*- always.

The forms jego (Gen./Acc. sing. masc., Gen. sing. neut.) and jemu (Dat. sing. masc. and neut.) are emphatic.

The forms jej (Gen. Dat. sing. fem.), ją (Acc. sing. fem.), ich (Gen. pl. all genders, Acc. pl. masc. pers.), im (Dat. pl. all genders), je (*Acc.*

sing. neut., Acc. pl. "other" genders) can be both emphatic and unemphatic.

The forms jego, jej, and ich are used for the Possessive Pronoun-adjectives of the third person when not referring to the subject of the sentence. They do not decline. Thus: jego = his, its, jej = her(s), its, ich = their(s).

ja = I; my = we; ty = thou; wy = you; siebie, się = self (Reflexive)

Nom.	ja	my	ty	wy	-
Gen.	mnie, mię*	nas	ciebie, cię*	was	siebie, się*
Dat.	mnie, mi*	nam	tobie, ci*	wam	sobie (dial. se)
Acc.	mnie, mię*	nas	ciebie, cię*	was	siebie, się*
Instr.	mną	nami	tobą	wami	sobą
Loc.	mnie	nas	tobie	was	sobie

The forms marked * are enclitics and cannot start a sentence.

mię, cię, się are pronounced mie, cie, sie (not with a nasal vowel). mnie is often used for mię unstressed.

ty and wy are only used in familiar address to a single person and to several people respectively.
In polite speech one uses for "you":—
Pan + 3rd pers. sing. of the verb—to a man
Pani + 3rd pers. sing. of the verb—to a woman
Panowie + 3rd pers. plur. of the verb—to several men
Panie + 3rd pers. plur. of the verb—to several women
Państwo + 3rd pers. plur. of the verb (or, colloquially, + 2nd pers. plur.)—to a married couple, or to a group of people of both sexes.
(This is a Polish feature unique in the Slavonic group of languages. Cf. Italian: Lei; Spanish: Vd. (usted); Hungarian: Maga, Ön.).

The corresponding Genitives are used for the polite "your" when not referring to the subject of the sentence: Pana, Pani, Panów, Pań, Państwa. For Pana, pański (adj.) can be used.

THE ADJECTIVES

Declension.—Polish adjectives are divided into two declensions: hard and soft stems. The soft are less numerous. Velar stems in Polish are declined like soft stems, except in Nom., Acc. and Instr. sing. fem., where they have hard endings. The differences

between the hard and soft stems may be summarized in
two main points: (1) where hard stems have -*y*- in the
endings, soft stems have -*i*-; (2) where hard stems
have -*e*- in the endings, soft stems have -*ie*-. Furthermore in the Nom. sing. fem., soft stems have -*ia*
instead of -*a*. In the masc. and neut. sing., Instr.
and Loc. are all identical. In the fem. sing. Gen. =
Dat. = Loc., and Acc. = Instr. In the plural the
oblique cases are identical for all genders and Gen.
= Loc. *Special attention* should be paid to the consonantal changes that take place before the soft ending -*i* in the Nom. plur. for the masc. personal gender. In the sing., Acc. = Gen. for masc. animates,
but = Nom. for inanimates, as in other Slavonic languages, but in the plur. Acc. = Gen. only for masc.
personal nouns.

Hard stem:—dobry = good

SING.

	Masc.	*Neut.*	*Fem.*
Nom.	dobry	dobre	dobra
Gen.	dobrego		dobrej
Dat.	dobremu		dobrej
Acc.	= Gen. or Nom.	dobre	dobrą
Instr.	dobrym		dobrą
Loc.	dobrym		dobrej

PLURAL

	Masc. Pers.	*Other Genders.*
Nom.	dobrzy	dobre
Gen.	dobrych	
Dat.	dobrym	
Acc.	dobrych	dobre
Instr.	dobrymi	
Loc.	dobrych	

Velar stem:—wielki = great, big

SING.

	Masc.	*Neut.*	*Fem.*
Nom.	wielki	wielkie	wielka
Gen.	wielkiego		wielkiej
Dat.	wielkiemu		wielkiej
Acc.	= Gen. or Nom.	wielkie	wielką
Instr.	wielkim		wielką
Loc.	wielkim		wielkiej

POLISH

	PLURAL	
	Masc. Pers.	*Other Genders.*
Nom.	wielcy	wielkie
Gen.	wielkich	
Dat.	wielkim	
Acc.	wielkich	wielkie
Instr.	wielkimi	
Loc.	wielkich	

Soft stem: —głupi = stupid

SING.

	Masc.	*Neut.*	*Fem.*
Nom.	głupi	głupie	głupia
Gen.	głupiego		głupiej
Dat.	głupiemu		głupiej
Acc.	= Gen. or Nom.	głupie	głupią
Instr.	głupim		głupią
Loc.	głupim		głupiej

PLURAL

	Masc. Pers.	*Other Genders.*
Nom.	głupi	głupie
Gen.	głupich	
Dat.	głupim	
Acc.	głupich	głupie
Instr.	głupimi	
Loc.	glupich	

In the Nom. plur. masc. pers., the following consonantal changes take place before the soft ending -*i*:—

                                      Nom. pl. masc. pers.

t is softened to *ć*, e.g.: prosty = straight, simple   prości
d is softened to *dź*, e.g.: twardy = hard   twardzi
n is softened to *ń*, e.g. konny = mounted, on horseback   konni
s is softened to *ś*, e.g.: łysy = bald   łysi
ł is softened to *l*, e.g.: wesoły = merry   weseli
p (*hard*) is softened to *p* (*soft*), e.g.: tępy = blunt, dull   tępi
b (*hard*) is softened to *b* (*soft*), e.g.: słaby = weak   słabi
w (*hard*) is softened to *w* (*soft*), e.g.: żywy = alive, living   żywi
m (*hard*) is softened to *m* (*soft*), e.g.: łakomy = greedy   łakomi
sz is softened to *ś*, e.g.: pieszy = (on) foot   piesi

This softening also occurs regularly in all Comparative adjectives: (see below).

    lepszy = better   lepsi
ż is softened to ź, e.g.: duży = big   duzi
    (but boży = God's   boży)
ch is softened to *ś* (2nd Palatalization),
    e.g.: głuchy = deaf   głusi

This ending *-i* becomes *-y* for adjectives with a stem ending in *cz*, *c*, *dz*, *k*, *g*, *r*.

Adjectives in *cz*, *c*, *dz* retain these consonants before this *-y* and in consequence the Nom. plur. masc. pers. is the same as the Nom. sing. masc., e.g.:—

              ochoczy = willing
              obcy   = foreign
              cudzy   = alien

Adjectives in *k* and *g*, change these to *c* and *dz* respectively in the Nom. plur. masc. pers. (2nd Palatalization); after these *c* and *dz*, *-i* becomes *-y*, e.g.:—

wielki = great, Nom. plur. masc. pers. wielcy
długi = long,   "   "   dłudzy

Adjectives in *-r*, change it to *rz* in the Nom. plur. masc. pers., e.g.:—

dobry = good, Nom. plur. masc. pers. dobrzy

Soft stem adjectives have the same form in the Nom. sing. masc. and Nom. plur. masc. pers., e.g.:—

              tani = cheap

(Before 1936, in the Instr. and Loc. sing. the ending -ym was used for masc. nouns and -em for neut. nouns. Similarly in the Instr. plur. -ymi, -imi were used for the masc. pers. gender, -emi for other nouns. This difference was abolished in the new orthography because it did not correspond to the normal pronunciation in the living language. The same applied to the pronouns.)

For a few adjectives a short, predicative form, with no ending, exists in the Nom. sing. masc. only. The closing of the syllable causes *o* to become *ó*. In other cases the fill-vowel *-e* or *-ie* is inserted between consonants which would otherwise make a final group:—

gotowy = ready,   Masc.predicative:(jestem) gotów =
                                                          (I am)ready
pełny = full,   "   "   "   pełen
wesoły = merry,   "   "   "   wesół

zdrowy	= healthy,	Masc.predicative:(jestem)			zdrów
mocny	= powerful,	"	"	"	mocen
łaskawy	= kind,	"	"	"	łaskaw
godny	= worthy,	"	"	"	godzien
żywy	= alive,	"	"	"	żyw
winny	= indebted,	"	"	"	winien
powinny	= obliged to, due	"	"	"	powinien, also powinno (neut.)

Rad = glad, wart = worth(y), kontent = satisfied, are used only in this form.

These forms were once declined like nouns (cf. the Indefinite declension of adjectives in O.S.) and have left traces in adverbs and adverbial expressions (see "Adverbs" below), e.g.:—

    wysoko (adv.) = high
    z rzadka = rarely
    po polsku = in Polish
    wkrótce = soon
    dobrze (an old Loc.) = well
Likewise—
    wysoce = highly

A fair number of nouns are adjectival in form, such as—

    leśny = forester
    złoty (Polish coin)
    luty = February
    służący (masc.) } = servant
    służąca (fem.)

So are all surnames in *-ski, -ska, -cki, -cka, -dzki, -dzka*, Christian names (of foreign origin) ending in *-i* or *-y*, e.g.: Antoni (= Anthony), fem. surnames in *-owa*,[1] place names and names of dues, assignments of money, etc. in *-e*, e.g. Zakopane (in the Tatras), strawne (= travelling allowance). These are all declined like adjectives in the sing. In the plur. foreign names, and titles and professions of men have the noun-ending *-owie* in the *Nom.* only.

Foreign names in *-e* and *-i* are also declined like adjectives, e.g.:—

    Goethe, Gen. sing. Goethego
    Papini, " Papiniego

There is no special declension for the few

---

[1]Fem. surnames of *unmarried* women in *-ówna* are declined like *a*-stem nouns.

possessive adjectives that exist in Polish: e.g. ojcowy, ojców = father's, siostrzyn = sister's, follow the hard adjectival declension.

THE COMPARISON OF ADJECTIVES

The Comparative degree is formed from the Positive degree in one of four ways:—

1. The commonest way in Polish is to add *-szy* (masc.), *-sza* (fem.), *-sze* (neut.) to the stem of the Positive adjective, which usually ends in a single consonant, e.g.:—

gruby	= thick,	Comp.:	grubszy
głupi	= stupid,	"	głupszy
twardy	= hard,	"	twardszy
ciekawy	= interesting, curious,	"	ciekawszy
prosty	= simple, straight,	"	prostszy (stem in -st!)

Adjectives in *-ki, -oki, -eki* drop these endings before adding the Comparative endings, e.g.:—

szybki	= fast,	Comp.:	szybszy
niski	= low,	"	niższy (s to ż by assimilation)
wysoki	= high,	"	wyższy (s to ż by assimilation)
daleki	= distant,	"	dalszy
szeroki	= broad,	"	szerszy

Adjectives with stems in *g, n,* and *ł* soften these consonants to *ż, ń,* and *l* before adding the Comparative endings, e.g.:—

drogi	= dear,	Comp.:	droższy
słony	= salty,	"	słońszy
miły	= nice, pleasant,	"	milszy

Some adjectives ending in *-ony, -oły* and *-iały* change the preceding vowel as well as softening the *n* or *ł*, e.g.:—

czerwony	= red,	Comp.:	czerwieńszy
wesoły	= gay,	"	weselszy
biały	= white,	"	bielszy
śmiały	= bold,	"	śmielszy

But most adjectives in *-ły* derived from verbs, leave the preceding vowel unaltered, e.g.:—

		from		Comp.:
dojrzały	= ripe,	dojrzeć	= to ripen,	dojrzalszy
trwały	= lasting,	trwać	= to last,	trwalszy

POLISH

2. If the stem ends in a group of consonants, the endings -(i)ejszy, -(i)ejsza, -(i)ejsze, with the softening of the preceding consonantal group, are preferred, e.g.:—

grzeczny	= polite,	Comp.:	greczniejszy
jasny	= bright,	"	jaśniejszy
łatwy	= easy,	"	łatwiejszy
piękny	= beautiful,	"	piękniejszy

A few adjectives can take either of the above endings, e.g.:—

częsty = frequent, Comp.: częstszy (or częściejszy)
mądry = wise, " mędrszy or mądrzejszy

3. A few adjectives and all Past Participles Passive used as adjectives, form their Comparative with bardziej (=more), preceding the Positive degree, e.g.:—

bardziej gorzki = more bitter
" mściwy = " vindictive
" kochany = " beloved
" zniszczony = " devastated, worn out

4. A few common adjectives form their Comparative from another root, irregularly, e.g.:—

dobry	= good,	Comp.:	lepszy
zły	= bad, evil,	"	gorszy
duży wielki	}= large, great,	"	większy
mały	= small,	"	mniejszy

Notice also the irregularities in:—

gorący = hot, Comp.: gorętszy
lekki = light, " lżejszy
wąski = narrow, " węższy

The Superlative degree is formed quite regularly from all types of *Comparative* adjectives by prefixing naj-, e.g.:—

		Comp.	Superl.
1. gruby	= thick, coarse,	grubszy,	najgrubszy
2. grzeczny	= polite,	grzeczniejszy,	najgrzeczniejszy
3. gorzki	= bitter,	bardziej gorzki,	najbardziej gorzki
4. dobry	= good,	lepszy,	najlepszy

All Comparative and Superlative adjectives decline regularly like ordinary hard adjectives.

Very = bardzo, nader, *or* wielce.

Than = (1) niż, with the same case after it as before it, e.g.:—
   Kościół był wyższy niż dom = The church was higher than the house.
 = (2) od + Gen., used mostly with Personal Pronouns, e.g.:—
   Tyś piękniejsza od niej = You are more beautiful than she
   Tyś piękniejsza ode mnie = You are more beautiful than I
 = (3) jak (= as), after a negative, e.g.:—
   Nie gorszy jak inni = no worse than others
 = (4) (po)nad + Acc., in a few emotional expressions, e.g.:—
   Droższy nad (ponad) życie = dearer than life

Rather better = trochę lepszy, nieco lepszy
Rather good = dosyć (dość) dobry
Less than = mniej niż
The bigger, *the* better = im większy, tym lepszy
As (big) *as* = tak (wielki) jak(o)
As soon as possible = jak (*or* co) najrychlej
The (very) best of all = najlepszy ze wszystkich
Too (long) = za *or* zbyt (długi)
The same (in quality) as = taki sam jak
The same *one* as (identical) = ten sam co

ADVERBS

Adverbs formed from adjectives, except from those in *-ski*, *-cki*, end either in *-o* or in *-e*, which latter causes the preceding consonant to be palatalized:—

słaby	= weak,	adv.	słabo
dobry	= good,	"	dobrze
wielki	= great,	"	wielce
otwarty	= open,	"	otwarcie
wysoki	= high,	{ "	wysoce = highly
		"	wysoko = high (up)
tani	= cheap,	"	tanio
ciemny	= dark,	"	ciemno

Adverbs formed from adjectives in *-ski*, *-cki* end in *-u* and are preceded by the preposition po:—

chamski = boorish, adv. po chamsku
niemiecki = German, " po niemiecku = in German (fashion)
polski = Polish, " po polsku

Comparison of Adverbs

Adverbs formed from adjectives other than those in *-ski*, *-cki*, can form Comparative degrees with the ending *-(i)ej*, which always causes palatalization of the preceding consonant:—

bardzo	= very,	Comp.	bardziej
ciemno	= darkly,	"	ciemniej
tanio	= cheaply,	"	taniej
długo	= long,	"	dłużej
krótko	= briefly,	"	krócej
czysto	= clean (adv.),	"	czyściej

As in the Comparative adjectives, Comparative adverbs formed from adverbs in *-ko, -oko, -eko*, lose these syllables in the Comparative degree; the palatalizations still occur:—

daleko	= far,	Comp.	dalej
szeroko	= widely,	"	szerzej
wysoko	= high,	"	wyżej

Likewise, Comparative adverbs formed from adverbs in *-ono, -'ało, -oło*, change the stem vowel in the Comparative degree:—

czerwono	= red(adv.),	Comp.	czerwieniej
biało	= white(adv.),	"	bielej
wesoło	= merrily,	"	weselej

The Superlative degree is regularly formed with the prefix naj- attached to the Comparative adverb:—

najsłabiej = most weakly; najdalej = furthest
najtaniej = most cheaply; najweselej = most merrily

Those adjectives that form their Comparative and Superlative degrees with bardziej, najbardziej, form their Comparative and Superlative adverbs likewise:—

gorzko = bitterly, Comp. bardziej gorzko, Superl. najbardziej gorzko

Adverbs formed from adjectives with irregular Comparatives, have similar irregularities in their Comparative adverbs:—

dobrze	= well,	Comp.	lepiej,	Superl.	najlepiej
źle	= badly,	"	gorzej		etc.
dużo } wiele	= much,	"	więcej		
mało	= little,	"	mniej		
gorąco	= hot,	"	goręcej		
lekko	= lightly,	"	lżej		
wąsko	= narrowly,	"	wężej		
nisko	= low,	"	niżej		

Adverbs of time, place, manner, degree and interrogative adverbs have the most various endings and derivations: —

PLACE
tutaj (pron. tutej)	= here
tam	= there, thither
tędy	= that way
stąd	= hence
stamtąd	= thence
dotąd	= up to here
tu i ówdzie (or owdzie)	= here and there
wszędzie	= everywhere
nigdzie	= nowhere
gdzieś	= somewhere

TIME
teraz	= now
wtedy	= then
dzisiaj pron. dzisiej dziś	} = to-day
wczoraj	= yesterday
jutro	= to-morrow
dawno	= long ago
rano	= in the morning
wieczór wieczorem	} = in the evening
wcześnie	= early
późno	= late
wkrótce niebawem niezadługo	} = soon
zaraz	= immediately
zawsze	= always
nigdy	= never
co dzień	= everyday
dopiero	= just, only
już	= already
wreszcie	= at last
kiedyś	= some time
czasem, czasami niekiedy	} = at times, sometimes
dotąd	= till now
tylekroć tylekrotnie	} = so many times
nieraz	= many a time

MANNER
tak	= thus, so

MANNER (Contd.)

prędko	}	= quickly
rychle		
powoli		= slowly
nagle	}	= suddenly
raptem		
w ten sposób		= in this way
celowo	}	= on purpose
naumyślnie		
daremnie	}	= in vain
napróżno		
chętnie		= willingly
jakoś		= somehow

DEGREE

wiele		= much
bardzo		= very
dużo		= much, a great deal
trochę		= a little
mało		= little, few
tylko	}	= only
li		
tyle		= so much
w ogóle		= in general
prawie	}	= almost
niemal		
przynajmniej		= at least
właśnie		= just, exactly
(za)ledwie		= hardly
nadzwyczaj		= extraordinarily, extremely
dosyć, dość		= enough, rather, considerably
wcale		= quite; with neg. = (not) at all
całkiem		
zupełnie	}	= quite, wholly
całkowicie		
zgoła		
bynajmniej nie		= not in the least
właściwie		= properly, actually
coraz + Comparative		=...-er and...-er
e.g. coraz większy		= larger and larger

INTERROGATIVE

czy?		— interrogative particle (*starting* a question)
kiedy?		= when?
gdzie?		= where?
dlaczego?		= why?
po co?	}	= what for?
na co?		
jak?		= how?
ile		= how many?
dokąd?		= whither?

INTERROGATIVE (Contd.)
skąd?   = whence?
chyba?   = I suppose, probably

Not = nie; no = nie; yes = tak; certainly = owszem.

CONJUNCTIONS

These present no special difficulties in Polish; but notice the many alternatives! The commonest are:—

Coördinating:
i   = and   albo...albo } = either...or
a   = and (contrasting)   czy...czy
ale } = but   lub   = or
lecz   tudzież = likewise, too
no   = well   również } = also
więc   = then, therefore   też
otóż   = now, so (then)   zarówno = likewise, as well
zatem   = consequently   to też = and so, therefore,
jednak = however   in consequence
                                 nawet   = even

Subordinating:
jeśli   } = if
jeżeli
gdyby   = if (in unreal conditions)
kiedy   } = when
gdy
póki   = while, so long as
ponieważ } = because, as
gdyż
skoro tylko = as soon as
jak gdyby } = as if
jak(o)by
chociaż   } = although
aczkolwiek
żeby   ⎫
aby   ⎬ = in order that
ażeby   ⎭
oby   = would that...!
że, iż   = that
bo, bowiem
  (encl.)   = for, because
odkąd   = since
zanim, nim = before
skoro   = as, since, after

PREPOSITIONS

Prepositions in Polish largely agree with those in other Slavonic languages as regards the cases they govern. "By" a person is in Polish przez + Acc., not the plain Instrumental. "Do" is used widely for "to", as in other West Slav languages, and governs the Gen. Some prepositions can govern two or more cases according to the meaning intended. Compound prepositions govern the Gen. (except poza).

With Gen.:
```
bez*          = without
dla           = for, towards (after adjs.)
od*           = from
z*            = off, from, out of
u             = at, near
do            = to
za            = in the time of
(po)mimo      = past, in spite of
prócz,oprócz  = except
blisko        = near
(o)koło       = round, about
obok          = beside
zamiast       = instead of
wśród    }
pośród   } = among
podczas       = during
wskutek       = because of
według   }
wedle    } = according to
wobec         = in view of
wzdłuż        = along(side of)
względem      = with regard to
```

With Dat.:
```
ku     = towards            przeciw(ko) = against
wbrew  = contrary to        dzięki      = thanks to
                            gwoli       = for the sake of
```

With Acc.:
```
przez* = through; by    po     = for (to fetch)
mimo   = in spite of    nad*   = over (motion)
na     = on to          pod*   = under (motion)
w*     = into           przed* = before (motion)
o      = for, against—  za     = 1.behind(motion)
         proszę o                2.for,on behalf of
       = I ask for      między = between(motion)
                        z*     = about(with numbers)
```

With Instr.:
```
   z*    = with
```

*See footnote on p. 304.

```
    między = among           przed*= before (rest)
    nad*   = above (rest)    za    = behind (rest)
    pod*   = below (rest)    poza  = outside, beyond
With Loc.:
    na   = on           o  = about, concerning
    w*   = in           po = 1. over, about
    przy = near              2. after
```

The verbal prefixes *ob-*, *wy-*, *prze-*, *roz-*, and *wz-* do not occur as prepositions.

Monosyllabic prepositions take the stress when followed by monosyllabic pronouns:—

```
        zà to     = for this
        dò nich   = to them
        ò co?     = for what?
```

THE CONJUGATION OF VERBS

Voices and Tenses

In Polish, as in Russian, the first three old classes of Slavonic verbs now really form one, owing to the fact that in Polish all *e*'s of whatever origin cause palatalization, except those derived from ь.

The Polish tense system is essentially the same as that of other West and East Slav languages. Its rarely used Pluperfect and Past Conditional are the only forms unknown to Russian. The Dual number in verbs has been entirely lost in literary Polish, leaving only traces (the 1st pers. *plur*. endings *-wa* and *-ma*) in certain dialects. The old Imperfect and Aorist tenses were lost by the sixteenth century. Polish has no *declinable* Past Participle Active, nor any Present Participle Passive, in contrast to Russian; but it has a Past Participle Active in *-ł* and a Present and a Past (indeclinable) Gerund. No Supine exists in Polish.(See also pp. 263-265 for other features.)

As in all other Slavonic languages, no Passive voice exists in Polish. This is variously rendered:—

1. By the verb być (= to be) + Past Participle Passive:

Miasto jest atakowane = the town is being attacked
Miasto było atakowane = the town was (being) attacked

2. by the verb zostać (= to remain) + Past

---

*Simple prepositions consisting of, or ending in, a consonant take an *-e* before difficult consonant groups, e.g.: bezè mnie = without me, przedè mną = before me, przède wszỳstkim = above all (lit. before all), first of all.

Participle Passive of *Perfective* verbs only; this form emphasizes the action expressed and is a uniquely Polish use:

>On został zamordowany = he was murdered

3. A reflexive verb can also be used[1]:

>Kosciół widzi się z domu = The church is seen from the house

Notice that a reflexive verb can be used impersonally, like the use of "one" in English, and can then govern an object, cf. Lusatian, p. 424-25:—

sprzedaje się (3rd pers. sg.!) książki (Acc. pl.) = Books are sold

4. The impersonal 3rd pers. plur. can also be used, as in other Slavonic languages:

>Mówią różne rzeczy o nim = Various things are said about him
>Chwalą go niezmiernie = He is greatly praised

5. A use shared by Polish with Ukrainian is that of the Past Participle Passive with the (neuter) ending -*o* to express an impersonal verb in the *Past*; the object goes in the case governed by the verb:

>Mówiono różne rzeczy o nim = Various things were said about him
>Widziano tam kobietę = A woman was seen there
>Szukano książki (Gen.s) ale nie znaleziono = The book was looked for, but was not found

The *Present* is the only true simple tense in modern Polish (the Past being really a compound tense, although written in one word). The personal endings of the Present are:—

>Sing. 1. -*ę*, or -*m* (for -*a*-verbs)
>2. -*sz*
>3. —(no ending)
>Plur. 1. -*my*
>2. -*cie*
>3. -*ą* (for all verbs! -*ją* after a vowel)

---

[1] In Polish the reflexive verb is formed by using the Active verb with the enclitic Accusative Reflexive Pronoun się, which is used for all persons, is written separately, and is pronounced sie (ɕɛ).

All these, except the -ę of the 1st pers. sing. and the -ą of the 3rd pers. plur. are preceded by -ie- (-e- after *chuintantes* and yot) or -i- (-y- after *chuintantes*) or -a-, which join the stem of the verb to the ending and distinguish the three main categories of Polish verbs. The verbs with -ie-(e) joining vowel can be further subdivided for etymological purposes into pure -ie-verbs (O.S. -є), -nie-verbs (O.S. -нє), and -je-verbs (O.S. -ю). The -a- type of verb is derived from verbs with -aje- and is to be met with in all South and West Slav languages. The old "athematic" verbs, four in number, survive in Polish and are best treated as irregular.

The Present tense of verbs of Class I (see below) with dental stems affords examples of the vowel alternation *io/ie*, e.g.:—

niosę = I carry, niesiesz = you (fam.) carry

Infinitives end in -*ć*, except for velar stems of Class I which have Infinitives in -*c*:

pisać = to write; nieść (Impfve.) = to carry

but—

piec = to bake; móc = to be able

The Infinitive is no guide as to the formation of the Present tense. For etymological and comparative as well as practical purposes we therefore give below a list of verbs classified according to their Present endings with subdivisions according to their Infinitives.

Classification of Polish Verbs according to their Presents, with Subdivisions according to their Infinitives

		3rd pers. sg. Pres.	Infinitive		
I.	A.a.	niesie	nieść	= to carry	Same stem in Pres. and Infin., consonantal stem.
		piecze	piec	= to bake	
Also:—					
		umrze	umrzeć	= to die (Pfve.). Infin. in -*rzeć*, from *-erti.	
		zacznie	zacząć	= to begin (Pfve.). Infin. in -*ąć* from -атн.	
	b.	—		(No vowel stems.)	
	B.a.	bierze	brać	= to take. Infin. in -*ać*, consonantal stem.	

POLISH

| | b. | rwie | rwać | = to pluck, tear. Infin. in -*ać*, originally a vowel stem. |

II. dźwignie dźwignąć = to lift(Pfve.). *n*-stems.

III. Presents with -*je*:—
  1. Primary verbs.
     A. a. czuje   czuć   = to feel. Same vowel stem in Pres. and Infin.
        b. miele¹   mleć   = to grind. Same conson-
                    (<*melti) ant stem in Pres. and Infin.
     B. Infinitives in -*ać*
        a. kraje   krajać = to cut. Infin. in -*ać*, vowel stem.
        b. orze   orać   = to plough. Infin. in -*ać*, consonant stem.
  2. Derived verbs. All vowel stems.
     A. siwieje   siwieć = to grow grey. Pres. stem. -*ie*-, Infin. in -*ieć*.
     B. kupuje   kupować = to buy. Pres. stem. -*u*-, Infin. in -*ować*.

IV. New Class, by contraction from -*aje*- in Present.
    zna   znać   = to know (Fr. connaître)
    działa   działać = to act
    kocha   kochać = to love

V. A. chwali   chwalić = to praise. *i*-stem throughout.
      uczy   uczyć   = to teach. *y*-stem throughout after *chuintante*.
   B. widzi   widzieć = to see. -*i*- Pres. stem, -*ieć* in Infin.
      krzyczy krzyczeć = to shout. -*y*- Pres. stem, -*eć* in Infin. after *chuintante*.

Athematic verbs:—
1st pers.sg. 3rd pers.sg.
  dam   da   dać(Pfve.) = to give ⎫ see "Irreg-
  jem   je   jeść   = to eat ⎬ ular Verbs"
  wiem   wie   wiedzieć   = to know ⎭ for full
                            (Fr.savoir) conjugation
  jestem   jest być   = to be

---

¹This verb does not represent a Class of verbs, being rather an exception in Polish.

Yotation takes place in the 1st pers. sing. and 3rd pers. plur. of Pres. of all verbs of (Polish) Class V, e.g.:—

		Pres.			3rd p. pl.
tracić	= to lose	tracę	but	tracisz etc.	tracą
widzieć	= to see	widzę	"	widzisz	widzą
prosić	= to request	proszę	"	prosisz	proszą
wozić	= to convey	wożę	"	wozisz	wożą
puścić	= to let go	puszczę	"	puścisz	puszczą
jeżdzić	= to travel (Freq.)	jeżdżę	"	jeździsz	jeżdżą

etc.

The Future Tense and the Aspects

There are two alternative ways of forming the Future of Imperfective (and Frequentative) verbs— with no difference of meaning.

1. The commonest way is with the Future of być (= to be), i.e.:—

1st p.sing. będę   1st p.plur. będziemy
2nd   "   będziesz   2nd   "   będziecie
3rd   "   będzie   3rd   "   będą

usually preceding the Past Participle Active in -ł (masc. sg.), -ła (fem. sg.), -ło (neut. sg.), -li (masc. pers. plur.), -ły (other genders pl.). This Past Participle Active is obtained by adding these endings to the Infinitive stem (Infinitive without the final ć) of verbs of Classes I.B, II, III, IV, V. In Class I.A these endings are added to the root of the verb, e.g.:—

piec = to bake, stem piek- (in piekę = I bake), Past. Part. Act.: piekł, piekła, etc.

The vowel alternations *ió/io/ie* occur here before dental stems, e.g.:—

nieść = to carry,
Past Part.Act. msc.sg.   niósł (with closed syll.)
  "   "   " fem.sg.   niosła,
  "   "   " neut.sg.   niosło
  "   "   " masc.pers. pl.   nieśli
  "   "   " other gend.pl.   niosły

In normal conversation the final ł is not often pronounced in masc. sing. forms with a consonant immediately preceding the ł, such as niósł, padł (= fell), and piekł.

Verbs with Infinitives in -*ieć* or -*eć* (O.S. -ѣти) show the alternation *ia/ie*, e.g.:—

widzieć = to see, Past.Part.Act.masc.sg.   widział
   "   "   "   fem.sg.   widziała
   "   "   "   neut.sg.   widziało
   "   "   "   masc.pers.pl.   widzieli
   "   "   "   other g.pl.   widziały

Verbs with Infinitives in -*ąć* show the alternation *ą/ę*, e.g.:—

ciągnąć = to pull, Past.Part.Act.masc.sg.   ciągnął
   "   "   "   fem.sg.   ciągnęła
   "   "   "   neut.sg.   ciągnęło
   "   "   "   masc.pers.pl.   ciągnęli
   "   "   "   other g.pl.   ciągnęły

Notice that not all verbs with Infinitives in -*nąć* preserve the syllable -*ną*- in the Past Participle Active. Some regularly drop it, others can drop it or need not. Those with a *vowel* directly before the -*nąć*, and monosyllabic verbs regularly preserve it, e.g.:—

ciągnąć = to pull; Past. Part. Act. ciągnął
    but—
marznąć = to freeze; Past. Part. Act. marzł (r and z
    are pronounced separately in this verb),
    while—
klęknąć(Pfve.) = to kneel down, has either klęknął,
    klęknęła, or kląkł, klękła;
    but—
płynąć = to float, *must* have płynął,
    and
tchnąć = to take a breath, has tchnął.

2. The other alternative way of forming the Future of Imperfective verbs is by using the Future of być,: będę, etc., with the Infinitive which, as often as not, precedes the auxiliary verb, e.g.:—

śpiewać będę = I shall sing
będę robić   = I shall do

The Future of Perfective verbs is in form their Present, which always has a Future meaning, as in other West and East Slav languages:—

robię = I do, am doing, but zrobię = I shall do
piszę = I write,   " napiszę = I shall write

The Formation of the Aspects:
Perfective from Imperfective

1. The last two examples illustrate one of the commonest ways of forming the Perfective aspect from a simple Imperfective verb in Polish, namely by the addition of a prefix:—

myć = to wash (Impfve.), Pres. myję
umyć = to wash (Pfve.), Fut. umyję

2. Another way of forming a Pfve. verb from an Impfve. is by using the ending *-nąć* to signify a single action:—

krzyczeć = to shout (Impfve.)
  Pres. krzyczę
krzyknąć = to shout (Pfve.)
  Fut. krzyknę

3. Some verbs merely change the Infinitive ending:—

chwytać = to catch (Impfve.), chwycić (Pfve.)

4. Occasionally, in the case of common verbs, a totally different root is used:—

widzieć = to see, Impfve.   zobaczyć or ujrzeć—Pfve.
mówić   = to say   "   powiedzieć—Pfve.
kłaść   = to lay   "   położyć—Pfve.
brać   = to take   "   wziąć or zabrać—Pfve.

Imperfective from Perfective

A few simple verbs are originally Pfve. in meaning. These also form Impfves. by changing the Infinitive ending, often by lengthening it:—

kupić = to buy,   Pfve., kupować —Impfve.
dać   = to give   "   dawać   —Impfve.
puścić = to let go   ".   puszczać—Impfve.
wrócić = to return   "   wracać —Impfve.

The numerous compound verbs used to express various shades of meaning beyond that of mere "perfectiveness" and which are Perfective because of their prefix, form their Imperfective aspect by various forms of lengthening:—

podpisać   = to sign,   Pfve., Impfve. podpisywać
nakryć   = to cover   "   "   nakrywać
dostać   = to get, receive   "   "   dostawać
poznać   = to get to know   "   "   poznawać
zabić   = to kill   "   "   zabijać
wybrać   = to choose   "   "   wybierać
nazwać   = to name   "   "   nazywać
przeprosić = to apologize   "   "   przepraszać
odmówić   = to refuse   "   "   odmawiać

Frequentative verbs are generally formed in this last way. They are somewhat more numerous in Polish than in other Slavonic languages apart from Czech and Slovak, e.g.:—

pisać   = to write, Impfve., Freq. pisywać = to write
                                              often or regularly
widzieć = to see   "   "   widywać
mieć   = to have   "   "   miewać
jeść   = to eat   "   "   jadać
pić   = to drink   "   "   pijać

From the above it will have been gathered that aspects are not formed automatically or regularly. The usage for each verb has to be learned separately by listening, reading, and observation.

The Past Tense

In contrast to the East Slav languages, the Past tense in Polish, besides varying according to gender, has personal endings. These endings (for 1st and 2nd pers. only) are added to the Past Participle Active in -ł and in the case of the masc. sing. a joining vowel -e- is used. (The Personal Pronouns are only used when emphasized.) The endings, derived from the old form of the Present of być used as an auxiliary verb (cf. French: je suis allé), are:—

            Sing. 1 -*m*   Plur. 1 -*śmy*
                  2 -*ś*   2 -*ście*
                  3 (none)   3 (none)

We thus have a great variety of forms for the various persons and genders, e.g.:—

	SING.			PLUR.	
	Masc.	*Fem.*	*Neut.*	*Masc.Pers.*	*Other Genders*
1	niosłem	niosłam	—	nieśliśmy	niosłyśmy
2	niosłeś	niosłaś	—	nieśliście	niosłyście
3	niósł	niosła	niosło	nieśli	niosły

It will be observed that the 3rd pers. sing. and plur. are identical in form with the Past Participle Active.

Notice that the 1st and 2nd pers. plur. are stressed on the *third* syllable from the end. This is due to the fact that the endings of the Past Tense are still partly felt to be independent auxiliaries, for they *can* be *transferred* and attached to other words in a sentence, such as subordinating conjunctions, pronouns, adverbs, adjectives, nouns, and numerals, e.g.:—

pisałem   = I was writing, but: kiedy
                                 pisałem *or* kiedym pisał
                                 = when I was writing
Gdzieś była?   = Where have you (fem.) been?
Myśmy już powiedzieli   = We have already said
Dalekom poszła   = I (fem.) went far

Powinienem to powiedzieć = I am obliged to say that.
W domuście to zrobili?   = Did you make it at home?
Jedeneśmy[1] miały   = We (fem.) had one

N.B.—These transferences are *not* obligatory.

The meaning of the Polish Past tense presents no difficulties. The Past of Impfve verbs generally corresponds to the English Imperfect, as it refers to an action, etc., continuing in the past: pisał = he was writing. The Pfve. Past refers to a completed action in the past and corresponds to the English Past or Perfect tenses: napisał list = he wrote, or has written, the letter.

The Pluperfect Tense

This tense has almost entirely disappeared from modern Polish, but is to be met with in older writers. It is formed by adding the Past Participle of być in the appropriate gender, but without personal endings, to the forms of the Past tense in the various persons, e.g.:—

widziałem był   = I (masc.) had seen
dałaś była   = you (fem. sg.) had given
poszedł był   = he had gone
kupiliśmy byli   = we (masc.) had bought
dostałyście były   = you (fem.) had received
ujrzeli byli   = they (masc.) had caught sight of...

The Conditional

The Conditional mood is formed by adding the endings: Sing. 1. -*bym*, 2. -*byś*, 3. -*by*, Plur. 1. -*byśmy*, 2. -*byście*, 3. -*by*, to the Past Part. Act. in the appropriate gender. We thus have two different sets of forms for the masc. and fem. genders respectively, with a third variant in the 3rd pers. sing. for neuter:—

Masc.	*Fem.*	*Neut.*
widziałbym	widziałabym	—
widziałbyś	widziałabyś	—
widziałby	widziałaby	widziałoby
widzielibyśmy	widziałybyśmy	—
widzielibyście	widziałybyście	—
widzieliby	widziałyby (f. and n.)	

It will be seen that the endings are the same as those of the Past tense with the auxiliary -*by*- inserted. Originally the Conditional endings were separate auxiliary verbs in Polish. It is not

[1] A joining vowel -*e*- is used when the word to which the ending is attached ends in a consonant.

surprising, therefore, that they too, like the endings of the Past tense, can be *placed after* other words in a sentence. They are written together only with conjunctions:—

jeżelibyśmy (*or* gdybyśmy) wiedzieli
  = if we should know, if we knew,
   also—if we *had* known
chętnie bym to zrobił = I would gladly do it
ja bym powiedział = *I* would say

Notice also the stresses on the 3rd and 4th syllable from the end, another sign of the separateness of these endings.

The Past Conditional
To emphasize that a condition is (unfulfilled) in the past, a Past Conditional *can* be formed by adding the auxiliary Past Participle, był, była, było, byli, były in the appropriate gender to the ordinary Conditional with its personal endings, as in the formation of the Pluperfect Tense. But if this auxiliary is put first the personal endings are attached to it and not to the main verb:—

widziałbym był   = I would have seen, *or*: byłbym widział
słuchałabyś była = you (f.) would have listened, *or*: byłabyś słuchała

But this tense, like the Pluperfect tense, is rarely used in modern Polish, the ordinary Conditional being used instead without loss of clarity. It is particularly rare in *both* clauses of an unfulfilled condition. (The conjunction for "if" in unfulfilled conditions is gdyby.)

The Imperative
True Imperative forms exist in Polish for the 2nd pers. sing. and the 1st and 2nd pers. plur. The 3rd persons sing. and plur. are rendered by niech (less commonly niechaj) + Pres. Impfve. or Pfve.

1. If the Present stem of the verb, as seen in the 2nd pers. sing., ends in a single consonant, no ending is added to form the 2nd pers. sing. Imperative and the consonant is merely softened or kept soft, except in the case of *chuintantes* (ex-palatals) which are retained, and labials which become hard:—

	2nd pers. sg. Pres.	2nd pers. sg. Imper.
nieść = to carry,	niesiesz,	nieś!
płynąć = to float,	płyniesz,	płyń!

		2nd pers. sg. Pres.	2nd pers. sg. Imper.
pisać	to write,	piszesz	pisz!
bronić =	to defend,	bronisz,	broń!
uczyć =	to teach,	uczysz,	ucz!
krajać =	to cut,	krajesz,	kraj!
robić =	to do,	robisz,	rób!

(with regular vowel alternation *o/ó* and hardening of final labial.)

2. But verbs with a Present stem ending in two or more consonants, add the ending -*ij* for the 2nd pers. sing. Imperative (-*yj* after *chuintantes*):—

		2nd pers. sg. Pres.	2nd pers. sg. Imper.
dąć	= to blow,	dmiesz,	dmij!
rwać	= to tear,	rwiesz,	rwij!
drzeć	= to rend,	drzesz,	drzyj!
ciągnąć	= to pull,	ciągniesz,	ciągnij!

3. Verbs with Pres. stems ending in a vowel add the ending -j:—

		2nd pers. sg. Pres.	2nd pers. sg. Imper.
kupować	= to buy,	kupu-jesz	kupuj!
działać	= to act,	działa-sz	działaj!
pokazywać	= to show,	pokazu-jesz	pokazuj!
wychowywać	= to bring up,	wychowu-jesz	wychowuj! *or* wychowywaj!
poznać (Pfve.)	= to get to know,	pozna-sz (Fut.)	poznaj!

The 1st and 2nd persons plural Imperative are obtained by adding -*my* and -*cie* respectively to the 2nd person sing. of all three types:—

		1st pers. pl.	2nd pers. pl.
nieś!	= carry!	nieśmy!	nieście!
dmij!	= blow!	dmijmy!	dmijcie!
kupuj!	= buy!	kupujmy!	kupujcie!
dzialaj!	= act!	działajmy!	działajcie!

3rd pers. sing. and plur.—examples:—

Sing. niech niesie! = let him carry! Plur. niech niosą!
" niech zrobi! = let him do! (Pfve.) " niech zrobią!

The Gerunds (*Active*)

As in other Slavonic languages, Gerunds in Polish are indeclinable verbal adverbs and can refer only to the subject of a sentence. They can qualify a verb in any tense. The *Present Gerund* is formed from all Imperfective verbs by adding -*c* to the 3rd pers. plur. Pres.; it expresses an action contemporary with that of the main verb. E.g.:—

Pres. Gerund
niosą = they carry, niosąc = while carrying
działają = they act, działając

The *Past Gerund* is formed only from Perfective verbs by adding the ending -*szy* to the masc. Past Participle Active in -ł, when the stem of the verb ends in a consonant:—

Past Part. Act. zniósł = carried down, stem zniós-;
Past Gerund: zniósłszy = having carried down

(The ł here is of fairly recent origin and is not usually pronounced.)
But if the stem ends in a vowel, the ending -*wszy* is added to the *stem*:—

Past Past. Act. zdziałał = performed, stem zdziała-;
Past Gerund: zdziaławszy
"   "   " zrobił = done, stem zrobi-;
Past Gerund: zrobiwszy

The Past Gerund is never declined, despite its apparently adjectival ending, and behaves like the Pres. Gerund above; but it expresses an action *preceding* that of the main verb. It is rarely used in conversation.

The Participles

Polish has only three participles (verbal adjectives)—the Present Participle Active, the Past Participle Active in -ł used only in the *Imperfective Future* and *Past* tenses and in the *Conditional* Mood (q.v.), and the Past Participle Passive.

The *Present Participle Active* is formed only from Imperfective verbs by adding the endings: sing. -*cy* (masc.), -*ca* (fem.), -*ce* (neut.), plur. -*cy* (masc. pers.), -*ce* (other genders), to 3rd pers. plur. Pres., e.g.:—

niosą = they carry; niosący, -a,-e,etc. = (who is) carrying
działają = they act; działający,-a-e,etc. = (who is) acting

They are declined exactly like adjectives and agree with their noun in gender, number, and case; but being verbal, they can also govern an object in the appropriate case. They express an action contemporary to that of the main verb and often replace a relative clause.

Kobieta, szukająca tej książki, przyszła do nas.
= The woman who was looking for this book, came
to us.

This participle is frequently used in modern Polish.

The *Past Participle Active* in *-ł* is never used
apart from the Imperfective Future and Past tenses
and the Conditional Mood. We have already dealt with
its formation under the heading "The Future Tense and
the Aspects". A few remnants of the participial use
of this form have become pure adjectives:

```
były      = former
doniosły  = important
roztyły   = gross, corpulent
zwiędły   = faded
ogłupiały = stupefied
```

A few remnants of an old *Present Participle Passive* have suffered the same fate, having become entirely adjectival and some even substantival, e.g.:—

```
ruchomy  = mobile
wiadomy  = known
rzekomy  = so-called, would-be
rodzimy  = natural, native
znajomy  = acquaintance
```

The *Past Participle Passive* is frequently used
in modern Polish, both independently and to form the
Passive Voice (see pp. 304-5). It is formed from the
Infinitive, mostly with the adjectival endings: sing.
- *ny* (masc.), *-na* (fem.), *-ne* (neut.), plur. *-ni*
(masc. pers.), *-ne* (other genders).

When the Infin. stem ends in a consonant, the
soft joining vowel *-io-* is used. This regularly becomes *-ie-* in the Nom. plur. masc. pers.:—

nieść = to carry; Past Part. Pass.: niesiony, -a,-e,
    Nom. plur. masc. pers. only—niesieni, other
    genders plural: niesione = (having been)
    carried.
zrobić = to do; Past Part. Pass.: zrobiony, -a,-e,
    Nom. plur. masc. pers. only—zrobieni, other
    genders pl.: zrobione = (having been) done.

Verbs of Polish Class V with Infin. in *-ić* or
-yć undergo *yotation* before the ending *-iony*. Hence
we have:—

prosić	= to request,	Past. Part.Pass.:	"	"	proszony,
wywozić	= to export,	"	"	"	wywożony,
urodzić się	= to be born,	"	"	"	urodzony,
stracić	= to lose,	"	"	"	stracony,
					etc.

Verbs with Infin. in -*ać* have Past Part. Pass. in -*any*, -*a*, -*e*, e.g.:—

czytać = to read, Past Part. Pass.: czytany, -a, -e; while verbs with Infin. in -*ieć* have Past Part. Pass. in -*iany*, -*a*, -*e*. The alternation *ie/ia* reminds one that the original vowel was ѣ(ĕ):—

zrozumieć (Pfve.) = to understand, Past Part. Pass.: zrozumiany, Nom. pl. masc. pers. zrozumiani (with -*ia*-!)

But verbs with Infin. in -*nąć*, -*ąć* and monosyllabic roots in -*ić*, -*uć*, and -*yć* and those going back to vocalic r have their Past Part. Pass. in: sing. -*ty*, -*ta*, -*te*, plur. -*ci*, -*te*, ą changing to ę, e.g.:—

		Past. Part. Pass.
dźwignąć	= to lift,	dźwignięty, -a, -e, plur. dźwignięci, -te
dąć	= to blow,	dęty, -a, -e, plur. dęci, -te
pić	= to drink	pity
odczuć	= to feel, (Pfve.)	odczuty
szyć	= to sew,	szyty
drzeć	= to tear,	darty

Some verbs have alternative forms, especially verbs in -*nąć*, e.g.:—

dźwigniony from dźwignąć (above);

and with

mleć = to grind, mielony is used in preference to mełty.

Some verbs in -*nąć* which are intransitive, have a Past Part. which is Passive in form but not in meaning, e.g.:—

zwiędnąć = to fade, zwiędnięty = faded

The Verbal Noun

The Verbal Noun in -*anie*, -*enie* or -*cie* is formed, when required, from the Past Participle Passive.

The ending -*anie* is used for verbs with Infinitives in -*ać* and Past Part. Pass. in -*any*, e.g.:—

pisać = to write, Past Part. Pass. pisany,—pisanie = writing

The ending -(*i*)*enie* is used for all verbs with Past Part. Pass. in -(*i*)*ony*, e.g.: nieść = to carry, Past Part. Pass. niesiony,—niesienie = carrying.

Verbs with Past Part. Pass. in *-ty* regularly have Verbal Nouns in *-cie*, e.g.:—

                           Past Part. Pass.
    pokryć = to cover,   pokryty,—pokrycie
    zamknąć = to close,   zamknięty,—zamknięcie
    otworzyć = to open,   otwarty,—otwarcie

A peculiarity of Polish (shared with Slovak) is that reflexive verbs can retain the się with the Verbal Noun, e.g.: spalić się = to get burnt down—spalenie się fabryki = the burning down of the factory.

All Verbal Nouns decline like soft neuter *o*-stems (see under "The Declension of Nouns," No. 4*b*, "zdanie," above).

Examples of the three main Conjugations of Verbs
   1. *-ie-* type (Clases I, II, and III).

	Class I. nieść = to carry (Impfve.)[1]	*Chuintante sub-type* Class III. pisać = to write
Present		
Sing. 1	niosę	piszę
2	niesiesz	piszesz
3	niesie	pisze
Plur. 1	niesiemy	piszemy
2	niesiecie	piszecie
3	niosą	piszą
Imperative		
Sing. 2	nieś	pisz
Plur. 1	nieśmy	piszmy
2	nieście	piszcie
Gerunds		
Present	niosąc	piszac
Past	zaniósłszy	napisawszy
Participles		
Past Act.	niósł	pisał
Past Pass.	niesiony	pisany

   2. *-a-* type (Class IV)
             kochać[2] = to love

Present
Sing. 1 kocham
    2 kochasz   Gerunds
    3 kocha   Present kochając

[1] So also Class II.
[2] Like kochać, umieć (= to know how to), and its compounds, e.g. rozumieć (= to understand), and śmieć (= to dare), substituting *-ie-* in the endings for *-a-*, except in the Past Participles Active and Passive which have *-ia-*: e.g. śmiał, rozumiany.

Present		Gerunds
	Past zakochawszy się[1]
Plur. 1	kochamy
2	kochacie	Participles
3.	kochają	Past Act. kochał
	Past Pass. kochany

Imperative
Sing. 2 kochaj
Plur. 1 kochajmy
2 kochajcie

3. -i(y)- type (Class V).

Chuintante sub-type

chwalić = to praise   krzyczeć = to shout

	chwalić	krzyczeć
Present		
Sing. 1	chwalę	krzyczę
2	chwalisz	krzyczysz
3	chwali	krzyczy
Plur. 1	chwalimy	krzyczymy
2	chwalicie	krzyczycie
3	chwalą	krzyczą
Imperative		
Sing. 2	chwal	krzycz
Plur. 1	chwalmy	krzyczmy
2	chwalcie	krzyczcie
Gerunds		
Present	chwaląc	krzycząc
Past	pochwaliwszy	(krzyknąwszy)
Participles		
Past Act.	chwalił	krzyczał
Past Pass.	chwalony	krzyczany

Irregular Verbs
The Athematic verbs:—

	być = to be	dać (Pfve.) = to give	jeść = to eat	wiedzieć = to know
Present				
Sing. 1	jestem		jem	wiem
2	jesteś		jesz	wiesz
3	jest		je	wie
Plur. 1	jesteśmy		jemy	wiemy
2	jesteście		jecie	wiecie
3	są		jedzą	wiedzą
Future				
Sing. 1	będę	dam		
2	będziesz	dasz		
3	będzie	da		
Plur. 1	będziemy	damy		
2	będziecie	dacie		
3	będą	dadzą		

[1] = having fallen in love.

Imperative
```
Sing. 2    bądź           daj         jedz        wiedz
Plur. 1    bądźmy         dajmy       jedzmy      wiedzmy
      2    bądźcie        dajcie      jedzcie     wiedzcie
```
Gerunds
```
Present    będąc          —           jedząc      wiedząc
Past       -bywszy        dawszy      zjadłszy    dowiedzia-
           (zdobywszy)¹                           wszy się²
```
Participles
```
Past Act.  był            dał         jadł        wiedział
Past Pass. -byty          dany        jedzony     zapowie-
           (zdobyty)                              dziany³
```

The most important other irregular verbs:—

	Pres. 1st p. sg.	3rd p. sg.	Imper. 2nd p. sg.
chcieć = to want	chcę,	chce;	chciej!

	Past Part. Act. m. sg.	m. pers. pl.	Past Part. Pass.
	chciał,	chcieli	

	Pres.		Imper.
mieć = to have	mam,	ma;	miej!
	miał,	mieli	

Class I

trząść = to shake	trzęsę,	trzęsie;	trząś!	
	trząsł,	trzęśli;		trzęsiony
leźć = to creep, drag	lezę,	lezie;	leź!	
	lazł,	leźli		
znaleźć (Pfve.) = to find	znajdę,	znajdzie;	znajdź!	
	znalazł,	znaleźli;		znaleziony
kłaść = to put	kładę,	kładzie;	kładź!	
	kładł,	kładli;		kładziony
prząść = to spin	przędę,	przędzie;	prządź!	
	prządł,	przędli;		przędziony
siąść (Pfve.) = to sit down	siądę,	siądzie;	siądź!	
	siadł,	siedli		
móc = to be able	mogę,	może;	—	
	mógł,	mogli		

[1] zdobyć = to capture, (Pfve.)
[2] = having found out.
[3] = announced.

	Pres.		Imper.	
	1st p. sg.	3rd p. sg.	2nd p. sg.	
dąć = to blow	dmę,	dmie;	dmij!	
	Past Part. Act.			Past Part.
	m. sg.	m. pers. pl.		Pass.
	dął,	dęli;		dęty
jąć = to start	-jmę,	-jmie;	-jmij!	
	jął,	jęli;		-jęty
wziąć(Pfve.) = to take	wezmę,	weźmie;	weź!	
	wziął,	wzięli;		wzięty
kląć = to curse[1]	klnę,	klnie;	klnij!	
	kląl,	klęli;		klęty
ciąć = to cut	tnę,	tnie;	tnij!	
	ciął,	cięli;		cięty
rwać = to tear	rwę,	rwie;	rwij!	
	rwał,	rwali;		rwany
zwać = to name	zwę or zowię,	zwie or zowie;	zwij!	
	zwał,	zwali;		zwany
łgać = to tell lies	lżę	łże;	łżyj!	
	3rd p.pl. lżą;			
	łgał,	łgali;		-łgany
brać(Impfve.) = to take	biorę,	bierze;	bierz!	
	brał,	brali;		brany
drzeć = to rend[2]	drę,	drze;	drzyj!	
	darł,	darli;		darty
żreć = to eat (of animals)	żrę,	żre;	żryj!	
	żarł,	żarli;		żarty
wrzeć = to boil	wrę,	wrze, or wre;	wrzej!	
	wrzał,	wrzeli		

[1] So also: zacząć = to begin (Pfve.)
[2] See also: umrzeć = to die (Pfve.).

POLISH

	Pres.		Imper.
	1st p. sg.	3rd p. sg.	2nd p. sg.
kaszleć = to cough	kaszlę,	kaszle;	kaszl! *or* kaszlaj! *or* kasłaj!

	Past Part. Act.		Past Part. Pass.
	m. sg.	m. pers. pl.	
	kaszlał,	kaszlali;	kaszlano
	or		*or*
	kasłał,	kasłali;	kasłano

Class II

	Pres. 1st	Pres. 3rd	Imper. 2nd
wstać(Pfve.) = to get up	wstanę,	wstanie;	wstań!
	wstał,	wstali;	wstano
pachnieć *or* pachnąć = to smell pleasant	pachnę,	pachnie;	pachnij!
	pachniał, pachnieli *or* pachnął, pachnęli (arch.)		
ciec = to flow	cieknę,	cieknie *or* ciecze;	cieknij!
	ciekł,	ciekli;	-cieczony
kraść = to steal	kradnę,	kradnie;	kradnij!
	kradł,	kradli;	kradziony
paść(Pfve.) = to fall	padnę,	padnie;	padnij!
	padł,	padli	
rość *or* rosnąć = to grow	rosnę,	rośnie;	rośnij!
	rósł,	rośli	
	(*Past 1st p.sg.masc.* rosłem)		
lec(Pfve.) =[1] to lie down	legnę,	legniesz;	legnij!
	legł,	legli;	-lężony
rzec(Pfve.) = to say	rzeknę,	rzeknie *or* rzecze	rzeknij! *or* -rzecz!
	rzekł,	rzekli;	-rzeczony

---

[1] Cf. ląc *or* lęgnąć = to hatch; lęgnę; wylęgła.

POLISH

Class III   Pres.   Imper.
                 1st p. sg.   3rd p. sg.   2nd p. sg.

pruć =
  to rip,cleave pruję,   pruje;   pruj!
  likewise: Past Part. Act.   Past Part.
  kłuć =   m. sg.   m. pers. pl.   Pass.
  to prick   pruł,   pruli;   pruty
mleć =
  to grind   mielę,   miele;   miel!
                 mełł,   melli;   mielony
                                                              (or
                                                              mełty)

słać =
  to send   ślę,   śle;   ślij!
                 słał,   słali;   słany

słać =
  to spread   ścielę,   ściele;   ściel!
                 słał,   słali;   słany

lać =
  to pour   leję,   leje;   lej!
                 lał,   lali;[1]   lany

Class IV
dawać (Impfve.) =
  to give   daję,   daje;   dawaj!
                 dawał,   dawali;   dawany
similarly—
poznawać = to get to know (Impfve.) and
stawać = to stop (intrans.—Iterative), the Pfve. of
  which—stanąć—is regular.
stawać *się* (Impfve.), with stać się, stanę się
  (Pfve.), = to become.
Cf. stać = to stand, Class V, below; cf. also
  stawiać (Impfve.), postawić (Pfve.) = to place
  (both regular!).

Class V
patrzeć or
  patrzyć (Impfve.) =
  to look   patrzę,   patrzy;   patrz!
                 patrzył,   patrzyli;   patrzono
                    or   or
                 patrzał   patrzeli;
spojrzeć = to look (Pfve.), has an irregular
              Imperative: spójrz!
bać się =
  to fear   boję się,   boi się;   bój się!
                 bał się,   bali się;   bano się

[1] In Warsaw speech: leli; likewise: śmieli (or śmiali) się
= they were laughing, from śmiać się, śmieję się.

	Pres.		Imper.	
	1st p. sg.	3rd p. sg.	2nd p. sg.	
stać (Impfve.) = to stand	stoję,	stoi;	stój!	

	Past Part. Act.		Past Part.
	m. sg.	m. pers. pl.	Pass.
	stał,	stali;	stano
spać = to sleep	śpię,	śpi;	śpij!
	spał,	spali;	-spany

Verbs of Going and Conveying

To go (on foot):
  Impfve.: iść   Pfve.: pójść
Pres.:   idę, idziesz   Fut.: pójdę, pójdziesz
Past Part.   poszedł, poszła
  Act. sg. szedł, szła, szło
      pl. szli, szły
Past Tense:
    sg. 1 szedłem, szłam, etc.
    pl. 1 szliśmy, szłyśmy
Imper.:   idź![1]   pójdź!
          Frequentative: chodzić
     Pres.:   chodzę, chodzisz
     Past Part. Act. sg.: chodził, chodziła
     Imper.:   chodź![2]

To go (be conveyed):
  Impfve.: jechać   Pfve.: pojechać
Pres.:   jadę, jedziesz Fut.: pojadę, pojedziesz
Past Part. Act.: jechał   pojechał
Imper.   jedź!   pojedź!
                Freq.: jeździć
     Pres.:   jeżdżę, jeździsz
     Past Part. Act.:   jeździł
     Imper.:   jeźdź!

To come (on foot):
  Impfv. *and* Freq.: przychodzić   Pfve.: przyjść
Pres.:   przychodzę,   Fut.: przyjdę,
           przychodzisz   przyjdziesz
Past Part.   przyszedł,
  Act.:   przychodził   przyszła
Imper.:   przychodź!   przyjdź!

---

[1] = odejdź! = go away!
[2] = przyjdź! = come (here)!

To come (conveyed):
  Impfve. *and* Freq.: przyjeżdżać   Pfve.: przyjechać
  Pres.:   przyjeżdżam,   Fut: przyjadę,
              przyjeżdżasz   przyjedziesz
  Past Part.
    Act.:   przyjeżdżał   przyjechał
    Imper.:   przyjeżdżaj!   przyjedź!

  Similarly:

To go away   = odchodzić, odejść, Fut. odejdę,
  (on foot)   Imper. odejdź! Past Part. Act.
                odszedł, odeszła
To go away
  (conveyed) = odjeżdżać, odjechać
To go out   = wychodzić, wyjść, Past Part. Act.
  (on foot)   wyszedł, wyszła
To go out
  (conveyed) = wyjeżdżać, wyjechać

  On the same model=
To carry:
  Impfv.: nieść   Pfve.: zanieść
  Pres.:   niosę,niesiesz   Fut.: zaniosę,zaniesiesz
  Past Part.
    Act. sg.: niósł,niosła   zaniósł,zaniosła
        pl.: nieśli,niosły
    Imper.:   nieś!   zanieś!
             Freq: nosić
        Pres.:   noszę, nosisz
        Past Part. Act.: nosił
        Imper.:   noś!
To bring:
  Impfve. *and* Freq.: przynosić   Pfve.: przynieść
  Pres.: przynoszę,przynosisz Fut.: przyniosę,
                                     przyniesiesz

To lead:
  Impfve.: wieść   Pfve.: powieść *or* zawieść[1]
  Pres.:   wiodę,wiedziesz Fut.: powiodę,powiedziesz
  Past Part.
    Act. sg.: wiódł,wiodła   powiódł,powiodła
        pl.: wiedli,wiodły
    Imper.:   wiedź!   powiedź!
             Freq.: wodzić
        Pres.:   wodzę, wodzisz
        Past Part. Act.: wodził
        Imper.:   wodź! *or* wódź!

[1] Pfve, also: zabrać, zaprowadzić, poprowadzić.

To bring (a person):
Impfve. *and* Freq.: przywodzić   Pfve.: przywieść
(*or*: przyprowadzać,   przyprowadzić—regular)
Pres.: przywodzę,   Fut.: przywiodę
    przywodzisz   przywiedziesz

To convey:
  Impfve.: wieźć   Pfve.: zawieźć
  Pres.:   wiozę, wieziesz   Fut.: zawiozę, zawieziesz
  Past Part.
    Act. sg.: wiózł, wiozła   zawiózł, zawiozła
        pl.: wieźli, wiozły
  Imper.:   wieź!   zawieź!
                Freq.: wozić
      Pres.:   wożę, wozisz
      Past Part. Act.:   woził
      Imper.:   woź!

To bring (in a vehicle):
Impfv. *and* Freq.: przywozić   Pfve.: przywieźć
Pres.: przywożę, przywozisz   Fut.: przywiozę,
                                                  przywieziesz

WORD ORDER WITH ENCLITICS

(For the list of enclitics, see above after "Pronunciation" under "Enclitics," p. 243.)

Although Polish has many enclitic words which occur frequently, it has no rigid rules about word order with enclitics such as exist in the South Slav languages.

Enclitics cannot, of course, start a sentence. And in sentences of more than two words they do not occur at the end either. Thus one says:—
    Spotykam go   = I meet him
but—Często go spotykam = I often meet him.

If two adverbs or adverbial expressions occur, the enclitic Personal Pronoun, which prefers to come early in the sentence, may be put after the first, especially colloquially, or after the second (which ordinarily also precedes the verb), e.g.:—

    Teraz go często spotykam = I meet him often now
or—
    Teraz często go spotykam (the more literary
                                                order)

When a negative verb occurs, the negative particle (which is a *pro*clitic) must immediately precede the verb. Hence in any but a three word negative sentence with an enclitic, the enclitic will still precede the (negative) verb, e.g.:—

    Nie spotykam go = I do not meet him

Teraz go nie spotykam = I do not meet him now
Teraz go nigdy nie spotykam = I never meet him now
or (more literary)—
   Teraz nigdy go nie spotykam

But the verb itself may be more stressed than some of the adverbs, and so occur towards the beginning of a sentence. Then the enclitic pronoun occurs as third, and not second, word in the sentence, e.g.:—

Często spotykam go w mieście = I often meet him in town
Nie spotykam go teraz = I do not meet him now

The Reflexive Pronoun się usually follows the verb with which it goes:—

Boję się to (colloq. tego) zrobić = I am afraid to do that

But it too avoids the final position colloquially:—

   Praca się zaczęła = Work began
as well as—
   Zaczęła się praca

It can also be separated from its verb by a Dative enclitic:—

Zdaje mi się że... = It seems to me that...

When a Dative or Genitive enclitic occurs with an Accusative enclitic, the Dative or Genitive usually precedes, e.g.:—

Dam ci go jutro = I shall give it to you tomorrow
Niech mi go Pani przeczyta = (Please) read it to me!
but:
Dlaczego się jej wstydzisz? = Why are you ashamed of it (fem.)?

When two reflexive verbs occur together, one się serves them both:—

Boję się spóźnić = I am afraid to be late

To, when used as a Demonstrative Pronoun, *may* also be enclitic, especially if in the Accusative, but it follows the enclitic Personal Pronouns, e.g.:—

Dam ci to jutro = I shall give you this tomorrow
Często chciałem mu to powiedzieć = I have often wanted to say that to him

But when *to* is used as a particle expressing interest, it precedes other enclitics:—

Dlaczego to mu jej nie dasz? = Why then won't you give it (fem.) him?
Gdzież to je chowa? = *Where* does he keep them then?

It will be observed that no part of the verb "to be" is treated as an enclitic.

The *detachable* Conditional endings, when not written with another word, take precedence over other enclitics, e.g.:—

Chętnie byśmy go zobaczyli = We would gladly see him
To by się mogło stać = That could happen
Nigdy by mi to na myśl nie przyszło = That would never occur to me

The interrogative particle czy is not an enclitic and always *starts* a question:—

Czy mi go nigdy nie dasz? = Will you never give it to me?

TEXTS

(printed as in source, not all in modern orthography)

I. Ś. Lukasz, VIII.

5. Wyszedł rozsiewca, aby rozsiewał nasienie swoje; a gdy on rozsiewał, tedy jedno padło podle drogi i podeptane jest, a ptaki niebieskie pozobały je.
6. A drugie padło na opokę, a gdy wzeszło, uschło, przeto iż nie miało wilgotności.
7. A drugie padło między ciernie; ale ciernie wespół z nim wzrosły, i zadusiły je.
8. A drugie padło no ziemię dobrą, a gdy wzeszło, przyniosło pożytek stokrotny.

To mówiąc wołał: Kto ma uszy ku słuchaniu, niechaj słucha!

II. J. Kochanowski.

Tren X

Orszulo moja wdzięczna! gdzieś mi sie podziała?
W którą stronę, w którąś sie krainę udała?
Czyś ty nad wszytki nieba wysoko wzniesiona
I tam w liczbę aniołków małych policzona?
Czyliś do raju wzięta? czyliś na szcześliwe
Wyspy zaprowadzona? czy cię przez tesklive
Charon jeziora wiezie i napawa zdrojem
Niepomnym, że ty nie wiesz nic o płaczu mojem?
Czy, człowieka zrzuciwszy i myśli dziewicze,

Wzięłaś na sie postawę i piórka słowicze?
Czyli sie w czyścu czyścisz, jeśli z strony ciała,
Jakakolwiek zmazeczka na tobie została?
Czyś po śmierci tam poszła, kędyś pierwej była,
Niżeś sie na mą ciężką żałość urodziła?
Gdzieśkolwiek jest, jeśliś jest, lituj mej żałości,
A nie możeszli w onej dawnej swej całości,
Pociesz mię, jako możesz, a staw sie przede mną,
Lubo snem lubo cieniem lub marą nikczemną.

III. A. Mickiewicz.

Dobrywieczór

Dobrywieczór! on dla mnie najsłodszem życzeniem;
Nigdy, czyto przed nocą dzieli nas zapora,
Czyli mię ranna znowu przywołuje pora,
Nie żegnam się, ni witam z takiem zachwyceniem,

Jak w tę chwilę, wieczornym ośmielony cieniem;
Ty nawet, milczeć rada i płonić się skora,
Gdy usłyszysz życzenie dobrego wieczora,
Żywszem okiem, głośniejszem rozmawiasz westchnieniem.

Niechaj dzieńdobry wschodzi tym, co społem żyją,
Objaśniać pracę, która ich ręce jednoczy;
Dobranoc niech szczęśliwych kochanków otoczy,

Gdy z rozkoszy kielicha trosk osłodę piją;
A tym, co się kochają i swą miłość kryją,
Dobrywieczór niech przyćmi zbyt wymowne oczy!

IV. A. Mickiewicz.

Bakczysaraj w nocy

Rozchodzą się z dżamidów pobożni mieszkańce,
Odgłos izanu w cichym gubi się wieczorze,
Zawstydziło się licem rubinowem zorze,
Srebrny król nocy dąży spocząć przy kochance.

Błyszczą w haremie niebios wieczne gwiazd kagańce,
Śród nich po safirowym żegluje przestworze
Jeden obłok, jak senny łabędź na jeziorze,
Pierś ma białą, a złotem malowane krańce.

Tu cień pada z menaru i wierzchu cyprysa,
Dalej czernią się kołem olbrzymy granitu,
Jak szatany, siedzące w dywanie Eblisa

Pod namiotem ciemności; niekiedy z ich szczytu
Budzi się błyskawica i pędem farysa
Przelatuje milczące pustynie błękitu.

V. E. Orzeszkowa.

From "Niziny"

Wiosenny wieczór spadał na pola, ziejąc mocną wonią świeżo zoranej ziemi. Mglisto było, pochmurno i cicho. Drogą, z rzadka osadzoną drzewami, szła kobieta bosa i w siermiędze. W zmroku i mgle szła prędko i prosto, nie omijając kałuż ani głębokich kolein, które z pod bosych stóp jej bryzgały wodą i rzadkiem marcowem błotem. Bose te stopy ciężkie były i silne, doskonale snadź zażyłe z ziemią, po której stąpały. Wszystko im jedno było, poczem szły, byleby tylko szły prędko. Wszystko jedno było idącej kobiecie, co ją otaczało, byleby jaknajprędzej doszła do tego, co było przed nią. Nie lękała się niczego: ani zwiększającej się coraz ciemności, ani obejmującej widnokrąg ciszy, ani rozsianych po polu i widmową postać przybierających grusz i topoli. Nie zachwycała się też niczem: ani sklepieniem nieba, nieruchomem i utkanem z białych szarych obłoków, ani wonią ziemi, którą z nad zagonów podnosiły ciepłe powiewy, ani gwiazdami, które tu i ówdzie błyskały z pomiędzy chmur. Nie lękając się niczego i na wszystko, co ją otaczało, obojętna, wyprostowana, silna, do pośpiechu czemś gnana, szła i szła...

VI. H. Sienkiewicz.

From "Ta trzecia"

Zacząłem go malować przed rokiem.

Było tak.

Idę sobie wieczorem nad Wisłą, patrzę: rozbił się galar z jabłkami. Andrusy wyławiają jabłka z wody, a nad brzegami siedzi cała rodzina żydowska w takiej rozpaczy, że nawet nie lamentują, tylko pozałamywali ręce i patrzą na wodę jak posągi. Jest stary Żyd, patrjarcha-nędzarz, stara Żydówka, młody Żyd, kolosalna bestja jak Machabeusz, młoda dziewczyna, piegowata trochę, ale z ogromnym charakterem nosa i ust, wreszcie dwoje Żydziąt. Wieczór zapada; rzeka ma miedziane refleksy—poprostu cudne. Drzewa na Saskiej Kępie całe w zorzy, dalej na Kępie szeroko rozlana woda, tony czerwone, tony ultramaryny, tony prawie stalowe, to znów przechodzące w purpurę i fiolet. Perspektywa powietrzna— rozkosz! przejście od jednych tonów do drugich takie niepochwytne a cudne, że aż dusza piszczy—naokół cicho, świetlisto, spokojnie. Melancholja nad wszystkiem, że się chce wyć—i ta grupa w smutku, siedząca tak jakby wszyscy od małego pozowali w

pracowniach....
   Odrazu mi w głowie zaświtało: oto mój obraz!

VII. T. Lenartowicz.

Kalina

Rosła kalina z liściem szerokiem,
Nad modrym w gaju rosła potokiem,
Drobny deszcz piła, rosę zbierała,
W majowem słońcu liście kąpała.
W lipcu korale miała czerwone,
W cienkie z gałązek włosy wplecione.
Tak się stroiła jak dziewczę młode
I jak w lusterko patrzyła w wodę.
Wiatr co dnia czesał jej długie włosy,
A oczy myła kroplami rosy.
U tej krynicy, u tej kaliny
Jasio fujarki kręcił z wierzbiny,
I grywał sobie długo żałośnie,
Gdzie nad krynicą kalina rośnie,
I śpiewał sobie: Dana! oj dana!
A głos po rosie leciał co rana.
Kalina liście zielone miała
I jak dziewczyna w gaju czekała.
A gdy jesienią w skrzynkę zieloną
Pod czarny krzyżyk Jasia złożono,
Biedna kalina znać go kochała,
Bo wszystkie swoje liście rozwiała,
Żywe korale wrzuciła w wodę,
Z żalu straciła swoją urodę.

VIII. J. Kasprowicz.

Nad książką nachylony

Nad książką nachylony,
Ni jednej nie widzę zgłoski.
A słucham jedynie, czy stamtąd
Szum nie zaleci boski.

Nie ślą mi swoich nowin
Potoki, wierchy, urwiska—
Turkot li wozów ulicznych
W moją tęsknotę się wciska.

Nie ślą mi swoich nowin
Płomienie z za krańca świata,
W to moje głuche pustkowie
Zwolna już mrok się wplata.

Hej! wyrwę się z jego więzów,
Raz jeszcze do lotu się zmuszę,
By spocząć, gdzie w blaskach szczytów
Bóg się wmiłował w duszę.

IX. Antoni Słonimski.

Liryka

Wiem, piechotą będę szedł ze stacji,
Choćby ciemnym to było wieczorem.
Zbłądzić trudno, kolejowym torem
I na lewo od dwu drzew akacji.

Kwiat tytoniu w ciemnościach pachnący,
Miodny zapach końskiego nawozu
I daleko gdzieś gwizd parowozu,
Długi, smętny, tęskliwie cichnący.

Tak jak nieraz to już było we śnie,
Poznam głos twój, gdy zapytasz: „Kto tu?"
I za gardło uchwyci boleśnie
Strach i rozpacz, i szczęście powrotu.

„Kto tu?" spytasz, powiem—„Ja—Antoni,
Tutaj jestem." Jeszcze krok, pół kroku.
I dłoń drżącą poczuję na skroni.
I usłyszę bicie serca w mroku.

„Nie myślałem, że cię tak przestraszę!
Nie pal światła, stójmy tak, w ciemności.
Po co patrzeć w oczy już nie nasze,
Kiedy serca biją jak w młodości?"

„Po coś wrócił? Tu źle."—„Ja wiedziałem,
Lecz nie było dla mnie ukojenia,
Zostawiłem tu wszystko, co miałem,
Nasze wspólne młodzieńcze marzenia."

SECTION 4. LUSATIAN (or Wendish), or SORBIAN

INTRODUCTION

No book on the modern Slavonic literary languages would be complete without a chapter on the ancient and interesting Lusatian Serb or Wendish tongue.

The Lusatians call themselves "Serbja" (Serbs-Upper Lusatian) and "Serby" (Lower Lusatian) and their country "Łužica" (Upper Lusatian) or "Łužyca" (Lower Lusatian) (Lusatia; in German—Lausitz). Hence the English name Lusatian Serbs. The Germans call them "Wenden" (slightly pejorative) or "Sorben" —hence the English use of "Wends" or "Sorbs." As the name "Serbs" can cause confusion with the Yugoslav Serbs of Serbia, while the term "Wend" or "Sorb" does not readily indicate a nationality at all to the English mind, we propose using the term "Lusatian" here. This name indicates the native land to which these Slavs are attached so passionately that they would never agree to being transferred to other areas where there is a higher proportion of Slav inhabitants. It is true, that there are also many Lusatian *Germans*, but we hold that to the English mind Lusatian will mean a Slav inhabitant of Lusatia, just as Scot or Welshman does not indicate an Englishman living in Scotland or Wales but a man of Scottish or Welsh family who may or may not know a Celtic language. The Lusatians themselves freely admit that there are not a few Lusatians, who no longer have a complete mastery of their mother tongue and have become Germanized, just as in Britain to-day some Welshmen do not speak Welsh.

The period of Germanization has been so long that it is really a wonder that any Lusatians at all have preserved their language. Actually they still number somewhere about 75,000, living in their remote corner of the German Democratic Republic. Their area is now on the borders of N.W. Czechoslovakia and S.W. Poland (Lower Silesia). Too small in numbers, in comparison with their neighbours, to make an independent state, the Lusatians have been victims in the game for power of strong neighbouring rulers. Nevertheless they have survived, holding fast to their language, their Christian religion and their ancient customs, patiently tilling their land and waiting doggedly for better days. After the two recent world wars they have made claims to autonomy and independence, but the statesmen of the Great Powers

have not even mentioned that they have considered
their case. So the Lusatian cause has remained on
the conscience of the very few who know anything
about them (under whatever name). Their case has
been passed over and ignored by the majority of the
Press, and they have been considered too insignifi-
cant to be worthy of any kind of independence.
Nevertheless, to the student of Slav languages, literatures and history they form a most interesting, if
obscure, group of Slavs. Because of their very survival and ancient character they deserve to be more
widely known, even apart from their literature, which
is no mean achievement for so small a people.

The home of the Lusatians lies east of a line
from Berlin to Dresden, and is centred for the most
part on the upper reaches of the River Spree
(Sprjewja). The two chief towns of Lusatia, Budyšin
(Bautzen), the capital of Upper Lusatia, and Chośebuz
(Cottbus), the capital of Lower Lusatia, are both on
the Spree. The eastern frontier of Lusatia runs from
Görlitz (Zhorjelc) northwards along the east bank of
the River Neisse (Nysa) and then along the Oder as
far as Fürstenberg (Přiběh), then west along the
canals to the River Spree. This river then forms
Lusatia's north-west boundary up to a point about 20
km. north of Lübben (Lubin). From this point the
frontier lies to the west of Lübben, Kalau (Kałava),
Ruhland (Rólany), Königsbrück (Kinsbórk), then runs
south-east to Bischofswerda (Biskopicy) to reach the
Czech frontier about 10 miles N.W. of Šluknov.[1] It
follows this frontier to Zittau (Žitawa), from where
it goes N.E. to Görlitz. The total area within
these boundaries is 6,242 km².

The greater northern half of this area is low-
land intersected by many rivers, the soil becoming
poorer and more sandy towards the north. North-west
of Chośebuz (Cottbus) is the marshy and wooded area
known as the Spreewald (Błota). South of Spremberg
(Grodk) Upper Lusatia begins, but the hills do not
rise before we reach Kamenz (Kamjenc) or Weissenberg
(Wóspork). There is more industry in these hillier
areas, but no part of Lusatia is really poor or bar-
ren. Good roads, numerous railways, and electricity
have brought a fair share of material "civilization"
to these parts. The population of the towns in
Lusatia everywhere shows a large German majority
(about 80 per cent), but the rural population in some

---

[1] Since the thirteenth century an ethnically and linguistically German strip of territory on both sides of the Czech
frontier has separated the Czech and Lusatian-speaking areas.

parts reaches about 75 per cent Lusatians. Census figures are unreliable owing to the pressure put on everyone to call themselves Germans, but in 1880 some 180,000 still declared themselves as having Lusatian as their mother tongue. The lowest recent estimate, by the Czech publicist Vladimír Zmeškal, put the total of Lusatians knowing their mother tongue in 1938 at 130,000. Many besides have been Germanized. More recent figures are not available. One of the frankest German estimates of the Lusatian-speaking area in Germany is contained in Andrees' book, *Wendische Wanderstudien*. This was removed from the libraries by the Nazis (some say even in America).

The process of Germanization has been going on for about 1,000 years. The English missionary, St. Boniface (Wynfrith) who died in A.D. 754, praised the Slavs of this area for their civic and domestic virtues and gentle character in contrast to the barbaric Germans. And the German historian, W. Jacobi, states that their trade and industries were highly developed in those days. Yet the Lusatians were not ruled by Slavs until, and only for a brief period from, 1002(-1032) when the Polish king, Bolesław Chrobry, incorporated Lusatia in his kingdom by conquest. Varying fortunes under German rulers followed till in the fifteenth century Lusatia came under the Bohemian Crown, under which it remained for three centuries. When Bohemia fell, in the seventeenth century, Lusatia was divided between Saxony and Prussia till the unification of Germany under Bismarck. During this period the Lusatians gradually became relegated to the peasantry and the poorest workers by discriminatory laws, expropriation and every other means. The Lusatian language was neglected and despised and only survived in the homes and in the churches. The pressure of Germanization was particularly severe under Prussia. In the Saxon part of Upper Lusatia, Lusatians enjoyed a certain amount of cultural freedom in the nineteenth century. The Royal House patronized the "Sorbs" and the Crown Prince was even obliged to learn their language, which could be taught in schools and used for religious instruction and in the Law Courts. It is not surprising, therefore, that in the nineteenth century literature developed far more in the Upper Lusatian dialect than in the Lower Lusatian one.

After the treaty of Versailles, despite the advocacy and support of Dr. E. Beneš, the Lusatians were not technically recognized as a minority on the grounds that they had no state outside Germany with which they could claim close affinity. They thus remained, as President T. G. Masaryk put it, "the only Slav people without their own state." They had no representative in the Reichstag. In 1931 only two schools in Lower Lusatia taught any Lusatian at all. The advent to power of Hitler was quickly followed by an intensification of their persecution. Many publications and cultural organizations, including the Sokols, were closed down. Several of their leaders were sent to concentration camps. The use of the Lusatian language in public was forbidden altogether. The Lusatian papers were muzzled and finally suppressed. At the end of the war some Lusatians joined the Resistance in small partisan groups, and it is said that paratroopers were glad to land near the quiet Lusatian villages, where cats were then more favoured than dogs and thus their arrival could remain unnoticed. But the Lusatian claims to a form of independence under the protection of Czechoslovakia were again ignored. However, the occupying Soviet forces allowed the Lusatians to rebuild their cultural centre in Budyšin, the Serbski Dom, which the Nazis had burnt down when retreating. They allowed the use of Lusatian in schools and newspapers, the *Nowa doba* (New Era) daily paper appeared, and publishing was restarted. Hope dawned again, though dispossessed Germans from Eastern Europe poured into Lusatia.

It is little wonder that the Lusatians, so long and consistently persecuted, should have developed a very reserved character, being always driven in on themselves. The Lusatian peasantry is famed for its great conservatism and deeply religious inclinations; and they have preserved many ancient Slav customs and traditions. Not the least interesting of their treasures is their very archaic Slav tongue, which still preserves the full use of the Dual number and the Aorist and Imperfect tenses.

Modern Lusatian is divided into two main literary languages, Upper Lusatian and Lower Lusatian, which are based on the two main groups of dialects, centred on Budyšin and Chośebuz respectively. These dialects are very similar in grammar and vocabulary, but their underlying phonetic basis is rather different; so that unless one has studied their main phonetic differences, the speaker or reader of one dialect does not always immediately understand a speaker of the other dialect or a book in it. But with an elementary study of both dialects, one can read them both without difficulty. Philological studies have shown that the differences between the two dialects must have started developing as early as the thirteenth century.

Modern Lower Lusatian is, on the whole, more unique and more unlike the other Slavonic languages than Upper Lusatian. Lower Lusatian is, in some respects, nearer Polish, as it retains the original Slav g and develops vocalic $ḷ$ and $ṛ$ similarly; but it has no nasal vowels. Upper Lusatian is nearer Czech, changing Common Slav g to h. It is still nearer Slovak and Old Czech, for the Czech "přehláska" (vowel mutation) is unknown in Lusatian. But in both dialects the stress accent falls on the first syllable of words and word groups, as in Czech and Slovak and in contrast to Polish.[1] The Lower Lusatian is called by Upper Lusatians "Gronjak" from kak śi groniś? = what are you called? (groniś = to call). The Upper Lusatian who inhabits the "hola" = heath, is called "Holan"; and he is also called "Hajak" from his word for "yes"—haj (cf. the Slovak "hej").

The oldest printed books, beginning with Albin Moller's Hymnal, were printed in Gothic type. Catholic writers until the nineteenth century also used the Gothic script, though with a different orthography using diacritics. The eventual acceptance of Latin type was due to the influence of the Maćica Serbska. This influential body adopted it for its publications in 1848, using the so-called "analogical" system of spelling based on Czech and Polish, which gained in popularity during the second half of the nineteenth century.

In the pages below we give the details of Upper Lusatian, and also a brief study of the differences between the two dialects. We do this because, owing to the greater oppression in Lower Lusatia under Prussia, there is a good deal more literature in Upper Lusatian, mainly from the last two centuries; and because Upper Lusatian is probably more alive as a spoken and printed language to-day. After the section on Upper Lusatian morphology, we also give a list of the main instances where Lower Lusatian morphology differs. The student will have no difficulty in understanding Lower Lusatian after this study. It seems almost superfluous to mention that all Lusatians are bilingual to-day, as they have to know German to earn their living and for other obvious reasons of geography, etc. The influence of German can naturally also be seen in their language,

---

[1] See below under "Features characteristic of Upper Lusatian" and "The Lusatian Dialects" for fuller details of their features and differences.

in their vocabulary, and in their word order particularly.

LUSATIAN LITERATURE

The oldest recorded example of Lusatian is an oath of loyalty of the burghers of Budyšin, dating from 1532, preserved in the town museum there.

The earliest example of literary Lusatian is the Protestant pastor M. Jakubica's translation of the New Testament into Lower Lusatian[1] of 1548, kept in the State Museum in Marburg. The text is remarkable, among other things, for the fact that Jakubica indicated the then still existing long vowels by his spelling, using double vowels or inserting h between two vowels: daa (= he gave), nehemy (= dumb—mod. Upper Lusatian: němy), spihy (= he sleeps—mod. Upper Lusatian: spi). A Psalter in Lower Lusatian of only slightly later date is preserved at Wolfenbüttel in Germany.

The oldest printed book in Lusatian appeared in 1574 in Budyšin. It was Albert Moller's book of religious songs and catechism in Lower Lusatian.[2]

The oldest printed example in Upper Lusatian is Pastor W. Warichius' (Worjech) translation of Luther's smaller catechism, dating from 1597.

In the seventeenth century a number of Lusatian grammars and dictionaries were written. In 1650 Jan Chójnan published in manuscript the first Lusatian grammar—of Lower Lusatian—entitled *Linguae Vandalicae ad dialectum districtus Cotbusiani formandae aliquis conatus*. In it Chójnan pointed out the many Germanisms used in Lower Lusatian then (the same was done by J. B. Hauptmann in 1761) and held up Czech and Polish writers as models. In 1679 the Jesuit Jakub Ticin published in Prague a printed grammar of Upper Lusatian entitled *Principia linguae Vendicae*, using in it the Slav (not German) spelling of Lusatian. J. A. Swětlik and Bohdan Fabricius became known at this period for their translations of the Scriptures. It was Fabricius' translation of the New Testament into the dialect of Chośebuz, published in 1709, as well as J. F. Fryco's translation of the Old Testament into the same dialect (both widely used and read), that finally caused this dialect to be chosen as the literary language of Lower Lusatia. J. Langa's translation of the Old Testament into the dialect of Budyšin, published in 1728, had the same

---

[1] Actually, the dialect of Žarow (Sohrau).
[2] This work is in the dialect of Lubnjow (Lübbenau).

effect for Upper Lusatian, causing the Budyšin dialect to be chosen as the standard for literary Upper Lusatian. This translation was produced jointly with Jan Běmar, Matej Jokuš and Jan Wawer.

The Protestant priest Michał Frencel is famous for having, in 1697, sent some of his own works to Peter the Great, who was then passing through Dresden. The books were accompanied by a letter which is still preserved and expresses loyal sentiments of Slav brotherhood. Frencel translated the New Testament and other parts of the Bible, and also published catechisms, grammars, and small dictionaries. In his later works he went over to the German spelling of his language, probably to demonstrate his loyalty and reach a wider public.

The year 1706 saw the foundation in Prague of the Catholic Lusatian Seminary of SS. Peter and Paul, and ten years later the Evangelical Preachers' Association (Serbske prědařske towaŕstwo) was founded in Leipzig. In these two institutions, many young Lusatian priests and teachers were trained and thereby the cultural development of the Lusatian people was greatly strengthened. As these two centres were beyond the bounds of Lusatia, it made it possible for cultural ideas from Western Europe and from other Slav countries to penetrate into the comparatively small and remote Lusatian world. It was in Leipzig, too, that the first (handwritten) Lusatian newspapers appeared during these years. The Prague seminary, on the other hand, produced some of Lusatia's most illustrious writers and scholars throughout the nineteenth century, and continued to exist till 1922, when the building was sold during the period of despair among the Lusatians after their disappointment at the treaty of Versailles.

Georg Körner, a German who worked all his life for the Lusatians in the religious, historical and literary fields, published the first bibliography of Lusatian books, covering 71 volumes, in the eighteenth century, thereby inaugurating the systematic study of Lusatian literature.

The number of writers in Lusatian grew at the end of the eighteenth and beginning of the nineteenth centuries. The most important were: C. Knauth (religious and literary history), P. Młońk (poetry), J. Hórčanski (folklore), and J. A. Janka and K. B. Šerach, who in 1790 started publishing a monthly journal of "instruction and diversion," which was forbidden by the authorities after the first issue, *Měsačne pismo k rozwučenju a k wokřewjenju*.

Nevertheless towards the end of the eighteenth

century the standard of written Lusatian undoubtedly fell, for it aroused the strictures even of Josef Dobrovský, the founder of Slavonic philology who took a lively interest in Lusatian and met many Lusatian students at their Prague Seminar. In a letter to V. Zlobický dated 15th February, 1798, Dobrovský wrote, probably referring mainly to Lower Lusatian: "It is a clumsy and mutilated (chyždený) language of which Czechs and Moravians would be ashamed." In the nineteenth and twentieth centuries the language was greatly developed, being modelled mainly on Polish and Czech, which were also the main sources for borrowed words. The big dictionaries of Pful (Lusatian Dictionary, 1866), Muka (Dictionary of Lower Lusatian and its dialects 1911-1928—see below), Řezak (German-Lusatian dictionary, 1920), and Kral (Upper Lusatian-German dictionary, 1927) illustrate well the richness of the language.

In 1809 Jan Dejka, a master carpenter, created a considerable stir by launching a paper entitled *Sserski Powedar a Kurier* (Lusatian Reporter and Courier), in which he expressed his faith in the viability of Lusatian culture. His paper continued appearing for four years before it was finally forbidden by the authorities because of its progressive and nationalistic ideas. Dejka was the herald and precursor of the Lusatian national revival in the nineteenth century.

Handrij Lubjenski, a Protestant pastor, and Tecetin Mět, a Catholic priest, further helped the national revival with their books for churches and schools, and songs. So did the poet and song-writer Rudolf Mjeń (1767-1841).

During the nineteenth century difficult tasks lay before the reformers, such as the purification of the language from alien influences and the improvement of its orthography. Throughout this period they maintained close contact with the Czech and Slovak "national awakeners."

The first widely known Lusatian poet of the nineteenth century was Handrij Zejler (1804-1872), who was a Protestant pastor by calling, and had been a pupil of Lubjenski. He abandoned dealing with language problems in favour of poetry. He loved Lusatian folksongs and stories, from which he drew much of his inspiration and his faith in his people and their language. He wrote the Lusatian national anthems *Rjana Łužica* (= Fair Lusatia) and *Hišće Serbstwo njezhubjene* (Lusatian Serbs are still alive), the latter on the model of the Polish national anthem; and also the famous poem beginning

"Trać dyrbi Serbstwo, zawostać" (Lusatians must survive and live). His poetry is remarkable for its purity of language, as can be seen from the four volumes of his collected works, edited by Muka (see below) who corrected only his orthography. Zejler used:—

cž	and *tsch* for modern		č
cz	"	"	ć
dž	"	"	dž
je	"	"	ě
ss	"	"	s
s	"	"	z } as in German
z	"	"	c

and *j* to indicate "yotation" (palatalization with *j*) in all instances. In 1825 he was the leader of the Evangelical Preachers' Association in Leipzig and in the following year he founded the *Serbske Nowiny*, which was then the sole Lusatian periodical and appeared in manuscript. His short grammar of Upper Lusatian in German appeared in 1830 and was based on Dobrovský's Czech Grammar.

In 1842 the weekly Lusatian newspaper *Jutrnička* (= Morning Star) made its appearance under the editorship of J.P. Jordan (v.infra). It ran for only twenty-six issues, failing for lack of support. But a week later on 25th June 1842, a new weekly, edited by Zejler, and entitled *Tydženska Nowina* (= Weekly News), appeared, catering for the same public. In 1849 the editorship passed to Smoler, and in 1854 its name was changed to *Serbske Nowiny*. It continued publication for nearly seventy years. (From 1920 to 1937 it came out as a daily, continuing with great difficulties for four years even under the Nazi régime, which finally forced it to close down.)

To this period also belong J. Radyserb-Wjela, the poet and collector of proverbs and author of the libretto of the first Lusatian opera *Smjertnica* (= The goddess of Death), composed by Jurij Pilk, b. 1858; and also the Catholic scholar and propagator of the Lusatian cause, J. P. Jordan (1818-1891). His grammar of Upper Lusatian in German was also founded on Dobrovský's Czech Grammar, and came out in 1841. In it he revived the use of ɓ, ƥ, ŧ, ŵ, ř. The letters s, z, č, ć were correctly used by him, but he used dž for dž and ė for modern ě. He also used small letters initially for common nouns in contrast to the German usage of capitals for all nouns, followed by other Lusatian writers then.

Jan Ernst Smoler (1816-1884) was one of the greatest leaders of the Lusatian national revival.

He was a pupil of the Czech, F. L. Čelakovský, at Breslau. In 1838, when he came there, he founded at the University a students' society whose first aim was the cultivation of the Lusatian language. He too, like Zejler, loved his native folk-songs and published a big collection of them in two volumes in the years 1841-43. In 1841 he also published a small handbook on Lusatian orthography proposing the use of forty-seven letters, which was still a far cry from J. P. Jordan's sensible orthography given in his grammar already mentioned. But two years later, when Smoler had become acquainted with Jordan's spelling, he adopted it and advocated its use (it had forty letters) in the preface to his German-Lusatian dictionary, only altering $è$ to $ě$ or je. He also published these views in a separate pamphlet in the same year. Unfortunately the spelling in the body of his dictionary was not consistent, though his selection of words is quite modern. In one of his most famous poems, *Wostań w kraju*, he appealed to his countrymen not to seek illusory fortunes beyond the bounds of Lusatia.

In 1847 he founded the Maćica Serbska in Budyšin (and also the first Lusatian bookshop there). The Maćica Serbska had as one of its main functions the care and development of the Lusatian language. In the year of its foundation it adopted the Jordan-Smoler spelling as its official orthography with only very slight changes introduced by the Lusatian philologist, Dr. Kř. Pful. They called it an "analogical" orthography because it was modelled analogically on Polish and Czech orthography, explaining this in the Časopis Maćicy Serbskeje of 1848. This orthography was then adopted by all Catholic Upper Lusatian writers and by Lusatian scholars generally, such as Jakub Buk and Michal Hórnik (see below). A special committee for the Lusatian language was established in 1854, but a separate one for Lower Lusatian was not created till 1880, under the direction and guidance of Hendrich Jordan (see below).

In 1848 the Lower Lusatians started publishing the *Bramborski serbski casnik* (= Brandenburg Lusatian journal) and a *Serbske towarišstwo* was founded in Chośebuz (Cottbus) and writers of modest talent started appearing.

K. A. Jenč (1828-1895) wrote the first history of the Lusatian language and people.

One of the most famous pupils of the Prague Seminar at this period was Michał Hórnik (1833-1894). Using as a model the Polish historian W. Bogusławski's *Rys dziejów serbołużyckich* Hórnik in collaboration with Bogusławski produced the classical *History of the Lusatian People*, a masterpiece of fine language and style. He was editor of the Časopis Maćicy Serbskeje and in the eighties began publishing a weekly paper for Catholics, the *Katolski Posoł*. He also carried through a spelling reform with Czech as his guide. He greatly disapproved of the lack of uniformity in Lusatian orthography in his day. For while the Maćica Serbska used the "analogical" spelling, popular works written for wider reading were still printed in the Gothic script, with one spelling for Catholics and with another spelling for Protestants. The Protestant popular press used:—

	for	c
cz, cž, ß	"	č
ß	"	s
ſ	"	z
ie	"	ě

Hórnik advocated a uniform spelling for all writings of the popular press of whatever denomination as early as 1859. The Catholics adopted his policy in the 1860's. Upper Lusatian Evangelical writers long refused to be convinced by him, but nowadays a uniform orthography is used for all publications.

Hórnik also interested himself in Lower Lusatian, regretting that the two dialects had drifted so far apart, and hoping that Lower Lusatian writers would try to bring their language nearer to Upper Lusatian and educate their sadly neglected people. Both Hórnik and Smoler encouraged the publication of Lower Lusatian texts in the periodical *Łužičan* (founded 1860) and added explanations to them, pointing out how different the two dialects had become. Hórnik also published an anthology (Čitanka) of Upper Lusatian folk and composed literature, adding a full vocabulary. He became the chief national leader when Smoler died.

His opposite number on the Protestant side was H. J. Imiš (1819-1897), writer, teacher, national organizer, and champion of his people against German accusations of "Panslav aggression."

H. Dučman, the poet (1836-1909), also wrote a history of Catholic Lusatian literature. The first Lusatian woman poet, Herta Wićazec (1819-1885), published her first poems during this period too.

In Lower Lusatian at this time one of the most noteworthy figures was J. B. Tešnař (1829-1898), who in 1860 published a version of the Bible and various Evangelical church books, in which he paid great attention to the purity of the language. In this way

he both created the modern literary Lower Lusatian
language and perfected the Lower Lusatian orthography,
basing himself on that of Fryco. He was also guided
not a little by the writings of M. Hórnik.

    Lusatia's greatest poet is undoubtedly Jakub
Bart, better known under his *nom de plume* of
Ćišinski. He lived from 1856-1909, and was a Catholic priest. He knew full well that his unfortunate
nation had only their language and their soul left to
call their own, and drew his inspiration from their
tragic and heroic history. He was also inspired by
the literature of other Slav peoples. Together with
A. Muka (see below) he started the Young Lusatian
movement. In 1875 Lusatian students from Upper and
Lower Lusatia united in a single association, the
aim of which was to foster national and cultural work
of all kinds. They also arranged during the vacations popular meetings known as "schadźowanki" in
villages threatened with Germanization. To these
meetings the local population was invited as well as
the students, and they became thus demonstrations of
national will and solidarity. This group of young
people attacked "the non-Lusatian atmosphere" of
Lusatian literature, which did not give free play to
the beauty and power of the Lusatian language. Their
greatest opponent was Professor Pful, the author of
the Lusatian dictionary. The disagreement came to a
head in the dispute between him and Ćišinski. In the
new periodical *Lipa Serbska*, Ćišinski attacked the
contemporary literary language chiefly for its lexical purism and also its syntax, which slavishly
copied German. They were tactfully supported by J. E.
Smoler and M. Hórnik. Michałk tried not to take
sides and to effect a reconciliation. In Lower
Lusatia meanwhile literary activities were led by M.
Kosyk, the poet. Their programme aimed at the liberation of their language from the influence of German
and the rousing of the Lusatian intelligentsia to
awareness of the fate of their less fortunate kin
in Lower Lusatia and the border regions at the hands
of the Germans.

    The Young Lusatian Movement triumphed over its
Lusatian opponents when in 1880 Ćišinski published
his play *Na Hrodźišću* (= At the Fortress), with its
most effective and beautiful Upper Lusatian language.
Four years later he started a new era in Lusatian
literature with the publication of his *Kniha Sonettow*
(= Book of Sonnets), which also started a new phase
for the Upper Lusatian literary language. In this
book he included also his translations of sonnets by

Petrarch, Shakespeare, Mickiewicz, Kollár, and
Vrchlický. In his *Formy* (1888) he tested the power
of his language in all the poetic forms known to
world literature. He produced in all about fifteen
collections of poems, and also the epic *Nawoženja* (=
The Bridegroom). In these works he raised Upper
Lusatian to the level of the other Slavonic languages. He also tried to rouse the common people of
Lusatia from their conservatism as well as to defend
his people against the Germans. His personality is
well expressed in his lines:—

    Mi žiwjenje bě bój a beda
    a broń a škit a puć bě pjero
(Life for me meant woe and strife with men,
My shield, my arms, my road was e'er the pen.)

    His ally, though temperamentally his opposite,
was Dr. Ernst Muka (1854-1932). He was a philologist
of distinction. In his historical grammar[1] of Lower
Lusatian (1891) he further perfected Tešnaŕ's orthography. On the other hand, for Upper Lusatian he carried through a series of minor reforms of the spelling of individual words in collaboration with Jurij
Libš (1857-1927), the author of the first book on
Upper Lusatian syntax. Muka co-operated later with
B. Šwela (see below) in publishing in 1903 a definitive Lower Lusatian orthography. This work outstripped anything similar then existing for Upper
Lusatian, and particularly with regard to the uniform
rendering of Common Slav ě it could well be a model
for Upper Lusatian as well.

    Muka's comparative dictionary, already mentioned,[2]
was published first in Petrograd in 1911-1915 (letters A-N) and then in Prague in 1926-28 (letters O-Ž). His output of works in the fields of philology,
ethnography and literary history was enormous. He
also organized the collection of funds for the establishment of a cultural and organizational centre for
Lusatians, called the Serbski dom. This was opened
in 1904, and housed an extensive library, a museum, a
printing press and a publishing house, besides a hall
for meetings. This "dom" was burnt down by the Germans at the end of the second world war, as we have
said, but the foundation stone for a new Serbski dom
was laid in 1947. The completed new Serbski dom
was opened in 1956.

    Another notable writer was Miklawš Andricki

---

[1] The full title is: *Historische und vergleichende Laut- und Formenlehre der Niedersorbischen (Niederlausitzisch-wendischen) Sprache.*   [2] p. 340.

(1871-1908), who also worked as a journalist and translator. He was an advocate of a realistic outlook on life.

In lower Lusatia Hendrich Jordan (1841-1910), a teacher, collected folksongs and folk tales and published a *Cytanka* (= Reader). He was one of the chief workers in the Lower Lusatian Committee of the Maćica Serbska, which he helped to establish in 1880. He wrote the Lower Lusatian words of the national anthem, *Rědna Łužyca*

M. Kósyk, one of the best poets in Lower Lusatian, was converted to writing poetry in his native language by reading Šafarík's *Geschichte der slawischen Sprache und Literatur*. He purged his native dialect of Germanisms, following the lines of Tešnaŕ's reforms of the prose language.

Bogumil Šwela (b. 1873), already mentioned for his collaboration with Muka, also produced several readers and anthologies in Lower Lusatian.

Efforts at unifying the two dialects, such as that started by the Circle of Lusatian Writers, founded in Budyšin in 1900, proved ineffective.

A notable champion of the Lusatians was the Catholic priest, Jurij Deleńk, who in the *Serbske Nowiny* and the *Katolski Posoł* asserted his people's right to call themselves Slavs. "We are subjects of the German Reich, but not of the German people," he wrote. He organized the publication of a cheap series of Lusatian books. He fell on the western front in the German ranks in 1918, as did some 6,000 other young Lusatians.

Among the Czechs, Adolf Černý (b. 1864) was one of the most active propagators of the Lusatian cause through his many writings on Lusatian subjects. He was the first Lektor in Lusatian at Prague University.

Ludvík Kuba (b. 1863), the notable Czech painter, musician and writer, also showed great interest in Lusatia by writing about her people, painting pictures of them and publishing their songs.

Among the Poles who interested themselves in Lusatia we should mention the lawyer, ethnographer, historian and publicist, Alfons Parczewski (1850-1933). He helped to found the Lower Lusatian Committee of the Maćica Serbska. He also provided money for the publication of Lower Lusatian books and "calendars" (an important item of varied reading for the masses), and with his sister wrote many historical articles popularizing the Lusatians.

Later, in the newly born Czechoslovaka, Dr. Josef Páta, a notable Czech scholar of Lusatian, produced an excellent anthology (Čítanka) of modern (mostly Upper) Lusatian poems and prose passages. He was the first Professor of Lusatian at Prague University. He also wrote an *Introduction to the Study of Lusatian Literature* (Czech and Lusatian editions), a grammar of Upper Lusatian, and a small dictionary: Upper Lusatian--Czech--Serbocroatian and Czech--Upper Lusatian. He was one of the hostages executed by the Nazis in retaliation for the assassination of the Nazi "Protector" Heydrich. We should also mention here the Czech publicist and publisher of Lusatian books, Vladimír Zmeškal (b. 1902).

Marko Smoler (1857-1941), the son of J. E. Smoler, played an important part as editor of the *Serbske Nowiny* and director of the Lusatian bookshop. He also directed the activities of the Language Committee of the Maćica Serbska, when it was revived after falling into abeyance after Muka's death.

After the first world war there was a considerable output of periodicals and papers, of which the journal of the Maćica Serbska was the most serious. Unfortunately not all the papers were at an equally high linguistic level because Lusatian writers were hampered through having no school training in their native language. The language of the newspapers also suffered because of hasty translation from German. Of the chief papers, the *Katolski Posoł* maintained the highest standard in language.

Of the later writers some of the most noteworthy in Upper Lusatian are:

Jozef Nowak (b. 1895), the poet and dramatist, follower of Ćišinski;

Jan Skala (1889-1945), poet and socialist; tried to publish a periodical in the central Lusatian dialect; editor of the paper of the national minorities in Germany, *Kulturwehr*;

Jan Lainert (1892-1974), modernist poet who wrote on love themes;

Jakub Lorenc-Zalěski (1874-1939), novelist and writer, who revived the "Circle of Lusatian Writers" in 1921. This Circle was more productive in Prague than in Budyšin.

Marja Kubašec (b. 1890), who has attained distinction in both prose and poetry;

Matej Urban (1846-1929), translator of the entire *Iliad* and *Odyssey*;

J. Libš, who made the fifth Lusatian translation of Thomas à Kempis' *Imitation of Christ*; (see also p. 345);

Ota Wićaz (1874-1952), historian, editor of *Łužica* and *Časopis Maćicy Serbskeje*;

Michal Nawka (1885-1968), writer of short novels, translator of Gogol's *Revizor*, musician (see below);
Mikławs Krječmar (1891-1967), literary historian, editor, Lektor at Prague University;
Jakub Wjacławk (1885-1951), historian, bibliographer, author of an orthographical dictionary;
Měrćin Nowak(-Njechornski) (b. 1900), writer, translator, journalist, and also painter.

We should also mention Jan K. Wałtaŕ (Walter) (1860-1922), a German who became by his own convictions a poet in Upper Lusatian.

The most notable writers of recent years in Lower Lusatia have been W. Nowy, B. Šẃela (already mentioned), the sisters Domaskojc, and particularly the poetess, Mina Witkojc (b. 1893), who was a pupil of Muka and also worked as an editor, translator and publisher.

The most important writers of the younger generation are Jurij Młynk, Marija Młynkowa, Kito Lorenc, Wilem Bjero, Jurij Koch, Jurij Brězan.

In 1928 Michal Nawka put forward proposals for a simpler and more phonetic and uniform spelling of both dialects. He was opposed, however, by both Muka and Šẃela, chiefly on the grounds that he would only cause greater confusion. Nawka proposed abolishing mute letters and writing soft consonants with an acute accent over them (as in Lower Lusatian) instead of putting a *j* after them in the Upper Lusatian manner. His proposals were supported two years later by M. Nowak, but were not generally adopted, the present partly historical spelling being retained. Nawka's little book on Lusatian style, *Pokiwy pyskej a pjeru* (= Guide for Tongue and Pen), 1936, was, however, more widely appreciated as a guide to correct writing and speech.

The seizure of power by Hitler in 1933 was soon followed by many blows at Lusatian cultural institutions, such as the disbandment of their Sokol organization, the closing down of several papers and publishing firms, and the trial of leading Lusatians. In 1936, the only publication in Lower Lusatia was a *Pratyja* (calendar with reading matter). Only in Saxon Upper Lusatia were any cultural activities at all tolerated—in the schools and churches.

Since the second world war the Lusatians (Sorbs) have been allowed a large amount of freedom and given support in cultural matters. Under the Constitution of the German Democratic Republic the rights of the Lusatian minority are fully protected in the fields of education, the development of their culture and the use of their language in the courts and in administration in the districts where there live any appreciable number of Sorbs. The work of the Sorbian national organization Domowina centred in the Serbski dom, and its publishing house, Domowina, has official support from the republic's government. And in districts where Sorbs live there are two kinds of schools, those with instruction mainly in Sorbian, relatively few in number, and those where Sorbian is taught as a language besides German. In the higher spheres of learning, the Sorbian Ethnological Institute (Institut za Serbski ludospyt) in Budyšin is an integral part of the German Academy of Sciences and does valuable research in the fields of dialectology, folklore, literature and history. In the districts with a sizeable Sorbian population, as well as in Budyšin (Bautzen) where Sorbs are only a small minority, street signs and inscriptions in public places, as well as all publicity literature, are regularly bilingual, the text being printed in German and Upper Lusatian (Sorbian). Thus, unlike in former days, the rights of the Sorbs are fully protected, and they are encouraged to keep up their language and develop their culture. The only threats to their language and culture are posed by the large influx of German settlers from regions to the east (now incorporated in Poland) who have settled in central Lusatia, and by the limited regional distribution of the Lusatian languages and their lack of economic "usefulness" and appeal as far as employment and earning a living are concerned, a common problem for minority groups everywhere. These features and the question of the very acceptance by the somewhat conservative Sorbian population of the enlightened policy of their government pose the only problems for the survival of the remarkably interesting Sorbian languages and Sorbian culture today. It is certainly true that in no period in their history has the publishing of books, newspapers and periodicals flourished as it has since 1945. And even a modest broadcasting service has been established from the stations in Cottbus and Görlitz. It is to be hoped that the work of cultural workers and teachers is not in vain, and that all classes and denominations of Sorbs will continue to welcome the chances their republic is offering them.[1]

[1] For fuller information, attractively and clearly presented, the reader is referred to Gerald Stone's *The Smallest Slavonic Nation - The Sorbs of Lusatia*, published by the Athlone Press of the University of London in 1972.

THE UPPER LUSATIAN ALPHABET

Upper Lusatian		Approximate English Equivalent
A	a	(more open and forward than) ah
B	b	b
	[b̆]	[1]p (only finally)]
C	c	ts in "bits"
Č	č	(medium) ch
D	d	(dental) d
Dź	dź	j
E	e	open e in "bet"
	ě	phon. ię, cf. Eng. ea in "dear"; like ie in Slovak but with prominence of i
F	f	[2]f
G	g	[2]g in "go"
H	h	voiced h, as in Czech and Slovak; unvoiced initially
Ch	ch	ch in "loch"; initially strongly aspirated kh
I	i	i in "machine"
J	j	y in both "yes" and "boy"
K	k	k
[Kh	kh	[3]aspirated k, initial only]
Ł	ł	w, like ł in colloquial Polish
L	l	l in "last"
M	m	m
	[m̆]	[1]m (only finally)]
N	n	(dental) n
	ń	yn preceded by a vowel, as in "Boyne"
O	o	o as in "for"
	ó	oo as in "poor"
P	p	p
	[p̆]	[1]p (only finally)]
R	r	r (rolled, or uvular as in German)
	[r̆]	[1](only finally), as for r]
	ř	[4]sh after k and p, soft s after t
S	s	s in "see"
Š	š	sh (fairly soft)
T	t	(dental) t
Ć	ć	medium ch, the same as for č
U	u	between u in "put" and oo in "boot"
(V	v)	[5]v (only in foreign words)
W	w	w, as in English
	[w̆	[1]y in "boy" (only finally, rare)]

Upper Lusatian		Approximate English Equivalent
	y	*y* in "Mary"; near to Polish *y*
Z	z	*z*
Ž	ž	*zh* (fairly soft), *s* in "pleasure"

Letters for which no capital is given do not occur at the beginning of words.
[ ] indicate letters now not used.

NOTES ON THE ALPHABET

Vowels occur initially only in exclamations and words of foreign origin. Native Upper Lusatian words have *w* prefixed to all Slav roots originally having an initial *o* or *u*. E.g.:—

        Och! = oh!, opera = opera

but—
    woko = eye, wón = he, wo = about, wucho = ear, wučer = teacher;

j is used before *a* and *e*, e.g.:—

        jandźel = angel, Jendźelska = England,

and *h* before *i*, e.g.:—

        hić = to go (Impfve.), hinak = otherwise

[1] [Accented (final) ƀ, m̃, p̃, r̃ were identical in pronunciation with their unaccented counterparts in final position. They, like ŵ, were preserved in spelling to indicate a soft stem and in flexion were replaced by *bj, mj, pj, rj,* and *wj* respectively, pronounced soft b, m, p, r, and w before a vowel. E.g.:—
        hołb = pigeon, Gen. sg. hołbja
        kowaŕ = a smith, " " kowarja
kreŵ, now written krej and always so pronounced, = blood, Gen. sg. (krwje or) kreje or krwě.]

ń also occurs in writing only finally and before consonants, changing to *nj* before vowels other than *i* and *ě*, e.g.:—
    dań, phon. dajn, = tax, Gen. sg. danje; přińć = to come (Pfve.) Before *i* and *ě*, *n* is written but soft ń is pronounced.

[2] *f* and *g* occur only in onomatopoeic and borrowed words:- fyrać = to buzz, snort; falš = deceit, fabrika = factory gagać = to cry like a goose, cackle; geograf = geographer, gmejna = community.
(Common Slav *g* has become *h*, as in Czech and Slovak.)

[3] [*kh* replaced original initial *ch* [x] in most Upper Lusatian words, e.g.:—
khlěb = bread, khodźić = to go (Freq.), khwalba or khwała = praise,
and also in compounds: přikhadźeć = to come, all now *written* with *ch*] but—chcyć = to want.

[4] ř is only preserved in Upper Lusatian spelling after *k* and

p when it is pronounced š (Eng. *sh*), e.g.: křik (= shouting), přecy (= always), and after t when the group is pronounced either soft ts̈, e.g. tři, phon. ts̈i, = three, or soft ts̈ (Eng. *ch* soft), e.g. třasć, phon. ts̈asts̈, (= to shake). Before ě it can also be pronounced hard ts, e.g. třeleć (= to shoot), pronounced cyleć, phon. tsɨlɛts̈.

[5]*v* i not really a Lusatian letter. It occurs in foreign words only, e.g.:—

    volleyball, volt, visavis, Vesuv = Vesuvius.

COMPARISON WITH OTHER SLAVONIC LATIN SCRIPTS

Long vowels, as in Czech and Slovak, do not occur in Lusatian.

ě, ó, ř, y have a different value in Upper Lusatian from that in Czech.

Czech d', t', ů are not used in Upper Lusatian.

ń is used for Czech and Slovak ň.

Slovak ä, ľ, ĺ, ô, ŕ are not used in Upper Lusatian.

Polish q, ę, ś, ź do not occur in Upper Lusatian (Lower Lusatian has ś, ź; see on Lower Lusatian below, under "The Lusatian Dialects", p. 370-373).

ć, dź, ó, w have a different value in Upper Lusatian and Polish.

Polish ż is rendered ž.

dź, *ch* [and *kh*] are the only digraphs used in Upper Lusatian. *Kh* was peculiar to Upper Lusatian.

Slovenian and Croätian h is rendered *ch* in Lusatian.

Serbocroätian đ or *dj* (ђ) is rendered dź.

Serbocroätian ć (ћ) is also rendered ć in Lusatian.

Serbocroätian and Slovenian *lj* (љ) correspond to Lusatian l (unbarred).

Serbocroätian and Slovenian *nj* (њ) correspond to Lusatian ń, *nj*, or n before i and ě.

dž occurs only in Lower Lusatian.

Vocalic l or r do not occur in Lusatian.

PRONUNCIATION

The *Accent* in Lusatian is a purely stress accent and falls on the first syllable of words, and word groups consisting of a monosyllabic preposition followed by a noun or pronoun, provided these have no more than two syllables.

    drjèwo = a tree

```
zèleny    = green
pòd dubom = under an oak
přì tebi  = near you
```

Certain monosyllabic pronouns, conjunctions and auxiliary verbs are used as enclitics or proclitics and have no stress, as in other West and South Slav languages (see "Word Order with Enclitics," pp. 460-61).

The negative *nje-* is always prefixed to its verb and therefore takes the stress, as in Czech and Slovak, e.g.:—

```
njèpłač! = do not cry!
njèjsym  = I am not
```

Njèleći ptačk k nanej, maćeri, ale . . . k ródnej zemi = A bird does not fly to its father (and) mother, but . . . to its native land

The Vowels

All vowels are short in Lusatian, and *a, e, i, o,* and *u* are similar to the corresponding Polish vowels and Czech *short* vowels. Only *e, ě, ó,* and *y* need further comment.

e is pronounced more closed before j and soft consonants.

ě is a peculiarly Lusatian sound, something like the *ea* of "dear", but instead of being phonetically represented Iə, it is nearer ^{i}e. It is similar to the diphthong *ie* in Slovak, phonetically rendered i̯e, but gives greater prominence to the *i* element, hence it is represented i^e, as in rěka (= river) phon.'ri̯eka. It is quite distinct in pronunciation from *je,* as in worjech, phon.'wɔɾɛx (= nut). (Both *ě* and *je* represent Common Slav *ě* (Old Slavonic ѣ) and other C.S. vowels—see "The Features characteristic of Upper Lusatian", especially Nos. 5, 6, and 7.) Consonants are pronounced soft before *ě* and *i.*

ó is also a glide diphthong, starting with a full *u* followed by an o or ə off-glide, hence it is represented u^o or u^e. It often corresponds in position to Slovak ô, Czech ů or Polish ó, but *not* always. E.g.:—

```
wóz     = waggon, Cz. vůz, Slk, voz, Pol. wóz
kóń phon.
 ku̯ɔjn  = horse,  "  ků̊ň,   "  kôň,   "  koń
    but—
dom     = house,  "  dům,   "  dom,   "  dom, etc.
```

y has a sound distinct from *i,* as in Polish. It is a vowel of ɨ (Russian ы) type, but is pronounced

with the tip of the tongue further forward in the
mouth, like the Polish *y* to which it is most similar.
Unstressed it tends to be centralized and pronounced
nearly as ə. E.g.:—

    być = to be
    syn = son

It is the continuation of Common Slav *y* (O.S. ⱻI) and
also represents C.S. *i* (O.S. и) and *other* vowels
after the regularly hard sibilants *s* and *z*. E.g.:—

    syno = hay O.S. сѣно
    zyma = winter " зима
    sym = I am " ѥсмь

 Before all palatal and formerly palatal consonants except *č* the vowels *a*, *e*, *ó* and occasionally
ě, *o* and *u* are pronounced with a *j* after them, e.g.:—

kaž = as, pron. kajš (with final *ž* unvoiced)
tež = also, " tejš (" " ")
kóždy = each, " ku°jždy
stož = which (rel). phon. ʃtɔjʃ
chěža = house, phon. khejʒa
tuž = therefore, so phon. tujʃ

 Diphthongs with *j* (= i̯) as the second element
can occur in Lusatian with all vowels. E.g.:—

   kraj = land napoj = a drink
   krej = blood mój = my; we two
   měj! = have! wuj! = howl! (also = uncle)
   pij!¹ = drink! myj! = wash!

 Diphthongs with *w* and *ł* (both pron. u̯) as the
second element can also occur with all vowels, except
that -*ów*- and -*uw*- do not happen to occur in one syllable in any word in Upper Lusatian; (cf. Polish,
Slovak, Slovenian, Ukrainian, and Byelorussian).
E.g.:—

prawda = truth, pron. prau̯da
šewc = cobbler
lěwc = left-handed person
hriwna = mark(coin) (h is silent!)
row = grave, phon. rou̯
syw = sowing(grain)
dał = gave, Past Part.Act.,Pfve.
wodźeł = put on, " " " "
hrěł = was warming, " " " Impfve.(h silent!)
pił = was drinking, " " " "
poł = half, almost " " " " phon. pou̯

  ¹Often pronounced pi.

kłół = was pricking, Past Part.Act.,Impfve.
duł = was blowing,   "   "   "   "
mył = was washing,   "   "   "   "

In žuwak (= ruminant animal), the Slavonic syllabic division after the vowel -u- causes w to be at the beginning of the next syllable: žu-wak. (See also below under ł and w in "The Consonants").

The Consonants.

Final voiced consonants, except h (which is silent finally), w, and ź, l, m [m̓], n, ń, r [r̓], are pronounced unvoiced, as in all other Slav languages except Serbocroätian and Ukrainian. E.g.:—

    dub is pron. dup = oak
    sad   "   sat = fruit
    muž   "   muš = man
    mróz   "   mrós = frost
    budź!   "   buć = be!

ć and dź are affricates, equivalent respectively to *ch* and *j* in English and pronounced harder than ć and dź in Polish. As in Polish, they are the soft counterparts of t and d respectively. But in contrast to the usage in Polish, they are written before *all* vowels as well as before consonants. E.g.:—

    ćĕło   = body
    ćah   = train
    ćma   = darkness
    ćišina   = quiet (noun)
    dźowka, phon. dẑou̯ka   = daughter
    dźak   = thanks
    dźeń   phon. dẑejn   = day
    dźiki or dźiwi   = wild

(They are the only consonants with ʼ which occur initially.)

l is the Lusatian version of *soft* l. It is pronounced palatalized before i, ĕ and e. (Cf. Polish.)

ł is the Lusatian hard l and is pronounced like w in English, that is: w or u̯ in all positions. E.g.—

dał, Past Part. Act. = gave, pron. dau̯
połny   = full,   "   pou̯ny
ławka   = bench,   "   wau̯ka
łža   = a lie,   "   u̯ža (Cf. Pol.
                                       łza = tear)

Both l and ł, as well as r, are silent finally after other consonants, e.g. in mysl (= thought), njesł (carried), wĕtr (= wind).

w can be silent medially, as in krwawy (= bloodstained) pron. krawy.

For C.S. vocalic *ḷ* and *ṛ*, Upper Lusatian has '*el* or *oł* and '*er* or *or* respectively, according to origin and surrounding consonants. (See below "The Characteristics of Upper Lusatian," No. 4.)

h, unvoiced initially, is pronounced as a weakly voiced *h* (phon. ɦ), similar to h in Czech and Slovak, medially between vowels:

               hasa = street,
but
               noha = leg,
               jeho = his

It represents C.S. *g* (O.S. г). It is silent finally and also initially before other consonants, e.g. in:—

    Bóh = God   hnězdo = nest
    hdźe = where   hród = castle
    hłós = voice   hwězda = star, pron. u̯i^ezda

But in a few words medially before other consonants it is now written and pronounced *ch* (phon. x), e.g.:—

lochki = light, (cf. Russian: лёгкий, г pronounced x)
mjechki = soft ("   "   мягкий, "   "   "
łochć = elbow
N.B. bahno = swamp, is pronounced with ɣ (= voiced
              x): 'baɣnɔ.

Initial *ch* is regularly pronounced [k^h]. Until 1948 it was spelt *kh*.

w is pronounced as in English, phon. w or u̯, whether it occurs initially, medially, or finally. It is never pronounced like labio-dental *v* but is bilabial. It is thus pronounced the same as Lusatian *ł*. E.g.:—

   wěsty = certain
   prawda = truth (cf. Slovak pravda)
   row   = grave
   Serbow = of the Lusatian Sorbs (Gen. plur.).

This is also true of prothetic *w*, always used in Upper Lusatian before original initial *o* and *u* e.g.:— wótc (= father), wuhlo (= coal), wutroba (= heart), cf. Russian утроба (= womb).

The velars *h*, *ch*, *k* are always followed by *i*, never by *y*. (Cf. Russian and Polish.) E.g.:—

hibot = movement, cf. Cz. pohyb
ćichi = quiet,   "   tichý, Pol. cichy, Russ.
    тихий

blizki = near, cf. Cz. blízký, Pol. bliski, Russ.
близкий

The sibilants s, z, and c are always followed by y (see on y under "The Vowels"). E.g.:—

cygan = gypsy, cf. Cz. cikán   Pol. cygan
cybla = onion,   "   cibule,   "   cebula

A soft z can be heard before i in foreign words and with silent h, e.g. telewizija = television, zhibnyć = to bend.

č, š, ž, on the other hand, are fairly soft in Upper Lusatian and are therefore followed by i and not y (in contrast to Lower Lusatian and Polish), e.g.:—

čisty = clean
šić = to sew
žiwić(so) = to feed

d and t are always hard in Lusatian and usually require y and not i after them, except in loanwords, e.g. dirigować = to conduct. (See ć and dź above.)

n is hard before all vowels except i and ě. Hence -ny in pyšny (= elegant) is pronounced hard. But n is soft in něhdźe (= somewhere), nihdy (= never). n is also soft before je, as in njesć (= to carry), pron ɲɛsʧ. n is regularly pronounced like ng in "sing", phon. ŋ, before k and g, e.g.: banka, pron. baŋka (= bank), spink (= spasm), gingawa = waterlily.

ń, finally and before consonants, is regularly pronounced jn, e.g. stań! = get up!, phon. stajn
dźeń = day,   "   dᴣejn,
kóń = horse,   "   kuɔjn,
wuńć = to get out "   wujnʧ

ř is written only after k, p, and t (for pronunciation see above on ř after the Alphabet, footnote 4). rj, as in rjany (= beautiful), is pronounced rj (not like soft r in Russian, but more like rj in Slovenian).[1]

[b̕, m̕, p̕, and ř used to indicate soft endings in further flexion and were themselves pronounced hard, not soft, in their always final positions in Upper Lusatian. (They were *derived* from originally soft consonants, of course.)

Final ŵ, also indicating a soft stem, was usually pronounced j, as in cyrkeŵ (= church), now spelt as well as pronounced cyrkej, Gen. sing. cyrkwje.]

---

[1] With uvular r the distinction between hard and soft r is difficult to hear.

VOWEL GRADATION AND VOWEL LENGTHENING

Examples of *Vowel Gradation* in Upper Lasatian can be seen in numerous series of words. E.g.:—

njesć = to carry (Impfve.); nosyć (Freq.)
wjesć = to lead (Impfve.); wodźić (Freq.)
smjerć = death, mrěć = to be dying (Impfve.), Pres. mrěju = I am dying; Pfve. Fut. wumru = I shall die, wumorić = to exhaust.
brać = to take (Impfve.); Pres. bjeru = I take
mjerznyć = to freeze; mróz = frost.
ležeć = to lie; łožo = couch, bed
ćec = to flow; Pres. ćeku = I flow, ćečeš, etc.; točić = to draw or tap (beer)
ćeć = to cut, hew; Pres. tnu, tnješ or ćnu, ćnješ
wisać = to hang (intrans.); wěšeć = to hang up (trans., Impfve.)
sedźeć = to sit (Impfve.), sydnyć so = to sit down (Pfve.)
duch = spirit; duša = soul; dych = breath

Vowel Lengthening survives only etymologically owing to the absence of long vowels in Lusatian. Examples are comparatively rare. E.g.:—

lećeć = to fly (Impfve.) ; lětać (Freq.), cf. Cz. letěti; létati
brać = to take (Impfve.); Pres. bjeru; zběrać = to collect
chodźić = to go (Freq.) ; přichadźeć = to come (Impfve.)
skočić = to jump (Pfve.) ; skakać (Impfve.)
prosyć = to request ; prašeć so = to ask (a question)
posłać = to send (Pfve.) ; posyłka = a parcel (sent)

The vowel correspondences o/ó and e/ě in the declensions of nouns (see below: Morphology. The Declension of Nouns, No. 4a, Masc. o-stems) are really relics of earlier lengthening, e.g.:—

Bóh (earlier long vowel) = God, Gen. sg. Boha, cf. Czech: Bůh, Boha; similarly:—

    kóń = horse, Gen. sg. konja
    hród = castle,   "   hrod-a or -u
    měd = honey,   "   mjedu

SLAVONIC CHARACTERISTICS

1. Metathesis of liquids. Lusatian, like Polish, has true West Slav forms with vowels o, ó or ě, 'e after the liquids. ě corresponds to an original rising intonation, 'e to a falling one. E.g.:—

<pre>
hród   = castle, Gen. sg. hroda or hrodu
wrota   = gate
mróčel(fem.) = cloud
hłód   = hunger, Gen. sg. hłoda or hłodu
hłowa   = head
włoha   = dampness
brěza   = birch tree (cf. Russ. берёза)
před   = before (prep.)
prědk   = front
prjedy   = before (adv.)
brěmjo   = burden
drjewo   = wood (cf. Russ. дéрево)
</pre>

and exceptionally—

<pre>
brjóh   = shore, Gen. sg. brjoha
mlěć   = to grind
</pre>

but—

<pre>
mloko   = milk
</pre>

Initially in:—

<pre>
łódź   = boat   ⎫
łochć = elbow   ⎬ from roots with origi-
robota = labour, corvée ⎭ nal falling intonation
roz-   = apart (prefix)

radło = plough   ⎫
ratar = ploughman ⎬ from roots with origi-
łakać = to (lie in) ⎭ nal rising intonation
         wait for
</pre>

2. The 1st Palatalization of velars, changing k, h, ch into $č$, $ž$, $š$ respectively, is common in Lusatian. E.g.:—

pjeku = I(also: they) bake, pječeš, pječe, etc. = you, he bake(s)
člowjek = person; Voc. sg. člowječe!
móc = to be able; Past Part. Act. móhł; Pres. móžu = I can ($ž$ by analogy with the other persons), móžeš, móže, etc., also 3rd pers. pl. móža
Bóh = God; Voc. sg. Božo!
paduch = thief; Voc. sg. paduše (*or* paducho)!
strachota = fear, danger; strašny = terrible, dangerous

2a. c and z, when derived from k and g respectively, also change to č and ž:

wótc = father, Voc. sg. Wótče naš! = Our Father!
hólc = boy   "   hólče! (or holco!)
knjez = gentleman, "   knježe (= Sir!)

3. The 2nd Palatalization of velars, by which k, h, ch become respectively c, z, and š (the last as in Czech and Polish), is also found in some instances in Upper Lusatian to-day. E.g.:—

ruka = hand,   Dat.,Loc.sg. and Nom.,Acc.Dual: ruce
mloko = milk,   Loc.sg. w mlóce
wojak = soldier, Nom.pl. wojacy
wulki = great,   "   " masc.pers. wulcy
sněh = snow,   Loc.sg. w sněze
brjóh = shore,   "   " na brjoze (or brjohu)
noha = foot,   Dat.,Loc.sg. and Nom.,Acc.Dual: noze
drohi = dear,   Nom.pl.masc.pers.: drozy
brjuch = belly, Loc.sg. na brjuše
proch = dust,   "   " w próše (or prochu)
Čech = Czech,   Nom.pl. Češi and Češa (or Čechojo)
suchi = dry,   Nom.pl.masc.pers.: suši

Where *g* occurs as the final consonant of a stem as in—figa (= a fig), it changes to *dz* or more commonly to *z* before *e*, cf. Polish, e.g.:—

fidze or fize—Dat., Loc. sg. and Nom., Acc. Dual;
Pol. figa, Dat., Loc. sg. fidze

4. Yotation or the palatalization of consonants before *j* has a rather more limited field in Lusatian than in Polish, Russian, and Serbocroätian. It is tending to be eliminated in some verbs in instances where one would expect it, by forms constructed on the analogy of other persons or forms of the verb. It can also be found in nouns and in a few Comparative adverbs. The *chuintantes* ć, dź, č, š, ž do not change before *j*. The Past Participles Passive are mostly formed from the same stem as in the Infinitive. Before *j*:—

k, h, ch change to č, ž, š respectively, as in other Slavonic languages:—

płakać = to cry; Pres. płaču, płačeš (as well as
                        płakam, płakaš)[1]
skakać = to jump;   "   skakam, skakaš or skačeš
łhać or= to tell   "   łžu, łžeš or łžiš
łžeć   lies;
lochko = lightly; Comparative: lóže or lóšo

[1] For the Present tense we give the 1st and 2nd pers. sing. in the following examples unless otherwise stated.

duša = soul, < duchja

t, d change to *c, z* respectively, as in Czech:—
klepotać = to knock; Pres. 3rd pers. sg. klepoce
                                   (or klepota)
błyskotać = to flash;   "   "   "   " błyskoce
                                   (or błyskota)
płakajucy = (who is) crying (Pres. Participle)
swěca   = candle
mjeza   = boundary
    But—
rodźeny = born; by analogy with Infin. rodźić
wodźić   = to lead (Freq.); Pres. 1st pers. sg.
        wodźu, by analogy with wodźiš
přichadźeć = to come (Impfve.), < *přichadjać,
        Pres. přichadźam, přichadźeš.

s, z change to *š, ž* respectively, as in other Slavonic languages:—
nosyć   = to carry (Freq.); Pres.1st pers.sg. nošu =
      I carry
prosyć = to request, Pres. 1st pers. sg. prošu, Past
      Part.Pass. prošeny
wysoko = high (adv.), Comparative: wyše = higher
wozyć = to convey (Freq.); Pres. 1st pers. sg. wožu
skazyć = to spoil; Pres. 1st pers. sg. skažu, Past
      Part.Pass, skaženy
wjazać = to bind; Pres. 1st pers. sg. wjazam, 2nd
      p.s. (arch.) wježeš, now wjazaš
blizko = near (adv.), Comp. bliže

n becomes soft before *j* (spelling e.g. nju, pronounced -ńu):—
    honić = to hunt, chase; Pres. honju, honiš
    mjenić = to change; Pres. mjenju, mjeniš

l remains, *ł* becomes *l*:—
chwalić = to praise; Pres. chwalu, chwališ
dźělić = to divide; Pres. dźělu, dźěliš
słać   = to send *and* to spread; Pres. sćelu, sćeleš

r becomes *rj*, pronounced rj:—
    wěrić = to believe; Pres. wěrju, wěriš
    kuric = to smoke; Pres. kurju, kuriš
    morjo = sea

p, b, w, m remain, preserving the *j* after them:—
    ćerpjeć = to suffer; Pres. ćerpju, ćerpiš
    kupić   = to buy (Pfve.); Fut. kupju, kupiš
    dyrbjeć = to have to; Pres. dyrbju = I must
    hłuboko = deep (adv.); Comp. hłubje or hłubšo
    žiwić so= to feed; Pres. žiwju so, žiwiš so
    rozumjeć= to understand; Pres. rozumju, rozumiš
    zlemic = to break (Pfve.); Fut. zlemju, zlemiš
When the root of the verb ends in -*j*- one *j* is lost:—

łójić = to hunt, catch; Pres. lóju, lójiš
prajić = to say; Pres. praju, prajiš

st and *sk* both become *šć*:—

pušćeć   = to let, < *pustjać
pišćeć   = to squeal, creak, < *piskjać
hnojišćo = dungheap, < *hnojiskje

zd becomes *zdź*:—

jězd = travelling (in a vehicle); jězdźić = to travel, Pres. jě*zd*žu, by analogy with jězdźiš.

5. The dropping of consonants.

The spelling of Lusatian is largely "historical" or etymological. Certain consonants are regularly mute in pronunciation, such as *l*, *ł*, and *r* finally after other consonants, *h* finally and before other consonants (often initially), as already explained under "Pronunciation: The Consonants".

A further feature characteristic of the Upper Lusatian consonantal system is the dropping of *w* between two vowels when the second one is *i* as in stajić[1] (= to place, stand something up), for stawić. Cf. Russian поставить, Czech postaviti. *w* is also dropped in some words after velars before *o*, as in hózdź = nail, cf. Russ. гвоздь, Pol. gwóźdź, etc. (See No. 11 under "Features Characteristic of Upper Lusatian" below.)

A curious result of the dropping of *t* in słać (= to spread), for stłać, has been its consequent coincidence in form with słać (= to send), as in Polish. But in Lusatian the identity has been carried further, into all the parts of the two verbs, the Present sćelu, the Imperative sćel!, etc., being regularly used with the meaning of "send" as well as with that of "spread".

6. Prothetic and epenthetic consonants.

We have already pointed out immediately after giving the Lusatian alphabet, that no native Lusatian words begin with a vowel, prothetic *w* being used in Upper Lusatian before *o* and *u*, prothetic *j* before *a* and *e*, and *h* before *i*.

In the 3rd person Personal Pronoun, epenthetic *n(j)*- is used after prepositions, as in Russian, Ukrainian, Polish, Czech and Slovak. E.g.:—

Gen.sg. jeho = of him; but: bjez njeho = without him
Dat.pl. jim = to them; "   k nim   = towards them

[1] *j* is inserted to avoid hiatus.

Dat.dual jimaj = to them but: k nimaj = towards them
           two;   two

 j is used prothetically in: jón = it (masc. impersonal Acc. sg.).
 Notice also: tajki = such, kajki = what kind of?, with inserted j.

FEATURES CHARACTERISTIC OF UPPER LUSATIAN

(From the notes below it will be seen that it is the vowel system of Upper Lusatian which presents the most numerous exclusively Upper Lusatian features.)
 * marks those points also true in a general way for Lower Lusatian (not necessarily for the particular examples).

1. The nasal vowels. *C.S. ǫ (O.S. ѫ) develops into u, as in East Slav, Serbocroätian, and when short, in Czech. E.g.:—

         ruka = hand
         muž = man
         dub = oak

  C.S. ę (O.S. ѧ) becomes:
    (1) 'a before hard consonants,
    (2) 'e before soft consonants,
    (3) 'o finally (like other final e's after soft consonants)

E.g.:—
  (1) jazyk = tongue, pjaty = fifth, hrjada = perch, beam, mysla = they think, < myslić, cf. O.S. мыслѧтъ
  (2) pjeć = five, dźewjeć = nine, započeć = to begin
  (3) brěmjo = burden, ćelo = calf

2. The semi-vowels.
  C.S. ъ, when developed, becomes o or ó before a hard consonant, but e before a soft consonant. E.g.:—

         moch   = moss
         són, Gen. sg. sona = dream
         won   = out
    but—
         krej   = blood
         dešć   = rain

  C.S. ь usually becomes 'e in Upper Lusatian, e.g.:—
         dźeń = day

     len = flax
     lesć = guile
     wjes = village
  but also—
     pos = dog
     law = lion

 *3. The fill-vowel is usually *e*, but can also be *y* and *o*; sometimes no fill-vowel is used. E.g.:—

    woheń = fire
but—
    sym = I am
    sy d om = seven (as well as sydm)
    Pětr = Peter

 4. C.S. vocalic ŗ (O.S. ръ) becomes *or*, e.g.:—

    kormić = to feed
    hordy = proud
    morchej = carrot

 C.S. ŗ̓ (O.S. ръ, рь) before hard dentals also becomes *or*, otherwise it becomes *'er*, e.g.:—

    čorny = black
    porst = finger
    zorno = seed

but—
 ćerpjeć = to suffer, čerw = worm, wjerch = top,
    ceiling; prince, wjerba = willow
and—
 smjerć = death, pjerść = soil, humus, žerdź = rod

 C.S. vocalic ļ becomes *oł*, as also does C.S. soft ļ' when it occurs before a hard consonant or after *č*, *ž*, *s*, *z*, *t*, *d*, e.g.:—

khołm = hill	połk = regiment	čołm = boat
žołty = yellow	połny = full	dołhi = long
tołsty= fat	wołma = wool	stołp = pillar

but exceptionally—

    słónco = sun

 Otherwise ļ' becomes *'eł*, e.g.:—

    mjelčeć = to be silent
    pjelnić = to fill;
  also—wjelk = wolf

 But C.S. rъ, rь, lъ, lь develop the semivowels normally, e.g.:—

   knot = mole (for krot, cf. Russ. крот)
   krej = blood

 Note the irregular:—

```
sylza       = tear
jabłuko     = apple
pcha or tcha = flea (losing ł)
```

*5. C.S. ě (O.S. ѣ) *usually* develops into ě in Upper Lusatian when it occurs in the first syllable of a word, but not invariably, e.g.:--

```
rěka   = river
měra   = measure
hnězdo = nest
pěsń   = song
```

In syllables other than the first, C.S. ě becomes *je* (Lower Lusatian *'e*):—

```
na dubje    = on the oak
žonje       = to the woman
mjedwjedź   = bear
```

But after *s*, *z*, *c*, C.S. ě becomes *y* in *any* syllable except finally in Upper Lusatian:—

```
         syno      = hay
         cyły      = the whole
but—     w ruce    = in the hand
         na brjoze = on the shore
```

(But Lower Lusatian: seno; cely; we ruce.)

But C.S. *e* is preserved as *e* after *s*, *z*, *c*, e.g.:—

sebje = oneself (Gen. Acc.), zeleny = green

*6. C.S. *e* often becomes *o* finally after soft consonants *in nouns* and sometimes medially in open syllables before hard consonants, e.g.:—

polo = field, morjo = sea, lico = face

but Upper Lusatian:—

budźe = he will be, budźeće = you will be, etc., in *verbs*.
sotra = sister, ćopły = warm, žona = woman

but—

zeleny = green, wjeseły *and* wjesoły = merry

7. *e* in Upper Lusatian becomes ě when it was originally long or had a rising intonation and often when it occurs after a soft consonant, e.g.:—

```
pěc    = stove
brěza  = birch, cf. Russian берёза
ćěmny  = dark
šěsć   = six
ně     = no
```

8. *ó* can occur in Upper Lusatian—

(1) in closed syllables, e.g.:—
hród = castle   płód = fruit   hóčka = hook
hnój = manure   wólša = alder   suhłós = harmony

(2) when derived from C.S. *or*, *ol* with rising intonation, e.g.:—
błóto = mud   mrózy = frosts   dróha = road
cf. Russian болóто = bog, морóзы, дорóга.

(3) in originally pretonic syllables, now stressed in Lusatian, e.g.:—
brózda = furrow   młóćić = to hammer
wróćić = to (re)turn tłóčić = to print, squeeze
bróny = harrow
Cf. Russian бороздá = furrow, боронá = harrow, воротúть = to return, молотúть = to hammer.

9. *o* can be changed to *e* before soft consonants, as in:—

dejić = to milk   lemić = to break   sel = salt
selić = to salt   zerja = dawn (pl.)   telki = so many a, so great (Low Lus. telik)

a can also become *e* between soft consonants, as in Czech (cf. No. 26):—

jejo   = egg, cf. Cz. vejce
zjewić = to reveal, cf. Cz, zjeviti
běžeć = to run, cf. Cz. běžeti
słušeć = to befit, belong, cf. Cz. slušeti se

*10. Final soft *ŵ* becomes *j*, e.g.:—

krej = blood   rjetkej = radish
domoj = home(ward) morchej = carrot

*11. *w* is lost—

(1) After a vowel and before *i* or *j*, e.g.:—
rukajca = glove
łójić   = to hunt, catch
prajić = to say
połojca = a half

(2) after a velar consonant and before, *o*, e.g.:—
chory = ill
hózdź = nail

(3) in the prefix *vъz* = up, e.g.:—

zróst = growth, cf. Cz. vzrůst
zdaleny = distant, cf. Cz. vzdálený

*12. s, z, and c are always hard, causing original i after them to become y and, in Upper Lusatian only, original ě to become y too except finally (cf. No. 5), e.g.:—

zyma = winter   syno = hay
prosyć = to request   syrota = orphan
wozyć = to convey   cyły = whole

*13. stj and skj both give šć, and zdj sometimes gives ždž (see on yotation, No. 4 of "Slavonic Characteristics" above).

*14. łn changes in some words to łm, e.g.:—

wołma = wool, cf. Czech vlna
čołm = boat, " Russian чёлн

15. initial ch (phon. x) is pronounced kh in Upper Lusatian but written ch, e.g.:—

chlěb = bread   chromy = lame
chłód = cold   přichadźeć = to come

(See also footnote 3 after the Alphabet.)

*16. The regular avoidance of initial vowels in all native Lusatian words by prefixing w before o and u, h before i, and j before a and e. (Cf. Byelorussian). E.g.:—

woko = eye   hinak = otherwise
wón = he   hić = to go
wucho = ear   jehnjo = lamb

Also in foreign words, e.g.:—

jandźel = angel
Jendźelska = England
Wódra = Oder
Wukrajina = Ukraine

But in modern loan words initial vowels remain: uniwersita = university, opera - opera

17. The prefix vy- (O.S. въ-) becomes wu- in Upper Lusatian, e.g.:—

wuchadźeć = to go out (Impfve.)
wupić = to drink up (Pfve.)

*18. C.S. suffixes -ъkъ, -ьcь, -ьsъ, -ъtь become -k, -c, -s, -ć, e.g.:--

zbytk = remnant
kónc = end, aim
wows = oats
łochć = elbow

This is due to analogy with the other cases, zby*tka*, etc. Cf. No. 2.

*19. In common with Czech, C.S. *dj* gives *z*, while C.S. *tj* gives *c*, as in all other West Slav languages, e.g.:—

U.L.	Cz.	Slk.	Pol.
mjeza = boundary,	mez(e),	medza,	miedza
swěca = candle,	svíce,	svieca,	świeca

*20. In common with Czech and Slovak, literary Lusatian has initial stress.

21. Common Slav *g* has become *h* (medially - *voiced* ɦ), cf. Czech and Slovak, e.g.:—

noha = leg, Cz. noha, Pol. noga, Russ. horá

*22. As in both Czech and Polish (but not in Slovak), *ch* (x) changes to *š* in the 2nd Palatalization (not to *s*), e.g.:—

w měše = in the sack, (Nom. sg. měch)

*23. In the metathesis of liquids, the vowels used are *o* and *e* and their variants (*ó* and *ě* or *je*), as in Polish. (See above "Slavonic Characteristics" No. 1.)

24. *ř* (from soft *r'*) after *k* and *p* is pronounced *š* in Upper Lusatian, like *rz* in Polish after all unvoiced consonants, e.g.:—

při	= near,	cf. Pol.	przy
před	= before,	"	przed
přećiwo	= against,	"	przeciw
křiž	= cross,	"	krzyż
křemjeń	= flint,	"	krzemień

But the pronunciation of *ř* as soft *s'* after *t* is a feature of Upper Lusatian only:

tři = three. In Lower Lusatian it is *spelt* as well as pronounced tśi.

25. The (in Upper Lusatian only slightly palatal) alveolar affricates *ć*, *dź* represent original palatalized *t'*, *d'*, as in Polish, e.g.:—

ćichi	= quiet,	Pol.	cichy
dźiki	= wild,	"	dziki
dźesać	= ten,	"	dziesięć

26. The vowel alternation 'a/ja (from C.S. *ę*) before hard consonants ><'e/je between soft consonants, figures in Upper Lusatian in the course of declension, conjugation, etc. Cf. Polish. E.g.:—

LUSATIAN

    rjad   = row,   Loc. sg. w rjedźe or w
                                   rjadu
    rjany = beautiful, adv. rjenje or rjano
    wjazać = to bind, Pres. 2nd pers. sg. wježeš

  Cf. Pol.: rząd   = row,   Loc. sg. w rzędzie,
                                          and also:
          miasto = town,   "   w mieście
  But U.L. nan   = father,   "   wo nanje

*27. In common with all West Slav languages, original *kw* and *gw* are preserved (in Upper Lusatian *gw* as *hw*), e.g.:—

    kwět   = flower
    hwězda = star (Lower Lusatian gwězda)

*28. The West Slav feature of preserving the combinations *tl*, *dl* is also a regular feature of Lusatian, e.g.:—

    pletła (fem. Past Part. Act.) = woven
    wjedła ("   "   "   ) = led
    mydło   = soap

*29. Labials followed by *j*, as in other West Slav languages, do not take *l* (in contrast to East and South Slav), e.g.:—

    zemja   = earth
    kupju   = I shall buy
    lubju so = I please

*30. The *j* after labials before the back vowels *a*, *o*, *u* is pronounced as a distinct *j* (cf. Ukrainian), e.g.:—

    słomjany = of straw
    w njebju = in the sky

  Cf. Ukrainian п'ять = five

*31. As in other West Slav languages, *sk* sometimes becomes *šk* in Lusatian, e.g.:—

    škra   = spark
    škŏrc   = starling
    škerjedny = disgusting

*32. As in other West Slav languages and in Ukrainian and Byelorussian, Lusatian drops an original initial *i*, e.g.:—

    mam = I have, hrać = to play

*33. Original C.S. -*ky*-, -*gy*- (O.S. кы, гы) always become -*ki*-, -*hi*- respectively, as in Russian and Byelorussian and in Polish, while in Upper Lusatian *only*, C.S. -*chy*- (O.S. хы) likewise becomes

-*chi*-, as in Russian and Byelorussian and in contrast to Polish, Czech, and Slovak. E.g.:—

kiwać	= to beckon,	wulki	= great
hibać	= to move	druhi	= second, other
chileć so	= to incline	muchi	= flies, Nom. pl.
		ćichi	= quiet

34. The group *str* sometimes loses the *s*, e.g. sotra = sister, cf. R. сестрá; wótry = sharp, cf. R. óстрый; třecha = roof, cf. Cz. střecha; truna = string (musical), cf. R. струнá ; tradác = to live in poverty, cf. R. страдáть = to suffer.

35. As in Polish, East Slav, and Bulgarian and Macedonian, there are no quantities (long vowels) or intonations ("musical" accents) in Lusatian. (The latter, of course, are absent also from Czech and Slovak.)

THE LUSATIAN DIALECTS

By far the most important Lusatian dialect after Upper Lusatian is *Lower Lusatian*, which has been used as a literary language from an even slightly earlier date than Upper Lusatian. (See "Lusatian Literature" above.)

Lower Lusatian is spoken in the northern half of Lusatia centred round Chośebuz (Cottbus). Owing to the more oppressive rule of Prussia, this area is far more Germanized, and consequently during the nineteenth century literature did not flourish in Lower Lusatia to the extent it did in Upper Lusatia. The language itself is also more Germanized.

In some respects Lower Lusatian is even more distinctive among the Slavonic languages than Upper Lusatian. We give below a list of its main phonetic features.

Its orthography differs from Upper Lusatian in that soft ŕ is indicated with ' in final position. *j* has its full jot value. Before back vowels preceded by *j* labials do not become soft themselves but are always followed by j in pronunciation, e.g.: wjacor (= evening), mjasec (= month) mjod, (= honey). Soft ŕ and *l* are fully palatalized in pronunciation, e.g. kuŕ = smoke, lampa (phon. ḷampa) = lamp. *w* is pronounced *v*, not *w*, in Lower Lusatian dialects. It is palatalized before *i* and *ě*.

The main phonetic features of Lower Lusatian

1. š, ž are hard, in contrast to Upper Lusatian. Hence they are followed by *y*, not *i*, as in Polish,

e.g.:—

šyja = neck, žyto = corn, Łužyca = Lusatia

c is also hard and always followed by y, e.g.:—

cysty = clean

2. č is almost always replaced by c, e.g.:—

cas = time, cłowjek = person, wjacor = evening
but—

lažčej = easier (adv.), or (ldžej)

3. Upper Lusatian ć, dź are regularly replaced by ś, ź respectively, except after s, z, š, ž, ś, ź, ć, dź, c, č, e.g.:—

śichy = quiet
źowka = girl, daughter
śopły = warm
źeń = day
daś = to give (Pfve.)
źěło = work

but—

dosć = enough
zwězćo = bind up!·
ku ćći = to the honour (of)
gozdź = nail
gośćina = feast
mjelčćo = be silent!
puš(ć)ćo = let! (2nd p. pl.)
pozdźe = late

4. C.S. g is retained, in contrast to Upper Lusatian, e.g.: grěch = sin.

5. C.S. chy is retained, in contrast to Upper Lusatian, e.g.: śichy = quiet.

6. After k, p, t—š often replaces Upper Lusatian r, while ś replaces ř (<ŕ), e.g.:—

pšawy = real, right   kśidło = wing
tšawa = grass   pśi = near
kšasny = fine   tśi = three

7. Prothetic h instead of prothetic w, e.g.:—

hogeń = fire, Upper Lusatian: wohen
hokno = window
hucho = ear
huzki = narrow
but woko = eye

However, since 1945 it has been the practice in the present day literary language to write w-.

8. The prefix vy- (O.S. въі) is rendered hu-,

(but *wu-* in the literary language) e.g.:—

    hugnaś = to drive out
    hugon = common pasture
    hugrono = pronunciation, expression

9. *e* becomes *'a* before hard consonants, e.g.:—

jazor = lake   wjacor = evening   mjaza = boundary
śamny = dark   pjas = dog   wjas = village
brjaza = birch

10. Final *e* becomes *'o* in the *verbs* as well as in the nouns, e.g.:—

    buźo = he will be
    buźośo = you (pl.) will be
    pišo = he writes

11. C.S. ę (O.S. ⱥ) becomes ě when stressed, and *e* when unstressed, e.g.:—

    jězyk = tongue
    grědka = vegetable bed
  but—
    kozle(tko) = kid

12. C.S. ъ becomes *e* before both hard and soft consonants, e.g.:—

    wen = out   mech = moss

and also:—

    kšej = blood

C.S. ь regularly becomes *'a* before hard consonants, e.g.:—

    pjas = dog   wjas = village
    lan = flax   lasć = guile

but before soft consonants it becomes *e*, e.g. źeń = day, pjeńk = tree-trunk, stump.

13. C.S. r̥ becomes *ar*, before which the velars *k* and *g* take a softening *j*:

    marchwej = carrot
    kjarmiś = to feed
    gjardy = proud

C.S. ŕ̥ becomes *ar* before hard dentals, otherwise it becomes *er* e.g.:—

    carny = black   cart = devil
    marznuś = to freeze   twardy = hard
  tarł = rubbed (Past Part. Act.—Old Lower Lusatian)
  but—
pjerwjej = before, first (adv.)   cerkwja = church
serp = sickle   žerź = rod

C.S. *ł* and *ľ* become *oł* after *c*, *ž*, and *p*, e.g.:—

    cołm = boat žołty = yellow połny = full

but after *t*, *d*, *s*, *ł* becomes *łu*

    dłujki = long tłusty = fat słup = pillar

otherwise, after a labial *ł* becomes *ał*, e.g.:—

            wałma = wool

and *ľ* becomes *el*, e.g.:—

        mjelcaś = to be silent wjelk = wolf

14. *ó* has a different pronunciation in Lower Lusatian: either ou͡ or oe͡. It occurs only in stressed syllables after labials, except bilabial *ł* (= w), and velars when no labial or velar comes after. It is no longer indicated in the orthography, e.g.:—

        gora = hill bosy = bare-foot

It is retained in pronunciation when prefixes and prepositions take away the stress on to themselves, e.g.:—

        po godach = after Christmas
        pogoniś = to drive

15. *ě* is pronounced i͡ə with a full *e* after a full *i*, e.g.:—

          rěka = river

Unstressed original *ě* (ь) becomes *'e*, e.g.:—

    mjadwjeź = bear na dubje = on the oak

16. co (= what) >< Upper Lusatian: što.

17. A tendency to develop a secondary stress on the penultimate syllable, as in the Eastern Lusatian dialects and Polish.

The two other main dialects of Lusatian are:—

(1) the Central (transitional) dialect spoken in the region of Terp, Zabrod, and Bluń, and also to the west around Zły Komorow (Senftenberg); and—

(2) the Eastern dialect, as exemplified in the dialect of Mužakow (Muskau) which was closely studied by the Russian philologist, L. V. Ščerba. It is now extinct.

The *Central* dialect contains features from both Upper and Lower Lusatian and is a blend of the two. Jan Skala made an attempt to use it as a literary language in a periodical which he edited; but he did not gain its acceptance.

The *Eastern* dialect was a transition to the Polish dialects further east, but it contained some features peculiar to itself which we give first in the list that follows:—

1. The C.S. nasal vowel ę becomes 'a before soft as well as before hard consonants, while finally it becomes -e, except in Present Gerunds where it becomes -o:—

  grjada= bed (for plants), pjać = five
but—
 ćele = calf; ležo = lying, stojo = standing

In other eastern areas ę becomes u:—
   juzyk = tongue

2. pŕ becomes pć, which is sometimes simplified to ć, while kŕ becomes sć, e.g.:—

  pći = near ćišła = (she) came
  sćiwda = wrong, injury

3. An epenthetic g is inserted in the combinations zr, žr, which become zgr, žgr, e.g.:—

  žgrebe or zgrebe = foal
  žgrjodło   = source, spring
  zgrjały   = ripe

4. w (pron. u̯) is lost after a closed ô, e.g.:—
  dubô = of oaks rô = grave

5. j (pron. i̯) is lost after e and i, e.g.:—
 kre = blood ce = whose (cf. Russ. чей)
 pi = drink! ki = a stick

6. č becomes c, as in Lower Lusatian.

7. C.S. ъ has become e, as in Lower Lusatian and Polish, e.g.:—

  dešć = rain weš = louse

8. r̥ becomes ar, as in Lower Lusatian and Polish, or är, e.g.:—

  karmi = feeds carny = black
but—
  twärdy = hard zärno = a seed

 l̥ becomes -oł- after c (from č) and ž, but -łu- after t, d, s as in Lower Lusatian and Polish, e.g.:—

  cołm = boat žołty = yellow
  kłusty (<tłusty) = fat
  dług (also dälgi) = long
  słup   = pillar

In other eastern areas l̥ becomes äł after labials, e.g.:—
   päłny = full

9. C.S. ě (O.S. ѣ) became 'a before hard dentals, otherwise e; e subsequently sometimes replaces 'a, where the latter would be expected—through the working of analogy, cf. Polish. E.g.:—

    klatka = cage
    belić = to whiten
    pjask = sand
    w leće = in summer
    dźad = grandfather

hence—

    beły = white
    leto = summer

10. š, ž are not soft, but also not as hard as in Lower Lusatian and Polish; they therefore approach š, ž in Czech and Slovak.

11. what? = co?, as in Lower Lusatian, Czech and Polish.

12. As in Slovak, Slovenian, Serbocroätian, and to a large extent in Lower Lusatian, the ending -m has been generalized for the 1st person sing. Present of all classes of verbs, with only three verbs as exceptions:—

    dźěłam = I do
    vidźim = I see
    sypem = I pour
    njesem = I carry
    kupujem = I buy

but—

    ja mogu = I can
    ja cu = I want
  ja budu *or* budźem = I shall be

13. C.S. initial jь (O.S. и) sometimes becomes *jo*, e.g.:—

    jogła = needle

14. As in Lower Lusatian, a secondary accent on the penultimate syllable could be heard in the Eastern dialects; cf. Polish.

THE MORPHOLOGY OF UPPER LUSATIAN

THE DECLENSION OF NOUNS

Lusatian morphology is notable for the fact, that, in common with Slovenian, it preserves the Dual number throughout the declensions and conjugations. Nevertheless, despite the number of forms thus still used, it is true to say that the system of Upper Lusatian noun declensions is simpler than that of Czech or Polish. There are only a few differences between the hard and soft versions of each type. And, of course, the Czech vowel mutations after soft consonants (přehláska) are absent from Lusatian.

The Instrumental case, as well as the Locative, can only be used with prepositions, as in Slovenian. The plain Instrumental of other Slavonic languages is regularly rendered by *z* (= with) + Instrumental in Upper Lusatian, e.g.:—

Pisa z wołojnikom = He writes with a pencil
Potom bu tam z fararjom = Afterwards he became vicar there

The Vocative has a distinctive form only for masculine nouns in the singular. In all other instances the Vocative is the same in form as the Nominative.

With masculine nouns the *Accusative* of *all* numbers is the same as the Genitive only for masculine personal nouns, while for inanimate nouns it is the same as the Nominative. For animate nouns not denoting persons, such as the names of animals, the Accusative is the same as the Genitive in the singular, while in the dual and plural it is the same as the Nominative.

In the dual the Nom., Voc. (and Acc. for masculine names of animals and inanimate, and also all feminine and neuter nouns) have one and the same form. The Genitive dual for nouns of all genders has the same ending as the Genitive plural of *all* genders:—*-ow*. (But in Lower Lusatian the Genitive dual has *-owu*.) The Dat., Instr. *and Loc.* dual for nouns of all genders ends in *-omaj* (Lower Lusatian *-oma*). In respect of the Loc. dual there is thus a difference with Slovenian.

In the plural the endings *-am, -ami* (soft stems *-emi*), *-ach* have been generalized for the Dat., Instr. and Loc. respectively of nouns of all genders, as in East Slav.

In the plural of feminine nouns the Nom., Voc. and Acc. are the same in form as the Gen. sing., as in other West (and South) Slav languages.

The old short ŭ-stems do not exist as a separate declension, but have left numerous traces in other declensions, as in all other modern Slavonic languages.

Of the other terminations the only distinctively Upper Lusatian ones are *-ej* for the Dat. sing. of masc. nouns, and *-o* for the Voc. sing. of some masc. nouns;

further -*u* for the Instr. sing. of fem. nouns, which occurs also in Lower Lusatian.

1. *i*-stems, feminine only. The vast majority of nouns formerly belonging to this declension have gone over to the fem. soft *a*(*ja*)-stems in Upper Lusatian (but not in Lower Lusatian), preserving only a distinctive *i*-stem Acc. sing., like the Nom., e.g.; kósć (= bone), below. Only a few nouns, mostly ending in -*c*, have preserved a semblance of the original *i*-stem declension, with -*y* replacing -*i* after the hardened *c* (or *s*). (In Lower Lusatian a separate *i*-stem declension exists for fem. nouns with other final consonants in the Nom.)

kósć = bone   nóc = night

SING.

Nom.	kósć	nóc
Gen.	kosće	nocy
Dat.	kosći	nocy
Acc.	kósć	nóc
Instr.	kosću	nocu
Loc.	kosći	nocy

DUAL

Nom./Acc.	kosći	nocy
Gen.	kosćow	nocow
Dat./Instr./Loc.	kosćomaj	nocomaj

PLUR.

Nom.	kosće	nocy
Gen.	kosćow	nocow
Dat.	kosćam	nocam
Acc.	kosće	nocy
Instr.	kosćemi	nocami
Loc.	kosćach	nocach

Notice the irregular sól (= salt), which changes its root vowel to -*e*- in declension, e.g.: Gen. sg. and Nom. pl. sele, etc.

Like kósć are declined the numerous abstracts in -*osć*, e.g.: wĕrnosć (= truth), lubosć (= love), etc.; also: česć (= honour), which can have an irregular Dat. sing. cći; woš (= louse), Gen. sg. wšě, Nom. pl. wši (pron. pši); and rož (= rye), Gen. sg. ržě, irregular Acc. sg. ržu.

Like nóc.: only móc (= power), pěc (= stove), other cases except Acc. sg. p*j*ecy, etc.; wěc (= thing); wjes (= village), dropping -*je*- in other cases, Gen. sg. wsy.

2*a*. Consonant stems. These, with the characteristic "inserted" syllable before the ending, survive

as a type in Upper Lusatian only in certain neuter nouns ending in -*jo*. These insert either -(*j*)*eć* in the sing. and dual and -(*j*)*at*- in the plural, or else -(*j*)*enj*- throughout; but their *endings* are those of the soft neuter *jo*-stems (save sometimes after -*t*- in the Instr. pl.).
E.g.:—

kurjo = chicken   znamjo = sign

SING.

Nom.	kurjo	znamjo
Gen.	kurjeća	znamjenja
Dat.	kurjeću	znamjenju
Acc.	kurjo	znamjo
Instr.	kurjećom	znamjenjom
Loc.	kurjeću	znamjenju

DUAL

Nom./Acc.	kurjeći	znamjeni
Gen.	kurjećow	znamjenjow
Dat./Instr./Loc.	kurjećomaj	znamjenjomaj

PLUR.

Nom.	kurjata	znamjenja
Gen.	kurjatow	znamjenjow
Dat.	kurjatam	znamjenjam
Acc.	kurjata	znamjenja
Instr.	kurjatami	znamjenjemi
Loc.	kurjatach	znamjenjach

Like kurjo are declined mainly the names of young animals:—

ćelo	= calf
žrěbjo *or* zrěbjo	= foal
młodźo	= young creature
jehnjo	= lamb
kózlo	= kid
ptačo	= birdling
libjo	= gosling
pilo	= duckling
proso	= pigling
huso	= gosling, goose

also zwěrjo = wild animal, swjećo, Gen. sg. swjećeća = holy image, and in the sing. swinjo = pig, which has an irregular plur., viz.:—
  Nom./Acc. swinje, Gen. swini, Dat. swinjom, Instr. swinjemi, Loc. swinjoch.
So also:—
holčo = girl, Gen.sg. holčeća, Nom./Acc.pl. holčata, and

LUSATIAN 379

hólčo = boy, Gen. sg. hólčeća, Nom./Acc.pl. hólčata, but
for hólčo in the oblique cases of the singular, forms from hólc (= boy), e.g. Gen. sg. hólca, are more frequently used.

Like znamjo: brěmjo = burden, płomjo = flame, ramjo = shoulder, symjo = seed, wumjo = udder, promjo = beam, stripe, tymjo = marsh; crown of the head.

njebjo (= sky), a soft *jo*-stem in the sing., Gen. sg. njebja, has an irregular *s*-stem plural, e.g.: Nom./Acc. njebjesa, Gen. njebjes, Dat. njebjesam, etc.

Notice the unique declension of mać or maćer (= mother), the only surviving *r*-stem in Upper Lusatian:

	Sing.	DUAL	
Nom.	mać,(maćer)	Nom./Acc.	maćeri
Gen.	maćerje	Gen.	maćerjow
Dat.	maćeri	Dat./Instr./Loc.	maćerjomaj
Acc.	maćer,(mać)		
Instr.	maćerju		
Loc.	maćeri		
Voc.	maći		

	PLUR.
Nom.	maćerje
Gen.	maćerjow
Dat.	maćerjam
Acc.	maćerje
Instr.	maćerjemi
Loc.	maćerjach

2*b*. The old long *ū*-stems survive in nouns formerly ending in *-eŵ*, now pronounced and spelt *-ej*, e.g.:—

    cyrkej = church   britej = razor blade
    morchej[1] = carrot   žerchej[1] = cress
    łahej = bottle   škorodej = crucible
    rjetkej[1] = radish

also in:—

    pónoj = frying-pan   Gen. sg. ponwje,
    gratej = shoemaker's thread   " grateje

---

[1]These are now sometimes declined also in the singular like fem. *ja*-stems, e.g. Gen. s. morcheje, Inst. s. morcheju.

LUSATIAN

SING.

Nom.	cyrkej
Gen.	cyrkwje
Dat.	cyrkwi
Acc.	cyrkej
Instr.	cyrkwju
Loc.	cyrkwi

The Dual and Plural follow the *ja*-stems, see zemja, below, No. 3.

krej, formerly spelt kreẃ (= blood), may have a Gen. sg. krwě. It declines:

	SING.	DUAL	PLUR.
Nom./Acc.	krej	krwi	krwje
Gen.	krwě (lit.lang.) or kreje		etc., like Dual and Plural of zemja (see below).
Dat./Loc.	krwi		
Instr.	krwju		

solotej = salad, can be similarly declined, or like morchej (see footnote, p. 379).

3. *a*-stems, mainly feminine. These are clearly subdivided into hard *a*-stems and soft *ja*-stems, as in Old Slavonic. The Instr. sg. ends in -(*j*)*u* by contraction. The Voc. sg. is the same as Nom. sg. New endings can be seen in the Gen. dual and plur.: -*ow*, Dat./Instr./Loc. dual: -*omaj*, and in the Instr. plur. for soft stems: -*jemi* (*a>e* between two palatal consonants). The Acc. pl. is *always* like the Nom. pl., even for animate nouns.

Velar stems undergo the 2nd Palatalization in the Dat./Loc sg. and Nom./Acc. dual.

Masculine nouns in -*a* are declined like *o*- or *jo*-stems in the plural—see nan (= father), and muž (= man), below, No. 4*a*.

žona = woman   ruka = hand   zemja = earth
duša = soul

	Hard stems	Velar stems	Soft stems	Chuintante stems
SING.				
Nom.	žona	ruka	zemja	duša
Gen.	žony	ruki	zemje	duše
Dat.	žonje	ruce	zemi	duši
Acc.	žonu	ruku	zemju	dušu
Instr.	žonu	ruku	zemju	dušu
Loc.	žonje	ruce	zemi	duši
DUAL				
Nom./Acc.	žonje	ruce	zemi	duši
Gen.	žonow	rukow	zemjow	dušow
Dat./Instr./Loc.	žonomaj	rukomaj	zemjomaj	dušomaj

PLUR.				
Nom.	žony	ruki	zemje	duše
Gen.	žonow	rukow	zemjow	dušow
Dat.	žonam	rukam	zemjam	dušam
Acc.	žony	ruki	zemje	duše
Instr.	žonami	rukami	zemjemi	dušemi
Loc.	žonach	rukach	zemjach	dušach

Hard stems

Those ending in -*ca*, -*sa*, and -*za* change the ending -*je* of the Dat./Loc. sing. and Nom./Acc. dual to -*y*, because *c*, *s*, *z* are always hard in Upper Lusatian (See "Features characteristic of Upper Lusatian," No. 12.) Thus these cases have the same form as the Gen. sg. and Nom./Acc. pl.:—

	Gen., Dat., Loc. sg.,	Nom., Acc. dual,	Nom., Acc. pl.	
ranca = pig,	" "	" "	" "	rancy
kosa = scythe,	" "	" "	" "	kosy
koza = goat,	" "	" "	" "	kozy

All other hard nouns regularly soften the final consonant of their stem before the ending -(*j*)*e* of the Dat., Loc. sg. and Nom., Acc. dual. E.g.:—

woda	= water,	Dat. sg.	wodźe
pata	= brooding hen,	"	paće
žona	= woman,	"	žonje
skała	= rock,	"	skale
kura	= hen,	"	kurje
kopa	= heap	"	kopje
žaba	= frog,	"	žabje
kruwa	= cow	"	kruwje
słoma	= straw,	"	słomje
harfa	= harp,	"	harfje
but—			
sotra	= sister	"	sotře (after *t*)

and monosyllables have the ending -*ě*:

hra	= game,	D., L.s., N., A. du.	hrě
ćma	= darkness,	" " " "	ćmě
škra	= spark	" " " "	škrě
stwa	= room,	" " " "	(we)jstwě

Velar stems

Like ruka = hand, Dat.,Loc.sg. and Nom.,Acc. dual ruce with 2nd Palatalization, we have:
noha = leg, Dat.,Loc.sg. and Nom.,Acc.dual noze
figa = fig, "   "   "   "   "   fidze or fize

wopuška or łopuška
= little tail Dat.,Loc.sg.and Nom.,Acc.dual wopušce
or łopušce

And nouns ending in -*cha* have the ending -*e* after the *š* which here replaces *ch* (see "Slavonic Characteristics", No. 3), hence we have:—

       třecha = roof, Dat. sg. třěše
       mucha = fly,   "   muše

Soft stems

Those ending in a *chuintante*, e.g.: -*ša*, -*ča*, have no *j* in the endings, see duša above.
Notice:—

łža = a lie,   has Gen.sg. łžě
mša = Mass,   "   "   mšě or mše
sla = breeching, "   "   slě; pl. slě, Gen. slow
                                                 = bracers
škla = dish   "   "   šklě

Nouns with Nom. sg. in -*eń* or alternatively -*nja* are declined as if they always ended in -*nja*, i.e. like zemja, e.g.: bróžeń or bróžnja (= barn), Gen. sg. bróžnje, Dat./Loc. sg. bróžni, Acc./Instr. sg. bróžnju, Gen. pl. bróžnjow or bróžni.

So also: móšeń = satchel, purse, studźeń or studnja = well, etc.

A few irregular fem. nouns have a Gen. plur. in -*i* instead of -*ow*, e.g.:—

       kokoš = hen, Gen. pl. kokoši
       konop or konopej f. = hemp,
            Gen. pl. konopi or konopjow

Others can have no ending in the Gen. pl., e.g.:—

       njedźela = Sunday, Gen. pl. njedźel

husa = goose, Gen. pl. husow or hus, hora = mountain, Gen. pl. horow or hór.

Names of domestic animals (and some other nouns) can also take the endings -*om*, -*omi*, -*och* in the Dat., Instr. and Loc. plur. respectively instead of the usual endings. Cf. the irregular plur. of swinjo (= pig) above under the neuter consonantal stems, No. 2*a*, p. 378.

knjeni (= lady, Mrs.) is declined like a soft stem ending in *n*, with an irregular Nom. *and Acc.* s. knjeni, Gen. s. knjenje, Dat./Loc. s. knjeni, Instr. s. knjenju. The other cases are regular.

So also the rare pani or pań (= lady).

Pluralia tantum decline according to their ending quite regularly:—

HARD:
    narodniny[1] = birthday
    nožicy = scissors
    prózdniny[1] = holidays
    widły = pitchfork

SOFT:
    durje = door
    kachle = stove
    klěšće = tongs, pincers
    pišćele = organ (musical instrument)
    sanje = sledge
    droždźe = yeast, (Gen. droždź-ow or -i)
    hrabje = rake
    husle = violin

žně (= harvest) has Gen. pl. žni or žnjow.

Masculine nouns ending in -*a* or -*ja* follow the corresponding masculine or feminine models in the sing. and dual. In the plur. they follow the *o*- or *jo*-stems (see below No. 4*a*) and therefore have varying Nom. plur. forms, e.g.:—

		Nom. pl.	
wójwoda	= duke		wójwodźi or wójwodojo
braška	= master of the ceremonies at wedding	"	braški or braškojo
starosta	= chairman, president	"	*usually:* starostojo
husita	= Hussite,	"	husići
ćěsla	= carpenter,	"	ćěslojo
hrabja	= count,	"	hrabjojo
wjesnjanosta	= village mayor	"	wjesnjanostojo
but			
herba	= heir,	"	herbja

Masculine names in -*o*, e.g. Kito, Nedo, follow this type.

Names of countries ending in -*ska* are declined like fem. adjectives. (See below under "The Adjectives".)

4*a*. Masculine *o*-stems. These also are subdivided into hard *o*- and soft *jo*-stems. These two types, however, differ only in three or four cases (apart from the *j* preceding the ending in soft stems when declined): the Nom. (and for inanimates the Acc.) dual ends in -*aj* for hard stems and in -*ej* for

---

[1] These nouns can have Gen. pl. with zero ending: narodninow *or* narodnin.

soft stems; the Instr. pl. ends in -*ami* for hard stems and in -*emi* for soft stems; in the Loc. sg. hard stems have -(*j*)*e* or -*u*, while soft stems have only -*u*. Only soft stems can have the ending -*je* in the Nom./Acc. plur. The Nom. plur. can have a great variety of endings. Note the typically Upper Lusatian ending -*ej* (<-*ewi*) in the Dat. sing.

The ending for the Acc. varies according to the rule differentiating personal animate, impersonal animate and inanimate nouns given above in the introduction to the declensions (p. 376).

nan = father   ptačk = (little) bird   dub = oak

SING.	*Hard* personal animate	*Hard* impersonal animate	*Hard* inanimate
Nom.	nan	ptačk	dub
Gen.	nana	ptačka	duba
Dat.	nanej	ptačkej	dubej
Acc.	nana	ptačka	dub
Instr.	nanom	ptačkom	dubom
Loc.	nanje	ptačku[1]	dubje
Voc.	nano	ptačko	dubje(dubo)
DUAL			
Nom./Voc.	nanaj	ptačkaj	dubaj
Gen.	nanow	ptačkow	dubow
Dat./Instr./Loc.	nanomaj	ptačkomaj	dubomaj
Acc.	nanow	ptačkaj	dubaj
PLUR.			
Nom./Voc.	nanojo	ptački[2]	duby
Gen.	nanow	ptačkow	dubow
Dat.	nanam	ptačkam	dubam
Acc.	nanow	ptački[2]	duby
Instr.	nanami	ptačkami	dubami
Loc.	nanach	ptačkach	dubach

muž = man   čerw = worm   mječ = sword

SING.	*Soft* personal animate	*Soft* impersonal animate	*Soft* inanimate
Nom.	muž	čerw	mječ
Gen.	muža	čerwja	mječa
Dat.	mužej	čerwjej	mječej
Acc.	muža	čerwja	mječ
Instr.	mužom	čerwjom	mječom
Loc.	mužu	čerwju	mječu
Voc.	mužo	čerwjo	mječo

[1]-*u* for velar stems, -*e* or -*je* for other stems.

[2]-*i* for some velar stems, -*y* for other stems, and e.g. řeznik = butcher, Nom. pl. řeznicy, with second palatalization.

	Soft personal animate	Soft impersonal animate	Soft inanimate
DUAL			
Nom./Voc.	mužej	čerwjej	mječej
Gen.	mužow	čerwjow	mječow
Dat./Instr./Loc.	mužomaj	čerwjomaj	mječomaj
Acc.	mužow	čerwjej	mječej
PLUR.			
Nom./Voc.	mužojo	čerwje	mječe
Gen.	mužow	čerwjow	mječow
Dat.	mužam	čerwjam	mječam
Acc.	mužow	čerwje	mječe
Instr.	mužemi	čerwjemi	mječemi
Loc.	mužach	čerwjach	mječach

Many monosyllabic nouns with *ó* as their root vowel change this *ó* to *o* in declension, e.g.:—

```
bóh  = a god,     Gen. sg. boha
hród = a castle,     "    hrodu or hroda
kóń  = horse,        "    konja
hósć = guest,        "    hosća
nóž  = knife,        "    noža,  etc.
```

Some others, on the other hand, keep the *ó* in declension, e.g.:—

```
kónc = end,      Gen. sg. kónca
wótc = father,      "    wótca
mróz = frost,       "    mróza
tkhór = polecat,    "    tkhórja, etc.
```

Dissyllabic nouns with -*o*- as their root vowel and ending in the Nom. sing. in -*oł*, used to drop the second *o* (before the *ł*) in declension and change the first *o* to *ó* (originally in compensatory lengthening), e.g.:—

posoł = messenger, Gen. sg. pósła, Nom. pl. pósły, pósli, or posłojo
kotoł = boiler,   "   kótła   "   kótly

But now forms retaining the second -*o*- are preferred: G.s. posoła, kotoła. Also: wosoł = donkey, G.s. wosoła.

    pos (= dog) does drop its *o* in declension:—

Sing. Gen./Acc. psa, Dat. psej, Instr. psom, Loc. psu, Voc. pso!

Dual Nom./Voc./Acc. psaj, Gen. psow, Dat./Instr./Loc. psomaj

Plur. Nom./Voc./Acc. psy, Gen. psow, Dat. psam, Instr. psami, Loc. psach

    Some masc. nouns ending in -*eń* drop the -*e*- in declension, e.g.:—

woheń = fire, Gen. sg. wohnja

Others retain the -*e*-, e.g.:—

   korjeń = root,   Gen. sg. korjenja
   wuheń = furnace, chimney,   "   wuhenja

In the *Gen. sing.* the commonest ending is -*a*. Some monosyllabic inanimate hard nouns, however, have an alternative ending -*u*. Such are:—

   dom = house,   doma or domu
   hłód = hunger,   hłoda or hlodu
   len = flax,   lena or lenu
   lód = ice,   loda or lodu
   lud = people,   luda or ludu
   bóz = lilac, elder-tree, boza or bozu
   kał = cabbage,   kała or kału
   hród = castle,   hroda or hrodu
   skót = cattle,   skota or skotu
   sad = fruit,   sada or sadu

Yet: moch = moss, G.s. only mocha; płat = linen, G.s. płata; mór = plague, G.s. mora; but měd = honey, G.s. mjedu.

In the *Dat. sing.* monosyllabic nouns occasionally have the ending -*u* as an alternative to the usual -*ej*, e.g.:—

   duch = spirit, Dat.sg. duchu and duchej
   lud = people,   "   ludu and ludej
   měr = peace,   "   měru and měrej

But bóh (= a god) has Dat. sg. bohu only.

Note that in the *Instr. sg.* -*om* is used for soft as well as hard stems, as in Slovak. This case is not used without a preposition.

In the *Loc. sg.* the ending -*u* is used for:—
1. almost all animate nouns, e.g.:—

   w Bóhu   = in God
   w knjezu = in a gentleman, priest
   w duchu   = in a (the) spirit)

2. inanimates with stem -*c*, -*s*, -*z*, e.g.:—

   čěpc = cap   Loc. sg. w čěpcu
   wows = oats,   "   we wowsu
   wóz   = waggon,   "   we wozu

3. some others, including some with velar stems, e.g.:—

   běh   = running,   Loc. sg. w běhu
   (za)počatk   = beginning, Loc. sg. na (za)počatku

Other inanimate nouns ending in formerly velar

-*h* have the ending -*e* (<*je*<ъ) before which *h* undergoes the 2nd Palatalization and becomes *z*, e.g.:—

  sněh = snow, Loc. sg. w sněze
  brjóh = shore, bank, " na brjoze

Inanimates ending in velar -*ch* have the ending -'*e* (<*je*<ъ) before which *ch* changes to *š* according to the 2nd Palatalization, e.g.:—

  próch = dust, Loc. sg. w proše or prochu
  brjuch = belly, " na brjuše

The ending -(*j*)*e* is used mainly with all other hard stem inanimates; the final consonant is softened before it in the usual way, as also in the *a*-stems, e.g.:—

   zub = tooth, Loc. sg. w zubje

Notice:—
són (= dream, sleep), Gen. sg. sona; Loc. sg. we słódkim sonje (= in sweet sleep), but—wosnje (= in one's sleep).
rjad (= row), Loc. sg. w rjadu or w rjedźe (with change of root vowel).

In the *Voc. sg.* all soft stems, some stems in velar -*k*, -*h*, or -*ch* and those in sibilant -*s*, -*z* or -*c* usually have the ending -*o*; but note:—

knjez	= gentleman,	Voc. sg.	knježe! = Sir! (respectful)
člowjek	= person	"	člowječe! (slightly ironical), otherwise: člowjeko!
hólc	= boy,	"	hólče! (slightly ironical), otherwise: hólco!
bratr	= brother,	"	bratře! (slightly ironical), otherwise: bratro!

Wótc = forefather, (solemn) father, has V.s. Wótče only in Wótče naš! = Our Father! stary wótco! means 'helpless old man!'.

But—
 Bóh = God, Voc. sg. Božo! (with 1st palatalization)

Hard stems in the Voc. sg. usually have -'*e*, before which final consonants are softened in the usual way and *ch* sometimes undergoes the 1st Palatalization to *š*, e.g.:—

  susod = neighbour, Voc. sg. susodźe! or susodo!
  had = snake, " hadźe! or hado!
  kał = cabbage, " kale!
  Pawoł = Paul, " Pawoło! or Pawle!

```
snop      = sheaf,  Voc. sg. snopje!
zub       = tooth,     "     zubje!
  but—
nan       = father has more usually nano! sometimes
                                          nanje!
syn       = son        "  regularly     syno!
Jan       = John       "       "        Jano!
lud       = people     "       "        ludo!
bur       = peasant    "       "        buro!
  and—
paduch    = thief      "  paducho! or paduše!
Chrystus  = Christ     "  Chrystuso!   but with Jězus:
                          Jězus Chrystus = Jesus
                          Christ, Voc. sg. Jězu
                          Chrysće!
```

In the *Nom. plur.* nouns denoting *persons* most often end in *-ojo*, formerly rarely in *-owje*. But such nouns can also have other endings, namely:—

1. *-i*, after *c -y*. Nouns ending *-k* undergo the 2nd Palatalization *k>c* and also have *-y*, while some of those ending in *-ch* keep *-i*, before which *ch* becomes *š*, e.g.:—

```
Žid       = Jew        Nom. pl. židźi, also židźa or
                                Židojo
čert      = devil,        "     čerći or čertojo
student   = student,      "     studenći
duch      = spirit,       "     duchi, but more often:
                                duchojo
   but—
paduch    = thief,        "     paduši or paduchojo
Čech      = a Czech,      "     Češi, also Češa, Čechojo
                                while: Čechi = Bohemia,
                                Gen. (pl.) Čech
pohan     = heathen,      "     pohani *and* pohanojo
herc      = musician,
            player,       "     hercy
rěznik    = butcher,      "     rěznicy
wojak     = soldier,      "     wojacy (wojaki—toy
                                 soldiers)
hrěšnik   = sinner,       "     hrěšnicy
```

2. Some names of persons in a collective sense can have the ending *-(j)a*, before which consonants are softened, e.g.:—

```
    bratr  = brother,   Nom. pl. bratřa
    kmótr  = godfather,    "     kmótřa
    susod  = neighbour,    "     susodźa
    bur    = peasant,      "     burja
    mnich  = monk,         "     mniša (*ch + j > š*)
```

Čech = Czech   Nom. pl. Česa (see above No. 1)
Serb = a Lusatian
      Serb, Sorb   "   Serbja
Žid = Jew,   "   Židźa (see above No. 1)

3. Nouns in -ar, -er, -el, end in -jo, e.g.:—

    kowar = smith, Nom. pl. kowarjo
    wučer = teacher, " wučerjo
    přećel = friend, " přećeljo

So also:—
    hósć = guest, " hosćo
    pachoł = boy, " pacholjo

4. Nouns in -an end in -enjo, e.g.:—

delan = valley dweller,
        lowlander, Nom. pl. delenjo
měšćan = townsman, " měšćenjo
Słowjan = Slav, " Słowjenjo

5. A few nouns denoting persons can have -e, e.g.:—

    muž = man, Nom. pl. mužojo, rarely also:
                                muže
    jandźel = angel, " jandźeljo, more
                            rarely: jandźele

Other animate and inanimate nouns with *hard* stems most often have -y (-i after velars), while other animate and inanimate *soft* stem nouns have -e, e.g.:—

    woł = ox, Nom. pl. woły
    ptačk = bird, " ptački
    čerw = worm, " čerwje

It will be seen, therefore, that many masc. nouns can have various (sometimes alternative) forms in the Nom. pl., e.g.:—

    bóh = a god, Nom. pl. bohojo, bohi, (bohowje), occasionally even: bozy (with 2nd Palatalization).

In the *Gen. plur.* a few soft-stem nouns can have the ending -i instead of the regular ending -ow, e.g.:—

    łochć = elbow, Gen. pl. łochći
    nochć = finger " nochći
    kóń = horse " koni

A few other nouns have no ending the Gen. plur., e.g.:—

pjenjez = coin, Nom. pl. pjenjezy = money, Gen. pl.
                                            pjenjez

tysac = thousand, Gen. pl. tysac (or tysacow)
hody = Christmas,   "   hód

In the Dat., Instr. and Loc. plur., instead of the usual endings, one occasionally used to meet the endings -*om* for Dat. pl., -*omi* for Instr. pl., -*och* for Loc. pl., especially in the names of domestic animals, e.g.: konjom = to the horses.

The form mužom for the usual mužam (= to men), was also used infrequently, presumably only in the language of women!

Notice the irregular:—

knjez = gentleman, Mr., Voc. sg. knježe!, otherwise regular in sing. and dual, but in the pl.: Nom./Vqc. knježa (phon. knejza), Gen./Acc. knježich, Dat. knježim, Instr. knježimi, Loc. wo knježich (= about ...).

lud = a people, nation, has regular plur. ludy, declined like duby, but the pl. ludźo = people, declines: Nom./Voc. ludźo, Gen./Acc. ludźi, Dat. ludźom, Instr. ludźimi, Loc. ludźoch.

hosćo, Nom. pl. of hósć = guest, is declined like ludźo.

dźeń = day, declines:—

	SING.	DUAL		PLUR.
Nom.	dźeń	Nom./Voc./Acc dnaj[1] or dnjej	Nom./Voc.	dny
Gen.	dnja	Gen. dnow[1] or dnjow	Gen.	dnow[1] or dnjow
Dat.	dnjej	Dat./Instr./Loc. dnomaj[1] or dnjomaj	Dat.	dnam[1] or dnjam
Acc.	dźeń		Acc.	dny
Instr.	dnjom		Instr.	dnami[1] or dnjemi
Loc.	dnju		Loc.	dnach or dnjach

wodnjo = by day

But tydźeń = week, declines regularly, Gen. sg. tydźenja, etc. In the du. and plur. it is usually replaced by: njedźele (N.pl.), njedźeli (N.du.).

4*b*. Neuter *o*-stems. These are also subdivided into hard *o*-stems, ending in -*o*, and soft *jo*-stems ending in -(*j*)*o* [<(*j*)*e*] and -(*j*)*e*, the latter mostly verbal nouns. But these two types really differ in declension only in the Nom./Acc. dual, which ends in -*je* in the hard stems and in -*i* in the soft stems and

---

[1]Forms with hard *dn*- are characteristic of the Catholic dialect.

and sometimes in the Loc. sing. In the Instr. plur. soft stems have -*emi*. The Gen. dual and plur. almost always ends in -*ow*. (Voc. = Nom.)

	słowo = word	polo = field
	Hard stems	*soft stems*
SING.		
Nom.	słowo	polo
Gen.	słowa	pola
Dat.	slowu	polu
Acc.	słowo	polo
Instr.	słowom	polom
Loc.	słowje	polu
DUAL		
Nom./Acc.	słowje	poli
Gen.	słowow	polow
Dat./Instr./Loc.	słowomaj	polomaj
PLUR.		
Nom.	słowa	pola
Gen.	słowow	polow
Dat.	słowam	polam
Acc.	słowa	pola
Instr.	słowami	polemi
Loc.	słowach	polach

In the *Dat. sg.* -*u* is now the usual ending.

In the *Instr. sg.* both hard and soft stems have -*om*, as in the masc. *o*-stems.

In the *Loc. sg.* nouns ending in -*so*, -*zo*, -*co* *always* have -*u*, while those ending in -*ko*, -*cho*, -*go* usually also have -*u*, e.g.:—

maso	= meat,	Loc. sg.	masu
železo	= iron	"	železu
pleco	= ham, leg(of meat),	"	plecu
wóčko	= eye,	"	wóčku
wucho	= ear,	"	wuchu
Kongo	= Congo	"	Kongu

But mloko = milk has Loc. sg., with *k* changing to *c* by the 2nd Palatalization before *e* (<*ě*):—

mloko = milk, Loc. sg. młóce

Jabłuko = apple, can also have Loc. sg. jabłuce, or jabłuku.

Other hard stems have -(*j*)*e* in the Loc. sg. with the usual softening of consonants before this ending, e.g.:—

hnězdo	= nest,	Loc. sg.	hnězdźe
čoło	= forehead,	"	čole
błóto	= mud,	"	błóće
město	= town, place,	"	mesće

In the *Nom., Acc. du.* note: wóčce = eyes, from wóčko, but płec*y* = legs of meat, from płeco, and kolesy = wheels, from koleso.[1]

In the *Gen. pl.* a few nouns have no ending, e.g.:—
lěto = year, Gen. pl. lět

Some soft stems have Gen. pl. in -*i*: jejo = egg, Gen. pl. jeji, chosćo = broom, Gen. pl. chosći.

Verbal Nouns end in -*nje* or -*će*: widźenje = seeing, biće = beating. A few other nouns also end in -*e*, e.g.: zbože, more often zbožo = happiness. They are declined exactly like polo.

Irregular neuter nouns:

Notice the irregular duals and plurals of woko (= eye), wucho (= ear):—

DUAL	Nom./Voc./Acc.	woči	wuši
	Gen.	wočow	wušow
	Dat./Instr./Loc.	wočomaj	wušomaj
PLUR.	Nom./Voc./Acc.	woči	wuši
	Gen.	wočow	wušow
	Dat.	wočam	wušam
	Instr.	wočemi	wušemi
	Loc.	wočach	wušach

But the regular duals and plurals mean:—
Du. woce Pl. woka = fat circles   Gen. pl. wok
                     on rich soup,
 " wuše " wucha = handles on   "   "   wuch
                     pots,

The diminutive wóčko is more often used than woko.

dźěćo = child:—

Sing. Nom./Voc./Acc. dźěćo, Gen. dźěsća, Dat./Loc. dźěsću, Instr. dźěsćom

Dual. Nom./Voc./Acc. dźěsći, Gen. dźěsćow, Dat./Ins./Loc. dźěsćomaj

Plur. Nom./Voc./Acc./Gen. dźěći, Dat. dźěćom, Instr. dźěćimi, Loc. dźěćoch.

The plural is feminine in gender.

sto = hundred:—

Sing. Gen. sta, Dat./Loc. stu, Instr. stom
Dual. Nom.   dwě sćě = 200
Plur. Nom./Acc. sta, Gen. stow, Dat. stam, Instr. stami, Loc. stach

Pluralia tantum such as dźasna (= gums), jatra (= liver), wrota (= gate), are declined quite regularly.

Men's Christian names in -*o* are of masc. gender and are declined in the plural like nan or like muž

---

[1] In pronunciation the difference in the final vowel is negligible. Both are pronounced near ə. Cf. p. 354.

LUSATIAN

according to their stem, e.g.: Mĕto, Warko, Kito. (Cf. p. 383.)

(See also under No. 2*a*, neuter consonantal stems.)

Proper names

These are regularly declined according to their ending and gender like common nouns. E.g.:—

Šewčik— a surname, Dual Nom. Šewčikaj, Plur. Nom. Šewčikojo
Nowak— a surname, Dual Nom. Nowakaj, Plur. Nom. Nowakojo
Lubij— a town, Germ. Löbau, Gen. sg. Lubija.
Praha = Prague, Gen. sg. Prahi, Loc. sg. w Praze
Stróžišćo— a place, Gen. sg. Stróžišća
Boranecy, pl.— a place, Gen. Boranec (no ending, N.B.), Dat. Boranecam.

Those with adjectival endings are declined like adjectives (q.v.), but in the Nom. pl. they may end also in -*y*, -*i*, -*ojo*, e.g.:—

Nom. sg. Hórčanski,— a surname, Nom. pl. Hórčanski, -scy, or -skojo
Gen./Acc. pl. Hórčanskich

The feminine form ends in -*cyna*: Hórčanscyna.

Neuter adjectival place-names ending in -*o* decline, e.g.:—

Nom./Acc.	Slepo
Gen.	Slepoho
Dat.	Slepomu
Instr./Loc.	Slepom

Place-names in -*ej* and -*oj* are feminine and decline:—

Kamjenej—	in all cases except Gen.
Gen.	Kamjeneje
Nom./Acc.	Łupoj
Gen.	Łupoje
Dat./Loc.	Łupoji
Instr.	Łupoju

Names of peoples are often used for names of countries, e.g.:—

do Němcow = to Germany
ze Serbow = from Lusatia
z Čech = from Bohemia
do delan = to the lowlands (in N. Upper Lusatia)

There are also names of countries ending in

-*ska*, declined like feminine adjectives (see "The Adjectives"): e.g. Jendźelska = England.

Foreign proper names are declined according to Upper Lusatian models of similar stem and gender, bearing in mind the stem of the name in the original language. Hence:—

        Plato,   Gen. Platona

but—

        Xenofon, "   Xenofonta

Latin names usually drop the final -*us* in declension, e.g.:—

        Vergilius, Gen. Vergilia

THE NUMERALS

Cardinals

The general pattern of the Cardinals in Upper Lusatian is similar to that in other West Slav languages. Whereas the Cardinals "one" to "four" are adjectival and agree with the noun they qualify in case, "five" onwards are usually treated as nouns if they are in the Nom./Voc. or Acc. and the noun they govern is put in the Gen. plur. But in the Gen., Dat., Instr., and Loc. they are adjectival and agree with their noun. On the other hand the special forms for masculine personal nouns are adjectival throughout, and have the complement in the plural.

Jedyn (= one) declines like the pronoun tón (= this). (See below, under "The Pronouns".)

	Masc.	*Fem.*	*Neut.*
Nom.	jedyn[1]	jedna	jedne
Gen.	jednoho	jedneje	jednoho
Dat.	jednomu	jednej	etc.

Dwaj (= two) is used for (all) masc. nouns, dwě for fem. and neut nouns. In the Acc. dweju applies to masc. *persons*, dwaj to other masc. nouns, dwě to fem. and neut. The other cases are the same for all genders.

Wobaj, wobě (= both) is declined like dwaj.

For "three" and "four" special forms for masc. personal nouns exist in the Nom. and Acc. only: Nom. třo, štyrjo, Acc. troch, štyrjoch, as opposed to tři, štyri for all other nouns. They are followed by the verb in the plural.

For the Cardinals from "five" onwards special forms ending in the Nom. in -(*j*)*o may* be used

---

[1] Žadyn = no, no one, is declined like jedyn.

LUSATIAN

pronominally when referring to masc. personal nouns.
They are only declined when thus used by themselves.
But the ordinary forms pjeć, šěsć, etc., can also be
and *are* in fact used for masc. personal nouns as well
as for all others in *all* the cases when the noun counted
is mentioned. The Nom. forms in *-o* require the
verb in the plural; the other Nom. forms always
govern the verb in the (neuter) singular.

Notice that šěsć (6) changes *ě* to *e* in declension.

The Cardinals 6-90 are declined like pjeć (= 5)
when used by themselves.

Compound Cardinals with tens and units are regularly in the form "three and twenty", and govern the
Gen. plur.

Sto is declined like słowo when used by itself[1]
(see "The Declension of Nouns", No. 4*b*, Neuter *o*-
stems). Sto and the other hundreds are left undeclined before nouns; před sto lětami = 100 years ago;
z dwě sćě ludzimi = with 200 people.

	NOM.		
	Masc.	*Fem.*	*Neut.*
1	jedyn	jedna	jedne

		Fem.-Neut.
2	dwaj	dwě

			ACC.			
GEN.	DAT.	*M.pers.*	*Other M.*	*F., N.*	INSTR.	LOC.
dweju	dwěmaj	dweju	dwaj	dwě	dwěmaj	dwěmaj

	Masc.,	*Masc.*				ACC.
	Fem., Neut.	*pers.*				*All*
						other
	NOM.		GEN.	DAT.	*M.pers.*	*nouns*
3	tři	třo	třoch	třom	třoch	tři

		INSTR.	LOC.
		třomi	třoch

4	štyri	štyrjo	štyrjoch	štyrjom	štyrjoch
					štyri

		štyrjomi	štyrjoch

5	pjeć	*pjećich	pjećim		
	pjećo	†pjećoch	pjećom	pjećoch	
	pjećimi	pjećich			pjeć
	pjećomi	pjećoch			

[1]Except Loc. sing.: stu.
*Now used only in expressions of time. †Masc.pers.

6	šěsć, šesćo, etc., declined like pjeć	
7	sydom, syd(o)mjo	
8	wosom, wos(o)mjo	
9	dźewjeć, dźewjećo	
10	dźesać, dźesaćo	
11	jědnaće, -aćo, etc.	
12	dwanaće	
13	třinaće	
14	štyrnaće	
15	pjatnaće	
16	šěsnaće	
17	sydomnaće	
18	wosomnaće	
19	dźewjatnaće	
20	dwaceći	
21	jedynadwaceći	
22	dwajadwaceći	
30	třiceći	
40	štyrceći	
50	pjećdźesat[1] or połsta	
60	šěsćdźesat[1]	
70	sydomdźesat[1]	
80	wosomdźesat[1]	
90	dźewjećdźesat[1]	
100	sto	
101	sto a jedyn	
200	dwě sćě	
300	tři sta	
400	štyri sta	
500	pjeć stow	
900	dźewjeć stow	
1,000	tysac—declined like dub	
2,000	dwaj tysacaj	
3,000	tři tysacy	
4,000	štyri tysacy	
5,000	pjeć tysac	
10,000	dźesać tysac	
100,000	sto tysac	
1,000,000	milion—declined like dub	

Ordinals

These are all declined like hard adjectives (see the declension of dobry under "The Adjectives"), except přeni (= 1st), třeći (= 3rd), which are declined like soft adjectives (see lětni under "The Adjectives"). In compound Ordinals only the last in the spoken and written order is an Ordinal in form.

[1]Colloquially these numerals are pronounced with a final -*ć*, instead of t, by analogy with dźesać.

LUSATIAN

1st	přěni	přěnja	přenje
2nd	druhi	druha	druhe
3rd	třeći	etc.	
4th	štwórty		
5th	pjaty		
6th	šěsty		
7th	sydmy		
8th	wosmy		
9th	dźewjaty		
10th	dźesaty		
11th	jědnaty		
12th	dwanaty		
13th	třinaty		
14th	štyrnaty		
15th	pjatnaty		
16th	šěsnaty		
17th	sydomnaty		
18th	wosomnaty		
19th	dźewjatnaty		
20th	dwacety		
21th	jedynadwacety		
22th	dwajadwacety		
30th	třicety		
40th	štyrcety		
50th	pjećdźesaty or połstaty		
60th	šěsćdźesaty		
70th	sydomdźesaty		
80th	wosomdźesaty		
90th	dźewjećdźesaty		
100th	stoty		
101st	sto a přeni		
200th	dwustoty		
300th	třistoty		
400th	štyristoty		
500th	pjećstoty		
1000th	tysacty		
2,000th	dwutysacty		
1,000,000th	milionty.		

Multiplicative Numerals denoting "of (so many) different kinds" are formed mostly with the adjectival endings *-ory* or *-aki*. They all decline like dobry, except dwoji and troji, which follow lětni.

1 jednory
2 dwoji, dwojaki, dwójny
3 troji, trojaki, trójny
4 štwory, štworaki
5 pjećory, pjećoraki
6 šesćory
7 sedmory

```
 10 dźesaćory
 11 jědnaćory
 20 dwacećory
100 story, stotory
1,000 tysacory
```

The *Collective Numerals* dwoje, troje, štwore can be used with *pluralia tantum*. In the oblique cases they have soft adjectival (plural) endings.

Fractions with a half are formed with poł (= half) prefixed to the Ordinals, as in other West Slav languages and Byelorussian. E.g.:—

```
½  = poł, also połojca or połojčka
1½ = połdra (by contraction for połdruha)
2½ = połtřeća
3½ = połštwórta
4½ = połpjata, etc.
```

The names of fractions end in -*ina*:—

třećina = a third	pjećina = a fifth
štwórćina = a quarter	stoćina = a hundredth

Distributive Numerals

These are formed, as in Czech, with po + Loc., e.g.:—

po jenym (masc. and neut.), po jenej (fem.)	= one each
po dwěmaj	= two each
po třoch mužach	= three men each
po pjećich stach	= 500 each

Numeral Adverbs

These are formed with the Cardinal Numerals followed either by the invariable word króć (= times) or by the declinable noun raz, which goes in the case demanded by the numeral. E.g.:—

jónkróć	*or* raz	= once, *also*: jónu
dwaj króć	" dwaj razaj	= twice, *also*: dwójce
tři króć	" tři razy	= thrice, *also*: trójce
štyri króć	" štyri razy	= four times
pjeć króć	" pjeć razow	= five times

Sprěnja, zdruha, střeća, etc. = Firstly, secondly, thirdly, etc.

THE PRONOUNS

In Upper Lusatian, only the Demonstrative Pronouns in the singular, and the words for who? (štó?), what? (što?), no, none (žadyn) and -self (samón) have a separate pronominal hard declension, with Gen. sg. masc. and neut. -*oho*, Dat. sg. masc. and neut. -*omu*, distinct from that of the *adjectives*, where the former soft pronoun endings, Gen. sg. masc. and neut. -*eho*, Dat. sg. masc. and neut. -*emu*, have predominated. (See under "The Adjectives" for full declensions of these.) The Personal Pronouns of the 1st and 2nd person, the Reflexive Pronoun sebje, and wšón(= all), have declensions of their own. All the other pronouns have the soft pronominal (and now hard and soft adjectival) endings -*eho, emu*, still seen in Upper Lusatian in wón (= he), Gen. sg. jeho, Dat. sg. jemu.

The declensional system and the uses of the pronouns in Upper Lusatian are largely similar to those in other West Slav languages with one important exception: there are no special enclitic forms for the Personal Pronouns of the *3rd* person. Acc. sg. masc. = Gen. sg. masc. for animate nouns, but = Nom. sg. masc. for inanimates; but in the dual and plural Acc. = Gen. for masc. personal nouns only.

The following list gives the main pronouns in the usual categories:—

Demonstrative:—
    tón = this
    tutón = this here (emphatic)
    tónle = this here (")
    wony = that (declined like hard adj. dobry)
    tamón[1] = that yonder
    tamny = that yonder (declined like dobry)

Interrogative:—
    štó? = who?
    što? = what?
    kelki? = how great? (declined like dobry)
    kotry? = which? (declined like dobry-Nom. pl. m. pers. kotři)
    kajki? = what kind of? (declined like dobry)
    čeji?-a, -e = whose? (declined like soft adj. lětni)

Indefinite (formed from the Interrogatives with prefixes or suffixes):—
    něchtó — someone
    něšto = something
    někajki = some kind of (declined like dobry)
    štóžkuli = whoever
    štožkuli = whatever
  Also:—
    něchtóžkuli = someone, any one
    něštožkuli = something, anything

---

[1]Characteristic of the Western Catholic dialect, Gen. sing. m., n. tamnoho, etc.

Relative (formed from the Interrogatives with the suffix -ž):—

    kotryž, kotraž, kotrež = who, which
    kiž (defective declension) = who
    čejiž, čejaž, čejež = whose
    štóž = he (who)
    štož = that which, what
    kajkiž = as, of the kind that

Possessive (pronoun-adjectives):—

    mój = my, mine
    naš = our(s)
    jeho = his, its ⎫
    jich = their(s) ⎬ indeclinable
    jeje = her(s) ⎭
    twój = your(s)(sing. possessor)
    waš = your(s)(plur. " and polite)
    naju = our(s)(of us two)
    vaju = your(s)(of you two)
    jeju = their(s)(of them two)
    also—
    jejny = her(s), declined like dobry
    samsny = of oneself, personal, own

Definitive:—

    wšón *or* wšitkón = all
    kóždy = every (declined like dobry)
    sam(ón), sama, samo = -self (declined like tón)
    samy = sheer, only, the very (declined like dobry)
    samsny = the same (declined like dobry)
    druhi = other, different
    jenaki = (of) the same kind of
    hinaši = different (declined like lětni)
    tajki = such (declined like dobry)
    telki = so great (declined like dobry)
    wšelki = many a
    cyły = the whole

Negative:—

    nichtó = no one
    ničo = nothing
    žadyn, žana, žane = no (declined like tón), Gen. s.m., n. žanoho, etc.

LUSATIAN

    nikajki   = no (declined like dobry)

Personal:—
- wón, wona, wono = he, she, it
- ja = I
- mój = we two
- my = we
- ty = you (sg. familiar)
- wój = you two
- wy = you (plur. and polite)

We give below the declensions of those pronouns which differ in any way from the declensions of the adjectives:—

tón = this

SING.	Masc.		Neut.	Fem.
Nom.	tón		to	ta
Gen.		toho[1]		teje
Dat.		tomu[1]		tej
Acc.	toho, tón		to	tu
Instr.		tym		tej
Loc.		tym		tej

DUAL	Personal/Impersonal			
Nom.	taj, tej		tej	tej
Gen.		teju		
Dat./Instr./Loc.		tymaj		
Acc.	teju, tej		tej	tej

PLUR.				
Nom.	ći, te		te	te
Gen.		tych		
Dat.		tym		
Acc.	tych, te		te	te
Instr.		tymi		
Loc.		tych		

Like tón (with or without prefixes or suffixes):—
wón, tamón (= that), tutón, tónle (= this),
samón (= -self).

N.B.— One says both: To je mój přećel, and *Tón je mój přećel* for "This is my friend".

---

[1] teho, temu were used for these cases until soon after the Second World War (1945).

LUSATIAN

štó (-chtó[1])? - who?; što? = what?

SING.

Nom.	štó (-chtó[1])	što
Gen.	koho	čeho
Dat.	komu	čemu
Acc.	koho	što, čo[2]
Instr.	kim	čim
Loc.	kim	čim

The relative kiž (= who— all genders, sg. and pl.) has only Inst. sg. (z)kimž, Loc. s. (wo)kimž, and Dat. pl. kimž.

wšón, wšitkón = all[3]

SING.	Masc.	Neut.	Fem.
Nom.	wšón, (wšitkón)	wšo, wšitko	wša, wšitka
Gen.	wšeho, wšitkeho, (wšoho)[4]		wšeje, wšitkeje
Dat.	wšemu, wšitkemu, (wšomu)[4]		wšej, wšitkej
Acc.	an. wšeho, wšitkeho, (wšoho)[4]	wšo, wšitko	wšu, wšitku
	inan. wšón, wšitkón		
Instr.	wšem, wšitkim		wšej, wšitkej
Loc.	wšem, wšitkim, (wšom)[4]		wšej, wšitkej
PLUR.			
Nom.	wšitcy pers.	wšě, wšitke	wšě, wšitke
	wšě, wšitke impers.		
Gen.		wšěch, wšitkich	
Dat.		wšěm, wšitkim	
Acc.	wšěch, wšitkich, pers.	wšě, wšitke	wšě, wšitke
	wšě, wšitke impers.		
Instr.		wšěmi, wšitkimi	
Loc.		wšěch, wšitkich	

mój = my

SING.	Masc.	Neut.	Fem.
Nom.	mój	moje	moja
Gen.		mojeho	mojeje
Dat.		mojemu	mojej
Acc.	mojeho, mój	moje	moju
Instr.		mojim	mojej
Loc.		mojim	mojej

[1] -chtó is used only in compounds.
[2] The form čo is used only after prepositions, e.g.:—
    na čo? = on to what?
    pře čo? = for what?
    wo čo = about (for) what?
    za čo? = for what (purpose)? Cf. Cz. -č
[3] For pluralia tantum and some nouns in the singular cyły is used more often: cyłe njebesa = the whole heavens, cyłe lěto = the whole year.
[4] The forms with medial -o- were typical of the Catholic dialect.

LUSATIAN

	Masc.	Neut.	Fem.
DUAL			
Nom./Voc.		mojej	
Gen.		mojeju	
Dat./Instr./Loc.		mojimaj	
	Personal/Impersonal		
Acc.	mojeju, mojej	mojej	mojej
PLUR.			
Nom./Voc.	moji, moje	moje	moje
Gen.		mojich	
Dat.		mojim	
Acc.	mojich, moje	moje	moje
Instr.		mojimi	
Loc.		mojich	

Like mój; twój = your(s), sing. familiar, swój = own (referring to subject of sentence), naš = our(s), waš = your(s).

Notice: mojedla = for me, twojedla = for you, swojedla = for oneself, našedla = for us, wašedla = for you; also: jehodla = for him, jichdla = for them, jejedla = for her.

Personal Pronouns

wón = he, wona = she, wono = it

	Masc.		Neut.	Fem.
SING.				
Nom.	wón		wono	wona
Gen.		jeho		jeje
Dat.		jemu		jej
	Personal/Impersonal			
Acc.	jeho, jón		je, jo	ju
Instr.		nim		njej
Loc.		nim		njej
DUAL				
Nom.	wonaj, wonej		wonej	wonej
Gen.		jeju		
Dat.		jimaj		
Acc.	jeju, jej		jej	jej
Dat./Instr.		nimaj		
PLUR.				
Nom.	woni, wone		wone	wone
Gen.		jich		
Dat.		jim		
Acc.	jich, je		je	je
Instr.		nimi		
Loc.		nich		

N.B.— Acc. sg. masc. jón is used for masc. inanimates and animals, while jeho is used for masc. persons.

Nom. dual wonaj, Nom. pl. woni, Acc. plur. jich are used for masc. personal nouns only. Otherwise: wonej, wone, je are used for the respective cases.

After prepositions *n* is prefixed before forms beginning with *je*, while with forms beginning with *ji*, *n* replaces the *j* (and is pronounced soft, as regularly in the combination *ni-*), e.g.:—

> bjez njeho = without him, bjez njeje = without her, bjez nich = without them
> k njemu = to him, k njej = to her, k nim = to them.
> Also: přes njón = across it, masc., přes nju = across it, fem., přes nje = across them, impers.

Instead of jeho, jemu, jej one can find joh', jom', ji in poetical and popular language.
ja = I, mój = we two, my = we; ty = you (sg. fam.), wój = you two, wy = you (pl. and polite sg.); sebje = -self.

SING.			
Nom.	ja	ty	—
Gen.	mnje, mje	tebje, će	sebje, so[1]
Dat.	mni, mi	tebi, ći	sebi, sej[2]
Acc.	mnje, mje	tebje, će	sebje, so[2]
Instr.	mnu	tobu	sobu[3]
Loc.	mni	tebi	sebi
DUAL			
Nom.	mój	wój	
Gen.	naju	waju	
Dat./Instr./Loc.	namaj	wamaj	
Acc.	naju	waju	
PLUR.			
Nom.	my	wy	
Gen.	nas	was	
Dat.	nam	wam	
Acc.	nas	was	
Instr.	nami	wami	
Loc.	nas	was	

The forms mje, mi, će, ći, so, sej are enclitic. (See pp. 460-461).

The corresponding full forms are used after prepositions, and at the beginning of sentences to express emphasis:—

[1] So as a Genitive is used only after prepositions: wot so = from oneself.
[2] Both so and sej are used with verbs: bojeć so = to fear, myslić sej = to think (to oneself).
[3] Sobu is used adverbially without a preposition, meaning 'together, with one':
> Přinjes to sobu! = Bring it with you!

bjez tebje = without you (sg.)
ke mni = to me.

In polite speech to single persons, using Wy, the Past Participle of the Compound Past (Perfect) tense is put in the *sing.*, in the appropriate gender, as in Czech, and also the adjectival complement, if any:—

Wy sće (tola) dyrb*jała* prjedy ke mni přińć.
= You should have come to me before (you know).

Wy sće była chora? = Have you been ill? (to a lady)
Wy sće był chory? = Have you been ill? (to a man)

THE ADJECTIVES

Declension.— The declension of adjectives in Upper Lusatian is divided into two main types: 1. hard, ending in -*y*, 2. soft, ending in -*i*. Velar stems, however, which end in -*ki*, -*hi*, or -*chi*, belong to the hard type and merely change all endings with -*y* (-*ym*, -*ych*, etc.) into endings with -*i* (-*im*, -*ich*, etc.).

The Acc. in the masc. behaves as in the masc. nouns, i.e. Acc. = Gen. in *all* numbers for masc. *personal* nouns, Acc. = Gen. in sing. but = Nom. in dual and plur. for masc. *animate non-personal* nouns, and Acc. = Nom. in all numbers for masc. *inanimate* nouns.

Note that in the sing. masc. and neut. Instr. and Loc. have the same form (as in Polish, and in contrast to Czech and Slovak).

The Nom. pl. masc. ends in -*i* for masc. persons only. See below for the consonantal changes before this ending. Cf. Polish and Czech.

HARD:
dobry = good

	Masc.	Neut.	Fem.
SING.			
Nom.	dobry	dobre	dobra
Gen.	dobreho		dobreje
Dat.	dobremu		dobrej
Acc.	dobreho, dobry	dobre	dobru
Instr.	dobrym		dobrej
Loc.	dobrym		dobrej
DUAL	*Personal/Impersonal*		
Nom.	dobraj, dobrej	dobrej	dobrej
Gen.		dobreju	
Dat./Instr./Loc.		dobrymaj	
Acc.	dobreju, dobrej	dobrej	dobrej

LUSATIAN

	Personal/Impersonal	Neut.	Fem.
PLUR.			
Nom.	dobri, dobre	dobre	dobre
Gen.		dobrych	
Dat.		dobrym	
Acc.	dobrych, dobre	dobre	dobre
Instr.		dobrymi	
Loc.		dobrych	

SOFT:
lětni = summer (adj.)

	Masc.	Neut.	Fem.
SING.			
Nom.	lětni	lětnje	lětnja
Gen.	lětnjeho		lětnjeje
Dat.	lětnjemu		lětnjej
Acc.	lětnjeho, lětni	lětnje	lětnju
Instr.	lětnim		lětnjej
Loc.	lětnim		lětnjej

DUAL.	
Nom.	lětnjej
Gen.	lětnjeju
Dat./Instr./Loc.	lětnimaj

	Personal/Impersonal		
Acc.	lětnjeju, lětnjej	lětnjej	lětnjej
PLUR.			
Nom.	lětni, lětnje	lětnje	lětnje
Gen.		lětnich	
Dat.		lětnim	
Acc.	lětnich, lětnje	lětnje	lětnje
Instr.		lětnimi	
Loc.		lětnich	

N.B.— In poetical and popular language one finds the endings -*oh'*, -*om'* instead of -*eho*, -*emu* respectively.

Before the ending -*i* in the Nom. pl. masc. pers. the usual softening of consonants takes place and velars undergo the 2nd Palatalization. Only the permanently hard sibilants *s*, *z*, and *c* do not change. At the same time a (*j*)*a*- in the root, if it then finds itself between two soft consonants, changes into -(*j*)*e*-. -*o*- in the root also somtimes changes to -*e*- before this ending -*i*. E.g.:—

Softening *t* > *ć* :—
    tołsty = fat,   Nom. pl. masc. pers. tołsći
    swjaty = holy,   " " " " swjeći
    jaty = captive,   " " " " jeći

Softening *d* > *dź* :—
    młody = young,   " " " " młodźi
    chudy = poor,   " " " " chudźi

Softening ł > l:—
  swětły   = bright, light Nom. pl. masc. pers. swětli
  wjesoły = merry,   "   "   "   "   wjeseli

Softening n > ń(ni):—
  rjany   = beautiful, "   "   "   "   rjeni

2nd Palatalization k+i > c+y:—
  wulki   = great,   "   "   "   "   wulcy
  kralowski = royal,   "   "   "   "   kralowscy

2nd Palatalization hi > zy:—
  drohi   = dear,   "   "   "   "   drozy

2nd Palatalization chi > ši:—
  suchi   = dry,   "   "   "   "   suši

No change -zy: cuzy   = foreign, Nom.pl.masc.pers. cuzy
No change -cy: swinjacy = piggish, "   "   "   " swinjacy
                          dirty,

For soft stem adjectives in the Nom. pl. the ending -i is also reserved exclusively for adjectives qualifying masc. pers. nouns. Thus lěni = lazy, Nom. sg. masc. and Nom. pl. masc. pers.

Many adjectives formed from the names of animals and a few from other names end in -i and are declined like lětni, e.g.:—

  ptači   = bird's
  wjelči = wolf's
  koči   = cat's
  psyči   = dog's

also:—

  boži   = God's, divine
  knježi = a gentleman's

Other adjectives of this kind end in -cy and are hard, e.g.:—

  konjacy = horse's
  zwěrjacy = wild animal's
  swinjacy = pig's, piggish

and also with -zy , howjazy = bull's, ox's

A few adjectives are indeclinable:— njeboh = the late, and the loan words: fajn = fine, blond = blond, stur = immovable, stubborn, nob(e)l = noble, refined, bankrot = bankrupt, lindyr = Dutch (dress).
Formerly also: bosy = bare-foot (now declined)
         ryzy = pure, real; chestnut;
              (now declined) e.g.:—
  ryzy złoto = pure gold
  ryzy kóń   = chestnut horse

There are *no* short, predicative adjectives in Upper Lusatian except— rad, rada, rado (= glad).

Possessive adjectives also do *not* have short, substantival endings, in contrast to those in Czech, Old Slavonic, Russian, Byelorussian and Serbocroatian in -*ov* (Cz. -*ův*), -*ova*, etc., and -*in*, -*ina*, etc. Possessive adjectives in Upper Lusatian end in -*owy*, -*owa*, -*owe* from masc. nouns and in -*iny*, -*ina*, -*ine* from fem. nouns, and are declined just like dobry. E.g.:—

    nanowy bratr = father's brother
Gen. nanoweho bratra
    nanowa šotra = father's sister
    nanoweje šotry
    nanowe polo = father's field
    Gen. nanoweho pola

But: nanowsky = fatherly!

    sotřiny bratr = sister's brother
Gen. sotřineho bratra
    sotřina kniha = sister's book
    sotřineje knihy
    sotřine polo = sister's field
    Gen. sotřineho pola

Notice the use of the Genitives, singular and plural, always *preceding* the noun qualified, as possessive adjectives. These Genitives cannot, of course, agree with the noun in gender, number or case. E.g.:—

susodźic dźowka	= the neighbours' daughter
wučerjec dźěći	= the teachers' children
fararjec ladko	= the cemetery, lit. the vicar's vacant lot
Šołćic młyn	= the Šołta family's mill
Domaškec pola	= the Domašk family's fields

These are by origin Genitives plural—see p. 410-411.

Examples of Genitives singular are:—

Šołćineje nan	= Mrs. Šołta's father (see p. 410)
susodźineje dźowka	= the (female) neighbour's daughter
Nowotneho awto	= Nowotny's car
Andrickeho kniha	= Andricki's book

This is the *only* correct order of words in this construction. The Genitive *cannot* follow.

Notice that when further qualifiers are used before the normal declinable possessive adjectives, these qualifiers go in the *Genitive* and *agree* with the *possessor* in *gender*! E.g.:—

       našeho nanowe pola   = our father's fields
       mojeje sotřine dźěći = my sister's children
cf. stareje Benadźineje syn = old Mrs. Benada's son

One can compare this to the general Slavonic use of the Genitives of the third person Personal Pronoun as possessives; e.g. jeho dom = his house, jeje dom = her house, jich dom = their house. Cf. e.g. Russ. его дом, её дом, их дом.

In the western Upper Lusatian (Catholic) dialect forms, originally Genitives plural of the names for the inhabitants of places are used as possessive-descriptive adjectives, e.g.:—

       Budyšćan piwo = Budyšin beer,
but in Budyšin one says: Budyske piwo.
       Radworčan kermuša = the Radwor fair,
- in the Budyšin dialect: Radworska kermuša.
       Chróšćan burja = the peasants of Chróšćicy,
       naše Radworčan cyrkej = our (Radwor) church in
                                               Radwor.

Notice also the occasional substitution of adverbial expressions for adjectives as in:—

       z ćicha čłowjek = a quiet person
       nazeleń kabat   = a greenish coat

Similarly:—

nažołć = yellowish   načerwjeń = reddish
načorń = dark   namódry   = bluish

The names of many countries end in -*ska* and are declined like fem. adjectives, e.g.:—

Česka (sc. zemja) = Bohemia, Gen. sg. Českeje; Sakska = Saxony, Pruska = Prussia, Jendźelska = England, Francozska = France, Němska = Germany, Ruska = Russia.

Feminine Surnames

The adjectival ending -*owa* is used only for the names of *married* women in Upper Lusatian (in contrast to Czech and Slovak). It is added to the husband's surname if this ends in a consonant. E.g.:—

              Kral, fem. Kralowa;
              Cyž,   "   Cyžowa

If the husband's name is adjectival in form, the fem. adjectival ending is substituted, e.g.:—

              Čorny, fem. Čorna
              Horni,   "   Hornja

But from men's surnames ending in -*a*, fem. forms

are made with the ending *-ina* (or *-yna* after *c*, *s*, *z*). Velar stems undergo the 2nd Palatalization, so producing *c* from *k*, *z* from *h*, *dz* from *g*; but *ch* gives *š*, followed by *-ina*. E.g.:—

      Raba — Rabina
      Krupa — Krupina
      Słoma — Słomina
      Grafa — Grafina
      Hora — Horina
but—
      Krasa — Krasyna
      Hoza — Hozyna
      Šweca — Šwecyna

with softenings:—
      Wałda — Waldźina
      Šołta — Šołćina
      Skała — Skalina
      Kotra — Kotřina

with 2nd Palatalization:—
      Mucha — Mušina
but—
      Muka — Mucyna
      Noha — Nozyna
      Klega — Kledzyna

All these types are declined like feminine adjectives.

Family Names

These are usually formed from the man's surname by adding *-ecy*. But if the surname ends in *-a* preceded by any consonant except *s*, *z*, *c*, *tr* or any velar, the family name ends in *-icy* (with softening of a preceding *t*, *d*, or *l*).

Surnames ending in a consonant or a vowel other than *-a*:—

      Mróz — Mrózecy
      Pjetaš — Pjetašecy
      Suchi — Suchecy

Surnames ending in *-a*:—

  Kubaša — Kubašicy   Wałda — Wałdźicy
  Šołta — Šołćicy   Skała — Skalicy
but:
  Krasa — Krasecy and: Muka — Mukecy
  Hoza — Hozecy   Noha — Nohecy
  Šweca — Šwececy   Mucha — Muchecy
  Kotra — Kotrecy   Klega — Klegecy

These are declined:—

Nom.	Mrózecy	Kubašicy
Gen./Acc.	Mrózec	Kubašic
Dat.	Mrózecom	Kubašicom
Instr.	Mrózecami	Kubašicami
Loc.	Mrózecach	Kubašicach

Unmarried women have as their surname their family name *in the Gen. plur.* for all cases, e.g.:—

Hańža Kubašic; Dat. sg. Kněžnje Mrózec (= to Miss Mróz)

THE COMPARISON OF ADJECTIVES

Those adjectives which can be compared, form their Comparative degree either with the ending *-iši*, the commonest ending, or with *-ši*. A few adjs. can take either ending. There are no rules as to which ending is used for any given adjective. *-iši* becomes *-yši* after *s, z, c,* but softens other preceding consonants. Root vowel *-ja-* sometimes becomes *-je-*.

1. *-iši* is used with:—

čisty	= clean,	Comp.	čisćiši
swjaty	= holy,	"	swjećiši
hordy	= proud,	"	hordźiši
swětły	= bright,	"	swětliši
zrjadny	= regular, orderly	"	zrjadniši
mudry	= wise	"	mudriši
hłupy	= stupid,	"	hłupiši
dźiwi	= wild,	"	dźiwiši
suchi	= dry,	"	sušiši
			(with ch > š)
cuzy	= foreign.	Comp.	cuzyši
horcy	= hot,	"	horcyši

2. *-ši* causes preceding *h* and *z* to become *ž* and preceding *s* to become *š*. Other consonants can also often be softened before *-ši*. It is used with:—

bohaty	= rich,	Comp.	bohatši
chudy	= poor	"	chudši
młody	= young,	"	młódši
twjerdy	= hard,	"	twjerdši
rad	= glad,	"	radši
běły	= white,	"	bělši
wjesoły	= merry,	"	wjeselši
rjany	= beautiful,	"	rjeńši
tuni	= cheap,	"	tuńši *or* tuniši
stary	= old,	"	starši
luby	= dear, beloved	"	lubši
słaby	= weak,	"	słabši
nowy	= new	"	nowši *or* nowiši!
drohi	= dear,	"	dróši

Adjectives in -*ki* and -*oki* drop these endings in comparison and also take -*ši*

krótki	= short,	Comp.	krótši
hładki	= smooth,	"	hładši
rědki	= rare,	"	rědši
słódki	= sweet,	"	słódši
daloki	= distant, far	"	dalši
ćeńki	= thin,	"	ćeńši
šěroki	= wide,	"	šěrši
hłuboki	= deep,	"	hłubši
lochki	= light (in weight), easy	"	lóši

but—

mjechki	= soft,	"	mjechši
wysoki	= high,	"	wyši
niski	= low,	"	niši
bliski	= near,	"	bliši
wuski	= narrow,	"	wuši
ćežki	= heavy,	"	ćeši

Also:
tołsty = fat, " tołši (dropping -*st*-)

The following adjectives have irregular Comparatives all ending in -*ši*:—

dobry	= good,	Comp.	lěpši
zły	= bad,	"	hórši
wulki	= big, great,	"	wjetši
mały	= small,	"	mjeńši
dołhi	= long,	"	dlěši

The Comparative is also sometimes formed with bóle or wjacy (= more) + the Positive adjective, e.g.:—

Twoja suknja je bóle žołta = Your skirt is more yellow than mine.
  hač moja

The Superlative degree is always formed by adding the prefix *naj*- to the Comparative, e.g.:—

najčisćiši = the cleanest
najmłódši = the youngest
najlěpši = the best

The Superlative can be further strengthened with the prefix *na*-: nanajłěpši = the very best

It should be pointed out that certain adjectives formed from adverbs also end in -(*i*)*ši*, but are not, of course, Comparatives, but merely soft-stem adjectives. Such are:—

LUSATIAN

dźensniši = to-day's
jutřiši = to-morrow's
wčerawši = yesterday's
něhduši = one time, former
tehdyši or = the then, ... of that time
  tehdomniši
nětčiši = the present, now
tamniši = of that place
hinaši = different

All Comparative and Superlative adjectives are declined like soft Positive adjectives, e.g. lětni.

"Absolute Superlatives" are formed from Positive adjectives with various prefixes, e.g.:—

    předobry = very good, kind
    wjelesławny = very famous, illustrious
    prastary = very old, ancient
    wšehomócny = almighty

Very = jara
Than = hač, dyžli, nežli, *also*: kaž (=as)

Also the preposition přez + Acc. (lit. = beyond, above) is used for "than", e.g. přez jandźelow čisćiši = more pure than the angels

Rather better	= mało / trochu } lěpši
Much better	= wo mnoho / wo wjele } lěpši
Rather good	= dosć dobry
Less than	= mjenje hač
The bigger ..., the better...	= čim wjetši ..., ćim lěpši
As (good) as	= tak dobry kaž
As soon as possible	= { po móžnosći bórzy, hač (na)najskerje, hač (na)najskeršo
As fast as possible	= hač (na)najchětrišo, nanajručišo (= as promptly as possible)
The very best of all	= najlěpši { ze wšěch (wšitkich), mjeze wšěmi (wšitkimi)
Too	= přejara, přewjele
The same as	= samsny kaž, runy kaž, tajki samsny kaž
In the same way as	= { runje (poruno, porno) kaž, tak samo kaž
The same one as (who)	= tón samsny, kotryž (kiž)

ADVERBS

Adverbs formed from adjectives in Upper Lusatian end most commonly in -(j)e or else in -o, except those formed from adjectives in -ski, which have the endings either -ski or -sce.

The ending -(j)e softens preceding consonants and causes velars to undergo the 2nd Palatalization with k and h changing to c and z respectively before the -e. E.g.:—

wjesele	= merrily,	from	wjesoły or wjeseły
bohaće	= richly,	"	bohaty
twjerdźe	= hard,	"	twjerdy
chětře	= quickly,	"	chětry
wótře	= loudly }	"	wótry = sharp, loud
wótrje	= sharply		
mjechce	= softly,	"	mjechki
słódce or słódko	= sweetly,	"	słódki
ćiše¹	= quietly,	"	ćichi
chroble	= bravely		
słabje	= weakly		
jednorje	= simply		
rjenje } krasnje	= beautifully		

The ending -o is used mostly for adverbs formed from adjectives in -ki or -chi and a few others:—

blisko	= near		ćicho	= quietly
daloko	= far		dołho	= long
hłuboko	= deep		tołsto	= fatly (or tołsće)
wysoko	= high		tunjo	= cheaply
nisko	= low		mało	= little
sucho	= dryly		horco	= hotly, warmly

A few adverbs can have either ending:—

jasno	or	jasnje	= brightly, clearly
wusko	"	wusce	= narrowly, closely
sna(d)no	"	snadnje	= easily

Adverbs from adjectives in -ski either keep -ski or have -sce:—

pohanski	or	pohansce	= in a heathen manner
katolski	"	katolsce	= in Catholic fashion
łaćanski	"	łaćansce	= in Latin
jendźelski	"	jendźelsce	= in (an) English (way)

The forms with po and ending in -u are more archaic:

---

¹See also next paragraph.

LUSATIAN

```
po serbsku = in Lusatian
po česku  = in Czech
po němsku = in German
```

Notice the irregular adverbs:—

```
derje = well   from dobry
zlě   = badly,  "   zły
```

The Comparison of Adverbs

The Comparative degree is formed very simply for most adverbs by changing the ending of the Comparative adjective to -o, i.e. -iši to -išo, and -ši to -šo:—

```
połniši   = fuller         Comp. adv. połnišo = more fully
wjeselši  = more merry,      "    "   wjeselšo
rjenšo    = more beautifully
radšo     = more gladly, from rady— adv.
```

But adverbs from adjectives in -ki and -oki and a few others have Comparative adverbs in -e or -o, before which the -ki or -oki is dropped and softening of the stem takes place:—

```
wysoko       = high,            Comp. adv. wyše
blisko       = near,              "    "   bliže[1] or bližo
nisko        = low,               "    "   niže[1] or nišo
ćežko or     = heavily, with      "    "   ćešo
  ćežcy        difficulty,
lohko        = lightly,           "    "   lóže[1] or łóšo
daloko       = far,               "    "   dale
hłuboko      = deep,              "    "   hłubje[1] or hłubšo
wusko        = narrowly           "    "   wušo
šěroko       = broadly, widely    "    "   šěršo
rědko        = rarely             "    "   rědšo
```

Notice the irregular comparisons of:—

```
derje        = well,            Comp. lěpje = better
zlě          = badly,             "   hórje = worse
wjele }
mnoho } = much,                   "   wjace = more (of quantity)
jara         = very (much),       "   bóle  = more (of degree)
mało  }
małko } = little,  ⎫
trochu }           ⎬              "   mjenje = less
trošku } = a little,⎭
dołho        = long,              "   dlěje = longer
bórzy }
skoro } = soon,                   "   prjedy, skerje, or
                                        skeršo = sooner
```

---

[1]The forms in -e are more archaic.

Superlative adverbs are formed from Comparative adverbs with the prefix *naj-*. This is sometimes strengthened with the prefix *na-*

    najrjeńšo = most beautifully, *and* nanajrjeńso, etc.
    najbliže = nearest
    najlěpje = (the) best
    najwjace = most

Adverbs of place, time, manner, quantity, etc., mostly not formed from adjectives, have the most various forms and origins, and many are distinctively Lusatian. We give the commonest below.

PLACE

tu, jow	= here	won	= out
tam	= there, thither	nutř	= in
dotam	= thither	preč	= away, gone
tudy	= this way	dotal	= as far as that
sem, jow	= hither	domoj	} = home(ward)
wotsal	= hence	dom	
wottudy } z tudy	= thence	doma(ch)	= at home
		horjeka(ch)	= upstairs
wottam	= from over there	deleka	} = downstairs
druhdže	= elsewhere	spody	
wšudže(n) wšudžom wšudy }	= everywhere	dele	= down
		horje	= up
		wotdeleka	= from below
nehdže	= somewhere, to some place	zhor(je)ka wot hor(je)ka }	= from above
nihdže	= nowhere	wróćo, wróćmo	= back
nutřka	= inside	wot spody wotspódka }	= from underneath
wonka	= outside		
zady	= behind	zwopředka	= from the front
srjedźa	= in the middle	wotzady	= from behind
předku	= in front	zpod	= along the bottom
		po wjeršcy	= along the top

TIME

nětko	= now	hnydom	= immediately
tehdy tehdom }	= then	přeco přecy }	= always
dźens(a) jutře jutřiši dźeń (na)zajtra }	= to-day = to-morrow	ženje nihdy }	= never
		něhdy	= sometimes
		junu jónu }	= once, once upon a time
pozajtra	= the day after to-morrow	raz	= once
		nastajnje njepřestajnje (po)spochi }	= all the time
wčera	= yesterday		
hižo(m) juž(o) }	= already	prjedy	= before, earlier

LUSATIAN

TIME— contd.

hišće	= yet, still	druhdy	} = sometimes
hižo } nje	= no longer	hdys a hdys	
juž } nje		zaso	
wjace		znowa	} = again
hišće nje	= not yet	na nowo	
potom	= afterwards, then	njedawno	} = recently
		wóndano	
dawno	= long ago	zdawna	= for a long time now
zposlěd(ka) } = finally			
naposlěd(y)		lětsa	= this year
skónčnje	= at last	loni	= last year
hakle	= only	klětu	= next year
runje } = just, only		zdobom	= at the same time
zruna		bórzy	} = soon
rano	= in the morning, early	skoro	
		mjeztym	= meanwhile
wječor	= in the evening	dołho	= (for) a long time
		tójhdy	= for quite a long time
dotal	= up to now		
wottal	= from now	nadobo	= suddenly
dotud	= till then	počasu	= gradually
z časom } = in time, punctually		porědko } = seldom	
w prawym		zrědka	
času		wospjet	= again, repeatedly
zahe	= early	často, husto	= often
pozdźe	= late		

MANNER

tak	= thus, so	klubu	= out of spite
někak	= somehow	z wotmyslenjom } = on purpose, deliberately	
hinak } = otherwise		ze zamysłom	
hewak		zdarma, nadarmo, } = gratis	
wopak	= wrong	podarmo, zadarmo	
nikak	= in no way	podarmo	= in vain
nawopak	= wrong way round	zwučnje	= usually
		poprawom	= really, actually
pomału } = slowly		woprawdźe } = truly, in truth, indeed	
pomałku		nawoprawdu	
chětře } = quickly		wěsće } = certainly	
chwatnje		zawěsće	
spěšnje	= in haste	njejabcy } = unexpectedly, by chance	
ruče	= promptly, quickly	njenadźicy	
(w) skoku	= fast; at a gallop; quickly	ćiše, ćicho, sćicha } = quietly	
		mjelčo	
skokšo	= faster	pěšce	= on foot
nahło, nahle, z nahła } = suddenly			
nadobo			

MANNER— *contd.*

wěso,[1] wězo	= of course, certainly	sobu	= together
tohorunja	= in the same way	změrom	= quietly, still

DEGREE

jara	= very	mał(k)o	= little
wulce	= greatly	telko	= so much, so many, as much
trochu, trošku, kusk	} = a little	někelko	= some
		lědma, lědom, lědy	= hardly
mnoho, wjele	} = much	dosć	= enough
tójsto	= quite a lot, considerably	pječa	= they say
jeno(ž)	= only	snadź, snano, traš	} = perhaps
nimale, bjezmała, skoro	} = almost, nearly	móžno	= maybe, possibly
		wosebje	= especially
		wokoło	= approximately
zdźěla	= partly	pomêrnje	= relatively
zwjetša	= mostly	po zdaću	= evidently
cyle, zcyła, docyła, dospołnje	} = quite, completely	powšitkownje	= in general, generally
		na žane wašnjo	= in no way, not at all
wšitko w hromadźe	= altogether	samo	= even
znajmjenša	= at least	woprawdźe	= indeed, really
zawěsće, zawěrno	} = definitely	jeniččy	= exclusively, solely
		chětro	= rather, sufficiently

INTERROGATIVE

-*li* is used as an interrogative particle only occasionally. E.g.:—

Přijima-li knjez? = Is the gentleman at home? (lit. Is he receiving?)

hdy?	= when?
hdźe?	= where? whither? which way?*
zwotkel? (z)wotkal?	} = whence?
Čehodla?	= why? what for?[2]
přečo?	= why? (archaic)
kak?	= how?
kelko?	= how much? how many?

*Corresponding Relative: hdźež

---

[1] *s* pronounced *z*!
[2] In popular speech also: čomu? *or* čom(a)?

LUSATIAN

dźě(n)? = but surely?
woprawdźe? = really?
štoda? štoha? = what then?,...not...really?

Not = *nje-*, used as a (stressed) prefix.
No = ně; nic = not at all; nawopak = on the contrary
Yes = haj; wězo = certainly.

CONJUNCTIONS

The conjunctions in Upper Lusatian correspond closest in their shades of meaning and usage to those of Czech, but their forms are in most cases quite distinctive.

Coördinating:—

a	= and
tež, pron. tejš	= also
tohorunja	= likewise, also
ale	= but
wšak } pak	= however
(abo...) abo...	= (either...) or
pak...pak	= either...or (exclusive)
ani...ani	= neither...nor
na jednej stronje... na druhej stronje	= on the one hand... on the other hand
nic jenož...ale tež	= not only...but also
dźě(n)	= still, yet
tola	= but, however
mjenujcy	= namely
móhł rjec	= so to speak
kak } kaž	= as, like
da, dha, ha dluž, tuž, no } tedy, tak, to	= then, so
hewak	= anyway (Fr. *du reste*)
drje	= it is true, indeed
za to	= but still, in compensation
tohodla } pře to potajkim	= therefore
přečož	= wherefore
přetož	= for

Subordinating: (those different from the interrogative adverbs):—

čehoždla	= for which reason
tohodla zo } přetož dokelž	= because, since (causal)
hdźež	= where

zwotkełž	= whence
hdyž	= when, after, since (of time)
hač	= when, (in the future), whether (in indirect questions), except
doniž, dóniž, dónž	= while; (with *nje-*) until
hdyžkuli	= whenever
kažkuli	= however
tak bórzy hač	= as soon as
lědma zo	= hardly
prjedy hač	= before
mjeztym zo	= while (expressing contrast)
-li (enclitic) jeli-to jeli-zo	= if
hdy bych, by, etc. (variable Conditional auxiliary, see under "The Conditional" in "The Verbs")	= if (in unfulfilled conditions)
njech	= even if; let
byrunje(ž), byrnje(ž) hačrunjež hačkuli	= although
zo bych, by (variable like hdy bych)	= that (after verbs of wishing, commanding, requesting, fearing), in order that
zo	= that (after verbs of saying, thinking, rejoicing; also to express consequences after *tak*)
jako	= as
kaž by, jako by	= as if
na čo	= why, wherefore
dalokož	= (in) so far as
tak dołho hač, dołhož	= as (so) long as
wjelež	= as much as

THE PREPOSITIONS

Prepositions in Upper Lusatian are similar in form and use, as a whole, to those in other West Slav languages. We have already mentioned that a preposition is invariably used with the Instrumental case of all declinable words, and that *z* (= with) + Instr. renders the plain Instr. of other Slavonic languages except Slovenian. (See "The Declension of Nouns" under "The Morphology of Upper Lusatian", p. 376.)

do + Gen. wholly replaces *w* + Acc., and means "to", "into", and "in" in such expressions as:—

wěrić do Boha = to believe in God

pola is used for "by, at, with" where other West Slav languages use *u* + Gen., and Russian has *y* + Gen., etc.

"By" with a person expressing the agent is rendered, as in Polish, with přez + Acc., and not by the Instr. case: przeze mnje = by me.

dla is used for "for, for the benefit of", also "because of".

Only *po* is used with *three* cases, Dat., Acc., and Loc.—with the Dat. only in fixed expressions.

Most adverbs used as prepositions take the Genitive.

If a preposition ends in a consonant and the next word begins with a difficult group of consonants the fill-vowel *-e* is used.

Monosyllabic prepositions are regularly stressed, drawing the stress off the following word.

With Genitive:—

bjez(e)	= without
do	= to, into, in (see above)
dla	= for (the benefit of)— someone; because of (used *after* as well as before a noun) Notice that the neut. sing. Possessive Pronoun-adjectíve often replaces a Personal Pronoun before dla, with which it is written in one word: mojedla = for me, twojedla = for you, swojedla = for oneself, našedla = for us, wašedla = for you, (plur. and polite).
nimo (*sic*)	= past, except, beyond
(na)mešto	= instead of
pódla	= next to, near; *but* podłu = along
pola	= by, at, near (see above)
wokoło	= round
wot(e)	= from, of: jedyn wot nas = one of us
(za) čas	= in the time of: čas Hadama = in the days of Adam, za čas wojny = during the war
blisko	= near; njedałoko = not far from
dale	= beyond: dale Lipska = beyond Leipzig
mjelčo	= unknown to: mjelčo nana = unknown to father
(s)kónc	= at the end of; spočatk = at the beginning of
wyše	= above
niže	= below
spody	= under
spod zespody	} = from under
(wo)srjedź	= in the middle of
dosrjedź	= into " " "
zesrjedź	= from " " "
zboka	= at the side of
wusłědk	= as a result of; because of

z (ze)		= out of *and* off, from: ze Serbow = from Lusatia, hrać z dypkow = to play from music, hrać z pomjatka = to play from memory.
zeza		= from behind; zady = behind

With Dative:—

k(e)		= to (of persons)
přećiwo		= against
napřećo		= opposite, towards, to meet: napřećo swojemu přećelej = to(wards) one's friend
por(u)no, pornjo		= compared with, by the side of: pornjo Parisej su Drježdźany małe město = compared with Paris Dresden is a small town
po (see above):		po serbsku = in Lusatian
dźakowano		= thanks to

With Accusative:—

přez(e)		= over; through, by (of persons—see above): přez móst = over the bridge; přeze mnje = by me
pře		= for (the sake of), because of: pře swojich lubych = for one's dear ones
wob		= round, every other, the next but one: wob chěžu hić = to go round the house; wob dźeń = every other day
na		= on to: na drobne rozpowědać = to recount in detail
wo		= concerning, for: wo někoho so starać = to take care of somebody; ničo wo to = that does not matter (lit. nothing for that)
nad(e)		= (to) above (motion)
pod(e)		= (to) under (motion)
před(e)		= (to) before (motion)
za		= (to) behind, beyond (motion), for: sydnyć so za blido = to sit down at (a) table; za hory = (to) beyond the hills; za přećela = for a friend; za kij přimać = to seize hold of a stick
mjez(e)		= (to) among, between (motion)
po		= to fetch, for: po wodu hić = to go for water; po někoho hić = to go to fetch someone

With Instrumental:—

z(e)		= (together) with; *also*: with (of the instrument— see above): ze złotom płaćić = to pay in gold
nad(e)		= (rest) over, above
pod(e)		= (rest) under, below
před(e)		= (rest) before

za	= (rest) behind: za blidom sedźeć = to sit at (a) table; za horami = beyond the hills (rest)
mjez(e)	= (rest) among, between

With Locative:—

při	= by, near (cf. pola): při tebe = near you; při blidźe = near the table; při puću = by the roadside
w(e)	= in (physically and metaphorically): we wěrnosći = in truth
na	= on. Notice also: na Bohatej ulicy = in Bohata street; kak je na času? = what is the time?
wo	= about, concerning
po	= 1. about (of place): po měsće so přechodźować = to walk about a town; po rěcy = along the river; po lěsu hić = to go through a wood; najbohatši po cyłym měsće = the richest in the whole town; poćmje or poćmě = in the dark
	2. up to: po łochćach = up to the elbows
	3. after, in (of time): po troch dnjach = in (after) three days; po chwili = in a minute
	4. according to: po zakonju = according to (by) law; po mjenje = by name; po dołhosći = according to length; po wobstojenjach = according to circumstances
	5. in (distributively); po kruchach = bit by bit (see also under "The Numerals"— Distributive Numerals)

The verbal prefixes *wu-* (from *wy-*) and *roz-* are not used as prepositions. C.S. *vъz* has been reduced to *z*, as in: zlećeć = to fly up.

THE CONJUGATION OF VERBS

In the conjugation of verbs in Upper Lusatian, as in the declensions, special forms for the Dual number exist in all tenses: in the 2nd and 3rd persons dual, however, gender and not person, is distinguished. The number of verbal forms is further increased by the preservation of the Aorist and Imperfect (simple) tenses, as in Macedonian and Bulgarian. (But special forms for "Renarration" are unknown in Upper Lusatian.) Despite this multiplicity of forms, however, the use of the verbs in Upper Lusatian presents no formidable difficulties of its own to the English student.

The classification of the verbs according to their Present is equally applicable to Upper Lusatian, though this has not been the usual practice in Upper Lusatian grammars. We find Presents

    I with -'e-   joining vowel
   II with -nje- 'joining vowel'
  III with -je-   joining vowel
   IV with -a-   joining vowel
    V with -i-   joining vowel, becoming -y- after s and z.

Category IV has a hard and a soft variety. The soft stems conjugate in a way peculiar to Upper Lusatian, -a- changing to -e- between palatal consonants. (See below.)

In the Present the ending -m for the 1st pers. sing. is confined to Class IV. The 1st pers. plur. has -my, as in Polish

The Future of Impfve. verbs is formed with budu, etc. + Infinitive, as in Czech and Russian, except in the case of a few verbs which use prefixes—mostly verbs of motion which have po- prefixed to their Present, as in Czech and Slovak. The Future of Pfve. verbs is a Present in form, as is usual in West and East Slav.

The Aorist and Imperfect tenses share the same personal endings, except in the 2nd and 3rd pers. singular.

The Compound Past or Perfect has the meaning of an English Perfect (e.g. "I have done"). The auxiliary verb, the Present of "to be" always *preceding* the Past Participle Active, is required with *all* persons, as in Serbocroätian and Slovenian and in contrast to Czech and Slovak. The negative nje- is prefixed to the auxiliary verb, as in Serbocroätian and Slovenian.

The Pluperfect is freely used.

The Infinitive ends in -ć, except for velar stems of Class I which have -c (cf. Polish). There is no Supine.

The Present Gerund ends in -o. For many verbs a rarer alternative form in -cy exists.

The Passive voice can be expressed in four ways:—

1. with the verb "to be" + Past Participle Passive[1] (usually perfective) e.g.:—

---

[1] There is a fifth way of expressing the Passive, used colloquially and in dialects, with wordować and the Past Participle Passive: worduju bity = I am beaten. Cf. p. 466, No. 20 fn.

Sym zawołany = I am called
Buch přeprošeny = I was invited

2. with a reflexive verb,[1] e.g.:—
Pozdźišo poča so pomjenować = Later it began to be called (named)...

3. with an Active verb in the 3rd person plural used impersonally, and making the subject in English into the object, e.g.:—

Wołaja mje = lit. they call me, i.e. I am called

4. by using a reflexive verb impersonally in the 3rd pers. singular (neuter) and governing a further object, e.g.:—

Kusk drjewa je so wotšćěpiło = A piece of wood was split off (lit. one split off a piece of wood)

The negative *nje-* is always treated as a prefix with any part of the verb and takes the stress. In compound tenses it is prefixed to the auxiliary verb.

The Present tense has the following personal endings:—

Sing.
1 -*u*(-*m* for Class IV)
2 -*š*
3 —

Dual
1 -*moj*
2 and 3 (masc. pers.) -*taj*
2 and 3 (fem., neut. and masc. impers.) -*tej*

Plural
1 -*my*
2 -*će*
3 -*u* or -(*j*)*a* for -*e*- and -*a*- verbs
   -(*j*)*a* for -*i*- verbs

These endings, except those of the 1st pers. sing. and 3rd pers. plur., are joined to the Present stem of the verb by one of the following "joining vowels" according to the class of the verb:—

Cl. I -*e*   Cl. II -*nje*   Cl. III -*je*
Cl. IV -*a*   Cl. V -*i* (after *s*, *z*: -*y*)

---

[1] Reflexive verbs are formed by adding the Accusative enclitic Reflexive Pronoun *so* to all parts of the Active verb. The pronoun is always written separately.

"For oneself" can be rendered by the Dative enclitic Reflexive Pronoun *sej*.

In Class I softening takes place before the -e where possible and velars undergo the 1st Palatalization, e.g.:—

wjedu = I lead   pjeku = I bake   njesu = I carry

Sing. 1 wjedu   pjeku   but: njesu
      2 wjedźeš,   pječeš,   njeseš,
        etc.   etc.   etc.
Plur. 3 wjedu or   pjeku or   njesu or
        wjedźeja   pječeja   njeseja

Móc (= to be able), Past Part. Active móhł has -ž- throughout the Present:

Sing. 1 móžu = I can, (by analogy with 2nd, 3rd pers. sg., 1st, 2nd, 3rd p. dual and 1st and 2nd p. plur.)
      2 móžeš, etc.
Plur. 3 móža, móžu or móžeja (by analogy with 2nd, 3rd pers. sg., 1st, 2nd, 3rd p. dual and 1st and 2nd p. plur.)

Class II have -nu in 1st pers. sg. and also, sometimes, 3rd pers. pl., -nje- in the other persons.

Verbs of Class III with polysyllabic stems and all verbs of Class IV have -ja in 3rd pers. pl., while monosyllabic stem verbs of Class III have -ja or -eja.

In soft-stem verbs of Class IV the joining vowel -a becomes -e- when interpalatal, i.e. in 2nd pers. sg. and pl. and 3rd pers. pl., e.g.:—

třěleć = to shoot, Pres. Sg. 1 třělam, 2 třěleš, Plur. 2 třěleće, 3 třěleja.

In verbs of Class V the ending -u of the 1st pers. sg. is always preceded by a *soft* consonant, as well as the endings of all the other persons. Only s,z undergo *yotation* before -u in 1st pers. sg. and before -a in 3rd pers. plur., and remain hard before y in the other persons. E.g.:—

widźeć = to see prosyć = to request wozyć = to convey

Pres. sg. 1 widźu *but*: prošu   wožu
          2 widźiš   prosyš   wozyš
     pl. 3 widźa   proša   woža

The Infinitive in Upper Lusatian ends in -ć, except for verbs of Class I with velar stem which have -c.

In Class I this ending is joined direct to the stem: njesć = to carry, wjesć = to lead (<wjed-ti), but pjec = to bake, móc = to be able.
   Notice: mrěć = to die, Class I (<*merti); počeć = to begin, Class I (<po-čęti).

Verbs of Class II have Infinitives in -nyć:
wuknyć = to learn.

Verbs of Class III either have vowel stems: pić = to drink, znać = to know, or consonant stems in the Infinitive: kupować = buy (Impfve.), Pres. kupuju.

Only a few verbs have Infinitive in -ać and an (alternative) Present of Class III, namely:—

                    Class IV   Class III

płakać = to weep,
Pres. sg. 1 płakam
       2 płakaš or płačeš[1] ⎫ *only these persons*
       3 płaka or płače[1] ⎬ also njepłač! =
                                 ⎭ don't cry!(Imper.)

So also: skakać = to jump (skačeš, skače), pisać = to write (pišeš, piše), wjazać = to bind (wježeš, wježe), and occasionally: mazać = to smear (mažeš, maže), kazać = to order, demand (kažeš, kaze). Verbs in -otać also have an alternative Class III Present ending in the 3rd pers. sg. only: -oce, e.g.:—

    klepotać = to knock, 3rd pers. sg. klepoce
    błyskotać = to flash, "   "   " błyskoce

All these verbs really belong to Class IV.1 with Infin. in -ać (hard stems).

Verbs of Class IV.2 with *soft* stems have Infin. in -eć. Throughout their conjugation, i.e. in Pres., Imperative and Imperfect, original joining vowel -'a- in the terminations becomes -e- between two palatal consonants. (See "Examples of the Conjugation of Regular Verbs" , p. 445.)   All verbs of Class IV.2 are Imperfective (deverbativa).

Verbs of Class V have Infin. either in -ić or in -eć (also after *chuintantes*): chwalić = to praise, widźeć = to see, běžeć = to run.

As in other Slavonic languages, in Upper Lusatian the two key principal parts of a verb are the Present and the Infinitive. From these the other parts of the verb are formed. Fewer different classes of verbs are obtained if we use the Present as the first criterion for classification. For this reason and for easy comparison with the other sections of this work, we give below a list of typical verbs classified according to their Present, with subdivisions according to their Infinitive. The frequent differences between the Present and Infinitive stems will be observed.

---

[1]The forms with -č- occur only in folk poetry.

Classification of Upper Lusatian Verbs according to their Presents, with Subdivisions according to their Infinitives

```
                 3rd pers. sg.
                 Present   Infinitive
I.  A.a.         njese     njesć      = to carry  ⎫
                 pječe     pjec       = to bake   ⎪ Same stem in
           also:                                  ⎬ Pres. and
                 mrje      mrěć       = to die    ⎪ Infin., conso-
                 počnje    počeć      = to begin  ⎭ nantal stem.
                                      (Pfve.)
    b.   (no vowel
           stems)
    B.a. bjerje    brać      = to take. Infin. in -ać, con-
                                sonantal stem.
    b.   (no vowel
           stems)
II.      wuknje    wuknyć    = to learn.  n-stem
III. Present with -je-.
  1. Primary verbs.
    A.a. žije      žić       = to heal(intrans.) ⎫ Same stem in
         znaje     znać      = to know(Fr.       ⎬ Pres. and
                               connaître)        ⎭ Infin., vowel
         syje      syć       = to sow(seed)        stem.
    b.   mjele     mlěć      = to grind. Same stem in Pres.
        (or vowel stem:                and Infin., consonantal stem.
          mlěje)
(III.1.) B. Infinitives in -ać
    a.   taje      tać(<tajać) = to melt. Infin. in -ać,
                                  vowel stem.
    b.   płače (or płakać¹   = to weep. Infin. in -ać,
         płaka)                 consonantal stem.
  2. Derived verbs. All vowel stems in the Present.
         kupuje    kupować   = to buy (Impfve.). Present
                               stem -u-, Infin. in -ować.
```

N.B.—Verbs formed from adjectives in Upper Lusatian belong to Class V.B, e.g.: zeleni, zelenjeć = to grow green

IV. New category, by contraction from -aje- in Present:—
  1. *Hard stems:*—
         dźěła   dźěłać   = to work, act
         woła   wołać   = to call

---

[1]There are only a few verbs of this type left in Upper Lusatian, with -je endings only in the 2nd and 3rd pers. sg. See above under *the Present*, p. 427.

2. *Soft stems* (see above pp. 426, 427 under *the Present*):—

2nd p. sg.

	wróca	wróćeš	wróćeć	= to return (Impfve.)
	sadźa	sadźeš	sadźeć	= to plant (Impfve.)
	trěla	trěleš	trěleć	= to shoot (Impfve.)
V. A.	chwali		chwalić	= to praise. *i*-stem throughout.
	prosy		prosyć	= to request. *y*-stem after (hard) sibilant throughout
	1st p. sg.: prošu			
	3rd p. pl. proša			
B.	widźi		widźeć	= to see ⎫ *i*-stem in
	(Past Part. Act.		widźał)	⎬ Pres., In-
	leži		ležeć¹	= to lie ⎭ fin. in -*eć*.
	(Past Part. Act.		ležał)	

Athematic verbs (see "Irregular Verbs" for full conjugation)

Pres. 1st p.sg. jěm 3rd p.sg. jě Infin. jěsć = to eat
            wěm   wě   wědźeć = to know (Fr. savoir)
            sym   je   być = to be
            dam   da   dać = to give (Pfve.)

The Future Tense and the Aspects

The Future of most Imperfective verbs is formed with the Future of "to be" (być) followed by the Impfve. Infinitive. E.g.:—

Sing.   *Dual*   *Plur.*
1 budu dźěłać   1 budźemoj dźěłać   1 budźemy dźěłać
  = I shall do, work
2 budźeš dźěłać   2, 3 masc. pers.   2 budźeće dźěłać
                         budźetaj dźěłać
3 budźe dźěłać   2, 3 fem., neut. and   3 budu dźěłać
                         masc. impers.   or budźeja dźěłać
                         budźetej dźěłac

Only a few verbs form their Impfve. Futures with prefixes added to the Present (cf. Czech and Slovak), namely:—

---

¹N.B.—*e* in the ending between two palatal consonants.

```
hić     = to go,¹              Fut. póńdu
jěć     = to go(conveyed),¹     "   pojědu
njesć   = to carry,¹            "   ponjesu
wjesć   = to lead,¹             "   powjedu
wjezć   = to convey,¹           "   powjezu
lězć    = to climb,             "   polězu
ćahnyć  = to draw, drag,        "   počahnu;
                 2nd pers. sg.  počehnješ
ćěrić   = to drive, chase, Fut. počěrju
słać    = to send,              "   posćelu
běžeć   = to run,               "   poběhnu;
 Also—
měć     = to have               "   změju (Pres. mam!)
```

The Future of Perfective verbs is a "Present-Future", i.e. it is Present in form but always Future in meaning. (Cf. other West and the East Slav languages and Old Slavonic). Thus:—

```
dać(Pfve.)      = to give,  Fut. dam    = I shall
                                           give
zdźěłać(Pfve.)  = to make,   "   zdźełam = I shall
                                           make
pusćić (Pfve.)  = to let go, "   pusću   = I shall let
                                           go
```

The compound formation of the Future of *Perfective* verbs with budu, etc. occurs in popular speech only.

Most simple verbs are Impfve. The Pfve. aspect is formed from them in one of three ways:—

1. With a prepositional prefix which changes only the aspect of the verb, but does not substantially change its meaning, e.g.:—

```
Impfve. dźěłać   = to make, work, Pfve. zdźěłać
   "    pisać    = to write,       "    napisać
   "    lutować  = to save(up),    "    zalutować
   "    wuknyć   = to learn,       "    nawuknyć
   "    čitać    = to read,        "    přečitać
   "    wołać    = to call out,    "    zawołać
   "    pić      = to drink,       "    wupić
```

2. By using the endings -nyć, Pres. -nu, -nješ, etc. (but not all verbs with these endings are Pfve.), e.g.:—

```
Impfve. padać   = to fall,    Pfve. padnyć
   "    duć     = to blow,      "   dunyć
   "    lizać   = to lick,      "   liznyć
   "    łapać   = to seize,     "   łapnyć
```

[1]See below under "Verbs of Going and Conveying" for full conjugation.

3. A few verbs change their ending in other ways, or use an entirely different root, e.g.:—

Impfve. stupać = to tread, Pfve. stupić
" brać = to take, " wzać
" kłasć = to put, " położić

A certain number of simple verbs, however, are *Perfective* in meaning. Impfve. forms are formed from them by changing the conjugation endings, mainly:—

1. either to -*eć* Pres. -*am, -eš, a,* etc.
2. or to -*owaćc* " -*uju, -uješ,* etc.
3. or to -(*w*)*ać,* " (*w*)*am,* -(*w*)*aš,* etc.

Compound verbs with "meaningful" prefixes are treated in the same way. Few verbs in Upper Lusatian alter their root vowels in the formation of aspects.

1. Pfve. sadźić = to plant, Impfve. sadzeć[1]
" wróćić = to return " wróćeć
(trans.),
" pušćić = to let go, " pušćeć
" stajić = to place, " stajeć
" třělić = to shoot, " třěleć
" nabić = to load,stuff " nabijeć[1]
" poručić = to order, " poručeć
2. Pfve. kupić = to buy, Impfve. kupować[1]
" zapisać = to write down, " zapisować[1]
" wuwjesć = to lead out, " wuwodźować[1]
3. Pfve. dać = to give, Impfve. dawać
" sydnyć so= to sit down, " sydać so
" skočić = to jump, " sk*a*kać(with lengthening of root vowel)
" stanyć = to get up, " stawać
" zadać = to set(a task) " zadawać
" počeć = to begin, " počinać
" zakćěć - to start flowering, " zakćěwać

[1]Many verbs of Class IV.2 in -*eć* and of Class III in -*ować* can be Iterative in meaning. Only a few verbs have special Iterative forms:—

Impfv. njesć = to carry, Iter. and Freq. nosyć ⎫
" wjesć = to lead, " " " wodźić ⎬ See "Verbs of
" wjezć = to convey, " " " wozyć ⎪ Going and
" hić = to go, " " " chodźić ⎭ Conveying".

It will be seen from the above that Upper Lusatian, in contrast to Czech and Slovak, does not usually distinguish between special Iterative and (double) Frequentative forms. To render a Frequentative verb in the past, a Conditional is used. (See below "The Conditional".) Notice the true Frequentatives:—

    donošowac = to keep bringing (Impfve. donosyć, Pfve. donjesć)
    poběhowac = to keep running about, (Impfve. běhać = to run, Pfve. poběhać = to have a run)

Notice also that compound verbs formed from simple *Pfve.* verbs remain Pfve., e.g.:—

    zadać above, and
    nakupić = to buy up

On the other hand compound verbs formed from Iteratives and Imperfectives are Imperfective, e.g.:—

    nakupować = to be buying up

A few compound verbs formed from Impfve. verbs are no longer felt as compounds and are Impfve., e.g.:—

    rozumjeć (rozumić) = to understand
    zawidźeć = to envy
    posłuchać = to listen, obey
    přisahać = to swear
    přisłušeć = to belong
    dosahać = to suffice

The Compound Past or Perfect Tense

This is formed with the Present of być (= to be) always preceding the Past Participle Active in -ł. The auxiliary verb varies according to person (except in the 2nd and 3rd pers. dual), while the Past Part. Act. varies according to gender and number, thus:—

		Masc.	*Fem.*	*Neut.*	
Sing.	1	sym dźěłał	dźěłała		= I have worked (been working), etc.
	2	sy dźěłał	dźěłała		
	3	je dźěłał	dźěłała	dźěłało	
Dual	1	smój dźěłałoj (all genders)			

                Masc. Pers.   *Fem., Neut. and Masc. Impers.*
  2 and 3   staj dźěłałoj   stej dźěłałoj

		Masc. Pers.	Fem., Neut. and Masc. Impers.
Plur.	1	smy dźěłali[1]	dźěłałe[1]
	2	sće dźěłali[1]	dźěłałe[1]
	3	su dźěłali[1]	dźěłałe[1]

The auxiliary verb is regularly used with the 3rd pers. sing. and plur., as in Serbocroätian and Slovenian, and in contrast to Czech and Slovak.

The negative is always prefixed to the auxiliary verb, e.g.:—

  njesym dźěłał = I have not been working
  njeje dźěłał = he has not been working

This tense expresses an action in the past with relation to the present and is therefore often the equivalent of the English Perfect with "have". It is also used in reported statements referring to the past (in preference to the Aorist). E.g.:—

Sym kupił (Pfve.)   = I have bought
Sym kupował (Impfve.)   = I have been buying
Je rjekł, zo je był chory   = He said that he had
                              been (was) ill

The Past Part. Active is formed from the Infinitive by substituting -ł, etc., for the final -ć, e.g.:—

njeść	= to carry,	Past Part. Act.	njesł
ćahnyć	= to pull,	" " "	ćahnył
pić	= to drink,	" " "	pił
kupować	= to buy(Impfve.)	" " "	kupował
dźěłać	= to work, do	" " "	dźěłał
kupić	= to buy(Pfve.)	" " "	kupił
prosyć	= to request,	" " "	prosył

Dental and velar-stem verbs of Class I restore the original consonant of the root, seen in the 1st pers. sing. Pres., e.g.:—

	1st pers. sg. Pres.	Past Part. Act.
wjesć = to lead,	wjedu,	wjedł
pjec = to bake,	pjeku,	pjekł

Verbs of Class I, IV.2, and V.B. with Infinitives in -ec, have the vowel -a- before the ł-endings in all forms except the masc. pers. plur. which ends in -eli (with soft l! cf. Polish), e.g.:—

[1]According to H. Šewc, *Gramatika hornjoserbskeje rěče*, distinction of gender in the plural is no longer obligatory in this tense, the masc. personal form in -li being now frequently used for nouns of all genders.

Cl. I počeć = to begin (Pfve.), Past Part. Act.:—

Sing. masc. počał fem. počała počało
Dual masc.pers. počałoj masc.impers.,fem.,neut. počałoj (also!)
Plur. masc.pers. počeći masc.impers.,fem.,neut. počałe

Cl IV.2 sadźeć = to plant, Past Part. Act.:—

sadźał, sadźała, sadźało, sadźałoj, sadźałe, but masc. pers. plur. sadźeli.

Cl. V.B. běžeć = to run, Past Part. Act.: běžał, etc., but běželi (masc. pers. plur.)

Exceptions:—

Cl. III wodźeć = to put on (Pfve.), Past Part. Act. wodźeł

Cl. V.B ćerpjeć = to suffer, Past Part. Act. ćerpjeł or ćerpjał

The Aorist

The Aorist, which expresses a completed action in the past without any reference to the present, is formed in Upper Lusatian from the Past Part. Active by dropping the -ł endings and adding:—

Sing. 1 -*ch*
2 ⎫ -*e* after a consonant or *no*
3 ⎭ ending (leaving the *vowel* in the Past Part. Act. before the -ł as ending).

Dual 1 -*chmoj*
2 ⎫ masc. pers. -*štaj*,
3 ⎭ masc. impers., fem., neut. -*štej*.

Plur. 1 -*chmy*
2 -*šće*
3 -*chu*

It is formed *only from Pfve. verbs*, as in Macedonian.

Consonant stem verbs of Class I use the joining vowel -*e*- before these endings. Before this *e* velar stems undergo the 1st Palatalization, e.g. wupječech = I baked.

A few verbs of Class II in -*hnyć* and -*dnyć* may drop the -*n*- and behave like verbs of Class I, adding the above endings with -*e*- joining vowel direct to the -*h*- or -*d*-. *h* then undergoes the 1st Palatalization to *ž*, e.g.:—

torhnyć = to pull, Aor. toržech *or* torhnych

d is softened, e.g.:—

sydnyć so = to sit down, Aor. sydźech so *or* sydnych so

The forms without -*ny*- are now less frequently used and are felt to be archaic.

Palatal stem verbs of Class IV.2 and V.B. (i.e. all the regular verbs of this class) change the vowel -*a*- before the -*š*- of the endings of the 2nd and 3rd pers. dual and 2nd pers. plur. to -*e*- (i.e. in interpalatal position).

We thus have:—

Cl. I.		donjesech	= I brought
		wupječech	= I baked
		počach	= I began
		wumrě	= he died
		wubrach	= I chose
Cl. II.		nawuknych	= I learnt
		dosahnych *or* dosažech	= I reached
		padnych *or* padźech	= I fell
Cl.III.	1.	wupich	= I drank up
		wuznach	= I confessed
		napisach	= I wrote
	2.	wumolowach	= I painted
Cl. IV.	1.	zdzěłach	= I made, 2nd p. pl. zdźěłašće
	2.	dotřělach	= I shot at, 2nd p. pl. dotřělešće
Cl.V.A.		kupich	= I bought
		wuchwalich	= I praised
		skazych	= I spoiled
B.		poběžach	= I ran, 2nd p. pl. poběžešće
		wusłyšach	= I heard, 2nd p. pl. wusłyšešće

The Imperfect

The Imperfect, which denotes a continuous action in the past without reference to the present, is formed *from Impfve. verbs only*, as in Macedonian.

It has the same personal endings as the Aorist except in the 2nd and 3rd pers. sing., which have -*še*, as in Old Slavonic, Macedonian, Bulgarian and Serbocroätian.

These endings are added to the *Present* stem (softened in Cl. I, II, and V), except for verbs with Infinitive in -*ować*, Cl. III 2. Velar stems of Cl. I undergo the 1st Palatalization. Verbs of Cl. I and II have the joining vowel -(*j*)*e*-, all others: -*a*- (-*ja*- for vowel stems of Cl. III and for verbs of Cl. V). -*a*/-*ja*- become -*e*-/-*je*- interpalatally in the 2nd and 3rd pers. sg., 2nd and 3rd pers. dual and

2nd pers. plur. We thus have:—

Cl. I. njesech = I was carrying, 2nd and 3rd pers. sg.
                                    njeseše, etc.
        wjedźech = I was leading
        pječech = I was baking
        bjerjech = I was taking
Cl. II. wuknjech = I was learning
Cl. III.1. pijach = I was drinking, 2nd and 3rd pers. sg.
                    piješe, 2nd and 3rd pers. dual: masc.
                    pers. pještaj, other genders pještej,
                    2nd pers. plur. piješće
        znajach = I knew,   2nd and 3rd pers. sg. znaješe
        pisach = I was writing," "   "   "   "   pisaše
     2 kupowach = I was buying, " "   "   "   "   kupowaše
Cl. IV.1. dźěłach = I was doing, " "   "   "   "   dźěłaše
     2. trělach = I was shoot-
                  ing   " "   "   "   "   treleše
Cl. V.A chwalach = I was praising" "   "   "   "   chwaleše
        prošach = I was request-
                  ing   " "   "   "   "   prošeše
        warjach = I was boiling," "   "   "   "   warješe
     B. widźach = I was seeing, " "   "   "   "   widźeše
        běžach = I was running," "   "   "   "   běžeše

The Pluperfect

This compound tense is frequently used in Upper Lusatian in contrast to Czech, Polish and Serbocroātian. It is formed with the Imperfect tense of być (= to be), followed by the Past Part. Act. in -ł.

		Masc.	(*Imperfective.*) *Fem.*	*Neut.*	
Sing.	1	běch	dźěłał	dźěłała		= I had been working, making; had worked, made, etc.
	2	běše (bě)	dźěłał	dźěłała	
	3	běše (bě)	dźěłał	dźěłała	dźěłało

Dual 1 běchmoj dźěłałoj (all genders)
         Masc. Pers. Fem., Neut., Masc. Impers.
  2⎫
  3⎭ = běštaj dźěłałoj   běštej dźěłałoj

Plur. 1 běchmy dźěłali[1]   dźěłałe[1]
      2 běšće   dźěłali[1]   dźěłałe[1]
      3 běchu   dźěłali[1]   dźěłałe[1]

Similarly *Pfve.*: běch zdźěłał, etc. = I had made, etc.

[1]See footnote on p. 433.

The negative *nje-* is prefixed to the auxiliary verb: njeběch zdźěłał = I had not made.

The Conditional

This mood is formed with the Conditional of być (= to be) followed by the Past Art. Act. in -ł of either aspect. Here, too the negative *nje-* is prefixed to the auxiliary verb.

			Masc.	Fem.	Neut.	
Sing.	1	bych	zdźěłał	zdźěłała		= I would make
	2	(ty) by	zdźěłał	zdźěłała		
	3	(wón) by	zdźěłał			
		(wona) by		zdźěłała		
		(wono) by			zdźěłało	
Dual	1	bychmoj zdźěłałoj (all genders)				

Masc. Pers.   Fem.,Neut.,Masc.Impers.

$\left.\begin{array}{c}2\\3\end{array}\right\}$ = byštaj   zdźěłałoj   byštej zdźěłałoj

Plur.	1	bychmy	zdźěłali[1]	zdźěłałe[1]
	2	byšće	zdźěłali[1]	zdźěłałe[1]
	3	bychu	zdźěłali[1]	zdźěłałe[1]

Negative: njeby zdźěłała = she would not make, etc.

The Conditional can be used to express a repeated or habitual action in the past, as in other Slavonic languages. E.g.: Wona by často wótře słowčko porěčała, hdyž by wón skoržił... = She would often say a word sharply, if ever he complained ...

The Past Conditional

The Past Conditional used to be formed by adding the Past Part. Active in -ł (Impfve. or Pfve.) of the verb used to the Past Conditional of być (= to be) — see p. 448. The negative was always prefixed to the (first) auxiliary verb. This tense is not used now and is regarded as archaic.

Sing. 1 bych zdźěłał(a)był(a)
        = I would have made (Pfve).
     2 ty by zdźěłał(a) był(a)
     3 wón by zdźěłał był
        wona by zdźěłała była

Dual 1 bychmoj zdźěłałoj byłoj (all genders)
      2 and 3 masc. pers.
        byštaj zdźěłałoj byłoj
      2 and 3 masc. impers., fem., neut.
        byštej zdźěłałoj byłoj

[1]See footnote on p. 433.

Plur. 1 bychmy zdźělali (-łe)[1] byli (-łe)
    2 byšće zdźělali (-łe)[1] byli (-łe)
    3 bychu zdźělali (-łe)[1] byli (-łe)

    Negative: njebych zdźělał był, etc. = I would not have made

The Imperative

Special Imperative forms exist in Upper Lusatian for the 2nd pers. sg., 1st and 2nd pers. dual, 1st and 2nd pers. plur. They are formed from the Present stem, in its softened form (where possible) when consonantal, as seen in the 2nd pers sg. Pres. (1st pers. sg. for *i*-verbs). Velar stems of Cl. I, therefore, retain the 1st Palatalization.

Consonantal stem verbs have no further ending in the 2nd pers sg. apart from the softened consonant, unless the resulting form (not counting prefixes) would be a word without any vowels, in which case -*i* is added. We thus have:

			2nd pers. sg. Pres
Cl. I	wjedź!	= lead!	cf. wjedźeš
	pleć!	= weave!	" plećeš
	pječ!	= bake!	" pječeš, (1st p. sg. pjeku)
	bjer!	= take!(Impfve.)	" bjerješ
but:—			
	kći!	= flower!	" kćeš
	njełži!	= don't tell lies!	" łžeš *or* łžiš
	zajmi!	= capture!	" zajmješ

The other few forms in -*i* will be found in the list of "Irregular Verbs", q.v.

Cl. II   wukń!   (*ń* not pronounced in this verb throughout Imperative)= learn
         ćehń!   (<ćahnyć) = pull!
         duń![2]   = blow!
         stań![2]   = get up!

---

[1] See footnote on p. 433.
[2] Final -*ń* is pronounced -jn, e.g. stajn, with anticipation of the palatalization.

LUSATIAN 439

  Cl. V.A. kup! = buy! (Pfve.)
     kur! = smoke!
     mjeń = change!
     haj! = defend!
     proš! = ask! request!
     rozum! = understand!
  Cl. V.B mjelč! = be silent!

 Vowel stems take -*j* in the 2nd pers. sg. This applies to verbs of Cl. III, IV.1 and IV.2. E.g.:—

  Cl. III pij! = drink!
     znaj! = know!
     kupuj! = buy! (Impfve.)
  Cl. IV.1 pisaj! = write!
     dźěłaj = work!
  Cl. IV.2 sadźej! = plant!
     prašej so! = ask! (a question)

 The other true Imperative forms are obtained by adding the following endings to the 2nd pers. sg. Imperative:—

 Dual 1   -moj   -my
   2 masc. pers.   -taj   -će
   2 masc. impers., fem., neut. -tej

e.g. kupmoj! = let us two buy!
   pjectej! = you two (fem.) bake!
   pijtaj = you two (masc.) drink!
   pijmy! = let us drink!
   pisajće! = write (regularly)!
   stańće = get up! (Pfve.)

 The other persons of the Imperative are expressed by a periphrasis: njech + Pres. or (Pfve.) Fut., e.g.:—

  njech pječe! = let him (her) bake!
  njech stanu! = let them get up! (Pfve.)

 Prohibitions are generally expressed, as in other Slavonic languages, by the negative *Impfve*. Imperative, unless they express a warning or caution:—

  njekur! = don't smoke!
  njepij! = don't drink!
but—
  njepadń! = (mind you) don't fall!
  njech njepadnje! = see that he(she) doesn't fall!

The Gerunds (Active)

 The *Present Gerund* is formed only from Impfve. verbs. It is invariable and refers always to the subject of the sentence, as in other Slavonic languages. Most verbs have two alternative forms, identical in meaning, ending either in (-*j*)*o* or -*icy*/-*jcy*. These endings are added to the Present stem. Of the two forms it is the one in -*cy* which is sometimes wanting and is now rarely used.

Cl.	I	wjedźo or wjedźicy	= leading
		njeso	= carrying
		pječo or pječicy	= baking
Cl.	II	bjerjo	= taking
		wuknjo	= learning
Cl.	III.1	pijo or pijicy	= drinking
	2	lubujo or lubujcy	= loving
Cl.	IV.1	wołajo or wołajcy	= calling
	2	třělejo or třělejcy	= shooting
CL.	V	činjo or činicy	= doing, performing
		prošo or prosycy	= requesting

The *Past Gerund* is formed only from Pfve. verbs. This, too, is invariable and is formed from the Perfective Infin. stem by dropping the -*ć* of the Infin. and adding -(*w*)*ši*. The full ending -*wši* is used with all types of verbs except consonant-stem verbs of Cl. I with no -*a*- joining vowel in the Infin. Dental and velar stem verbs of Cl. I restore the original consonant of the root. Thus:—

Cl.	I	donjesši	= having brought (<donjesć)
		dowjedši	= having brought (a person) (<dowjesć, Fut. dowjedu)
		napjekši	= having baked (<napjec, Fut. napjeku)
but—			
		nabrawši	= having taken, gathered (<nabrać)
Cl.	II	nawuknywši	= having learnt
Cl.	III.1	wupiwši	= having drunk
	2	wumolowawši	= having painted
		donakupowawši	= having bought up
Cl.	IV.1	zawołeawši	= having called
	2	zatřělawši	= having shot (dead) (<zatřěleć)[1]
Cl.	V.A	pochwaliwši	= having praised
		poprosywši	= having requested
	B	zdźeržawši	= having detained (<zdźeržeć)[1]

The Participles— verbal adjectives (Present and Past Active, Past Passive)

The *Present Participle Active* is formed from Impfve. verbs, usually from their Present stem. It ends in: Sing. masc. -*acy*, fem. -*aca*, neut. -*ace*, (and, as an adjectival form, in: Sing. masc. -*aty*, fem.

---

[1] It will be observed that verbs of Cl. IV and V with Infin. in -*eć* restore the earlier *a* of this form before the *hard* *w* of the Past Gerund.

-*ata*, neut. -*ate*¹) and is to be distinguished from the Present Gerund in -(*i*)*cy*. Both forms are variable according to gender, number and case, and the form with -*acy*, etc. is equivalent to a relative clause. They are declined like dobry.

I	wjedźacy, -a, -e	=	(who is)	leading
	pječacy, etc.	=	"	baking
	njesacy, etc.	=	"	carrying
	bjerjacy *or* bjerucy	=	"	taking
Cl. II	wuknjacy	=	"	learning
Cl.III.1	pijacy	=	"	drinking
2	kupujacy *or* kupowacy	=	"	buying
	kedźbujacy or kedźbowacy	=	"	paying attention
Cl. IV.1	wołacy	=	"	calling
2	třělacy	=	"	shooting
Cl. V.A	khwalacy	=	"	praising
	činjacy	=	"	doing
B	dźeržacy	=	"	holding

The *Past Participle Active*, ending in -*ł*, is only used in compound tenses (see above—Compound Past, Pluperfect and Conditional). Its formation has been fully dealt with under "The Compound Past or Perfect Tense", q.v.

The *Past Participle Passive* is formed from the Infin. stem of verbs of either aspect but far more frequently from perfective verbs. It is declined like dobry, and usually ends in: Sing. masc. -*ty*, fem. -*ta*, neut. -*te* for all verbs of Cl. III 1.A.a. and III 1.B.a. (monosyllabic vowel stems), e.g.:—

pić = to drink, Past Part.Pass. wupity = drunk (down)
znać = to know, " " " znaty = known
tać = to melt, " " " roztaty = melted

For all other verbs with Infin. in -*ać* and -*eć* (from -*ać*) it ends in -*any*, -*ana*, -*ane*, e.g.:—

Cl. I wubrać = to choose, Past Part.Pass. wubrany = chosen
Cl.III.2 kupować = to buy " " " kupowany = bought
(Impfve.)
Cl. IV.1 wołać = to call, " " " zawołany = called
Cl. IV.2 třěleć = to shoot, " " " třělany = shot
Cl. V.B dźeržeć = to hold, " " " zadźeržany, (rarely: dźerženy) = held up

---

¹E.g. wijata rěka = a winding river; stejata lampa = a standard lamp.

Other verbs of Cl. I (consonantal stems with no joining vowel in Infin.) and all verbs of Cl. II (-nyć) and Cl. V.A (-ić) have Past Part. Pass. ending in -(j)eny, -(j)ena, -(j)ene. (The -j- occurs in verbs of Cl. II and Cl. V.A and causes yotation of the preceding consonant where possible (see p. 360, No. 4). E.g.:—

				Past Part. Pass.	
Cl. I	njesć	= to carry,	zanjeseny	= carried
	wjesć	= to lead,	zawjedźeny	= led
	pjec	= to bake,	napječeny	= baked
Cl. II	wuknyć	= to learn,	nawuknjeny	= learnt
Cl. V.A	chwalić	= to praise,	pochwaleny	= praised
	kazyć	= to spoil,	skaženy	= spoilt
	kurić	= to smoke,	wukurjeny	= smoked

Verbal Nouns

These are formed from the Infinitive or Present stem, or from the Past Participle Passive by changing -ty to -će, or -ny to -nje. By analogy, (neuter) Verbal Nouns with these endings are also formed from intransitive verbs which have no Past Participle Passive.

pićе	= drinking(noun)	nesenje	= carrying
wolanje	= calling	widźenje	= seeing
kupowanje	= buying	hajenje	= defending
wuknjenje	= learning	wěrjenje	= believing
třělenje	= shooting	dźerženje	= holding

and therefore also—
    byće = being   łhanje = lying, telling lies

Examples of the three main Conjugations of Regular Verbs

1. -(j)e type (Classes I, II, III.1 and III.2):—
Class I.   wjesć = to lead   njesć = to carry
               (Impfve.),   (Impfve.)
                                    with hard -s- stem

PRESENT
Sing.	1	wjedu	njesu
	2	wjedźeš	njeseš
	3	wjedźe	njese
Dual	1	wjedźemoj	njesemoj
	2 and 3, masc. pers.	wjedźetaj	njesetaj
	2 and 3, masc. impers., fem., neut.	wjedźetej	njesetej

Plur. 1	wjedźemy	njesemy
2	wjedźeće	njeseće
3	wjedu, wjedźeja	njesu, njeseja

IMPERATIVE
Sing. 2	wjedź	njes
Dual 1	wjedźmoj	njesmoj
2, masc. pers.	wjedźtaj	njestaj
2, masc. impers., fem., neut.	wjedźtej	njestej
Plur. 1	wjedźmy	njesmy
2	wjedźće	njesće

FUTURE
Sing. 1	powjedu	ponjesu

IMPERFECT
Sing. 1	wjedźech	njesech

AORIST
Sing. 1	zawjedźech	zanjesech

GERUNDS
Present	wjedźo, wjedźicy	njeso
Past	zawjedši	zanjesši

PARTICIPLES
Present Active	wjedźacy	njesacy
Past Active	wjedł	njesł
Past Passive	zawjedźeny	zanjeseny

Class II.   wuknyć = to learn (Impfve.)

PRESENT
Sing. 1	wuknu
2	wukneš
3	wuknje
Dual 1	wuknjemoj
2 and 3, masc. pers.	wuknjetaj
2 and 3, masc. impers., fem., neut.	wuknjetej
Plur. 1	wuknjemy
2	wuknjeće
3	wuknu, wuknjeja

IMPERATIVE
Sing. 2	wukń, wuk
Dual 1	wukńmoj
2, masc. pers.	wukńtaj
2, masc.impers., fem., neut.	wukńtej
Plur. 1	wukńmy
2	wukńće

} with -ń- not pronounced

FUTURE
Sing. 1	budu wuknyć

IMPERFECT
Sing. 1   wuknjech
AORIST
Sing. 1   nawuknych
GERUNDS
Present   wuknjo, wuknicy
Past   nawuknywši
PARTICIPLES
Present Active   wuknjacy, wuknucy
Past Active   wukny ł
Past Passive   nawuknjeny

Class III. pić = to drink (Impfve.) kupować = to buy (Impfve.)

PRESENT
Sing. 1   piju   kupuju
      2   piješ   kupuješ
      3   pije   kupuje
Dual 1   pijemoj   kupujemoj
      2 and 3, masc.
        pers.   pijetaj   kupujetaj
      2 and 3, masc.
        impers.,
        fem., neut.   pijetej   kupujetej
Plur. 1   pijemy   kupujemy
      2   piječe   kupuječe
      3   pija, pijeja   kupuja
IMPERATIVE
Sing. 2   pij   kupuj
Dual 1   pijmoj   kupujmoj
      2, masc. pers.   pijtaj   kupujtaj
      2, masc.impers.,
         fem., neut.   pijtej   kupujtej
Plur. 1   pijmy   kupujmy
      2   pijće   kupujće
FUTURE
Sing. 1   budu pić   budu kupować
IMPERFECT
Sing. 1   pijach   kupowach
AORIST
Sing. 1   wupich   donakupowach
GERUNDS
Present   pijo, pijicy   kupujo, kupujcy
Past   wupiwši   donakupowawši
PARTICIPLES
Present Active   pijacy   kupowacy
Past Active   pi ł   kupowa ł
Past Passive   wupity   kupowany

2. -*a*- type:—

CLASS IV. 1.(Hard): wołać = to call   2. (Soft): třĕleć = to shoot
              (Impfve.)   (Impfve.)

PRESENT
Sing. 1   wołam   třĕlam
      2   wołaš   třĕleš
      3   woła   třĕla
Dual 1   wołamoj   třĕlamoj
      2, masc. pers.   wołataj   třĕlataj
      2, masc.impers.,
         fem., neut.   wołatej   třĕlatej
Plur. 1   wołamy   třĕlamy
      2   wołaće   třĕleće
      3   wołaja   třĕleja
IMPERATIVE
Sing. 2   wołaj   třĕlej
Dual 1   wołajmoj   třĕlejmoj
      2, masc. pers.   wołajtaj   třĕlejtaj
      2, masc.impers.,   wołajtej   třĕlejtej
         fem., neut.
Plur. 1   wołajmy   třĕlejmy
      2   wołajće   třĕlejće
IMPERFECT
Sing. 1   wołach   třĕlach
AORIST
Sing. 1   zawołach   (třĕlich)[1]
GERUNDS
Present   wołajo, wolajcy   třĕlejo, třĕlejcy
Past   zawoławši   (třĕliwši)[1]
PARTICIPLES
Present Active   wołacy   třĕlacy
Past Active   wołał   třĕlał
Past Passive   zawołany   třĕlany

3. -*i*- type:—

Class V.   A. chwalić[2] = to   B. dźeržeć = to
               praise (Impfve.).   hold (Impfve.)

PRESENT
Sing. 1   chwalu   dźeržu
      2   chwališ   dźeržiš
      3   chwali   dźerži

[1] From třĕlić, Pfve.
[2] So also e.g. prosyć = to request, beg, Pres. prošu, prosyš, prosy, etc., 3rd p.pl. proša, P.P.A. prosył; hrozyć = to threaten, Pres. hrožu, hrozyš, hrozy, etc., 3rd p.pl. hroža, P.P.A. hrozył. After the hard *s* and *z*, *y* is substituted for *i* wherever it occurs.

Dual	1	chwalimoj	dźeržimoj
	2, masc. pers.	chwalitaj	dźeržitaj
	2, masc. impers., fem., neut.	chwalitej	dźeržitej
Plur.	1	chwalimy	dźeržimy
	2	chwaliće	dźeržiće
	3	chwala	dźerža

IMPERATIVE

Sing.	2	chwal	dźerž
Dual	1	chwalmoj	dźeržmoj
	2, masc. pers.	chwaltaj	dźeržtaj
	2, masc. impers., fem., neut.	chwaltej	dźeržtej
Plur.	1	chwalmy	dźeržmy
	2	chwalće	dźeržće

IMPERFECT

Sing.	1	chwalach	dźeržach

AORIST

Sing.	1	pochwalich	zdźeržach

GERUNDS

Present	chwalo	dźeržo
Past	pochwaliwši	zdźéržawši

PARTICIPLES

Present Active	chwalacy	dźeržacy
Past Active	chwalił	dźeržał
Past Passive	pochwaleny	zdźeržany (-eny)

Irregular Verbs

The Athematic Verbs:—

być = to be

	PRESENT[1]			IMPERATIVE	
Sing.	1	sym			
	2	sy	Sing.	2	budź
	3	je	Dual	1	budźmoj
Dual	1	smój		2, masc. pers.	budźtaj
	2 and 3, masc. pers.	staj		2, masc. impers., fem., neut	budźtej
	2 and 3, masc. impers., fem., neut.	stej	plur.	1	budźmy
				2	budźće
Plur.	1	smy			
	2	sće			
	3	su			

[1] After the negative *nje-* these forms begin with an additional *j* except in 3rd pers. sing., i.e.

njejsym, njejsy, njeje, etc. Njeje is pronounced neje.

LUSATIAN

		FUTURE	IMPERFECT[1,2]
Sing.	1	budu	běch
	2	budźeš	běše, bě
	3	budźe	běše, bě
Dual	1	budźemoj	běchmoj
	2 and 3, masc. pers.	budźetaj	běštaj
	2 and 3, masc. impers., fem., neut.	budźetej	běštej
Plur.	1	budźemy	běchmy
	2	budźeće	běšće
	3	budźeja	běchu

PERFECT (COMPOUND PAST)

Sing. 1 sym był, była
2 sy był, była
3 je był, była, było, etc.

PLUPERFECT

Sing. 1 běch był, była
2 běše był, była
3 běše był, była, było, etc.

CONDITIONAL

Sing.	1		bych
	2, 3		by
Dual	1		bychmoj
	2 and 3, masc. pers.		byštaj
	2 and 3, masc. impers., fem., neut.		byštej
Plur.	1		bychmy
	2		byšće
	3		bychu

[1] But in compounds: pobych, poby, etc., Aorist from pobyć (Pfve.) = to be (or stop) for a while.

[2] Note that in expressing the Passive Voice by a Past Part. Pass. with być in the Imperfect, the special forms: buch, bu, bu, buchmoj, buštaj, buštej, buchmy, bušće, buchu, are used instead of běch, bě(še), etc. E.g.:—
                Buch wołany = I was called
Buch, etc., can also mean "became", e.g.:—
  Potom bu tam z fararjom = Afterwards he became vicar there

LUSATIAN

PAST CONDITIONAL

Sing.1		bych był, (or budźich[1] był, or budźech[1] był była	
2		by był, " budźiše etc. " budźeše etc. była	
3		etc. " budźiše " budźeše	
Dual 1		" budźichmoj " budźechmoj	
	2 and 3, mas. pers.	" budźištaj " budźeštaj	
	2 and 3, masc. impers., fem., neut.	" budźištej " budźeštej	
Plur.1		" budźichmy " budźechmy	
2		" budźišće " budźešće	
3		" budźichu " budźechu)	

GERUNDS
Present   bywajo[2], bywajcy[2]
Past   pobywši
PARTICIPLES
Present   bywacy[2]
Past Active   był
Past Passive wotbyty (= lost)

	dać = to give (Pfve.)	jěsć = to eat (Impfve.)	wědźeć = to know (Fr. savoir)
PRESENT			
Sing. 1		jěm	wěm
2		ješ	wěš
3		jě	wě
Dual 1		jěmoj	wěmoj
2 and 3, masc. pers.		jěstaj	wěstaj
2 and 3, m. impers., f., n.		jěstej	wěstej
Plur. 1		jěmy	wěmy
2		jěsće	wěsće
3		jědźa	wědźa
IMPERATIVE			
Sing. 2	daj	jěs	wěs
Dual 1	dajmoj	jěsmoj	wěsmoj
2, masc. pers.	dajtaj	jěstaj	wěstaj
2, masc. impers., f.,n.	dajtej	jěstej	wěstej
Plur. 1	dajmy	jěsmy	wěsmy
2	dajće	jěsće	wěsće

---

[1] These forms are archaic.
[2] From the Frequentative bywać.

LUSATIAN

```
FUTURE
Sing. 1              dam              budu jěsć    budu wědźeć
      2              daš                 etc.         etc.
      3              da
Dual  1              damoj
      2 and 3, masc.
        pers.        dataj
      2 and 3, m. im-
        pers., f.,n. datej
Plur. 1              damy
      2              daće
      3              dadźa(daja)
IMPERFECT
Sing. 1              dawach¹          jědźach      wědźach
AORIST
Sing. 1              dach             zjěch        powěch²
GERUNDS
Present              dawajo,¹dawajcy¹ jědźo        wědźo
Past                 dawši            zjědši
PARTICIPLES
Present Active       dawacy¹          jědźacy      wědźacy
Past Active          dał              jědł         wědźał
Past Passive         daty             zjědźeny
```

Other irregular and noteworthy verbs

```
                     měć = to have        móc = to be able
PRESENT
Sing. 1              mam                  móžu
      2              maš                  móžeš
      3              ma                   móže
Dual  1              mamoj                móžemoj
      2 and 3, masc.
        pers.        mataj                móžetaj
      2 and 3 m. im-
        pers., f., n. matej               móžetej
Plur. 1              mamy                 móžemy
      2              maće                 móžeće
      3              maja                 móža, móžeja, mohu
IMPERATIVE
Sing. 2              měj³                 wumóž(= liberate!)
Dual  1              mějmoj               wumóžmoj
      2, masc. pers. mějtaj               wumóžtaj
      2, mas. im-
        pers.,f.,n.  mějtej               wumóžtej
```

¹From dawać (Impfve.), reg.
²From powěsć or powědźeć = to say, tell, relate (Pfve.).
³Pronounced: mej.

Plur.	1	mějmy	wumóžmy
	2	mějće	wumóžće
FUTURE			
Sing.		změju, změješ, etc.	budu móc, etc.
IMPERFECT			
Sing.	1	měJach	móžach
AORIST			
Sing.	1	wotměch	wumóžech *or* wumóch
GERUNDS			
Present		mějo	móžo
Past		wotměwši	zamóžiwši (= having been able)
PARTICIPLES			
Present Active		mějacy	móžacy
Past Active		měł	móhł, móhli, móhłe
Past Passive		wotměty	přemóženy (= overcome)

Negative Pres. of měć: nimam, nimaš, etc. wotměć = to hold (a meeting).

chcyć = to want: Pres. chcu, chceš, chce, chcemoj, chcetaj, chcetej, chcemy, chceće, chcedźa; Imperat. chcyj!; Imperf. chcych, chcyše; Pres. Ger. chcyjo; Past Ger. zechcywši; Pres. Part. Act. chcyjacy; Past Part. Act. chcył; negative forms: Infin, nochcyć, Pres. nochcu, etc., or njecham, -aš, etc.

směć = to dare: Pres. směm, směš, smě, směmoj, smětaj, smětej, směmy, směće, smědźa, Imperat. směj!; Imperf. smědźach; Pres. Ger. smědźo; Pres. Part. smědźacy, Past Part. Act. směł.

stać so[1] = to happen, become (Pfve.): Pres. stanu so, stanješ so, stanje so, stanjemoj so, stanjetaj (-tej) so, stanjemy so, stanjeće so, stanu so; Imperat. stań so!; Aor. stach so; Pres. Ger. stawajo so[2]; Past Ger. stawši so; Pres. Part. stawacy so[2]; Past Part. Act. stał so; Past Part. Pass. -staty.

spać = to sleep: Pres. spju, spiš, spi, spimoj, spitaj, spitej, spimy, spiće, spja; Imperat. spi!; Imperf. spach; Pres. Ger. spicy; Past Ger. wuspawši so; Pres. Part. spjacy; Past Part. Act. spał; Past Part. Pass. wuspany.

dźeć = to say, has only Imperfect: dźach, dźeše, dźachmy, dźešće, dźachu, of which dźeše is the only form frequently used.

---

[1]To be distinguished from: stać = to stand, Pres. stoju, stojiš, or steju, stejiš (see below).

[2]From stawać so (Impfve.), reg.

N.B.— dźeć so = to seem: mi so dźije = it seems to me, dźiješe so = it seemed, mi je so dźało = it seemed to me.

For hić (= to go, Impfve.) and jěć (= to go—conveyed), see "Verbs of Going and Conveying" below.

The following verbs, many irregular or seemingly so only in certain parts, should also be noted. We include some verbs which are regular in Upper Lusatian, but are interesting for comparison with other Slavonic languages. Of these we give only the Infin., meaning, and aspect, if Perfective.

Class I

Infin. Present	Imperat.	Imperf.	Aor.
mjasć = to press			
mjatu, mjećeš	mjeć	mjećech	
	Past Part. Act.		
	mjatł		
zajeć = to capture (Pfve.)			
zajmu, zajmjmeš	zajmi		zajach
	zajał		
wzać = to take (Pfve.)			
wozmu, wozmješ[1]	wzmi (wozmi)		wzach
	wzał		
poćeć = to begin (Pfve.)			
počnu, počnješ	počni (započ)		počach
	počał		
napjeć = to stretch (Pfve.)[2]			
napnu, napnješ	napni		napjach
	napjał		
wotćeć = to cut off (Pfve.)			
wotetnu, wotetnješ	wotetni		wotćach
	wotćał		
or wotećnu, wotećnješ	wotećni		
žeć[3] *or* žnjeć (more frequent) = to reap			
wužnu, -žnješ	-žni	-žnjach	
žnjeju, žnjeješ	žnjej	žnjejach	
	žnjał		
dréć = to flay			
dréju, dréješ	drěj	drějach	
	drěł		
dru, drješ	zadri		zadrěch

[1] In the colloquial language wzać now belongs entirely to Class IV, Pres. wzam, wzaš, etc.

[2] zapjeć = to button up (Pfve.) has Fut. zapinu, zapinješ, etc.

[3] Form rarely used.

Class I

Infin.	Present	Imperat.	Imperf.	Aor.
mrěć = to die				
	mrěju, mrěješ	mrěj	mrějach	wumrěch
	Past Part. Act.			
	mrěł			
	wumru, -mrješ	mri		
(za)prěć = to deny				
	(za)pru, (za)prješ	zapri		zaprěch
	or prěju, prěješ		(za)prěł	
trěć = to rub				
	tru, trješ			
	or trěju, trějes	tri, trěj		wutrěch
		(wu)trěł		
wrjeć, wrěć so = to boil				
	wru, wrješ			
	or wrěju, wrěješ	wri	wrějach	
		wrěł		
zawrěć = to close (Pfve.)				
	zawru, zawrješ			
	or zawrěju, zawrějes	zawri		zawrěch
		zawrěł		
kćěć = to flower				
	ktu, kćeš	kći		zakćech
	more frequently:		kćěł	
	kćěju, kćěješ	kćěj	kćějach	
ćec (reg.) = to flow				
	ćeku, ćečeš	ćeč	ćečech	
		ćekł		
syc = to hew, mow				
	syku, syčeš	syč	syčech	
		sykł		
tołc = to pound, crush				
	tołču, tołčes	tołč	tołčech	
		tołkł		
lac = to set traps				
	laku, lečeš	leč	lečech	
		lakł		
wlec so = to drag, trail				
	wleku so, wlečeš so	wleč so	wlečech so	
		wlekł so		
rjec = to say (Pfve.)	Other forms from rjeknyć,			
	Cl. II, q.v.	rjekl		
brać = to take				
	bjeru, bjerješ	bjer	bjerjech	pobrach
		brał		

Infin.	Present	Imperat.	Imperf.	Aor.
hnać, ćerić = to drive				
	ćerju, ćeriš (Class V.A)[1]	ćer	ćerjach	-hnach
		Past Part. Act.		
		hnał		
prać = to chop, strike				
	pjeru, pjerješ	pjer	pjerjech	wuprach
		prał		
žrać = to eat (of animals)				
	žeru, žerješ	žer	žerjech	zežrach
		žrał		
słać = 1. to send, 2 to spread				
	scélu, sćeleš	sćel	sćelech	posłach
		słał		

Class II

ćahnyć = to draw				
	ćahnu, ćehnjes	ćehń	ćehnjech	{začahnych / začežech}
		ćahnył		
dosahnyć = to reach (Pfve.)				
	dosahnu, dosahnješ	dosahń		{dosahnych / dosažech}
		dosahnył		
padnyć = to fall (Pfve.)				
	padnu, padnješ	padń, padni or pań		{padžech / padnych}
		padnył		
rjeknyć, rjec = to say (Pfve.)				
	rjeknu, rjeknješ	rjekń		rjeknych
		rjekł		
(See rjec, the more usual Infinitive, above, Class I)				
sydnyć so = to sit down (Pfve.)				
	sydnu so, sydnješ so	sydń so or syń so		{sydžech so / sydnych so}
		sydnył		
torhnyć = to tear (Pfve.)				
	torhnu, torhnješ	torhń		{torhnych / toržech}
		torhnył		
zapřahnyć = to harness (Pfve.)				
	zapřahnu, zapřehnješ	zapřehń		{zapřahnych / zapřežech}
		zapřahnył		
zběhnyć = to lift (Pfve.)				
	zběhnu, zběhnješ	zběhń		{zběhnych / zběžech}
		zběhnył		

---

[1] Future: počerju, etc.

Notice also:—
chelpnyć   = to gallop off (Pfve. reg.)
kradnyć   = to steal (Impfve. reg.)
minyć so   = to pass (Pfve. reg.)
płaknyć   = to start crying (Pfve. reg.)
přimnyć   = to seize (Pfve. reg.)
stanyć   = to get up (Pfve. reg.)
šlapnyć   = to swallow (Pfve. reg.)
wusnyć   = to go to sleep (Pfve. reg.)
začknyć so = to choke (Pfve. reg.)

Class III

Infin.   *Present*   *Imperat.*   *Imperf.*   *Aor.*
nadźeć so, nadźijeć so = to hope (for)
  nadźiju (or -jam) so,   nadźij so   nadźijach so
  nadźiješ so   *Past Part. Act.*
                                 nadźijał
kleć = to curse
  kliju, kliješ   klij or klej ·klijach or klejach
  or kleju, kleješ   klał
leć = to pour
  liju, liješ   lij   lijach
                                    lał
plěć = to weed (reg.)
  plěju, plěješ   plěj   prějach
                                    plěł
přeć = to wish
  přeju, přeješ   přej   přejach
                                    přał
smjeć so = to laugh
  smě̌ju so,[1] smě̌ješ so[1]   smě̌j so[1]   smě̌jach so[1]
                                  smjał
tkać = to weave (reg.)
  tkaju, tkaješ   tkaj   tkajach
                                  tkał
syć = to sow (reg.)
  syju, syješ   syj   syjach
                                   sył
wuć = to howl (reg.)
  wuju, wuješ   wuj   wujach
                                   wuł
próć = to rip
  próju, próješ   prój   prójach
                                   prół
wobróć = to ward off, restrain (Pfve.)
  wobróju,[2] wobróješ[2]   wobrój   wobróch
                                  wobrół

[1]-ě- is pronounced like e in these forms before the *j*.
[2]or: woboru, woborješ.

LUSATIAN

Infin.	Present	Imperat.	Imperf.	Aor.	Past Part. Act.
žwać, žuć = to chew					
	žuju, žuješ	žuj	žujach	wužuch	žwał
mlěć = to grind					
{	mlěju mlěješ	mlěj	mlějach	wumlěch	mlěł
	mjelu, mjeleš	mjel	mjelech		
kłóć = to prick (Pfve. *and* Impfve.)					
{	kolu, koleš (archaic)	kól	kołech	kłóch	kłół
	kłóju, kłóješ	kłój	kłójach		

Notice also:—

šić	=	to sew
kać so	=	to repent
tać	=	to melt
trać	=	to last
ruć	=	to roar, bellow
dwělować	=	to doubt
dźakować so	=	to thank
kedźbować	=	to pay attention
lubować	=	to love
prócować so	=	to exert oneself
wobžarować	=	to pity
zdychować	=	to sigh
žarować	=	to regret, mourn

Class IV. 1

Infin.	Present	Imperat.	Imperf.	Aor.	Past Part. Act.
kazać = to arrange, order					
{	kazam, kazaš	kazaj	kazach		kazał
	kazam, kažeš				
mazać = to smear[1]					
{	mazam, mazaš	mazaj	mazach		mazał
	mazam, mažeš				
pisać = to write					
{	pisam, pisaš	pisaj	pisach		pisał
	pisam, pišeš				
skakać = to jump[2]					
{	skakam, skakaš	skakaj	skakach		skakał
	skakam, skačeš				
wjazać = to bind					
{	wjazam, wjazaš	wjazaj	wjazach		wjazał
	wjazam, wjezeš				

---

[1] Similarly: rězać = to cut.
[2] Similarly: plakać = to weep.

Notice also:—

čitać	= to read	płokać	= to launder
jebać	= to deceive	pytać	= to seek
chelpać	= to gallop	spěwać	= to sing
		stonać	= to groan

Class IV.2 (reg.)

pokłonjeć so	= to bow	zaražeć	= to beat in, kill
prašeć so	= to ask (a question)	zbudzeć	= to arouse
wobaleć	= to wrap	měnjeć	= to change

Class V. A

Infin.	Present	Imperat.	Imperf.	Aor.	Past Part. Act.
ćmić so = to grow dark					
	ćmi so (3rd pers.)		ćmješe so		ćmiło
dnić so = to dawn					
	dni so (3rd pers.)		dnješe so		dniło
krčić = to christen					
	{krču, krčijes / krčiju	krči	krčijach		krčił
radźić so = to do well (of fruit); *also* to advise (without 'so')					
	radźi so (3rd pers.)		radźeše so		radźiło

Notice also:

lubić	= to promise
lubić so	= to please
łójić	= to catch
měnić	= to intend
morić	= to kill
myslić	= to think
poźčić	= to lend (Pfve.)
prajić	= to say
skomdźić	= to miss, be late for (Pfve.)
stajić	= to put (Pfve.)
tepić	= to heat, burn; to drown (trans.)
trělić	= to shoot (Pfve.)
wěrić	= to believe
wučić	= to teach
žiwić so	= to live (also: žiwy być = to live)

Class V. B

Infin.	Present	Imperat.	Imperf.	Aor.	Past Part. Act.
bojeć so = to fear					
	boju so, bojiš so	boj so	bojach so		bojał
ćerpjeć = to suffer					
	ćerpju, ćerpiš	ćerp	ćerpjach or ćerpjech		ćerpjeł[1]

[1] Or ćerpjal.

LUSATIAN

Infin.	Present	Imperat.	Imperf.	Aor.	Past Part. Act.
dyrbjeć = to have to, must					
	dyrbju, dyrbiš		dyrbjach		dyrbjał
łžeć, łhać = to tell lies					
	łžu, łžiš *or* łžeš	łži		łžach	łžal *or* łhał
rozumjeć(rozumić) = to understand					
	rozumju, rozumiš	rozum		rozumjach	rozumjał *or* rozumił
schorjeć = to fall ill (Pfve.)[1]					
	schorju, schoriš	schor		schorjech[1] *or* schorjach	schorjeł[1]
widźeć = to see					
	widźu, widźiš	widź[2]	widźach		widźał
zawidźeć = to envy (Impfve.)					
	zawidźu, zawidźiš	zawidź	zawidźach		zawidźał
	{ zawidźam, zawidźeš (modern lit. lang.)	zawidźej			
stać, stejeć, *or* stojeć = to stand					
	stoju, stojiš	stój		stojach	stał
	steju, stejiš	stej		stejach	
ržeć[3] = to tremble					
	ržu, ržiš	rži		ržach	ržał
tčeć = to stick out					
	tču, tčiš (pron. tčju, tčiš)	tči (pron. tci)		tčach	tčał

Notice also:—

ćišćeć = to press, print
mjelčeć = to be silent
sedźeć = to sit
słodźeć = to taste good

Verbs of Going and Conveying

To go (on foot) = Impfve. *and* Pfve.	hić	Freq.	chodźić
Pres.1st,2nd p.sg., 3rd p.pl.	du, dźeš, du *or* dzeja[4]		chodźu, chodźiš, chodźa
Fut. Impfve. *and* Pfve.	póńdu		budu chodźić
Past Part. Act. Impfve. *and* Pfve.	šoł, šła, šło, šli, šłe		chodźił, -ła
Imperfect	dźech		chodźach

---

[1]In popular speech: schorich, schorił. Similarly słodnjeć = to become sweet.
[2]More usually: hladaj, *or* hlej!
[3]ržeć is pronounced: žrjeć!
[4]Negative form: njeńdu, njeńdźeš, 3rd p.pl. njeńdu. Imperat. njeńdź, etc.

LUSATIAN

Imperative *Impfve*. and *Pfve*.	dźi! or pój! -my, -će		chodź!
Pres. Gerund	ducy	Pres. Part.	chodźacy
Past Gerund	(při)šedši (= having come)		
Past Part. Pass.	hity		

To go (be conveyed) = Impfve. and Pfve. jěć   Freq. jězdźić

Pres. 1st,2nd p.sg., 3rd p.pl.	jědu, jědźeš, jědu or jědźeja		jězdźu, jězdźiš, jězdźa
Fut. *Impfve*. and *Pfve*.	pojědu		budu jězdźić
Past Part. Act. *Impfve*. and *Pfve*.	jěł,-ła		jězdźił, -ła
Imperfect	jedźech		jězdźach
Imperative *Impfve*. and *Pfve*.	jědź!		jězdźi!
Pres. Gerund	jědźo		
Past Gerund	(při)jěwši = having arrived		
Pres. Part. Act.	jědźacy or jěducy		
Past Part. Pass.	jedźeny		

N.B.— jěchać (Impfve.) = to ride (on horseback)

To come (on foot) = Impfve. and Freq. přichadźeć (reg.)
           Pfve. přińć

Pres. 1st,2nd p.sg. 3rd p.pl.	přichadźam, přichadźeš, přichadźeja (Cl. IV.2)	Fut.	přińdu, přińdźeš
Past Part. Act.	přichadźał		přišoł, přišła
Imperfect	přichadźach	Aor.	přińdźech
Imperative	přichadźej!		přińdź!
Past Gerund			přišedši

So also: to go away = Impfve. wotchadźeć, Pfve. woteńć
         to go out = Impfve. wuchadźeć Pfve. wuńć
         not to go = Freq. njechodźić, Impfve. and Pfve. njeńć[1]

To come (conveyed), arrive = Impfve. prijězdźować Pfve. prijěć
                             (Cl. III.2)
To go away (conveyed)   = Impfve. —   Pfve. wotjěč
To go out, off (conveyed) = Impfve. wujězdźować Pfve. wujěč

[1] See footnote No. 4, p. 457.

To carry = Impfve. njesć   Pfve. zanjesć   Freq. nosyć
  Pres. njesu, njeseš, Fut. zanjesu   Pres. nošu, nosyš, noša
  Fut.   ponjesu   budu nosyć
  Past Part.
    Act.   njesł, -ła   zanjesł   nosył
  Imperfect   njesech   Aor. zanjesech   Imperf. nošach
  Imperative   njes!   zanjes!   noš!
  Pres. Gerund njeso   —   Pres. Part.
                                           Act. nošacy
  Past Gerund (do)njesši
            (= having brought)
  Past Part.
    Pass.   njeseny

To bring = Impfve. přinošeć (Cl. IV. 2)   Pfve. přinjesć
                  přinošować (Cl. III.2)

To lead = Impfve. wjesć   Pfve. zawjesć   Freq. wodźić
  Pres.   wjedu,   Fut. zawjedu   Pres. wodźu, wodźiš
             wjedźeš   wodźa
             wjedu *or* wjedźeja
  Fut.   powjedu   budu wodźić
  Past Part. Act. wjedł, -ła   zawjedł   wodźił
  Imperfect   wjedźech Aor. zawjedźech Imperf. wodźach
  Imperative   wjedź!   zawjedź!   wodź!
  Pres. Gerund wjedźo *or*   —
             wjedźicy
  Past Gerund (do)wjedši (= having brought *a person*)
  Pres. Part. Act. wjedźacy
  Past Part. Pass. wjedźeny

To bring (a person) = Impfve. přiwodźować   Pfve. přiwjesć

To lead out = Impfve. wuwodźować   Pfve. wuwjesć

To convey = Impfve. wjezć   Pfve. zawjezć   Freq. wozyć
  Pres.   wjezu,   Fut. zawjezu   Pres. wožu, wozyš,
             wjezeš   woža
             wjezu *or* wjezeja
  Fut.   powjezu   budu wozyć
  Past Part.Act. wjezł, -ła   zawjezł   wozył
  Imperfect   wjezech   Aor. zawjezech Imperf. wožach
  Imperative   wjez!   zawjez!   wož!
  Pres. Gerund wjezo
  Past Gerund přiwjezši (= having brought *in a vehicle*)
  Past Part.Pass. wjezeny

To bring (in a vehicle) = Impfve. přiwožować   Pfve. přiwjezć

To export = Impfve. wuwožować   Pfve. wuwjezć

    N.B. łećeć = to fly, lězć = to climb, also have Futures with the prefix po-: polećú = I shall fly (Impfve.), polězu = I shall climb (Impfve.).

WORD ORDER WITH ENCLITICS

In Upper Lusatian, in contrast to Czech, Slovak, Serbocroätian and Slovenian, the auxiliary verbs of the Compound Past (Perfect) and Pluperfect tenses, sym, sy, etc., and of the Conditional Mood, bych, by etc., are *not* enclitic and must always *precede* the Past Participle Active. In consequence of this, in short sentences they frequently occur as the first word, e.g.:—

Sym hizo wupowědź dał	= I have already given notice
Sy so nazymnił	= You have caught a cold
Bych rad to widzał	= I would gladly see it.
Je so wujasniło	= It was cleared up (of the weather)

The only regularly enclitic words are:—

1. The particle -*li* (= if; or acts as interrogative particle):

Dowoliće-li, wostanu na wjecer	= If you pėrmit, I shall stay to supper
Maće-li znamku?	= Have you a stamp?

2. The short forms of 1st and 2nd person sing. Personal Pronouns and of the Reflexive Pronoun, i.e. in the Gen., Acc. and Dat. cases, viz.:—

	1st pers. sg.	2nd pers. sg.	Reflexive
Acc., Gen.	mje[1]	će	so
Dat.	mi[1]	ći	sej

(Notice that in Upper Lusatian, as in Old Slavonic, and in contrast to other West and South Slav languages, no special enclitic forms exist for the *3rd* pers. Personal Pronoun.) The above pronouns regularly come directly after the first stressed word or word group of a sentence, e.g.:—

Dźakuju so (reflex. verb)	= I thank (you)
Widźu će	= I see you
Boli mje žołdk	= My stomach aches
Dyrbju sej nowu drastu kupić	= I must buy myself a new suit

If two such enclitic pronouns occur in the same clause, then the Reflexive usually takes precedence over the other, e.g.:—

Chce so wam jědźe?	= Do you want food? i.e. Have you an appetite?
Zda so mi, (zo ...)	= It seems to me (that)

---

[1] Both mi and mje can occur in initial position, especially in poetry. E.g. Mje mocnje ćehnje wutroba (Marja Kubašec) = My heart is strongly drawn...Mi žiwjenje bě boj a běda (Ćišinski) = Life for me meant (lit. was) struggle and woe.

But also:
Mi so dźije = It seems to me

If these pronouns occur with the auxiliary verbs, however, they are usually put after them, even when the auxiliary verb is not the first word in the sentence:

Dosć smy so zapozdźili	= We are rather late
Snadź by wam kurotwa lěpje słodzała?	= Perhaps you would prefer partridge?
Sobustawy su sej wšitcy runi	= The members are all equal (to one another)
Štó je ći prajił?	= Who told you?
Njerady bych so wróćil	= I would not like to come back
Njebyšće sej přał kusk twarožka?	= Would you not like a piece of cheese?
Miliduch je so za blido sydnył	= Miliduch has sat down at the table
Što je so stało?	= What has happened?

But notice:—

Mi je so dźało = It seemed to me

The other (often monosyllabic) Personal Pronouns may also be without emphasis in a sentence, but they are regularly put after the true enclitics:

Tak mi jón tola daj!	= But *give* it (masc.) to me then!
Rjeknu jej to	= I shall tell her that

Notice that -*li* takes precedence over other enclitics:—

Dowoliće-li mi ... = If you will allow me ...

3. The conjunctions: da (dha) = then, drje = it is true, indeed (like Cz. sice), and dźě = but (in remonstrance), are also regularly treated as enclitics:

Wy drje hižo wěsće	= You, it is true, already know
Što dha je z našim wjerchom?	= What then has happened to our prince?

Likewise often with: tola = but (cf. Germ. doch), and usually with :pječa = they say, e.g.:—

To tola stań!	= But get up then!
Wy sće tola dyrbjała prjedy ke mni přińć	= You should have come to me before, you know
To pječa wěrno njeje	= They say (or: I've heard) that's not true

LOWER LUSATIAN
MAIN DIFFERENCES IN MORPHOLOGY WHEN COMPARED WITH UPPER LUSATIAN

In the tables below we give the *main* instances in the morphology of Lower Lusatian in which it differs from Upper Lusatian apart from purely graphic differences due to differences of orthography and basic phonetic system.[1] For the sake of brevity we give the minimum of material on those forms in which the two dialects agree. We follow, as far as possible, the same order as in the preceding summary of Upper Lusatian morphology.

It should be noted that the Vocative case is not used in Lower Lusatian, except with a very few masc. nouns which have -*o*, e.g.: kněžo! = Sir!, synko! = sonny!, wujko! = uncle!, bratśiko! = little brother!, and some proper names.

In the Nom. dual and plural of all adjectives and pronouns (except Personal Pronouns) Lower Lusatian has the same ending for all genders *including* masc. personal: Nom. dual -*ej*, Nom. pl. -*e*.

1. Dual endings for all noun declensions:—

   Gen. dual   -*owu*
   Dat., Instr., Loc. dual -*oma*

2. Feminine *i*-stems:

   Gen. sing. -*i/y*. Upper Lusatian -*e* in nearly all nouns

3. Neuter consonantal stems:

   znamje   = sign   zwěrje(Gen. zwěrjeśa) =
   Instr. sg. znamjenim   beast
                              zwěrjeśim

4. Masculine *o*-stems:

   Dat. sg. -*oj*(*u*)   Upper L. -*ej*
   Nom. dual -*a*   "   "   -*aj*

5. Neuter *o*-stems:

   Instr. sg. -*im* for those with Nom. sg. in -*e*, e.g.: daśe = giving, Instr. sg. daśim

---

[1] See *The main phonetic features of Lower Lusatian* under "The Lusatian Dialects", pp. 370-373.

6. Numerals:

	Cardinals	Ordinals
1	jaden, jadna, jadno	prědny
2	dwa, dwě	drugi
3	tśo, tśi	tśeśi
4	styrjo, styri	stworty
5	pěś	pěty
6	šesć	šesty
7	sedym	sedymy
8	wosym	wosymy
9	źewjeś	źewjety
10	źaseś	źasety
-teens	-asćo	jadnasty, etc.

tens:
20-40	-źasća	dwaźasty, etc.
50-90	-źaset	pěśźasety, etc.
100	sto or hundert	hundertny, stoty
1,000	{ źaseś stow, źaseś hundertow, or towzynt or tysac	towzyntny, tysacny

both = wobej

7. Demonstrative Pronouns:

(toś) ten (ta, to) = this
    Loc. sg. masc. neut. tom
    Instr. sg. fem. teju
    Dat. Instr. Loc. dual tyma (-ma for *all* pronouns)

8. Interrogative Pronouns:

chto? = who?   co? = what?   ceji? = whose?
                                            kaki? what kind of?

        Gen. cogo
        Dat. comu
        Instr. cym
        Loc. com

9. Indefinite Pronouns:
něcht(en) = someone

10. Relative Pronouns:

chtož = who, což = what
kotaryž, kotaraž, kotarež, and kenž (invariable) = which

11. Possessive Pronouns:

        masc. moj = my, fem. moja
- Gen. sg. m.n. mojogo, etc.
- Instr. sg.f.   mojeju
- Loc. sg. m.n. mojom

So also the other Possessive Pronouns: twoj, naš, etc.

12. Definitive Pronouns:
- wšen, wša, wšo = all, Gen.s.m.,n. wšogo, etc.
- wšyken, wšykna, wšykno = all, " " " " wšyknogo, etc.
- młogeraki } = of many kinds
- wjelesery
- hynakšy   = different
- teliki   = so great
- teliko   = so much
- kuždy   = each
- taki, kaki   = such, as
- wotery   = many a
- samski   = the same
- sam, sama, samo = alone, self
  - Gen. s.m.,n. samego, etc.

13. Negative:
- nicht(en)   = no one
- žeden, Gen. sg. masc., neut. žednogo, = no

14. Personal Pronouns:

3rd pers.—
- Sing. Nom.   won = he   wono = it   wona = she
- Gen.   jogo, etc.
- Instr.   njeju
- Loc.   njom
- Dual Nom.   wonej (*all* genders)
  - Dat., Instr., Loc. jima/nima
- Plur. Nom. woni (*all* genders)

ja = I, Gen.,(Dat.,)Acc.,(Loc.) mnjo,
    Dat., Loc. also mnje, Instr. mnu

ty = thou, Gen., Dat., Act., Loc. tebje,
    Instr. tobu

Enclitics: mě Dat. *and Acc.* sg. from ja
          śi " " " " from ty

Dual Nom. mej = we two, wej = you two

Reflexive:
    Acc.,Gen.,Dat. and Loc. sebje, enclitic se = self

15. Adjectives:
   Loc. sg. masc. and neut.   -em but Instr. sg. -ym/
                              -im (Upper L. Instr.
                              and Loc. sg. m.n. -ym/
                              -im)
   Instr. sg. fem.   -eju
   Nom. (Acc.) dual   -ej for all genders
   Dat. Instr. Loc. dual   -yma (-ima)
   Nom. plur.   -e for all genders

16. Superlatives: nej(ž) + Comparative
   nejwušy = highest, nejkrotšy = shortest,
            nejmocnjejšy = strongest

17. Adverbs from adjectives in -ski have only -ski:
   němski = in German (fashion)
      Comparative adverbs all end in -'ej:
   dalej = further, šyrjej = more widely,
   dłymjej = deeper, wěcej = more
      Notice:
   źo? = where?, how, toś or tudy = here, gdy? =
   when?, něnt(o) = now, cora = yesterday, witśe =
   to-morrow, žednje = never; jo = yes, ně = no;
   cogodla? = why?

18. Conjunctions

   teke, tež   = also
   lěc(...lěc)   = whether(...or)
   žgan   = indeed, really
   weto   = despite, nevertheless
   gaž, gdyž   = when, if; ga = then*
   toś   = then, so
   až   = that
   aby   = (in order) that
   gaby   = if
   joli až, jolic   = in case, if
   (lěc) rownož
   rownož   }   = although
   dokulaž   = because
   daś(i)   = would that
   lěc, lic   = whether

19. Prepositions:
   With Gen.:   bźez(e)   = without
                pódla, pla = near
   With Acc.:   wob   = during
                mjaz(y)   = (to) between, among
   With Instr.: mjaz(y)   = between, among
Notice: mojogodla = for my sake, etc., with Gen.
        form of Possessive Pronoun.

   *in the main clause, cf. German so, Russian то

20. Verbs[1]:

Infinitive in -ś (or -ć after a sibilant, e.g. njasć = to carry, or -c for velar stems of Class I, e.g. pjac = to bake).
Supine: in -t, e.g.: njast = to carry, but Cl. I velar stems have -c, e.g.: pjac. The Supine is used only after verbs of motion, e.g. Du tam glědat = I am going there to have a look.
Negative: nje-.
Conditional auxiliary verb: by, for *all* persons.

21. Endings:

(A)
Pres. and Imperative: dual 1 -*mej*, 2 and 3 (all genders) -*tej*, plur. 2 -*šo*. In the Imperative the form for the 2nd pers. sg. is also used for 3rd pers. sg. For 3rd pers. plur. daś(i) with the 3rd pers. plur. of the Pres. is used.
Imperfect: 2nd and 3rd pers. sing. -*šo*
Imperfect and Aorist: dual 1 -*chmej*
                          2 and 3 -*štej* (all genders)
                 plur. 2 -*śćo*

22. Cl. I-III have -o- joining vowel in Pres., except in 1st pers. sing. and 3rd pers. plur., e.g.:—

Class I. njasć = to carry, II. wuknuś = to learn, III. piś = to drink
        pisaś = to write

Pres. sg. 1	njasu *or* njasom	wuknu *or* wuknjom	piju *or* pijom	pišu
2	njasoš	wuknjoš	pijoš	pišoš
pl. 2	njasośo	wuknjośo	pijośo	pišośo
3	njasu	wuknu	piju	pišu
Imperfect	njasech	Aor. nawuknuch	wupich	
Fut.	ponjasu			

Past Part. Act.
  sg. masc. njasł   wuknuł
  pl. (*all* genders) njasli

Pres. Part. (uncertain):[2]
        njasecy *but* wuknjecy   pijucy   pisajucy *or* mogucy   pišucy

---

[1]In popular speech only, the passive can also be formed with wordowaś (or werdowaś) instead of byś, followed by the Past Participle Passive as in Upper Lusatian popular speech.

[2]It should be noted that the Present *Gerund* in Lower Lusatian is the same in form as the Nom. sing. masc. of the Present Participle.

Past Part. Pass.
                njasony   wuknjony   pity   pisany

Cl. I. Note:
  naceś = to broach(Pfve.), Fut. nacnu, nacnjoš, etc.
                              or   naceju, nacejoš, etc.
  w(e)ześ´ = to take(Pfve.)   Fut. wezmu, wezmjoš, etc.
                              or   wzeju, wzejoš, etc.

  Like pić, verbs in -owaś; Inf. žałowaś = to
  mourn, Pres. žałuju or žałujom, Imperf.
  žałowach

  Like pisaś, e.g.:
    płakaś = to weep   Pres. płacom or płaku,
                                 płacoš[1]
    šepotaś = to whisper,   "   šepocu, šepocoš
    drapaś = to scratch,   "   drapju, drapjoš

  (and many other labial stem verbs in -aś)

    woraś = to plough, Pres. worju, worjoš

23. Class IV: *no* soft stems. źěłaś (= to work),
    identical with Cl. IV.1 in Upper L., but with
    above endings (A in No. 21) as for Cl. I-III
    of Lower L. Only Pres. Participle has -*ajucy*:
    źěłajucy.

  Compound verbs formed from verbs of Cl. IV require an *uncontracted Present*:—

    pytam = I seek, pśepyt*ajom* = I am looking
    through; *but* pśepyt*am* = I *shall* look through.

24. Cl. V: Infin. paliś = to burn, pšosyś = to re-
    quest; also: leśeś = to fly, zasłyšaś = to
    hear (Pfve.)

    Pres. sg. 1   palim   pšosym
          pl. 3   pale   pšose
    Imper. sg. 2   (pal!)   pšos!
    Imperfect   (palach)   pšosach   leśech
    Aorist formed from Infin., by replacing -*ś* with
    -*ch*, etc.:
                   spalich wupšosych wulećech zasłyšach
    Pres.Part.:palecy   pšosecy
    Past Part. palony   pšosony (topjony from topiś =
    Pass.   to heat)

[1]So also: pałkaś = to wash, launder.

25. Verbs with Infin, in *-ojaś*, *-ejaś*, and *-ojś* have contracted Present and Aorist without *i*, thus: stojaś = to stand:—

    Pres.sg. 1 stojm   dual 1 stojmej   plur. 1 stojmy
             2 stojš   2, 3 stojtej   2 stojśo
             3 stoj   3 stoje

         zakłojś = to prick, Aor. zakłojch

So also:

     se bojaś = to fear, łojś = to catch,
     dejaś   = to have to, etc.

Compound verbs formed from verbs of Cl. V, like compound verbs of Cl. IV, also have uncontracted Present endings and contracted Future endings:

     se gorjeś   = to burn (intrans.)
     se zagorjejo = it burns up (intrans.)
     se zagorjo   = it will burn up (intrans.)
     wucym   = I learn
     powucyju   = I teach
     powucym   = I shall teach

Athematic verbs:

26. byś = to be

     Pres. sg. 1 som   Imperat. buź   Aor. buch
                3 jo   bu
           pl. 2 sćo   etc.
     Fut. sg. 1 budu *or* buźom
                2 buźos
           pl. 1 buźomy
               3 budu

Neg. Pres.: njejsom, njejo, etc.

Conditional: *by*—for all persons, preceded by pers. pronoun.
Past Conditional: sg. 1   buźach *or* ja by był
                        2 and 3 buźašo *or* ty by był, etc.
Fut. Participle: buducy

27.
	weźeś	jěsć	daś
	= to know	= to eat	= to give (Pfve.)
Pres. sg. 2	weš	ješ	daš
pl. 3	weźe	jěźe	daźe *or* daju
Imperative	wěz	jěz	daj
Imperfect	wěźech	jěźech	
Aorist	(powěch[1] *or* powjeźech[1])	(zjěch)	(wu-dach)
Pres. Part.	wěźecy	jěźecy	dajucy
Past Part. Act.	wěźeł	(jědł)	(dał)
Past Part. Pass.	wěźony	zjěźony	dany

[1]= I announced

Verbal Noun: dańe *or* daśe

Irregular verbs:

28. hyś = to go (Impfve.)
    Pres. sg. 1 du   Imperative źi   Imperf. źěch
                (Aor. pśiźech = I came)
    2 źoš
    3 źo
    pl. 3 du
    Past Part Act. šeł, šła Fut. pojdu, pojźoš,
    etc. Imperat. pojź! Negative Pres.
    nje*j*du, etc.

    So also: wujšeł = gone out (Past Part. Act.),
    from wujś; Imperat. wujź(i); pśiź(i) = come!

29. kśěś = to want
    Pres.sg. 1 cu *or* com   neg. njok   Imperfect: kśěch
             2 coš   njocoš
    pl. 3 kśě *or* coju   njekśě

30. měś = to have, Pres. mam, maš, etc. (reg.) has
    the negative form: njamam, njamaš, etc. Im-
    perat.: měj! Future: změju, změjoš, etc.

31. łdgaś = to tell lies
    Pres.sg.1 łdžu   Imperative (nje)łdžy *or*
             2 ldžoš   (nje)łdgaj
    pl.3 łdžu *or*
         łdgaju

32.   mjasć   wjasć   mlaś
        = to sweep   = to lead   = to grind
    Pres. sg. 1 mjetu   wjedu   mjelu or mleju
              2 mješoš,etc. wježoš,etc.   mjeloš " mlejoš
    Imperat.   mješ!   wjeź!   mjel!   " mlej!
    Imperf.   mješech,etc. wježech,etc. mjelach " mlejach

                        Aor. zemlach
    But
    Past Part.
        Act. mjatł   wjadł   mlał
                   P.P. Passive mlaty

33. moc - to be able, Pres. mogu (*or* možom), možoš,
    Past Part. Act. mogał *or* mogł; Imperfect
    možach; neg. njamoc

34. rjac = to speak
    Pres. sg. 1 rjacom or rjaknu Imperative rjac!
              2 rjacoš " rjaknjoš
                              etc.
         pl. 3 rjaku

35. Irregular verbs, Cl. V:

držaś = to tremble
  Pres. sg. 1 držym, etc. Imperative drži or držaj!
       pl. 3 držyju or držaju
gorjeś se = to burn   but goriś = to anger
              (intrans.),
  Pres. sg. 1 gorju se   gorim
         2 gorjoš se   goriš
  Pres. Part. gorjecy   gorucy = burning,
                                       rutting
  Imperf.   gorješo se   gorjašo se = (he) was
                                      getting angry
spaś = to sleep
  Pres. sg. 1 spim
       pl. 3 spě (spje)
  Pres. Part. spicy or spijucy
spomnjeś = to remember (Pfve.)
  Fut. sg. 1 spomnjeju or spomnu or *rarely* spomnim
         2 spomnjejoš or spomnjos or *rarely*
                                        spomniš
  Aor. sg. 1 spomnjech
  Imperat.   spomnjej!
zněś = to sound
  Pres. sg. 3 zni (or znějo)
       pl. 3 zně (or zněju)

LOWER LUSATIAN WORD ORDER WITH ENCLITICS

1. Enclitic Personal Pronouns are always put second (never first) word in the sentence, in contrast to occasional usage in Upper Lusatian.

2. With reflexive verbs the Reflexive Pronoun *se* is kept as near to its verb as possible, usually preceding it.

TEXTS
UPPER LUSATIAN

I. Swjate Evangelium Jězusa Chrystusa po Lukašu, Staw VIII.

5. Syjer wuńdźe, zo by swoje symjo wusywał. A hdyž syješe, padźe někotre při pući, a bu rozteptane, a ptaki njebja zjěchu je. 6. A druhe padźe na skału, a zeschadźawši wuschny, dokelž włóhi njeměješe. 7. A druhe padźe mjez ćernje, a ćernje sobu rosćechu a podusychu je. 8. A druhe padźe do dobreje zemje, a hdyž bě narostło, přinjese stotory płód. To prajiwši

zawoła: Štóž ma wuši k słyšenju, njech słyši.

(Translated from the Vulgate by Juri Łusčanski and Michał Hórnik; Budyšin, 1896.)

II. H. Zejler.

Hola

Hdyž chce nas zyma spóžerać,
Hdyž wějo ćmi so w polu:
Štó lěsa chwalbu njespěwać,
Štó chcył mi zacpić holu?
   Stup, towaršo mój předuty,
   Do jstwički ćišišeje,
   Do stołpatej' pój drjewiny,
   Hdyž w polu wućek njeje.

O hola, zymy skludźerka,
Štó njewě, kak nam słužiš?
Přez wopor twojoh' bohatstwa
Najhórkšu zymu stužiš;
   Hdyž chwatajo do ćopłej' jstwy
   Połmódri huhotamy:
   Dha wěmy, što ći dołžimy,
   A što na tebi mamy.

Dha hordź so w włóskach zelenych,
Kiž twoje dźěći pyša;
Hordź so do časow šedźiwych,
A kaž će sněhi tyša
   Twój njewjestny wěnc njezblědnje,
   Hdyž lěta chód so minje,
   Hdyž wo krónu haj žaruje
   A krasnosć łukow zhinje!

III. H. Zejler.

Při kolebcy

Do zahrodki wětřik duł
A lisćička tam zelene je hnuł,
Z ćicha zynčeše;
Lisća spinkajće! Haj!

Jandźelko naš lubozny,
Nětk spinkaj, złoty hołbiko, tež ty!
   Lubosć maćerna
   Njespi, njedrěma. Haj!

Na hałzy spja ptačatka,
Je kryje štom a z lisćom wodzěwa,
   Stražu na tebi.
   Dźerža jandźelki. Haj!

Tuj, tuj, złote dźěćatko,
Nank, maćerka za tebje stara so,
  Strachi zdaluje
  Mjechcy pósćele. Haj!

W zbóžnym měrje, kurko, spi,
Nětk hišće swěći złote słónčko ći,
  Dóńž će njebudźa
  Rany žiwjenja. Haj!

Dóńž će starosć njebudźi,
Zamkń módre kukulatko, změrom spi,
  Nasa róžička,
  Naša lilija! Haj!

IV. Herta Wićazec

Čista wutroba

Čista wutroba
Je ta róžička,
Kiz na kóždym pućú kćěje,
Hdźež so boža lubosć směje,
Hdźež so zjednoća
Z wěru nadźěja.

Čista wutroba
Je ta studnička,
Kiž nam dawa móc a sylnosć,
K dobrym skutkam prawu swěrnosć,
A we hórkosći
Dušu wokřewi.

Čista wutroba
Je ta hwězdźička,
Kiž we ćmowej smjertnej nocy,
Hdyž nam zańdu naše mocy,
Miłu jasnosć da
Na puć do njebja.

Čista wutroba
Słódke spanje`da,
Hdźež po sprócnym ćežkim dźěli,
Kiž smy tudy dźělać měli,
Smjerć nas powoła
K měrej do rowa.

Čista wutroba
Wjedźe do njebja,
Pyši nas pri božim trónu
Z njezachodnej krasnej krónu;
Čista wutroba
Wěčnu zbóžnosć ma.

V. Jakub Ćišinski.

> Kak naleco nas slepić znaje!

Kastanija tam přede wsu
Je tysac swěcow zaswěćiła,
Na bozu módre kiće ktu,
Hdźež ze wsy kołsa rěčka čiła.

W nim sołobik sej pišćeli,
A bóle z bozu wóń so roni,
Kastanija so wjeseli
A žołma wyska, žołma zwoni ...

A do wutroby padnyło
Mi sonow bě a róžow rjanych,
Kaž w lětach před tym njebyło
By wichorow a sněhow žanych.

A we wutrobje nadźija
Sej zaswěća, hdyž lód w njej taje,
Kaž přede wsu kastanija—
Kak naleco nas slepić znaje!

VI. Jakub Ćišinski.

> Tužne połdnjo

Na polach leži mjelčina,
A žadyn wětřičk njezadunje;
Na hłowu słónco pali runje,
A stysknje soni ćišina.

A zemja dycha z tužnotu
Wot kćěwa, spěwa pohłušena!
A wote zboža podušena
Je zdrěmnyła sej z mučnotu.

VII. Jakub Ćišinski.

> Wosud wutroby

Sam doma sedźu, sedźo sam sej płakam,
Mi šěri něšto wutrobu a spina,
Mje wabi zbože a mje traši wina;
Před winu ćěkam a na zbože čakam.

Kaž worjoł wysoko ja w myslach łakam
A nizko jimatej mje próch a hlina.
Kaž škowrončk zběhnyć a do zemje klina
Kaž błysk mohł wrjesnyć so!— Tuž sam sej płakam—

Chcył lećeć z wichorom, ze słóncom horić
A chodźić z hwězdami a rěčeć z róžu
A wobraz duše namkać we krystalu!

O hrozna hra! Hač zymny sym hač palu
So, ničo njejsym, ničo njezamóžu,
Haj ani sebje znjesć a wjesć a tworić!

VIII. Jakub Ćišinski.

Worjołej

Mój worjoło, to bědne běchu časy,
Hdyž z lesću jachu će a do ćmy spnychu—
Straš z křidłow nóc! Kiž skóncować će chcychu,
Su do ćmy bjezdna zwjazani kaž djasy.
Drje wuzespinać móžachu na pasy
Ći křidłow móc a kamjeń walić k dychu
A rozcychnować hordych pjerjow pychu,
Nic chrobłosć pak a krej a krutosć rasy—
Leć do hór nět' a z duchom móc a jasnosć
Pij, kotraž ćeče z njebjeskeho stoła,
A z hwězdow sebi do pjerjow pleć krasnosć!
Staj na wjerch horow swojej' sławy krónu
A z horda zanjes do palčikow doła:
Štó móc ma w pjasći, sčinić ze mnje—wrónu?!

IX. Jakub Ćišinski.

Budyšin

Budź witane mi, stare město njepowalne!
Drje třepotało sy, hdyž z Frankom w dźiwim boju
stał Serb, hdyž w smjertnej bolosći sy piło swoju
krej; tola hišće stojiš, Serbstwa sydło skalne!

Drje zapusćał je cuzbnik twoje domy spalne,
krej twojich synow nječłowjeski teptał w hnoju,
a tola wutroby, hlej přez Łužicu dwoju
ći serbske serbski hišće bija njerozwalne!"

Hłós zańdźenych stolětow na tebje so roći:
„Stój kruće," hnuće prosy,„ Serbow swědko mócny,
zo stara sława wot tebje so njewobroći!"

Stój, o stój kruće, Serbstwa strážniko ty wótcny,
broń so, zo žadyn wichor tebje njerozkoći;
budź jasna hwězda Serbej, hdyž chce padnyć spróćny!

X. Jakub Ćišinski.

Zdźerž serbski lud!

Słyš, knježe, hdyž swój paćer praju:
    Zdźerž serbski lud!
We wótcnym mojim lubym kraju
    Zdźerž serbski lud!
Kiž módre hory nam a hona nam zelene
A ptačkow spěwy škitaš w haju,
    Zdźerž serbski lud!

Hdyž wótcow rěč a ród a rolu zańč nimaju,
Na mać a statok zabywaju,
    Zdźerž serbski lud!
Daj lubosć do wutrobow z njebjes, móc do stawow,
Hdyž swěrne woci zapłakaju:
    Zdźerž serbski lud!
Ty ludy wodźiš, kraje škitaš a sudźiš bróń;
Hdyž dźiwje mocy zahrimaju,
    Zdźerž serbski lud!
Njech tebi hłós mój šepta přeco tu modlitwu,
Hdyž do procha tež w rowje stłaju:
    Zdźerž serbski lud!

XI. (Folk Tale.)

Wucho abo kurjatko

    Borkač přiwjedźe sebi kmótra Hansa na kermušu. Jeho za blido sadźiwši, počina nože rjedźić a točić. Žona pak pječe w kuchini kurjatko, a po kucharsku woptawa a woptawa, hač běchu so kurjatka minyłe. Ale kak mohła so nětko wuřečeć? Zbožowna myslička ji připadźe. Muž zańdźe na najstwu, zo by tam po něčo dóšoł. Spěšnje suny so žona do jstwy a poča: „Hdy byšće wědźał, kmótře, što mój muž z wami chce. Chce wam wuši wotrězać—wbohi je druhdy přemysleny. Ćekńće, kmótře, ale spěšnje!" Kmótr naboja so a chwataše z dwora won. Po chwili přińdźe muž dele. „Hdźe je kmótr?" wopraša so. „O," dźeše žona, „ty sy sebi praweho njeplecha do domu přiwjedł; přilěze tón čłowjek do kuchinje a wzawši kurjatka ćekny z dwora." Muž njewotpołožiwši noža, kotryž měješe w ruce, běžeše hnydom za kmótrom wołajo: „Kmótře! jenož jedne mi daj!" Kmótr mysleše na wucho a nóžkowaše bóle dyžli prjedy.

XII. J. Radyserb-Wjela.

Herc

Sym herc we Serbach znajomy,
Mje wšudźom witaja,
A maju dźeń hdźe wjesoły,
Mój smyk jim zejhrawa.

Kaž włosancki 'nož smykowe
Na truny pomasnu,
So hnuja črjowka wjerćane
A jasnje wyskaju.

Ja hudźu młodej njewjesći
A spěšnym kwasarjam,
A kmótram hlej po wječeri
Ja žiły wubudźam.

Su ćěslojo hdźe zběhali
Sej po mnje sćeleja;
Jim zajusknu te truny tři
Na reju do koła.

A wječor na mnje wjesela
So młode třiharki.
Jim lóžka nóžka wjertliwa
Po huslach poskoči.

Ma rychły ludźik swjatoka
Na trawnym radniku,
Ja zahudźu— a młodźina
So wjerći pod lipu.

Wšě rjane dźowki korčmarske
Mi rady porjedźa,
Pak njepowěm ja, kotra je
Mi ze wšěch najlubša.

XIII. K. A. Fiedler

Hudźba

Ty wodźiš mje na hona jasne,
Čěr ludaprózdnu ćich'omnu,
A moje pŕeća, sony krasne
So swěća tebi we wočku.

Njech swět mje tyši, přepóznawa,
Ty wěš, što pjelni wutrobu.
Wšak twoja rěč mi wěstosć dawa,
Zo znaješ radosć, stysknotu.

A sym ja přišoł chudy k tebi,
Tu nabych drohich kubłow dosć:
Hlej, pokoj duše dobych sebi,
Móc a horjo a zbožownosć.

XIV. M. Andricki.

From „Zyma"

Minyłe su so lubozne dny lětnjeje krasnosće; zemje płody su hižo dawno pod rólnikowej třěchu schowane, wšě jeho dźěła na polu dokonjane; nowe zorno hižo wusyte, zo by k lětu ćim rjeńše płody přinjesło. W lěsu a w holi je woćichnył lubozny spěw wjesołeje ptačiny, kotraž je nas wopušćiła a do čoplišich krajinow so wróćiła. Štomy su młódne lisćo zhubiłe, pola a łuki krasnych kwětkow wotbyłe. Dźiwi wětr honi čorne mróčele po zaćmowjenym njebju; pastyr ćěri swoje stadło z trawneje podhórki do wowčernje; tyšna ćěka dźiwja zwěrina před hańskimi třělbami, ze smjerću a zahubenjom ji hrožacymi, a zaběhnje drje sebi husto do blizkosće čłowjeskich wobydlenjow, zo by nuzneje picy nadešła.

Husto je njebjo cyły dźeń z tołstymi mróčelemi pokryte a słónco so často ani njepokaza. Dny su ćmowiše přecy a krótše. Młóccy dźěłaju nětk dźeń wob dźeń w bróžni, žony a młode holcy pak schadźeja so na dołhich wječorach k přazy a bjesadźe. Čmowe njebjo saje sněh, kotryž kaž mjechka płachta młode sywy pokrywa a wohrěwa. Hatk a rěka mjerznje a z tym nastanje za dźěći nowe wjesele: ćahaja sebi na hornjej łubi sanje z kuta a wjesele woža so na nich přez hórki a dólčki. Často drje tón abo tamny pachołk wotleći a so do zymneho sněha kuli; to wšak so lochce zabudźe. Woprawdźe, tež zyma ma swoje wjesela, wosebje za dźěci!

XVś M. Andricki.

From „Pytach hospodu"

Wšak su tež druhdźe hišće rozswětlene wokna— rozumiće: bohaće rozswětlene, kaž su w hosćencach, a hołk a hara za nimi, kaž w hosćencach bywa.

A njewuběrach dołho, ale zaměrich hnydom na přeni tajki dom, kotryž mi do wočow padźe. Ale z krutym zamysłom, zo jim złameneho pjenježka njepopřeju, jelizo mi jene njepopřeja, štož bě mi nětkle najwažniše: hospodu. Tuž njeńdźech hakle do jstwy mjez hosći, ale wostach hnydom w chěži. Běše ćmowa, ale na druhim kóncu miškorješe so latarnja. Mi bě tale latarnja hwězda nadźije: snadź je při njej sam hosćencar; pońdu k njemu a porěču z nim mudre słowčko. Hosćencar tam njeběše, bě pak tam knjeni korčmarka, štož běše mi skónčnje tež prawje. Na nizkim stólčku tam sedźeše a sebi w dójńccy noze myješe. Žona kaž řeznik, skoro strašna, tak wulka bě a tołsta. Mój respekt bě wězo wulki a tohodla přednjesech swoju próstwu rjenje a ponižnje, kaž jenož móžno. Ale njepobych lěpje, hač we prjedawšimaj hosćencomaj.

„My žanych hosći na nóc njebjerjemy!" wotrubny tón řeznik, kaž by ze sekeru rubał.

„Ale njebudźće tola hrozna"— wobarach so ja zaso cyle pokornje— „Wsako ja ničo wosebne njeźadam. Ja sym ze wšěm spokojom. Jenož zo mohł něhdźe hłowu položić. Zo njemóžu na dróze ležo wostać, to tola sama widźiće. Nimaće dha nihdźe kućika za mnje!"

Žónka bu přećelniša— ale pomhać mi njemóžese. Woni hewak scyła nikoho na nóc njebjeru, tola dźensa by mi skónčnje rad k woli była. Ale dźensa njemóžeše. Runje je so jim daloki wuj z cyłej swójbu nawalił, a tak budźa dźensa sami na syno dyrbjeć. „To hižo dyrbiće dźensa dale hić. Móže być, zo maju pola Taborskeho hišće łožo. Dźiće tam pohladać: je to štwórte twarjenje wot nas dele. Runje před Wami smy tam jenoho knjeza pósłali."

XVI. Jan Skala.

Přećiwo Wšoněmcam

Smy njewólnicy byli, bići, chudźi
Přez tysac lět, a ze wšěch stron sće dřěli
Nam krej a kraj, kiž w pazorach sće měli
Nas, zacpětych a sćerpnych serbskich ludźi!

Nětk, hdyž waš hrěch was ze wšěch stronow smudźi,
Nas wot was narodny duch razny dźěli,
Nam swěri k serbskosći so w duši želi
A mozach, a nas z mortwych staću błudźi!

Pod chorhoj, bratřa, módru, čerwjenu a bělu
So stupmy! Njedajmy so zastrašić, so zabić
A z wšoněmskosću pohłušić a słabić!

My móc smy, z kruteju hdyž wolu
Sej wobaramy serbski dom a rolu
A ruce wšě sej zawdawamy k dźělu!

XVII. Měrćin Nowak-Njechorński.

Adwent!

Šěre dny leniwje so wlečeja wot nocy k nocy, husta kurjawa je zapopada, we swojich šlewjerjach, hrozy je zadusyć z nimi jako z łojawkami złowólneho demona.

Płowe lisćo storhane wot štomow, tłaje po dornje a dešćikowe kapki bubnuja jemu pohrjebne přezpolo.

A na njedźelu zemrětych— jako hdy by chcyło wusnyć, haj mrěć wšitko— přiroda, žiwjenje, swět, njebjesa ...

Njeje-li nadźije?

A je—přetož tu je adwent!

A d w e n t— přichad— kelko tajneho kuzła, kelko mócneho powaba chowa tuto słowo!

Je jako zernička po dołhej, dołhej nocy, jako přeni spěwčk ptačika po dołhej surowej zymje, je znamjo nadźije, dowěry k přichodej.

A d w e n t tu je— nam je, jako bychmy po dołhim wobćežnym pućowanju skónčnje we ćmowej nocy nadešli swój wukónc— škitacy wućek, wuchow. Hižo stejimy před durjemi, hižo swětło so k nam dobywa přez wokna a my słuchamy a čakamy a wěmy: „Bórze, bórze nam wotčinja, bórze budźemy wuchowani ...

A d w e n t; — hišće tu čakamy, ale čakamy z ćichej radosću, přetož nam je so dóstało znamjo

nadźije. Wěmy, zo podarmo nječakamy ...
 Njech złowólna kurjawa spyta zadusyć běłe dny
ze šěrej pawčinu, njech dešć a šwihel šrumi pohrjebne
přezpolo přirodźe, njech wichor bóle howri— my wěmy,
přińdźe k nam swětło.
 A d w e n t, a d w e n t! Štó móhł so přećiwjeć
twojemu mócnemu kuzłu?
 Hižo po zemi so znošuja cunje potajne zwuki,
njewidźomne mocy, kiž potajnje skutkuja a přihotuja
žedźace čłowjestwo na radostny dźeń— hody ...
 A d w e n t— pomałku jimaš a sputaš tež
najstruchlišeho zadwělowarja, małomyslneho, tak zo
zasy wěrić dokonja a nawuknje měć zasy dowěru a
nadźiju.
 Zbože so nam dóstanje, wumóženje— to nam
připowěduje adwent.
 A serbski narod?
 Wón je so předrěł přez ćmowe mhły přećiwnych
mocow. Wichor howrješe a torhaše lisćičko po druhim
wot hałozow serbskeje lipy. A zdaše so, jako by
surowy wichor chcył bórze šumic nad rowom serbskeje
narodnosće ...
 S e r b s k i a d w e n t!
 Hišće přećiwny wichor hrózbnje ruje a wuje, ale
serbsku lipu hižo njewuwróći. My so jeho njebojimy!—
 S e r b s k i a d w e n t!
 My smy přećerpili surowy dóńt, keluch z jěrym
napojom smy wupili hač do dna— nětk hladamy
wumóženja, wukupjenja, spomoženja ...
 A wěrimy do serbskeho přichoda.
 A pomałku nadźija so nam wróći do strušenych,
strašenych wutrobow.
 A pomałku dwěl a małomyslnosć so kradnje z
našich mysličkow, a dowěry nabywamy.
 A dwent, a dwen t!
 Čakajmy na přikhad wumóženja, přihotujmy so,
budźmy hotowi, hotowi ...!

LOWER LUSATIAN

I. (Folk Tale.)

Wodny muž a mjadwjeź

 I. W starodawnych casach pšiźe raz mjadwjeźař z
mjadwjeźom na wjacor do Kozlikojc młyna a wosta tam
pšez noc, dokulaž młynik běšo jogo stary znaty.
Zwěrje běšo do tłukarnje zawrěte. Na zajtšo pšiłěze
wodny muž do tłukarnje a kśasašo wogeń, aby sebje
snidanje zwarił; togodla běšo sebje brodatu karpu a
někotare śćipjeły sobu pšinjasł. Mjadwjeźa wubuźi
swětło. Cujašo a glědašo, co to by było. Zaprědka

se njewěrjašo, ale naslědku pśilěze k wogńu, źož wodny muž w kotle z jagłoweju měšawku swojo snidanje měšašo a wobraśašo. Gdyž běchu dosć warjone, wuśěgnu nyks (wodny muž) karpu a zachopi ju kusaś. Mjadwjeź to wiźecy tyknu też pazory do kotlika a wuśěgnu sebje śćipjeła. Něto akle wupytnu jogo wodny muž, pozwignu měšawku a rjaknu: „Kac, abo śi dam plac!" To pak jogo njewotegna; won sebje hyśći raz rybu wuśěgnu. Zasej jomu wodny muž rowno tak grozašo, ale podermo; dokulaž lěbda běšo mjadwjeź śćipjeła požrěł, wustrě južo zasej pazoru. Ale něto jogo wodny muž z łopatku kšuśe pśepraska. Ale chej! Lěbda jogo klapnu, wobojmje jogo rozgněwane zwěrje tak kšuśe, až won z bolosću zakśika a tak dłujko wołašo, až młynik a jogo gosć to słyšaštej a mjadwjeźa wotegnaštej. Wodny muž pak chwatajcy do wody zlěze.

Młynik běšo južo dawno na to wšo zabył, ako pśichodne lěto na Mariju naraz zasłyša wołaś: „Luby młyniko, maš ga hyśći tu groznu kocku?"—

„To se wě," wotgroni młynik, „a mam hyśći styri młode wot njeje, kotarež su źewjeś raz gorše nježli ta stara."— „Ga potom božemje!" źašo wodny mužyk a njebu źednje wěcej we młynje wiźony.

II. Jan Greško.

Grod „Sedym dubow" pla Mišna

Mjazy Drježdźanami a Mišnom na lěwem brjoze Łobja rozpadańki grodu „Sedym dubow" laže; na tom měsće nět mała cerkwja „Pšosarikowa cerkwja" pomějona stoj.

Wokoła lěta 1000 tam stojašo mocny grod, na kotremž sejźašo kněz Wrośisław. Ten južor běšo pśijaśel německego kejžora, kotaryž pśiźo raz na woglědy ku Wrośisławoju. Ten kejžoroju pokaza swoj grod a potom jogo wjeźašo do gumna, źož jomu pśedstawi swojich šesć synow. „Ja měnim, až ty maš sedym synow," źašo kejžor.— „Nic," jo rjakł Wrośisław; „mam jich jano šesć!"— No! wotegroni kejžor: „jo-li tak, potom tuder sajźim šesć dubow na wopomnjeśe, až som was wopytał." Potom kejžor wury šesć dubow a je sajźi. Na to kejžor grod wopuśći, a Wrośisław ze swojimi synami za nim na wojnu pśeśiwo Łužycanam śěgnješo.

W prěnjej bitwje pak bu jadyn jogo synow zabity wot někakego carnego ryśarja łužyskego. Gaž pak bu we drugej bitwje drugi syn z ruki togo samego ryśarja zabity, Wrośisław wěźašo, chto ten ryśar jo, kotaryž jomu synow zabija. To běšo jogo staršy syn, kotaregož won běšo zaprěł pśed kejžorom. Tak w kuždej bitwje jadyn syn Wrośisława zginu až do

nemłodšego, kotryž běšo doma wostał. Wrośisław z
tužyce a njespokojoneje wědobnosći wumrě. Tak bu
nejmłodšy syn kněz na wośćojskem groźe.

III. F. Rocha.

    Mojo gole

  Gdyž wjacor do postole
  Na swojo glědam gole,
  Kak rědnje z měrom spi;
  We zbožnej styknjom gluce
  Ja k njebju swojej ruce:
  Bog, gole zdźarž a zwarnuj śi!

  Gaž zajtša zasej rano
  Mě gole strowe stanjo
  A ruce styknijo:
  „Wośc-nas" swoj wubjatujo,
  Se k šuli pśigotujo,
  Mě swěta stysnosć wobojźo.

  A gaž pon we dnjo grajo,
  We gumnje zajuskajo,
  Kaž roža zakwita:
  Se cujom zas ak gole,
  Ned zajdu wšykne bole—
  Och cas ty złotneg' źiśestwa!

IV. F. Rocha.

    Noc

  Złotne słyńco zejźo domoj,
  Sledny błyść juž zgasujo;
  Noc se milna pušća dołoj
  A wša stworba k měru źo.

  Gwězdźina pśez njebjo kšaca
  Ako rědna njewjesta,
  Z swětłym pasom se wokasa,
  Kenž jo polny dejmanta.

  Wona sypjo słodke spanje
  Na wšych mucnych cłowjekow
  A podawa žognowanje
  Do wšych chamnych cłonaškow.

  W polach, w golach, wšudy spanje,
  Słodki měr wšo pśikšywa,
  Spokojne wotpocywanje,
  Wšudy swěta śišyna.

Noc, ty luba, och pśesćěraj
Twoje kśidła też na mnjo,
Nowe mocy zasej zběraj
A daj słodki měr do mnjo!

V. Mato Kosyk.

Maśerna rěc

Stare knorate štomisko
njewužytne se zezdanjo—
ale z jog' sprojtych korabjow
stwarje se žywy wot twarcow.

Młogi ma swoju maśernu rěc
za zestaranu sukatu wěc:
weto se wot njeje wuwiju
spěwne wěnaški z lažkosću.

Maśerna rěc jo też wot Boga
k sławjenju ducha nam darjona;
cuze ju do wěnkow splěśuju,
doma pak młoge ju stergaju.

VI. Mato Kosyk.

Nocne jagarje

Hajsa, hoj, hoj!
Jagarje nocne tšochtaju mocnje.
Pšec tud, pšec z puśa,
Jim won jan słuša,
Pši wašej gluce njepowjedajśo
Sromośejuce;— njewuźěrajśo!
Lichosć dej zgubiś,
Chtož bźo se zubiś!
Jagarje tšochtaju,
Psy z nimi nochtaju.
Hajsa, hoj, hoj!
Lej, drěmotka mychańc swoj pśestrějo
A Carnego Boga ryśarstwo
Se pokažo nět
A śěgnjo pśez swět.
Ta mań se nět zejźo.
Ta źiwa, a pśejźo.
Wot tłusteje kurjawy zawobalona.
A prězy tam sowy leśe,
Jich wocy ga jagarjam swěśe.
A mjazy zas' njetopyrje se wiju,
Kenž z kśidłoma zašwigaju
A chłodnosć jim pśiduwaju.
Toś z razom wětšy kaž zwěrina riju,
A kśudy pśez powětš wyrce;
A tuder praska

A klaska a rjaska;
Na puśu kamjenje byrce.
A tamkor se šwicy
A byrcy a ricy,
Až źiwno wšo klincy
A w wušyma bincy.
Psy pśipodla skokaju,
Kenž wsakorak łajkocu.
Lej! slězy wicharje wuju,
Kenž jagarje dopśewozuju.
A zwiju
A zryju
Jich źiwny a dłymoki slěd,
Až wšykno zas' minjo se nět,
Źož jagarje nocne
Tam tšochtaju mocnje.
    Hajsa, hoj, hoj!

FOR NOTES

FOR NOTES

FOR NOTES

FOR NOTES

FOR NOTES

OTHER BOOKS FROM SLAVICA PUBLISHERS

Charles E. Townsend: *The Memoirs of Princess Natal'ja Borisovna Dolgorukaja*, viii + 146 p., 1977.

Daniel C. Waugh: *The Great Turkes Defiance On the History of the Apocryphal Correspondence of the Ottoman Sultan in its Muscovite and Russian Variants*, ix + 354 p., 1978.

Susan Wobst: *Russian Readings & Grammar Terminology*, 88 p., 1978.

Dean S. Worth: *A Bibliography of Russian Word-Formation*, xliv + 317 p., 1977.

OTHER BOOKS FROM SLAVICA PUBLISHERS

Alexander Lipson: *A Russian Course,* xiv + 612 p., 1977.

Thomas F. Magner, ed.: *Slavic Linguistics and Language Teaching,* x + 309 p., 1976.

Mateja Matejić & Dragan Milivojević: *An Anthology of Medieval Serbian Literature in English,* 205 p., 1978.

Vasa D. Mihailovich and Mateja Matejić: *Yugoslav Literature in English A Bibliography of Translations and Criticism(1821-1975),* ix + 328 p., 1976.

Alexander D. Nakhimovsky and Richard L. Leed: *Advanced Russian,* xvi + 380 p., 1980.

Felix J. Oinas, ed.: *Folklore Nationalism & Politics,* 190 p., 1977.

Hongor Oulanoff: *The Prose Fiction of Veniamin A. Kaverin,* v + 203 p., 1976.

Jan L. Perkowski: *Vampires of the Slavs* (a collection of readings), 294 p., 1976.

Lester A. Rice: *Hungarian Morphological Irregularities,* 80 p., 1970.

Midhat Ridjanović: *A Synchronic Study of Verbal Aspect in English and Serbo-Croatian,* ix + 147 p., 1976.

David F. Robinson: *Lithuanian Reverse Dictionary,* ix + 209 p., 1976.

Don K. Rowney & G. Edward Orchard, eds.: *Russian and Slavic History,* viii + 311 p., 1977.

Ernest A. Scatton: *Bulgarian Phonology,* 224 p., 1975.

William R. Schmalstieg: *Introduction to Old Church Slavic,* 290 p., 1976.

Michael Shapiro: *Aspects of Russian Morphology. A Semiotic Investigation,* 62 p., 1969.

Rudolph M. Susel, ed.: *Papers in Slovene Studies,* 1977, 127 p., 1978.

Charles E. Townsend: *Russian Word-Formation, corrected reprint,* xviii + 272 p., 1975 (1980).

OTHER BOOKS FROM SLAVICA PUBLISHERS

Dorothy Disterheft: *The Syntactic Development of the Infinitive in Indo-European*, 220 p., 1980.

Ralph Carter Elwood, ed.: *Reconsiderations on the Russian Revolution*, x + 278 p., 1976.

Folia Slavica, a journal of Slavic and East European Linguistics. Vol. 1: 1977-78; Vol. 2: 1978; Vol. 3: 1979; Vol. 4: 1980-81.

Richard Freeborn & others, eds.: *Russian and Slavic Literature*, xii + 466 p., 1976.

Victor A. Friedman: *The Grammatical Categories of the Macedonian Indicative*, 210 p., 1977.

Charles E. Gribble, ed.: *Medieval Slavic Texts, Vol. I, Old and Middle Russian Texts*, 320 p., 1973.

Charles E. Gribble: *Russian Root List with a Sketch of Word Formation*, 55 p., 1973.

Charles E. Gribble: Словарик русского языка 18-го века/ *A Short Dictionary of 18th-Century Russian*, 103 p., 1976.

Charles E. Gribble, ed.: *Studies Presented to Professor Roman Jakobson by His Students*, 333, p. 1968.

William S. Hamilton: *Introduction to Russian Phonology and Word Structure*, 187 p., 1980.

Pierre R. Hart: *G. R. Derzhavin: A Poet's Progress*, iv + 164 p., 1978.

Raina Katzarova-Kukudova & Kiril Djenev: *Bulgarian Folk Dances*, 174 p., 1976.

Andrej Kodjak: *Pushkin's I. P. Belkin*, 112 p., 1979.

Demetrius J. Koubourlis, ed.: *Topics in Slavic Phonology*, viii + 270 p., 1974.

Michael K. Launer: *Elementary Russian Syntax*, xi + 140 p., 1974.

Jules F. Levin & Others: *Reading Modern Russian*, vi + 321 p., 1979.

Maurice I. Levin: *Russian Declension and Conjugation: a structural sketch with exercises*, x + 160 p., 1978.

OTHER BOOKS FROM SLAVICA PUBLISHERS

American Contributions to the Eighth International Congress of Slavists. Zagreb and Ljubljana, Sept. 3-9, 1978. Vol. I: Linguistics and Poetics, ed. by Henrik Birnbaum, 818 p., 1978; *Vol. 2: Literature*, ed. by Victor Terras, 799 p., 1978.

Balkanistica: Occasional Papers in Southeast European Studies, ed. by Kenneth E. Naylor, I(1974), 189p., 1975; II(1975), 153p., 1976; III(1976), 154p., 1978.

Henrik Birnbaum: *Common Slavic Progress and Problems in Its Reconstruction*, xii + 436 p., 1975.

Henrik Birnbaum and Thomas Eekman, eds.: *Fiction and Drama in Eastern and Southeastern Europe Evolution and Experiment in the Postwar Period*, ix + 463 p., 1980.

Malcolm H. Brown, ed.: *Papers of the Yugoslav-American Seminar on Music*, 208 p., 1970.

Ellen B. Chances: *Conformity's Children: An Approach to the Superfluous Man in Russian Literature*, iv + 210 p., 1978.

Catherine V. Chvany: *On the Syntax of Be-Sentences in Russian*, viii + 311 p., 1975.

Frederick Columbus: *Introductory Workbook in Historical Phonology*, 39 p., 1974.

Dina B. Crockett: *Agreement in Contemporary Standard Russian*, iv + 456 p., 1976.

R.G.A. de Bray: *Guide to the Slavonic Languages. Third Edition, Revised and Expanded*, in three parts: *Guide to the South Slavonic Languages*, 399 p., 1980; *Guide to the West Slavonic Languages*, 483 p., 1980; *Guide to the East Slavonic Languages*, 254 p., 1980.

Paul Debreczeny and Thomas Eekman, eds.: *Chekhov's Art of Writing A Collection of Critical Essays*, 199 p., 1977.

Bruce L. Derwing and Tom M.S. Priestly: *Reading Rules for Russian A Systematic Approach to Russian Spelling and Pronunciation With Notes on Dialectical and Stylistic Variation*, vi + 247 p., 1980.